Corruption and Anticorruption in Modern China

Corruption and Anticorruption in Modern China

Edited by
Qiang Fang and Xiaobing Li

LEXINGTON BOOKS
Lanham • Boulder • New York • London

Published by Lexington Books
An imprint of The Rowman & Littlefield Publishing Group, Inc.
4501 Forbes Boulevard, Suite 200, Lanham, Maryland 20706
www.rowman.com

6 Tinworth Street, London SE11 5AL, United Kingdom

Chapter 13 was previously published as Q. Fang, "Xi Jinping's Anticorruption from a Historical Perspective," *Modern China Studies* 24, no. 2 (2017): 112–38.

British Library Cataloguing in Publication Information Available

Library of Congress Cataloging-in-Publication Data Available

ISBN 978-1-4985-7431-0 (cloth: alk. paper)
ISBN 978-1-4985-7432-7 (ebook)

∞™ The paper used in this publication meets the minimum requirements of American National Standard for Information Sciences—Permanence of Paper for Printed Library Materials, ANSI/NISO Z39.48-1992.

Contents

Acknowledgments

The research in this book reflects almost four years of continuous collaborative endeavors made between the authors and civilian administrators, governmental officials, college professors, and institute researchers in China, Taiwan, and the United States. In the period from 2014 to 2018 the Association of Chinese Historians in the United States (CHUS) has organized several scholarly, academic conferences, and on-the-spot social and legal surveys in China and Taiwan. The majority of the authors of this book joined those delegations and had spent time, often during the summertime, to compile data and sources. Some of the chapters in this volume are drawn from several CHUS conferences. In both scope and content, this book is indeed a wealth of splendid scholarly presentations. The heartfelt thanks from the two editors go to each of the authors for their significant contributions to this book that should be welcome by both academics and general readers who intend to explore the corruption issue and anticorruption policy inside the People's Republic of China (PRC) and its recent historical evolution.

Qiang Fang wants to express his gratitude to the generous financial support from a number of grants provided by the University of Minnesota Twin Cities and the University of Minnesota Duluth. These grants include but are not limited to the University-wide Imagine Fund, and special supports from Professor Susan Maher, dean of College of Liberal Arts. In particular, we greatly appreciate the invitation to travel to Taiwan and the valuable anticorruption materials of Ge Yongguang, professor at the National Taiwan University and head of the China Youth National Salvation Corps. In addition, Qiang Fang would like to thank Ms. Jing Duan for her crucial assistance throughout the writing of this book.

Many people at the University of Central Oklahoma (UCO) have contributed to this volume and deserve recognition. First, Xiaobing Li would like to thank President Don Betz; Provost John F. Barthell; dean of the College of Liberal Arts, Catherine S. Webster; and chairperson of the Department of History and Geography, Katrina Lacher. They have been very supportive of the project over the past three years. The UCO faculty merit-credit program sponsored by the Office of Academic Affairs, as well as travel funds from the College of Liberal Arts, provided funding for our research and trips to conferences. The UCO Student Research, Creative, and Scholarly Activities (RCSA) grants sponsored by the Office of High-Impact Practices led by Director Michael Springer, made student research assistants available for the project during the past three years. Brad Watkins prepared the maps Travis Chambers proofread some chapters. Annamaria Martucci provided secretarial assistance. Li's special thanks go to Director Peter D. Hershock, Asian Studies Development Program, East-West Center, and Dr. Shana Brown, Department of History, University of Hawaii, as co-directors of the 2017–2018 Faculty Development Seminar of the USDoE/UISFL. The program offers a prized addition to the existing literature on the most important topics of China Studies.

Finally, the two editors offer thanks to Mr. Brian Hill and Mr. Eric Kuntzman for their excellent professionalism and their always timely support during the editorial progress of this book. Of course, the two editors are grateful to the editors, peer reviewers, copy-editors, and staff at Lexington and Rowman & Littlefield Publishers for their first-class editorial expertise, without which this book could not have been presented to the readers on time.

Qiang Fang (University of Minnesota Duluth)
Xiaobing Li (University of Central Oklahoma)

Note on Transliteration

The *Hanyu pinyin* romanization system is applied to Chinese names of persons, places, and terms. A person's name is written in the Chinese way, surname first, such as Mao Zedong. Some popular names have traditional Wade-Giles spellings appearing in parentheses after the first use of the *Hanyu pinyin* in the entry, such as Mao Zedong (Mao Tse-tung), as do popular names of places like the Yangzi (Yangtze) River, Huang (Yellow) River, and Guangzhou (Canton). Exceptions are made for a few figures, whose names are widely known in reverse order such as Sun Yat-sen (Sun Zhongshan, or Sun Yixian), and names of a few places and institutions, such as Tibet (Xizang) and Peking (Beijing) University.

Introduction

Who to Blame: Party, State, or Society?

Qiang Fang and Xiaobing Li

Without doubt, since China's new communist leader Xi Jinping launched an anticorruption campaign in late 2012, the scope and scale of the campaign has been so massive and sweeping that it is certainly unprecedented in the history of the PRC. According to a report of the *New York Times* in January 2016, roughly three years after Xi Jinping took power, over 140 tigers (high-ranking corrupt officials) and thousands of flies (low-ranking corrupt officials) had fallen.[1] Clearly, this figure is far fewer than reports of other major media. In October 2017, a BBC report entitled "Xi Jinping's Anticorruption Campaign: How Big Is Its Scope? What Is Its Goal?" estimated that a total of 170 minister-level officials had been demoted or imprisoned and around 1.34 million officials had been dismissed or punished since 2012.[2] But a *New York Times* commentary published in May 2017 disagreed with the numbers of BBC and it claimed that over 200 minister-level officials including Zhou Yongkang, former member of the standing committee of the Politburo, and Guo Boxiong and Xu Caihou, both of whom were once vice chairmen of the standing committee of the military. In addition, the commentary noted that Xi Jinping's anticorruption campaign contained some defects that might have drawn criticism of its true motive. One of the problems was that almost no official belonging to the class of princelings (*taizidang*) or officials whose parents were previous communist leaders had been punished. The author argued that the anticorruption campaign of Xi Jinping, who himself was a princeling, had probably attempted to shield the class, the "natural supporters of the communist Party."[3]

In hindsight, however, the ongoing anticorruption campaign is not the first or the largest in China's long history. As a matter of fact, so long as corruption exists, there will likely be anticorruption. According to the *Anti-corruption White Paper* (*fantanfu baipishu*) published by the United and

Self-strengthening Association, an organization sponsored by the GMD in Taiwan, officials are the principal body (*zhuti*) of corruption and a corruption activity refers to a behavior seeking "unlawful interest." Any corruption, the White Paper states, "will undercut a nation's competition capability, violate human rights, erode democracy, and result in political chaos and even *coup d'état*."[4]

In comparison to most other social classes/groups, officials who have the power are more susceptible to graft by trading their power to money. This kind of corruption can be applied to most countries and most bureaucrats. For example, as Gary Goodpaster has noted, corruption is a form of "seeking personal gain" and it is "natural for individual[s] to seek their own advantage and that of their family or relatives." "If the government controls access to economic opportunities or has large, exploitable resources, I would, of course, approach the government to gain access to them."[5] Yet, in 2014, Justice Robert of the US Supreme Court rendered a different meaning of corruption. In the case of *McCutcheon v. FEC*, Robert wrote that bribery should be quid pro quo, which, in other words, meant "explicit exchange of something of value."[6]

In this book, we would like to argue that corruption often appears in a variety of forms and in many fields such as government, business, academia, and judiciary. In the words of Xiaobo Lu, corruption is the "deviation from prescribed norms."[7] Any activity, no matter how trivial it is, could be corruption so long as it breaks the existing norms and laws, albeit some forms of corruption have the backing of the government, or the ruling class per se is the source of corruption. In that regard, corruption as an illicit or abnormal activity has a long history in China and many rulers from at least the Han dynasty till the PRC have launched numerous anticorruption campaigns.

According to the *Ancient Book*, when Zhou Wuwang started his military assault against Shang Zhouwang, the last king of the Shang dynasty (ca. 1600–1046 BCE) in the eleventh century BCE, he denounced the Zhouwang as corrupt, wasteful, and brutal. "Today's king of the Shang, disrespects heaven, imposes disasters on the people, indulge in alcohol, and inflicts cruelty," Wuwang said, "[Zhouwang also] brings disaster to the people by building palace, terrace, pond and wearing beautiful dresses."[8] The eventual success of Wuwang's campaign could in part be regarded as one against Zhouwang's excessive corruption. In the spring and autumn periods (770–476 BCE), Shuxiang, an official of Jin, one of the most powerful states in the period, warned Han Xuanzi, a Jin minister, that Huanzi, the son of former Jin military minister Luan Shu, was nearly executed for his extravagant lifestyle, haughty personality, and bribe-taking activities.[9]

In 74 BCE, the great generalissimo Huo Guang of the former Han dynasty (206 BCE–8 CE) forced the king of Changyi to abdicate for his promiscuity, wastefulness, and depravity. But, in less than two years after Huo Guang's death, most of Huo's remaining family including his wife had been executed for charges similar to that of the king of Changyi. Taking advantage of her husband's paramount power in the state, Huo's wife and other family members were allegedly extremely "arrogant and prodigal." Not only did Huo's wife build many mansions but she also ordered to add massive cosmetics such as embroidery and gold to her carriages. In addition, many of Huo Guang's children and cousins had occupied high-ranking governmental posts and had indulged themselves in building lavish houses and playing with pets rather than serving the state.[10]

The above cases in the early periods of China are merely a tip of the iceberg of corruption and corruption-related crackdown campaigns in China's past. As shown in the chapters of Stella Xu and Qiang Fang, more anticorruption campaigns were launched in the Tang (618–907) and Ming (1368–1644) dynasties. Most chapters in this edited volume examine the corruption and anticorruption cases from the late imperial China (esp. the Qing, 1644–1911) to the twenty-first century, a period that many historians in the West have done superb jobs examining. But most of them have centered their attention on either one short period or one corruption and anticorruption case. Up to now, there has yet been any book that strives to cover this entire period.

For example, in a study of the late Qing peasant uprising, Roxann Prazniak discusses the local official corruption and the adverse impact of the New Policies in the late Qing. When the water buffalo of Qu Shiwen's son Hongfu accidentally ate the grass of his neighbor, his neighbor who had the support of the magistrate confiscated the buffalo and beat Hongfu. Qu Shiwen tried to help his son. But the powerful neighbor and the local constables arrested Qu Shiwen and brought him to the county jail. Unable to bear the loss of the buffalo, Hongfu hanged himself. Upon his release from the prison, Qu Shiwen realized that "poor people had no defense against corrupt officials and wealthy gentry." He later transformed himself into an uprising leader.[11]

While the first several years of the new Republic of China continued the reform of the late Qing, China quickly turned into chaos shortly after Yuan Shikai died in 1916. The subsequent ten plus years were dominated by brutal and corrupt warlords. In the words of John E. Schrescher, in this period "power often came into the hands of a coalition of the rich and influential, backed by minor military men." Warlords at both low and top levels "developed a bad reputation as a group of petty tyrants, rapacious in their behavior and uninspired by high ideals."[12] Likewise, James E. Sheridan writes that, due to the constant need of money, the taxes levied by warlords as "extraordinary tax burdens" on the people. Warlords who often sought personal accumulation of wealth created the Opium Suppression Bureau to monopolize opium production and trade and to tax opium with the "guise of fines." When the warlords fought, "either the victors or the defeaters would loot nearby communities" and the "opportunity to loot" became one of the key reasons for the warlords to recruit soldiers.[13]

The republic under the leadership of Chiang Kai-shek has drawn the interest of many historians and in particular its grave corruption has been a hot topic in numerous books. In two studies, the late historian Frederic Wakeman Jr. remarks that the special tax bureau of Chiang Kai-shek's brother-in-law and the Opium Suppression Bureau under Du Yuesheng, a Green Gang leader and Chiang's sworn brother, had made China the "biggest opium producer" in the world. Much of the funds generated from the opium production and trade helped fund Chiang's military campaigns. Moreover, legal corruption was bold and rampant as the Special Service Department led by spymaster Dai Li could violate law at will and detain, kidnap, torture, and even murder those they suspected to be communist.[14]

Like Wakeman Jr., other historians also lash out at the serious corruption of Chiang's family. In *The Soong Dynasty*, Sterling Seagrave invokes a rumor that T.V. Soong had amassed "larger personal holdings in General Motors and DuPont, among others." An informant even revealed that T.V. and the Soong family had probably embezzled "a large part" of the $500 million from the lend-lease provided by the United States to support China's war against Japan during World War II.[15] In disagreement with Seagrave on the amount of money that the Soong family had taken during the war, Jonathan Fenby asserts that the Soong family had taken an estimated $3.5 billion through "their various enterprises during the war years." T.V. Soong's sister, Ailing, was accused by General Stilwell of making a good deal of money at the expense of the state. "[Ailing] controls a bank through which she bought American dollars at the ridiculously low official rate," Fenby writes, "just before a fresh splurge of printing of banknotes sent the Chinese currency plunging even further."[16]

Unlike other historians who tend to expose the family corruption of Chiang, Lloyd E. Eastman attempts to probe into the root and fundamental problem of GMD (aka KMT)'s corruption. The seed of corruption began after the Northern Expedition in 1926 when many warlords and opportunists flocked to join the GMD who "were totally indifferent to the revolutionary principles of the party and aspired only to obtain power and wealth." Due to no "new blood from within" and "effective criticism from without," the GMD regime had putrefied, which "immeasurably eased the task of Mao Tse-tung." After the GMD retreated to Taiwan, Chiang blamed corruption for his party's loss of mainland China. "From the latter part of the war against Japan to the present," Chiang noted, "the corruption and degeneracy manifested within our revolutionary army has been truly fantastic, simply unimaginable."[17]

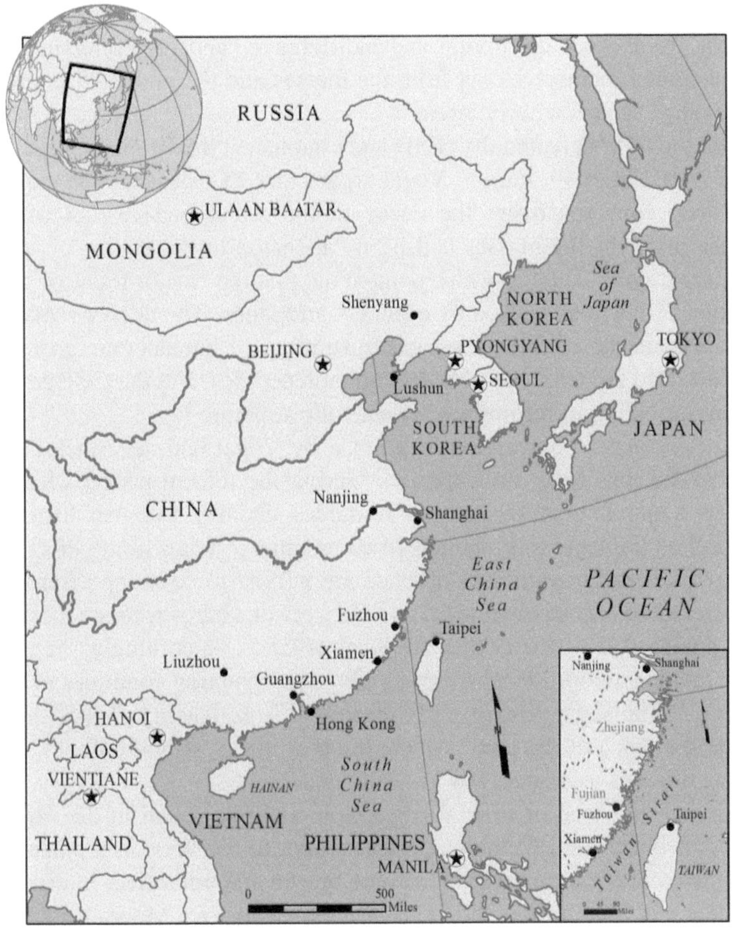

Figure 0.1 Map of East Asia. *Source*: Courtesy of Dr. Brad Watkins.

Many historians generally agree that the Chinese Communist Party (CCP) was more popular among Chinese commoners than the corrupt and decadent GMD, which helped to put the Party in control of most China.[18] However, recent studies show that the CCP was not without its corruption and in as early as the 1940s, the CCP had seen certain corrupt signs. In his banned book entitled *How the Red Sun Rises*, the late historian Gao Hua states that the CCP had established a hierarchy of official benefits around 1941 that gave high-ranking CCP officials much better food and residence.[19] Jonathan Spence also looks into the Yan'an period and, through the criticism of some revolutionary writers such as Ding Ling and Xiao Jun, uncovers a corruption picture synonymous to that of Gao Hua. The writers said that there was darkness over

Yanan, CCP's capital, as well as over Chongqing, GMD's capital. The CCP had not "rooted out corruption and indifference" and the communist leaders "separated themselves out from the masses and the young by enjoying a whole range of special privileges."[20]

After the CCP defeated the GMD and established the People's Republic of China (PRC) in 1949, Ezra F. Vogal argues that CCP leaders had expressed their deep concerns over "the decay in the moral behavior of officials" because many of the masses had been "alienated in the course of socialist transformations." The Party also pointed out that the "major focus of popular discontent" had been caused by officials' arrogance. The deeper roots of the problem were the inefficiencies and frustrations of bureaucratic growth that had "attracted the annoyance of the common people." But the CCP could not or were unwilling to reform the bureaucratic structure.[21]

The bureaucratic corruption mentioned by Vogal had nevertheless intensified in the post-Mao era, especially during the reform period when local officials acquire more power and resources. Stanley Lubman focuses his attention on the legal misconducts of communist officials in the PRC. As he put it, "CCP and government officials are willing to cover up offenses and are reluctant to accuse other officials." As a result, cadres who are most likely to be punished for their crimes are local officials. Accordingly, "regardless of the [anticorruption] mechanism employed, corruption continues to plague the CCP." The separation of Party discipline from legality "keeps the CCP beyond the reach of the law," which, in other words, would embolden high-ranking officials to neglect law and take graft.[22]

Although the seed of official corruption could be found in the early rule of Mao, it is not until China reopened its door to the West in the late 1970s that bureaucratic corruption has become brazen and unbridled. In his studies on China under both Mao and Deng Xiaoping, Maurice Meisner argues that the "crown princes and princesses" or children of top communist leaders took advantage of their privileges in benefiting themselves. They became "the most prominent symbols of the official profiteering and corruption that overwhelmed the Communist bureaucracy in the late 1980s." The official corruption in the 1990s was so rampant that its scope and scale "shocked even the most hardened of political cynics." For Meisner, corruption was one of the "unintended consequences" of Deng's economic reform. Unfortunately, Deng, with his own kids doing lucrative businesses, responded to the rampant corruption with a policy that was "confused, contradictory, and above all, ambiguous."[23]

As China's economic reform entered the twenty-first century, official corruption had become increasingly serious and prevalent until Xi Jinping launched an anticorruption campaign in late 2012. In a recently published book, Minxin Pei, a political scientist and a critic of Communist China, uses "collusive corruption" to identify China's systematic official corruption. In his argument, collusive corruption or collusion between power and money is more destructive than individual corruption because it "destroys the organizational and normative fabric of the state, increases the difficulty of detection, and produces greater financial gains for its perpetrators." In the worst scenario, corruption networks, including officials, businessmen, and gangsters, "seize control of these jurisdictions and turn them into local mafia states." Pei also notes that collusive corruption or crony capitalism is not limited to China, it could also be found in Russia, Ukraine, and the former Soviet Central Asian Republics.[24]

The idea of editing this book came out of a trip to Taiwan in the summer of 2017 organized by Chinese Historians in the United States and funded by the Grand Alliance of the Nationalist Party in Taiwan. During the trip, most of the authors of this book, such as Qiang Fang, Xiaobing Li, Zhi Guoyang, and Xiaojia Hou, had made preliminary discussion of this book. In the fall, more scholars expressed their interest and were willing to contribute their valuable insights. In addition, some authors organized a panel entitled "Corruption and Anticorruption in Modern China" at the 132nd American Historical Association annual conference at Washington D.C.

This book differs from the current scholarship in the following four respects. In the first place, this book will be the first one with a concentration on the corruption and anticorruption in the entire period of modern China, particularly from the late Qing to the present. Unlike other scholars who study one period or one case of corruption or anticorruption in modern China, the chapters in this book cover a variety of corruption- and anticorruption-related topics since the Qing dynasty. With a longer and broader perspective, this book will be in a better position to assist readers to grasp the continuities, commonalities, and dissimilarities of corruption and anticorruption in at least three main periods.

Another striking feature of the book is that some of the researches are cutting-age and based on newly released primary sources. One good example is Patrick Shan's study on Yuan Shikai's efforts opposing corruption, which mostly builds up on latest sources of Yuan's letters and documents. Xiaojia Hou's research on the Lake Wei is the first study on the local strife in the area of the Lake Wei. Thirdly, most of the contributors are West-based historians who not only have inalienable personal and family connections but also keep a close eye on the daily developments in China. Such kind of cross-cultural national sentiment can rarely be found among scholars who study China simply as a career or interest. Finally, at the end of this book, we seek to place corruption in a global context that is beyond the boundary of China. It is because we are keenly aware that corruption is a thorny issue faced by all nations, and no nation, be it democratic or authoritarian, can get rid of corruption completely. A good example is the United States, the so-called republican and democratic exemplar and defender, which has a long history of corruption and, worse, tries to legitimize some political corruptions.

The chapters in the book can be roughly divided into four parts under different themes. The first part "Centralized Power and Authoritarianism" contains only two chapters that examine the corruption and anticorruption in the Qing dynasty and the early republic. The Qing dynasty is the last dynasty in China with the minority Manchu in power. By studying and sorting out sixty-one anticorruption cases entailing exclusively first- and second-ranking officials in the Qing dynasty, Qiang Fang finds that most of the anticorruption report came from upper-level governments such as superiors in the province or region, censors in the capital, and the emperor or at least from peer-level officials. It was rather difficult for lower-ranking officials to check the corruption of their superiors. Fang concludes that, despite harsh punishment and multiple ways of exposing corruption, a combined cronyism, official mutual protection, the inferiority of law, and the almighty power of the emperors made anticorruption a more daunting task if not an impossible mission in the dynasty.

As a specialist on Yuan Shikai, the first de jure republican president, Patrick Shan investigates Yuan Shikai's governorship in Shandong, his general-governorship in Zhili, and his presidency during the early years of the republic by a particular focus on his management of officials. Yuan's efforts to reach the goal of clean yet effective government prompted him to implement his anticorruption measures. He championed for an incorrupt officialdom, adopted a number of policies to guarantee their enforcement, and assumed strict rules to punish dishonest officials. During his presidency, he endeavored to institutionalize official management by establishing new state organs. The analysis of his efforts points to his innermost commitment to identify, train, employ, and discipline talented prospective officials to reach the lofty goal of national revival. Unfortunately, the problem could not be solved by one determined man like Yuan Shikai, as corruption emerged and reemerged here or there. Corruption, more or less, is the cancer of all governments. Although Yuan tried to eradicate it and the subsequent regimes have continued to do so with vigorous endeavors, corruption has resurfaced as a headache to them all, because those regimes, including Yuan's, were centralist in nature, were not transparent enough, and were not effectively balanced. Nevertheless, this is not to deny Yuan's contributions to modernize China's administrative system.

There are three chapters dealing with corruption and anticorruption in the second part "Political Parties and Legitimacy." The first chapter authored by Sherman Lai has a focus on the role of corruption in Chiang Kai-shek's loss to the CCP. In his chapter, Lai states that the defeat of Chiang Kai-shek and his Nationalist government by the seemingly much weaker Chinese Communists in 1949 is an event that still affects the current China-US relations and the international security in East Asia and Western Pacific. And it has been a constant topic among the people interested in modern China. As Chiang enjoyed much more resources than his opponent Mao Zedong and had had a reputation of corruption prior to the outbreak of the Chinese Civil War in 1946, his defeat in 1949 was attributed to corruption. However, as the corruption in China is rampant, it is natural to question the previous view that the Nationalist government deserved its destruction because of its corruption. Lai's chapter is an attempt to answer this question through exploring and analyzing Chiang's wartime diaries. He argues that the principal reason for Chiang's defeat was his war against Japan. Although he developed a grand strategy of total and protracted war against the Japanese invasion and made it possible for China to emerge victorious at the end of World War II, Chiang underestimated the war's catastrophic impacts on his government and society. His underestimation let him make one mistake after another. When he realized it, it was too late to make up. The fate of the Nationalist government in mainland China was sealed in 1944, a year before Japan's surrender in August 1945.

Xiaobing Li's chapter is crisscrossed with that of Sherman Lai as he too examines GMD's corruption in its final years on mainland China. He argues that it was the failure of the takeover and economic reconstruction after World War II that cost the GMD state its "legitimacy"—if indeed the "loss of legitimacy" is the best way to interpret the GMD defeat. Corruption of the GMD played an important role in promoting the anti-GMD movement in China and became one of the major grievances of the forces of undermining the GMD regime in China. The decline in institutional trust partially resulted from failed anticorruption policy and corruption tolerance in and outside the government. Li's study attempts to address the relationship between postwar corruption and institutional trust. By exploring the relationship between corruption and institutional trust, Li notes that the institutional trust is a key linkage between a government and society and a foundation for democracy.

Generally speaking, corruption in the Mao era is less a cause of common discontent than in the reform era after 1978. Zhiguo Yang studies the so-called first anticorruption case in the PRC in which two high-ranking officials, Liu Qingshan and Zhang Zishan, were executed for their alleged crime of corruption. Yang points out that this incident epitomizes the Three-Anti Movement (1951–1952) in every possible way. Linking the first big case to the CCP effort to legitimize its party governance in China by giving an anticorruption focus to the movement, Yang seeks to reconstruct a historical narrative of the first big case in that context. He endeavors to argue that, despite the anachronization and decontextualization of the case in the CCP

Figure 0.2 Map of China. *Source*: Courtesy of Dr. Brad Watkins.

anticorruption account, it will remain an indispensable contraction block in the legitimation of the CCP party rule under normal circumstances but particularly when a legitimation crisis is perceived.

The bulk of the chapters are lumped in the third part "Government, Individuals, and Conflict Interest" that includes five chapters, almost half of the book. Like Zhiguo Yang, Xiaojia Hou's chapter also probes into a specific corruption case related to Lake Weishan, a middle-sized lake by Chinese standard, but her research stretches to the entire period of Mao and after. The lake of Weishan, lying between the border of Shandong and Jiangsu provinces, has suffered from endemic flooding for centuries and its ecological changes have consistently created complicated problems for local administrations. In the 1950s, severe disputes regarding the lakeside land and lake resources broke out between two adjacent provinces: Shandong and Jiangsu. Competing to control the lake, both disregarded laws and local customs, instead, using their native networks to amend, and even defy, the decisions from Beijing. For four decades, local officials switched their loyalties, made arbitrary decisions, mobilized mass violent support from below, and engaged in frequent armed confrontations that resulted in heavy casualties. Hou's chapter looks into the case of Lake Weishan and examines an extended understanding of corruption. She argues that money had played only a minor role under Mao's reign: the corruption in Mao's China was less a result of bribery, than a lack of prescribed norms and lack of accountability.

Due mostly to his tough stance in the 1989 Tiananmen incident, former president Jiang Zemin won over the trust and backing of Deng Xiaoping who succeeded Deng to be the paramount leader of the CCP. Centering his research on the Shannxi Province in the era of Jiang Zemin, Yang Dongyu argues that China's reform, opening up and modernization drive continued to be moving forward. The modernization of China achieved a rapid development in the 1990s. However, with a rapid development of the economy coupled with an absence of effective legal and social supervising mechanism, official corruption that had been one of the targets in the 1989 Tiananmen demonstration exacerbated and expanded to more industries and governments. Moreover, in a short period of time, corruption has reached alarming levels, which has become a public hazard to China's social improvement, economic development, and political stability. Against this backdrop, China had embarked on a vast and enduring national "anticorruption storm."

In their chapter on escaping corrupt officials, Yue Li and Chen Liu track some of those runaway officials who have absconded abroad with large sums of public funds and the Chinese law enforcement overseas. To avoid discipline and punishment in China and protect their cash and properties overseas, more and more corrupt Chinese officials looked for opportunities to flee the country and travel overseas. From the 1990s to 2000s, corrupt Chinese officials fled to foreign countries as it was the safest way to evade laws and responsibilities. In particular, developed countries such as the United States, Australia, and Canada have become a paradise for fugitives. In 2015, the Central Anticorruption Commission of the CCP launched the "Skynet project," which is an important project to capture the corrupt criminals hiding abroad and bring them back to China for justice. In particular, both Li and Liu examine the case of Yang Xiuzhu, former mayor of Wenzhou, who was the first one of the 100 Most Wanted on the Red List of the Skynet Project, and explains how China coordinated with international courts, foreign law enforcement, and local financial institutes to force corrupt officials like Yang to return to China. The authors also show the strong impact of Yang's case and China's international hunt for the corrupt officials. As Xi Jinping points out, "No matter where the corrupt elements are hiding in the world, the Chinese judiciary must chase them down and arrest them."

Specializing in Chinese literature and folk rhymes, Hellen Xiaoyan Wu explores the rich rhymes on official corruption from the late 1970s to the present. Her chapter first tries to demystify the myth that popular rhymes targeting corruption, a sensitive topic, are not officially published in print. She then examines the popular rhymes about corruption from the people's perspective and in the name of officials, followed by some poems created by officials themselves, which are supported by the real-life corruption cases reported in the media. After a discussion of the tradition that anonymous verses spread widely whenever corruption becomes serious, and the social value that this type of rhymes has in contemporary anticorruption efforts, Wu argues that *minyao* helps to understand today's China, its corruption and anticorruption in particular.

Stella Xu eyes corruption and anticorruption in the early history of China. It is well known among the Chinese that both the Han and Tang dynasties have been the golden ages; Xu, however, argues that corruption, which is not uncommon in many administrations and societies, was present even in these dynasties, and so it may be asked why and how corruption occurred during China's golden ages, and how similar or different were their corruption cases in terms of the social background, motivation, and manner of those involved during these periods? In addition, how did the Han and Tang dynasties, during which governmental control was relatively strong, try to prevent corruption, and identify, prosecute, and punish officials involved in corruption? It could be said that the government, with its legal codes and policies to prevent corruption, and corrupted officials are like a cat and mouse who keep on tracking and evading each other. Indeed, Han emperors realized the potential problems of corruption and issued edicts to legally prevent the possibility of corruption. A well-known example of their severe penalties for corruption was that punishment was extended to three generations through the stipulation that the descendants of corrupted officials could not be appointed to government positions.

The last part of the book is "New Century, New Struggle" in which three chapters target CCP's anticorruption efforts in the Hu Jintao and Xi Jinping administrations. Hu Jintao is the CCP leader who succeeded Jiang Zemin in 2002. In the early 2012, the year that Hu was set to retire and transfer his power to Xi Jinping, Wang Lijun, the powerful head of Chongqing Police Bureau and a longtime follower of Bo Xilai, the then Party secretary of the city, suddenly fled to US Consulate in Chengdu, Sichuan province. This political episode shocked almost everyone in China, which eventually helped Xi Jinping, a key rival of Bo Xilai, to remove and disgrace him with a punishment of life sentence. What had caused Wang's flight? What might have happened between him and his boss Bo Xilai? Recently (summer 2017), another top official of the party, Sun Zhengcai, who was appointed by the new Xi administration to be Bo Xilai's successor as the party boss in Chongqing ("rumored" to be the next party chief after Xi) also went down with possible trials pending. What happened to this "cursed" position in Chongqing? Was Hu Jintao able to do anything to stop the rampant corruption among the officials? Is the ongoing anticorruption campaign pushed by the party a success?

Or is it used simply to remove Xi's political opponents within the party? Is the Xi administration going to launch any political reform long overdue? For the above questions, Xiansheng Tian will address them with a look into the root of the two political scandals. Drawing recent online disclosure of more alleged scandals at the top of the CCP by a self-exiled businessman named Guo Wengui, Tian tries to do a relatively in-depth analysis on the issue and hopes to inspire more discussions that would healthily lead to the serious effort in promoting the "rule of law" in China.

As we have mentioned at the beginning of this book, since Xi Jinping launched his anticorruption campaign in late 2012, the campaign has drawn much attention from scholars. In this part, two authors will devote their analyses to it. One of Xi's anticorruption policies is the Eight Regulations that are meant to restrict extravagant and unnecessary government spending. These regulations have set up strict rules to be followed by every official in China and have become basic standards for official promotion. For those who first view Xi's anticorruption approach as a temporary and short-term movement that would sweep over like a tornado have now to admit that five years after the anticorruption campaign started, what Xi Jinping has been trying to do is clearly a necessary process of institution building and will help strengthen the Chinese economic development and national rejuvenation. Xiaoxiao Li asserts that Xi has paid more attention to institution building in China and has attempted to do more than his predecessors in constructing the rule by law.

Since Xi Jinping launched his unprecedented anticorruption campaign, scholars around the world have made many valuable arguments on Xi's anticorruption campaign. Some of them dismiss the anticorruption campaign as selective because most of the charged corrupt officials were Xi's political enemies; others see the campaign as a movement or power struggle. Regardless of their views, almost all of them have paid attention to Xi's anticorruption campaign or contemporary China and none has made effort to compare Xi's anticorruption campaign with the past similar practices. The contribution of Qiang Fang's chapter is to place Xi's campaign in a historical backdrop and draw a comparison between Xi's campaign and anticorruption campaigns under three notable rulers in the Tang, Ming, and Qing dynasties. Fang argues that while Xi's anticorruption campaign is comparable in many aspects to precedence in the dynasties, they have significant differences. The success and failure of dynastic anticorruption campaigns may provide readers with a better perspective in both understanding the nature and anticipating the likely outcome of Xi's ongoing anticorruption campaign.

As we have mentioned above, corruption and anticorruption have had a long history in China. The insatiable pursuit of power and wealth has accompanied China ever since its earliest empires. The chapters in this book hope to cast light on the continuity of corruption and anticorruption between early dynasties such as Han and Tang and the three polities since the late Qing. Although rulers in different periods have all tried to crack down corruption, some fundamental institutional defects such as the supremacy of the law and the virtually omnipotent rulers/Party have vitiated most of the efforts against bureaucratic corruption.

NOTES

1. Michael Forsythe, "Database Tracks 'Tigers and Flies' Caught in Xi Jinping's Corruption Crackdown" in *The New York Times*, January 21, 2016.
2. "Xi Jinping's Anticorruption Campaign: How Big Is Its Scope? What Is Its Goal (*Xi Jinping defanfu yundong: fanwei youduoguang Mubiao shishenme*)" in the *BBC*, October 23, 2017. http://www.bbc.com/zhongwen/simp/chinese-news-41719314.
3. Deng Yuwen, "Comment" in *The New York Times*, May 9, 2017.
4. *Anticorruption White Paper* (*fantanfu baipishu*), United and Self-Strengthening Association in the Republic of China, June 30, 2010.
5. Gary Goodpaster, "Reflections on Corruption in Indonesia" in Timothy Lindsey and Howard W. Dick, eds., *Corruption in Asia: Rethinking the Governance Paradigm* (Australia: The Federation Press, 2002), 88.
6. Zephyr Teachout, *Corruption in America: From Benjamin Franklin's Snuff Box to Citizens United* (Cambridge, MA: Harvard University Press, 2014), 7.
7. Cited in Xiaojia Hou's Chapter 6. Xiaobo Lu, *Cadres and Corruption: The Organizational Involution of the Chinese Communist Party* (Stanford: Stanford University Press, 2000), 12.
8. Liang Hong, ed., *The Ancient Book* (*shangshu*) (Hunan: Shidai wenyi chubanshe, 2003), 236–40.
9. "Discourse of Jin No. Eight (*jinyu ba*)" in *Discourses of the State* (guoyu) http://www.guoxue.com/book/guoyu/0014.htm.
10. Sima Guang, *Comprehensive Mirror for Assisting Government* (*zizhi tongjian*) (Beijing: Zhonghua shujü, 1956), Vols. 24–25.
11. Roxann Prazniak, *Of Camel Kings and Other Things: Rural Rebels against Modernity in Late Imperial China* (Lanham, MD: Rowman & Littlefield, 1999), 46.
12. John E. Schrecker, *The Chinese Revolution in Historical Perspective* (New York: Praeger, 1991), 138–39.
13. James E. Sheridan, *Chinese Warlord: The Career of Feng Yu-hsiang* (Stanford, CA: Stanford University Press, 1966), 16–27.
14. Frederic Wakeman jr, *Policing Shanghai: 1927–1937* (Stanford, CA: Stanford University Press, 1995), 205; Spymaster: *Dai Li and the Chinese Secret Service* (Stanford, CA: Stanford University Press, 2003), 144–61, 238–40.
15. Sterling Seagrave, *The Soong Dynasty* (New York: Harper & Row Publishers, 1986), 327, 407.

16. Jonathan Fenby, *Chiang Kai-shek: China's Generalissimo and the Nation he Lost* (New York: Carroll & Graf Publishers, 2004), 404.
17. Lloyd E. Eastman, *Seeds of Destruction: Nationalist China in War and Revolution, 1937–1949* (Stanford, CA: Stanford University Press, 1984), 120–29.
18. Philip Short, 1999, 418; Eastman, *Seeds of Destruction*, 170; Derk Bodde, *Peking Diary: 1948–1949 A Year of Revolution* (Minnesota: Fawcett Publications, 1967), 240.
19. Gao Hua, *How the Red Sun Rises? (gongtaiyang shiruhe shengqide)* (Hong Kong: Hong Kong Chinese University Press, 2011), 206–7.
20. Jonathan Spence, *The Gate of Heavenly Peace: The Chinese and Their Revolution, 1895–1980* (New York: Penguin Books, 1981), 328.
21. Ezra F. Vogal, *Canton under Communism: Programs and Politics in a Provincial Capital, 1949–1968* (Cambridge, MA: Harvard University Press, 1969), 189.
22. Stanley Lubman, *Bird in a Cage: Legal Reform in China after Mao* (Stanford, CA: Stanford University Press, 1999), 171.
23. Maurice Meisner, *Mao's China and After: A history of the People's Republic* (New York: Free Press, 1999): 475–76; Maurice Meisner, *The Deng Xiaoping Era: An Inquiry into the Fate of Chinese Socialism, 1978–1994* (New York: Hill & Wang, 1996), 304–21.
24. Minxin Pei, *China's Crony Capitalism* (Cambridge, MA: Harvard University Press, 2016), 9–15.

BIBLIOGRAPHY

1968. *Verifiable Records of Qing Shengzu* (*Daqing shengzu shilu*) vol. 39.

1984. *Documents of the Guangxü Reign* (*Guangxüchao donghualu*). Beijing: Zhonghua shujü.

Alexander, Herbert E. 1984. "Making Sense About Dollars in the 1980 Presidential Campaigns" in Michael J. Malbin, ed., *Money and Politics in the United States: Financing Elections in the 1980s*. New Jersey: Chatham House Publishers.

Anticorruption White Paper (*fantanfu baipishu*), United and Self-Strengthening Association in the Republic of China, June 30, 2010.

Arnsdorf, Isaac. "Trump Rewards Big Donors with Jobs and Access." *Politico*, December 27, 2016.

Ballhaus, Rebecca and Mulins, Brody. "Corporations Bet on GOP Senate Control." *The Wall Street Journal*, November 7, 2016.

Barboza, David. "Billions in Hidden Riches for Family of Chinese Leader." *The New York Times*, October 25, 2012.

Barboza, David and Lafraniere, Sharon. "'Princelings' in China Use Family Ties to Gain Riches." *The New York Times*, May 17, 2012.

Bartlett, Beatrice S. 1990. *Monarchs and Ministers: The Grand Council in Mid-Ch'ing China, 1723–1820*. Berkeley: University of California Press.

Berg, Larry L., Hahn, Harlan and Schmidhauser, John R. 1976. *Corruption in the American Political System*. New Jersey: Central Learning Press.

Blinder, Alan. "U.S. Ends Corruption Case against Former Virginia Governor." *The New York Times*, September 8, 2016.

Bodde, Derk. 1967. *Peking Diary: 1948–1949 A Year of Revolution*. Minnesota: Fawcett Publications.

Branigan, Tania. "The Guardian Politburo, Army, Casinos: China's Corruption Crackdown Spreads." *The Guardian*, February 2015.

Bu, Xianqun. 2014. *Corruption and Anticorruption in Chinese History (Zhongguo lishishangde fubai yufanfubai)*. Fujian: Lujiang chubanshe.

Chen, Zhiping. "The Seeing Clearly the Customary Fees of Late Qing Learning Officials in the Case of Wang Kaitai (*cong Wang Kaitaian kanqing qingmo xueguande lougui*)." *Zhongguo shehui jingjishi yanjiu*, Vol. 3, 2013, pp. 84–87.

Chin, Josh. "Chinese Lawyer Sentenced to Seven Years in Prison." *The Wall Street Journal*, August 4, 2016.

Choi, Chi-yuk. "Chinese Officials Facing Corruption Charges are Being Tempted by Suicide." *South China Morning Post*, June 15, 2016.

Cohen, Paul. "Changes over Time in Qing History: The Importance of Context." *Late Imperial China*, Vol. 37, No. 1, June 2016, pp. 10–13.

Confessore, Nicholas and Luo, Michael. "Perry Mines Texas System to Raise Cash." *The New York Times*, August 20, 2011.

Condon, George E. Jr. "Disgraced Congressman Randy 'Duke' Cunningham Is a Free Man Again." *The Atlantic*, July 10, 2014.

Dardess, John. *Confucianism and Autocracy*. California: University of California Press.

Deng, Yuwen. "Comment." *The New York Times*, May 9, 2017.

Denyer, Simon. "China's Ousted Official Bo Xilai Convicted of Corruption." *The Washington Post*, September 22, 2013.

Eastman, Lloyd E. 1984. *Seeds of Destruction: Nationalist China in War and Revolution, 1937–1949*. Stanford: Stanford University Press.

Editorial Board. "A Deadly Landslide Exposes the Depths of China's Corruption and Censorship." *The Washington Post*, December 29, 2015.

Elliot, Mark C. 2001. *The Manchu Way: The Eight Banners and Ethnic Identity in Late Imperial China*. Stanford: Stanford University Press.

Fang, Qiang. 2013a. *Chinese Complaint Systems: Natural Resistance*. London: Routledge.

———. 2013b. *A Short History of Chinese Petition* (*zhongguo shangfang zhidu shihua*). Beijing: China Youth Press.

———. "A Silent 'Revolution': The Late Qing Reform on the Jumping Appeals." *The Journal of Asian History*, Vol. 46, 2012, No. 1, pp. 97–116.

———. "Hot Potatoes: Chinese Complaint Systems from Early Times to 1898." *Journal of Asian Studies*, Vol. 68. No. 4, November 2009, pp. 1105–35.

Fang, Qiang and Des Forges, Roger. "Were Chinese Rulers Above the Law? Toward a Theory of the Rule of Law in Chinese History." *Stanford Journal of International Law*, Vol. 44, No. 1, 2007, pp. 101–146.

Fang, Qiang and Li, Xiaobing. 2017. *Power Versus Law in Modern China: Cities, Courts, and the Communist Party*. Lexington: University Press of Kentucky.

Farmer, Edward. 1983. *Zhu Yuanzhang and Early Ming Legislation*. Leiden: E.J. Brill, 1995, 2.

Fenby, Jonathan. 2004. *Chiang Kai-shek: China's Generalissimo and the Nation He Lost*. New York: Carroll & Graf Publishers.

Fu, Zhengyuan. 1993. *Automatic Tradition and Chinese Politics*. Cambridge: Cambridge University Press.

Ferguson, Charles H. 2012. *Predator Nation: Corporate Criminals, Political Corruption and the Hijacking of America*. Crown Publishing Group.

Feuer, Alan. "Why Are Corruption Cases Crumbling? Some Blame the Supreme Court." *The New York Times*, November 17, 2017.

Forsythe, Michael. "Database Tracks 'Tigers and Flies' Caught in Xi Jinping's Corruption Crackdown." *The New York Times*, January 21, 2016.

Forsythe, Michael. "Database Tracks 'Tigers and Flies' Caught in Xi Kinping's Corruption Crackdown." *The New York Times*, January 21, 2016.

Gao, Hong, "The Fundamental Cause of Lost 1895 War Is Qing Corruption (*jiawu zhanzheng shibaide genben yuanyinshi Qingchaode fubai*)." *The Journal of Qiqihaer Normal College*, Vol. 5, 1995, pp. 158–60.

Gao, Hua. 2011. *How the Red Sun Rises?* (*gongtaiyang shiruhe shengqide*). Hong Kong: Hong Kong Chinese University Press.

Goodpaster, Gary. 2002. "Reflections on Corruption in Indonesia" in Timothy Lindsey and Howard W. Dick, eds., *Corruption in Asia: Rethinking the Governance Paradigm*. Australia: The Federation Press.

Gore, Al. 2013. *The Future: Six Drives of Global Change*. New York: Random House Publishing Group.

Guy, R. Kent. 2017. *Qing Governors and Their Provinces: The Evolution of Territorial Administration in China, 1644–1796*. Seattle: University of Washington Press.

He, Qinglian. "Government Monopolized Anticorruption Explicitly Reveals the Backwardness of China's Institutions (Zhengfu longduan fanfu tuxian zhongguo zhidu luohou)." *The Voice of America*, February 7, 2014.

Helderman, Rosalind S. and Vozzella, Laura. "Va. Gov. McDonnell on Two-Way Street with Chief Executive of Struggling Company." *The Washington Post*, March 30, 2013.

Ho, Ping-ti. 1964. *The Ladder of Success in Imperial China*. Columbia: Columbia University Press.

Hofstadter, Richard. 1989. *The American Political Tradition and the Men Who Made It*. New York: Vintage Books.

Hucker, Charles. 1966. *Censorial System of Ming China*. Stanford: Stanford University Press.

Ingraham, Christopher. "Somebody Just Put a Price Tag on the 2016 Election. It's a Doozy." *Washington Post*, April 14, 2017.

Jacobs, Andrew. "China Appears Set to force Times Reporter to Leave." *The New York Times*, January 27, 2014.

Jacobs, Andrew, Hernandez, Javier C. and Buckley, Chris "Behind Deadly Tianjin Blast, Shortcuts and Lax Rules." *The New York Times*, August 30, 2015.

Ji, Shenying. 2015. *The Remaining Members: The Lurker of the "New Gang of Four"* (*Yudang: xinsirenbang deqianfuzhe*). Hong Kong: Neimu chubanshe.

———. 2015. *Party Remnants: The Lurker of the New "Gang of Four"* (*yudang: xinsirenbang deqianfuzhe*). Hong Kong: Neimu chubanshe.

Keliher, Macabe. "Administrative Law and the Making of the First *Da Qing Huidian*." *Late Imperial China*, Vol. 37, No.1, June 2016, pp. 55–108.

Keliher, Macabe and Wu, Hsinchao. "Corruption, Anticorruption, and the Transformation of Political Culture in Contemporary China." *The Journal of Asian Studies*, Vol. 75, No. 01, February 2016, pp. 5–18.

Ketcham, Ralph, ed. 2006. *Selected Writings of James Madison*. Indianapolis: Hackett Publishing.

Leggett, Karby. "In a Land Where Bribes are Commonplace, a Chinese Millionaire Pushed the Envelope." *The Wall Street Journal*, November 23, 2001.

Levin, Dan. "China Tells Schools to Suppress Western Ideas, with One Big Exception." *The New York Times*, February 9, 2015.

Li, Boyuan. 2013. *Exposure of the Official World* (guanchang xianxingji). Zhejiang: Zhejiang chuabn jituan.

Li, Chunmei. "A Preliminary Study on the Customary fee Income of Governors in Early Qing (*shitan qingchao qianqi dufude lougui shouru*)." *The Journal of Neimenggu Social Science*, Vol. 26, No. 4, July 2005.

Liu, E. 2017. *The Travels of Lao Can* (laocan youji). Zhejiang: Zhejiang wenyi chubanshe.

Liang, Hong, ed. 2003. *The Ancient Book* (*shangshu*). Hunan: Shidai wenyi chubanshe.

Liu, Xu. 1975. *The Old History of the Tang* (*jiutangshu*). Beijing: Zhonghua shujü.

Lin, Qian. 2013. *Power and Law in Traditional China* (*Chuantong zhongguo dequanyufa*). Beijing: Law Press.

Lubman, Stanley. 1999. *Bird in a Cage: Legal Reform in China after Mao*. Stanford: Stanford University Press.

Lichtblau, Eric. "Lawmakers' Ties to Toyota Questioned at Start of Inquiries." *The New York Times*, February 23, 2010.

Ma, Jun. "Corruption Defeated Late Qing Army: Elite Eight Banners Could Not Ride Horses and Half of them Fell (*fubai jikua qingjundui: baqi jingbing buhui qima shiren shangma banshuluo*)." *Wenhui dushu zhoubao*, December 13, 2010.

Marcus, Robert D. Burner, David, and Marcus, Anthony, eds. 2007. *American Firsthand: Vol II. Readings from Reconstruction to the Present*. New York: Bedfor/St. Martin's.

Markon, Jerry. "Ex-Rep. Jefferson (D. La) Gets 13 Years in Freezer Cash Case." *The Washington Post*, November 14, 2009.

Meisner, Maurice. 1999. *Mao's China and After: A History of the People's Republic*. New York: Free Press.

———. 1996. *The Deng Xiaoping Era: An Inquiry into the Fate of Chinese Socialism, 1978–1994*. New York: Hill & Wang.

Murong, Xuechun. "Xi's Selective Punishment." *The New York Times*, January 16, 2015.

Myers, Steven L. and Landler, Mark. "Frenzied Hours for U.S. on Fate of a China Insider." *The New York Times*, April 17, 2012.

Ni, Shawn and Van, Pham Hoang. "High Corruption Income in Ming and Qing China." *Journal of Development Economics*, 2006.

Nie, Da. "Corruption behind the Frivolity: The Relationship between Governmental and Cultural Corruption in the Dream of Red Mansion (*fuhua beihoude fubai: cong Hongloumeng kan guanchang fubai yuminfeng fubai deguanxi*)." *Zhongguo jijian jianchabao*, November 14, 2014.

Niu, Chuangping and Niu, Jiqing, eds. 2000. *Verifiable Records of the Economic Criminal Cases of Qing First and Second Ranking Officials (Qingdai yierpin guanyuan jingji fanzui anjian shilu)*. Beijing: Zhongguo fazhi chubanshe.

Park, Nancy E. "Corruption in Eighteenth-Century China." *The Journal of Asian Studies*, Vol. 56, No. 4, November 1997.

———. "Unofficial Perspectives on Torture in Ming and Qing China." *Late Imperial China*, Vol. 37, No. 1, 2016, pp. 17–54.

Patrick, Odsseus. "For a Century, the Mansion Sat above Sydney Harbor. Then China's Nouveau Riche Arrived." *The Washington Post*, June 17, 2014.

Pei, Minxin. 2016. *China's Crony Capitalism*. Harvard: Harvard University Press.

———. "China's War on Corruption Could Hasten Communist Party's Decline." *Nikkei Asian Review*, May 19, 2015.

———. "Crony Communism in China." *The New York Times*, October 17, 2014.

Perdue, Peter C. 2010. *China Marches West: The Qing Conquest of Central Eurasia*. Harvard: Harvard University Press.

Phillips, Tom. "China Behaving Like 'Gangster' State with Bookseller Kidnap, Say Hong Kong Politicians." *The Guardian*, June 17, 2016.

Prazniak, Roxann. 1996. *Of Camel Kings and Other Things: Rural Rebels against Modernity in Late Imperial China*. Lanham: Rowman & Littlefield.

Rauhala, Emily. "As Panama Leaks Spread, China's 'Red Nobility' Would Rather Not Talk About It." *The Washington Post*, April 7, 2016.

Reed, Bradly. 2000. *Talons and Teeth: County Clerks and Runners in the Qing Dynasty*. Stanford: Stanford University Press.

Rowe, William T. 2010. *China's Last Empire: The Great Qing*. Harvard: Harvard University Press.

Sha, Lu. "Several Officials of the Development and Reform Commission have been Punished due to Violations of the Rules Regarding Banquet with Public Money and Accepting Gifts (*Fagaiwei duoming guanyuan gongkuan chihe weigui shouli beichufen*)." *Xinjingbao*, April 17, 2016.

Shankar, Sneha. "Li Xiaolin, Former Chinese Premier Li Peng's Daughter, Hid over $2M In HSBC Swiss Account." *The International Business Times*, February 10, 2015.

Shi, Ping. "Fanfubai bushi quanli douzheng (Anticorruption Is Not Power Struggle)." *Qiushi*, July 2016.

Smith, Richard J. 2005. *The Qing Dynasty and Traditional Chinese Culture*. Rowman & Littlefield.

Sonmez, Felicia. "Free Speech in China Gets an Unlikely State-Media Backer." *The Wall Street Journal*, February 17, 2016.

Sun, Yat-sen. 1981. *The Complete Works of Sun Yat-sen* (*Sun Zhongshan quanji*). Beijing: Zhonghua shujü.

Schrecker, John E. 1991. *The Chinese Revolution in Historical Perspective*. New York: Praeger.

Seagrave, Sterling. 1992. *Dragon Lady: The Life and Legend of the Last Empress of China*. New York: Vintage Books.

———. 1986. *The Soong Dynasty*. New York: Harper & Row Publishers.

Sheridan, James E. 1966. *Chinese Warlord: The Career of Feng Yu-hsiang*. Stanford: Stanford University Press.

Sima, Guang. 1956. *Comprehensive Mirror for Assisting Government* (*zizhi tongjian*). Beijing: Zhonghua shujü.

Spence, Jonathan. 1981. *The Gate of Heavenly Peace: The Chinese and Their Revolution, 1895–1980*. New York: Penguin Books.

———. 1991. *The Search for Modern China*. New York: W.W. Norton & Company.

———. 2001. *Treason by the Book*. New York: Viking Press.

Shi, Minglei and Li, Xueyin. "An Investigation of Gifts on the Teachers' Day (*jiaoshijie songli diaocha*)." *Xinjingbao*, September 10, 2013.

Transparency International. "Corruption Perfections Index 2015." https://www.iaca.int/images/news/2016/Corruption_Perceptions_Index_2015_report.pdf.

Teachout, Zephyr. 2014. *Corruption in America: From Benjamin Franklin's Snuff Box to Citizens United*. Harvard: Harvard University Press.

Thiessen, Marc A. "Crony Capitalism Exposed." *The Washington Post*, November 14, 2011.

Teachout, Zephyr. 2014. *Corruption in America: From Benjamin Franklin's Snuff Box to Citizens United*. Harvard: Harvard University Press.

Tipton, Frank B. 2008. *Asian Firms: History, Institutions and Management*. London: Edward Elgar Publishing.

Twitchett, Denis. 1996. "How to Be an Emperor: T'ang T'ai-tsung's Vision of His Role" in *Asia Major* (3rd Series), Vol. 9, No. 1/2, pp. 1–10.

Veg, Sebastian. "China's Political Spectrum under Xi Jinping." *The Diplomat*, August 11, 2014.

Vogal, Ezra F. 1969. *Canton under Communism: Programs and Politics in a Provincial Capital, 1949–1968*. Harvard: Harvard University Press.

Wakeman, Frederic jr. 1985. *The Great Enterprise: The Manchu Reconstruction of Imperial Order in Seventeenth-Century China*. Berkeley: University of California Press.

———. 2003a. *Policing Shanghai: 1927–1937*. Stanford: Stanford University Press.

———. 2003b. Spymaster: *Dai Li and the Chinese Secret Service*. Stanford: Stanford University Press.

Wang, Tianyou and Xu, Daling. 1991. *Sixteen Emperors in the Ming Dynasty* (*mingchao shiliudi*). Beijing: Zijincheng chubanshe.

Wan, William. "China Broadcasts Confession of Chinese-American Blogger." *The Washington Post*, September 15, 2013.

Wang, Qishan. "Grasping and Utilizing the 'Four Patterns' in Supervising and Disciplining." *The Xinhua News Agency*, September 26, 2015.

Wong, Chun Han. "Chinese Court Issues Life Sentence to Former Presidential Aide for Corruption." *The Wall Street Journal*, July 4, 2016.

Wu, Han. 2001. *A Biography of Ming Taizu* (*Ming Taizuzhuan*). Tianjin: Baihua wenyi chubanshe.

Wu, Han. 2000. *Biography of Zhu Yuanzhang* (*Zhu Yuanzhangzhuan*). Zhejiang: Baihua wenyi chubanshe.

Xu, Beina. "Media Censorship in China." *Council on Foreign Relations*, April 7, 2015.

Yang, Fan. "The Latest Hearsay: Zeng Qinghong's Secret Detention Place Is Exposed (*Zuixin chuanwen: Zeng Qinghong mimi guanya didian baoguang*)." *Secret China*, July 13, 2014. http://m.secretchina.com/node/546794.

Yang, Jia Lynn, Hamburger, Tom and ElBoghdady, Dina. "Ways Investors Gain 'Political' Facing Public Scrutiny." *The Washington Post*, May 9, 2013.

Yang, Hegao. 1979. *Selected Works of Ancient Politics and Law (gudai zhengfa wenxuan).* Beijing: Beijing zhengfa xueyuan.

Yuen, Samson. "Disciplining the Party: Xi Jinping's Anticorruption Campaign and Its Limits." *China Perspectives* 2014/3 (2014).

Zhang, Jixin. 2016. *Things Seen and Heard about Bureaucracy in both the Daoguang and Xianfeng Reigns* (*daoxian huanhai jianwenlu*). Beijing: Zhonghua shujü.

Zeleny, Jeff and Thee-Brenan, Megan. "New Poll Finds a Deep Distrust of Government." *The New York Times*, October 25, 2011.

Zhang, Tingyu. 1974. *The History of the Ming* (*Mingshi*). Beijing: Zhonghua shujü.

Zhang, Yuxue. "Former Vice Head of the Logistic Department Gu Junshan Is Exposed to Be Involved in a Case of More Than 20 billion (*Yuanzonghouqingbu fubuzhang Gu Junshan beibao shean 200 duoyi*)." *Caijin net*, April 1, 2015.

Zhao, Erxun. 1982. *The Draft History of the Qing* (*qingshigao*). Beijing: Zhonghua shujü,

Zhang, Zhiguang. "Anticorruption in Chinese History (*Zhongguo lishishang defanfu*)." *Shanghai guancha*, May 29, 2014.

Zhang, Lun. "The Increasing Appearance of the Drawbacks in China's Movement-type Anticorruption (*Zhongguo yundongshi fanfu biduan riyi chengxian*)." *The French International Broadcast*, February 8, 2015.

Zheng, Yongnian. 2015. *China Entering the Xi Jinping Era*. London: Routledge.

Zhong, Chenfang. "People Unhappy to See the Remodeling of a Sydney Mansion by Zeng Qinghong's Son (*Zeng Qinghong zhizi Xini haozhai gaijian yincemu*)." *Voice of America*, June 19, 2014

Zhou, Yahui. "The Objective of Xi Jinping's Anticorruption is to Deal with Civilian Party (Xi Jinping fanfude mubiao shiduifu pingmindang)." August 15, 2014. www.boxun.com.

"*Zhu Yuanzhang chengtan bubiqin: weifanfu chusi qinzhizi yuqinnuxu*)." *Fenghuang lishi*, July 1, 2014. http://news.ifeng.com/a/20140701/40965124_0.shtml.

Zhu, Yuyang and Gui, Jie. "A Record of State Governing under Tang Taizong: Discussing How the Tang Dynasty Opposed Corruption (*Tang Taizong zhiguo fengyunlu: tantao tangchao ruhe fanfu*)." *The China Youth Daily*, August 22, 2014.

Part I

CENTRALIZED POWER AND AUTHORITARIANISM

Chapter 1

Fundamental Flaws

Corruption Reporting and Tackling in the Qing

Qiang Fang

CORRUPTION IN QING WRITINGS

If compared with the Ming dynasty (1368–1644), its immediate predecessor, the Qing dynasty (1644–1911), was arguably less corrupt and most emperors prior to the Opium War seemed to be more competent and diligent in terms of their internal governance and external policies.[1] Yet, corruption in the Qing remained and, in a handful of well-known cases, corruption was more serious than ever before (e.g., He Shen). Many popular novels and official accounts in the Qing had either explicitly or implicitly depicted a rather depraved and wicked picture of contemporary government and officialdom. As Nancy Park remarks, "Like popular proverbs, many Qing novels and short stories suggested that corruption was the norm and that virtuous officials were the exception rather than the rule in government."[2]

For example, in *Strange Stories from a Chinese Studio* (*liaozhai zhiyi*), a well-known collection of supernatural tales appeared in the mid-eighteenth century, Pu Songlin who had failed repeatedly to pass the provincial civil examination used numerous stories to satirize and expose the grave corruption inside the government/court and the civil examination. In one story entitled "Xi Fangping," Xi's father is said to have been killed by a rich local landlord. To satisfy his father's grievance, Xi tries to accuse the landlord in the underworld. But the landlord has already bribed most officials there and accordingly officials, including the underworld king, not only do not back Xi but also brutally torture him. It is not until the desperate Xi complains to the Erlangshen, an upright and powerful god who supervises the underworld, that the grievance of his father is finally redressed. Although it was safer for Pu to single out and expose the rampant underworld corruption in a period of stringent literary inquisition, the stories nonetheless hinted that collective bureaucratic corruption also occurred in the secular world.[3]

In the *Dream of Red Mansion*, one of the most renowned novels in the Qing, the author Cao Xueqin also reports unbridled corruption inside the government. In one case, Jia Yucun, a prefect who takes charge of a murder case involving a man from one of the most powerful families, pardons the murderer by "abusing law and practicing favoritism (*xunqing wangfa*)." Jia is subsequently rewarded and promoted to be the minister of military.[4] Similar accounts of Qing corruption also appear in contemporary novels such as *The Travels of Lao Can* (*laocan youji*) and *Exposure of the Official World* (*guanchang xianxingji*).[5]

The serious corruption claimed in Qing fictions could be testified in some more credible personal accounts of contemporary Qing officials as well as government documents. In 1711, after the famous writer Fang Bao was imprisoned in the late Kangxi reign (1661–1722), one of the best periods in the Qing, for his alleged involvement in a case of literary inquisition, he was able to disclose the firsthand exorbitant corruption and torture in the prison of the Board of Punishment. Rich or powerful prisoners could avoid death penalty and floggings by bribing the jailers, while poor prisoners were tortured and often died leaving behind many grievances.[6]

In the nineteenth century when the Qing dynasty was being battered by foreign invasions and domestic chaos, another official named Zhang Jixin, the Shanxi provincial grain intendant (*liangdao*), recorded massive corruption and torture among officials at the county and prefecture levels. According to Zhang, during birthday celebrations or other festivals, the grain intendant had to give 800 taels to the generals and 40 taels to the guards. Whenever there was an official visit, local officials including the grain intendant had to greet their guests with expensive banquets, rare fish, and gifts. In many legal cases, the magistrates would simply beat and even kill any alleged bandits without first verifying the charges.[7]

On March 1, 1897, Sun Yat-sen, the father of the Chinese republic, who was in exile, discussed the systematic corruption in Qing China. He mentioned one case in which a police head in Canton led his men and robbed a local cocoon factory. When the factory petitioned the city government for compensation, the military governor punished the petitioner instead of the police robbers. Sun argued that such crimes of police abuse of power rooted in corruption were not merely ingrained but also omnipresent in China. "Unless [Qing bureaucracy] undergoes a fundamental reform," Sun wrote, "regional and gradual reforms are hopeless." In addition, Sun lambasted the customary fees (*lougui*) of "door bag (*menbao*) or entrance fee," a traditional bribe extracted by guards, as one of the Qing corruptions. According to Sun, even the great victorious general Zuo Zongtang was denied a meeting with the emperor by the guards for failing to pay the "door bag."[8]

In its last years, Qing government documents admitted in 1901 and 1904 that the corruption at the local levels was so harmful that county runners and clerks were "like tigers and wolves in extorting money" and "preying" on commoners (*yurou baixing*). In 1902, an edict chastised an associate military director in the Shuntian prefecture for his "despicable corruption" and "wasteful living style." Another edict lamented that most county and prefect leaders could not "serve people wholeheartedly" and demanded to punish all "corrupt and cruel" officials and dismiss derelict officials who "cared nothing about people's plight."[9]

Scholarly Views on Qing Corruption

To what extent were the claims made in those Qing writings reflecting the real contemporary Qing official circle? And to what extent do scholars in China and the West agree or disagree on them?

Indeed, most studies inside and outside China intend to support the Qing writings and argue that corruption in the Qing and especially in the late Qing was serious and omnipresent. To cite a few examples, Richard J. Smith points out that there was "organized corruption within the Qing bureaucracy." One of the most notorious forms of corruption was "extraction of revenue in the form of 'gifts' from subordinates," which was being "encouraged by the central government fiscal system." Even honest officials were not exempt from taking gifts and one official received thirty percent of his stipends in the form of gifts.[10]

In his book entitled *The Manchu Way*, Mark C. Elliot states that during the late Kangxi reign the lifestyle of the elite banners in both the capital the local garrisons had become so lavish and extravagant that Emperor Yongzheng blamed them with "making eating and drinking the only important things" and "having forgotten frugality."[11] The late Frederic Wakeman Jr. is also highly critical of corrupt clerks in the early Qing period. He argues, "Everyone knows that this same lower bureaucracy was guilty of many of the worst crimes of the ancient regime. Scratch a clerk and you would find a felon."[12]

Shortly after Yongzheng enthroned in 1723, he greatly raised official salaries with the supplement of so-called honesty nourishment (*yanglianyin*) in hopes of curbing official corruption. However, the salary reform turned out to be disappointing as the additional salary remained "negligible compared to incomes from corruption." According to Shawn Ni and Pham Hoang Van, the most corrupt official in the Qing went unpunished because gift-taking, acceptance of bribes and extortion by government officials were so common and widespread that the Qing rulers chose not to take action.[13]

In the late Qing, bureaucratic corruption became more rampant and many officials took advantage of the weak central government for personal gains. Being the governor of Zhili and head of the Beiyang fleet, Viceroy Li Hongzhang was arguably the most powerful person in the late Qing. But in the words of Sterling Seagrave Li was also the "richest man in [Qing] China" who had almost "total control over the development and exploitation of North China's resources." Adding to his ability to amass wealth, Li used to keep a "chunk of stock in venture" in deals involving Chinese and foreign investment. Through lending state funds allocated to navy development to spendthrift but powerful Manchu princes such as Prince Chun, father of the emperor, and Prince Ching, Li was able to prevent them from interfering in his affairs.[14]

Chinese scholars are more likely to share the views of Qing novels and writings of Fang Bao, Zhang Jixin, and Sun Yat-sen that corruption was unrestrained and widespread in the Qing. Like Sun Yat-sen, for example, Li Chunmei criticizes the Qing customary fees. She argues that revenues from the customary fees such as door bag and holiday gifts constituted a big proportion of local official income. The governor of Henan received 200,000 taels a year from the customary fees.[15] Lai Huimin, a researcher at the Academia Sinica in Taiwan, argues that the Qing had the most corruption cases. In particular, she states that the banners were fond of lavish lifestyle and "considered it a shame for not being dressed as good as others."[16]

In her article titled "The Fundamental Cause of the Lost 1895 War Is Qing Corruption," Gao Hong attributed Qing's defeat in the First Sino-Japanese War to its corruption in three areas: politics, military, and system. Gao argued that the Qing spent lavishly on Empress Cixi's birthday, military officers took illegal means to steal public funds, gamble, and go whoring, and the central government was unable to control the army. "In fact, from the central court to local leaders, the Qing dynasty was completely dark in its last years," Gao writes.[17]

Other scholars study the corruption in more specific fields such as the banners, the civil service exam, and legal system. Ma Jun discusses the significant decadence of the eight banners in the late Qing prior to the Opium War. Like Lai Huimin, Ma notes that since Qing's conquest of China, the banners had indulged themselves in luxury life and lost their original warrior spirit. Long before the Opium War, smoking opium and gambling had become prevalent in Qing armies and many generals could not even ride horses. Without doubt, the corruption of the hereditary banners resulted in Qing's loss in the war.[18] In a paper on the tragic death of a poor student named Wang Kaitai during the Tongzhi reign (1862–1874), Chen Zhiping argues that it was the extortion of customary fees by local learning officials (*xueguan*) that forced Wang Kaitai to kill himself. This case unveils the corrupt civil examination in the late Qing.[19] Through his research of the four big cases in the late Qing, Hu Ming concludes that one of the causes of the false judgments is corruption inside the Qing bureaucracy that has not only triggered those grievances but also obstructed their correction.[20]

While most scholars, be they China-based or West-based, have a consensus about the embedded and comprehensive corruption in the Qing, particularly in the late Qing, a few historians have voiced different opinions and they argue that the extortion of fees by local runners and clerks, which had been denounced in many Qing writings and official documents, should not be deemed as corruption. For instance, Bradly Reed argues that the fee collection at the local level "constituted not a shadowy world of corruption, but rather an openly acknowledged feature of the Yamen court." The charges against runners' corruption were actually "a strategy, or resource, employed in the competition between elites and magistrates for local power and influence."[21]

In a well-researched article on the eighteenth-century Qing corruption, Nancy Park studies the harsh law against corruption and the loopholes in tackling corruption in the Qing. In line with Reed's argument on Qing corruption, Park also asserts that the rampant and abominable corruption at the local level as revealed in most Qing novels and writings, "although not wholly inaccurate, may have been overstated by commoners and local elites who resented the power that clerks and runners wielded."[22]

In this chapter, I am going to study sixty-one primary corruption cases all of which involved top Qing officials from the Shunzhi reign (1643–1661) till the very end of the dynasty, unlike other scholars who have either made general research on the Qing corruption or focused on specific graft within certain fields or levels. Although the sheer number of the sixty-one corruption cases may be only a fraction of the overall Qing corrupt cases, their concentration on numerous top-ranking officials could nonetheless be representative. All charged officials in these cases were such first- or second-ranking officials as ministers, governors, military governors, provincial administration commissioners (*buzhengshi*), or grain intendants, who, in other words, formed the backbone of the empire.[23]

A better and more nuanced understanding of the corruption of top officials especially the methods with which the Qing court adopted to tackle those corrupt officials will certainly help us address important questions such as: Why were there still so many corrupt officials despite rather severe punishment? Why were some officials executed for bribes of several thousands of taels and others pardoned for taking millions of taels? Why did some corruption cases entail hundreds of officials? Why did many corrupt officials have to await their successors to accuse them? And why did lower-ranking officials dare not accuse their superiors when they were extorted for money? I shall first classify the exposure and punishment of corrupt officials in the Qing into a number of categories. Then, I shall explore in detail the internal mechanism the Qing court used to deal with bureaucratic corruption and the effectiveness of each category. I would argue that, despite harsh punishment and multiple ways of exposing corruption, a combination of cronyism, official mutual protection, the inferiority of law, and the almighty power of the emperors make anticorruption a more daunting task if not an impossible mission.

Anticorruption Mechanism in the Qing

In the Qing dynasty, the law was very draconian toward official graft. Taking a bribe of a single tale could be punished by as many as seventy strokes of the heavy bamboo. If the bribe was more than eighty taels, the punishment would be strangulation (*jiao*). Officials who had stolen or embezzled 1,000 taels would be executed.[24] While the punishment against official corruption was relatively light in comparison with those in the reigns of Sui Wendi (581–604) and Ming Taizu (1368–1398),[25] the Qing was still highly ruthless on official corruption.

Aside from harsh laws, the Qing also inherited and developed about ten different avenues to report or accuse corrupt officials. Among the sixty-one cases of high-ranking official graft, five of them have been used more often than the others.

Reported by Censors

Created as rulers' eyes and ears, censors for a long time in the Chinese history had acted on behalf of the rulers to check and investigate local officials.[26] One of their missions was to expose corrupt officials to the rulers and bring them to the Board of Punishment. In one case, Gali, the military governor of Jiangxi in the Kangxi reign (1662–1722), was accused of taking graft and trying to murder his own mother. Since he was appointed as the Shanxi governor in 1699, Gali had been charged several times by censors with taking bribes over hundreds of thousands of taels and harming people. As soon as he heard about the charges, Gali would dispatch his followers to write to the Ministry of Revenue (*hubu*) and Emperor Kangxi to praise him as an upright official. Accordingly Kangxi shielded him every time. In 1709, Kangxi promoted Gali to be the military governor of Jiangxi. In 1714, however, Gali's mother accused his son to Kangxi of trying to murder her, a grave crime in Chinese filial piety and one of the ten abominations, and asked the emperor to execute Gali. After a joint interrogation and trial by central officials, Gali admitted his crimes of taking bribes and attempted murder of his mother. According to Qing law, Gali should be sliced for being "extremely disloyal and unfilial." Yet, once again, Kangxi reduced his punishment and simply demanded his suicide and confiscation of his properties.[27] As one of the most able rulers in the Qing, Kangxi in this case seemed to be too credulous to have been easily blinded and deceived by an evil and corruptible governor.

On March 13, 1741, censor Liu Wulong reported that Lu Zhuo, the Zhejiang governor, had accepted two bribes totaling at least 52,000 taels. In one instance, a Jiaxing prefect accepted 30,000 taels from a rich man who wanted the prefect to make favorable decision for him in a dispute of property inheritance. To also obtain the support from the provincial governor, the rich man whose surname was Wang asked the prefect to give the governor 50,000 taels. When the covert corruption was disclosed, governor Lu immediately exposed the corruption of the prefect to the central government so as to protect himself. The censor also charged that governor Lu had routinely taken graft from newly appointed officials in Zhejiang province and the amount was unknown. Emperor Qianlong praised the censor for his report and ordered him to ferret out tangible evidence about governor Lu's graft.

On June 16, upon receiving enough evidence about the corruption, Qianlong terminated Lu Zhuo's governorship and asked the military governor in Zhejiang to investigate the case and report back to him. In early August, Qianlong told the grand councilors, the most powerful officials in the Qing who had "extralegal" privileges and the utmost trust of the emperor,[28] that it was clear that governor Lu had taken large sums of bribes. In the case of Wang alone, he had acquired 50,000 taels, not to mention other grafts. The confiscation of governor Lu's house in Beijing had discovered over 10,000 gold taels. Qianlong then ordered two councilors to check governor Lu's residence in Zhejiang to prevent him from transferring his "private dirty graft (*sizang*)." When Governor Lu was not cooperative, the interrogators asked permission to use torture. In April 1742, the Board of Punishment reported that, according to the law for taking bribes, Governor Lu should be sentenced to deferred death of strangulation, a much less harsh punishment than the Qing law. Qianlong approved the board decision. One year later, the disgraced Lu paid back all his bribes to the government. Accordingly, the Board of Punishment mitigated his death sentence and sent him to the military for hard labor. In 1751, Qianlong was reminded of Lu's previous good work of building the seawall as Zhejiang governor and therefore he ordered to free Lu from hard labor. In 1755, impressed by Lu's good behavior, Qianlong appointed Lu as the governor of Shanxi.[29] The emperor's paramount power was conspicuously demonstrated in this case. The emperor could punish an official but he could also acquit him and promote him as he wished.

The censor in this case exerted his duty in charging Governor Lu with graft and Emperor Qianlong backed the charge. But in some other cases, the emperor would neglect censors' accusations. In 1882, censor Deng Qinglin reported to the court (Empress Cixi was the de facto ruler) that Cui Zunyi, the

Yunnan grain intendant, had committed twelve crimes such as taking bribes, violating law, and harming people. But the court simply did not respond. Ironically, in a county-level official evaluation, Cui won one of the top awards and was promoted to be the provincial administration commissioner, the second rank in the Qing bureaucracy. When the Yunnan governor asked the new commissioner Cui to send the regular provincial financial accounts to the central government for reimbursement, Cui was afraid that central officials might purposely cause trouble. He secretly tried to use over 107,000 taels to bribe dozens of officials in both Ministry of Revenue and Ministry of Works (*gongbu*). Cui took the rest of 23,000 taels for himself. Unfortunately, the Censorate received report about the collection corruption and censor Chen Qitai accused Cui of bribing central officials in reimbursement.

On July 23, the court asked imperial commissioners Linshu and Pan Zuyin to investigate the case and explore the truth. After detaining and interrogating several officials who had taken Cui's bribes, the court ordered to arrest Cui and his collaborators. Yet, Cui had died en route to Beijing. Thus the central government could not punish Cui but it still deprived Cui's official title posthumously and demanded his family to pay back his 23,000 taels kickback. Most officials involved in the case received punishment in accordance with the amount of their bribery. For example, the head of Yunnan department in the Ministry of Revenue took 7,000 taels and was to be sentenced to death by strangulation. But after he returned all the bribes, the court punished him with 100 strokes of bamboo sticks and banished him to 2,000 li. Although some clerks in the Ministry of Revenue had returned their bribes, the court insisted that they be beaten by 100 strokes and banished to 3,000 li because their threats of making trouble to Cui forced Cui into bribing them.[30]

In this case, the Qing court chose to ignore the first report of a censor of Cui's alleged evil activities as a grain intendant in Yunnan and even promoted him to be the administration commissioner. Without the exposure of Cui's bribing of so many central officials, the Qing court might not have discovered his serious crimes and misconducts.

Accused by Ruler/Central Government

In the Qing, many rulers would directly intervene by initiating either an overt or a covert investigation of an alleged corruption case or punishing a corrupt official. In some of these cases, rulers might have used corruption charges as a pretext to eliminate potential political enemies or challengers.

For instance, appointed as the Great General and Shanxi military governor, Niang Gengyao, a Han bannerman holding a top civil service degree, had accomplished major military campaigns in Tibet in the late Kangxi reign when he and Yinti, reportedly Kangxi's fourteenth and favorite son, suppressed the

Mongol rebellion in Tibet and expanded Qing territory by annexing a large territory in east Tibet (Amdo). After Yongzheng won a succession battle against his younger brother, Nian Gengyao continued his campaigns in the west to attack Mongol rebels. In 1723 and 1724, Yongzheng awarded Nian the titles of Great General and first-rank duke (*yidenggong*) respectively for his successful military service.[31] In April 1725, just one year after Nian's promotion to the first-rank duke, however, Yongzheng suddenly demoted Nian to be the general of Hangzhou, a much lower rank. In September, Nian was arrested under an imperial edict and three months later he was forced to kill himself and his property was confiscated. His father and brother lost their official posts and most of his sons over fifteen years were banished to the border regions. Number of people involved in the case was more than 100.

One of Yongzheng's charges against General Nian was his corruption. It was alleged that Nian had stolen funds and accepted bribes totaling 4 million taels, albeit the whole confiscated properties of Nian was "about one million taels." Another charge was Nian's ambition to plot a rebellion and to dethrone Yongzheng, an allegation that few would agree with. But Nian was said to be quite arrogant and unruly.[32] To justify his punishment of Nian Gengyao, Yongzheng claimed that he did this to safeguard the law: "To govern the state well, I have to bestow rewards and punishments fairly. If I ignore the law to pardon such rebels as Nian Gengyao, how will I be able to publicize the laws and win the hearts of the people"?[33]

As a matter of fact, Nian's fall and death mainly resulted from political reasons rather than his graft and the defense of law. Yongzheng had long suspected Nian's loyalty because of Nian's close tie to Yingti, his younger brother and key rival to the throne. One year after becoming the new ruler, Yongzheng began to criticize Nian for his "arrogance" and "monopolizing power." In 1724, Nian accused an official of graft and the Board of Punishment sentenced that official into deferred death with strangulation. But Yongzheng chose to meet the official who exposed Nian's alleged "crimes." Yongzheng then acquitted the official and even promoted him from second rank to first rank, an ominous sign for Nian. In the same year, Yongzheng secretly asked the military governor of Yunnan and Guizhou to accuse Nian. After the Board of Punishment suggested slicing for Nian's dozens of grave crimes and treason, Yongzheng noted that Nian was rebellious which was caused by his "frenzy and delirium." Due to his accomplishments in Tibet, Yongzheng ordered Nian to commit suicide instead of a death sentence with slicing.[34]

Unlike his father, Qianlong did not face any succession problem when he assumed the emperorship in 1735. As the longest-serving emperor in power in Chinese history, Qianglong's reign was the heyday of the Qing. While the latter part of Qianlong reign was troubled by uprisings and official grafts,

Qianlong in general was an able administrator. Through his acute observation and insight of his officials, Qianlong was able to uncover several major corruption cases.

In one case, when Qianlong in 1773 ordered Aertai, the military governor of Sichuan, to assume his new post in the capital and appointed Guilin to replace him, Aertai reported that Guilin had tried to camouflage his previous military failure. The central government quickly fired Guilin and banished him to Xinjiang. Meanwhile, Aertai found himself in hot water. Before he was prepared to leave Sichuan for Beijing, Aertai had made military suggestions to solve the dearth of ammunition in the front. Unfortunately, the suggestions inadvertently exposed Aertai's serious dereliction in military supply. Upon receiving Aertai's suggestions, Qianlong angrily questioned why he had not solved the problem long before. Some armies in the southwest had complained that they had been waiting for supply for a month. In addition to terminating Aertai's new appointment, Qianlong also ordered his arrest. While Aertai was in custody, some officials from Sichuan reported that Aertai had taken large sums of graft by buying nanmu, a rare, valuable tree that grew in southwest China and was in high demand by the central government. It was reported that Aertai had asked local magistrates and prefects to buy nanmu but refused to pay full price for it. Aertai took the rest of money at the amount of over 10,000 taels that he should have paid for nanmu. The grand councilors and the justice departments demanded that Aertai be beheaded. But Qianlong ordered Aertai to commit suicide.[35] While Peter C. Perdue called Qianlong a "desk general" because he disliked joining military campaigns,[36] Qianlong in this case seemed to have possessed a keen understanding of important military needs. With direct orders from Qianlong, the investigation and solution of the case went pretty smoothly.

Shortly after punishing Aertai, Qianlong discovered another much bigger and prevalent graft in which over 200 officials had been involved, easily making it one of the biggest grafts in Chinese history. The prime culprit Wang Tanwang was the administration commissioner in Gansu. In 1777, Wang was promoted to be Zhejiang governor. During his tenure as Gansu administration commissioner, Wang had garnered a total of more than 1 million taels of bribes. As the result of this case, three first-rank officials including Wang were executed, sixty-six officials got deferred death penalty, six officials were banished to the farthest border to do hard labor, more than fifty of them were assigned to defend the border, and the remaining fifty officials paid fines.

The credit of discovering this giant graft should be rendered to Qianlong. Like Sui Yangdi (604–618), Qianlong also loved his southern tour. During his tour to Zhejiang in 1780, local officials greeted him with large red lanterns and colorful silk signs wishing the emperor longevity. Qianlong clearly knew the cost was huge and he immediately scolded Governor Wang Tanwang for the wastefulness. But Wang blamed Yu Sheng, a lower-ranking official and tried to dodge the responsibility. In the next year, when grand secretariat Agui went to Zhejiang to inspect the seawall project, he found that Prefect Wang Sui had taken bribes in the name of welcoming Qianlong. After he reported the graft to Qianlong, the emperor told him that Governor Wang Tanwang certainly had encouraged and shielded the prefect. In about the same time, a couple of memorials from Gansu, where Wang Tangwang had formerly served as the administration commissioner for three years, finally forced Qianlong to kick off the investigation. The memorials said that the recent delay of the army in Gansu was caused by heavy rain, which was contrary to Wang's previous requests for aid due to Gansu's persistent drought. In May 1781, Qianlong appointed Agui as the imperial commissioner to lead the investigation who later reported that Governor Wang had obtained sizable bribes by selling university student titles in the imperial academy. According to Ping-ti Ho, the Qing limited the number of university students to less than 300, which was a stark contrast to the Ming when over 10,000 students enrolled in the imperial academy. University students in the Qing "were unable to enter government service without further purchase of Official titles."[37]

As a poverty- and disaster-ridden province, Gansu normally experienced different natural disasters. To have sufficient resources for the poor in a disastrous year, Wang Tanwang's predecessors had decided to sell titles of university student to whoever was willing to donate grain. But Wang changed the donation of grain to taels. Taking advantage of this new policy, many local officials used pretexts to extort money from the buyers. Families who wanted to purchase the title for their sons had no choice but to accept the charge. Because selling titles was lucrative, many local officials would bribe Wang for more titles. It was said that a bribe of 1,000 taels could only meet Wang and 2,000 taels could have a dinner with Wang. Wang also used his power to appoint officials in accordance with the amount of the bribes. Due to the large number of officials and sums of graft, the prosecutors, mostly grand secretariats and other central officials, found it difficult to apply the Qing law that any graft over eighty taels should be sentenced to strangulation. As a makeshift, the court made 20,000 taels as a threshold for death sentences. Otherwise, almost all the officials involved should be executed. Qianlong's edict denounced Wang and his collaborators as "despising law, looting public funds, and harming people."[38]

Without Qianlong's direct suspicion and meddling, the case of Wang Tanwang would have not been dug out. Local officials in Gansu had good reasons to protect each other so that they could continue to benefit from the selling of university student titles after Wang left Gansu for Zhejiang. They knew that the buyers of the titles who were relatively wealthy would not file complaints against the corruption to the central government. They, after all, harbored the dream that their sons could eventually become government officials with the title.

The biggest graft in Chinese history arguably occurred in the Qing and the corrupt official was Heshen, Qianlong's favorite servant and a grand councilor. In the case of Wang Tanwang, governor Wang only took 1 million taels. But when Heshen's home was confiscated, his total wealth and properties were astronomical – well above 100 million taels. According to Zhengyuan Fu, the annual revenue of the Qing in the late Qianlong reign was only about 70 million taels. Heshen's family wealth was about twice as much as the Qing's annual revenue.[39]

When Jiaqing took the throne in 1796 after his father Qianlong stepped down to show his filial piety to grandfather Kangxi, Jiaqing dared not touch Heshen who was then both the grand secretariat and the head of the Ministry of Revenue. Three years later, Qianlong died at the age of eighty-eight. Jiaqing was able to take action against Heshen. On January 8, 1799, just five days after Qianlong's death, several officials including one censor accused Heshen of abusing his power and violating law. Ostensibly, this accusation was motivated by Jiaqing in that the emperor promptly ordered to have Heshen arrested and sent to the Board of Punishment awaiting further investigation. Jiaqing also allowed soldiers to confiscate Heshen's properties. Shortly after Heshen was put into custody, Jiaqing publicly exposed Heshen's twenty crimes. Although Heshen's confiscated properties were bigger than the state income, most of his crimes seemed to emphasize his "rebellious and disloyal mind" and "greed and licentious behavior." Jiaqing also pointed out that many jewels, constructions, or pearls owned by Heshen were unseen even in the palace. In other words, Heshen failed to behave like a minister and his belongings exceeded that of the throne, a grave sedition in the Qing. On January 18, ten days after Heshen's arrest, Jiaqing ordered him to commit suicide, which was lighter than official suggestion that Heshen be publicly sliced for sedition.

To what degree was Heshen's punishment due to his corruption? In his comment on the memorial of Jiangxi governor, Jiaqing disclosed his actual intention in punishing Heshen: "If I do not eliminate Heshen, all people under heaven will only know Heshen and not me. I really have no choice [but penalizing Heshen]," Jiaqing wrote, "people will make their judgment on this case and there is no need for me to defend [my decision]." Even though Heshen was the biggest corrupt official in the Qing, if not in entire Chinese history, Jiaqing punished him for his seditious activities more than his corruption. If Heshen had continued to enjoy the same trust and favor from Jiaqing as from his father Qianlong, Heshen would have easily been pardoned. Like many other powerful officials in the history, Heshen's enviable power eventually led to his downfall.[40]

In the graft case of Heshen, who posed a potential challenge to the ruler, Jiaqing was able to act swiftly and proactively to detain and punish him. But in corruption cases of less or no challenge to his power, Jiaqing seemed to be numb and passive. In 1806 and 1807, due to numerous commoner petitions against provincial verdicts in Shandong and Henan, Jiaqing dispatched Guang Xing, vice minister of the Board of Punishment, to cope with cases in Shandong. Instead of fulfilling his duty as an imperial commissioner, Guang Xing demanded exquisite and luxurious food and lodging from local officials. During the two months of Guang's tour in Shandong, local officials had spent almost 50,000 taels on Guang and his entourage, most of the money came from the state revenue in the province.

In addition to his wasteful trips, Guang Xing also sought bribes from local officials in several major cases. In 1807, for example, there was a dispute of splitting family property among four rich brothers living in Jining, Sahndong province. One Li Lin sued his elder brother Li Han for monopolizing the family property. As the imperial commissioner, Guang Xing signaled to the Li brothers that he might be willing to solve the case with 70,000 to 80,000 taels of bribery. Having been sent to custody by Guang Xing, Li Han, the elder brother, immediately asked his servant to give 80,000 taels to Guang Xing. In the next day, Li Han was released. While in Shandong and later in Henan, Guang Xing not only spent lavishly but also accepted thousands of taels of bribery from local officials.

Despite Guang Xing's extravagant lifestyle and corruption, no official in the two provinces was bold enough to expose his misconducts. As a reward of his trips to Henan and Shandong, Guang Xing got a promotion and moved up to become the head of the Imperial Household Department (*neiwufu*) and take charge of the palace budget. Yet, in 1808, when Guang Xing attempted to cut the quota of silk and cloth to the ladies of the court (*gongnu*), Jiaqing dismissed him and opened an investigation of his other misconducts. Until then, Guang Xing's past corruption finally came to light. Yet Guang Xing still tried to deny some of his crimes. An infuriated Jiaqing in early 1809 ordered to have Guang Xing strangulated for "despising law (*miaofa*)" and "extorting [local officials] for tens of thousands of dirty taels." Guang Xing's son was banished to northeast border to do hard labor.[41]

Similar to what his father had done in the case of Wang Tanwang, Jiaqing was instrumental in investigating Guang Xing and bringing him to justice. Without Jiaqing's order of further investigation, no local or central officials who had known Guang Xing's malfeasance or had bribed him would have dared to accuse him. It seems that the whole anticorruption mechanism in the

Qing sometimes solely relied on the emperor's personal wisdom, judgment, and will.

Superiors Charging Subordinates

In Qing China, it was easier and safer for a higher-ranking official to report and punish the misconduct of his subordinates than the opposite. In May 1793, Chai Zhen was promoted from Zhejiang salt commissioner to Lianghuai salt commissioner, a third-ranking official post. But no sooner did Chai assume in his new post than he began to borrow money from salt traders to offset his loss in Zhejiang. Local salt traders then gave Chai a total of 170,000 taels, the annual tax they were supposed to pay the state. When Quan De, Chai's superior, heard about the borrowing, he quickly conducted a covert interrogation of officials involved in this case. After he found enough evidence, Quan De stripped off Chai's official title and imprisoned him. In the meantime, Quan De reported the case to the court. Qianlong ordered the military governor and the governor in the region to further investigate the corruption. Both officials were curious why Chai Zhen who had served as the salt commissioner in Zhejiang for just little more than a year had owed such large sums of money.

Under further pressure and interrogation, Chai admitted that it was Zhejiang governor Fu Song who had extorted him of the money. All the expenses of the governor's office, *inter alia*, building of temples, digging the West Lake, and other river projects would be paid first by the salt commissioner. But Fu Song refused to reimburse Chai of the money. Worse, Fu Song even asked Chai to pay his five trips to Beijing and other costs of his family and the provincial government. In addition, the governor asked Chai for precious gifts such as jade, antique, pearl, and gems totaling 58,000 taels. With no stamina to ask the governor to return his money let alone to report the governor's extortion to the court, Chai had to borrow money from salt traders. Accordingly, the investigators believed that Fu Song was the real culprit for the loss of so much state money. In compliance with the Qing law that any theft of 1,000 taels of state funds would be sentence to deferred decapitation, the imperial commissioners suggested in their report to Qianlong to sentence Fu Song to immediate execution. Qianlong responded that he was too old to conduct the interrogation of Fu Song and he deemed unworthy to be angry with such a demeaning (*xialiu*) governor. He ordered to have some officials inspect the execution of Fu Song in Zhejiang. Although Chai was forced to borrow money, Qianlong also ordered his beheading probably for his not reporting earlier.[42]

During the last year of the Kangxi reign (1722), Sichuan governor Cai Ting appointed Cheng Rusi to be the prefect of Bianzhou, a prefecture where salt was usually managed by traders. As soon as Cheng became the new prefect, he closed down the salt market and wanted to buy out all salt from private traders. Some traders did not follow the order and tried to smuggle salt out of the region. Cheng decided to block the waterway but it encountered fierce protest. When many traders attempted to pass the official blockade, the soldiers opened fire that killed some traders. After Shangan military governor Nian Gengyao was told about the tragic incident, he reported to the new emperor Yongzheng. Yongzheng acted swiftly by asking Nian to arrest Cheng. Before Nian came to capture him, Sichuan governor Cai Ting had already informed Cheng who sent his servants to portray himself as an upright official. Cai Ting also allegedly fabricated stories to praise Cheng in his memorial to Yongzheng. Cai accused Nian of framing "honest officials."

In 1724, Cai Ting was charged with forcing Chongqing prefect Jiang Xingren to kill himself. But Cai Ting lied to Yongzheng that Jiang's death was caused by a disease. Nian Gengyao told Yongzheng the truth. After Yongzheng interrogated Cai, the latter had to acknowledge his misbehavior. The Board of Punishment suggested that Cai be sentenced to a deferred strangulation. Fortunately, Cai Ting's accuser Nian Gengyao was catching Yongzheng's ire and worry for his arrogance and military successes. Instead of punishing Cai as Nian suggested, Yongzheng met Cai from the prison and let Cai have the chance to charge Nian and defend himself. Having had what he sought, Yongzheng not just acquitted Cai but also promoted him to be the head of the Censorate, which was first rank in the Qing.

After the downfall and death of Nian, Yongzheng appointed General Yue Zhongqi to take Nian's post as Shangan military governor. But Cai Ting, who was now the military governor of Zhili, secretly spread rumor to calumniate Yue. Because Yue won the trust of Yongzheng,[43] Yongzheng chastised Cai. In 1726, Yongzheng happened to read the report of Nian on the clash between Bianzhou prefect Cheng Rusi and salt traders in 1722 and Cheng's giving bribery to Cai. Yongzheng realized that he might have been duped by Cai in the case. He sent a clandestine order to Yue Zhongqi along with the Board of Punishment to investigate the case. When the report came, Yongzheng was astonished by the corruption. As a matter of fact, Bianzhou's annual tax should be around 60,000 taels and the tax of only eighty days was more than 20,000 taels, but prefect Cheng and his successor had lied to the throne that the tax was only 20,000 taels. The solid evidence forced Cheng to admit his corruption. While in his two year tenure as the prefect the total tax of Bianzhou was over 100,000 taels, Cheng had only sent the state 40,000 taels and the rest had been sent to Cai Ting as bribery. In July 1727, the Board of Punishment suggested that both Cai and Cheng be sentenced to immediate decapitation and their families also be punished. In September, Yongzheng approved most of the decision made by the board except that Cai Ting should be put to deferred strangulation rather than immediate beheading.[44]

In the Qing, officials in charge of civil examination used to have little chance to take bribe. In Yongzheng's words, he was glad that the government managing civil examination had not heard any graft since he took the power. But when Yongzheng read the corruption charges against Yu Hongtu, a civil examination official in Henan, he was very surprised and furious because Yu was the first one to be indicted in his reign. The charges showed that Yu had taken bribes in the provincial examinations. After receiving bribes, Yu would accept poor-quality exams. As a result, some well-known good students would have lower scores than ordinary students. But Yu amassed a total of more than 10,000 taels of bribery. In his edict demanding severe punishment of Yu (immediate beheading), Yongzheng wrote that he would no longer trust civil examination officials in the province. He also blamed provincial governors for shielding them. He ordered to punish governors whose provincial civil examination officials were caught for corruption.[45]

Yongzheng may have been disingenuous when he claimed that civil examination officials were largely honest. In some satirical stories of Pu Songlin who lived in the Kangxi reign, the civil examination in the Qing was also corrupt. In one story entitled "Yu Qu'e," Yu is a very diligent and excellent student, yet he has failed several civil examinations. Yu blames the corrupt civil examination officials for his failure and hopes that Duke Zhang Fei (a famous and upright general in the Three Kingdoms, 220–280 CE) would come and punish those officials. Yu finally wins the praise of Duke Zhang Fei who appoints Yu to be an official.[46] Pu Songling's story might have been a mirror of his own experience in the civil examination. Despite his outstanding writing skill and knowledge, Pu Songling, like Yu Qu'e, had repeatedly lost his attempts in civil examination. His dream that someone like Duke Zhang Fei would come and punish corrupt civil examination officials could only become true in his novels about ghosts and fox spirits in the underworld.[47] Additionally, the case of the corrupt civil examination official in the Yongzheng reign serves to demonstrate that, contrary to Park's argument, the official misconducts in popular novels could also reflect the real contemporary world.

Subordinates Charging Superiors

While it was easier and safer for superiors to accuse their subordinates of corruption, it was not uncommon for subordinates to charge their superiors with graft, albeit facing a much higher risk. On October 19, 1655, Zhang Mian, a clerk in the Ministry of Personnel, used knife to cut his hair and neck outside the Forbidden City. Zhang accused Gu Ren, the regional inspector of Shuntian prefecture, of taking bribes and persecuting innocent people. Zhang alleged that Gu Ren was trying to kill him. Emperor Shunzhi ordered the grand secretariat to detain Gu Ren who finally told the truth. After Gu Ren heard that Zhang Mian wanted for a promotion, he promised Zhang that he would help if Zhang could give him 200 taels. But Zhang rebuked the request. He believed that it was illegal to have a promotion by paying a bribe. In order to get the money, Gu had He Shenlie, an official in the Board of Punishment, pledged to promote Zhang if he would give the money. When Zhang again refused to pay, Gu retaliated by recriminating Zhang for bribing him for promotion and also tried to kill Zhang. Managing to escape, a desperate Zhang rushed to the palace to complain. With Shunzhi's approval, the central government sentenced both Gu Ren and He Shenlie to immediate decapitation.[48] Using self-mutilation in front of the imperial palace to draw attention is nothing new in Chinese history. In as early as the Tang dynasty (618–907), the court issued at least two edicts to ban self-mutilation close to the imperial palace. In the Ming and Qing dynasties, the law also severely punished anyone who shouted outside the palace or mutilated himself/herself.[49] Despite the price he had paid, Zhang Mian was still luckier than many other petitioners as his self-mutilation eventually led to the redress of his grievances. It might have been because he was working in the central government, and was thus treated differently from commoners.

In late February 1701, Shaanxi governor Wu Bingqian lodged a capital appeal to the Forbidden City against Wu He, the Shangan military governor, a higher-ranking official than the Shaanxi governor. In his appeal, Wu Bingqian accused his superior of embezzling military forage and falsely charging him with deducting military materials and money. Kangxi asked the judiciary to investigate the case. The judiciary reported that Governor Wu Bingqian had done nothing wrong and he was right that his superior Wu He had framed him with fabricated evidence. The judiciary told the emperor that Wu He should be deprived of his official power and punished with the embarrassing cangue. But Kangxi only approved the strip of Wu He's military governorship and not the cangue.[50]

In 1715, the vice general of the bordered white banner reported to the Censorate that Zhu Mala, the general and his superior, and Bage, the grand secretariat, had embezzled state funds. After an investigation, the Censorate told Kangxi that each of the officials had embezzled 300 taels. According to the law, they should be sentenced to deferred decapitation. Kangxi approved the punishment.[51] This case shows that Kangxi in his later years could still strictly enforce the law and punish high-ranking officials.

In the Qianlong reign, while Qianlong could, as aforementioned, discover some official corruption by himself and implement the law, he would try to protect others if those accused officials were close to him. In January 1781, Hai Ning, the grain commissioner in Yunan, boldly exposed the extortion of the Yungui military governor, the highest-ranking official in both Yunnan and Guizhou provinces. According to Hai, Li Shiyao, the military governor, had extorted lots of money from his subordinates. Upon hearing the report, Qianlong quickly sent three central ministers including Heshen as imperial commissioners to investigate the case. The imperial commissioners found that Li had taken bribery totaling 31,000 taels plus some precious jewels. In Qing law, that amount of graft was sufficient for a deferred decapitation. In May, officials from all the main central ministries concluded that the suggested punishment by the three imperial commissioners was too lenient for such a large amount of graft. They recommended an immediate beheading for Li Shiyao.

But Qianlong actually disliked both suggestions and only wanted to demote Li while still retaining him. In his comment on the case, Qianlong first blamed Li Shiyao for having letting him down. Yet, the emperor then hinted that Li "has worked hard" in dealing with Thailand and capturing thieves and robbers. Furthermore, Qianlong mentioned that Li's ancestor had helped the founding of the Qing. Instead of directly ordering officials to reduce the punishment, Qianlong asked all governors in the empire to submit their views on the two suggested punishments. Anhui governor Min He was intelligent enough to grasp the true intention of Qianlong. He told the emperor that Li Shiyao should not have a capital punishment. Qianlong praised governor Min He and ordered the Ministry of Personnel to conduct another investigation. The new punishment was a deferred decapitation. In 1782, Qianlong reappointed Li Shiyao to be the Shangan military governor, albeit his rank was not first but third. Three years later, when Li was sentenced to immediate decapitation for hindering military operation (*yiwu junji*), Qianlong once again pardoned him and reduced the punishment to deferred death sentence.[52]

Peer Reporting and Accusation

Using peer reporting and accusations was another method to curb official corruption. For example, in 1654, Grand Secretariat Ning Wan,[53] a Manchu grand secretariat, charged his Han colleague, Grand Secretariat Chen Mingxia with hogging property and taking graft. In his reports, the first alleged "crime" of Chen was his resistance to a Manchu-style haircut, which demonstrated Chen's rebellious attitude toward the ruling Manchu regime. Chen's second "crime" was hogging the highly expensive Jiangning Garden (worth over 100,000 taels), an unclaimed property that should have belonged to the government. Moreover, Chen had reportedly tried to protect his relative named Shi Rugang, a former local official who had confiscated a student's property and forced him to commit suicide. After Shi Rugang agreed to transfer his fine property to Chen, the grand secretariat promised Shi to reinstate his official post. Central ministries such as the Ministry of Personnel confirmed that Ning Wan's accusations were all correct. They suggested that Chen Mingxia should be decapitated and his wife be banished to the northern border. Emperor Shunzhi decreed to have Chen strangulated due to his long-time service to the ruler.[54]

In another case that took place in Shanxi province in May 1759, Puxi, a civil commissioner (*tongzhi*) in charge of the civil examination, reported that his colleague Hushitu and a lieutenant general Baode had embezzled 18,000 taels of public funds to cover the loss of budget. Qianlong appointed Liu Tongxun as the imperial commissioner and sent him to Shanxi to investigate the charge. Liu discovered that not only had Baode taken a bribe of 1,500 taels in a case of chopping state-owned lumber, but the accuser Puxi was himself a corrupt official who had allegedly accepted a bribery of over 10,000 taels. Liu suggested that both Baode and Hushitu be beheaded and Puxi be strangulated. Upon receiving Liu Tongxun's report, Qianlong was so infuriated that he immediately ordered the execution of Baode with the on-site inspection of an imperial commissioner. Qianlong also scolded Liu for his harsher punishment on Hushitu whose crime was only trying to cover the budget loss with state funds than Puxi who had taken over 10,000 taels of dirty money. Although initially hesitant, Qianlong finally sided with the imperial commissioner by sentencing Hushitu and Puxi to decapitation.[55]

Here, Qianlong depended on his trusted officials as his "ears and eyes" in investigation of a charge and, while he at first disagreed with their recommended punishment, he chose to support them eventually.

Charging Predecessors

Another less usual method to dig out corruption was newly appointed officials accusing their predecessors. In one case, shortly after E Leshun, the son of a powerful minister in three reigns and the governor of Zhejiang for three years, was appointed as the governor of Shandong in November 1755, the new Zhejiang governor named Fu Lehun reported to Qianlong that E Leshun had extorted 6,000 taels from Zhejang merchants when he was the governor. According to Qing law, an illicit amount of 6,000 taels taken by an official was sufficient for a capital punishment. While the investigation report of the imperial commissioners argued that governor Fu Lehun might have falsely charged E Leshun, Qianlong insisted that E Leshun's crime was indisputable and should not be pardoned simply because he was also a grand secretariat and the son of a duke. Qianlong then ordered E Leshun to commit suicide.[56]

In the Qing, it was rather common for local officials to extort money from salt merchants. As Li Chunmei has remarked, all levels of local officials tried to levy different kinds of taxes to fill their own pockets.[57] In this case,

E Leshun did what many local officials had done. Qianlong could defend the law by showing no mercy to a governor and a son of an important duke.

In July 1757, Qianlong appointed Jiang Zhou, the Shanxi governor, to be the Shandong governor. The new Shanxi governor, Ta Yongning, immediately accused Jiang Zhou of corruption and greed and of siphoning off the provincial coffer during his tenure as governor. Qianlong ordered the cabinet and the Ministry of Personnel to investigate the charge. In October, the court stripped Jiang Zhou's official title and the imperial commissioner arrested officials related to the case. For all the charges by Governor Ta Yongning and the imperial commissioner, Jiang Zhou could do nothing but admit his corruption and embezzlement of state funds totaling thousands of taels. The central investigators also accused Yang Longwen, the provincial inspector (*jiansi*) of being obsequious to and colluding with Jiang Zhou. With the approval of Qianlong, the investigators sentenced both Jiang and Yang to immediate decapitation.[58]

Other Corruption Reporting Channels

Aside from the above six methods of anticorruption in the Qing, there are some other ways that were used less frequently or the accusers were unclear. For example, as a long-lasting but consistent means to check local official misconducts, people's complaints remained popular in the Qing, though many, if not most, of them would go unnoticed or unresponded by the central government. In one case during the late Kangxi reign, General Lanli in Fujian was allegedly evil and dictatorial and had levied very heavy taxes on merchants and peddlers. In protest against the intolerable taxes, many people petitioned the provincial and central governments. Fortunately, the sea of protests forced the provincial leaders to expose Lanli's crimes to the throne and demanded his dismissal and arrest. Kangxi acted swiftly and ordered the arrest and sent Lanli to Fujian for further investigation. Investigators found that Lanli had taken bribes as much as tens of thousands of taels and his predatory policies had hurt numerous people. But due to Lanli's audacious fight in the conquest of Taiwan in 1683, Kangxi saved the life of Lanli and asked his tribe in Beijing to supervise him.[59] In this case, Kangxi reneged his own emphasis on the importance of law in managing a state.[60]

In March 1756, Huanwen and Guo Yiyu, Shanxi's military governor and governor respectively, planned to make a gold stove as a tribute to the emperor. They told local officials to sell gold to them but only agreed to pay the gold with two-thirds of the market value. Dissatisfied and unwilling to lose money themselves, local officials forcibly used the same ratio to buy gold from local merchants and commoners. Outraged, local merchants and commoners submitted joint petitions to provincial, regional, and central governments. Governor Guo Yiyu was scared by people's uproar, he immediately drafted a memorial charging military governor Huanwen with the money change. The imperial commissioner discovered that Guo Yiyu actually had collaborated with Huanwen and that Huanwen had extorted thousands of taels from his subordinates since he took the military governorship three years ago. To rectify the bureaucracy and defend the state law, Qianlong ordered Huanwen to commit suicide and pardoned his old mother. For Governor Guo Yiyu, Qianlong found his behavior despicable because of his secret report against his collaborator Huanwen. Yet he chose only to dismiss Guo and send him to the military fort to serve rather than to kill him.[61] This might be because Qianlong did not want to discourage future official exposition of corruption or sedition.

In these two cases, it seems that commoners' petitions worked well in pressuring the provincial and central governments to take quick action against the corrupt officials. But we should note that the petitions made in the two cases were collective involving many local people. If the petitions to the capital were lodged individually, the result could have been much less sanguine and effective. Indeed, in most periods of the Qing as in other post-Tang dynasties, the law was rather harsh toward capital complaints regardless of the truth or falsity of their complaints.[62] After 1899, although single capital complainants were no longer punished except for blocking royal carriage (*lanyujia*), almost no charged officials were punished. To cite one case, in 1904, Zhu Zhaolian, a county student (*tongsheng*), from Shangcheng county, Henan province, presented a charge at the capital against one Zhu Changrui for stealing his property. According to the student, thanks to the former magistrate Jiang, he had retrieved his land, but a new magistrate Zheng, who was corrupt, had been persuaded by Zhu Changrui that he (the student) was a "bandit" and had sent runners to his home to confiscate his property and arrest five members of his family. The student had appealed to the prefect to rein in the magistrate, but the magistrate delayed any review of the case. The student had then appealed to the governor. Meanwhile, Zhu Changrui, emboldened by the magistrate's support, attacked and wounded two of the student's brothers. The student, feeling his family was in danger, "begged his way over 2,000 li [over 600 miles]" to the capital where he charged the magistrate with "neglecting state law (*daxian*)."

The Board of Punishment instructed the governor of Henan to review the case. After a detailed investigation, the governor reported that the "student's land" had actually been earmarked by his mother as the "family's burial land (*jitian*)." When the mother died in January 1901, Zhu Changrui and his brothers, who were relatives of the student, sold the burial land for 540,000 taels to pay for her burial. The student's father opposed the sale of the family property and complained about Zhu Changrui to the magistrate. Another relative, who was also unhappy with Zhu Changrui's sale of the burial land, flooded his land to prevent him from planting. It was at that point that Zhu Changrui accused the student and his uncle of colluding with local bandits to bring harm to his property. The magistrate sent armed men to put down the "uprising." According to the Board's inquiry, when the magistrate was investigating the case, someone else took the occasion to steal some of the student's property. When the student charged Zhu Changrui with the theft and the magistrate rejected the charge, the student had a complaint written out and taken to the Censorate in Beijing.

The governor concluded that the student had no connection to bandits and that his charges against the magistrate were partially correct. His principal crime, therefore, was mounting a skipping-level appeal on the basis of some false information and without waiting for the decision of the governor. The governor recommended that the complainant be acquitted and allowed to return home without penalty due to a new legal reform in the late Qing.[63] In this case, the governor's report blamed the student for his quasi-false complaint and nothing about the magistrate. It was partially because the student acted alone and not collectively, which had little pressure on the central government and the governor.

Mutual accusations among corrupt officials were not rare in Qing China. In 1712, the wife of former Xining prefect Yao Honglie and the wife of Qingyang prefect Chen Hongdao went to the capital to charge each other with corruption. Because the mutual charge involved higher-ranking officials such as Gansu administration commissioner Wu Shi and Chuanshan military governor Yin Tai, it caught the attention of Kangxi who ordered the Censorate and the Ministry of Revenue to look into the case. Through talking with local farmers, the imperial commissioners obtained hard evidence that Wu Shi had augmented farmers' tax and kept it in their own pocket. Yin Tai, the military governor, was criticized of dereliction for failing to stop the tax increase and graft. Because Wu Shi was a Manchu banner who could enjoy some legal privileges,[64] the court removed Wu's post and punished him with cangue but allowed him to redeem himself with money.[65]

In some cases, corrupt officials were dug out simply by chance. For instance, Long Keduo was a bannerman in the bordered yellow banner, first-ranking official, and brother-in-law of Kangxi. In 1727, one of Long's house servants was accused of trying to capitalize on his master's power to extract bribes from officials. When the investigation proceeded further, the graft of Long Keduo was also exposed. The investigators charged him with forty-one crimes including, among other crimes, five sedition crimes, four deceit crimes, seven law violations and the like. Despite all his grave crimes, Long was largely pardoned because he was a royal relative and trusted by Kangxi. Yongzheng noted in his decree of the case,

> While Long Keduo should be executed for his forty-one serious crimes, my father [Kangxi] had called and talked to my brothers and Long Keduo before he asked me to be the new emperor. . . . Today, if I kill Long for his crimes, it would conform to the law but my heart will feel sad.

The court finally only executed Long's servant and removed his post as the head of the Ministry of Revenue. Yongzheng assigned Long to conduct survey and discuss the Sino-Russian border.[66] No one knows whether Yongzheng told the truth that his father actually had made him the heir. Not being "the obvious favorite" of Kangxi, Yongzheng's ascending to the throne has long been clouded by conspiracy and usurpation and thus he had ruthlessly eliminated anyone including many of his brothers who might be a threat.[67] But Yongzheng in this case showed his leniency toward Long Keduo, both for Long's royal connection and the legitimacy of his own throne.

There were many graft cases that did not have any accusers or the identity of the accuser was vague or missing. In one case that occurred in 1757, the so-called Midday of the Qianlong reign as well as the Qing,[68] Yang Hao, the administration commissioner of Hunan, was charged with taking more than 3,000 taels by manipulating state grain prices. The official document did not say who had lodged the charge and it only noted that the Board of Punishment had conducted the investigation and proposed a deferred capital punishment. Upon receiving the report and the proposed punishment from the board, Qianlong was enraged at the light punishment with a fear that the punishment was not harsh enough to deter future official embezzlement of state funds. He ordered an immediate arrest and severe punishment of the investigator. As a result, Yang Hao was sentenced to immediate execution and his investigator who was condemned as "seeking personal gains and fame (*yingsi guyu*)" was sent to work in the military fortification.[69] As the emperor and a far-sighted state leader, Qianlong was right in this case to toughen his mercilessness to official theft of state money.

Fundamental Flaws

As I have argued in the chapter, the Qing took official misconducts and corruption very seriously and accordingly developed highly comprehensive and rigorous mechanism to expose, deter, and punish corruption. A top official could be strangulated for taking mere 80 taels and 1,000 taels of bribery would suffice to have the official beheaded. Although in many cases, the emperor treated the culprits more leniently by ordering them to commit suicides, the loss of life was indeed very harsh and ruthless. In addition to its stringent and cruel laws, the Qing also directly or indirectly created around ten anticorruption methods to report corruption.

Table 1.1

Corruption Reporter(s)	*Shunzhi*	*Kangxi*	*Yongzheng*	*Qianlong*	*Jiaqing*	*Daoguang*	*Xianfeng*	*Tongzhi*	*Guangxu*	*Total No.*
1. Upper-Level Officials		1	1	4				1	3	10
2. Censors	1	2		3					2	8
3. Emperor		1	1	3	2					7
4. Reporting against Predecessors				5					1	6
5. Lower-Level Officials	1	2		3						6
6. Peer Officials	2	1		2					1	6
7. Official/Commoners	1	1		1						3
8. Mutual Exposition		1		1						2
9. Other Reporters		1	2	1						4
10. Unknown		3	1	1	3	1				9
Total No.	4	13	5	24	5	1		1	7	61

To better understand the internal operation and effectiveness of the Qing anticorruption mechanism, I have divided the sixty-one top-official corruption cases into roughly ten categories in terms of their reporters or accusers of corruption from Shunzhi to Guangxu. This chart helps mirror the complete operation of the Qing anticorruption apparatus and I am going to examine the methods more useful or more often used in the Qing anticorruption mechanism.

According to the chart, the number of corruption cases exposed by superior officials is ten, the biggest among the sixty primary corruption cases. Official graft reported by censors is the second biggest. Cases discovered by Qing emperors and peer officials are the same, each has seven cases. Corruption exposed by subordinates is six, which was much fewer than cases reported by superiors. This is easy to comprehend as it would be less risky for an upper-level official to expose the corruption of his subordinates because the ruler normally trusted upper-level officials more than lower-level officials and upper-level officials tended to have more power or means to find out the misconduct of his subordinates. To be sure, there are some exceptions to this general rule. In the case of Nian Gengyao, whose alleged arrogance and close connection with Kangxi's fourteenth son, Yongzheng's most formidable challenger to the throne, had led to his speedy downfall and disgrace. When Nian reported the corruption of Cai Ting, the Sichuan governor and his subordinate, Yongzheng, not only pardoned Cai but also encouraged him to countercharge Nian. Having got what he sought, Yongzheng promoted Cai to the first rank and used his mostly false testimonial against Nian and ordered his suicide.[70]

As rulers' spies, central censors represented the throne in the provinces to inspect and expose any official malfeasance. In the case of Zhejiang governor Lu Zhuo, it was a censor's report that had brought him down.[71] In 1687, censor Chen Zizhi accused Hubei governor Zhang Gan of taking bribes of more than 90,000 taels, which prompted Kangxi to remove Zhang's governor post and appointed several imperial commissioners including a head of the Censorate to detain Zhang and interrogate him. The investigation ended up with substantial evidence of most corruption charges against governor Zhang. In addition to sentencing Zhang into deferred strangulation, Kangxi also dismissed several central officials who had recommended Zhang in the past.[72]

However, the significance of censorship in checking bureaucratic corruption is not without its limitations. The origin of censors' power came from the throne and it was up to the emperor to deny or accept their reports. If the emperor ignored their report for personal reasons, there was nothing that the censors could do. In some cases, censors even became accomplices to corrupt officials. In the case of Sichuan military governor Gali, Kangxi had neglected a censor's accusation and continued to shield Gali until Gali's mother charged her son with attempted murder. In 1880 when the Qing was facing threats from both inside and outside, the young emperor Guangxu and the regent empress Dowager Cixi paid no attention to a censor's report against the serious corruption of one Cui Zunyi, the Yunnan grain intendant. Ironically, Cui in the meantime won the highest appreciation in the annual evaluation of medium-level officials and therefore was promoted to the provincial administration commissioner. It was not until 1882 when Cui tried to bribe officials in ministries of revenue and works that his crimes had finally become public.[73] Had the ruler investigated Cui upon hearing the first censor's charge, Cui would have been punished in 1880 and would not have committed another graft crime later.

Peer reporting was not uncommon in the Qing. There were about six peer accusations in the sixty-one cases. Officials at the same rank were inclined to compete with their peers for promotion or the favor of their superiors and the ruler, especially after Yongzheng gave officials a green light for secret memorials in order to strengthen the power of the throne.[74] Once an official found out any wrongdoing of his peer or competitor, he was very likely to report unless he and the peer were in fact collaborators. In particular, the case of Chen Mingxia reflected the competition, contempt, or distrust between a Manchu grand secretariat and his ethnic Han colleague. One of the allegations against Chen was merely his desire to hairstyle to retain the ethnic haircut of Han Chinese to preserve peace between the conquering minority (Manchu) and the conquered majority (Han). Additionally, Chen's occupation of a Han Chinese's garden could be a gift and should not be regarded as malpractice.[75] This accusation could not be made at a worse time as the regent Oboi had been trying to strengthen the Manchu identity and dominance since the Ming conquest, a stark contrast to Hongtaiji's earlier and more conciliatory policies toward the Han majority. Partly due to their hatred toward Han officials or Manchu superiority, the mostly Manchu investigators and decision makers sentenced grand secretariat Chen to strangulation.[76]

The stakes were high for lower-ranking officials to expose the corruption of their superiors. It was because their superiors had more networks in the court and more resources to retaliate. In the case of Gu Ren, Zhang Mian, the desperate clerk of the Ministry of Personnel, had to mutilate himself in front of the Forbidden City to charge his superior. In 1701, Wu Bingqian lodged a capital appeal against the Shangan military governor for false charge and deliberate persecution. Although Governor Wu had a much higher post and power than the small clerk Zhang Mian, he still had to face grave threat and reprisal from the accused superior. Indeed, if governor Wu had not faced a life threat, he would very much likely have tried to avoid a direct confrontation with his superior, much less filing a capital appeal.[77] Like thousands of other desperate capital complainants with strong belief in natural resistance, both Zhang Mian and Wu Bingqian hoped that the emperor and the son of heaven would be their last hope and savior.[78]

Unsurprisingly, the most effective anticorruption method in the Qing was the direct intervention of the throne. Without Qianlong's acute intuition and insight in the cases of Zhejiang governor Wang Tanwang and Jiangxi governor Hao Shuo, both corrupt officials would have never been dug out. In the case of Wang Tanwang, for instance, more than 200 local officials had been entailed through intertwined and lucrative interests. No official, from provincial leaders to magistrates, wanted to expose the massive corruption to the central government. Owing to the tremendous amount of graft and large number of official involvement, Qianlong felt compelled to raise the minimum graft for immediate decapitation from 1,000 taels to 20,000 taels, otherwise, dozens of high-ranking local officials would be executed. In the case of Hao Shuo, the Jiangxi governor had capitalized his power in the province to extort tens of thousands of taels from local officials and no one dared to accuse him. If Hao Shuo had not caused suspicion of Qianlong, the governor could have easily retained his governorship and continued to take money from his subordinates most of whom were either afraid of his power or seeking his favor. To local officials, central officials, especially those imperial commissioners appointed by the ruler, were more intimidating. As shown in the case of Guang Xing, no matter how insatiable and demanding the imperial commissioner had been during his trips to Shandong, no local official was courageous enough to accuse him. All they could do was to satisfy his extravagant requests and to please him. Because there was no report against Guang Xing, Emperor Jiaqing continued to trust Guang Xing until the emperor himself discovered the misconduct of Guang Xing.[79]

The relative effectiveness of Qing rulers' direct action in exposing and punishing corrupt officials, however, reveals a fundamental flaw in the whole Qing anticorruption system. Despite the extremely harsh laws against bureaucratic corruption, despite a total of about ten methods designed to report and check official graft, and despite some Qing rulers' direct and forceful meddling in anticorruption, corruption in the Qing was anything but an effectively restrained practice among officials. Given a top-down bureaucratic system with the emperor on the top, virtually omnipotent and above the law,[80] all government officials were appointed by their superiors or the ruler and lower-ranking officials were subject to the leadership and supervision of their superiors. If a higher-ranking official (e.g., provincial governor or military governor) extracted money or demanded bribery from his subordinates, few subordinates would risk their life or career to accuse his superior at the court unless they have encountered lethal threats. In the sixty-one corruption cases, many more of the corruption reports had been made by peer officials or by high-ranking officials and only a fraction of them came from lower-ranking officials. As shown in the case of Hao Shuo, the local officials refrained from reporting after governor Hao had extorted them for money. The corruption of the governor would very likely have remained to be covert if Qianlong had not found out himself. Moreover, local officials tended to protect each other if they could jointly benefit from the corruption. In so doing, the corruption became systematic and ingrained in the Qing. If central agents such as the censors or imperial commissioner failed to conduct serious and meticulous research, it was rather difficult for them to uncover graft at the local level.

Even though the Qing ruler could weigh enormous impact on a case, an emperor could be unpredictable in dealing with individual corruptions. As I have shown, rulers such as Qianlong in some cases were able to discover a corrupt official themselves and act quickly to bring them to justice. But in other cases, especially if the corrupt official had made extraordinary military accomplishment in the past or was still enjoying the emperor's trust and favor, being the son of an important former minister, or belonging to the royal families, the Qing rulers would often put law behind and choose to grant special pardon to those officials no matter how corrupt they had been. In the case of Heshen, Qianlong's favorite official and grand councilor, Heshen was by far the most corrupt official in Qing history, but so long as he enjoyed the trust and favor of the emperor, the emperor would keep his eyes closed to him. In one case, Qianlong sent Heshen to investigate an official graft, which was almost minimal in comparison with that of Heshen. After Jiaqing arrested Heshen and forced him to commit suicide, Heshen's astronomical corruption was not even his principal crime. Heshen's biggest crime was nothing but his challenge and potential threat to Emperor Jiaqing. Accordingly, to Jiaqing and pretty much to Qianlong as well, corruption, no matter how big it was, was less important than a threat to his very imperial power.[81]

Conclusion

Unlike conventional scholarship that studies different aspects of the corruption in the Qing, this chapter sought to focus on sixty-one primary cases of anticorruption in the Qing. Officials in these cases were either first rank or second rank who should have been the pillar of the dynasty. While the total number of the cases per se may not include all grafts of top officials, we could still draw a rough picture of the anticorruption methods and solution through the sixty-one cases. Among them, we have seen most of the anticorruption report coming from upper-level governments such as superiors in the province or region, censors in the capital, and the emperor or at least from peer-level officials (thirty-one out of fifty-one known reporters or 60 percent). If we treat those reports against predecessors as peer accusations, the total number will be thirty-seven or more than 72 percent. This percentage is phenomenal as it proves that a corrupt official in the Qing was less likely to be accused by his subordinates. The reason is that the Qing, like periods before and after it (including the PRC), was a top-down political system in which almost all officials obtained their post and power from their superiors or the ruler. As Beatrice S. Bartlett aptly writes,

> [In the Qing] provincial officials below the highest ranks tended to be overshadowed by their superiors and were rarely able to use the palace memorial system to circumvent those in charge of their work and recommendations of their own promotions.[82]

To secure their post and power, they had to please and obey their superiors. In return to the submission of their subordinates, upper-level officials would try to protect them. In that regard, lower-level officials would tolerate whatever their superiors had done to them including extortion of money and bribes unless their lives were being threatened. In some cases, both upper- and lower-level officials collaborated in mutually beneficial business (e.g., selling quota of university students in the Wang Tanwang case). This intertwined connection among different levels of officials laid the basis of systematic corruption in the Qing, which created an almost insurmountable barrier for aggrieved individual commoners or lower-ranking officials to redress their grievances at the local level.

The emperor and central inspectors would be the only and last hope for a clean bureaucracy and grievance satisfaction. Yet, even capable emperors such as Kangxi and Qianlong could be mercurial as they had sharp intuition in some cases to ferret out corrupt officials, while in other cases they would suddenly become blinded to grafts committed by their favored and trusted officials or relatives. Because emperors in the Qing, as in most other periods, were quasi-divine (son of heaven with a mandate) and mostly above the law, no one could or dared to alter an emperor's decision to pardon a corrupt official. Without a legal supremacy and a relatively effective and functional constitutional check of power, a mixture of systematic bureaucratic corruption and inconsistent rulers was the fundamental flaw in the Qing that would hopelessly thwart whatever well-designed anticorruption efforts and mechanism.

NOTES

1. Qiang Fang, 2013; and *A Short History of Chinese Petition* (*zhongguo shangfang zhidu shihua*) (Beijing: China Youth Press, 2013), chapter 7.
2. Nancy E. Park, "Corruption in Eighteenth-century China" in *The Journal of Asian Studies*, Vol. 56, No. 4, November 1997, 967–1005: 992.

3. "Xi Fangping" in Pu Songling, *Strange Stories from a Chinese Studio*, http://duguoxue.cn/yuedu/lzzybhw/.

4. Nie Da, "Corruption behind the Frivolity: The Relationship between Governmental and Cultural Corruption in the Dream of Red Mansion (*fuhua beihoude fubai: cong Hongloumeng kan guanchang fubai yuminfeng fubai deguanxi*)" in *Zhongguo jijian jianchabao*, November 14, 2014.

5. Both novels have exposed grave corruption among Qing officials. For details see Liu E, *The Travels of Lao Can* (laocan youji) (Zhejiang: Zhejiang wenyi chubanshe, 2017); Li Boyuan, *Exposure of the Official World* (guanchang xianxingji) (Zhejiang: Zhejiang chuabn jituan, 2013).

6. As Nancy Park has argued, even though the judiciary was rigged in favor of the wealthy, both officials and the public in the Ming and Qing dynasties had a consensus that torture was "an indispensible tool of justice." See Nancy Park "Unofficial Perspectives on Torture in Ming and Qing China" in *Late Imperial China*, Vol. 37, No. 1, 2016: 17–54: 42–3; for Fang Bao see Yang Hegao, *Selected Works of Ancient Politics and Law (gudai zhengfa wenxuan)* (Beijing: Beijing zhengfa xueyuan, 1979), 2: 325–28.

7. Zhang Jixin, *Things Seen and Heard about Bureaucracy in both the Daoguang and Xianfeng Reigns* (*daoxian huanhai jianwenlu*) (Beijing: Zhonghua shuju, 2016), 79, 96–104.

8. Sun Yat-sen, "China's Presence and Future (zhongguo dexianzai heweilai)" in *The Complete Works of Sun Yat-sen* (*Sun Zhongshan quanji*) (Beijing: Zhonghua shuju, 1981), 1: 95–97.

9. *Documents of the Guangxü Reign* (*Guangxüchao donghualu*) (Beijing: Zhonghua shujü, 1984), 4742, 5113, 5193.

10. Richard J. Smith, *The Qing Dynasty and Traditional Chinese Culture* (Lanham, MD: Rowman & Littlefield, 2015), 121.

11. Mark C. Elliot, *The Manchu Way: The Eight Banners and Ethnic Identity in Late Imperial China* (Stanford, CA: Stanford University Press, 2001), 286–87.

12. Frederic Wakeman, Jr. *The Great Enterprise: The Manchu Reconstruction of Imperial Order in Seventeenth-Century China* (Berkeley: University of California Press, 1985), 447.

13. Shawn Ni and Pham Hoang Van, "High Corruption Income in Ming and Qing China" in 2005, *Journal of Development Economics*, 2006. Vol. 81, No. 2, December 2006, 316–336.

14. Sterling Seagrave, *Dragon Lady: The Life and Legend of the Last Empress of China* (New York: Vintage Books, 1992), 170–81.

15. Li Chunmei, "A Preliminary Study on the Customary Fee Income of Governors in Early Qing (*shitan qingchao qianqi dufude lougui shouru*)" in *The Journal of Neimenggu Social Science*, Vol. 26, No. 4, July 2005, 26–30.

16. Lai Huimin, "The Judicial Trial and Corruption Cases in Early Qing (*Qingqianqi detanwuan yusifa shenpan*)" in *Six Reading Meeting of the Unit of the Legal History at the Academia Sinica*, 2004; http://saturn.ihp.sinica.edu.tw/~AdjTP/LaiOnCorruptionCases.pdf.

17. Gao Hong, "The Fundamental Cause of Lost 1895 War Is Qing Corruption (*jiawu zhanzheng shibaide genben yuanyinshi Qingchaode fubai*)" in *The Journal of Qiqihaer Normal College*, Vol. 5, 1995, 158–60.

18. Ma Jun, "Corruption Defeated Late Qing Army: Elite Eight Banners Could Not Ride Horses and Half of Them Fell (*fubai jikua qingjundui: baqi jingbing buhui qima shiren shangma banshuluo*)" in *Wenhui dushu zhoubao*, December 13, 2010.

19. Chen Zhiping, "The Seeing Clearly the Customary Fees of Late Qing Learning Officials in the Case of Wang Kaitai (cong Wang Kaitaian kanqing qingmo xueguande lougui)" in *Zhongguo shehui jingjishi yanjiu*, Vol. 3, 2013, 84–87.

20. The four big cases in the late Qing are Taiyuan cases, Horse-stabbing case, famous musician case, and the Yang Naiwu and Xiaobaicai case. Hu Ming, "The Procedural Logic behind the Grievances: Perceiving the Legitimate Legal Procedure through the Four Big Cases in the Late Qing (*yuan'an beihoude chengxu luoji: cong wanQing sida'an toushi zhengdang falu chengxu*)" in *Tribute of Political Science and Law*, Vol. 27, No. 4, July 2009, 96–103.

21. Bradly Reed, *Talons and Teeth: County Clerks and Runners in the Qing Dynasty* (Stanford, CA: Stanford University Press, 2000), 200: 242.

22. Park, 1997: 995.

23. Paul Cohen argues that Qing dynasty is quite different from Qing Empire, which is very appropriate when dealing with the Qing in East Asia or as a part of the world. But in this chapter, I still regard both terms interchangeable. See Paul Cohen, "Changes over Time in Qing History: The Importance of Context" in *Late Imperial China*, Vol. 37, No. 1, June 2016, 10–3: 12.

24. See Niu Chuangping and Niu Jiqing, eds., *Verifiable Records of the Economic Criminal Cases of Qing First and Second Ranking Officials (Qingdai yierpin guanyuan jingji fanzui anjian shilu)* (Beijing: Zhongguo fazhi chubanshe, 2000), 112, 157; also see Park, 1997: 971.

25. Sui Wendi once made a law to execute any person who stole only one tael, while Ming Taizu would skin a corrupt official and filled with grass to scare his successors. For Sui Wendi see Qiang Fang, *Chinese Complaint Systems: Natural Resistance* (London: Routledge, 2013), Chapter 1; for Ming Taizu see Wu Han, *Biography of Zhu Yuanzhang* (*Zhu Yuanzhangzhuan*) (Zhejiang: Baihua wenyi chubanshe, 2000); Wang Tianyou and Xu Daling, *Sixteen Emperors in the Ming Dynasty* (*mingchao shiliudi*) (Beijing: Zijincheng chubanshe, 1991), 23.

26. For a detailed study of the censorial system in Chinese history see Charles Hucker, *Censorial System of Ming China* (Stanford, CA: Stanford University Press, 1966).

27. Niu Chuangping, 2000: 29–32.

28. A good study on the Qing grand council is Beatrice S. Bartlett, *Monarchs and Ministers: The Grand Council in Mid-Ch'ing China, 1723–1820* (Berkeley: University of California Press, 1990).

29. Niu Chuangping, 2000: 321–23.

30. Ibid., 375–92.

31. For the succession battle after Kangxi's death see R. Kent Guy, *Qing Governors and Their Provinces: The Evolution of Territorial Administration in China, 1644–1796* (Seattle: University of Washington Press, 2017), 222–23; also see Peter C. Perdue, *China Marches West: The Qing Conquest of Central Eurasia* (Harvard: Harvard University Press, 2010), 226–48.

32. See Zhongguo diyi lishi danganguan, ed., *Complete Translation of the Palace Memorials in Manchu in the Yongzheng Reign* (*Yongzhengchao manwen zhupi zouzhe quanyi*) (Anhui: Huangshan shushe, 1998), 1. 1222–227.

33. *Verifiable Records of Qing Shengzu* (*Daqing shengzu shilu*), 1968, 39. 576.

34. Niu Chuangping, 2000, 38–48.

35. Ibid., 146–52.

36. Peter C. Perdue, 2010: 424.

37. Ping-ti Ho, *The Ladder of Success in Imperial China* (Columbia: Columbia University Press, 1964), 33–4.

38. Niu Chuangping, 2000: 162–86.

39. Frank B. Tipton argues that the Qing annual income was only 43 to 44 million taels. For Fu's number see Zhengyuan Fu, *Automatic Tradition and Chinese Politics* (Cambridge: Cambridge University Press, 1993), 146; for Tipton see Frank B. Tipton, *Asian Firms: History, Institutions and Management* (London: Edward Elgar Publishing, 2008), 116.

40. Niu Chuangping, 2000: 223–47.

41. Ibid., 364–74.

42. Ibid., 209–22.

43. Yongzheng continued to trust Yue Zhongqi in the case of Zeng Jing who tried to persuade Yue to rise against the Qing. For more detail about the case see Jonanthan Spence, *Treason by the Book* (New York: Viking Press, 2001).

44. Niu Chuangping, 2000: 306–13.

45. Ibid., 314–15.

46. "Yu Qu'e" in Pu Songling, http://duguoxue.cn/yuedu/lzzybhw/

47. Zhang Yanfang, "The Defects of the Civil Service Examination in the Qing as Seen in *Strange Stories from a Chinese Studio* (*cong liaozhai zhiyi kan qingdai kejuzhi zhiliubi*)" in Study of *Strange Stories from a Chinese Studio*, 1002–3712 (2004) 02-0067-03, 67–69.

48. Niu Chuangping, 2000: 300–02.

49. See Qiang Fang, *Chinese Complaint Systems: Natural Resistance* (London: Routledge, 2013), Chapter 1.

50. Niu Chuangping, 2000: 15–6; "Hot Potatoes: Chinese Complaint Systems from Early Times to 1898" in *Journal of Asian Studies*, Vol. 68. No. 4 (November) 2009: 1105–35.

51. Niu Chuangping, 2000: 33.

52. Niu Chuangping, 2000: 156–61.

53. In the Kangxi reign, grand secretariat was second rank and in the Yongzheng reign, the emperor promoted it to first rank. See Bartlett, 1990: 33–4.

54. Ibid., 3–8.

55. Ibid., 324–27.

56. Niu Chuangping, 2000: 61–3.

57. Li Chunmei, 2005: 28.

58. Niu Chuangping, 2000: 77–85.

59. Ibid., 24–5.

60. When Kangxi approved the publication of the Qing administrative law in 1690, he said "the way to manage the state is to put forth the statutes." See Macabe Keliher, "Administrative Law and the Making of the First *Da Qing Huidian*" in *Late Imperial China*, Vol. 37, No.1, June 2016, 55–108: 95.

61. Niu Chuangping, 2000: 64–75.

62. Qiang Fang, 2013: Chapter 1.

63. Archives from the First Historical Archives in Beijing. Xingbu anhuisi [Board of Punishment, Anhui division]. Category: "*Toudao qiangjie ji zhapian anjian* [Cases of Theft, Robbery, and Froud]." Case no. 13827; also from Qiang Fang, "A Silent 'Revolution': The Late Qing Reform on the Jumping Appeals" in *The Journal of Asian History*, Vol. 46, No. 1, 2012, 97–116.

64. For the Manchu banners' legal privileges see Mark C. Elliot, 2001.

65. Niu Chuangping, 2000: 34–7.

66. Ibid., 49–3.

67. See Perdue, 2010: 230; William T. Rowe, *China's Last Empire: The Great Qing* (Cambridge, MA: Harvard University Press, 2010), 66.

68. Jonathan Spence, *The Search for Modern China* (New York: W.W. Norton & Company, 1991), 97–101.

69. Niu Chuangping, 2000: 86–8.

70. See ibid., 306–13.

71. See ibid., 321–23.

72. Ibid., 12–4.

73. Ibid., 375–92.

74. Bartlett, 1990: 63.

75. Niu Chuangping, 2000: 3–8.

76. For the ascendancy of Manchu under Oboi see Richard J. Smith, 2015: 68 and Mark Elliot, 2001.

77. Both cases see Niu Chuangping, 2000: 300–02; 15–16.

78. For a comprehensive study of the capital petition in Chinese history and the theory of natural resistance see Qiang Fang, 2013; and *A Short History of Chinese Petition* (*zhongguo shangfang zhidu shihua*) (Beijing: China Youth Press, 2013).

79. See three cases respectively in Niu Chuangping, 2000: 162–86;198–208; 364–74.

80. For the discussion of the relationship between Chinese rulers and the law see Qiang Fang and Xiaobing Li, *Power Versus Law in Modern China: Cities, Courts, and the Communist Party* (Lexington: University Press of Kentucky, 2017), Chapter 1; and Qiang Fang and Roger Des Forges, "Were Chinese Rulers Above the Law? Toward a Theory of the Rule of Law in Chinese History" in *Stanford Journal of International Law*, Vol. 44, No. 1, 2007, 101–46.

81. Some scholars argue that Jiaqing's crackdown of Heshen was to seize his mammoth properties. See Lai Huimin, 2004.

82. Bartlett, 1990: 51.

BIBLIOGRAPHY

1968. *Verifiable Records of Qing Shengzu* (*Daqing shengzu shilu*) vol. 39.

1984. *Documents of the Guangxü Reign* (*Guangxüchao donghualu*). Beijing: Zhonghua shujü.

Alexander, Herbert E. 1984. "Making Sense About Dollars in the 1980 Presidential Campaigns" in Michael J. Malbin, ed., *Money and Politics in the United States: Financing Elections in the 1980s*. New Jersey: Chatham House Publishers.

Anticorruption White Paper (*fantanfu baipishu*), United and Self-Strengthening.

Arnsdorf, Isaac. "Trump Rewards Big Donors with Jobs and Access." *Politico*, December 27, 2016.

Association in the Republic of China, June 30, 2010.

Ballhaus, Rebecca and Mulins, Brody. "Corporations Bet on GOP Senate Control." *The Wall Street Journal*, November 7, 2016.

Barboza, David. "Billions in Hidden Riches for Family of Chinese Leader." *The New York Times*, October 25, 2012.

Barboza, David and Lafraniere, Sharon. "'Princelings' in China Use Family Ties to Gain Riches." *The New York Times*, May 17, 2012.

Bartlett, Beatrice S. 1990. *Monarchs and Ministers: The Grand Council in Mid-Ch'ing China, 1723–1820*. Berkeley: University of California Press.

Berg, Larry L., Hahn, Harlan and Schmidhauser, John R. 1976. *Corruption in the American Political System*. New Jersey: Central Learning Press.

Blinder, Alan. "U.S. Ends Corruption Case Against Former Virginia Governor." *The New York Times*, September 8, 2016.

Bodde, Derk. 1967. *Peking Diary: 1948–1949 A Year of Revolution*. Minnesota: Fawcett Publications.

Branigan, Tania. "The Guardian Politburo, Army, Casinos: China's Corruption Crackdown Spreads." *The Guardian*, February 2015.

Bu, Xianqun. 2014. *Corruption and Anticorruption in Chinese History (Zhongguo lishishangde fubai yufanfubai)*. Fujian: Lujiang chubanshe.

Chen, Zhiping. "The Seeing Clearly the Customary Fees of Late Qing Learning Officials in the Case of Wang Kaitai (*cong Wang Kaitaian kanqing qingmo xueguande lougui*)" in *Zhongguo shehui jingjishi yanjiu*, Vol. 3, 2013, pp. 84–7.

Chin, Josh. "Chinese Lawyer Sentenced to Seven Years in Prison." *The Wall Street Journal*, August 4, 2016.

Choi, Chi-yuk. "Chinese Officials Facing Corruption Charges are Being Tempted by Suicide." *South China Morning Post*, June 15, 2016.

Cohen, Paul. "Changes over Time in Qing History: The Importance of Context" in *Late Imperial China*, Vol. 37, No. 1, June 2016, pp. 10–3.

Condon, George E. Jr. "Disgraced Congressman Randy 'Duke' Cunningham Is a Free Man Again." *The Atlantic*, July 10, 2014.

Confessore, Nicholas and Luo, Michael. "Perry Mines Texas System to Raise Cash." *New York Times*, August 20, 2011.

Dardess, John. *Confucianism and Autocracy*. California: University of California Press.

Deng, Yuwen. "Comment." *The New York Times*, May 9, 2017.

Denyer, Simon. "China's Ousted Official Bo Xilai Convicted of Corruption." *The Washington Post*, September 22, 2013.

Eastman, Lloyd E. 1984. *Seeds of Destruction: Nationalist China in War and Revolution, 1937–1949*. Stanford: Stanford University Press.

Editorial Board. "A Deadly Landslide Exposes the Depths of China's Corruption and Censorship." *The Washington Post*, December 29, 2015.

Elliot, Mark C. 2001. *The Manchu Way: The Eight Banners and Ethnic Identity in Late Imperial China*. Stanford: Stanford University Press.

Fang, Qiang. "Hot Potatoes: Chinese Complaint Systems from Early Times to 1898" in the *Journal of Asian Studies*, Vol. 68. No. 4, November 2009, pp. 1105–35.

———. "A Silent 'Revolution': The Late Qing Reform on the Jumping Appeals" in *The Journal of Asian History*, Vol. 46, 2012, No. 1, pp. 97–116.

———. 2013a. *Chinese Complaint Systems: Natural Resistance*. London: Routledge.

———. 2013b. *A Short History of Chinese Petition* (*zhongguo shangfang zhidu shihua*). Beijing: China Youth Press.

Fang, Qiang and Des Forges, Roger. "Were Chinese Rulers Above the Law? Toward a Theory of the Rule of Law in Chinese History" in *Stanford Journal of International Law*, Vol. 44, No. 1, 2007, pp. 101–46.

Fang, Qiang and Li, Xiaobing. 2017. *Power Versus Law in Modern China: Cities, Courts, and the Communist Party*. Lexington: University Press of Kentucky.

Farmer, Edward. 1983. *Zhu Yuanzhang and Early Ming Legislation.* Leiden: E.J. Brill, 1995, 2.

Fenby, Jonathan. 2004. *Chiang Kai-shek: China's Generalissimo and the Nation he Lost*. New York: Carroll & Graf Publishers.

Ferguson, Charles H. 2012. *Predator Nation: Corporate Criminals, Political Corruption and the Hijacking of America*. Crown Publishing Group.

Feuer, Alan. "Why Are Corruption Cases Crumbling? Some Blame the Supreme Court." *The New York Times*, November 17, 2017.

Forsythe, Michael. "Database Tracks 'Tigers and Flies' Caught in Xi Jinping's Corruption Crackdown." *The New York Times*, January 21, 2016.

Forsythe, Michael. "Database Tracks 'Tigers and Flies' Caught in Xi Jinping's Corruption Crackdown." *The New York Times*, January 21, 2016.

Fu, Zhengyuan. 1993. *Automatic Tradition and Chinese Politics*. Cambridge: Cambridge University Press.

Gao, Hong. "The Fundamental Cause of Lost 1895 War is Qing Corruption (*jiawu zhanzheng shibaide genben yuanyinshi Qingchaode fubai*)" in *The Journal of Qiqihaer Normal College*, Vol. 5, 1995, pp. 158–60.

Gao, Hua. 2011. *How the Red Sun Rises?* (*gongtaiyang shiruhe shengqide*). Hong Kong: Hong Kong Chinese University Press.

Goodpaster, Gary. 2002. "Reflections on Corruption in Indonesia" in Timothy Lindsey and Howard W. Dick, eds., *Corruption in Asia: Rethinking the Governance Paradigm*. Australia: The Federation Press.

Gore, Al. 2013. *The Future: Six Drives of Global Change*. New York: Random House Publishing Group.

Guy, R. Kent. 2017. *Qing Governors and Their Provinces: The Evolution of Territorial Administration in China, 1644–1796*. Seattle: University of Washington Press.

He, Qinglian. "Government Monopolized Anticorruption Explicitly Reveals the Backwardness of China's Institutions (Zhengfu longduan fanfu tuxian zhongguo zhidu luohou)." *The Voice of America*, February 7, 2014.

Helderman, Rosalind S. and Vozzella, Laura. "Va. Gov. McDonnell on Two-Way Street with Chief Executive of Struggling Company." *The Washington Post*, March 30, 2013.

Ho, Ping-ti. 1964. *The Ladder of Success in Imperial China*. Columbia: Columbia University Press.

Hofstadter, Richard. 1989. *The American Political Tradition and the Men Who Made it*. New York: Vintage Books.

Hucker, Charles. 1966. *Censorial System of Ming China*. Stanford: Stanford University Press.

Ingraham, Christopher. "Somebody Just Put a Price Tag on the 2016 Election. It's a Doozy." *Washington Post*, April 14, 2017.

Jacobs, Andrew. "China Appears Set to force Times Reporter to Leave." *The New York Times*, January 27, 2014.

Jacobs, Andrew, Hernandez, Javier C. and Buckley, Chris. "Behind Deadly Tianjin Blast, Shortcuts and Lax Rules." *The New York Times*, August 30, 2015.

Ji, Shenying. 2015. *Party Remnants: The Lurker of the New "Gang of Four" (yudang: xinsirenbang deqianfuzhe)*. Hong Kong: Neimu chubanshe.

———. 2015. *The Remaining Members: The Lurker of the "New Gang of Four" (Yudang: xinsirenbang deqianfuzhe)*. Hong Kong: Neimu chubanshe.

Keliher, Macabe. "Administrative Law and the Making of the First *Da Qing Huidian*" in *Late Imperial China*, Vol. 37, No.1, June 2016, pp. 55–108.

Keliher, Macabe and Wu, Hsinchao. "Corruption, Anticorruption, and the Transformation of Political Culture in Contemporary China." *The Journal of Asian Studies*, Vol. 75, No. 01, February 2016, pp. 5–18.

Ketcham, Ralph, ed. 2006. *Selected Writings of James Madison*. Indianapolis: Hackett Publishing.

Leggett, Karby. "In a Land Where Bribes are Commonplace, A Chinese Millionaire Pushed the Envelope." *The Wall Street Journal*, November 23, 2001.

Levin, Dan. "China Tells Schools to Suppress Western Ideas, with One Big Exception." *The New York Times*, February 9, 2015.

Li, Boyuan. 2013. *Exposure of the Official World* (guanchang xianxingji). Zhejiang: Zhejiang chuabn jituan.

Li, Chunmei. 2005. "A Preliminary Study on the Customary fee Income of Governors in Early Qing (*shitan qingchao qianqi dufude lougui shouru*)" in *The Journal of Neimenggu Social Science*, Vol. 26, No. 4, July 2005.

Liang, Hong, ed. 2003. *The Ancient Book* (*shangshu*). Hunan: Shidai wenyi chubanshe.

Lichtblau, Eric. "Lawmakers' Ties to Toyota Questioned at Start of Inquiries." *The New York Times*, February 23, 2010.

Lin, Qian. 2013. *Power and Law in Traditional China* (*Chuantong zhongguo dequanyufa*). Beijing: Law Press.

Liu, E. 2017. *The Travels of Lao Can* (laocan youji) Zhejiang: Zhejiang wenyi chubanshe.

Liu, Xu. 1975. *The Old History of the Tang* (*jiutangshu*). Beijing: Zhonghua shujü.

Lubman, Stanley. 1999. *Bird in a Cage: Legal Reform in China after Mao*. Stanford: Stanford University Press.

Ma, Jun. "Corruption Defeated Late Qing Army: Elite Eight Banners Could not Ride Horses and Half of them Fell (*fubai jikua qingjundui: baqi jingbing buhui qima shiren shangma banshuluo*)." *Wenhui dushu zhoubao*, December 13, 2010.

Marcus, Robert D., Burner, David, and Marcus, Anthony, eds. 2007. *American Firsthand: Vol II. Readings from Reconstruction to the Present*. New York: Bedfor/St. Martin's.

Markon, Jerry. "Ex-Rep. Jefferson (D. La) Gets 13 Years in Freezer Cash Case." *The Washington Post*, November 14, 2009.

Meisner, Maurice. 1996. *The Deng Xiaoping Era: An Inquiry into the Fate of Chinese Socialism, 1978–1994*. New York: Hill & Wang.

———. 1999. *Mao's China and After: A History of the People's Republic*. New York: Free Press.

Murong, Xuechun. "Xi's Selective Punishment." *The New York Times*, January 16, 2015.

Myers, Steven L. and Landler, Mark. "Frenzied Hours for U.S. on Fate of a China Insider." *New York Times*, April 17, 2012.

Ni, Shawn and Van, Pham Hoang. "High Corruption Income in Ming and Qing China" *Journal of Development Economics*, Vol. 81, No. 2, 2006, pp. 316–336.

Nie, Da. "Corruption behind the Frivolity: The Relationship between Governmental and Cultural Corruption in the Dream of Red Mansion (*fuhua beihoude fubai: cong Hongloumeng kan guanchang fubai yuminfeng fubai deguanxi*)." *Zhongguo jijian jianchabao*, November 14, 2014.

Niu, Chuangping and Niu, Jiqing, eds. 2000. *Verifiable Records of the Economic Criminal Cases of Qing First and Second Ranking Officials (Qingdai yierpin guanyuan jingji fanzui anjian shilu)*. Beijing: Zhongguo fazhi chubanshe.

Pei, Minxin. 2016. *China's Crony Capitalism*. Harvard: Harvard University Press.

———. "China's War on Corruption Could Hasten Communist Party's Decline." *Nikkei Asian Review*, May 19, 2015.

———. "Crony Communism in China." *The New York Times*, October 17, 2014.

Park, Nancy E. "Corruption in Eighteenth-century China" in *The Journal of Asian Studies*, Vol. 56, No. 4, November 1997.

———. "Unofficial Perspectives on Torture in Ming and Qing China" in *Late Imperial China*, Vol. 37, No. 1, 2016, pp. 17–54.

Patrick, Odsseus. "For a Century, the Mansion Sat above Sydney Harbor. Then China's Nouveau Riche Arrived." *The Washington Post*, June 17, 2014.

Perdue, Peter C. 2010. *China Marches West: The Qing Conquest of Central Eurasia*. Harvard: Harvard University Press.

Phillips, Tom. "China Behaving Like 'Gangster' State with Bookseller Kidnap, Say Hong Kong Politicians." *The Guardian*, June 17, 2016.
Prazniak, Roxann. 1996. *Of Camel Kings and Other Things: Rural Rebels against Modernity in Late Imperial China*. Lanham: Rowman & Littlefield.
Rauhala, Emily. "As Panama Leaks Spread, China's 'Red Nobility' would rather not Talk about it." *The Washington Post*, April 7, 2016.
Reed, Bradly. 2000. *Talons and Teeth: County Clerks and Runners in the Qing Dynasty*. Stanford: Stanford University Press.
Rowe, William T. 2010. *China's Last Empire: The Great Qing*. Harvard: Harvard University Press.
Schrecker, John E. 1991. *The Chinese Revolution in Historical Perspective*. New York: Praeger.
Seagrave, Sterling. 1986. *The Soong Dynasty*. New York: Harper & Row Publishers.
———. 1992. *Dragon Lady: The Life and Legend of the Last Empress of China*. New York: Vintage Books.
Sha, Lu. "Several Officials of the Development and Reform Commission have been Punished due to Violations of the Rules Regarding Banquet with Public Money and Accepting Gifts (*Fagaiwei duoming guanyuan gongkuan chihe weigui shouli beichufen*)." *Xinjingbao*, April 17, 2016.
Shankar, Sneha. "Li Xiaolin, Former Chinese Premier Li Peng's Daughter, Hid over $2M In HSBC Swiss Account." *The International Business Times*, February 10, 2015.
Sheridan, James E. 1966. *Chinese Warlord: The Career of Feng Yu-hsiang*. Stanford: Stanford University Press.
Shi, Minglei and Li, Xueyin. "An Investigation of Gifts on the Teachers' Day (*jiaoshijie songli diaocha*)." *Xinjingbao*, September 10, 2013.
Shi, Ping. "Fanfubai bushi quanli douzheng (Anticorruption is not Power Struggle)." *Qiushi*, July 2016.
Sima, Guang. 1956. *Comprehensive Mirror for Assisting Government* (*zizhi tongjian*). Beijing: Zhonghua shuju.
Smith, Richard J. 2005. *The Qing Dynasty and Traditional Chinese Culture*. Rowman & Littlefield.
Sonmez, Felicia. "Free Speech in China Gets an Unlikely State-Media Backer." *The Wall Street Journal*, February 17, 2016.
Spence, Jonathan. 1981. *The Gate of Heavenly Peace: The Chinese and Their Revolution, 1895–1980*. New York: Penguin Books.
———. 1991. *The Search for Modern China*. New York: W.W. Norton & Company.
———. 2001. *Treason by the Book*. New York: Viking Press.
Sun, Yat-sen. 1981. *The Complete Works of Sun Yat-sen* (*Sun Zhongshan quanji*). Beijing: Zhonghua shuju.
Teachout, Zephyr. 2014. *Corruption in America: From Benjamin Franklin's Snuff Box to Citizens United*. Harvard: Harvard University Press.
Thiessen, Marc A. "Crony Capitalism Exposed." *The Washington Post*, November 14, 2011.
Tipton, Frank B. 2008. *Asian Firms: History, Institutions and Management*. London: Edward Elgar Publishing.

Transparency International. "Corruption Perfections Index 2015." https://www.iaca.int/images/news/2016/Corruption_Perceptions_Index_2015_report.pdf.

Twitchett, Denis. How to Be an Emperor: T'ang T'ai-tsung's Vision of His Role, in Asia Major (3rd Series), Vol. 9, No. 1/2, pp. 1–10.

Veg, Sebastian. "China's Political Spectrum under Xi Jinping." *The Diplomat*, August 11, 2014.

Vogal, Ezra F. 1969. *Canton under Communism: Programs and Politics in a Provincial Capital, 1949–1968*. Harvard: Harvard University Press.

Wakeman, Frederic jr. 1985. *The Great Enterprise: The Manchu Reconstruction of Imperial Order in Seventeenth-century China*. Berkeley: University of California Press.

———. 2003a. *Policing Shanghai: 1927–1937*. Stanford: Stanford University Press.

———. 2003b. Spymaster: *Dai Li and the Chinese Secret Service*. Stanford: Stanford University Press.

Wan, William. "China Broadcasts Confession of Chinese-American Blogger." *The Washington Post*, September 15, 2013.

Wang, Qishan. "Grasping and Utilizing the 'Four Patterns' in Supervising and Disciplining." *The Xinhua News Agency*, September 26, 2015.

Wang, Tianyou and Xu, Daling. 1991. *Sixteen Emperors in the Ming Dynasty* (*mingchao shiliudi*). Beijing: Zijincheng chubanshe.

Wu, Han. 2001. *A Biography of Ming Taizu* (*Ming Taizuzhuan*). Tianjin: Baihua wenyi chubanshe.

Wong, Chun Han. "Chinese Court Issues Life Sentence to Former Presidential Aide for Corruption." *The Wall Street Journal*, July 4, 2016.

Wu, Han. 2000. *Biography of Zhu Yuanzhang* (*Zhu Yuanzhangzhuan*). Zhejiang: Baihua wenyi chubanshe.

Xu, Beina. "Media Censorship in China." *Council on Foreign Relations*, April 7, 2015.

Yang, Fan. "The Latest Hearsay: Zeng Qinghong's Secret Detention Place is Exposed (*Zuixin chuanwen: Zeng Qinghong mimi guanya didian baoguang*)." *Secret China*, July 13, 2014. http://m.secretchina.com/node/546794.

Yang, Hegao. 1979. *Selected Works of Ancient Politics and Law (gudai zhengfa wenxuan)*. Beijing: Beijing zhengfa xueyuan.

Yang, Jia Lynn, Hamburger, Tom and ElBoghdady, Dina. "Ways Investors Gain 'Political' Facing Public Scrutiny." *The Washington Post*, May 9, 2013.

Yuen, Samson. "Disciplining the Party: Xi Jinping's Anticorruption Campaign and its Limits." *China Perspectives* 2014/3 (2014).

Zeleny, Jeff and Thee-Brenan, Megan. "New Poll Finds a Deep Distrust of Government." *The New York Times*, October 25, 2011.

Zhang, Jixin. 2016. *Things Seen and Heard about Bureaucracy in both the Daoguang and Xianfeng Reigns* (*daoxian huanhai jianwenlu*). Beijing: Zhonghua shuju.

Zhang, Lun. "The Increasing Appearance of the Drawbacks in China's Movement-type Anticorruption (*Zhongguo yundongshi fanfu biduan riyi chengxian*)." *The French International Broadcast*, February 8, 2015.

Zhang, Tingyu. 1974. *The History of the Ming* (*Mingshi*). Beijing: Zhonghua shujü.

Zhang, Yuxue. "Former Vice Head of the Logistic Department Gu Junshan is Exposed to be Involved in a Case of more than 20billion (*Yuanzonghouqingbu fubuzhang Gu Junshan beibao shean 200 duoyi*)." *Caijin net*, April 1, 2015.

Zhang, Zhiguang. "Anticorruption in Chinese History (*Zhongguo lishishang defanfu*)." *Shanghai guancha*, May 29, 2014.

Zhao, Erxun. 1982. *The Draft History of the Qing* (*qingshigao*). Beijing: Zhonghua shuju,

Zheng, Yongnian. 2015. *China Entering the Xi Jinping Era*. London: Routledge.

Zhong, Chenfang. "People Unhappy to See the Remodeling of a Sydney Mansion by Zeng Qinghong's Son (*Zeng Qinghong zhizi Xini haozhai gaijian yincemu*)." *Voice of America*, June 19, 2014.

Zhou, Yahui. "The Objective of Xi Jinping's Anticorruption is to Deal with Civilian Party (Xi Jinping fanfude mubiao shiduifu pingmindang)." August 15, 2014. www.boxun.com.

"*Zhu Yuanzhang chengtan bubiqin: weifanfu chusi qinzhizi yuqinnuxu*)" in *Fenghuang lishi*, July 1, 2014. http://news.ifeng.com/a/20140701/40965124_0.shtml.

Zhu, Yuyang and Gui, Jie. "A Record of State Governing under Tang Taizong: Discussing How the Tang Dynasty Opposed Corruption (*Tang Taizong zhiguo fengyunlu: tantao tangchao ruhe fanfu*)." *The China Youth Daily*. August 22, 2014.

Chapter 2

Accountability, Supervision, and Penalty

Yuan Shikai as a Watchdog in Managing Government Officials

Patrick Fuliang Shan

INTRODUCTION

Historians often struggle to find a balance between historical value and popular opinion when evaluating the legacy of historical figures. For multiple reasons, an influential man may retain a permanent stain on his name. Nevertheless, a careful study enables scholars to find his historical contributions to social progress and national modernization. Yuan Shikai (1859–1916) is such a man. He was born in the turbulent nineteenth century and went through the vicissitudes of national turmoil and transformation. Throughout his life, he acquired numerous vicious enemies who condemned him and labeled him with negative nomenclatures. In particular, he was denounced as a national thief who stole the country after the 1911 Revolution. Indeed, he was demeaned by all the rulers of the party-state during the twentieth century. Consequently, his "notoriety" stalled serious studies and delayed unbiased research on him for decades. Only after China embraced reform over the past thirty years did Chinese scholars start to assess Yuan from a relatively objective standpoint. As a result, Yuan is now seen as a talented official and a devoted reformer in China's transition from empire to republic.

A commitment to redress historical wrongs should urge scholars to explore Yuan Shikai's vital role in China's military modernization, economic advancement, cultural progress, educational improvement, and other fields. Yet, his lifelong endeavors to change China's officialdom has been neglected. Yuan was an official throughout his life, first serving the Qing Empire and then working for the Republic of China. To reach the goal of an efficient and effective administration, he spent a great deal of his life interacting with officials below him, training them to be competent administrators, and penalizing them in case of violations. Official management was an important component of his career and an inseparable part of his political life during the long period when he first served as the governor of Shandong Province, then as the governor-general of Zhili Province, and finally as the first president of the Republic of China.

The aim of this chapter is to demonstrate Yuan Shikai's efforts to clean up the officialdom from within, purporting to prevent corruption, disciplining administrators, penalizing fraudulent power-holders, and ensuring productive governance. Because his skill as an administrator was overshadowed by his other accomplishments in military modernization, economic advancement, and cultural progress, few scholars have devoted to this topic to date. This chapter intends to explore the other side of the story by focusing on his official management as an important part of his career and maintains that he has left a rich legacy to China's administrative modernization. Engaging with abundant primary sources, notably the newly published *Yuan Shikai quanji* [The Complete Works of Yuan Shikai] along with other secondary sources, including biographies and scholarly articles, this chapter demonstrates that Yuan had achieved a great deal in this area. From three different aspects, this chapter analyzes Yuan's creative notions of official management, his provincial implementation of his ideas, and his continual administrative reform during his presidency.

Yuan Shikai's Philosophy of Official Management

Sifting through Yuan Shikai's works, both his official documents and his private correspondence, one can easily find that he spent a great deal of time managing officials below him. He had developed systematic ideas on this matter. In a few ways, he exemplified the complete bureaucratic administrator of modern China during the transition from empire to republic. In fact, there is no element of mystery in his thought, which was a direct response to the existing ineffective bureaucracy and national catastrophes. Seeing China's disastrous defeat in the hands of Japan in 1895, Yuan blamed the outdated bureaucracy as one of the reasons, asserting that the Qing Empire was short of talents (talented individuals) and that Qing officials were deficient in modern knowledge. He saw the prevalent corruption of the late Qing regime as a result of the Taiping Rebellion after which local officials expanded their power base and acted presumptuously. More disastrously, a lot of officials, as Yuan witnessed, did not open their eyes to the outside world and grew into ultra-conservative bureaucrats.[1] Without knowledge of the treaties China had signed, those conservative officials only instigated clashes with foreign powers and brought new catastrophes to the nation.[2] In contrast, Yuan's interest in official management started with his childhood ties. When he was young, his adopted father served as an official in Shandong and Jiangsu, exposing young Yuan to the officialdom. In other words, Yuan's thought on official management had deep-rooted and profound backgrounds.

A close examination shows that Yuan Shikai started to voice his creative ideas on officialdom after the First Sino-Japanese War. He actively participated in the reform movement, vehemently responding to China's recent national defeat. While he paid special attention to the issue of China's bureaucracy, he offered his own proposals for improvement. In his memorial to Emperor Guangxu on August 20, 1895, he pinpointed China's conservative bureaucracy as ineffective and bloated, simply because numerous conservatives held positions, stuck to the old ways, and refused to acquire practical learning. Henceforth, he asserted, new talent should be trained, recommended, and employed.[3] In late 1897 and early 1898, he lobbied the emperor's tutor and a high-ranking official, Weng Tonghe, intending to press the imperial court to employ new and properly prepared administrators. Yuan linked the reform of officialdom with national salvation, national survival, and national development. Amazingly, Yuan asserted all these ideas before even becoming a governor, although he was then the commander with a special task of training China's first modern army.

Subsequently, Yuan Shikai continued to underscore the importance of official management and viewed it as an essential component in statecraft. Although an official position was just one of many occupations, as Yuan understood, officials once hired had automatically signed a contract with the state.[4] Official behaviors had an intimate link with the rise and the fall of the state. On many occasions, Yuan declared that "the fall of a state is usually caused by corrupt officials."[5] When he became president of the Republic of China, he used the Qing's fall as a warning, "The late Qing collapsed due to the sale of official positions and its prevalent bribing habits."[6] As a result, in Yuan's eyes, the Qing officialdom was full of impotent power-holders and corrupt wrongdoers. He argued that only talented officials in the government could enable China to establish a solid foundation for self-strengthening and reach the goal of a powerful statehood.[7] In a nutshell, Yuan optimistically asserted that China could reach the objective of national recovery, growth, and prosperity, if talented officials staffed the government.[8]

Throughout his political career, Yuan Shikai valued the qualifications of officials who needed not all be geniuses, but who must possess a certain level of education, moral value, sound fitness, a diligent attitude, and other basic traits. In his eyes, their knowledge of more advanced nations should be a part of qualification. He once suggested that talented officials could be selected from the youth in the coastal region, because of their direct exposure to Western culture.[9] He advised that good officials should listen to diverse opinions, including sharp criticism. Only in this way could pure politics be promoted and bad tendencies avoided.[10] Corrupt officials must be punished but those who made mistakes unintentionally could be pardoned and rehired so long as they behaved well during the probationary period.[11] In any case, an official should be familiar with Chinese culture, have administrative experience, and more importantly, know about Western culture. Once he remarked that "the best officials should be well versed in traditional learning, possess a certain level of expertise, and additionally strive to pursue the new learning."[12]

It is not easy to identify qualified officials, let alone make full use of their talent. Yuan Shikai suggested adopting a two-track selection system. First, candidates completed a written examination which enabled the government to determine writing aptitude, critical thinking, cultural familiarity, and the ability to respond within a short time. However, he did not recommend the traditional Civil Service Examination System because of its narrow focus on the ancient classics. Instead, Yuan promoted including Western science, technology, and other practical learning as a part of the examination. The reliance on examination alone was not sufficient; additionally, he demanded personal on-the-ground experience. He said that "examination determines the future, but experience underscores the importance of the past. The two must be valued without dropping either one."[13] Yuan further remarked that "a candidate must be scrutinized to ascertain his talent and be judged to see if he is fit for the assigned job."[14] According to the ability of candidates, those with the greatest talent would be assigned to important positions, while the more ordinary would be given regular jobs.[15]

According to Yuan Shikai, all the selected candidates were assets of the country and should be put into a selection pool for official positions. He further asserted that it would be ideal if the state could obtain more contenders, examine them, train them, and cultivate them to expand their knowledge and to enhance their skills. In this way, the officialdom would not encounter a shortage of qualified officials and the future government would not worry about the deficiency of eligible candidates. In case of the unavailability of official positions, those candidates would be able to land jobs in other fields easily. Yuan even proposed establishing a four echelon formation with different groups of talented candidates. The first included ready-to-use candidates, who could be immediately employed. The second included those of preparatory status for imminent use. The third were those reserved status while the fourth were those of affiliated status for future use.[16] With such a huge reservoir, Yuan expected to employ and manage officials at will.

Yuan Shikai always required officials to make a clear distinction between private interests and public service, because private matters could seduce officials to corruption and lead them to abuse their power. If an official worked for the benefit of his own family, hunted for privileges for his own relatives, and sought positions for his own kin, he inevitably would be a corrupt official due to nepotism and favoritism. Yuan demanded that family members or relatives should not be given priority, even if they were qualified, when an official was handling the employment issue.[17] Yuan himself "did not employ relatives. In the case a relative came to beg for help," he would use a portion of his own salary as a monthly subsidy to help him out and support him. In this way, Yuan did not add any burden to the public fund.[18] Furthermore, he did not allow personal animosity to cloud administration in order to reach the goals of justice, righteousness, and uprightness. He once demanded that an official should not bring his own favor or distaste into governance, stating, "In hiring new officials, one should not bear in mind old aversion."[19]

Throughout his political career, the phenomenon he hated most was the corpulence of government, as manifested by a huge force of officials and assistant officials. The large number of governmental employees seemed to be a help, yet they hampered the effectiveness of governance. Not only did it add a burden to state finance, but it also lowered the salaries of all employees. In the long run, this bloated bureaucracy led to low income, inadequate efficiency, and poor returns. Limited resources were wasted while officials bickered over trivial issues. A simple case might be delayed while officials passed the buck without a sense of responsibility. Even worse, officials in the redundant system colluded with each other and collaborated with criminals to oppress the people for a lion's share.[20] Yuan said that "redundant officials receive low salary which compels them to live in desperation," leading to further corruption.[21] Thus, he proposed to streamline the government and to make it simpler, smaller, more effective, and more serviceable. Indeed, a major area Yuan focused on in his long career was fighting the swelling ranks of administrators for an efficient yet right-sized administration.

One approach by Yuan to fight corruption was his offer of a higher salary to officials. It was hard for low-salaried officials to avoid the temptation of monetary lures. "After eliminating the redundant official positions, the saved money should be offered to the existing officials so that they would receive higher income." Yuan termed it "money for sustaining incorrupt officials." Of course, this is not Yuan's invention, as high salaries were offered during the imperial period by various dynasties, also to prevent corruption. Yuan simply carried it on, as he remarked that a "high salary should be offered to officials in order for their family to live a relatively comfortably life without worrying about food, clothes, and other necessities. Henceforth, officials would devote themselves whole-heartedly to public services, be away from potential distress of their family needs, and thus become incorruptible."[22] Furthermore, a high salary would attract more highly qualified candidates, giving the government more options while selecting officials.

Yuan Shikai's vision for successful official management for high-quality governance was closely interlocked with local governance. Besides the provincial officials who were under the direct control of the central government, Yuan believed that the key was the county-level government, because it connected with the upper structure above and more importantly it was posited above the 90 percent of Chinese population below. He remarked that "county magistrates are crucially vital officials in the entire government."[23] "The closest to the people are no more than those magistrates at the prefectural and county levels. Once a region receives a good magistrate, it is blessed with peace while the local people rejoice. Once a region receives a bad magistrate, it is damned with corrupt officials while bandits proliferate."[24] "One good official means that one region is endowed with countless fortunes."[25] He demanded that local officials work diligently for the local people, because "each fraction of energy a magistrate devotes to the region will enable him to bring one more bit of vigor to support the local people."[26]

Heavy were the burdens on Yuan Shikai when he became the first president of the Republic of China in 1912. As the chief executive of the most populous country in the world, he continued to work diligently to manage officials at all levels of administrations and carried on his ideas through to his presidency. Yet, the sudden switch to republic posed a challenge, because the republic itself could not solve all problems. Many expected that this first democracy would be a panacea. In reality, Yuan had to cope with new and tough issues. His personal tragedy lay in his disbelief of the democratic institution and in his continual faith in strong, efficient, and effective government. He said that "now republic is established and national polity is changed. A careful examination reveals that the political transition was actually caused by a certain reason as it did not originate in a creative move for institutionalization. Although empire now becomes republic, the ordinary people in their own hearts still expect to rely on the government rather than to lean on Congress."[27] He personally detested Congress as he noted that "Congress is an unsustainable state organ. Among the eight hundred congressional members, two hundred are good men, another two hundred are noisy 'sparrows,' and the remaining four hundred are feeble individuals. What can they do?"[28] The only solution, according to him, was to make the government more efficient through official management.

In response to the sudden change of national polity, Yuan Shikai believed that normal governmental function should not be interrupted. Rather, officials must labor diligently and cooperate closely to ensure public safety and safeguard social order. In particular, during those days of transition from empire to republic in early 1912, Yuan ordered that "the governmental operation could not be suspended for a single day," and officials must protect public property, state funds, and other governmental valuables.[29] To guarantee administrative continuity, Yuan proposed to employ these old officials of the Qing dynasty. He even cited historical precedents to justify it, as he remarked that "the best ministers of the Han Dynasty were those old officials of the late Qin. The famous ministers of the Tang were the officials of the collapsed Sui. Political administration does not rely on imagined fabrication; rather, it requires accountability while an official cannot obligate his responsibility without experiences."[30] Of course, those who would like to serve the republic must support the change and be willing to serve the new state.

Many old problems persisted into the new republic. In addition, Yuan witnessed serious new issues, as he saw bribery become so prevalent that some officials only set their eyes on profits. As their governance became weak, bandits proliferated and some officials even collaborated with outlaws to exploit the local people.[31] While China had entered the new era, the quality of officials could not satisfy the needs of the time. He commented that "the junior officials lack proper strategies and basic experience in handling cases, while the senior yet conservative officials are insufficient in wisdom and knowledge to catch up with the new global trend."[32] In terms of rules, ever since the dramatic political change, "valuable rules are discarded so that many officials work for personal gains, disobey orders, act arrogantly, break laws, and become public hazards."[33] Henceforth, he believed that institutional change must be implemented for effective governance.

It is interesting to take notice of Yuan's new notion of official loyalty to the new state. In the old imperial days, political loyalty was reserved for the emperor, who was deemed the Son of Heaven and who held the Mandate of Heaven to rule the land. This old doctrine had perished, because the target vanished along with the transition from empire to republic. Yuan did not bring forth a systematic theory in this regard, but he had formulated his ideas on it. For the transition to republic, he required officials to carry out relevant measures to maintain peace and order, serve the people wholeheartedly, and give full support to the new state.[34] Later on, he made it clear that the ultimate loyalty of all officials should be given to the new state, as he remarked that "all officials for today's republic must pledge allegiance to the state."[35] However, "the state" is an abstract term. As Yuan disbanded his rival the Nationalist Party in late 1913 and abolished the uncooperative Congress in early 1914, this abstract term was often interpreted as loyalty to Yuan himself as the head of state.

Yuan Shikai's Provincial Implementation

Prior to late 1899, Yuan Shikai had fashioned his creative ideas on efficiency in administration. Yet, he did not have an opportunity to implement them. For nearly two years between late 1899 to late 1901 he was the chief executive of the Shandong Province. It was in this capacity as a provincial governor that he had an opportunity to enforce a series of measures to discipline officials to create an efficient provincial administration. From late 1901 to early 1907, he served as the governor-general of Zhili Province where he continued to implement his official control, reform, and penalty. Altogether, Yuan was a provincial leader for more than eight years, during which he performed quite well. When he assumed those two positions in Shandong and Zhili, both provinces were encountering unbearable difficulties; however, when he departed from them, both Shandong and Zhili were seen as model provinces in North China. A careful examination shows that his diligent management contributed to his accomplishments there.

As soon as Yuan arrived in Shandong in late 1899, he faced an ominous situation—provincial disorder. He had to deal simultaneously with the growing Boxer Uprising and accommodate the Germans who recently built a colony in the Qingdao area. He promised the imperial court that he "would supervise officials . . . eliminate bandits, pacify the land, and establish amity with the foreign power to avoid disasters."[36] After his careful analysis of the origin of the Boxer Uprising, he found that "the clash between civilians and Christians was caused by local officials who did not handle cases fairly."[37] Facing this clash, Yuan's attitude was firm: "Christian proliferation is allowed by the treaties China had signed. Therefore, the church should be protected."[38] He ordered local officials to use extreme means to wipe out the uprising from the land and he deployed troops to suppress the Boxers. Here, Yuan's job was a mixed one, as he combined domestic issues with diplomacy, integrated civilian affairs with military actions, and merged secular matters with religious matters. Under his firm leadership and his harsh campaigns, the Boxers soon virtually vanished from Shandong, as his administration killed four thousand Boxers while no foreigners died during his governorship.

In Yuan's eyes, the Boxer Uprising was a tragedy to China, as North China was ravaged by both rebels and foreign troops and China then had to pay a huge amount of reparation. Thus, he proposed to punish those officials responsible for inciting the peasants to join the Boxer Uprising. In particular, he targeted the former governor of Shandong, Yuxian, who vehemently inspired the Boxers while adopting a xenophobic stance. Under Yuan's direction, Yuxian and many other officials were either executed or removed from their official positions. By punishing those officials, Yuan wanted to warn other administrators to abide by the treaties China had signed with international powers, and to not provoke the foreign powers to invasion. During the suppression of Boxers in Shandong, Yuan punished quite a few local officials for not being able to exterminate Boxers in a timely fashion. Previously, Yuan's move was seen as evidence of his status as a national traitor, but is now regarded as a rational move to protect

China's national interests and to avoid further national catastrophe from a potential German invasion.[39]

In dealing with officials and in examining their performance, Yuan tried to collect timely yet accurate information concerning their routine conduct as well as the local people's appraisal of them. According to the testimony of Yuan Shikai's daughter, Yuan often dispatched "secret examiners" to obtain reliable data. Whenever a case occurred, he would send a first examiner closely followed by a second one to do the same investigation into the same official. The two examiners did not know each other but were required to deliver separate reports to Yuan at different times. After reading the two reports, he would be able to get a more impartial image of that official. Once Yuan remarked that "the most important thing for an executive is to know what is going on in the local region. Only with the unerring information can he respond properly. If he was duped by his subordinates, he would be a blind man making mistakes."[40] Within half a year after his arrival in Shandong, Yuan relied on those secret examiners to impeach about ten local magistrates while recommending four individuals to be magistrates.[41]

In particular, Yuan Shikai hated officials' debauched behaviors, immoral sexual misconduct, and visits to prostitutes. Yuan demanded officials to be administrators with integrity while devoting their time and energy to public service. In his eyes, a perverted life wastes energy and leaves less time for governance. According to Qing rule, officials were allowed to take in concubines as long as he was able to support his big family. In this regard, Yuan Shikai took the lead as he had one wife and nine concubines, all considered members of his huge family. A visit to the brothel would discredit an official's reputation. If such a visit was found, that official might be admonished or even dismissed. For gathering accurate information, he sent out plainclothes investigators to monitor an official's visit to a brothel or simply catch him on the spot, as he did with one official, Mr. Wu, whose visit to a prostitute resulted in impeachment. Yuan exposed several other officials' similar visits and warned them of impending severe punishment if such a behavior continued.[42]

Naturally, Yuan proposed to penalize officials in Shandong for a number of other reasons, including their failure to prevent Boxers, to forestall a bandit attack, or to suppress both of them. For example, when the magistrate of Lijin County did not take timely actions to forestall a Boxer attack, he received a penalty of a bad record. Furthermore, this magistrate was ordered to eliminate the Boxers inside his county within a couple of weeks.[43] Some magistrates were penalized because of their extortion, abuse of power, complicity with bandits, spreading unfounded rumors, physical inability, or other misconduct.[44] Nevertheless, Yuan would reexamine certain cases to determine if those penalized officials could be given a second chance. For example, Yuan regarded Gaomi County magistrate Ji Guifen a timid man who mishandled the railway case with the Germans. For this reason, Ji was dismissed from his position and was put on probation.[45] After more than a year's meticulous reexamination, Yuan proposed to reemploy Ji, because he believed that Ji was a talented man of high personal quality.[46]

Two years' governorship in Shandong enabled Yuan to see through the weakness of the officialdom. In his report to the central government, he lamented that "among the over one thousand magistrates and alternate magistrates in Shandong, many were occupied not with business but idleness, while indulging themselves in dainty food, tasty wine, and mundane joyfulness. And, some started to curry favor with their superiors for personal gains." Because they were not able to handle official routines, they relied on their secretaries who often made mistakes. In fact, they became harmful and hazardous to the state. In October 1901, Yuan proposed that the central government establish a special school called the Official Instruction Academy in Shandong and required officials in groups to be trained in politics, foreign affairs, state revenue, and canal control. Obviously, the purpose was to nurture officials in practical learning.[47]

When Yuan arrived in Zhili in late 1901 as its governor-general (with other concurrent titles such as the Commissioner of Trade at Northern Ports), Yuan turned out to be a state leader but was charged with a particular responsibility to govern Zhili Province. He inherited a devastated province; with the Boxer Uprising just suppressed there, foreign troops still stationed in Zhili, and a displaced local population awaiting resettlement, it was a daunting task to rule over this province.[48] Among a few priorities, Yuan saw effective government with efficient officials as a key to stabilize the land, recover the local economy, and improve people's livelihood. He remarked that "Zhili has poor soil on which people live in poverty. After the recent military catastrophe, people's hearts are not pacified and bandits still roam. Now, the province will have to rely on officials for gentle nurturing, exterminating evils, creating a safe environment, revitalizing people's energy, and preventing perversion."[49]

The quality of the officials was not satisfactory, leading Yuan Shikai to order the establishment of the Official Instruction Academy in Zhili to train officials, in particular those alternate officials at county and prefecture levels. Discipline was implemented at the academy, diverse courses offered, and examinations administered to see if the objectives were reached. In Yuan's words, this training academy would enhance the quality of officials with new learning in order to prevent official corruption and administrative ineffectiveness.[50] Major courses included Politics (exposing officials to administration, justice system, and educational management), Foreign Affairs (allowing officials to understand foreign culture, foreign economy, and Sino-foreign treaties), Revenue (urging officials to protect the local economy while collecting taxes), and Canal Control (requiring them to pay attention to the maintenance of rivers and canals, in particular the Yongding River in Zhili). All those courses directed local officials to practical learning and pragmatic solutions to the existing problems. Besides this academy, Yuan also established others such as the Assistant Official and Staff Academy to train minor officials for the same purpose.[51]

It is worthwhile exploring Yuan's contributions to abolish the tradition of selecting officials through the Civil Service Examination System, which had been in place for a millennium. Ever since the Sui dynasty (581–618), this system had significantly shaped Chinese imperial rule. As a meritocracy, it enabled the Chinese Empire to make full use of brilliant talent. Yet, it did not pursue a wider curriculum due to its narrow focus on the ancient classics. It did not give any emphasis to science, technology, and mathematics. As a result, it was seen as a barrier to modernization, because officials who succeeded within these parameters were quite conservative with the old worldview. By the late nineteenth century, the call to abolish it was loud and well heard. Yuan always saw it as an obstruction to national modernization and demanded its elimination. He linked this system to China's backwardness, and argued that China could not be prosperous if it continued to exist.[52] With his advocacy and persuasion, the Qing dynasty in 1905 finally abolished it. Its eradication prompted office seekers to study science, modern education, and practical problem-solving skills, and compelled them to devote themselves to Western learning, which was what Yuan really anticipated.

Yuan focused on founding new venues for training officials, such as the Zhili College of Politics and Law. As he explained, the institution's aim was to "prepare its students to be officials at prefecture and county levels" and to replace the previous Official Instruction Academy. The difference between the two was that the academy tended to be informal while the new college functioned as a higher-level institution with comprehensive curriculum, including constitutional studies, economy, ethnics, history, geography, mathematics, education, law, foreign language, and international treaty.[53] The college offered two programs, one lasting for half a year as preparatory study, and another lasting for one and a half years of advanced study. Yuan even invited foreign instructors to tutor students about Western learning. When the college was initiated in October 1905, about 160 individuals were admitted, far above the original target of 120. After graduation and further examination, many of those graduates became officials in Zhili.[54]

While hiring new officials who had gained modern education, Yuan Shikai ordered the reduction of the bloated officialdom in Zhili, as it had a lot of redundant positions consuming a huge amount of state budget. Minor officials and staff, according to Yuan's observation, actually became "tigers and wolves" to harass, harm, and damage the local community, because of their misuse of power and their collaboration with bandits. Not surprisingly,

Yuan called for shrinking the local government by eliminating redundancies. Within a year from October 1902 to October 1903, under Yuan's orders, the Tianjin county government enforced two major elimination measures. As a result, the original huge county bureaucracy of more than 3,000 men was reduced to only 250 or so. In other words, less than 10 percent of the former personnel remained, which significantly minimized the county government and enhanced its effective performance.[55]

Even after the streamlining, Yuan did not stop working for a more efficient and less bloated bureaucracy. In 1907, under his guidance, Zhili Province established two agencies for that purpose. One was the Investigation Bureau to probe people's complaints and study officials' charges against other officials. The second was the Tryout Bureau, which supervised new officials and delivered a report twice a month to offer recommendations in regard to promotion, demotion, and dismissal of officials.[56] In overseeing officials' hiring and retention, Yuan was inclined to keep individual character and personal disposition at the forefront of his personnel decisions. He justified his rejection of eleven kinds of individuals into the government with the following characters: cunningness, ostentation, indiscretion, arrogance, greediness, boastfulness, hesitation, indecision, nonchalance, unfaithfulness, and shamelessness. He believed that those individual traits often led officials to make mistakes and commit crimes, resulting in weak administration and iniquitous governance.[57]

Yuan Shikai implemented a policy to broaden the scope of officials by sending them overseas to acquire new knowledge and to expose them to the culture of industrialized countries. For young officials, the journey was to learn and for senior officials it was to experience new things. By mid-1905, Yuan dispatched over one hundred Zhili officials overseas, with each individual's journey lasting approximately three months, during which some were required to attend short-term programs at different schools. The destination was usually Japan or some Western country, where they visited local officials, judges, teachers, and entrepreneurs. Yuan required them to keep a diary and report on their experience upon returning.[58] The expense was paid by the provincial government. As more joined the journey, Yuan required the local county government to raise more money for this study abroad program. Later on, he even allowed certain individuals to sponsor their own journey. Those who did well would be appointed with a higher position upon return. Yuan penalized those who squandered public funds. For example, Deng Yongkui, a country magistrate, was sent to Japan to attend a specially designed program in law and politics. While in Japan, Deng spent his days seeking personal pleasure, flunked his short-term courses, and was expelled by the university authorities. After a brief verification, Yuan dismissed Deng from his position, purporting to warn others to study hard during the overseas program.[59]

One unprecedented move by Yuan Shikai was his promotion of local autonomy by allowing a popular election in Tianjin to organize an assembly in mid-1907. After setting qualifications, such as the qualifying age of twenty-five, property valued at $2,500 (Chinese dollars), no criminal record, an elementary school education, among others, Yuan vehemently promoted this first election in Chinese history. Although it had a limited representation, it allowed the local elites to participate in local governance.[60] The result of election was the formation of the Tianjin Assembly with thirty members. The assemblymen would work with local administrators to handle issues, offer advice, and take part in other local matters.[61] When the assembly was convened on August 20, 1907, Yuan congratulated the assemblymen and praised this first successful election as the future model of the whole nation. He encouraged assemblymen to work diligently for the benefit of the local populace.[62] Without a doubt, this election was a breakthrough in China's political life. Changing practice that had lasted a millennium, its limited scope did not allow the majority of the population to participate and it could not be called a democratic institution. At least, those local elites got a chance to work with local officials to handle local affairs.

The official violations of imperial rules pained Yuan Shikai, who in turn was resolute in his efforts to punish transgressors. Embezzlement or stealing of public funds was penalized without mercy. Extortion or adding illegal levies burdening the local people was not tolerated. Bad habits and laziness were taboo.[63] Unfair or perfunctory verdicts to local cases would not be accepted. If an official could not complete his duties, he would be removed from his position. Guangzong County magistrate Wang Yujun delayed the collection of the local tax of more than 3,500 taels, for which he was dismissed. Under Yuan's order, Wang was required to pay that amount within two weeks; otherwise, his family property would be confiscated as collateral.[64] The use of the kangaroo court often resulted in severe penalties. For example, Zhili alternate prefectural magistrate Xu Fuli tried to control a mining area while disrespecting state rules. Even worse, he unlawfully arrested the state inspector and tortured him during an illegal detention. For this matter, Xu was dismissed and further punished as a criminal.[65] Pretension with a fake identity could cost an official his position. One prefectural magistrate, Zhu Xilin, pretended to be a higher-ranking official during his travel in northeast China (Manchuria), which was viewed as a dishonest act. For this very reason, Zhu was fired from his job.[66]

Presidential Institutionalization

Yuan Shikai never expected that he would be the first president of the Republic of China while he was serving the Qing Empire. After nearly a decade of holding high-ranking positions as the governor of Shandong, the governor-general of Zhili, and a brief tenure as minister of foreign affairs, he was dismissed by Prince Regent Zaifeng in early 1909 due to a power struggle at the imperial court. As a result, he retired from politics for nearly three years and resided in his home province of Henan. It was the outbreak of the 1911 Revolution that offered him a chance to reemerge as one of the most powerful men of the empire. Of course, during the change from empire to republic, Yuan was instrumental in turning this revolution into a less bloody and less violent transition, becoming the first president through political compromise. After the imperial abdication, Yuan served as president between 1912 and 1916. During his four-year presidency and with the exception of his fleeting monarchical endeavors in early 1916, Yuan carried his official management to this young republic, where he endeavored to institutionalize it. He created a brand-new mechanism, allowing his government to be mindful of official selection and to be alert to officials' routine performance.

As soon as Yuan assumed his position as president of the republic, he began to implement his reform to transform the traditional official system into a new civil servant system. Besides legislators in Congress and officers in the army, all other officials would be "civil servants." Yuan categorized officials into a few categories and divided them into professional power-holders: executives, diplomats, techno-officials, tax collectors, court judges, police officers, and so on. He ordered different salaries for each group and used state law to guarantee payment. Through the system, he hoped to establish an efficient yet modern bureaucracy full of competent officials carrying out their official duties. Yuan hoped the newly institutionalized positions, along with the corresponding higher incomes, would stimulate the interests of gifted individuals to be qualified officials and would encourage them to work enthusiastically for the young republic.[67]

The selection of civil servants would be conducted through examinations, as Yuan's rules specified on January 9, 1913. The coverage of the examinations contained Chinese learning and Western learning, including language, history, geography, civil law, international law, economics, finance, politics, justice, international treaties, and so forth.[68] The examination consisted of preliminary and advanced examinations, oral and written tests, and other special requirements. Successful candidates would be further reviewed before appointment as officials. For administering the examinations, Yuan established a committee and the Examination Bureau to take charge of officials' examinations and appointments.[69] Yuan advised the examiners to avoid prejudice, bias, bribery, favoritism, nepotism, and other unfair measures in order to obtain qualified, moral, and upright public servants.[70] Of course, the implementation of this new system took time, yet it epitomizes Yuan's orchestration to choose officials with a high level of expertise.

Yuan initiated the bestowal of various awards and honors, such as the Jiahe, Jinhe, and Wenhu medals to outstanding officials and to encourage them to be more diligent in their positions. A careful reading of the primary sources shows that this bestowal was an oft-heard story. The purpose was to use models to inspire other officials to follow suit. Naturally, this was done in addition to the governmental routine recognition of the officials' yearly achievements. The honor, of course, attracted the people's respect to the awardees, and served as an incentive for them to be more cautious and more diligent. An awardee could be one of the state leaders, such as Li Yuanhong, who received the first-grade Jiahe Medal on the New Year's Day in 1914, or just a local official, such as Li Ji, who was Fangcheng County magistrate in Henan. The reason why Li got the honor was because he captured nearly sixty bandits while seizing their weapons during a local rural pacification campaign. Thus, Li received the fifth-grade Jiahe Medal on August 2, 1914.[71] To recognize the contributions of over thirty magistrates for collecting tax in a timely manner, Yuan ordered the bestowal of fifth-grade Jinhe Medals on September 6, 1914.[72] Altogether, Yuan conferred hundreds of different kinds of medals during his presidency.

Yuan Shikai demanded long-term service, as short term meant a waste of the enormous investment of governmental resources and could cause troubles to a region or a particular administration. Citing the ancient official stint of a ten-year period, Yuan valued lengthy service in one position to maximize an official's capability to serve the state. For the longer service, an official could shoulder an array of responsibilities by making full use of his expertise to obtain a more satisfactory result. As the young republic encountered chaos and unpredictability, an official's durable work in one position would be congenial to the local people. Yuan ordered on August 2, 1914, that "once an appointment is made, an official should not be relocated to another place at will. In case a relocation is necessary, it must be approved by the government through a normal procedure." Hopefully, as Yuan expected, all officials would diligently complete their duties in their positions for a longer time.[73]

Yuan Shikai emphasized the importance of local officials, once remarking that people's welfare could not be guaranteed if grassroots politics did not move onto the right track. He ordered that the provincial government report the performance of its officials once every three months, while the county government deliver a report about its official performance once a month.[74] In late 1913, Yuan's government required local administrators, in particular county magistrates, to go to Beijing in groups for a special training program to enrich their knowledge, enhance their familiarity with modern politics, and improve their management skills. The successful ones received certificates while a small number of unsuccessful ones would be warned or dismissed due to poor performance.[75] As the local officials served as intermediates between the central government and the overwhelming majority of the Chinese population, Yuan saw them as a pillar of the successful Chinese government. On May 15, 1914, during his meeting with the county magistrates, Yuan advised them to be clean, cautious, and diligent. The magistrates were expected to perform well at grassroots politics while never alienating themselves from the local populace.[76]

Yuan Shikai always warned the officials to be on guard against undesirable behaviors. On March 30, 1915, he proposed his "Four Admonitions" to them against laziness, nepotism, extravagance, and pleasure-seeking. He told them that "if every official does his duty, the country that is not strong will be strong. If every official neglects his responsibility, the state that should not perish will perish."[77] He asked officials to place a plaque with a political motto on it and to hang it in their offices as a serious warning to secure them from going astray.[78] He advised officials to be frugal as the young republic encountered a financial difficulty, implying that "one penny less for expenditure means one penny more for the benefits of the civilian administration."[79] He demanded that provincial officials during their inspection tours in the local community not burden civilians by bringing less escorts and less guards and by paying their own meals. He made it clear that any violations would be punished severely.[80]

In terms of handling official violations, Yuan Shikai made a breakthrough in China's administrative history, because he promulgated the first administrative procedural law and established the Political Correction Board, the first such body in modern China, to handle related cases concerning officials' crimes, violations, and accusations.[81] The board was established on March 31, 1914, with fifteen arbitrators to offer verdicts on different cases. The arbitrators were mostly legal experts who had many years' experience in handling judicial cases. Now, their new job was to target corrupt officials and penalize them according to the legal code. To highlight the importance of this board, Yuan inserted one article in the Constitution of the Republic of China promulgated on May 1, 1914, to declare the board's duty as accepting people's complaints and legal cases against any corrupt officials.[82] In case of a criminal case, the board would work with the judge of a criminal court to offer a verdict. An overall survey of the board's operations displays its sound mechanism and its systematic procedures. In its existence for fourteen years from 1914 to 1928, the board handled a number of tough cases and punished many corrupt officials.[83] The board is now hailed as the first administrative procedural legal system in Chinese history.[84]

Within the Political Correction Board, Yuan Shikai ordered the establishment of the Political Supervision Council with one chief impeacher along with sixteen other impeachers whose job was to bring charges against corrupt officials and send them to trial by the board and by the criminal court.

Anybody, either civilian or official, could lodge complaints to this council against any official. After receiving a case, the chief impeacher, after working with other impeachers, would report it to the president who would send it to the board for a deliberation and further actions. According to the impeachment act, four issues were serious problems: officials' violation of constitution and laws, receipt and payment of bribes, abuse of power, and negligence of people's suffering.[85] In its short existence from 1914 to 1916, the council brought a number of cases and assisted the president to punish corrupt officials. Nevertheless, Yuan wrote a note to the council to advise the impeachers to collect reliable yet convincing evidence before filing a formal impeachment, to refuse to listen to erratic rumors, and to act impartially without any personal bias.[86]

In the midst of institutional reform, Yuan still found that corruption among officials remained prevalent. In the past, he blamed the rotten regimentation for allowing officials room for debasement. Now, he blamed the corrupt officials for their own personal characters. As he saw it, senior officials tended to be conservative, while junior officials were predisposed to be arrogant. Both conservativism and arrogance led them to behave dishonestly, dishonorably, and fraudulently. Consequently, hedonism, greediness, and extravagance became officials' behaviors. The abuse of power occurred. Some officials carried their personal love and hatred into their handling of public issues and others judged cases according to their own contentment and rage. Some utilized the state law to work for their families' well-being, while others ignored the state law behaving as hegemons in the local community.[87] No matter how Yuan's government prohibited evil habits, some officials continued to indulge themselves in unethical living. As a result, gambling, sexual immorality, and luxurious wastefulness were persistent. Even in the national capital, which was supposed to be the model for the entire country, the above problems were rampant.[88] While the hedonistic life of officials hampered their performance as public servants, their assistants would utilize the chance to commit sinful acts. Facing this situation, Yuan decided to enforce draconian measures to punish those unscrupulous administrators.

Yuan Shikai matched his words to his actions. At first, his actions were modest as he established the Civil Servant Penalty and Admonition Committees at the central government and provincial levels to handle official violations, including not fulfilling responsibilities, defilement of identities, and loss of popular trust. The penalty included dismissal, demotion, salary reduction, and admonition.[89] A careful examination shows that this action of discipline tended to be too broad while the penalty was too light. As Yuan continued to witness widespread corruption, he announced the Official Corruption Penalty Act on June 5, 1914. In it, he stipulated that any officials who intentionally yet illegally seized $500 would be penalized by a capital sentence, that any official who embezzled $1,000 unintentionally would be penalized by life imprisonment, and that any official who escaped with $5,000 of public funds even after return would be sentenced to capital punishment. The act made it clear that capital punishment must be carried out by gunshot, and that those who received other punishment would be exiled to Xinjiang or other remote frontier regions.[90] He hoped that the new act would achieve its objective as a warning to all officials.[91]

Yuan Shikai offered no mercy to even high-ranking officials regardless of their previous contributions to his government. The Wang Zhixin case is an instance to the point. Wang Zhixin (1868–1914), a native of Shandong, had been a follower of Yuan Shikai for over a decade during which he assisted Yuan to suppress the Boxers in Shandong and helped organize the first police force in modern China. After the republic was established, Wang served as the vice minister of internal affairs and then the superintendent of the patrolling police in Beijing. In 1913, Wang was promoted to be the executive chief of Shuntian prefecture with more than twenty counties around the Beijing Area. In fact, his position is equivalent to today's mayor of Beijing.[92] Wang abused his power by selling official positions, extorting local businessmen, smuggling opium, and padding the bills to steal state funds.[93] Altogether, the money Wang seized illegally amounted to over $50,000. For Yuan, "this was a heinous crime, worse than a bandit waylaying property and murdering the owner." Under Yuan's order, Wang was quickly arrested and sentenced to death, which was swiftly carried out by execution. Yuan circulated a notice about this case to warn officials of the serious consequence in case of corruption.[94]

Because Yuan Shikai stressed the importance of local officials, he punished many violators in different provinces, in particular those at the county level. According to one source, between 1914 and 1916, Yuan's government handled 153 cases and punished 470 men, including 431 county magistrates, or 91.5 percent of the total.[95] Some magistrates were punished severely, for example, Yang Dao, Rongxian County magistrate in Guangxi Province, was executed under Yuan's order due his illegal seizure of local money.[96] Hanyuan County magistrate Chen Xi in Sichuan Province, besides his greediness for money, did not handle a bandit attack on the county seat well, resulting in colossal losses after bandits looted the public funds. Chen was handed a capital sentence.[97] Liu Dingxi, Baxian County magistrate in Zhili Province, because of fraud and illegal taking of money over $500, was punished by a swift execution.[98] Other local officials were penalized for different reasons. Wen Dingxiang, the manager of Hubei Mint, who intentionally reduced the purity of copper coins and illegally made silver coins for his own profit, was dismissed from his position even after he returned what he seized.[99]

Yuan's other measures for official management deserves our attention. As he did in his Zhili years, he intended to make the republican government efficient yet not elephantine. When his government encountered financial straits, he proposed cutting down redundant and titular positions in order to both make ends meet and reach the objective of effective administration. In early 1915, when Zhou Ziqi, the minister of finance, delivered a report about the budget issue, Yuan issued an order to the whole country to eliminate unnecessary positions. Offices with idle officials must be streamlined. Specially established governmental bodies, once finished with their tasks, should be eradicated. Overlapping offices should be combined. For example, the local mining supervisory office should be integrated into the provincial department of finance or department of agriculture and commerce. Step by step, after careful elimination, the government, he hoped, could be more productive. Those officials who were removed could be hired again once new vacancies became available.[100]

Although the students returning from overseas programs constituted a modest fraction of the administration, Yuan always paid special attention to them. While he was elated to see the returning students bringing knowledge back to China, he saw problems in their employment in the government. Quite a few did not do what they had studied. Some were forced to assume official positions as a decoration for an administration. Some became a waste as they were appointed in an unfamiliar field. Now, Yuan ordered the hiring of those returned students according to their expertise, making sure that their talent matched their new positions. He suggested that it would be better if they served as officials in schools, railways, banks, mining, hospitals, postal services, urban management, or other relevant fields. The Examination Bureau would keep an archive of their files and would offer promotion according to their performance. In this way, he wanted to see to it that returned the students who returned wield a particular influence through imparting their specially acquired knowledge into the Chinese statecraft. He even expected that some of them would continue to develop their own expertise in their fields so that they could be excellent specialists just like their counterparts in the industrialized countries.[101]

Conclusion

Since the late 1970s, as China embraced the age of reform, the Chinese attitude toward Yuan Shikai has enormously changed. Yuan is no longer a historical villain as previously believed. Rather, the collective memory of Yuan tends to be quite objective. He is now remembered not only as a man who made a grave mistake in his monarchical endeavors, but also as a man who contributed to China's modernization in a number of ways. Without a doubt, Yuan's monarchical move has bred controversy which was detrimental to the nation and fatal to his own life. In many other respects, however, Yuan was a contributor to his nation's overall modernization, including his reform on the existing bureaucracy as discussed here. Although Yuan is not officially rehabilitated, as some scholars have intended to do, his image has become more positive than ever. No intention in this chapter is made to rehabilitate this man's image. Nevertheless, one major aspect of his political career should not be neglected. Here, his official management is explored, purporting to display the intricate political mechanism around the time of China's transition from empire to republic during which Yuan put his efforts to build an efficient and clean government.

The history of Yuan's official management could be roughly partitioned into two phases. The first one was his provincial reform in Shandong and Zhili as a provincial chief executive. Motivated by patriotism after China's defeats at the hands of great powers, Yuan desired to modernize his country and blamed corruption in an ineffective government as a factor leading to his nation's backwardness. It was in Shandong and Zhili that he got a chance to implement his creative ideas to reconstruct the administration, to transform officials, and to discipline violators. He pioneered his firm actions, including the abolition of the Civil Service Examination System. During his presidency, he even institutionalized his official management by promulgating relevant laws and by establishing new state bodies. He posited official management to be a part of his state-building and nation-building. Now, under the pen of historians, Yuan is the man who initiated the first civil servant system in modern China, issued the first administrative procedural law, and established the first administrative judging institution.[102] All those should be seen as his contributions to his nation's administrative modernization.

In a sense, Yuan Shikai devoted a considerable amount of his life to official management. The analysis of his efforts points to his innermost commitment that talented prospective officials must be identified, trained, employed, and disciplined to reach the lofty goal of national revival. Recently, a scholar commented that Yuan respected meritocracy, cherished personal ability, and valued individual integrity. "Whether an individual was a returned student or a member of the traditional gentry, whether he came from a humble background or was born in a prestigious family, and whether he was a literati or a military commander, Yuan would employ him according to his ability so long as he had a special expertise. Yuan's approach was comprehensive, open-minded, progressive, and flexible, which contributed to the successful rise of his Beiyang Clique."[103] Indeed, Yuan was obsessed with handling official management as demonstrated by his trying to retain relevant information in his own mind. He always showed his acute sensitivity to any wrong information. As one of his contemporaries commented, "Yuan has a good memory . . . . Yuan can memorize those details about local affairs, long after his officials from different provinces visited him and reported to him. His familiarity with local politics somehow and sometimes surpasses those local officials, making them very frightened in front of him."[104] Indeed, his dedication to official management persisted until the last minute of his life, as the two documents he approved before his death on June 6, 1916, were his decisions to promote one person to be the vice minister of communication and to appoint another individual to be the treasurer of Heilongjiang Province.[105]

Although Yuan Shikai intended to deliver sound official policies and endeavored to institutionalize official management, to his disappointment, corruption remained endemic as scandals were exposed. It seemed that the situation did not improve, as he received reports concerning the scandals wrought by shameless officials who horrified the nation and hurt the people living under them. The corruption issue was more complex than his proposed solutions promising overnight triumph. This study raises a question about the perpetual nature of official corruption and proves that official management has been a constant theme in China's long political history. The problem could not be solved by one determined man like Yuan Shikai. As long as power centralism exists, officials will utilize their authority to seize benefits. As long as the political operation is not transparent, corruption will inevitably reemerge. As long as the lack of effective checks on power persists, fraud will emerge. Corruption, more or less, is the cancer of all governments. Although Yuan Shikai tried to eradicate it and the subsequent regimes have continued to do so with vigorous endeavors, corruption resurfaced as a headache to them all because those regimes, including Yuan's, were centralist in nature, were not transparent enough, and were not effectively balanced effectively. Nevertheless, this is not to deny many of Yuan's valuable contributions to modernize China's administrative system.

NOTES

1. Yuan Shikai, "Shang Weng Tonghe xulun bianfa shuotie" (January 16, 1898), *Yuan Shikai quanji* [to be abbreviated YSKQJ] Vol. 4, 61.

2. Yuan, "Zhi xinjianlujun xingwuchu Xu Shichang han" (January 6, 1900), *QSKQJ*, Vol. 5, 42.

3. Yuan, "Zunfeng mianyutiaochen shijia qingdai zouzhe" (August 20, 1895), *YSKQJ*, Vol. 3, 536–538.

4. Yuan, "Wenguan baozhangfa caoan liyou" (July 20, 1912), *YSKQJ*, Vol. 20, 205.

5. Yuan, "Xuejie suzhengshi zhi yanci" (May 26, 1914), *YSKQJ*, Vol. 26, 479.

6. Yuan, "Jiejian pingzhengyuan renyuan zhi xunci" (June 6, 1914), *YSKQJ*, Vol. 27, 63.

7. Yuan, "Zhi shu liangjiangzongdu Zhang Zhidong dian" (February 17, 1903), Vol. 11, 24.

8. Yuan, "Shang Weng Tonghe bianfa shuotie" (December 30, 1897), *YSKQJ*, Vol. 4, 60.

9. Yuan, "Zunfeng mianyutiaochen shijian qingdai zouzhe" (August 20, 1895), *YSKQJ*, Vol. 3, 536.

10. Yuan, "Xuzhong najian ling" (June 24, 1914), *YSKQJ*, Vol. 27, 219.

11. Yuan, "Qing kaifu beican zhixian Ji Guifen pian" (June 10, 1901), *YSKQJ*, Vol. 9, 545.

12. Yuan, "Dui moyaoyuan zhi yongren fangzhen tan" (June 17, 1915), *YSKQJ*, Vol. 31, 593.

13. Yuan, "Wenguan renyongfa caoan liyou" (July 20, 1912), *YSKQJ*, Vol. 20, 205.

14. Yuan, "Duiyu yongren zhi tongyu" (March 9, 1915), *YSKQJ*, Vol. 30, 600.

15. Yuan, "Mizou qingganjin shixing yubeilixian jinchenguanjian shitiao" (July 26, 1907), *QSKQJ*, Vol. 16, 335.

16. Li Zhongping, "Qingmo xinzhengshiqi Yuan Shikai rencai sixiang tanxi" [An analysis of Yuan Shikai's ideas on talents during the New Administration of Late Qing], *Anhui shixue* [Anhui History] (No. 3, 2008), 53.

17. Yuan, "Yongren yuanze" (July 31, 1915), *YSKQJ*, Vol. 32, 227.

18. Zhang Qiwen, "Qianxi Yuan Shikai de rencai sixiang" [An analysis of Yuan Shikai's ideas on talents], *Fazhi yu shehui* [Law and Society] (No. 11, 2009), 306.

19. Li Zhongping, ibid., 53.

20. Chu Shuangzhi, "Xinzhengshiqi Yuan Shikai dui Zhili lizhi de zhengdun" [Yuan Shikai's official management during the new administration in Zhili], *Beijing-kejidaxue xuebao* [Journal of University of Science and Technology of Beijing] (Vol. 18, No. 2, June 2002), 28.

21. Yuan, "Zunfeng mianyutiaochen shijia qingdai zouzhe" (August 20, 1895), *YSKQJ*, Vol. 3, 538.

22. Ibid., 538.

23. Yuan, "Xianling gesheng minzhengzhang yanxing kaohe xianzhishi ling" (October 17, 1913), *YSKQJ*, Vol. 24, 73.

24. Yuan, "Jingjuxianneng gezhixian kenqing zhuoyong zhe" (February 6, 1901), *YSKQJ*, Vol. 8, 239.

25. Yuan, "Geminzhengzhang shenze xianneng ling" (November 7, 1913), *YSKQJ*, Vol. 24, 194.

26. Yuan, "Xianling gesheng minzhengzhang yanxing kaohe xianzhishi ling" (October 17, 1913), YSKQJ, Vol. 24, 73.

27. Yuan, "Gongbu Zhonghuaminguo yuefa zhi bugao" (May 1, 1914), *YSKQJ*, Vol. 26, 211.

28. Wang Birong, *Bainian Yuanjia* [The Yuan family in the one hundred years] (Guilin: Guangxishida Chubanshe, 2013), 18.

29. Yuan, "Bugao neiwai daxiao wenwu guanya" (February 13, 1912), *YSKQJ*, Vol. 19, 566.

30. Su Quanyou, He Kewei, *Yuan Shikai zhuan* [Biography of Yuan Shikai] (Hangzhou: Zhejiangdaxue Chubanshe, 2013), 336.

31. Deng Yiwu, "Lun Yuan Shikai zhengfu de wenguan zhidu" [On the civil servant system of the Yuan Shikai Government], *Jinandaxue xuebao* [Journal of Jinan University] (Vol. 12, No. 1, 2002), 48.

32. Chen Guanghua, "Beiyang zhengfushiqi wenguan chengjiezhidu tanxi" [An analysis of the penalty and admonition of civil servants during the Beijing Government Era], *Heilongjiang shizhi* [History of Heilongjiang] (No. 23, 2008), 18.

33. Yuan, "Culing zunxing guanli weiling chenghualing zhi ling" (August 19, 1914), *YSKQJ*, Vol. 28, 158.

34. Yuan, "Tongyu bailiao ling" (March 13, 1012), *YSKQJ*, Vol. 19, 633.

35. Yuan, "Zhengdun guanchang ling" (October 20, 1913), *YSKQJ*, Vol. 24, 84.

36. Yuan, "Gongbao didong jieshufu zhuanzhe" (December 26, 1899), *YSKQJ*, Vol. 5, 3.

37. Yuan, "Zhi xinjianlujun yingwuchu Xu Shichang han" (January 6, 1900), *YSKQJ*, Vol. 5, 42.

38. Yuan, "Tongchigao" (January 19, 1900), *YSKQJ*, Vol. 5, 98.

39. Yang Tao, "Gengzishibian hou Yuan Shikai lizhu 'chengban huoshou' zhuzhang tanxi" [An analysis of Yuan Shikai's vehement proposal after 1901 to punish those chief officials who were responsible for the Boxer Uprising], *Guizhou wenshi congkan* [Journal of Guizhou literature and history] (No. 4, 2010), 16.

40. Yuan Jingxue, *Nueryanzhonglingmian Yuan Shikai* [Seeing Yuan Shikai from daughter's eyes] (Beijing: Zhongguowenshichubanbshe, 2012), 18.

41. Liu Yijiang, *Yuan Shikai pingzhuan* [A critical biography of Yuan Shikai] (Vol. 1) (Beijing: Jingjiribaochubanshe, 2004), 349.

42. Niu Jinkui, "Yuan Shikai qiaozhi guanchang buzhengzhifeng" [Yuan Shikai's wise way of correcting the evils of the officialdom], *Wenshi bolan* [Broadview of literature and history] (No. 12, 2015), 70.

43. Yuan, "Pi Lijinxian bing" (July 26, 1900), *YSKQJ*, Vol. 6, 11.

44. Yuan, "Tecan yonglie buzhi wenwugeyuan zhe" (December 31, 1900), *YSKQJ*, Vol. 8, 54.

45. Yuan, "Qingjiang zhixian Ji Guifen zhaiding chakan pian" (May 19, 1900), *YSKQJ*, Vol. 5, 445.

46. Yuan, "Qing kaifu beican zhixian Ji Guifen pian" (June 10, 1901), *YSKQJ*, Vol. 9, 545.

47. Yuan, "Kaiban keliguan pian" (November 4, 1901), *YSKQJ*, Vol. 9, 640.

48. Stephen MacKinnon, *Power and Politics in Late Imperial China: Yuan Shikai in Beijing and Tianjin* (Berkeley, CA: University of California Press, 1980), 37.

49. Yuan Shikai, "Kaocha shuli fenbie juhai zhe" (July 3, 1904), *YSKQJ*, Vol. 12, 264.

50. Yuan Shikai, "Pi keliguan bing keli diyi anqingce you" (June 23, 1904), *YSKQJ*, Vol. 12, 234.

51. Yuan Shikai, "Keli timu" (June 4, 1905), *YSKQJ*, Vol. 13, 499. Yuan Shikai, "Changshe lixuxuetang tongchi zhuoliang sheli zha" (July 16, 1905), *YSKQJ*, Vol. 13, 576.

52. Yuan Shikai, "Zhi liangjiangzongdu Zhang Zhidong dian" (February 17, 1902), *YSKQJ*, Vol. 11, 25.

53. Yuan Shikai, "Niding fazhengxuetang zhangchengtiaogui zhe" (July 29, 1906), *YSKQJ*, Vol. 15, 212.

54. Tian Zhengping, Xia Yijun, "Yuan Shikai yu Qingmo guanshen jiaoyu" [Yuan Shikai and official education during the late Qing Dynasty], *Zhejiangdaxue xuebao* [Journal of Zhejiang University] (No. 10, 2010), 71.

55. Chu Shuangzhi, "Xinzhengshiqi Yuan Shikai dui Zhili lizhi de zhengdun," ibid., 29.

56. Yuan Shikai, "Zhafa diaochachu zhangcheng wen" (May 20, 1907), *YSKQJ*, Vol. 16, 132. Yuan Shikai, "Zhafa kaoyanchu zhangcheng wen" (May 22, 1907), *YSKQJ*, Vol. 16, 138.

57. Chu Shuangzhi, "Xinzhengshiqi Yuan Shikai dui Zhili lizhi de zhengdun," ibid., 39.

58. Yuan Shikai, "Fengchi guanshen fu Riben youli pian" (July 20, 1905), *YSKQJ*, Vol. 13, 585.

59. Yuan Shikai, "Zhiguan Deng Yongkui zai Ri youxue huangfei qingyugezhi pian" (May 20, 1906), *YSKQJ*, Vol. 15, 51.

60. Jerome Ch'en, *Yuan Shih-k'ai* (Stanford, CA: Stanford University Press, 1972), 73.

61. Su Quanyou, "Yuan Shikai yu Tianjin defang zizhi" [Yuan Shikai and Tianjin local autonomy], *Liaochengshifanxueyuan xuebao* [Journal of Liaocheng Teachers' College] (No. 2, 2001), 74.

62. Yuan Shikai, "Tianjin yishihui chenglizhiri tixueshi Lu Jing daiweizhici wen" (August 20, 1907), *YSKQJ*, Vol. 16, 432.

63. Yuan Shikai, "Fuchen yige zhizhou Yao Yuqing weiguanqingxing zhe" (July 25, 1902), *YSKQJ*, Vol. 10, 358.

64. Yuan Shikai, "Zuijiao yige zhixian Wang Yujun kuiqian pian" (May 31, 1902), *YSKQJ*, Vol. 10, 261.

65. Yuan Shikai, "Qingjiang zhizhou Xu Fuli gezhi xunban pian" (December 29, 1905), *YSKQJ*, Vol. 14, 386.

66. Yuan Shikai, "Qingjiang Zhu Xilin gezhi shenpban pian" (September 27, 1904), *YSKQJ*, Vol. 12, 470.

67. Yuan Shikai, "Gongbu zhongyang xingzhengguan guandeng faling" (October 16, 1912), *YSKQJ*, Vol. 20, 507.

68. Yuan Shikai, "Gongbu guanyu wenguan renmian zhixing ling" (January 9, 1913), *YSKQJ*, Vol. 21, 353.

69. Ji Liping, "Beijing zhengfushiqi wenguan kaoshi yu renyong zhidu pingxi" [An analysis of the mechanism for civil servant examinations and appointments], *Shixue yuekan* [History Monthly] (No. 12, 2005), 55–56.

70. Yuan Shikai, "Lijin kaoshi exi ling" (January 31, 1914), *YSKQJ*, Vol. 25, 205.

71. Yuan Shikai, "Yu Li Ji xunzhang ling" (August 2, 1914), *YSKQJ*, Vol. 28, 9.

72. Yuan Shikai, "Yu Xu Jiayan deng jiangzhang ling" (September 6, 1914), *YSKQJ*, Vol. 28, 303.

73. Yuan Shikai, "Shenzhong rongdian zhengdiao zhiguan ling" (August 2, 1914), *YSKQJ*, Vol. 28, 11.

74. Yuan Shikai, "Dianling gesheng chabao lizhi chengji" (April 18, 1914), *YSKQJ*, Vol. 26, 126.

75. Ji Liping, ibid., 57.

76. Yuan Shikai, "Diyici xianzhishi jinjian xunci" (May 15, 1914), *YSKQJ*, Vol. 26, 351–353.

77. Yuan Shikai, "Mingcui sijie yongzuo guanzhen ling" (March 30, 1915), *YSKQJ*, Vol. 30, 786.

78. Yuan Shikai, "Zhengdun lizhi ling" (September 22, 1914), *YSKQJ*, Vol. 28, 419.

79. Yuan Shikai, "Yancheng guanshi xuxiang erxi ling" (November 6, 1914), *YSKQJ*, Vol. 29, 284.

80. Yuan Shikai, "Qinqiu minmo ling" (January 7, 1915), *YSKQJ*, Vol. 30, 44.

81. Ernest Young, *The Presidency of Yuan Shih-k'ai: Liberalism and Dictatorship in Early Republican China* (University of Michigan Press, 1977), 161.

82. Yuan Shikai, "Gongbu Zhonghuaminguo yuefa ling" (May 1, 1914), *YSKQJ*, Vol. 26, 205.

83. Zhao Yong, Wang Xuehui, "Zhongguo xingzheng shenpan zhidu de diyici shijian—Pingzhengyuanzhidu de chuangli yu yanbian" [The first experiment of China's administrative legal system—the establishment and evolution of the Political Correction Board and its system], *Renmin luntan* [People's Tribune] (Vol. 432, No. 2, 2014), 103.

84. Li Weiyi, "Minchu Pingzhengyuan xingshi xingzhengjiancha zhineng de zhidu changshi lun" [An analysis of the function and judging system of the Political Correction Board during the early years of the Republic of China], *Zhengzhoudaxue xuebao* [Journal of Zhengzhou University] (Vol. 39, No. 3, May 2006), 66.

85. Yuan, "Gongbu jiutanfa ling" (July 20, 1914), *YSKQJ*, Vol. 27, 484.

86. Yuan, "Shouyu suzhengting" (March 11, 1915), *YSKQJ*, Vol. 614.

87. Yuan, "She Pingzhengyuan chengxu guanfang ling" (April 2, 1914), *YSKQJ*, Vol. 26, 8.

88. Yuan, "Yanjin guanli judu yeyou ling" (August 29, 1914), *YSKQJ*, Vol. 28, 239.

89. Yuan, "Gongbu guanyu wenguan renmian zhixing ling" (January 9, 1913), *YSKQJ*, Vol. 21, 359.

90. Yuan, "Guanyuan fanzang zhizui tiaoli ling" (June 5, 1914), *YSKQJ*, Vol. 27, 44.

91. Chen Guanghua, "Beiyang zhengfushiqi wenguan chengjiezhidu tanxi," ibid., 19.

92. Si Gong, "Yuan Shikai fantan cengqiangbi buxia 'Beijing shizhang'" [Yuan Shikai's anti-corruption and his execution of his subordinate who was the mayor of Beijing], *Beijing nongye* [Beijing agriculture] (No. 1, 2012), 39.

93. Zhang Yaojie, "Yuan Shikai da 'laohu' de beihou yinqing" [The scene behind Yuan Shikai's anti-corruption campaign], *Lianzheng liaowang* [Vision for Clean Administration] (No. 10, 2015), 68.

94. Yuan, "Yancheng nahuilanzang zhi Wang Zhixin yi chengqianbihou ling" (October 24, 1914), *YSKQJ*, Vol. 29, 178.

95. Chen Guanghua, "Yuan Shikai zhengfu shiqi de zhishi chengjie zhidu shulun" [An analysis of the penalty system to target the county magistrates under the Yuan Shikai government], *Jiamusi jiaoyuxueyuan xuebao* [Journal of Jiamusi Teacher's College] (Vol. 107, No. 5), 41.

96. Yuan, "Jiang Yang Dao chuyi sixing ling" (August 4, 1915), *YSKQJ*, Vol. 32, 251.

97. Yuan, "Chu Chen Xi sixing ling" (July 10, 1915), *YSKQJ*, Vol. 32, 69.

98. Yuan, "Chu Liu Dingxi sixing ling" (September 17, 1914), *YSKQJ*, Vol. 28, 386.

99. Yuan, "Wen Dingxiang jiao wenguan gaodeng chengjie weiyuanhui yichu ling" (December 28, 1914), *YSKQJ*, Vol. 29, 629.

100. Yuan, "Cai rongyuan ling" (March 12, 1915), *YSKQJ*, Vol. 30, 616.

101. Yuan, "Liuxue biyesheng liangcai shiyong ling" (April 5, 1915), *YSKQJ*, Vol. 31, 34.

102. Deng Yiwu, "Lun Yuan Shikai zhengfu de wenguan zhidu," ibid., 51.

103. Deng, "Hongxian dizhiqian Yuan Shikai yu bushu de guanxi—jianlun Yuan Shikai de yongrenshu" [Yuan Shikai's relations with his subordinates before his Hongxian Monarchy—An analysis of Yuan Shikai's way of using talents], *Wuhanligongdaxue xuebao* [Journal of Wuhan Technological University] (Vol. 17, No. 6, December 2004), 738.

104. Bai Jiao, *Yuan Shikai yu Zhonghuaminguo* [Yuan Shikai and the Republic of China] (Beijing: Zhonghuashuju, 2007), 4.

105. Yuan, "Pishuduli Heilongjiang junwu jian xun'anshi Bi Guifang chengbao caizhengtingzhang Kui Sheng jieyinrenshi riqi you" (June 6, 1916), *YSKQJ*, Vol. 35, 570.

BIBLIOGRAPHY

Bai, Jiao, *Yuan Shikai yu Zhonghuaminguo* [Yuan Shikai and the Republic of China], (Beijing: Zhonghuashuju, 2007).

Chen, Guanghua, "Beiyang zhengfushiqi wenguan chengjiezhidu tanxi" [An analysis of the penalty and admonition of civil servants during the Beijing Government Era], *Heilongjiang shizhi* [History of Heilongjiang] (No. 23, 2008), 18.

Chen, Guanghua, "Yuan Shikai zhengfu shiqi de zhishi chengjie zhidu shulun" [An analysis of the penalty system to target the county magistrates under the Yuan Shikai government], *Jiamusi jiaoyuxueyuan xuebao* [Journal of Jiamusi Teacher's College] (Vol. 107, No. 5), 41.

Ch'en, Jerome, *Yuan Shih-k'ai* (Stanford, CA: Stanford University Press, 1972).

Chu, Shuangzhi, "Xinzhengshiqi Yuan Shikai dui Zhili lizhi de zhengdun" [Yuan Shikai's official management during the new administration in Zhili], *Beijingkejidaxue xuebao* [Journal of University of Science and Technology of Beijing] (Vol. 18, No. 2, June 2002), 28.

Deng, Yiwu, "Lun Yuan Shikai zhengfu de wenguan zhidu" [On the civil servant system of the Yuan Shikai Government], *Jinandaxue xuebao* [Journal of Jinan University] (Vol. 12, No. 1, 2002), 48.

Deng, Yiwu, "Hongxian dizhiqian Yuan Shikai yu bushu de guanxi—jianlun Yuan Shikai de yongrenshu" [Yuan Shikai's relations with his subordinates before his Hongxian Monarchy—An analysis of Yuan Shikai's way of using talents], *Wuhanligongdaxue xuebao* [Journal of Wuhan Technological University] (Vol. 17, No. 6, December 2004), 738.

Ji, Liping, "Beijing zhengfushiqi wenguan kaoshi yu renyong zhidu pingxi" [An analysis of the mechanism for civil servant examinations and appointments], *Shixue yuekan* [History Monthly] (No. 12, 2005), 55–56.

Li, Weiyi, "Minchu Pingzhengyuan xingshi xingzhengjiancha zhineng de zhidu changshi lun" [An analysis of the function and judging system of the Political Correction Board during the early years of the Republic of China], *Zhengzhoudaxue xuebao* [Journal of Zhengzhou University] (Vol. 39, No. 3, May 2006), 66.

Li, Zhongping, "Qingmo xinzhengshiqi Yuan Shikai rencai sixiang tanxi" [An analysis of Yuan Shikai's ideas on talents during the New Administration of Late Qing], *Anhui shixue* [Anhui History] (No. 3, 2008), 53.

Liu, Yijiang, *Yuan Shikai pingzhuan* [A critical biography of Yuan Shikai] (Vol. 1) (Beijing: Jingjiribaochubanshe, 2004).

MacKinnon, Stephen, *Power and Politics in Late Imperial China: Yuan Shi-kai in Beijing and Tianjin* (Berkeley, CA: University of California Press, 1980).

Niu, Jinkui, "Yuan Shikai qiaozhi guanchang buzhengzhifeng" [Yuan Shikai's wise way of correcting the evils of the officialdom], *Wenshi bolan* [Broadview of Literature and History] (No. 12, 2015).

Si, Gong, "Yuan Shikai fantan cengqiangbi buxia 'Beijing shizhang'" [Yuan Shikai's anticorruption and his execution of his subordinate who was the mayor of Beijing], *Beijing nongye* [Beijing Agriculture] (No. 1, 2012), 39.

Su, Quanyou, "Yuan Shikai yu Tianjin defang zizhi" [Yuan Shikai and Tianjin local autonomy], *Liaochengshifanxueyuan xuebao* [Journal of Liaocheng Teachers' College] (No. 2, 2001), 74.

Su, Quanyou and He Kewei, *Yuan Shikai zhuan* [Biography of Yuan Shikai] (Hangzhou: Zhejiangdaxue Chubanshe, 2013).

Tian, Zhengping and Xia Yijun, "Yuan Shikai yu Qingmo guanshen jiaoyu" [Yuan Shikai and official education during the late Qing Dynasty], *Zhejiangdaxue xuebao* [Journal of Zhejiang University] (No. 10, 2010), 71.

Wang, Birong, *Bainian Yuanjia* [The Yuan family in the one hundred years] (Guilin: Guangxishida Chubanshe, 2013), 18.

Yang, Tao, "Gengzishibian hou Yuan Shikai lizhu 'chengban huoshou' zhuzhang tanxi" [An analysis of Yuan Shikai's vehement proposal after 1901 to punish those chief officials who were responsible for the Boxer Uprising], *Guizhou wenshi congkan* [Journal of Guizhou Literature and History] (No. 4, 2010), 16.

Young, Ernest, *The Presidency of Yuan Shih-k'ai: Liberalism and Dictatorship in Early Republican China* (Ann Arbor: University of Michigan Press, 1977).

Yuan, Jingxue, *Nueryanzhonglingmian Yuan Shikai* [Seeing Yuan Shikai from daughter's eyes] (Beijing: Zhongguowenshichubanbshe, 2012).

Yuan, Shikai, *Yuan Shikai quanji* [The complete works of Yuan Shikai] (Vol. 1–36), (Kaifeng: Henan University Press, 2013).

Zhang, Qiwen, "Qianxi Yuan Shikai de rencai sixiang" [An analysis of Yuan Shikai's ideas on talents], F*azhi yu shehui* [Law and Society] (No. 11, 2009), 306.

Zhang, Yaojie, "Yuan Shikai da 'laohu' de beihou yinqing" [The scene behind Yuan Shikai's anticorruption campaign], *Lianzheng liaowang* [Vision for Clean Administration] (No. 10, 2015), 68.

Zhao, Yong and Wang Xuehui, "Zhongguo xingzheng shenpan zhidu de diyici shijian—Pingzhengyuanzhidu de chuangli yu yanbian" [The first experiment of China's administrative legal system—the establishment and evolution of the Political Correction Board and its system], *Renmin luntan* [People's Tribune] (Vol. 432, No. 2, 2014), 103.

Part II

POLITICAL PARTIES AND LEGITIMACY

Chapter 3

Chiang Kai-shek versus Guomindang's Corruption in the Republic Era

Sherman Xiaogang Lai

In the summer of 1949, the Chinese Nationalist government was collapsing. The victorious armies of the Chinese Communist Party (CCP) were sweeping across the country while the defeated Nationalists were fleeing to the island of Taiwan. In tremendous chaos, Chiang Kai-shek, the leader of the Guomindang (the GMD, the Nationalists or Kuomintang) publicized an open letter to his comrades. He confessed in the letter that the root of GMD's humiliating defeat was its "notorious factional struggles" since its first day in 1905.[1] He vowed to remove it. Chiang's acknowledgment echoed the comments of the British prime minister Winston Churchill in January 1942. In response to the US president Franklin D Roosevelt's prediction of China's potential contributions to the war, Churchill claimed, "I would of course always be helpful and polite to the Chinese, whom I admire and liked as a race and pitied for their endless misgovernment."[2]

In 1949, the State Department of the United States reiterated Churchill's view when it explained to the American public about the loss of China in the "China White Paper." This controversial document reviewed the United States' engagement with China, especially with the Nationalist government since the Pearl Harbor in 1941. It attributed the collapse of the Nationalist government to the loss of the revolutionary zeal that brought it to power in the 1920s in addition to the tremendous losses in the war against Japan.[3] The White Paper, however, turned out to be the beginning of what is called as a "[p]olitical [o]dyssey of an [i]ntellectual [c]onstruct."[4] It gave birth to McCarthyism that blamed the Communists' plots and moles in the State Department for the collapse of the Nationalist government. McCarthyism dominated the United States' China policy until the Vietnam War. When the United States was trapped in the jungles of Vietnam, it began seeking rapprochement with the People's Republic of China (PRC). In the wave of re-considering the

United States' Asia policy in the postwar de-colonization, the White Paper's argument resurged. Lloyd Eastman proved that GMD's defeat was out of its post-revolution military dictatorship and corruption.[5] Nevertheless, the post–Cold War studies on the Chinese Revolution, which John King Fairbank termed as "The Great Chinese Revolution"[6] unrolled a kind of extraordinary complexity. China's transition from the world's largest agrarian empire into a kind of nation-state was intertwined with the CCP revolution and the Japanese invasion in addition to urbanization and industrialization.

While the CCP's dark side was revealed,[7] the achievements of the Nationalist government were re-appraised and appreciated.[8] In the meantime, Deng Xiaoping's market-oriented reforms resulted in prosperity. The rapid economic growth in an authoritarian CCP's party-state means rampant corruption. The CCP was so corrupt that the question about the collapse of the Nationalist government was raised: Was the GMD so corrupt that it deserved being destroyed by the CCP?[9] This chapter is not intended to question the legitimacy of the CCP's revolution. Instead, it is an attempt to examine the corruption issue of the Nationalist government in the contexts of its contemporary domestic and international politics by investigating Chiang's wartime diaries in reference to the CCP's anti-GMD accusations and to scholarly works. It argues that corruption was a problem in the Nationalist government but became serious only after the Japanese occupied Burma in 1942, cutting off China's last communication line with the West. Chiang, however, was not well aware of the catastrophic impacts of this defeat until the Japanese launched Operation *Ichigo* in 1944. This offensive campaign critically damaged his reputation inside and outside of China. It left Chiang no other option but to seek compromise with the CCP after Japan surrendered. Chiang, however, overestimated the capacity of his government and tried to solve the CCP problem with force.[10] He thus sealed the fate of the Republican China.

DEFINITION AND METHODOLOGY

The word "corruption" is a word of broad meanings and varied definitions. A clear-cut definition of "corruption" helps investigate the issue of corruption. According to *Oxford English Dictionary*, "corruption" has physical, moral, and purity-perversion meanings. At physical levels, it refers to actions that lead to the "destruction or spoiling of anything, esp. by disintegration or by decomposition with its attendant unwholesomeness; and loathsomeness; putrefaction."[11] It can also be applied to the "Destruction, dissolution of the constitution which makes a thing what it is."[12] At moral level, corruption refers to "a making or becoming morally corrupt; the fact or condition of being corrupt; moral deterioration or decay; depravity."[13] It can also refer to misconducts in public affairs: "Perversion or destruction of integrity in the discharge of public duties by bribery or favor; the use or existence of corrupt practices, esp. in a state, public corporation, etc." These definitions in general match the contexts in which Chiang mentioned the issue of corruption in his wartime diaries. Nevertheless, the Republic of China was an entity unified only in name. It did not have a unified administrative and parliamentary institution. It was actually a GMD-led coalition of various kinds of Chinese states ruled by local militarists who used to be called "warlords."

In addition, in striking contrast to the CCP, the GMD itself was a nationwide coalition of various political entities. It did not have a hierarchy administrated by disciplined members as the CCP did. The core of the GMD-led Nationalist government was an army officered by graduates of Whampoa Military Academy that Chiang served as its first commandant. As China did not have a unified nationwide bureaucracy, corruption did not always relate to the Nationalist government under Chiang's leadership. And it did not refer to the institutional integrity that did not exist. Chiang's use of the term "*fubai*" (corruption) was therefore casual and vague. He often used the term to express his frustration with local politics. On the whole, the issue of corruption is not a prominent subject in his wartime diaries. A statistical analysis of Chiang's wartime diaries shows that Chiang's primary concern was on diplomacy, financial affairs, institutional development, and self-cultivation. The amount of his words about corruption was so tiny in comparison with these issues mentioned above that it cannot be catalogued independently.[14] Nevertheless, this does not mean that corruption was unimportant to the fate of the Republican China. Rather, it reflects the complicated linkage between corruption and the collapse of the Republican China. It also highlights the necessity to adopt an appropriate approach to describe and analyze this problem and then to evaluate its impacts. In his study of the rise of European nation-states and their competitions, John Brewer's theory about the rise of the English fiscal-military state in its wars against France during the seventeenth and eighteenth centuries provides a valid model.[15]

Brewer proves that Britain's victory over France came from its solid fiscal institution of checks-and-balances based on its parliamentary system. This institution prevented embezzlement while integrating Britain's society. The British economy at that time was agrarian. Land was the government's principal source of revenue. Based on thorough and precise census and land surveying, tax collectors visited each landowners, traders, and retailers regularly and in high frequency.[16] In parallel to the tax-collecting system was a system of auditing. It could discover tax collectors' any wrongdoing immediately.[17] The authority of budget-approving and tax-raising was in the Parliament. The cabinet must submit its budget plan to the Parliament for approval. In order to have its plan approved, the cabinet must explain to the parliamentarians its reasons. The latter would then discuss and debate openly before voting. Because this process was transparent, landowners who were the constituents of the parliamentarians were well informed. Therefore, either approval or rejection or revision reflected the society's maximum consensus.[18] The integration of the society enabled the British society to sustain higher tax rate than France.[19] In addition, the Royal Navy commanded the sea. It not only prevented Britain from invasion but also ensured the access to the resources overseas.[20] It therefore placed Britain in an undefeatable position. This situation enabled the British government to sell governmental bonds to finance its war efforts, turning protracted wars into good investments. In contrast, France did not have this system of checks-and-balances. The outcome of the absence of balances-and-checks was the rampant corruption in addition to its unfair revenue system.[21] Although France was more resourceful than the British Isles, its competition against Britain finally bankrupted it and led to the French Revolution.

In comparison with the seventeenth- and eighteenth-century Britain, the Nationalist government's situation was not good at all. Facing the encroachments of Japan, an overwhelmingly powerful foe, Chiang resorted to total and protracted war. China's victorious emergence at the end of World War II came from the successful implementation of this strategy.[22] The foundation of this strategy was the vastness of China's territory, the rise of China's nationalism and the accessibility to international assistance. The territorial vastness and nationalism meant that Japan could not defeat China unless it occupied entire China. But this was unlikely because the West and the Soviet Union would not allow Japan to defeat China. They would find ways to help China as long as China kept fighting. The combination of these three determinants of China's vastness, nationalism and international assistance meant that China would become undefeatable if its government and army could sustain Japan's initial military strikes. In order to make up for China's military weakness, Chiang selected the mountainous and underdeveloped southwestern China centered on Sichuan province as his home base. That Nationalist government survived World War II proved that Chiang's strategy worked. His diaries show, however, that he did not predict that a total and protracted war would put his government, army, and the societies in Free China, the zones under Nationalist government's rule, under extreme pressure. The impacts of this pressure gradually altered the society, turning corruption, which was an occasional topic in Chiang's diaries, into a demoralizing catalyzer, making him feel helpless. A question therefore appeared: How did Chiang lead a coalition of Chinese states of pre-industrial economy live through the Japanese relentless onslaughts? It would be difficult to examine and assess the extent of corruption and its impacts without reviewing how China moved to the stage when the Japanese launched Operations *Ichigo* that imposed critical damage on the Nationalist government. It is therefore necessary to review how Chiang viewed corruption prior to Operation *Ichigo*.

Corruption in Chiang Diaries Prior to 1942

The issue of corruption appeared in Chiang diaries more often in his pre-1933 entries than afterward. It reflects that corruption had not been among Chiang's top concerns. In the early days after the Japanese seizure of Manchuria in September 1931 until the Tanggu Truce in May 1933, Chiang complained often, in his diaries, of the corruption within the GMD. His complaints during this period were focused on the loss of revolutionary zeal among senior members. On June 30, 1932, he blamed that "senior [GMD] members are corrupt,"[23] and that the corruption was "rampant in the GMD apparatus in Hubei province."[24] He moaned further in September 1932: "Every [GMD] member is corrupt. Most recently recruited are either scums or useless thugs. In the meantime, it is hard [for GMD's good members] to approach non-GMD people and observe them [for future appointments]."[25] The GMD party-state was therefore "hopeless."[26] He lamented that the Chinese public were "walking dead," intoxicating themselves.[27] The tones of his diaries, however, altered after the Japanese humiliated his proud Central Army along the Great Wall in May 1933. This defeat led to the Tanggu Truce that prohibited the deployment of the Central Army in Beijing and Tianjin area. Having recognized that this disastrous battle came from his miscalculation, Chiang began considering an appropriate strategy to counter the Japanese encroachments in the contexts of domestic and international politics.

The outcome of his consideration was his grand strategy against the Japanese invasion mentioned earlier. During the process of shaping his grand strategy, Chiang kept complaining of corruption. The contexts of his blames altered. Rather than mere laments, Chiang was working hard to unify his country, a precondition that he believed for a successful war against Japan. His efforts soon resulted in two milestone achievements in 1934 and 1935, respectively. The first achievement was the Central Army's peaceful entry into southwestern China, Chiang's future home base in a total war against Japan. Chiang first concentrated his resources and destroyed CCP's Jiangxi Soviet in the fall of 1934. In the name of pursuing the defeated Reds, Chiang sent the Central Army into southwestern China. The second achievement was the issue of *fabi*, China's first nationwide banknotes, in November 1935. *Fabi* was the product of the collaboration between the governments of China and Britain to establish a unified administrative system across China. To the former, national unification was its determined goal. To the latter, it was a strategy to counterbalance the aggressive Japan. In order to avoid antagonizing

Japan, the British government adopted an indirect approach to helping the Nationalist government. By offering its guarantee, the British government encouraged those British banks (such as Hong Kong and Shanghai Bank) that had commercial ties with China to provide credits to the Nationalist government. The Nationalist government could use the credits from British banks to start its financial reform by issuing *fabi*.[28] It gained overwhelming financial superiority over its domestic rivals and accelerated the program of national unification. As *fabi* enabled the Nationalist government to concentrate China's limited resources to its war efforts against Japan, it is termed as one of China's essential preconditions to live through the war.[29] The success of *fabi* brought the Nationalist government to its peak. *Fabi*, however, depreciated tremendously during the war. Thanks to American assistance, it survived the war. But the depreciation catalyzed various kinds of wartime tension, including corruption, and turned out to be one of the principal reasons for the collapse of the Nationalist government in 1949. It was a process that began with the Nationalist government's military defeats by the Japanese during 1937–1938.

Chiang had predicted these military defeats and made appropriate preparations. These defeats were a part of the first stage of his total and protracted war against Japan. As described earlier, Chiang selected Sichuan as his home base. In order to complete the strategic evacuation from the Yangzi Valley to Sichuan and to prove China's worthiness for international assistance, Chiang launched the Battle of Shanghai, trying to wipe out the Japanese garrison in the Japanese concession in this international city. He committed to the battle all his German-trained crack troops armed with German weapons. Many provinces' ruling militarists followed Chiang and sent their provincial troops to participate. Nevertheless, the Chinese army was routed after three months of fierce fights. Although the strategic evacuation to Sichuan went on orderly, Chiang was appalled that his routed soldiers were raging against civilians. "It had by no means occurred to me prior to the outbreak of the ongoing war that routed soldiers would be raging in this productive area, my source of revenue. It hurts indeed. It might be a critical wound in [my] war [efforts] against Japan. I should have taken into account that routed soldiers would raging including rubbering and raping."[30] On his way to retreat to Wuhan, Chiang saw numerous fleeing refugees. He felt very guilty and did not know how to comfort them.[31] He did not blame the Chinese public again. Words like "walking dead" no longer appear in his diaries. In addition to the sense of guilt, Chiang worried about keeping various factions together in a common war against Japan, especially after he had to give up his national capital of Nanjing. If the war against Japan ceased, Chiang predicted that China would fall into civil wars.[32] But it would be impossible to continue the war if Japan offered a generous term for peace. To his relief, the Japanese condition was too harsh for anyone in power to accept. The war therefore went on as he hoped.[33] By the end of October 1938, Chiang's strategic evacuation completed. After Chiang retreated to Sichuan from Wuhan at the end of October 1938, the war entered its second stage of attrition.

The mood of Chiang's diaries during the period from the defeat in Shanghai in November 1937 to the fall of Wuhan in October 1938 altered remarkably. It gradually moved from sadness and depression to confidence. In the meantime, financial and economic problems were growing and catching Chiang's increasing attention (See Graph 3). He found that Chinese public servants and private citizens often contacted Japanese soldiers or civilians in private. These contacts obviously involved commercial activities because Eastern China had close economic ties with Japan before the war. It was normal the Chinese and Japanese businessmen tried to remain or restore their prewar trade relations as long as the situation permitted. But these private contacts were beyond Chiang's tolerance.[34] He was also upset to find that many governmental agencies were seeking comfort and using government's automobile to move furniture[35] while military men enjoyed themselves in ballrooms.[36] The term "horrible situation of corruption" began appearing in his diaries.[37] From this time onward, he used terms such as "coward and incompetent" to criticize against his governmental agencies and diplomats.[38] In addition, he found himself involving into the local politics of Sichuan elites, a situation that he had not predicted. Chiang was happy to know that Liu Xiang, the most powerful militarist in Sichuan, died of cancer in January 1938. "Liu's passing away [helped] to put the province under the central government's direct administration. The foundation of the war against Japan has therefore laid down. This situation is powerful enough to deter the Japs," Chiang wrote, "it was the turning point [for the Nationalist government] to move from crisis to safety."[39] However, Chiang gradually realized that the situation was not that simple at all. It took him a year and half to start engaging the local politics in October 1939. He wrote helplessly in November 1940, "These old-style warlords in Sichuan are incompetent and intellectually poor. They are a bunch of greedy cowards. But I cannot be either harsh or tolerant to them. It is indeed a difficult situation."[40]

When Chiang wrote down his tricky relations with Sichuan local elites mentioned above in November 1940, his most difficult time since the outbreak of the war in July 1937 was over. This difficulty came from the Nazi's victory in Europe in the summer of 1940. Prior to that moment, Britain was the Nationalist government's principal supporter. When Britain itself was in danger and fighting against the Nazis for its survival, Japan asked Britain to close the Burma Road, China's last communication line with the West. In order to test the stand of the United States, the only country that was capable to rescue the situation, Britain decided to suspend the Burma Road for three

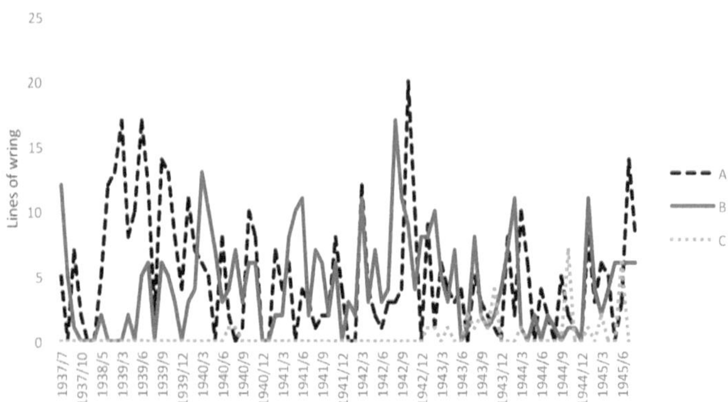

Legend:

A: Institutional improvements (domestic politics and regional authorities)

B: Finances and economics

C: Postwar plans

Figure 3.1 Volume of Writing on Organizational Affairs in Monthly Reflection and Monthly Plans.

months in the name of maintenance on July 18, 1940. If the United States adopted a firm stand against the Japanese aggression, Britain would follow. If it did not, Britain would make a deal with Japan. Chiang was caught off balance and became desperate. A ceasefire accord between the Nationalist government and Japan was imminent. It went without saying that the first victim of this potential accord would be the CCP. In order to improve CCP's strategic situation, Mao Zedong, the CCP's leader, ordered his guerrilla forces in the Yangzi Valley to launch a series of preemptive offensives against local National security forces.[41] Ironically, the Japanese saved Chiang from desperation. In order to deter the United States from intervening Japan's expansion, the Japanese government formed a formal alliance with Germany and Italy on September 27, 1940. Until this moment both Britain and the United States were cautious in helping China lest their assistance push Japan to Germany. Japan's formal alliance with Germany meant that Britain and the United States were eager to help China for the approaching Pacific War in which China would be one of their principal allies.[42] Fifteen months later, the Japanese attacked Pearl Harbor on December 7, 1941, driving the United States, Britain, and China into formal alliance.

The outbreak of the Pacific War was the moment that Chiang had been looking forward to. He termed the Pearl Harbor as "the nadir of China's war against Japan" in the entry of his diaries on December 8, 1941. He also reminded himself of caution, warning himself of the danger out of compliments. These warnings, however, as his flee to Taiwan in 1949 showed, proved invalid. Allying with the United States and Britain guaranteed that China would emerge victorious at the end of the global war. But it also implied a series of unprecedented challenges. Chiang and his government disproved their ability to handle these challenges. One of the first challenges was the rapid depreciation of *fabi*. As described earlier, *fabi* was a product of the collaboration between the Chinese and British governments to serve their individual and shared interests in resisting Japan's aggression. Because *fabi* was founded on the British credits, it was an international currency. After the Japanese occupied large areas of Chinese territory, their occupation authorities in China did their best to collect *fabi* in order to purchase in the international market what the Japanese economy needed.[43] But the Japanese could no longer access the international market after the Pearl Harbor. In the meantime, they seized tremendous amount of *fabi* from the international exchange centers in Hong Kong and the International Settlement in Shanghai. The Japanese then used the *fabi* in their possession to purchase materials in Free China and the CCP territories. Their snapping-up of resources fueled the already serious inflation in China.[44] The already-existing inflation came from the Nationalist government's wartime financial demand.[45] Yangzi Valley was China's most productive area on which the Nationalist government's revenue was dependent. But it was lost to the Japanese in November 1937, four months after the war broke out. In the meantime, the Japanese started naval blockade by occupying China's principal ports, trying to bring the Nationalist government to its knees by strangling its economy.

After Germany defeated France in June 1940, Japan forced the French government to close Haiphong-Kunming Railway, leaving the Burma Road as China's last communication line with the West. Because of the Japanese strangling strategy and the relatively stable frontline, financial affairs gradually rose to Chiang's top concern. Thanks to the Burma Road, the inflation rate was not too bad before the Japanese cut it off in the First Burma Campaign in April 1942. The loss of Burma placed China under siege. China's only communication line with the outside world was the Hump Fly through the Himalayas. The Hump tonnage was far less than what China needed, inflation became the Nationalist government's principal method available to finance its war efforts. A vicious circle therefore began: the more the *fabi* depreciated, the more resources the Japanese could purchase; the more materials flowed out of Free China and CCP territories, the more serious the inflation would become. In order to stop the flow, some CCP base areas began expelling *fabi* and establishing exclusive zones of their banknotes. However, the Nationalist government could not terminate its own banknotes. Moreover, in contrast to the CCP banknotes that were compartmentalized, the circulation of *fabi* was nationwide. Each CCP base area had its own independent and unconvertible banknotes. A CCP banknote did not affect another one. And the economy of one base area did not affect others. The leaders of each CCP base area could select a monetary policy that best served their interests regardless of others, including relentlessly taking advantage of the depreciation of *fabi*.[46] Among the top victims of *fabi*'s depreciation were salary earners ranging from public servants and military people to teachers.[47] These people were the mainstay of the Nationalist government. And Chiang Kai-shek was appalled to see them struggling on the edge of survival.

The entries of Chiang's diaries in 1942 and 1943 were full of his anxiety over the financial situation and the livelihood of salary earners. In order to ensure salary earners' survival, the Nationalist government ordered in September 1942 that the pay of *tianfu*, a combination of property tax and corvée, must be rice rather than cash.[48] In addition to this significant reform, Chiang thought that the poor institution of the Nationalist government was responsible for the situation. Institutional improvement was therefore among his top priority in 1942. In his view, his government was poorly organized and overstaffed with disqualified employees.[49] In order to rationalize China's banking institution, he concentrated the authority of issuing banknotes to the Central Bank, one of the four members of the Headquarters of Four Joint Banks (*silian zongchu*), an association of four dominant banks under Chiang's chairmanship. Although these two reforms enabled the Nationalist government to stay through the war, Chiang underestimated the devastating impacts of China's wartime inflation. His principal attention was on military and diplomatic affairs. He did not recognize the seriousness of inflation until mid-September 1942. In striking contrast, the CCP leadership had warned its regional agencies and base areas of *fabi*'s forthcoming dramatic depreciation and potential impacts as early as at the beginning of February 1942. "The prices are going up fast," Chiang wrote in the entry of his diaries on September 17, 1942, "*fabi* is flowing back from the occupied zones. The economic situation in the future will be more threatening than military and diplomatic issues. If I do not take in charge of the economic affairs, the crisis will not be overcome."[50]

While envisaging the potentially fatal threats in the next year of 1943, Chiang listed "rapid price raising, inflation and economy collapsing" as the third one after the potential raids into northwestern China by either the Japanese or the CCP.[51] As later events showed, none of these two envisaged threats by Chiang existed. And Chiang's preparations for the predicted economic crisis were far from satisfactory. He recognized correctly that economic crisis directly related to the morale declination of his army and civilian officials.[52] Chiang did not pay sufficient attention to economic affairs and figured out a solution. Instead, he regarded himself as the leader of postwar

Asia. He was over-concerned with the nationalist movement in India and gave Mahatma Gandhi extraordinary support regardless of Britain's strong but tactical warnings. The West's suspicion did not disappear until Chiang openly denied his intention to become Asia's postwar leader in November 1942.[53] In the meantime, he enjoyed composing his chauvinist work of *China's Destiny*.[54] In this work, he attributed China's plight to foreign invaders ranging from Manchus in the seventeenth century and the British in the nineteenth century to the ongoing Japanese invasion and Bolsheviks's infiltration. He was so happy with this work that he tried to indoctrinate Chinese people with his ideas. He ordered to issue a copy of the book to every class of each elementary school.[55] In addition, he had it translated into English in late spring 1943, even though he had noticed the rapid deterioration of the economy and its impacts on government employees[56] as well as the famine in Henan province.[57] He also knew well that there was some kind of linkage between economic deterioration, widespread misconduct of governmental officials, the increased governmental budget, and the expansion of airfield construction projects for the operations of the US Army Air Force (USAAF) in China.[58]

As the USAAF increased its operations in China, it required for more airfields; as the Nationalist government constructed new airfields, it had to increase its expenditure. Because its revenue was already dependent on inflation, expenditure increase meant further inflation. As the entire economy was going down and became increasingly dependent on the governmental expenditure, widespread spread of corruption was inevitable in a country like wartime China where the governmental institution did not have checks-and-balances. Instead of searching for a solution, Chiang seemed more concerned with the attitudes toward his government by the Westerners in China. Their criticism strongly affected their home countries' public opinion on the Nationalist government, which was moving from sympathy to contempt. Rather than checking his government and himself, Chiang attributed the public opinion changes to his diplomats abroad, Chinese media, and Western journalists in China. He even tried to restrain the latter's movements. Chiang blamed Winston Churchill while avoiding discussing the issue of *fabi*'s exchange rates with US dollar and British pound, a bitter controversial question between the Nationalist government and its Western allies that affected the entire Western communities in China and Western leaders. This was an issue that Chiang hardly mentioned in his diaries[59] as he did with the issues that he felt bad or guilty about, such as his order to break the Yellow River banks in June 1938. Nevertheless, Arthur Young, Chiang's financial advisor, explained Chiang's dilemma in the exchange rate, his solution to the dilemma, its relations with corruption, and the devastating impacts on the Nationalist government's image in the West.

As explained earlier, the British government's prewar efforts to counterbalance the Japanese aggression was the financial foundation of *fabi*. Its guarantee to the British banks to loan the Nationalist government integrated Britain's political interests with investors' commercial interests. Both governments of Britain and the United States responded actively to the Nationalist government's appeals for help after China's all-out war against Japan broke out. Among the major helps was Henry Morgenthau's maneuver in close collaboration with Sir Frederick Maze, the inspector general of the Chinese Maritime Customs Service, through the US Congress and government to convert into cash the silver that the Nationalist government stored in the United States.[60] This cash was essential for the Nationalist government to finance the war. After the war became protracted conflicts of attrition and the silver was draining out, the British and US governments worked with the Nationalist government and established two foundations to stabilize the *fabi*.[61] But the two foundations could not halt the growing speed of the *fabi*'s depreciation and were disbanded. The Nationalist government then responded with an artificial exchange rate of USD 1= C$ 20 *fabi*.[62] This was a safe option to Chiang's financial dilemma. Had he let the *fabi*'s exchange rate flow freely, its depreciation would have been plunged and would have damaged investors' confidence. The artificial rate, however, became a serious problem when the gap between the official exchange rate and black-market rates was being rapidly widened.

In February 1944, the black-market price of the US dollar rose to C$ 215.[63] Westerners in China felt that they were relentlessly exploited.[64] Many agencies found their operations in China increasingly difficult. The US and British governments then asked the Nationalist government to raise the exchange rates. But the latter refused, declining to give specific reasons. The mood of Westerners in China toward the Nationalist government became hostile. This mood altered the Nationalist government's public image in the West. To keep their agencies running in China, the US and British governments tacitly permitted them to exchange money in the black market. On the Chinese side, the existence of a huge gap between the official and black-market exchange rates meant tremendous profits and stimulated corruption. Because financial assistance to China from the United States and Britain was provided in Western currencies, any Chinese official who had access to Western aid could profit immensely through the black market. By diverting American financial assistance into private use, some Nationalist officials even sent their children to the United States for education,[65] and reportedly purchased property in the United States.[66] Such activity poisoned working relationships between Western agencies and the Nationalist government. The Nationalist government's international image changed dramatically. During and after the Battle of Shanghai, it looked to represent a new China that was fighting for independence, dignity, and justice. By early 1944, it had degenerated to a symbol of corruption.

Chiang did not deny the existence of rampant corruption in his government. But he did not take any measure to stop the spread of corruption beyond complaining of his bureaucrats in his diaries. Before the end of his travel to Cairo for his meetings with Churchill and Roosevelt, Chiang blamed Churchill for China's difficulties. In his view, the top enemy of the United States was Japan rather than Germany. He thought that Churchill was the person who persuaded Roosevelt to adopt the strategy of Europe First because of his jealousy of China. Chiang's travel to Cairo opened his eyes. "I witnessed Britain's global influence and the vastness of her Empire," he wrote in his diaries after the visit. "This was my biggest accomplishment in travelling to Egypt. It is fascinating that the British turned the rebellious Muslims in Asia and Africa into obedient servants. They must have some magic power."[5] Chiang had a strong feeling of inferiority in his communications with the Western leaders. In striking contrast to his trust in Roosevelt prior to the Pearl Harbor, Chiang thought Roosevelt was either cunning or being cheated by Churchill. He therefore avoided communicating with them as much as possible.[67] Nevertheless, he believed that his huge army was essential in the Allies' efforts to defeat Japan. As China was under besiege by the Japanese, Chiang thought that the Allies' top priority was to break the blockage by regaining Burma. Because the most difficult part of military operations in Burma was logic supports, Chiang asked Britain and the United States to send a powerful fleet to the India Ocean to win the command of sea there. As the Allies were concentrating their resources on the forthcoming invasion into continental Europe, they did not have extra resources for an all-out Burma campaign and just wanted a limited offensive campaign in northern Burma, but they could not tell Chiang directly about the reason lest he leaked the vital information. Field Marshall Alan Brook, the chief of the Imperial General Staff, explained to Chiang the Allies' strategy, but he found that Chiang did not understand and felt frustrated.[68] Alan Brook's frustration was in fact a reflection of Chiang's distrust of Britain because of his defeat in the First Burma Campaign in 1942. Chiang wrote, "If this campaign [of limited offensives] is not postponed, it will be surely another defeat . . . . My country cannot afford being cheated again by the British."[6]

Instead of the British, however, it was the Americans that he would have bitter controversies with over the issues of the United States' financial aid to China and his command over the Chinese army. Chiang put forward to Roosevelt a request for a one billion dollar loan during the Cairo Conference, but the latter did not give him a definite answer. Soon after his return to China, Chiang found that his financial situation was rapidly deteriorating because of the airfield construction projects, especially those for B-29 long-range bombers against Japan's home islands. He found that he could not afford the projects at all. He therefore believed that Roosevelt would give him his required loans. He was caught off balance when he learned that his request has been turned down.[69] While he was arguing with Roosevelt, his army in Xinjiang province in northwestern China along the border with Russia and Mongolia was bombed and strafed repeatedly by the Red Army's airplanes. Chiang was confused. While protesting to Moscow, Chiang appealed to the United States for help. Before he found any clues for the reasons behind the Red Army's bombing, the Japanese launched Operation *Ichigo*, the largest military operation in Japan's history. This offensive campaign broke the frontline stalemate since the fall of 1938. It sliced through Free China from the northern bank of the Yellow River in Henan province into Vietnam 2,000 miles away. In addition to the immense losses in life and material in China, Operation *Ichigo* catalyzed the existing tension between the United States and the Nationalist government into a crisis that would seal the latter's fate.

Operation *Ichigo* was the Japanese response to their gradual loss of command over the sea after they were forced out of Salomon Islands by the fall of 1943. In order to secure the supplies of essential materials from Southeast Asia to their home islands, the Japanese decided to launch an unprecedented offensive campaign to slice through Free China along the railways of Pinghan (from Beijing to Wuhan), Yuehan (from Guangzhou to Wuhan), and Xianggui (from Hengyang to the border with Vietnam), linking their colony of Korea with Southeast Asia under their occupation. In the meantime, they would destroy USAAF bases nearby. They would then build an overland railway system from Singapore to Pusan on the narrow Tsushima Strait.[70] The Japanese started the military buildup of a half million men and equipment as early as the fall of 1943. It was implemented through the railway systems in North China under the eyes of millions of Chinese people among whom large numbers of Chinese intelligence agents were working. That Chiang did not make appropriate preparations against Operation *Ichigo* and that he did not even identify the Japanese intention a month after the Japanese offensives began reflected the condition of his government and army after warring Japan for nearly seven years. It is not exaggerating to attribute the Chinese army's defeats in Operation *Ichigo* to the rampant corruption throughout the entire apparatus of the Nationalist government. Although it is difficult to blame specific persons or agencies for the catastrophe, Chiang, as the leader of the GMD and the Nationalist government, must be held responsible. And he acknowledged his responsibility in July 1944 when Roosevelt asked him to transfer his command over the entire Chinese army to General Joseph Stilwell. "The period of the last three years was my golden time to solve thoroughly [China's] domestic problems and [its] diplomatic quarrels with the Unite States and Russia," Chiang wrote, "but I did not use well this valuable window of opportunity. I hesitated all the time and dare not make many major decisions. I [often] regretted after I made decisions and dared not to implement them. It was indeed a kind of stupidity termed as 'Try to beat a snake without killing it.'. . . How ignorant and silly I have been!"[71] Chiang did not explain why he blamed himself so. Nevertheless, the following statistical analysis of the entries of his wartime diaries reveals the reasons.

Chiang kept his journal in a standard diary pad for elementary school students. His entries of diaries are regular. He also wrote down his considerations in the pages of "Monthly Plan," "Monthly Reflection," "Annual Plan," and "Annual Reflection." When the pages of these categories in a standard diary pad were not sufficient, he would use an extra pad. If the contents of the sections of Chiang's diaries mentioned above are categorized and the amount of lines of each category is compared, his varied concerns over various issues can be identified. Figure 3.2 is a comparison of the amount of lines of four categories in the sections of reflection and plan in Chiang's wartime diaries. These four categories are "Self-evaluation and reminding," "Self-encouragement and outlet of stress," "Study of traditional philosophy," and "Family affairs." In figure 3.2, the amount lines of "Self-encouragement and outlet of stress" and "Study of traditional philosophy" form two overlapping spikes. The spike of the former could be interpreted as Chiang's response to the stress out of the international and domestic situations in the aftermath of the Nazis' victory in Europe. How can the spike of the start of his study of traditional philosophy in December 1940 be explained? It must be out of Chiang's assessments of the changed international situation. He recognized from the visit to Germany by Vyacheslav Molotov, the foreign minister of the Soviet Union, in November 1940 that the two countries were going toward war. The Soviet resumed supply of weaponry to the Nationalist government, which had been suspended for eleven months because of China's refusal to support Moscow during the Russo-Finish War, in the aftermath of the visit. In Chiang's view, the resumption was a sign that a war between the Soviet Union and Germany was approaching.[72] In the forthcoming struggle for survival, Joseph Stalin would desperately need China to continue its war of resistance, pulling back Japan from invading Siberia. He therefore shipped a remarkable quantity of weapons, which he would need soon, to China whose resistance capacity had declined significantly since the suspension of weaponry supplies. When the Soviet Union was fighting for its survival, Chiang predicted, Japan would not be standing idly. It would either invade Siberia or intensify its aggression to Southeast Asia. In either scenario, it would provoke a war against the West and push them to ally China. As a member of the Western alliance, China would be emerging victorious at the end of the global war. Chiang's top priority was therefore switching to postwar China rather than conducting the ongoing war. By that time, Chiang was sure that Mao Zedong, who released his agenda in January 1940, was his deadly rival after the war. Mao's agenda was addressed in Marxist discourse in his article

"On New Democracy." Chiang's study of traditional philosophy was his preparation to counter "On New Democracy." And the outcome of his efforts was *China's Destiny* mentioned above.

Chiang's diaries show that he enjoyed the processes of composing, revising, and delivery of *China's Destiny*. He wrote on April 2, 1943, "I listened to the broadcast of [some text of] *China's Destiny* after supper. I am pretty happy with myself."[73] He termed Britain "envious" of China when he learned that *China's Destiny* was banned in Britain.[74] He did not care the CCP's sharp criticism either. "I read the Reds' pamphlet on *China's Destiny*. It is full of abusive words and does not affect me at all. I just ignore it."[75] However, the impacts of *China's Destiny* went beyond Chiang's expectation. "I predicted the strong influence of *China's Destiny*. The most affected would be Britain and the next would be the Reds. But I did not expect that their response could be so strong. Every achievement has its price. I believe that as time goes, the influence of this book on our

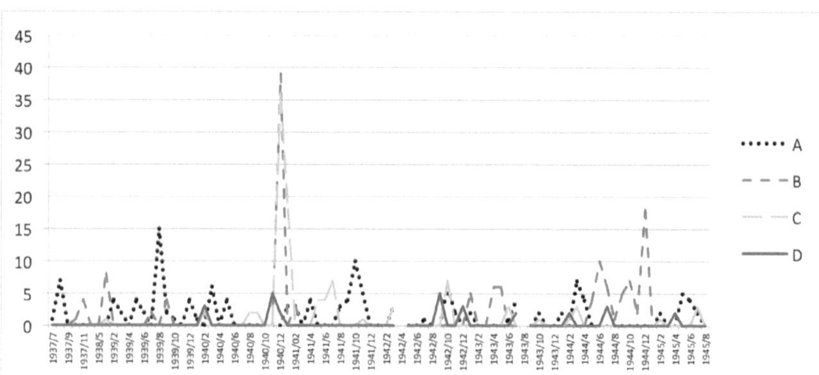

Legend

X axis: Lines of writing

Y axis: Year/month

A: Self-evaluation and reminding

B: Self-encouragement and outlet of stress

C: Study of traditional philosophy

D: Family affairs

Note: Chiang did not write Monthly Plans or Monthly Reflections in 1938.

Figure 3.2 Volume of Writing on Self-Cultivation in Monthly Plans and Monthly Reflections.

state and nation will be growing. I must be the beginning of the reemergence of sages."[76] Chiang did not realize something fundamentally wrong with *China's Destiny* until he met a few times with US vice president Henry Wallace who was visiting China in June 1944. In one of their last meetings, Wallace told Chiang that the latter was not what *China's Destiny* presents: a narrow-minded harsh man of paranoia. Chiang suspected that the bad impression of the book must be out of the translation that must be sabotaged.[77]

When Chiang came to realize the real influence of his *China's Destiny*, his armies in China were losing one battle after another in the Japanese offensive *Ichigo*.

Prior to beginning of Operation *Ichigo* in April 1944, the Japanese in Burma launched a desperate offensive operation into India, trying to seize the area of Imphal-Kohima, the gateway to Bengal and the Hump's terminal, in the previous month of March. The Japanese were as invincible as they had been in the First Burma Campaign in 1942 and approaching Imphal and Kohima. Being anxious with the situation and being impatient with Chiang's inaction, Roosevelt asked Chiang to help the British through offensives in northern Burma by the Chinese troops in India (X Force) and Yunnan province (Y Force). The X Force was based on those troops that retreated to India with the British in 1942. They were reinforced with the soldiers airlifted through the Hump. They were supplied, equipped, and trained to the US Army's standard under Joseph Stilwell's direct supervision. The Y Force was also equipped with American weapons and trained by American instructors. Although the X Force started advancing into northern Burma as early as October 1943 and performed well, the Y Force did not move. Chiang did not order the Y Force to launch offensives until Roosevelt threatened to cut off supplies. Despite the tremendous difficulties out of terrain, monsoon, leaks of information, and the resulting heavy casualties, the Y Force made impressive advances.[78]

The good performance of Chinese forces in Burma formed a striking contrast with their comrades in China. Being reinforced by Chiang's reluctance to commit to the offensives in Burma and demand for more aid, it convinced Roosevelt that Chiang's leadership was the root of problems in China. He therefore asked Chiang to let Stilwell command the entire Chinese army.

Chiang opted a strategy of dodge. But under Roosevelt's repeated asking, he decided to accept and began listing the key points in commanding the Chinese army as a suggestion to Stilwell, his incoming successor.[79] On the top of his listed points was the reality that the Chinese army, the so-called Nationalist Revolutionary Army, was not a single national army. It was a combination of over twenty armies of various kinds except the CCP's.[80] The leadership to command this type of an army was therefore different from commanding a single national army. Chiang did not tell Roosevelt about his decision and his preparation for the power transfer, hoping that the latter would alter his mind.

Nevertheless, Roosevelt sent him his ultimatum. This ultimatum outraged Chiang so much so that he was determined to kick Stilwell out of China regardless of the costs. Chiang's determination came from Stilwell's insult.[81] Their mutual relations had been so bad that Stilwell wanted to insult Chiang by himself. He pushed away Ambassador Patrick Hurley and brought Roosevelt's ultimatum to Chiang himself. Facing Chiang's fury, Roosevelt stepped back. For the purpose of face-saving, Roosevelt tried to keep Stilwell in China, but Chiang replied that he could not guarantee Stilwell's safety. As their common war against Japan was ongoing, Roosevelt could not afford to lose Chiang and called Stilwell back. Nevertheless, Operation *Ichigo* and the Stilwell crisis fatally damaged Chiang's reputation in the United States, making it impossible for the US government to launch large-scale aid program to help Chiang. By the time of Stilwell crisis, the Nationalist government had been increasingly dependent on American gold. Roosevelt's calling back of Stilwell was, in Arthur Young's opinion, a "major event affecting Chinese-American relations" that "Washington became more ready to consider playing with the Chinese Communists."[82] Although the American gold helped Chiang's government go through the war against Japan, it revealed to Mao Zedong Chiang's critical weakness.

The Nationalist government's dependence on American gold came from *fabi*'s rapid depreciation out of its inflation policy. As mentioned earlier, this policy was carefully managed prior to the Pearl Harbor and was under control. But it was out of control after the Japanese could no longer use *fabi* to purchase in the international market and placed China under siege by cutting off the Burma Road. By this time, the United States had replaced Britain as the Nationalist government's principal financial supporter and began shipping supplies to China as early as March 1941 according to the Lend-Lease Act. It could not, however, solve the problem of shortage of various kinds of materials in the besieged Free China. Worse still was that "a very large proportion of supplies flown into China" was "destined for the United States military forces then operating in China."[83] This meant the Lend-Lease program helped little to reduce *fabi*'s depreciation.

Because the Nationalist government was responsible for the construction of required airfields and other facilities, the American military operations in China worsened the Nationalist government's financial situation. As the war had been going on for over six years, it was impossible to raise funds from the middle class whose members were struggling to survive. How to finance China's war efforts became an urgent and tricky issue to the Chinese, American, and British financial experts. They thought of all kinds of available options and preferred currency reform at first. But they found this option too risky to implement. They finally targeted the wealthy class throughout China regardless of whether they were located in Free China or in the occupied zones.[84]

These experts predicted that in the chaos of a war full of uncertainties, gold was appreciated because of its stable value. Wealthy people would like to hoard gold. Other people would also do their best to buy gold. Gold would therefore absorb some banknotes of *fabi* and slow down the rate of inflation. The gold was out of the budget of the US government's financial assistance to the Nationalist government.

Because of emergency, the first gold was airlifted. One ton of gold went by rail from New York City to Miami where it was flown to India via South America, Africa, and the Middle East. In November 1943, it arrived in China.[85] When the gold was delivered into the market, *fabi*'s depreciation rate was remarkable reduced. *Fabi* was therefore saved. But it became completely dependent on the US government's financial aid. As the Stilwell crisis critically damaged Chiang's relations with the US government, this aid would come to an end when Japan was defeated. If Chiang wanted American aid for postwar reconstruction, he would have to negotiate a new deal with the US government. As the CCP had grown into a powerful political-military entity during the war against Japan, Chiang's negotiation with the United States would definitely involve the CCP. As the George Marshall's unsuccessful mission to mediate the GMD-CCP conflict showed, no one could prevent Chiang and Mao from fighting out. This meant that the United States would not keep *fabi* from collapsing in a renewed GMD-CCP civil war as it was doing now. Chiang would therefore be in a very dangerous financial situation if he went to war against the CCP. The outbreak of the civil war and Chiang's defeat in 1949 demonstrate that Chiang did not know his situation when Marshall was trying to mediate. Nor did he know that two officials in charge of the gold program in the Department of Treasury of the US government were arguably Communist moles under Moscow's direction.[86] These two officials were roommates during their education at Columbia University. They did as much as possible to delay the process of gold transfer to the Nationalist government.[87] They ignored the Nationalist government's urgent calls for quick shipment of gold and did not arrange airlifting any more. They were also roommates of Ji Chaoding, a CCP mole. Ji would later become a secretary of H. H. Kung[88] and was under the immediate direction of Zhou Enlai, the founder and head of the CCP's intelligence service who was serving as the leader of the CCP legation in Chongqing.

It goes without saying that Ji informed Zhou about the financial situation of the Nationalist government. The possession of extraordinary amount of gold among GMD officials reflected the extent of fragility of Nationalist government. Mao therefore composed a poem full of contempt after his forty-day negotiation with Chiang in Chongqing from late August to early October 1945. Two sentences of this poem are "Each government official in Chongqing is corruptive; each piece of [human] excrement in Yan'an (the CCP's wartime capital) is more valuable than the gold [over there]" (重庆有官皆墨吏，延安无屎不黄金).[89]

Conclusion

Sixty-eight years later, in March 2013, one of the top soldiers of the CCP army, the Chinese People's Liberation Army, was put under custody because of corruption. Tons of cash was found in his house. He was involved in one of the first publicized scandals involving staggering amounts of cash.[90] Being measured in quantity, the extent of CCP's corruption exceeded tremendously the GMD's prior to the latter's collapse in 1949. The reasons behind of the collapse were no doubt more than corruption. The catastrophic war against the Japanese invasion was obviously the turning point between the GMD-CCP competition, a point that the CCP does not accept. As early as 1944, the CCP asserted that it was the mainstay of China's war against Japan. Its acknowledgment on this historical issue would demythologize its national victory and fundamentally alter its relations with Taiwan. The topic of the linkage between the war against Japan and the collapse of the Nationalist government is therefore still a taboo in China. In the meantime, the issue of "Who lost China?" has been such a painful and emotional controversy in the American politics and academia that it was not until the early 1990s that scholars in the West began reinvestigating Republican China. In their renewed research efforts, the issue of corruption has been ignored. Perhaps, the extent of corruption in Republican China was trivial in comparison with the People's Republic's. Possibly also, they found so many fascinating achievements during Chiang's period that it was not worthwhile at all to reexamine the corruption in the Nationalist government.

NOTES

1. Qin Xiaoyi, ed., *Jiang zong tong da shi chang bian* (蒋总统大事长编) (Taibei: Zhongshan tu shu gong ssŭ, 1968), Vol. 6, 395, 404.

2. Winston S. Churchill, *The Second World War* (Boston, MA: Houghton Mifflin, 1950), Vol. 4, 119.

3. "The Department of State, "Letter of Transmittal," in the Department of State, "The China White Paper" (Originally issued as "United States Relations with China: With Special Reference to the Period of 1944–1949," August 1949) (Stanford, CA: Stanford University Press, 1967), vii.

4. Suzanne Pepper, "The Political Odyssey of an Intellectual Construct: Peasant Nationalism and the Study of China's Revolutionary History—A Review Essay," *The Journal of Asian Studies*, Vol. 63, No. 1, February 2004, 105–25.

5. Lloyd E. Eastman, *The Abortive Revolution: China under Nationalist Rule, 1927–1937* (Cambridge, MA: Harvard University Press, 1974).

6. John King Fairbank, *The Great Chinese Revolution, 1800–1985* (New York, NY: Harper and Row, 1986).

7. Tony Saich and Hans Van de Ven, eds., *New Perspectives on the Chinese Communist Revolution* (Armonk, NY: M.E. Sharpe, 1995).

8. *The China Quarterly*, No. 150 (1997), Special Issue: Reappraising Republic China.

9. Yang Kuisong, "The complicated reasons behind the GMD's defeat" (杨奎松, "国民党败给共产党的原因其实非常复杂,") *Weilaiwang*, April 12, 2017, http://news.china.com/history/all/11025807/20170412/30412879_all.html; He Qinglian, "Corruption was not the reason for the GMD's Collapse" (何清涟,"国民党之败并非缘于腐败,"), *VOA*, November 22, 2014, https://www.voachinese.com/a/heqinglian-blog-history-notes-20141121/2530061.html.

10. Jay Taylor, "Chiang Kai-shek and Chinese Modernization," in Ramachandra Guha ed., *Makers of Modern Asia* (Cambridge, MA: The Belknap Press of Harvard University Press, 2014), 55.

11. *Oxford English Dictionary* (Oxford: Oxford University Press, 2000). http://www.oed.com.proxy.queensu.ca/view/Entry/42045?redirectedFrom=corruption&.

12. Ibid.

13. Ibid.

14. Chiang Kai-shek kept his diaries for over fifty years, rarely missing a day. In his diaries, Chiang recorded the happiness, confusion, worries, and frustrations that common people experience during their lifetime, providing a unique source from which historians could re-explore the familiar stories and re-explain old questions. He used standard diary pads and kept his daily diary entry to within twelve lines of writing. Chiang mentioned the issues that caught his attention and his feelings in his daily entry. If he felt that an issue warranted additional attention, he would write about it in his *Zalu* (miscellaneous notes) at the end of the diary pad. In addition to *Zalu* and his regular daily diary entry, Chiang wrote a *Benxingqi yuding* (Weekly Plan) and a *Benxingqi fanxing* (Weekly Reflection) each week and a *Bengyueyuding* (Monthly Plan) and a *Bengyue fanxing* (Monthly Reflection) each month. And at the beginning of each year, he listed the issues that needed his attention in his *Bengnian yuding* (Annual Plan). At the end of each year, he conducted an annual self-review in his *Bengniandu fanxing* (Annual Reflection). Because Chiang's written records of his issues of concern were of various lengths, the priority of his concerns and the time that he spent on them can be measured by the number of lines of writing in his diaries once the contents of his diaries have been categorized (See Sherman Xiaogang Lai, "What concern Chiang Kai-shek? A survey and analysis of Chiang Kai-shek's wartime diaries," in *The International Conference on the Second Sino-Japanese War in the Global Context of World War II*," Chongqing, China, September 14, 2013).

15. John Brewer, *The Sinew of Power: War, Money and the English State, 1688–1783* (London: Routledge, 1989).

16. Ibid., 95, 101–07.

17. Ibid., 112–13.

18. Ibid., 223.

19. Ibid., 91.

20. Paul Kennedy, *The Rise and Fall of the Great Powers: Economic Change and Military Conflict from 1500 to 2000* (New York, NY: Random House, 1987), 73–99.

21. Brewer, *The Sinew of Power*, 20–22, 126–34.

22. Wego W.K. Chiang, *How Generalissimo Chiang Kai-shek Won the Eight-Year Sino-Japanese War, 1937–1945* (Taipai: Li Ming Culture Enterprice CoLt, 1979); Mao Zedong, "Assessment of the postwar situation and directive on current tasks), Mao Zedong's Telegram to Peng Dehuai, January 25, 1943," in Central Archives (中央档案馆) ed., *Selected Documents of the Chinese Communist Party Centre, 1943–1944* (中共中央文件选集), Vol. 14 (Beijing: Zhonggong zhongyang dangxiao chubanshe, 1992), 14.

23. Chiang Kai-shek, Diaries, Hoover Institution Archives, Stanford, CA [hereafter "Chiang diaries"], Box 36, Folder 6, June 30, 1932.

24. Chiang diaries, Box 36, Folder 7, July 1, 1932.

25. Chiang diaries, Box 36, Folder 9, September 1, 1932.

26. Chiang diaries, Box 36, Folder 9, September 11, 1932.

27. Chiang diaries, Box 36, Folder 9, September 13, 1932. Chiang had similar complaints until May 1933. See Chiang diaries, Box 36, Folder 13, January 30, 1933; Chiang diaries, Box 36, Folder 16, April 3, 1933.

28. Anthony Best, *Britain, Japan and Pearl Harbor: Avoiding War in East Asia, 1936–41* (London: Routledge, 1995), 79; Wu Jinping (吴景平), "Britain and China's Monetary Reform in 1935" (英国与1935年的中国币制改革), *Historical Studies*, No. 6 (1988), 175–90.

29. Xu Fenghua (徐锋华), "A historiography of *fabi* study during last two decades (近二十年来法币改革研究综述)," *Minguo dai'an* (Archives of the Republican China), No. 3 (2007), 130–38.

30. Chiang diaries, Box 39, Folder 17, Monthly Reflection, November 1937.

31. Chiang diaries, Box 39, Folder 17, November 25, 1937. See also: Chiang diaries, Box 39, Folder 28, September 3, 1938.

32. Chiang diaries, Box 39, Folder 18, December 29, 1937.

33. Chiang diaries, Box 39, Folder 18, December 26, 1937.

34. Chiang diaries, Box 39, Folder 27, August 20, 1938.

35. Chiang diaries, Box 40, Folder 2, December 2, 1938.

36. Chiang diaries, Box 40, Folder 2, December 18, 1938.

37. Chiang diaries, Box 40, Folder 2, December 20, 1938.

38. Chiang diaries, Box 39, Folder 29, October 1, 1938.

39. Chiang diaries, Box 40, Folder 2, Miscellaneous, January 22, 1938.

40. Chiang diaries, Box 40, Folder 27, Weekly Reflection, November 10, 1940.

41. Sherman Xiaogang Lai, "A War Within the War: The Road to the New Fourth Army Incident in January 1941," *Journal of Chinese Military History*, Vol. 2, No. 1, 18.

42. In order to retaliate Mao's preemptive offensives, Chiang destroyed the headquarters of the New Fourth Army, one of the CCP's principal guerrilla forces in January 1941.

43. Ai Chu'nan (艾楚南), "On wartime financial and economic policies (战时财政经济政策), August 1940," *Selected Archival Materials on the Revolution in Shandong* (山东革命历史档案资料选编) (Jinan: Shandong renmin chubanshe, 1981), vol. 3, 298–306.

44. "Directive of Central Financial and Economic Department on *fabi*'s depreciation and proper responsive strategies in anti-Japanese base areas (中共中央财政经济部关于法币贬值和各根据地应采取的对策的指示), February 5, 1942," in *Selected documents of the Chinese Communist Party Centre*, Vol.13, 301–04.

45. Felix Boecking, "Select Unmaking the Chinese Nationalist State: Administrative Reform among Fiscal Collapse, 1937–1945," *Modern Asian Studies*, Vol. 45, No. 2 (February 2011), 277–301.

46. "A primitive review on currency warfare (对敌货币斗争初步检讨)," in Finance Institute of the Chinese People's Bank (中国人民银行金融财政研究所) ed., *Historical Materials of North Sea Bank in the Chinese Revolutionary Base Areas* (中国革命根据地北海银行史料) (Jinan: Shandong renmin chubanshe, 1986), vol. 1, 277.

47. Arthur N. Young, *China and the Helping Hand* (Cambridge, MA: Harvard University Press, 1963), 410, 423.

48. Hao Yinjia (郝银侠), "Re-think about the Nationalist government's *Tianfu* reform" (新视角: 国民政府田赋征实制度之再探讨), *Republican Archives* (民国档案), no. 2, 2011, 110–20.

49. Chiang diaries, Box 42, Folder 18, General, The Chronology of 1942.

50. Chiang diaries, Box 42, Folder 14, September 17, 1942.

51. Chiang diaries, Box 42, Folder 22, General, 1943.

52. Chiang diaries, Box 42, Folder 14, Weekly Reflection (after September 19) and November 22, 1942; Chiang diaries, Box 42, Folder 14, December 23, 1942.

53. Chiang diaries, Box 42, Folder 16, Monthly Reflection, November 1942.

54. Chiang diaries, Box 42, Folder 16, November 7, 1942; Chiang diaries, Box 42, Folder 14, Monthly Reflection, December 1942; Chiang diaries, Box 42, Folder 23, 7, 9, January 25, 1943.

55. Chiang diaries, Box 42, Folder 2, March 31, 1943.

56. Chiang diaries, Box 42, Folder 3, 1, 6, 11 and Weekly Reflection, April 1943.

57. Chiang diaries, Box 42, Folder 3, April 5, 1943.

58. Chiang diaries, Box 42, Folder 3, 6 and Weekly Reflection, April 1943.

59. Chiang diaries, Box 43, Folder 14, February 23, 1944.

60. Young, *China and the Helping Hand*, 31–34.

61. Ibid., 181–83; Song Peiyu (宋佩玉), "Chen Guangfu and the Stabilization Board of China" (陈光甫与中英美平准基金委员会), *Social Science Research* (社会科学研究), No.4, 2006, 154–59.

62. Young, *China and the Helping Hand*, 258.

63. Ibid., 303.

64. Ibid., 293.

65. Ibid., 294–95.

66. Ibid., 387–88.

67. Chiang diaries, Box 43, Folder 7, August 19, 1943.

68. Hsiao-ting Lin, "Chiang Kai-shek and the Cairo Conference," in Joseph W. Esherick and Matthew T. Combs eds., *1943: China at the Crossroad* (Ithaca, NY: East Asia Program Cornell University, 2015), 445–46.

69. Chiang diaries, Box 43, Folder 13, January 11, 1944.

70. Hara Takeshi, "The Ichigo Offensive," in Mark Peattie, Edward J. Drea and Hans van de Ven eds., *The Battle for China: Essays on the Military History of the Sino-Japanese War of 1937–1945* (Stanford, CA: Stanford University Press, 2010), 392–402.

71. Chiang diaries, Box 43, Folder 19, Monthly Reflection, July 1944.

72. Chiang Kai-shek diaries, Box 41, Folder 7, Weekly Reflection (Second Week of January 1941). See also, Sherman Xiaogang Lai, "A War Within the War: The Road to the New Fourth Army Incident in January 1941," *Journal of Chinese Military History*, Vol. 2, No. 1, 2013, 1–27.

73. Chiang diaries, Box 43, Folder 3, April 2, 1943.

74. Chiang diaries, Box 43, Folder 5, Monthly Review, June 1943.

75. Chiang diaries, Box 43, Folder 9, October 4, 1943.

76. Chiang diaries, Box 43, Folder 9, October 17, 1943.

77. Chiang diaries, Box 43, Folder 18, June 25, 1944.

78. Asano Toyomi, "Japanese Operations in Yunnan and Northern Burma," in *The Battle for China*, 361–85.

79. Chiang diaries, Box 43, Folder 20, August 29, 1944.

80. Chiang diaries, Box 43, Folder 21, September 7 and 8, 1944.

81. Jay Taylor, *The Generalissimo: Chiang Kai-shek and the Struggle for Modern China* (Cambridge, MA: The Belknap Press of Harvard University Press, 2009), 287–88; Barbara W. Tuchman, *Stilwell and the American Experience in China, 1911–1945* (New York, NY: The Macmillan Company, 1970), 493–94.

82. Young, *China and the Helping Hand,* 316.

83. The Department of State, "The China White Paper" (originally issued as "United States Relations with China: With Special Reference to the Period of 1944–1949," August 1949) (Stanford, CA: Stanford University Press, 1967), 27.

84. Young, *China and the Helping Hand,* 317–18.

85. Young, *China and the Helping Hand,* 321.

86. Bruce Craig, *Treasonable Doubt: The Harry Dexter White Spy Case* (Lawrence, KS: University Press of Kansas, 2004).

87. Young, *China and the Helping Hand,* 323–32.

88. Young, *China and the Helping Hand*, 188; Zong Daoyi (宗道一), "Ji Chaoding: An Unforgettable Communist" (冀朝鼎:一位永远不能被遗忘的杰出共产党人), *Extensive Reading About CP'S History* (党史博览), No. 3, 2002, 46–50.

89. Wu Zhengyu (吴正裕), "A Political Poem by Mao Zedong during the Chongqing Negotiation" (毛泽东在重庆谈判期间创作的一首七律政论诗), December 21, 2016, http://dangshi.people.com.cn/n1/2016/1221/c85037-28964889.html.

90. Charles Clover and Jamil Anderlini, "Chinese General Caught with Tonne of Cash," *Financial Time*, November 31, 2014, https://www.ft.com/content/4883f674-7171-11e4-818e-00144feabdc0.

BIBLIOGRAPHY

Ai Chu'nan (艾楚南). "On Wartime Financial and Economic Policies (战时财政经济政策), August 1940." *Selected Archival Materials on the Revolution in Shandong* (山东革命历史档案资料选编), vol. 3. Jinan: Shandong renmin chubanshe, 1981, pp. 298–306.

Best, Anthony. *Britain, Japan and Pearl Harbor: Avoiding War in East Asia, 1936–41*. London: Routledge, 1995.

———. "The Leith-Ross Mission and British Policy towards East Asia, 1934–37." *International History Review* 35.4 (2013): 681–701.

Boecking, Felix Boecking. "Select Unmaking the Chinese Nationalist State: Administrative Reform among Fiscal Collapse, 1937–1945." *Modern Asian Studies* 45.2 (February 2011): 277–301.

Brewer, John. *The Sinew of Power: War, Money and the English State, 1688–1783*. London, England: Routledge, 1989.

Callahan, Raymond. "The Illusion of Security: Singapore 1919–42." *Journal of Contemporary History* 9.2 (1974): 69–92.

Chiang Kai-shek. *China's Destiny*. New York: Macmillan, 1947.

———. *Diaries*. Stanford, CA: Hoover Institution Archives.

Chiang, Wego W.K. *How Generalissimo Chiang Kai-shek Won the Eight-year Sino-Japanese War, 1937–1945*. Taipai: Li Ming Culture Enterprice CoLt, 1979.

Churchill, Winston. *The Second World War*. Vol. 4: The Hinge of Fate. London: Cassell, 1951.

Connell, John. *Wavell, Supreme Commander, 1941–1943*. London: Collins, 1969.

Craig, Bruce. *Treasonable Doubt: The Harry Dexter White Spy Case*. Lawrence, KS: University Press of Kansas, 2004.

Department of State of the United States. "The China White Paper (Originally Issued as 'United States Relations with China: With Special Reference to the Period of 1944–1949')." Stanford, CA: Stanford University Press, 1967.

Eastman, Lloyd E. *The Abortive Revolution: China under Nationalist Rule, 1927–1937*. Cambridge, MA: Harvard University Press, 1974.

Esherick, Joseph W. and Combs, Matthew T., ed. *1943: China at the Crossroad*. Ithaca, NY: East Asia Program Cornell University, 2015.

Fairbank, John King. *The Great Chinese Revolution, 1800–1985*. New York, NY: Harper and Row, 1986.

Hao Yinjia (郝银侠). "Re-think about the Nationalist Government's *Tianfu* Reform" (新视角: 国民政府田赋征实制度之再探讨). *Republican Archives* (民国档案) 2 (2011): 110–20.

He Qinglian (何清涟). "Corruption was not the Reason for the GMD's Collapse" ("国民党之败并非缘于腐败.") *VOA*, November 22, 2014, https://www.voachinese.com/a/heqinglian-blog-history-notes-20141121/2530061.html.

Kennedy, Paul. *The Rise and Fall of the Great Powers: Economic Change and Military Conflict from 1500 to 2000*. New York: Random House, 1987.

Kirby, S. Woodburn. *The War Against Japan*. London: Her Majesty's Stationery Office, 1957–58.

Lai, Sherman Xiaogang. "What Concern Chiang Kai-shek? A Survey and Analysis of Chiang Kai-shek's Wartime Diaries." In "The International Conference on the Second Sino-Japanese War in the Global Context of World War II," Chongqing, China, September 14, 2013.

———. "A War Within the War: The Road to the New Fourth Army Incident in January 1941." *Journal of Chinese Military History* 2.1 (2013): 1–27.

Mitter, Rana. *China's War with Japan, 1937–1945: The Struggle for Survival.* London: Allen Lane, 2013.

Oxford English Dictionary (Oxford: Oxford University Press, 2000). http://www.oed.com.proxy.queensu.ca/view/Entry/42045?redirectedFrom=corruption&.

Peattie, Mark Peattie, Drea, Edward J. and van de Ven, Hans, ed. *The Battle for China: Essays on the Military History of the Sino-Japanese War of 1937–1945.* Stanford, CA: Stanford University Press, 2010.

Pepper, Suzanne. "The Political Odyssey of an Intellectual Construct: Peasant Nationalism and the Study of China's Revolutionary History—A Review Essay." *The Journal of Asian Studies* 63.1 (February 2004): 105–125.

Qin, Xiaoyi, ed. *Jiang zong tong da shi chang bian* (Annals of President Chiang). Taibei: Zhongshan tu shu gong ssŭ, 1968, Vol. 6.

———. *Zhonghua minguo zhongyao shiliao chubian* (Important Historical Documents of Republic of China), vols 2 and 3. Taipei: Guomindang Zhongyang Zhixing Weiyuanhui Dangshi Weiyuanhui, 1981.

Romanus, Charles F. and Sunderland, Riley. *Stilwell's Mission to China.* Washington, DC: Office of the Chief of Military History, Dept. of the Army, 1953.

Saich, Tony and Van de Ven, Hans, eds. *New Perspectives on the Chinese Communist Revolution.* Armonk, NY: M.E. Sharpe, 1995.

Song Peiyu (宋佩玉). "Chen Guangfu and the Stabilization Board of China" (陈光甫与中英美平准基金委员会). *Social Science Research* (社会科学研究) 4 (2006): 154–159.

Taylor, Jay. *The Generalissimo Chiang Kai-shek and the Struggle for Modern China.* Cambridge, MA: Harvard University Press, 2009.

The China Quarterly, 150 (1997), Special Issue: Reappraising Republic China.

Tuchman, Barbara W. *Stilwell and the American Experience in China, 1911–1945.* New York, NY: The Macmillan Company, 1970.

Wu Jinping (吴景平). "Britain and China's Monetary Reform in 1935" (英国与1935年的中国币制改革). *Historical Studies* 6 (1988): 175–190.

Wu Zhengyu (吴正裕). "A Political Poem by Mao Zedong during the Chongqing Negotiation" (毛泽东在重庆谈判期间创作的一首七律政论诗," December 21, 2016. http://dangshi.people.com.cn/n1/2016/1221/c85037-28964889.html.

Xu Fenghua (徐锋华). "A Historiography of *fabi* Study during Last Two Decades (近二十年来法币改革研究综述)." *Minguo dai'an* (Archives of the Republican China) 3 (2007): 130–138.

Yang, Kuisong. "The Complicated Reasons Behind the GMD's Defeat" (杨奎松, "国民党败给共产党的原因其实非常复杂,"). *Weilaiwang*, 12 April 2017. http://news.china.com/history/all/11025807/20170412/30412879_all.html.

Young, Arthur N. *China and the Helping Hand*. Cambridge, MA: Harvard University Press, 1963.

Zhongguo renmin yinhang jinrong caizhen yanjiusuo (Finance Institute of the Chinese People's Bank) ed., *Historical materials of North Sea Bank in the Chinese Revolutionary Base Areas* (中国革命根据地北海银行史料), vol. 1. Jinan: Shandong renmin chubanshe, 1986.

Zhonghua minguo zhongyao shiliao chubian (Important Historical Documents of Republic of China) ed. Qin Xiaoyi, vols 2 and 3. Taipei: Guomindang Zhongyang Zhixing Weiyuanhui Dangshi Weiyuanhui, 1981.

Zhongyang Dan'an guan (Central Archives), ed. *Selected Documents of the Chinese Communist Party Centre, 1943–1944* (中共中央文件选集), vol. 14. Beijing: Zhonggong zhongyang dangxiao chubanshe, 1992.

Zong Daoyi (宗道一). "Ji Chaoding: An Unforgettable Communist" (冀朝鼎:一位永远不能被遗忘的杰出共产党人). *Extensive Reading About CP'S History* (党史博览) 3 (2002): 46–50.

Chapter 4

Anticorruption Policy and Party Politics

The Lost Political Battle and the Fate of the GMD

Xiaobing Li

Japan's surrender in August 1945 did not automatically bring peace and independence to Chinese people, who soon found themselves returning to civil war in 1946. Both Nationalist and Communist Parties approached postwar issues from an exclusive, China-centered, absolute nationalist calculation for an "independent and strong China."[1] They expected neither US or Soviet hegemony, nor restoration of prewar European colonial powers in China. General Chiang Wei-kuo (Jiang Weiguo), former secretary general of the ROC's Council of National Security and ROC president Chiang Kai-shek's son, said that his father was convinced that the Roosevelt administration did not have a strategic plan for postwar China, nor did it consider China as a new power that would replace Japan in the position of dominance in East Asia after the war.[2]

Even though the United States and the ROC fought as allies during the war, the leaders of the two countries found it extremely difficult to establish a partnership for a postwar order due to conflicting backgrounds and beliefs and incompatible visions for the future of East Asia. Moreover, Truman administration's aid to Jiang has largely been ignored, or treated only briefly by historians, because the GMD (Guomindang, or Kuomintang, KMT), as well as Truman, "lost China" to the CCP (Chinese Communist Party) by the end of the Chinese Civil War. This joint effort is all too commonly dismissed as a solely sterile phase of the wartime alliance or as a precursor of the upcoming CCP takeover, both of which have been given more detailed attention.

Some historians in the West argue that the Chinese Communists' victory over the GMD in the Chinese Civil War of 1946–1949 was politically predestined, given the conflicts between two parties, the failure of American involvements, the critiques from intellectuals of GMD leaderships, student movements against the GMD, and the popularity of CCP land reforms. Some, however, have questioned whether the Chinese Civil War is best examined through the use of these categories of analysis.

Joseph Esherick observes that early works on the civil war and land reforms had a partial analysis with rosy descriptions. Esherick suggests not to think the Chinese revolution explainable by "anti-pole" structures such as "China and the West, state and society, urban-rural or class contradictions."[3] Suzanne Pepper stresses that, although the CCP land reform succeeded in gaining support to match the GMD, people's attitudes toward the two were not totally either advantageous or disadvantageous for either party during the war. Nevertheless, the CCP was one of the minority parties and was not accused of being responsible for the war, an accusation which the GMD, already powerful, could not escape.[4] It is conceivable that the draconian rule of the Japanese caused the Chinese people to turn against the Chinese state. In fact, it appears more likely that it was the failure of state-building during the GMD's control in the mainland that cost the Chinese state its "legitimacy"—if indeed the "loss of legitimacy" is the best way to interpret the GMD defeat. The GMD had a chance to promote major changes short of revolution. The failure to do so accounts for the rise of communism in the mainland China. Edward Dreyer explains the outcome of the civil war in conventional military-historical terms: "The Nationalists sent their best formations into a series of traps in Manchuria and North China, lost them, and afterwards never had a chance. Mao's revolution was a consequence, rather than a cause, of the communist victory on the mainland."[5]

This chapter argues that it appears more likely that it was the failure of the takeover and economic reconstruction after World War II cost the GMD state its "legitimacy"—if indeed the "loss of legitimacy" is the best way to interpret the GMD defeat. Corruption of the GMD played an important role in promoting the anti-GMD movement in China and became one of the major grievances of the forces undermining the GMD regime in China. The GMD had a chance to promote major changes short of revolution. Chinese people's trust in the GMD government through the war against Japan's invasion had been eroding rapidly. The decline in institutional trust partially resulted from failed anticorruption policy and corruption tolerance in and outside the government.

This study addresses the relationship between postwar corruption and institutional trust. First, it provides an overview of corruption of the GMD in 1945–1946. Second, it explains why the government's anticorruption policy failed in the major cities like Shanghai in 1947–1948. Third, our finding affirms that corruption eroded political trust in China, even though Chinese people tolerated individuals who involved in corruption and scandals. Fourth, the chapter provides some reasons on why the failure to deal with the corruption so accounts for the rise of communism in China in 1948–1949. Our conclusion explores the relationship between corruption and institutional trust. The institutional trust is a key linkage between a government and society and a foundation for democracy. In other words, tolerance for corruption undermines people's trust in government and interests in participating in politics, and slows down, if not totally stops, democratization.

"TAKEOVER" AND CORRUPTION AFTER WORLD WAR II

By 1937 armed clashes between the Japanese and Chinese troops at Lugouqiao, or the Marco Polo Bridge outside Beijing, had escalated into all-out war between China and Japan. Japan's imperialist attempt to turn North China into a second Manchukuo led to the full-scale military confrontation between these two East Asian countries. Unlike the First Sino-Japanese War in 1894–1895, the Second Sino-Japanese War, or the Anti-Japanese War in China, was a long struggle of attrition that ended only with Japan's unconditional surrender to the Allies in 1945. After the total war broke between China and Japan in July 1937, in September, the GMD made public a declaration for GMD-CCP cooperation and recognized the legal status of the CCP. Thus, an anti-Japanese united front formally came into existence.[6] This front is often called the Second United Front (1937–1945) to distinguish it from the First United Front of GMD-CCP cooperation (1924–1927).

From 1939 to 1945, China was divided into three distinctive regions. The first region were the Japanese-occupied territories (*Lunxuanqu* in Chinese), including strategic areas in Manchuria, northeastern China, southeastern China, Hainan Island, and major coastal cities including Shanghai, Nanjing, Wuhan, Hong Kong, and Guangzhou—the most industrialized urban areas. In the occupied region which had about 36–40 percent of national population, some local warlords and their armies collaborated with the Japanese. Many Chinese in the occupied region accepted Japanese military administration and the puppet government of Wang Jingwei "because they had no choice, or because they saw the possibility of profiting from cooperation with Japan."[7]

The second region was the Nationalist-controlled region (*Guotongqu*), also known as "Free China," including Chongqing, the wartime ROC capital, and a few rear base cities such as Chengdu, Kunming, Guilin, and central and southwestern China. Under Chiang Kai-shek and his GMD government, the

GMD-controlled region had about 48–50 percent of the total population and 60 percent of China's rice production. US aid to the Nationalists increased after December 1941, but China was a distant part of the China-Burma-India Theater. In April 1942, Japanese forces in Burma took Lashio and cut the Burma Road, the Nationalist-controlled region's only land route to the outside world. Thereafter, American aid had to be flown over "the Hump" of the Himalayas to reach Chongqing. Chiang's US military adviser, Lieutenant General Joseph Stilwell, tried to train and organize new Chinese divisions equipped by the United States, but he became increasingly frustrated with Chiang's refusal to commit them to fight the Japanese in Burma or in southeastern China. There was also disagreement among US generals about aid to China. Major General Claire Chennault wanted to build on the success of the Flying Tigers and their high kill ratio against Japanese pilots to commit most aid to the new US Fourteenth Air Force in China.

The third region in wartime China was the Communist-controlled region, or the "liberated regions" (*Jiefangqu*) according to the historians in China. This region loosely incorporated scattered rural areas in remote northern and northwestern regions under the influence of the CCP with Yan'an as the political center through the war. When Jiang lost some of his best troops in the war against the Japanese invasion, Mao's successful guerrillas recruited a large number of peasants into his forces. The units of the CCP's Eighth Route Army marched to the enemy-occupied territories, where they carried out guerrilla operations and established military and political bases.[8] The Eighth Route Army in North China increased from 46,000 men in 1937 to 220,000 men in 1939, and to 500,000 men in 1940. In the south, the CCP's New Fourth Army moved north and south of the Yangzi (Yangtze) River and established bases in southern Jiangsu and also north of the river. In each of the bases, the CCP established a government, reduced the peasants' rents and interests, returned land to poor peasants, and armed the masses.

At the end of the Anti-Japanese War in 1945, the levels of public trust in the government of the Republic of China (ROC) were high since Chinese people had a strong confidence in the GMD which had achieved the final victory of the war over Japan after eight years of bloody fighting. While the Chinese armies lost three million soldiers in the war, the civilian population suffered ten million casualties. In the wake of the Allied Forces' offensive campaign against the fascists and militarism across the globe, Chinese people developed a new vigor of nationalism which revealed a profound change taking place in the former semi-colony and occupied territories. This new nationalism was no longer a traditional, Eastern cultural or Han-Chinese ethnic nationalism, but a modern, Western-style state nationalism that emphasized national independence, self-government, state interests, and territorial sovereignty. Moreover, during the war, the ROC government under the leadership of Chiang Kai-shek actively participated in the international diplomacy and became one of the Allies leaders with Franklyn Roosevelt, Winston Churchill, and Josef Stalin. Chinese people had a good reason to believe their national leader and trust his government of the GMD.

After Japan suddenly surrendered in August 1945, there was a power vacuum in the "occupied territories," especially in cities such as Shanghai, Beijing, and Guangzhou. Chiang found himself far away from the country's economic and population centers and facing many unprecedented challenges. Chiang's armies began to occupy all the large cities and controlled most of the railroads, highways, seaports, and transportation hubs.[9]

The GMD officials followed the troops to rush to "takeover" (*jieshou*) the occupied areas, including land, industries, transportation, communication, businesses, and banks in late 1945 and early 1946. In that winter, before any form of effective administration had been established in the cities, finance and commerce in the urban areas came under threat from newcomers from Chongqing who tried to use their government connections to enrich themselves. Although a large number of GMD officials avoided being entrapped by the riches of the cities, the government's inability to deal with corruption tore into its legitimacy.[10]

The US government wanted to maintain the wartime coalition between the ROC and Mao's communists. In the fall of 1945, President Harry Truman sent Patrick Hurley, the US ambassador to China, to Yan'an, the CCP capital, to pick up Mao and escort him to Chongqing for negotiations with Chiang.[11] The Chongqing Talks lasted forty-three days. In October 1945, Chiang and Mao signed an agreement which provided for a joint coalition government under Chiang's leadership.[12] However, since both sides had different political agenda, the negotiations failed, and the two parties resumed their military conflicts in North China.

Following Hurley's resignation, Truman appointed General George Marshall, secretary of state and former head of the JCS, as his envoy to China in December 1945. Marshall tried to use US aid, which the ROC desperately needed, as a negotiating tool to force Chiang to accept terms which would also be acceptable to Mao. Marshall believed that even the threat of a reduction of US aid to China would bring Chiang around. In fact, neither Chiang nor Mao would compromise and they refused to cooperate with one another. The Chinese Civil War began on June 26, 1946, when Chiang launched an all-out offensive against CCP-held areas, culminating in a major attack in central China and other attacks throughout the country.[13] Seeing the momentum of civil war growing, Marshall announced in January 1947 that his mission had failed.[14]

The GMD officials used the opportunities of takeover to benefit themselves by confiscating businesses, seizing banks for private financial gains, controlling market and transportation, misusing public funds, illegal business practice, smuggling, bribery, and kickbacks in the "occupied areas." For instance, in Xiamen, the GMD officials demanded all local businesses to apply for a "patriotic certificate" to verify their nationalistic attitude rather than pro-Japanese stand during the occupation. Those who failed to get a certificate would lose their business licenses and their companies would be confiscated by the GMD authorities. Most of the local business owners lost their companies, shops, and properties to the GMD officials.[15]

In Shanghai, the GMD government failed to reconstruct the prewar national market, since the officials enjoyed collecting huge amount of money for merchants to transport their goods by the state-controlled railways. From 1946 to 1947, the railroads connecting the cities were held up by factional infighting within the government. Even Chen Lifu, head of the GMD Organization Department, could not get government ministries to work together in developing any railway plan for the future. Valuable time was lost while ministries and individual ministers had their own positions in the party.[16] In Manchuria, General Liang Huasheng, governor of Jilin, did his best to exploit the remaining industries of what had been the region's most developed area for his own profit, rather than seeing to the repair of the many factories and plants that had been incapacitated by Soviet looting. That the northeastern headquarters was unable to deal with corrupt officials like General Liang made it difficult for the GMD to put the industrial potential behind its military efforts.[17]

Chinese people began to lose their confidence and trust in the GMD government when it seemed to them that public resources and even private properties transferred to serve certain individual interests. GMD corruption spawned personal connections and made the government and bureaucracy personal instruments or vehicle of politicians. Therefore, the GMD government began to lose its credibility. But even more important, these revenues went to individual officials, who then prevented the state from developing a free market economy. These "official corruption" stopped the state from generating vital income, reducing its ability to decrease the portion of its revenue, and increasing its dependence on extortion, foreign aid, and higher taxes.[18] It is interesting to note that the corruption itself in China in the 1990s–2000s was not necessarily an impediment to economic growth. Some pundits argue that corruption was the grease that kept the political and economic wheels moving. And Chinese people seem to trust political institutions as long as their living standard has been improved, even though corruption reigns. The problem in the late 1940s was that few of the basic incentives for growth were present, and that official corruption prevented some of these incentives from being formed.

In the summer of 1946, the Chinese Communist and Nationalist armed forces began a full-scale war against each other for supremacy in the country.

Chinese military historians divide the civil war into three phases. The first phase of the Civil War began on June 26, when Jiang launched an all-out offensive campaign against Mao's "liberated regions" with a major attack in central China and other offensive campaigns from south to north.[19] From September to November, the GMD troops moved northward along four major railroads, and tried to advance into the CCP liberated regions. Jiang believed that if he could squeeze the CCP forces out of their bases within three to six months, he could win the war. The Communist forces made full preparations for fighting a new war against the GMD. The CCP forces totaled 1.68 million troops by the beginning of the war, even though the Red Army was, in fact, an army equipped with "millet plus rifles." They controlled the countryside with a population of about 100 million, while the GMD held the cities with larger population. Mao adopted a new strategy in late 1946, "giving them tit for tat and fighting for every inch of land,"[20] and "offense in the north; defense in the south."[21] The goal was to maintain and concentrate a superior force to destroy the GMD's effective strength.

"Great Tiger Hunt": Anticorruption Efforts

The GMD-CCP postwar struggle focused on the northeast, the location of China's heavy industry, coal, oil, and chemistry sources, established by the Japanese from 1931 to 1945. Japan's surrender, along with the Russian Red Army's withdrawal, created a power vacuum in that strategic region and invited GMD-CCP competition over its cities, industrial and commercial centers, and key points of transportation. In 1946, Chiang Kai-shek reinforced the northeast with a large number of his best troops. For the first time in its history, the CCP Central Committee transferred 110,000 troops with 20,000 party cadres with the goal of transforming its military from a regional to national level. The northeast thereafter became its strategic base, which secured communications and transportation between the Soviet Union and the CCP.

In 1946, the CCP successfully reserved most of its troops and stayed in its "liberated areas" during Jiang's all-out offensive campaign. Soon after, the CCP's offensive campaign began in the north and soon swept into the south. The CCP managed to maintain their control of one-quarter of the country. Westad points out that the key to the CCP's success in mobilizing the Chinese masses was their ability to manage local politics.[22] It was because Chinese people came to see the Jiang regime as a "bad government" which allowed, tolerated, and even encouraged the high level of corrupt practices. As a consequence, the elimination of corruption came to be one of the major expectations from the masses in the war, making the absence of corruption germane to the definition of a "good government."

Therefore, it seems possible to explain how institutions interacted and changed. We may have learned from this main lesson of Chinese history that political institutions were decisive in shaping economic and social institutions.[23] In the Chinese Civil War, official corruption had played a significant part in the public indictment of the GMD regime. One may agree that in China petty corruption permeated society, encouraging a culture of bribery and connections as the mechanisms for getting things done. It is still true today. However, government and official corruption corroded confidence and trust of the Chinese people because they believed the state assets and their properties were stolen through illegal activities and transactions. The marriage between the oligarchs and the Jiang regime maintained a system in which political power ensured economic advancement and vice versa.

In terms of the regime's survival, it is uncertain how much harm corruption did. But it caused GMD mismanagement, which became a direct cause of its collapse on the mainland. Granted, in part as a result of the war, the GMD government failed to control inflation, which by mid-1947 had reached record levels. Between 1947 and 1948, inflation rose to an annual average of about 230 percent.[24] Corruption inside and outside the party became a major problem as inflation rose and central control weakened. Therefore, the key political institutional decline brought the society to the point where the public lost their confidence and trust in the government.

The result of the GMD's difficulties in handling the takeover of the occupied areas, especially the cities, was a steady erosion of popular support for the central government. The party failed in their urban policies and thereby destroyed much of the party's legitimacy in the occupied areas. By 1946, the GMD government was getting desperately short of cash with which to fund its plans for the civilian and military buildup of postwar China. It was no surprise to business owners in Shanghai, Guangdong, and Tianjin that the GMD returned to the same forms of extortion and confiscations that they had experienced before the war.[25]

The second phase of the Chinese Civil War started in March 1947 and ended by August 1948. Since his all-out offensive campaign was failing, Chiang changed his war strategy from broad assaults to attacks on key targets. Jiang concentrated his forces on two points: the CCP-controlled areas in Shandong and Shaanxi, where the CCP Central Committee and its high command had been since 1935. Jiang failed again.

During the war, the CCP's massive propaganda campaigns helped the communists form a united front in opposition to the Chiang regime. Corruption within the ROC, spiraling inflation, and the factional struggles within the GMD also assisted in making communist propaganda popular and successful. Exploiting widespread complaints about Chiang's government and also the strong desire for peace after World War II, the CCP organized a second front against Jiang in major cities through student-led anti-government and anti-war movements to politically isolate the ROC. In 1947, for instance, students from more than sixty cities demonstrated for the patriotic and democratic movement, opposing hunger, civil war, and persecution. Regarding these demonstrations, Vincent reported to Washington that "the Chinese university students would inevitably be swayed in their attitudes and approaches by any widespread campaign, whether of Communist or other origin, directed against American military aid to the Jiang regime and would in turn become strongly anti-American. The anti-American feeling in China might possibly take an even more serious turn than at present."[26] In twenty-nine cities, including Shanghai and Tianjin, 3.2 million workers staged strikes and demonstrations in early 1947. As Westad concludes, the CCP's skillful propaganda juxtaposed a "new China" against the deeply flawed old China headed by Jiang. Mao mobilized the Chinese masses, especially the peasants, by exploiting Jiang's weaknesses and mistakes, and by expanding his revolution across the country.[27]

In that year, the peasant movement spread to seventeen provinces and 1 million peasants participated in armed uprisings against the GMD government. In May 1946, the CCP stated that the policy of rent and interest reduction, which had been carried out during World War II, would change to a policy of confiscation of land from the landlord class and its redistribution among the peasants. In September 1947, the "Outline of the Agrarian Law of China" became public. It abolished the old land rental system and the land system incorporating the concept of "land to the tillers" would take its place. Landlords' land was to be confiscated without compensation for equitable redistribution among the rural population.[28] Through the land reform, over 96 million peasants in the "liberated areas" support the PLA or joined the army themselves. From July 1946 to June 1948, the PLA enlisted 1.6 million peasants, as new landowners, into their troops. The peasants' enthusiasm brought about an early victory of the CCP in the Civil War.[29]

To make the anti-Jiang campaign effective and successful, Zhou Enlai drafted a Central Committee telegram and sent it to all regional party bureaus, sub-bureaus, and front committees on January 20, 1947. He instructed the local party leaders "to coordinate all of the propaganda and protesting activities and carry them out immediately."[30] Deng Xiaoping issued a bureau instruction to the Central Plain party officials: "Carry out the Party Central Committee's Directive." Deng emphasized on June 6, 1948, that "strengthening propaganda and education is a task that demands immediate attention both in the army and in all areas" and "party committees and political organs at all levels should provide more effective leadership over propaganda and education, so as to be sure they are fully in keeping with the Party's principles and policies. They should put a stop to such erroneous practices as writing slogans and conducting propaganda at will."[31]

In October 1947, the PLA issued a manifesto calling upon the people to "overthrow Jiang Jieshi and liberate all China." It put forward this political program: "United workers, peasants, soldiers, intellectuals and businessmen, all oppressed classes, all people's organizations, democratic parties, minority nationalities, overseas Chinese and other patriots; from a national united front; overthrow the dictatorial Jiang Jieshi government; and establish a democratic coalition government."[32] In December, through its economic policy, the party again promised the peasants that the CCP would confiscate land from the landlords and redistribute it among the peasants. Not surprisingly, the new policy received wide support of the peasants. Some Western historians attribute Mao's victory over Chiang's offensives during the early years of the civil war due to CCP popularity, political propaganda, and land reforms continuing to gain peasants' support.

Facing the economic difficulties and mass protesting, Jiang began his economic reform in 1947, including an anticorruption policy in 1948. The pressure also came from the US government which continued to support the Jiang's regime after World War II. Chiang Ching-guo, son of Chiang Kai-shek, and several leading generals urged Jiang Jieshi with a crackdown on corruption and the misuse of public funds. The reform policy was finally announced on August 19, 1948, with a new currency, the Gold Yuan (*Jinyuanjuan*). Jiang Jingguo was sent to Shanghai, the main battleground against corruption and mismanagement in the GMD. Westad describes, "The young Jiang went to his new task with determination and substantial public support. More than most GMD leaders, Jingguo realized that the campaign which he was at the helm of might be his party's last chance to stabilize the political and economic situation before the military showdown with the CCP."[33] Chiang Ching-guo struck hard on the corruption in Shanghai by putting more than 3,000 officials and businessmen in jail within two weeks. Some of those in prison were Shanghai's best known Chinese businessmen, who were called as the "big tigers."[34] Among others were Green Gang leader Du Yuesheng's own son, charged with black-market stock-exchange trading. Jiang Jingguo also organized paramilitary forces to raid warehouses and suspects' homes, placed "secret-report boxes" in the streets, and issued new laws and regulations. They had contributed significantly to the local dissatisfaction with the regime and the mobilization of opposition groups.

Although Jiang Jingguo's "Great Tiger Hunt" (*Dahu*) was successful in price control against inflation, solving corruption cases against political protection and cover-ups, and slowing down public complaints against the government, his anticorruption efforts did not stimulate the economy and could not last long in Shanghai. In September, only four or five weeks of the anticorruption movement, the shelves of shops became empty since the retailers could sell goods at rates eight or even ten times higher in the surrounding provinces and other cities. The manufacturing factories were closed because the owner could not keep up with the cost of production when they had to purchase the raw materials at high prices from other regions. By October, Chiang Ching-guo's anticorruption movement was over.

Thereafter, corruption continued and further impeded governmental performance, which in turn escalated the decline of the public trust. GMD corruption diverted administrative resources and activities to areas where marginal gains from graft were maximized, and the public suffered from the increasing cost as well as the poor quality of public works. It also led to the ROC overspending on certain areas at the expense of the public's welfare. What lost the GMD government adherents in the cities and among elites elsewhere was its aggressive policies to exploit all classes of citizens for its own purposes that led to the breakdown of trust between Jiang's regime and the people it had been seen to represent, especially landlords, business owners, and urban professionals. Eventually, GMD corruption hindered post–World War II economic reconstruction and development by lowering investment, reducing the effectiveness of American aid, and undermining tax revenues.

Save the GMD and Lost China

While corruption fundamentally betrayed public trust, eroded people's confidence, and lowered the governmental performance, the GMD party somehow survived postwar takeover and corruption problems, which facilitated the development of the party after the war. Party membership was not only a political protection or promotion at the working place, but also an inside connection to the business center and powerful authorities. In the party-state like the ROC, the state-business relationship benefited the GMD, party leaders like Song Ziwen and Kong Xiangxi, and the party member. Therefore, corruption encouraged political participation and promoted the party membership after the war. It also maintained the personal loyalty and political trust of the GMD members.

The Guomindang as a party was seriously weakened by the Japanese invasion and occupation for eight years. Because of the war, Jiang was pre-occupied with the war-fighting and had less time for the party and its organization in 1937–1945. The attempts at revamping the GMD into an elite party with a strictly hierarchical organization were dropped, and the party's policies suffered under the thousands of big and small compromises it had to strike with local power-holders, including warlords and CCP guerrilla forces. It became the GMD culture to use public resources to cater to particularistic loyalty, even if the same activities would be perceived as corrupt in the West. In particular, the norm of reciprocity embedded in GMD political culture socialized people to treat corrupt exchanges as neutral and acceptable. Moreover, the

Chinese culture emphasizes hierarchical relationships, order, and harmony, which might also consolidate Chinese people's trust in political parties and the government.

While public opinion in the cities was turning increasingly critical of the GMD's handling of reunited China, the GMD party's leadership became more centralized around Jiang Jieshi. No other leader in the party had the authority to make any important decisions. In terms of public legitimacy, official corruption had a negative effect. It represented the state as unjust, and it prompted the regime to take highly unpopular actions to add to its office-holders' incomes. Both resulted in the increasing criticism and public protesting against the government in 1948–1949. Newspapers and magazines highlighted a wide range of cases that were often not merely individual examples of fraud, but large-scale plans for ripping off businesses or companies.

Chiang Kai-shek, however, did not launch a much-needed political reform to clean the GMD party by stopping corruption and mismanagement. A political reform could weaken or even collapse the party during the Civil War. Corruption continued to be rampant in the GMD-held regions in the last year of the Chinese Civil War. The corrupt system was made possible by a broad network of personal network and patron-client relationships whose focal point was, naturally, the presidency. Many top governmental appointments were distributed to Chiang's followers, while the bulk of the provincial administration was filled by family and friends of the senior officials. Then, various problems that corruption raised led to the failure to provide representations, basic welfare, and, mostly important, protection and safety of the civilian population in the Chinese Civil War.

The third phase of the war lasted from August 1948 to October 1949. In the fall of 1948, the CCP-armed forces reorganized as the People's Liberation Army (PLA) and began launching offensives from rural areas against GMD defenses in urban areas. This phase included three of the most important PLA campaigns in the war: the Liao-Shen Campaign (in northeastern China), Ping-Jin Campaign (in the Beijing-Tianjin region), and Huai-Hai Campaign (in Eastern China). The three campaigns lasted altogether 142 days, during which 1.54 million GMD troops were killed, wounded, captured, or had revolted against Jiang's regime.[35] In terms of scale, or the number of enemies destroyed, the three campaigns were unprecedented in Chinese military history. As a result of these offensive campaigns, all of northeast, most of north, and the rest and central China areas north of the Yangzi River were liberated. Nearly all of Chiang's best troops were wiped out. In early 1949, the PLA had fifty-eight infantry armies, numbering 4 million men.[36]

To save the party, Jiang retired from his presidency on January 21, 1949, but continued to serve as the chairman of the GMD. In fact, it was his personal network rather than a well-organized party to maintain his power in the

GMD. Therefore, Jiang continued to tolerate the corruption, malfeasance, and fraud that existed in his political party. Although Chiang was aware of negative impact of corruption, he knew that the termination of personal network and loyalty, party's power and control of the government, and party-owned and -run businesses (*Dangchan*) would destroy the GDM political base and eventually destroy the party itself. GMD political culture tended to emphasize group harmony and hierarchical relationships. Access to the state resources was achieved through political network; having loyal party members in positions of authority, in turn, allowed for the incumbent to control and benefit from the illegal exchange of public decision for money and political support. This was clearly the case inside the GMD, where corruption, personal favoritism, loyalty, and patronage were closely entangled. Party members socialized, even if it meant sacrificing their personal life, to serve the interest of the political group and party.

After Jiang's retirement, Vice President Li Zongren (Li Tsung-jen) came to the forefront. The peace talks between the GMD and CCP began on April 1 and ended on April 20 when both sides failed to reach an agreement.[37] The PLA then ordered 1 million troops to cross the Yangzi (Yangtze, or Changjiang) River on April 21. Two days later, Nanjing, the capital of the ROC, fell and Chiang removed the seat of his government with 1 million troops and government officials to Taiwan. The PLA pressed on in its drive into the northwest, southwest, and central China. By September, the PLA occupied most of the country except for Tibet, Taiwan, and various offshore islands.

Politically, the CCP strove to form a united front among all the people for opposition to Jiang. Spiraling inflation, government corruption, and factional struggles within the GMD made elimination of the Communist forces impossible. The CCP was also able to use US aid programs in its political propaganda to describe the Jiang regime as America's puppet and an international imperialist agent in China. The Communist Party Center launched massive propaganda campaigns in 1948–1949, which had developed at least three political points against US aid programs to the Chiang government. Secondly, according to the CCP, the reason for the US government paying for Chiang's war was a US attempt to take over China. The CCP was attempting to identify its political and military agenda as anti-imperialistic, nationalistic, and patriotic in comparison with Chiang's pro-American policy. Thirdly, therefore, the CCP should end the Chiang regime as the puppet of the American imperialists to stop its fighting and killing more Chinese people. Mao told the Chinese public, "This situation is now coming to an end," and he called for the Chinese masses to join the CCP to "finish" the civil war by defeating Chiang's army.[38] Thus, the CCP was able to attack pro-American Chiang's regime and blame US aid for the death of millions of Chinese people in their civil war.

By September 1949, Mao's PLA occupied most of the country except for Tibet, Taiwan, and various offshore islands. The GMD lost several million troops as well as its control of mainland China to the Communists in the civil war. On October 1, 1949, Mao Zedong declared the birth of the People's Republic of China (PRC). After Chinese Nationalist forces were ousted from mainland China, on December 8, 1949, Jiang moved the seat of his government to Taiwan. News of the Communist "takeover" of China swept across the United States like wildfire. The politicians, media, and public opinion criticized the Truman administration, stating that the United States did not give enough support to Jiang's government, and therefore, Truman "lost China."

In retrospect, the disregard for corruption and the state's failure to stop it contributed to the end of the Jiang regime in China. It became a central issue for the critics of the GMD government; this was manifested by the centrality of issue for the political and military struggles during the Chinese Civil War. As popular dissatisfaction with these problems continued, the opposition, represented by the CCP, made anticorruption a major issue in its popular appeal, and was able to attract much support with its promise to end the practices of corruption. After the founding of the PRC, the Three Antis and Five Antis Campaigns expressed the will of the new regime to impose order in industry and commerce. The Three Antis Campaign that targeted corruption, waste, and obstructionist bureaucracy reflected concerns of the CCP leadership about the moral decay of the rank and file of the revolution.[39] This policy sought to embrace the war in Korea, which required a solid base and stable economic growth. In Shanghai, voluntary confessions by business owners amounted to over one thousand daily. Noncompliance meant humiliation, trial, and even betrayal by their own families. Most private entrepreneurs were found guilty one way or another.[40] Zhou Jingwen, for example, claimed that about 200,000 Chinese committed suicide during the Three and Five Antis Movements.[41] Frederick C. Teiwes concludes that "these campaigns indicated to broad sections of society the full extent of the Party's aims for social transformation. As the emphasis shifted from reassurance to tightening control, many groups that had hitherto been left basically alone were now drawn into the vortex of directed struggle. By the end of the 1950s the CCP had become, for the majority of China's urban population, a force to be reckoned with."[42] The Soviet-like high-handed measures certainly made China a party-state again under the CCP rather than under the GMD.

NOTES

1. Lanxin Xiang, *Recasting the Imperial Far East: Britain and America in China, 1945–1950* (Armonk, NY: M. E. Sharpe, 1995), 30–31.

2. General Jiang Weiguo (Chiang Wei-kuo) (GMD Army, ret.), son of Jiang Jieshi, and adoptive brother of Jiang Jingguo (Jiang Ching-kuo), president of the ROC from 1978–1988, interview by the author at Rongzong [Glory's General] Hospital in Taipei, Taiwan, on May 25–27, 1994.

3. Joseph W. Esherick, "Revolution in a Feudal Fortress," *Modern China* 24, no. 4 (October 1998):370.

4. Suzanne Pepper, *Civil War in China: The Political Struggle, 1945–1949* (Berkeley, CA: University of California Press, 1978), 75.

5. Edward L. Dreyer, *China at War, 1901–1949* (New York: Longman, 1995), 7.

6. Bruce A. Elleman, *Modern Chinese Warfare, 1795–1989* (London: Routledge, 2001), 205–6.

7. Harold M. Tanner, *China: A History from the Great Qing Empire through the People's Republic of China* (Indianapolis, IN: Hackett, 2010), 2: 169.

8. There are rich examples of CCP military operations behind the enemy lines in literature focused on the Resistant War against Japan. For example, in Feng Chih, *Behind Enemy Lines* (Beijing: Foreign Languages Press, 1979), Chapters 2–5.

9. Peter Zarrow, *China in War and Revolution, 1895–1949* (New York: Routledge, 2005), 330–31.

10. Pepper, *Civil War in China*, 155–60.

11. In 1944, to avoid a collapse of the CCP-GMD coalition, US ambassador Hurley visited Yan'an, Mao's wartime capital, and proposed a joint postwar government in China. See Patrick Hurley, "Aide Memoirs," September 25, 1944; and his letter to President Roosevelt accompanying the memoirs, September 25, 1944, *Ambassador Patrick Hurley Papers*, University of Oklahoma Library, Norman, Oklahoma.

12. Compilation Committee of ROC History, *A Pictorial History of the Republic of China* (Taipei, Taiwan: Modern China Press, 1981), 2: 259.

13. Xiang, *Recasting the Imperial Far East*, 142.

14. Xiaobing Li, *A History of the Modern Chinese Army* (Lexington: University of Kentucky Press, 2007), 71–77.

15. Zhang Wenzhen, *Buxi de langtao: Xiamen daxue Jiefang geming douzheng fengmao* [Spare No Effort: The Characteristics of Xiamen University's Struggle for Liberation and Revolution] (Xiamen: Xiamen daxue chubanshe [Xiamen University Press], 1991), 270–79.

16. Wang Xueqing, *Jiang Jieshi he Chen Lifu Chen Guofu* [Jiang Jieshi and Chen Lifu and Chen Guofu] (Changchun: Jilin wenshi chubanshe [Jilin Historical and Archival Publishing], 1994), 24–26, 113–15.

17. Pepper, *Civil War in China*, 169.

18. Arvind K. Jain, ed., *Economics of Corruption* (Boston, MA: Kluwer Academic, 1998).

19. For the detailed events in the Chinese Civil War, see Xiaobing Li, *The Cold War in East Asia* (London: Routledge, 2017), 53–54, 57–59.

20. Mao, "The Situation and Our Policy after the Victory in the War of Resistance against Japan," in *Selected Works of Mao Tse-tung* (Beijing: Foreign Languages Press, 1977), 4: 14.

21. Mao, "Greet the New High Tide of the Chinese Revolution," ibid. 4: 119–24.

22. Odd Arne Westad, *Decisive Encounters: The Chinese Civil War, 1946–1950* (Stanford, CA: Stanford University Press, 2003), 107.

23. Alina Mungiu-Pippidi, "The Quest for Good Governance: Learning from Virtuous Circles," *Journal of Democracy* 27, no. 1 (January 2016): 95.

24. William C. Kirby, "The Chinese War Economy," in *China's Bitter Victory: War with Japan, 1937–1945*, eds. James C. Hsiung and Steven I. Levine (London: Routledge, 1992), 185–87.

25. Lu Yangyuan and Fang Qingqiu, eds., *Minguo shehui jingji shi* [A Social and Economic History of the Republic] (Beijing: Zhongguo jingji chubanshe [China Economics Press], 1991), 794–802.

26. Vincent, "Memorandum by the Director of the Office of Far Eastern Affairs (Vincent) to the Secretary of State," February 5, 1947, in *Foreign Relations of the United States (FRUS), 1947*, ed. US Department of State (Washington, D.C.: Government Printing Office, 1989), 7: 787.

27. Westad, *Decisive Encounters*, 279.

28. Mao, "Present Situation and Our Tasks," a report made by Mao to a meeting of the Central Committee on December 25–28, 1947, in *Selected Works of Mao*, 4: 164.

29. Military History Research Division, China Academy of Military Science (CAMS), *Zhongguo renmin jiefangjun quanguo jiefang zhanzhengshi* [History of the PLA in the Chinese Civil War] (Beijing: Junshi kexue chubanshe [Military Science Press], 1997), 4: 14–16, 649–51.

30. CCP Central Archival and Manuscript Research Division, *Zhou Enlai nianpu, 1898–1949* [A Chronological Record of Zhou Enlai, 1898–1949] (Beijing: Zhongyang wenxian chubanshe [CCP Central Archival and Manuscript Press], 1990), 717.

31. Deng, "Carry out the Central Committee's Directive on the Work of Land Reform and of Party Consolidation," a directive drafted by Deng for the Central Plains Bureau of CCP Central Committee on June 6, 1948, *Selected Works of Deng Xiaoping* (Beijing: Foreign Languages Press, 1994), 1: 130.

32. "Manifesto of the Chinese People's Liberation Army," in *Selected Works of Mao*, 4: 150. This political manifesto was drafted by Mao at Shenchuanpao, northern Shaanxi, for the General Headquarters of the PLA. It was issued on October 10, 1947, and known as the "October 10 Manifesto."

33. Westad, *Decisive Encounters*, 184.

34. Wang Zhangling, *Jiang Jingguo Shanghai dahu ji: Shanghai jingji guanzhi shimo* [Jiang Jingguo's Great Tiger Hunt in Shanghai: A Full Record of the Shanghai Economic Reform] (Taipei: Zhizhong chubanshe, 1999).

35. Westad, *Decisive Encounters*, 205–11.

36. Qian Haihao, *Jundui zuzhi bianzhixue jiaocheng* [Graduate Curriculum: Military Organization and Formation] (Beijing: Junshi kexue [Military Science Press], 2001), 40.

37. Mao, "Order to the Army for the Country-wide Advance," in *Selected Works of Mao*, 4: 387–97.

38. Mao, "Farewell, Leighton Stuart!" ibid. 4: 438.

39. Peng Deng, "The Impact of the Korean War on the Chinese Society: The Mass Campaigns in 1951–52," conference paper at the Association of Asian Society (AAS) annual meeting, Chicago, IL, March 22–25, 2003.

40. Kenneth Lieberthal, *Revolution and Tradition in Tientsin, 1949–1952* (Stanford, CA: Stanford University Press, 1980), 168 and table 8.

41. Zhou Jingwen, *Ten Years of Storm: The True Story of the Communist Regime in China* (Westport, CT: Greenwood, 1960), 115 and 133.

42. Frederick C. Teiwes, "Establishment and Consolidation of the New Regime," in *Cambridge History of China*, vol. 14, part 1: *The Emergence of Revolutionary China, 1949–1965* (Cambridge: University of Cambridge Press, 1967), 88.

BIBLIOGRAPHY

CCP Central Archival and Manuscript Research Division. *Zhou Enlai nianpu, 1898–1949* [A Chronological Record of Zhou Enlai, 1898–1949]. Beijing: Zhongyang wenxian chubanshe [CCP Central Archival and Manuscript Press], 1990.

Compilation Committee of ROC History. *A Pictorial History of the Republic of China.* Taipei, Taiwan: Modern China Press, 1981.

Deng, Xiaoping. "Carry out the Central Committee's Directive on the Work of Land Reform and of Party Consolidation." A Directive Drafted by Deng for the Central Plains Bureau of CCP Central Committee on June 6, 1948. In *Selected Works of Deng Xiaoping*. Beijing: Foreign Languages Press, 1994.

Dreyer, Edward L. *China at War, 1901–1949.* New York: Longman, 1995.

Elleman, Bruce A. *Modern Chinese Warfare, 1795–1989.* London: Routledge, 2001.

Esherick, Joseph W. "Revolution in a Feudal Fortress." *Modern China* 24, no. 4 (October 1998): 360–78.

Feng, Chih. *Behind Enemy Lines*. Beijing: Foreign Languages Press, 1979.

Hurley, Patrick. "Aide Memoirs," September 25, 1944; and his letter to President Roosevelt accompanying the memoirs, September 25, 1944. In *Ambassador Patrick Hurley Papers*, University of Oklahoma Library, Norman, Oklahoma.

Jain, Arvind K, ed. *Economics of Corruption*. Boston, MA: Kluwer Academic, 1998.

Jiang, Weiguo (Chiang Wei-kuo) (GMD Army General, ret.), son of Jiang Jieshi, and adoptive brother of Jiang Jingguo (Jiang Ching-kuo), president of the ROC from 1978–1988, interview by the author at Rongzong [Glory's General] Hospital in Taipei, Taiwan, on May 25–27, 1994.

Kirby, William C. "The Chinese War Economy." In *China's Bitter Victory: War with Japan, 1937–1945*. Eds. James C. Hsiung and Steven I. Levine. London: Routledge, 1992.

Li, Xiaobing. *A History of the Modern Chinese Army*. Lexington: University of Kentucky Press, 2007.

Li, Xiaobing. *The Cold War in East Asia*. London: Routledge, 2017.

Lieberthal, Kenneth. *Revolution and Tradition in Tientsin, 1949–1952*. Stanford, CA: Stanford University Press, 1980.

Lu, Yangyuan and Fang Qingqiu, eds. *Minguo shehui jingji shi* [A Social and Economic History of the Republic]. Beijing: Zhongguo jingji chubanshe [China Economics Press], 1991.

Mao, Zedong. "Greet the New High Tide of the Chinese Revolution." In *Selected Works of Mao Tse-tung*, 4: 119–26. Beijing: Foreign Languages Press, 1977.

Mao, Zedong. "Order to the Army for the Country-wide Advance." In *Selected Works of Mao*, 4: 387–97. Beijing: Foreign Languages Press, 1977.
Mao, Zedong. "Present Situation and Our Tasks." A Report Made by Mao to a Meeting of the Central Committee on December 25–28, 1947. In *Selected Works of Mao*, 4: 146–69. Beijing: Foreign Languages Press, 1977.
Mao, Zedong. "The Situation and Our Policy after the Victory in the War of Resistance against Japan." In *Selected Works of Mao Tse-tung*, 4: 1–25. Beijing: Foreign Languages Press, 1977.
Military History Research Division, China Academy of Military Science (CAMS). *Zhongguo renmin jiefangjun quanguo jiefang zhanzhengshi* [History of the PLA in the Chinese Civil War]. Beijing: Junshi kexue chubanshe [Military Science Press], 1997.
Mungiu-Pippidi, Alina. "The Quest for Good Governance: Learning from Virtuous Circles." *Journal of Democracy* 27, no. 1 (January 2016): 72–98.
Pepper, Suzanne. *Civil War in China: The Political Struggle, 1945–1949*. Berkeley, CA: University of California Press, 1978.
Qian, Haihao. *Jundui zuzhi bianzhixue jiaocheng* [Graduate Curriculum: Military Organization and Formation]. Beijing: Junshi kexue [Military Science Press], 2001.
Tanner, Harold M. *China: A History from the Great Qing Empire through the People's Republic of China*. Indianapolis, IN: Hackett, 2010.
Teiwes, Frederick C. "Establishment and Consolidation of the New Regime." In *Cambridge History of China*, vol. 14, part 1: *The Emergence of Revolutionary China, 1949–1965*. Cambridge: University of Cambridge Press, 1967.
Vincent. "Memorandum by the Director of the Office of Far Eastern Affairs (Vincent) to the Secretary of State," February 5, 1947. In *Foreign Relations of the United States (FRUS), 1947*, ed. US Department of State, 7: 779–788. Washington, DC: Government Printing Office, 1989.
Wang, Xueqing. *Jiang Jieshi he Chen Lifu Chen Guofu* [Jiang Jieshi and Chen Lifu and Chen Guofu]. Changchun: Jilin wenshi chubanshe [Jilin Historical and Archival Publishing], 1994.
Wang, Zhangling. *Jiang Jingguo Shanghai dahu ji: Shanghai jingji guanzhi shimo* [Jiang Jingguo's Great Tiger Hunt in Shanghai: A Full Record of the Shanghai Economic Reform]. Taipei: Zhizhong chubanshe, 1999.
Westad, Odd Arne. *Decisive Encounters: The Chinese Civil War, 1946–1950*. Stanford, CA: Stanford University Press, 2003.
Xiang, Lanxin. *Recasting the Imperial Far East: Britain and America in China, 1945–1950*. Armonk, NY: M. E. Sharpe, 1995.
Zarrow, Peter. *China in War and Revolution, 1895–1949*. New York: Routledge, 2005.
Zhang, Wenzhen. *Buxi de langtao: Xiamen daxue Jiefang geming douzheng fengmao* [Spare No Effort: The Characteristics of Xiamen University's Struggle for Liberation and Revolution]. Xiamen: Xiamen daxue chubanshe [Xiamen University Press], 1991.
Zhou, Jingwen. *Ten Years of Storm: The True Story of the Communist Regime in China*. Westport, CT: Greenwood, 1960.

Chapter 5

Crime (or No Crime) and Punishment

The Making of the First Big Case in New China and Legitimation of CCP Party Governance, 1950–1991

Zhiguo Yang

In discussing the relationship between anticorruption campaigns and legitimation crisis in the Communist nations in the 1980s, Leslie Holms, an Australian political scientist, draws the following conclusion:

> Recent leadership concerns about and reactions to official corruption in so many communist states, and the notable increase in the reporting of corruption in the official media, were neither fortuitous nor necessarily simply reflective of a growing incidence of corruption in these societies. Rather, they reflected, at least to some extent, a change in the leaders' perception of their own and their system's legitimacy and an attempt to alter the balance between different modes of legitimation—especially popular legitimation.[1]

So far as the Communist leadership in China was concerned, such a change in perception occurred in 1987, when the Chinese Communist Party (CCP) held its 13th Congress in the midst of economic reforms. During the Congress, Zhao Ziyang, then general secretary of the CCP's Central Committee, spelled out the need to conduct inner-party struggle against official corruption in the reform and opening-up (改革开放) era:

> The people complain a great deal now that a small number of Party members, particularly leading cadres, have abused their power for private gain at the expense of the people's interests, hindering the smooth progress of the reform and implementation of the open policy and damaging the party's prestige. This is a grave problem which we must take seriously and tackle in earnest . . . . The inner-Party struggle against corruption is unavoidable when we are carrying out

the reform and open policy. If we tolerate decadent elements in the Party, the whole Party will decline.[2]

By the time when Zhao Ziyang sounded the alarm of decline in the leadership ability of the party through his speech, the CCP had maintained its position as China's sole ruling party for thirty-eight years. While during this period of time it had to withstand and survive crises such as the Cultural Revolution of 1966–1976, only twice did the CCP have to deal with the challenge to its legitimacy through nationwide anticorruption campaign: before the one kicked off in the late 1980s, the only other such campaign was the Three-Anti Movement of 1951–1952 (三反运动), a movement that has been presented in the CCP version of the history of the People's Republic of China (the PRC) as the first effort at "combating corruption and building an honest government."[3] Launched at a moment when the CCP just emerged as the victor in the Nationalist-Communist civil war and when it was trying to balance its Communist ideology with the reality of governing a massive nation whose socioeconomic order could not be more distant from the Communist ideal, the movement served as an important means for the CCP to legitimize its newly established party governance to the people by eradicating from its rank those party officials who were inflicted with one of the evils of the "old society": corruption. During this short but stormy movement, many party officials of primarily middle- and low-rank status were publicly tried and swiftly convicted and punished for their alleged crimes of corruption. While most of these cases have faded from the collective memory in China, one case, the first big case in new China as it has been called, is an exception and remains the hallmark of the Three-Anti Movement. Depending on perspectives, it can be labeled the first big case of corruption in the PRC or the first big case of the first anticorruption campaign in new China; but no matter how it is defined, the case has perpetuated the notoriety of Liu Qingshan and Zhang Zishan (刘青山, 张子善), two veteran Communist revolutionaries who were "made" corrupt party officials during the Three-Anti Movement. More importantly, the passage of time and change in circumstances have not diminished the significance of the case as an indispensable component of the CCP's self-claimed anticorruption record.

An important episode in the history of the PRC, the Three-Anti Movement and the first big case as a part of it are yet to be further studied. The existing scholarship is scarce and it is primarily from China.[4] Partly for ideological reason, while this scholarship has laid down a solid foundation for further historical inquiry of the topic, it has to stay within the confines of official interpretation, creating a need to depoliticize the case and study it from a historical perspective. This chapter will take up the task.

A study of the first big case as part of CCP effort to accomplish its grand enterprise of establishing and legitimating its party governance in the early years of the PRC, this chapter will shed light on the historical circumstances under which the Three-Anti Movement was launched and two committed Communist revolutionaries were demonized to propagate the goal of the movement as an anticorruption campaign. In addition, relating the first big case to the CCP legitimation effort in 1950–1952 when the new Communist state saw itself as confronted with domestic and international foes, it will illuminate how such an effort predetermined the corruption attribute of the case and the way to close it. Moreover, given the fact that all the "corrupted perpetrators" exposed during the movement have ceased to be part of the CCP narrative of its anticorruption history but the case involving Liu Qingshan and Zhang Zishan,[5] this chapter will explore why they—and their stigma as corrupted party officials—have become one of the cornerstones of the CCP anticorruption discourse despite the legal controversies surrendering their case. In sum, the purpose of the chapter is twofold: reconstructing the first big case by relating it to the legitimation of the CCP party governance in the early 1950s and detaching it from the manufactured anticorruption discourse.

CONSOLIDATING CCP PARTY GOVERNANCE AND THE THREE-ANTI MOVEMENT, 1949–1952

The period of 1948–1952 was a crucial moment in the history of the Chinese Communist movement. In 1948, seeing the light at the end of the tunnel of Chinese civil war, the CCP combined once scattered "liberated areas" in North China into a united territory and organized a centralized administration to govern it. There were still Nationalist holdouts in Beiping and Tianjin in the area, and the People's Liberation Army was yet to drive the Nationalist forces out of the major cities in Manchuria and cross the Yangtze River to destroy the last Nationalist bastion in southern China. However, confident that the fall of the Nationalist regime was now only a matter of time, the CCP quickened its steps to extend its nation-building enterprise from North China to the rest of China, especially its cities and industrial and commercial centers. In March 1949, Mao Zedong met with other veteran Communist leaders in the Second Plenary Session of the CCP's Seventh Congress to map out a plan building a Communist state in China. When he declared the founding of the PRC in Beijing on October 1, 1949, the first step for the realization of the plan had been completed. The CCP party governance now replaced the party governance by the Nationalists.

As one of the high-ranking Communist leaders directly involved in charting a course of transition for the party and the new state it aspired to create,

Bo Yibo (薄一波) was central to major CCP decisions in this crucial moment. Because of that, when he published his memoir entitled, in English translation, *A Few Important Decisions and Historical Events in Retrospect* in 1991, it became the most cited primary source for researchers on the CCP policies throughout Mao's era and after. Although his reminiscences may not be taken at their face value and must be used together with other historical records whenever it is possible to do so, given the crucial role Bo Yibo played in the transition of the CCP in 1948–1952, his memoir can shed more light on the significance of this eventful period of CCP history to the legitimization of CCP party governance than any other sources.

Bo Yibo's career as one of the architects of a new Communist state began in 1948 when he was appointed secretary of the CCP Central Committee's North China Bureau (中共中央华北局). From that position, he not only took charge of the administration of a large portion of northern China where the Nationalist control had been completely eradicated, but also participated in the takeover of Beiping and Tianjin after these two major northern China cities fell to the People's Liberation Army forces in early 1949, the organization of the new PRC government on the basis of alliance with non-Communist parties, the making of economic policies to ease the anxiety of the urban bourgeoisie and the landholding peasants (the "rich peasants") over the collectivization of their property, and the implementation of price and currency reforms to curb the uncontrollable inflation that had plagued the Nationalist regime.[6] As he points out in his memoir, although there was disagreement among the CCP leaders about how long the "new democratic social order" should last, both Mao Zedong, who wanted to move China quickly to socialism, and Liu Shaoqi, who advocated a more moderate approach, saw a transitional period as necessary to generate strong enough support for the new government and the socialist revolution it pledged to undertake. Among all the measures that Bo Yibo and other CCP leaders implemented to ease the transition, the Three-Anti Movement was the only attempt to prevent the legitimacy of the CCP as a ruling party from being questioned as a result of official corruption.[7]

It is no coincidence that the Three-Anti Movement occurred after the deployment of People's Volunteer Army in North Korea to fight the Korean War, the initiation of land reform to eradicate the landlord class in China's vast rural area, and the crackdown of the Nationalists and their supporters as "counterrevolutionaries." With the looming threat from the external and domestic foes to the new Communist state still on the horizon, the CCP leadership decided to strengthen its capacity to deal with it through the Three-Anti Movement that, similar to the wartime rectification movements that radical CCP leaders launched to remove the unwanted elements from the party, would purge those officials who were considered to have jeopardized that capacity by their corruption. After the movement got underway throughout the nation, the CCP Central Committee appointed Bo Yibo to oversee it. Thus, just like his narrative of and reflection on the other events in the formative stage of the CCP party governance that he personally got involved in, his narrative of and reflection on the Three-Anti Movement in his memoir can lend credible insight to not only the origin and impact of the movement but also the making of the first big case as a result of it.

To Bo Yibo, the need to sustain China's war effort in Korea contributed to the beginning of the movement. Facing the unfinished task of economic recovery and fiscal deficit, Mao Zedong devised a plan in October 1951 to win the war while curbing inflation and increasing production all at the same time. To realize the plan, Mao decided to reduce the size of the army, shrink governmental bureaucracy, and tighten expenditure.[8] Aiming at "increasing production through practicing austerity," these measures did not initially include an anticorruption component until November 1951, when the CCP central leadership received a report from Gao Gang (高岗), secretary of CCP Central Committee's Northeast (Manchuria) Bureau (中共中央东北局).

One of the most important industrial bases in China, Manchuria, and its main manufacturing and transportation centers such as Changchun and Shenyang (Mukden) saw the shift of power from the Nationalists to the Communists in 1948.[9] After their decisive military victory over the Nationalists, the Communist leaders in Manchuria quickly turned their attention to reviving the economy and the early start of postwar industrial reconstruction—and the Soviet assistance to it—enhanced the position of Manchuria as a primary source of supply of industrial technology, manufactured goods, and raw materials in China.[10] When the Korean War broke out in June 1950 and the CCP leadership decided to intervene by sending the People's Volunteer Army to Korea in October 1950, however, Manchuria's economy was strained as it was geared to support the war effort. To maintain the momentum of growth and meet the needs of Chinese troops fighting in Korea all at the same time, Gao Gang and the party apparatus under his control started in May 1951 an Increasing Production and Reducing the Cost movement to maximize productivity through efficient use of resources. Five months later, this seemingly mundane managerial measure was given a political dimension when Gao Gang determined that three obstacles stood on the way to the success of his movement: official corruption, waste, and bureaucratic spirit of the party administrators. To remove them, he called upon the CCP members and the general public to participate in an anticorruption, anti-waste, and anti-bureaucratic spirit campaign. Thus, in October 1951, the Three-Anti Movement first began in Manchuria.[11]

But the movement did not remain a regional phenomenon for long. On November 1, 1952, Gao Gang submitted a report on his Three-Anti

Movement to the CCP Central Committee in Beijing. In his report, Gao first painted a picture of widespread corruption in Manchuria and then described the approaches he adopted to end it. To him, the most effective way to expose official corruption and combat it was to launch a "massive democratic movement" through which ordinary citizens were encouraged to help the party identify governmental officials who had committed corruption.[12] Having already warned the party of the danger of bourgeois influences on party officials who now became the administrators in cities, Mao Zedong saw in Gao Gang's report both a proof of what he had feared and a way to safeguard the party's credibility and he acted quickly. On November 20, 1952, Mao forwarded the report to party officials at every administrative level, asking them to continue the nationwide drive to increase production by reducing cost on the one hand and by waging an unwavering struggle of the three-anti on the other hand.[13] The call was met with frenzy response from all corners of China, transforming a regional initiative from Manchuria into a national upheaval.

It was a short but vehement movement lasting from November 1951 to October 1952 and its primary target was the corrupted officials known as "tigers." After a brief account of the Three-Anti Movement as a CCP effort to consolidate its control over the cities in her comprehensive history of the PRC, Maurice Meisner identifies three groups of people who were hit as tigers: the "old Guomindang officials who had been retained in the urban administrations and who now were dispensable, new Party members hastily recruited during the final years of the civil war who proved unsuited to the new tasks of post-revolutionary administrative work, and older Party cadres who were seen as corrupted by urban bourgeois influences."[14] Being part of the bureaucracy of the CCP party government, a large number of them were purged to make it cleaner and purer. According to An Ziwen, a veteran Communist leader who recommended the end of the Three-Anti Movement in October 1952, by the time when the CCP Central Committee accepted An's recommendation, about 100,000 officials had been found guilty of corruption and economic crimes. Among them, 9,942 were sentenced to prison terms, 67 were punished with life sentence, 47 were sentenced to death, and 9 were given suspended death sentence.[15] While most of the 47 executed "corrupt officials" have faded from China's collective memory of the movement, two of them, Liu Qingshan and Zhang Zishan, have never been forgotten.[16] Rather, they have been integrated into the CCP official historical narrative of its anticorruption campaigns.

Belonging to the "older Party cadres who were seen as corrupted by urban bourgeois influences," Liu Qingshan and Zhang Zishan were perfect targets for a movement with a goal to showcase the CCP resolve to legitimize its rule through an anticorruption campaign against its own members. They had an impeccable record as Communist revolutionaries and that credential won them high administrative positions when the Nationalist China was replaced by a new China. They matched Mao's stereotype of the party veterans who became susceptible to "bourgeois influences" after they left rural area and moved to cities. More importantly, their alleged corruption harmed the peasant laborers most, the social group whose support the CCP still could not afford to lose. As the accused and the condemned in the first big case in the Three-Anti Movement and in new China, Liu Qingshan and Zhang Zishan have been portrayed as committed revolutionaries falling from grace and corruption has been blamed for that fall. For historians, reconstructing the first big case and assessing its significance to the CCP party governance involves depoliticizing an official narrative that mixes facts with anticorruption rhetoric.

Let's begin the "historicization" of the first big case with an account of Liu Qingshan's and Zhang Zishan's early career as Communist rebels.

From Revolutionaries to Corrupted Officials: Origins of the First Big Case, 1949–1951

Like so many cases in the mass movements in the PRC history, the first big case is full of ambiguities and controversies. However, when it comes to the credential of Liu Qingshan and Zhang Zishan as Communist revolutionaries, the discrepancy between the official version of the case and the version in which Liu and Zhang are presented as victims of a vicious political movement ceases to exist. Based on different perspectives, the two versions begin the telling of their story from the same threshold: Liu's and Zhang's commitment and devotion to the Communist revolution in China.

As shown in Bo Yibo's memoir, the primary reason for Liu's and Zhang's revolutionary career to be made part of the official account of the case is to validate the argument that without extreme vigilance even veteran revolutionaries could become corrupt officials in urban environment.[17] Because of that, the biographic information in Bo's account is brief about their pre-1949 activities but detailed about the two short years during which they allegedly committed the crime of corruption. Recently, an alternative but "unofficial" version of the case emerged to challenge the validity of the official account. In the name of restoring reputation of and seeking justice for Liu Qingshan and Zhang Zishan, Liu Tieqi, Liu Qingshan's oldest son, and Liu Zejun, a member of Liu Qingshan's linage, have strenuously researched the case. However, since their interpretation questions the official verdict in the case, they could not find a publisher in China to print their findings, forcing them to go online and publish their research on the case in their internet blogs in early 2010. Although they are non-conventional sources, their online publications nevertheless present us with impressionist but credible evidence to add flesh and blood to the biographical sketch of Liu's and Zhang's early life as Communist rebels that is only mentioned in passing in the official account.[18]

Born in the 1910s, Liu Qingshan and Zhang Zishan grew up in two destitute peasant families in southern Hebei Province. For Liu, the turning point in his early life as a poor and uneducated farm hand hired by a landlord in his hometown of Anguo County occurred in 1931. In that year, as a result of the influence of underground Communist recruiters, Liu joined the CCP and became a party member at age fifteen.[19] In August 1932, he joined other new Communist recruits in an armed rebellion against the Nationalist administration in the county seat of Li County. Known as the Li County Rebellion in the CCP history, it began on August 27, only to be crashed by the Nationalist forces three days later. As the youngest rebel captured alive, Liu Qingshan escaped a certain execution only because his grandparent, a renowned doctor in the area, bribed the Nationalist county head to save his grandson's life.[20]

Shenxian County was located about 40 miles south of Liu Qingshan's hometown and Zhang Zishan was born there in 1914. The youngest of four siblings who lost their parents to poverty and illness, Zhang enrolled in a village elementary school when he was eight years old. It was a rare educational opportunity that the rural youth of Zhang's socioeconomic background could hardly afford, but his two older brothers and one older sister created it for him through savings from their hard labor, hoping that at least one of them could be freed from the spell of poverty through education. Upon finishing his elementary education, Zhang was admitted into a four-year normal college in the county seat of Dingxian and it was in there that his life took a radical turn, largely due to Japanese aggression in China and the relentless Nationalist campaigns against the Communist forces even after the Manchuria Incident of 1931. Like many educated young Chinese at the time, Zhang became a student activist and got involved in protests against Japanese imperialism and Nationalist policy of "defeating domestic foes before resisting external enemies." Impressed by his charismatic leadership to his peers and his public speech skill, the underground CCP organization in the college approached Zhang for the purpose of making him one of their own. In 1933, Zhang Zishan joined the party at age nineteen.[21] Starting a dangerous revolutionary's career in an urban setting, Zhang Zishan did not rub shoulders with death as did Liu Qingshan in the failed Li County Rebellion, but he spent more than a year in Nationalist prison for leading a protest against Nationalist civil war policies.[22] Just like in the case of Liu Qingshan, when Zhang Zishan fell in the Three-Anti Movement, this episode of his revolutionary career was juxtaposed with his alleged corruption to show how far removed he had become from his original commitment to the cause of the party.

The rank of Liu Qingshan and Zhang Zishan in the party rose steadily afterward and they crossed paths with each other during the Second

Sino-Japanese War (1937–1945). Leading guerrilla warfare against Japanese troops and their Chinese collaborators in Communist base area in northern China called Shanxi-Chahar-Hebei Border Region, they came to work in the eighth military district in the Hebei part of the Region toward the end of the war, with Liu Qingshan heading the intelligence department of the district's government and Zhang Zishan serving as its director for party organizations.[23] When the war against Japan was over in 1945, both Liu Qingshan and Zhang Zishan were promoted to the position of party secretary but in different districts. While Liu remained in the eighth military district, Zhang left it to lead the tenth military district.[24] They did not join each other as comrades-in-arms again until the end of the CCP-GMD civil war.

Taking charge in central Hebei that was relatively free from civil war fighting in 1945–49, Liu Qingshan was able to devote his political career to implementing CCP policies of purging those who had cooperated with the Japanese or the Nationalists and carrying out land reform by confiscating landlords' land and then distributing it to the landless peasants. However, when the Communist forces launched offensives against Nationalist holdouts in major cities of Manchuria and North China, Liu was directed to recruit new soldiers and procure supplies for the troops in the front, a job that was made easier by the land reform beneficiaries who were the source of both the new recruits and the supplies. When the Nationalist influence had been removed from all of North China except for a few cities in mid-1948, a confident CCP called upon its local organizations to shift their priority to "production" so as to lay down the ground for postwar economic reconstruction. Liu enthusiastically heeded the call and worked hard to fulfill it, adding another qualification for his future upward movement in the CCP leadership hierarchy.[25] Although information about Zhang Zishan's whereabouts during this time was not as revealing as that for Liu Qingshan's activities, given the fact that both of them were in central Hebei area under the same command, their responsibilities should be more parallel to each other than different from each other.

And their wartime devotion to the cause of the CCP paid off. When the dust of the civil war settled down in Hebei in August 1949, the CCP Committee of Hebei Province and the Provincial People's Government replaced the wartime military command system, and Liu Qingshan was appointed secretary of the CCP Committee in the newly established Special Prefecture of Tianjin (天津专区), a huge rural area in central Hebei surrounding Tianjin, the second largest industrial center in China at the time, next only to Shanghai. Since the prefecture also included the previous ten military districts that Zhang Zishan had led, when Liu was given the opportunity to choose his lieutenant, he picked Zhang and made him chief executive of the prefecture and deputy secretary of its party committee.[26] Working as a team once again, they now stepped into an unchartered territory of running CCP party governance at the local level. Together with the party they had so brilliantly served, Liu and Zhang began the transition from Communist rebels deeply rooted in rural areas to wielders of state power.

Although it was the outcome that the CCP had been fighting for, when the transition occurred it became a source of anxiety for the CCP leadership, too. As mentioned earlier, in March 1949, about a month before the capture of the Nationalist capital Nanjing by the People's Liberation Army, Mao Zedong and other major CCP leaders met in the cafeteria of the CCP headquarters in Hebei and outlined their plan for the transformation of the CCP from a revolutionary party with its bastion in the countryside to a party that would move to the cities and administer them. It is in this meeting, the Second Plenary Session of the Seventh Central Committee of the CCP, that Mao Zedong somberly warned his fellow revolutionaries of the challenges they would face in the cities. In particular, anticipating that the bourgeois would come to flatter the victorious Communists, Mao voiced his concern over "some Communists, who were not conquered by enemies with guns and were worthy of the name of heroes for standing up to these enemies, but who cannot withstand sugar-coated bullets; they will be defeated by sugar-coated bullets."[27] A prophecy at the time, it would underline CCP policies in the Three-Anti Movement. To Bo Yibo, the case of Liu Qingshan and Zhang Zishan proved the accuracy of Mao's prediction, even though they never moved to cities for their responsibilities as CCP administrators.[28]

The Special Prefecture of Tianjin and the city of Tianjin were in the vicinity of each other but they belonged to two separate jurisdictions. For those Communists who took over the municipal government of Tianjin from the Nationalists, the change in their role was swift and drastic. Fresh from the civil war battleground, they now had to concern themselves with the restoration of the city's infrastructure and revival of its commerce and industry. In addition, in order to make up for their lack of experiences in operating a municipal government for a major metropolis in China, they had to keep their ideological rigor under check and work together with the capitalist entrepreneurs and civil servants who had worked for the Nationalist regime before.[29] As the top administrators of a largely rural area, however, Liu Qingshan and Zhang Zishan experienced a much less dramatic change in their role. During the wartime they had been part of a peasant revolution in central Hebei and now their new job required them to continue their tie with the same peasant population in the same area but with a different purpose: serving the needs of cities like Beijing and Tianjin. Heading the prefectural government from Yang Liuqing, an ancient rural township along the Grand Canal, Liu and Zhang were never situated in the burgeoning ground of "sugar-coated bullets" like the city of Tianjin.[30]

And what Liu and Zhang did from Yang Liuqing was hardly different from what governing a rural area had always required of its administrators, like Huang Liu-hung, a Qing dynasty county magistrate described by Jonathan Spence in *The Death of Woman Wang*.[31] For example, as soon as the new prefectural government opened its door for business, it found itself confronted with the time-honored issue of disaster relief and resettlement of the dislocated farmers. As a result of the record-breaking flooding in central Hebei during the summer of 1949, a large portion of the rural population under the jurisdiction of Liu and Zhang had to abandon their home and be relocated in Manchuria so that they could survive the current disaster and rebuild their home away from home. As the two top party and civil administrators in their prefecture, Liu and Zhang spent their first year in Yang Liuqing on overseeing water control projects, migration of the dislocated farmers to Manchuria and the parts of Hebei Province that were not severely affected by the flooding, and the distribution of food and other relief materials from Beijing to the homeless and the hungry.[32]

Continuing a wartime practice, Liu Qingshan and Zhang Zishan also had to secure a budget for the prefectural government, primarily through the profits from the industrial and commercial enterprises owned and managed by the government itself. These governmental enterprises, known as *jiguan shengchan* (机关生产) in Chinese,[33] were indispensable financial assets for Liu and Zhang when the allocation of budget from the provincial or central government was either not available or not guaranteed, and managing them almost became a full-time job for these two party administrators. In early 1951, for example, the prefectural government received permission to leave Yang Liuqing and relocate to Tianjin. Although this meant Liu, Zhang, and their staff would finally place themselves in an urban environment, before that could happen they had to first construct their own office buildings in the city proper with their own resources. To get things started, Liu and Zhang invested public fund under their disposal in factories to manufacture cable line, aluminum, machinery, and so on, so the profits from them could be used to pay the construction cost. When the proceeds from the government enterprises proved inadequate, they secured bank loans with which to buy lumber from Manchuria and build kilns to bake bricks. In the meantime, Liu Qingshan also founded a construction company with government fund and investment from privately owned businesses in Tianjin, hoping that after the completion of the current project the company would make more money for the prefecture by picking up other construction contracts.[34]

Not everything Liu Qingshan and Zhang Zishan did was solely related to earning the "bread and butter" for the prefectural government. After the outbreak of the Korean War, for example, the Chinese air force decided to build a military airport in Wuqing County as it was close to the Bohai over which

Chinese planes would cross before reaching their destinies in North Korea. Since Wuqing County was under the jurisdiction of the Special Prefecture of Tianjin, the construction of the airport was delegated to the prefectural government, with state funding transferred to Liu and Zhang to allow them to purchase land for the airfield, compensate the peasants who would lose their land because of the construction, and pay the labor for the construction. The job was done in July 1951, just on time to meet the strenuous demand of logistics supply from the Chinese troops fighting along the Thirty-Eighth Parallel. For Liu and Zhang, the project was also a profitable business deal. When the prefectural accountants found that the state payment for the airport exceeded the actual construction cost and offered to return the balance to the air force, the latter asked the prefecture to keep the money as a token of the air force's gratitude. Liu and Zhang obliged and the surplus was invested in their governmental enterprises.[35]

Similar to what local Yamen did during the Qing dynasty or earlier, the aforementioned mundane and routine activities turned these two wartime Communist veterans into adroit businessmen. Although gray areas existed in how they managed the finance for the local and national projects under their supervision and although some prefectural officials questioned some of their superiors' financial transactions,[36] Liu's and Zhang's political career continued its upward movement. In May 1951, for example, Liu Qingshan was promoted to the position of deputy secretary of the CCP Committee in Shijiazhuang, provincial capital of Hebei, a promotion that also created a vacancy for the top party position in the prefecture. Zhang Zishan filled in it.

However, a series of unexpected events turned the world of Liu Qingshan and Zhang Zishan upside down. In early October 1951, Li Kecai, a high-ranking party administrator in the prefecture who was disdained with Liu's and Zhang's handling of the governmental enterprises, reported his superiors' "criminal activities" to the party authorities in Hebei Province. Alerted, the provincial CCP Committee formed a task force and sent the team to the prefecture to investigate the alleged wrongdoings. After spending a week conducting closed-door interviews with a small number of prefectural government employees, the task force submitted its report to the CCP Committee of Hebei. In concluding the report, the task force stated: "We believe there are many severe problems regarding the governmental enterprises in the Special Prefecture of Tianjin and recommend that the provincial CCP Committee take action to solve them as quickly as possible."[37] On November 21, 1951, ten days after receiving instruction from the CCP central leadership in Beijing to battle corruption in party organizations, the Hebei CCP Committee called more than 800 party administrators to Baoding for a special meeting. Soon after the meeting started, the task force's report was presented to its participants for deliberation. Although it is unknown to what had happened to it, when the deliberation was concluded on November 29, 1951, Zhang Zishan, who was representing his prefecture in the meeting, was arrested. Liu Qingshan had gone to Europe to attend the World Peace Council conference in Vienna as a "peasant" representative from China before the Baoding meeting was convened. But as soon as the unsuspicious peasant representative returned to Tianjin from his overseas mission, he was arrested as well. Together, they were charged as "big embezzlers" (大贪污犯).[38]

In their book entitled, in English translation, *A Study of the "Three-Anti" Movement*, Chinese scholars Wang Shunsheng and Li Jun tried to link the case of Liu Qingshan and Zhang Zishan to the Three-Anti Movement as a cause-effect relationship. To them, while the investigation of Li Kecai's allegations had begun before Mao Zedong expanded what Gao Gang had done in Manchuria to the whole nation, the punitive phase of Liu's and Zhang's case coincided with the movement and was tremendously impacted by it.[39] We do not know whether or not Liu Qingshan and Zhang Zishan had had time to assert their innocence—even if they had, there is no evidence of it—but the tense whirlwind that the Three-Anti Movement stirred up led to the severe and swift punishment of two Communist revolutionaries as corrupt party officials.

Crime (or No Crime) and Punishment: The Making of the First Big Case, 1951–1952

Based on the evidence collected by the task force, the provincial party authorities sent Liu Qingshan and Zhang Zishan to prison. Before another round of investigation to base their punishment as criminals on, the CCP Committee of Hebei first expelled Liu and Zhang from the party and the rationale for this decision was spelled out as such:

> In the two-year long peaceful environment resulted from [Communist] victory in China, [Liu Qingshan and Zhang Zishan] succumb to the temptation of selfish bourgeois behavior, thought, and decadent [way of life]. They now have irrevocably become unforgivable traitors to the party, the nation and the people . . . . [They] are not just two ordinary criminals and thieves. As predicted [by the CCP leadership] in the Second Plenary Session, as a result of their failure in resisting the attack from sugar-coated bullets and surrender to enemies, they have turned themselves into the agents of counter-revolutionaries, corrupting and dividing the party from inside.[40]

Thus, declared the Committee, not only would they be expelled from the party, they would be punished for their economic crimes according to the law as well.

Such a law, however, had yet to be written.[41] In the absence of it, the fate of Liu and Zhang was put in the hands of party officials and administrators. In early December 1951, the provincial CCP Committee created a commission to investigate the case and recommend punishment to the central CCP leadership in Beijing. To build their case, the commission went to the prefectural government, interrogated those who had got involved in "illegal activities" of Liu and Zhang, and obtained confessions from them. On December 14, 1951, the commission concluded its investigation and submitted its report to Bo Yibo, head of the CCP Central Committee's North China Bureau that had jurisdiction over both Hebei Province and the Special Prefecture of Tianjin. The report asked for death penalty.[42]

Situated between the CCP Central Committee in Beijing and the CCP Provincial Committee of Hebei in the party power structure, the North China Bureau had to make its own decision on the basis of the report before submitting its recommendation to Beijing. Death sentence was favored, but there was no unanimous support for it. To legitimize such an extreme punishment, the Bureau returned the ball to those who had worked with or under Liu Qingshan and Zhang Zishan in the prefectural government, asking them to vote on whether or not they should be put to death. The Bureau received a total of 552 votes and 535 of them endorsed capital punishment. Conducted amid massive political pressure resulted from the Three-Anti Movement, such a voting outcome was not unpredictable, but it provided the Bureau with the mandate it needed to request Beijing's approval of the death sentence. In the meantime, however, it also suggested that the CCP Central Committee may suspend the death sentence for two years if it wanted to.[43]

Mao Zedong did not take the cue when the case reached his desk. Instead, he approved the death sentence. When Huang Jing, whom Liu Qingshan and Zhang Zishan reported to during the civil war and who was now the party chief in the municipal government of Tianjin, approached Bo Yibo and asked him to persuade Mao Zedong to spare the lives of his wartime subordinates on the ground of their contribution to the Communist cause, Mao bluntly rejected the attempt. According to Bo Yibo, Mao Zedong was determined to put Liu and Zhang to death because he saw it as serving a weightier purpose than just punishing corruption:

> We must execute [Liu Qingshan and Zhang Zishan] exactly because they are high-ranking party leaders, have made great contributions, and are influential. Only by executing them could we save 20, 200, 2,000, or even 20,000 party cadres who have made all kinds of mistakes of different degrees [but could be detained and stop them].

Meant to be preemptive, Mao Zedong's decision sealed the fate of Liu Qingshan and Zhang Zishan.[44]

Only slightly more than two months elapsed between the arrest of Liu and Zhang and the finalization of the decision to punish them for their "crime" with death. Jailed in solitude, they had been kept in dark about what was going to happen to them. On February 9, 1952, one day before their scheduled execution, Liu Qingshan and Zhang Zishan were informed of the corruption accusation against them and the punishment for their alleged crime. Shocked, they vehemently protested and requested an appeal. However, when they were told that an appeal was out of the question because Mao Zedong had approved the death sentence, they felt silent, resigning to what had become inevitable.[45]

Liu Qingshan and Zhang Zishan spent the last day of their lives in Baoding Sports Stadium. Built in the 1930s, the stadium was now turned into the site of a public trial that unfolded in front of more than 20,000 spectators on February 10, 1952. As the trial proceeded to the point where Song Zhiyi, chief justice of the supreme court of Hebei Province, announced the court's findings and its sentence, Liu and Zhang learned the specific crimes they had been accused of for the first time. Together with those who had worked with them in the prefectural government and those who had labored for the water control projects and governmental enterprises under their supervision, Liu Qingshan and Zhang Zishan heard the enumeration of their "crimes" through a loudspeaker:

> As a result of being heavily influenced by the decadent bourgeois thought, [Liu Qingshan and Zhang Zishan] took advantage of their position to embezzle and steal state fund for airport construction, flood disaster relief, labor for water control projects, and grain rations for the families of governmental employees. In addition, they withheld part of the grain rations for the water control laborers and obtained bank loans through deception. Altogether, 17.1 billion yuan has been embezzled in these ways and then spent on operating the governmental enterprises that they secretly controlled.[46]
>
> They openly engaged in illegal business deals with the embezzled and stolen state fund. In April 1951, for example, they forged a business relationship with an unscrupulous merchant called Zhang Wenyi and paid her 4.9 billion yuan to buy iron and steel. Instead of fulfilling the order, Zhang spent the money speculating in the market, losing 2.1 billion yuan. In May of the same year, [the defendants] spent 400 million yuan that was part of the state flood disaster relief fund on buying lumber from Manchuria at a discount price, ignoring the hardship and suffering of the flooding victims.
>
> In order to expand their governmental enterprises, they got themselves involved in construction business by buying a private lumber factory and then merging it with their own government construction company in March 1951. Afterward, they violated state policies by luring with an offer of high salary

> 31 engineers and technicians from enterprises of state or public ownership in Tianjin and Manchuria to work in their company.
>
> Between 1950 and the spring of 1951, water control projects were under way in river valley areas of Chaobai, Yongding, Daqing, Longfeng, and Haihe that are under the jurisdiction of the Special Prefecture of Tianjin. [Taking advantage of the opportunity], they opened supplying stations for the peasant laborers as a way to make money. In operating these stations, they substituted rotten grains for the high-quality grains the laborers were supposed to receive from the state-run work-for-food program and raised the price for grain, cooking oil and vegetable, robbing the exploited peasant laborers of 2.2 billion yuan.
>
> They supported their extravagant life style, including drug consumption, by putting into their own pockets 307 million yuan of the state fund Liu and Zhang embezzled through the aforementioned activities.

And Song Zhiyi wrapped up the verdict with the announcement of capital punishment for Liu Qingshan and Zhang Zishan, confirming in front of an agitated crowd what they had learned the night before.[47] Afterward, they were transported to the cadet field training ground of Baoding Military Academy and executed.

Liu Qingshan died at age thirty-six and Zhang Zishan at age thirty-four. Despite their young age, since they had started their revolutionary career in their teens, by the time of their death they had indeed become the "older Party cadres who were seen as corrupted by urban bourgeois influences."

Conclusion: Michel Foucault and *The First Big Case in New China*

Broadly defined, corruption is the "use of public office for private advantage."[48] The two groups of people who have tried to shape our understanding of the first big case by writing about it do not dispute the fact that Liu Qingshan and Zhang Zishan did take advantage of their position of power to grow the governmental enterprises under their control, but they disagree on whether or not doing so was motivated by private advantage and thus constituted corruption. To Liu Tieqi and Liu Zejun and those who had been persecuted as Liu's and Zhang's accomplices during the Three-Anti Movement, what Liu Qingshan and Zhang Zishan did was nothing but generating a budget for the prefectural government to operate on. Although some of their "measures of expediency," such as transferring fund for public projects to the governmental enterprises, could be considered dubious or even erroneous practice, they were meant to be for the public good of the prefectural government and its employees. At the very least, nothing Liu Qingshan and Zhang Zishan had done can be characterized as corruption because it did not lead to private advantage for themselves and for their immediate and extended families, either in terms of pecuniary gains or in terms of status and influence.[49]

To those historians and scholars whose writings about Liu Qingshan and Zhang Zishan are in conformity with Bo Yibo's official version of the case, one point in the argument of Liu Tieqi and Liu Zejun is impossible to refute and that is the legality of governmental enterprises. Actually, Beijing did not take the authority to run governmental enterprises away from its local administrations until March 12, 1952, a month after Liu and Zhang had been put to death for "being obsessed with pursuing profits" from their enterprises.[50] Still, in an attempt to validate the case as the first big anticorruption case in the history of the PRC, they assert that Liu and Zhang overstepped the legal limit and turned governmental enterprise from a means to stay financially self-reliant for the work unit into a tool to enrich themselves.[51]

For Mao Zedong and other CCP leaders, however, the legality of the case was probably not as much a concern as using the case to justify and expand the Three-Anti Movement, as Wang Shunsheng and Li Jun point out in their book.[52] On the surface, it seems that the CCP Committee of Hebei's reports rationalized Mao's decision to mete out a punishment that fitted the offenses, but then Mao's comments on Huang Jing's last effort to save the lives of Liu Qingshan and Zhang Zishan shed a different light. If Bo Yibo's reminiscence of the event can be trusted as a credible evidence, then we have reason to believe that Mao Zedong wanted to alarm the party cadres with the death of two decorated revolutionaries who had placed their regional interest over that of the party and the nation. Moreover, Mao had predicted that after the Communist victory some CCP veterans would fall to the sugar-coated bullets fired by the bourgeois, and he also invoked the failure of Li Zicheng in building a long-lasting dynastic rule after his rebellion had overthrown the Ming dynasty in 1644 to warn his own party of a similar outcome if vigilante was not practiced.[53] With that perspective in the background, when the case of Liu Qingshan and Zhang Zishan was brought to Mao Zedong's attention, he probably could not resist the inclination to see it as a confirmation of his prediction or fear and then acted accordingly. As a result, Liu Qingshan and Zhang Zishan were placed as human sacrifices on the altar of the CCP party governance to be consolidated and perpetuated.

The politicization of the case occurred against a particular historical background. First, when the Three-Anti Movement was launched at the national level in December 1951, only two years had gone by since the fall of Nationalist regime and one reason for the fall has been said to be the rampant corruption by Nationalist officials. Thus, to differentiate itself from its predecessor, the CCP needed to create an anticorruption focus for the movement and nothing could be more effective in creating such a focus—and showing its resolve to prevent what had fallen on the Nationalists from falling on itself—than putting to death two loyal but now corrupted Communists. Put in another way, public denouncement of the alleged corruption and public trial and execution for such a crime served the need of the CCP to legitimize its party governance to the people and the party bureaucrats alike. Second, even though the corruption accusation against Liu Qingshan and Zhang may not stand a chance of passing a legal scrutiny both then and certainly now, for the CCP leadership that struggled to reinstate political centralization and initiate a centrally controlled economy in the early 1950s, the centrifugal tendency that Liu and Zhang unmistakably displayed in their fixation with their governmental enterprises had to be stopped. Death was an extreme way to stop it but it was also necessary to apply this time-honored Legalist method to the strengthening of a new Communist state: bearing the stigma of official corruption that may seem groundless, or *moxuyou* (莫须有) in Chinese, under normal circumstances, Liu Qingshan and Zhang Zishan were put to death as much to punish their "crime" as to instill fear into those party cadres who would otherwise continue to "seek selfish gains or advance the small-group interests of their own units or departments at the expense of the Party and the people."[54]

If the Three-Anti Movement and its anticorruption theme defined through the first big case reflect the urgency with which the CCP pursued the consolidation and legitimization of its rule in 1951–1952, over the ensuring decades the case has been decontextualized and anachronized. For example, in the anticorruption campaign in China in the 1980s to 1990s, the CCP official media lost no opportunity to emphasize the "current relevance" of the Liu Qingshan and Zhang Zishan case, linking it to the recent official corruption cases that have resulted from totally different socioeconomic circumstances and that dwarfed the first big case in terms of pecuniary gains for corrupt party officials like Zhou Yongkang.[55] Still, as long as official corruption remains a threat to the legitimacy of CCP party governance in China, the first big case will probably remain a component of the CCP anticorruption discourse. An unfillable hole would have emerged if that component were pulled out from the official party history of relentless and never-ending combat against corruption.

In discussing the relationship between popular consciousness and the production of truth by political regime, French historian and philosopher Michel Foucault argues that emancipating truth from every system does not matter as much as "detaching the power of the truth from the forms of hegemony, social, economic, and cultural, within which it operates at the present time."[56] So far as the first big case is concerned, the official truth about it was first forged during the Three-Anti Movement. However, since the essential theme of that truth is official corruption and its harm to the people, it has been removed from its historical context and remanufactured to serve the party's timeless need for legitimation. After all, the CCP party governance is supposed to be for the people and thus official corruption is not supposed to be tolerated, especially when a legitimation crisis seems to be on the horizon.

One of the most recent examples of such maneuver is a Chinese movie titled *Xin zhongguo diyi daan* (The First Big Case in New China). Produced by Changchun Film Studio in 1992, the movie dramatizes the case of Liu Qingshan and Zhang Zishan along the official line and its plot revolves around the alienation of Liu and Zhang from the peasants under their jurisdiction. In one of the scenes of the film, the peasant coolies are showed to have fallen to illness en masse. When a righteous Communist cadre from the prefectural government finds out that the illness is caused by the rotten food the peasants have eaten and that the quality food originally allocated to them has been sold by Liu and Zhang to fund their governmental enterprises, he delivers an angry lecture to his two superiors:

> You should think about [what you have done] with your conscience! How compliant the common people are! Why are they so compliant? Because they believe in the party and the government. Being a part of this party and government, how could you do what you've done? Do you not fear that these common people will rise up against you?[57]

We may wonder how much the audience of the film would resonate with its depiction of the first big case and the anticorruption rhetoric in that depiction. To historians, however, a more relevant question to ask is how such a propagation through popular media, such as film, has contributed to the validation and perpetuation of a truth that meets the need of the CCP to constantly legitimize itself.

Being associated with such a truth, Liu Qingshan and Zhang Zishan, and the first big case in new China itself, will continue to be an indispensable component of the CCP's anticorruption discourse, even though that discourse is oftentimes presented as a historical narrative.

NOTES

1. Leslie Holmes, *The End of Communist Power: Anticorruption Campaigns and Legitimation Crisis* (Cambridge: Polity Press, 1993), 10.
2. Cited in Holmes, *The End of Communist Power*, 7; also see Li Xueqing and Weiluo, eds., *Xin zhongguo fanfubai tongjian* (The Chronicle of the Anticorruption campaigns in New China) (Tianjin: Tianjin renmin chubanshe, 1993), 435–36.
3. Huang Rongxiu and Liu Songbin, eds., Zhongguo gongchandang lianzheng fanfu shiji (The Chinese Communist Party's historical records of building an honest government and combating corruption) (Beijing: Zhongguo fangzheng chubanshe,

1997), 3–4; Wang Shunsheng and Li Jun, *"Sanfan" yundong yanjiu* (A study of the "Three-Anti" Movement) (Beijing: zhonggong dangshi chubanshe, 2006), 1.

4. Two examples of such scholarship that have informed this study are Wang Shunsheng and Li Jun's, *"Sanfan" yundong yanjiu* and Xie Yijing's, "Sanfan yundong zhi yanjiu" (A study of the Three-Anti movement, a master thesis) (Taipei: Guoli zhongyang daxue tushuguan, 2015).

5. For example, on February 1, 1952, two party and governmental officials in Beijing, capital of the PRC, were executed for their alleged crime of corruption in a public trial mass meeting, ten days before the execution of Liu Qingshan and Zhang Zishan. Like Liu and Zhang, these two officials, Song Degui and Xue Kunshan, were among a few dozens of party officials executed during the Three-Anti Movement. But unlike Liu and Zhang, they have never been accorded with the notoriety in the CCP narrative of its anticorruption campaigns as Liu and Zhang have, despite the similarities between the two cases. Xueqing and Weiluo, *Xin zhongguo fanfubai tongjian*, 24.

6. Bo Yibo, *Ruogan zhongdajuece yu shijiande huigu* (A few important decisions and historical events in retrospect) (Beijing: zhonggong zhongyang dangxiao chubanshe, 1991), 1–137.

7. Ibid., 65–66.

8. Ibid., 139.

9. Liaoning-Shenyang Campaign, one of the three major campaigns in the CCP-GMD civil war, ended in November 1948 with a decisive Communist victory and led to the unchallenged Communist control of all of Manchuria, including its main industrial and urban centers such as Changchun and Shenyang. Dai Maolin and Zhao Xiaoguang, *Gao Gang zhuan* (A biography of Gao Gang) (Xian: Shanxi renmin chubanshe, 2011), 194–95.

10. Ibid., 198–9, 205, 219–20.

11. Ibid., 229–30.

12. Ibid., 229.

13. Ibid., 230. Also see Bo Yibo, *Ruogan zhongdajuece yu shijiande huigu*, 140.

14. Maurice Meisner, *Mao's China and After: A History of the People's Republic* (New York: The Free Press, 1999), 87.

15. Xueqing and Weiluo, *Xin zhongguo fanfubai tongjian*, 32.

16. For example, in the anticorruption campaign that Zhao Ziyang called upon the CCP to participate in in 1987, Liu Qingshan and Zhang Zishan were often mentioned as an example of what could have happened to party officials if they relaxed their vigilance against the influence of bourgeoisie thoughts. "Liu Qingshan Zhang Zishan tanwuan shi zengmohuishi"? (What happened in the corruption case of Liu Qingshan and Zhang Zishan?) *Jiefangjun bao* (the PLA Daily), May 19, 1986.

17. Bo Yibo, *Ruogan zhongdajuece yu shijiande huigu*, 140–49.

18. Liu Zejun's book, *Liu Qingshan Zhang Zishan de duanzan rensheng* (Short lives of Liu Qingshan and Zhang Zishan), was published in Hong Kong in 2013. In the meantime, he also posted his book in his blog, creating an online audience for it. In this article, all the citations from this book are from its online version. Since it is not page-numbered, when a citation is made, the note will only list the title of the chapter from which it comes and the internet link to the chapter.

19. Liu Zejun, *Liu Qingshan Zhang Zishan de duanzan rensheng*, chapter 3 canjia lixian baodong (participating in the Li County Rebellion). http://blog.sohu.com/s/NjAyMzg1NDE/235805277.html.

20. Ibid.

21. Liu Zejun, *Liu Qingshan Zhang Zishan de duanzan rensheng*, chapter 4 Zhang Zishan jiashi (the family history of Zhang Zishan), http://blog.sohu.com/s/NjAyMzg1NDE/235805530.html.

22. Ibid., chapter 5 beipu ruyu ningsi buqu (rather die in prison than give up the faith).

23. Ibid., chapter 15 diaoren bafenqu chenggongbuzhang (appointment as head of the intelligence department in the eighth military district), http://blog.sohu.com/s/NjAyMzg1NDE/300439006.html; also see Zhou Jiqiang, "Jinchaji junqu jianshi" (a concise history of the Shanxi-Chahar-Hebei military region), *Junshi lishi* (military history), no. 1 (1995), 44–48.

24. Liu Zejun, *Liu Qingshan Zhang Zishan de duanzan rensheng*, chapter 15 diaoren bafenqu chenggongbuzhang.

25. Ibid., chapter 16 churen bafenqu diweishuji (as the secretary of the CCP Committee in the eighth military district); also see Bo Yibo, *Ruogan zhongdajuece yu shijiande huigu*, 3–4.

26. Liu Zejun, *Liu Qingshan Zhang Zishan de duanzan rensheng*, chapter 17 jiuren Tianjin diweishuji (becoming secretary of the CCP prefectural committee for the special prefecture of Tianjin).

27. Mao Zedong, "Report to the Second Plenary Session of the Seventh Central Committee of the Communist Party of China," March 5, 1949. Transcription from the Maoist Documentation Project, https://www.marxists.org/reference/archive/mao/selected-works/volume-4/mswv4_58.htm.

28. Bo Yibo, *Ruogan zhongdajuece yu shijiande huigu*, 148.

29. About the initial moderate approach to the middle class and former employees of the Nationalist municipal government by the Communist administrators in Tianjin, see Bo Yibo, *Ruogan zhongdajuece yu shijiande huigu*, 10–13. For the measures implemented by the Communist administrators to restore commerce and industry in Tianjin and stabilize its financial market in 1949, the first year for Communist administration in Tianjin, see Compiling Committee of Tianjin Gazette, ed., *Tianjin tongzhi dashiji* (a chronicle of Tianjin history) (Tianjin: Tianjin shehui kexueyuan chubanshe, 1991), 296–309.

30. Liu Zejun, *Liu Qingshan Zhang Zishan de duanzan rensheng*, chapter 17 jiuren Tianjin diweishuji.

31. Jonathan Spence, *The Death of Woman Wang* (New York: Penguin Books, 1979), 9–13.

32. Ibid.

33. About the origins and history of governmental enterprises, see Wang Shunsheng and Li Jun, *"Sanfan" yundong yanjiu*, 80 and Liu Zejun, *Liu Qingshan Zhang Zishan de duanzan rensheng*, chapter 18 shengchan zijiu yu jiguan shengchan (self-reliance through production and government enterprises), http://blog.sohu.com/s/NjAyMzg1NDE/300439132.html.

34. Liu Zejun, *Liu Qingshan Zhang Zishan de duanzan rensheng*, chapter 18 shengchan zijiu yu jiguan shengchan.

35. Ibid., chapter 17 jiuren Tianjin diweishuji.

36. Liu Zejun, *Liu Qingshan Zhang Zishan de duanzan rensheng*, chapter 20 dui Liu Qingshan Zhang Zishan wenti de chachu jingguo (investigation of the Liu Qingshan and Zhang Zishan case and their punishment), http://blog.sohu.com/s/NjAyMzg1NDE/300439310.html; also see Wang Shunsheng and Li Jun, *"Sanfan" yundong yanjiu*, 81.

37. Liu Zejun, *Liu Qingshan Zhang Zishan de duanzan rensheng*, chapter 20 dui Liu Qingshan Zhang Zishan wenti de chachu jingguo.

38. Ibid.

39. Wang Shunsheng and Li Jun, *"Sanfan" yundong yanjiu*, 81.

40. "Zhonggong Hebei shengwei guanyu kaichu Liu Qingshan Zhang Zishan daji de jueding" (resolution by the CCP Provincial Committee of Hebei to expel Liu Qingshan and Zhang Zishan from the CCP), Appendix 1 in Liu Zejun, *Liu Qingshan Zhang Zishan de duanzan rensheng*, http://blog.sohu.com/s/NjAyMzg1NDE/301270784.html.

41. Bo Yibo, *Ruogan zhongdajuece yu shijiande huigu*, 138.

42. Liu Zejun, *Liu Qingshan Zhang Zishan de duanzan rensheng*, chapter 20 dui Liu Qingshan Zhang Zishan wenti de chachu jingguo.

43. Bo Yibo, *Ruogan zhongdajuece yu shijiande huigu*, 151.

44. Ibid., 152.

45. With the official case file of Liu Qingshan and Zhang Zishan still classified, the only available source for this narrative is Liu Tieqi's biography written on the basis of public documents and, more importantly, interviews with Liu Qingshan's and prison guards. See Liu Zejun, *Liu Qingshan Zhang Zishan de duanzan rensheng*, chapter 21 daipu, jianyu, gongshen, gucheng qiansheng (arrest, prison, public trial, and firing squad in the ancient city), http://blog.sohu.com/s/NjAyMzg1NDE/301270750.html and Liu Qingshan Zhang Zishan de duanzan rensheng: houji (short life of Liu Qingshan and Zhang Zishan: postscript), http://blog.sohu.com/s/NjAyMzg1NDE/301270808.html.

46. Chinese currency at the time was called "the old yuan." In 1955, the old yuan was replaced by the new yuan and the conversion rate was 10,000 old yuan versus 1 new yuan. Thus, measured in new yuan that has evolved into today's renminbi, the 17.1 billion yuan that Liu Qingshan and Zhang Zishan had been accused of embezzling was equivalent to 1.71 million renminbi, more or less. Bo Yibo, *Ruogan zhongdajuece yu shijiande huigu*, 76.

47. "Hebei sheng renmin fayuan linshifating panchu datanwufan Liu Qingshan Zhang Zishan sixing panjueshu," February 10, 1952 (death sentence verdict for big embezzlers Liu Qingshan and Zhang Zishan from the special court appointed by the supreme court of Hebei Province), appendix 2 Liu Zejun, *Liu Qingshan Zhang Zishan de duanzan rensheng*, http://blog.sohu.com/s/NjAyMzg1NDE/301270784.html. Also see Bo Yibo, *Ruogan zhongdajuece yu shijiande huigu*, 149 and Xueqing and Weiluo, *Xin zhongguo fanfubai tongjian*, 11–12.

48. Leslie Holmes, *The End of Communist Power*, 65.

49. According to Liu Zejun, when the commission formed to investigate the "crimes" of Liu Qingshan and Zhang Zishan arrived in Yang Liuqing, the first thing it did was to confiscate personal properties of Liu and Zhang but no valuables were found. More importantly, those who had been punished as accomplices of Liu and Zhang in 1951 but were still alive in the 1980s were exonerated and rehabilitated, signifying an overturn of their corruption charges that Liu and Zhang had been accused of as well. See Liu Tieqi and Liu Zejun, *Xin zhongguo diyi daan jiemi* (the untold history of the first big case in new China), chapter 7 Liuzhangan de shean congfan (the accomplices of Liu Qingshan and Zhang Zishan) http://blog.sohu.com/s/NjAyMzg1NDE/309078161.html and chapter 16 Liu Zhang fuhua duoluo lema? (Were Liu Qingshan and Zhang Zishan corrupted and decadent?) http://blog.sohu.com/s/NjAyMzg1NDE/309078261.html.

50. Citing it as a breeding ground for corruption and waste of national resources, the Government Administration Council of the PRC (政务院) revoked the right of its local administrations to run governmental enterprises on March 12, 1952, and centralized their management. See Xueqing and Weiluo, *Xin zhongguo fanfubai tongjian*, 29.

51. Wang Shunsheng and Li Jun, *"Sanfan" yundong yanjiu*, 80.

52. Ibid., 81.

53. In all the Chinese works about the Three-Anti Movement and the first big case in new China, Mao Zedong's expression of hope that the CCP could pass the test of victory that Li Zicheng and the peasant rebellion under his leadership had failed to pass has been cited as a primary reason for his decision to radicalize the movement by meting out extreme punishment to Liu Qingshan and Zhang Zishan. See Bo Yibo, *Ruogan zhongdajuece yu shijiande huigu*, 153–56; Wang Shunsheng and Li Jun, *"Sanfan" yundong yanjiu*, 23–25; and Xie Yijing, Sanfan yundong zhi yanjiu (a study of the Three-Anti Movement) (a master thesis, National Central University in Taipei, 2015).

54. Speech of Hu Yaobang in June 1986, cited in Leslie Holmes, *The End of Communist Power*, 67.

55. An example of such an anachronized reference to the first big case can be found in "Liu Qingshan Zhang Zishan tanwuan shi zengmohuishi"? *Jiefangjun bao*, May 19, 1986.

56. Paul Rabinow, *The Foucault Reader* (New York: Pantheon Books, 1984), 74–75.

57. Changchun Film Studio, *Xin zhongguo diyi daan* (the first big case in new China) (1992), https://www.youtube.com/watch?v=Lhi_1XGxaoA.

BIBLIOGRAPHY

Bo Yibo 薄一波. *Ruogan zhongdajuece yushijian de huigu* (A few important decisions and historical events in retrospect). Beijing: Zhonggong zhongyang dangxiao chubanshe, 1991.

Dai Maolin and Zhao Xiaoguang 戴茂林、赵晓光. *Gao Gang zhuan* (A biography of Gao Gang). Xian: Shaanxi renmin chubanshe, 2001.

Holmes, Leslie. *The End of Communist Power: Anticorruption Campaigns and Legitimation Crisis*. Cambridge: Polity Press, 1993.

Huang Xiurong and Liu Songbin 黄修荣、刘宋斌, eds. *Zhongguo gongchandang lianzhengfanfu shiji* (The Chinese Communist Party's historical records of building an honest government and combating corruption). Beijing: Zhongguo fangzheng chubanshe, 1997.

Li Xueqin and Weiluo 李雪勤、魏洛, eds. *Xin zhongguo fanfubai tongjian* (The Chronicle of anticorruption campaigns in new China). Tianjin: Tianjin renmin chubanshe, 1993.

Liu Tieqi and Liu Zejun 刘铁骑、刘泽军. *Xin zhongguo diyidaan jiemi* (The untold history of the first big case in new China). http://blog.sohu.com/s/NjAyMzg1NDE/309078346.html, 2014.

Liu Zejun 刘泽军. *Liu Qingshan Zhang Zishan de duanzan rensheng* (Short lives of Liu Qingshan and Zhang Zishan). Hong Kong: Xianggang wenji chubanshe, 2013.

Meisner, Maurice. *Mao's China and After: A History of the People's Republic*. New York: The Free Press, 1999.

Tianjin difangzhi bianxiong wuyuanhui 天津地方志编修委员会 (Commission for composing and editing Tianjin Gazette), ed. *Tianjin tongzhi dashiji* (A comprehensive history of Tianjin: A list of significant historical events). Tianjin: Tianjin shehui kexueyuan chubanshe, 1991.

Wang Shunsheng and Li Jun 王顺生、李军. *"Sanfan" yundong yanjiu* (A study of the "Three-Anti" Movement). Beijing: zhonggong dangshi chubanshe, 2006.

Xie Yijing 谢易菁. "*Sanfan yundong zhi yanjiu*" (A study of the Three-Anti movement, a master thesis). Taipei: Guoli zhongyang daxue tushuguan, 2015.

Part III

GOVERNMENT, INDIVIDUALS, AND CONFLICTING INTERESTS

Chapter 6

Connection, Corruption, and Confrontation

Lake Weishan

Xiaojia Hou

In 2002, *Map of the Administrative Divisions of the People's Republic of China* was published.[1] It is the first authoritative map since the Qin dynasty (221–206 BC) that legally demarcates all the borders of provinces and counties in China. But this map has three undecided provincial borders. Two of them were involved with military bases, the only civilian undefined border was the Lake Weishan area which "has not yet be surveyed due to special reasons . . . [and therefore] is a temporary delimitation."[2] By "special reasons," they refer to the protracted border disputes between Shandong and Jiangsu provinces over Lake Weishan, for which frequent armed confrontations burst out, gun shots fired, and dead bodies lay. These border disputes originated and were deeply entrenched with Chinese communist government's organizational corruptions.

Today corruption has become a plague to the Chinese Communist Party (CCP). The current Xi administration is making anticorruption the top priority of its political agenda. In China, the term "corruption" is often narrowly understood as the transaction between power and wealth: it has been widely assumed that corruption was a new phenomenon that began during Deng Xiaoping's Reform. However, the concept of corruption in China is far beyond monetary exchange. Mao's China (1949–1976) was never free of corruption.

The classical notion of corruption can be traced back to Greek philosophies. Plato viewed the phenomenon that sectional interests prevailed as corruption; Aristotle regarded "corrupted" constitutions served the interest of the rulers instead of being bounded by law.[3] Different people have different understanding of corruption at different times, thus the spirit of corruption is ambiguous. Lu Xiaobo, after extensively examining the organizational history of the CCP, suggests that in nature, corruption is the deviation from prescribed norms, legal or organizational, for private gains involving both material gains and practices such as nepotism, patronage, and statistical falsification.[4] This broad interpretation helps us much better to study corruption in China. In Mao's China, the absence of the market economy and the ideological danger associated with wealth caused money to be inessential. This meant that officials often used their power to pursue personal, non-monetary gains.

Organizationally, what plagued the CCP cadres from the beginning of the People's Republic of China (PRC) was the lack of a definition of their prescribed norms. Chinese Communist officials were supposed to conform to party rules, government regulations, revolutionary goals, and to focus on serving the local people. Waves of political campaigns consistently changed rules and regulations: these new doctrines often conflicted with revolutionary goals. Local interests were at times at odds with the interests of the central government. Conformance to the prescribed norms was not easy for Chinese officials. For example, prioritizing local interests, over the greater public, could be labeled as corruption. This could lead to being purged, similar to what happened in the Three-Anti Campaign (see chapter 6). The Three-Anti Campaign was the party's vehicle to rearrange the organizational resources and redistribute power, not just to eradicate embezzlement.[5] The other side of the coin, however, is the absence of accountability. Because there were no defined prescribed norms, officials had a wide range of actions to cope with local needs from below and with demands from the central government above. What happened when the local interests clashed with central orders? How did local cadres amend their understanding of prescribed norms? What was the main form of corruption in Mao's China? The case of disputes over Lake Weishan sheds lights on these questions.

CREATION OF LAKE WEISHAN

Lake Weishan lies between Shandong and Jiangsu Provinces. It is the southernmost lake of four interlocking sub-lakes, with Zhaoyang, Dushan, and Nanyang lakes to its north, see figure 6.1.[6] Those four lakes together are customarily called Lake Nansi (Southern Four Lakes); sometimes they are also called Lake Weishan. In this chapter, the term "Lake Weishan" is used to refer to the southernmost lake of the four sub-lakes and the term "Lake Nansi" is used to refer to all four lakes together. Today, Lake Nansi is the largest freshwater lake in northern China, approximately 120 km long and 1266 square km in area. One and half centuries ago, it was almost double the size; yet, a millennium ago, it did not exist all at. For centuries, the drastic physiographic changes have challenged local administrations.

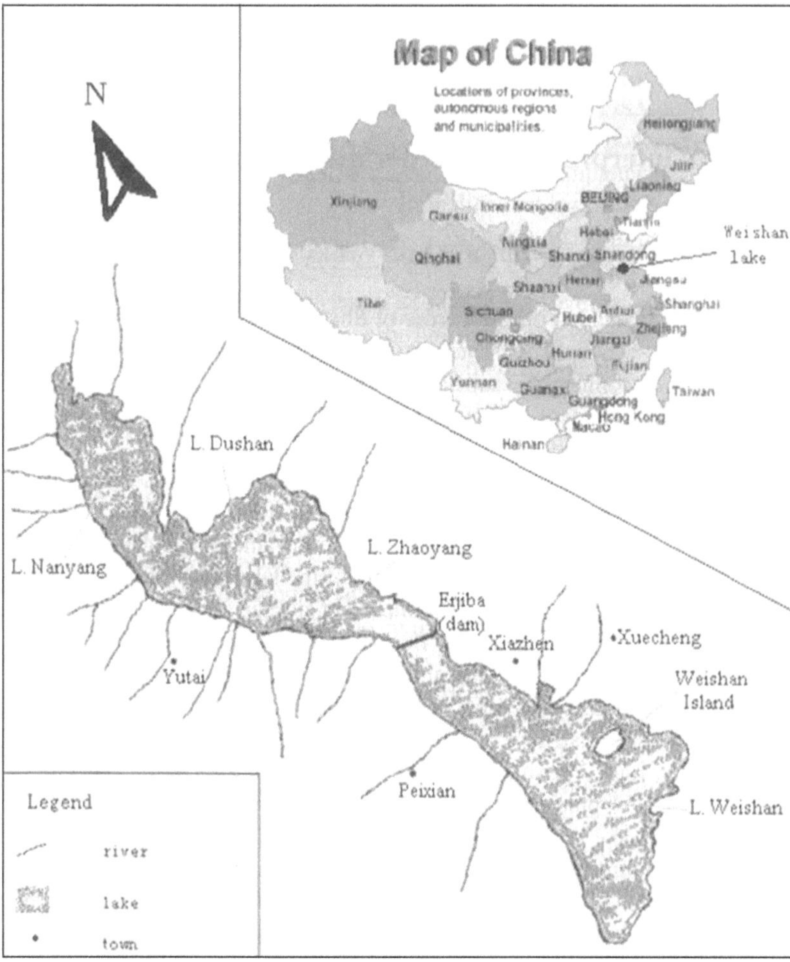

Figure 6.1 Sketch Map of "Lake Nansi". Drawn by Guo Rongxing with assistance by Guo Liqing. *Source*: Rongxing Guo, Cross-Border Resource Management, Volume 10 (Netherland: Elsevier Science, 2005), 198.

Prior to 1194, the Lake Nansi area was a fertile low-lying land between Shandong and Jiangsu provinces. On its west the Si River ran into the Huai River. The area was approximately 34–35 meters above sea level and the lowest part in altitude was in southwest of Shandong province. In 1194, the Yellow River broke its banks and changed the river's course. The new course took over the water channel of the Si River, ran into the Huai River, and flowed into the sea. The new course lasted for 660 years, until another major course change in 1855. Year after year, the Yellow River sediments accumulated, the river bed rose up. This buildup stopped the old Si River from entering the Huai River. Hard to trespass, the Si River water spread out across low-lying lands and gradually formed scattered depressions. The Yellow River continued to break dikes in its new course; flooded water further fed the depressions, which turned into small lakes. As the Yuan Dynasty (1271–1368) began, there were more than twenty lakes dotting the area.[7] The construction of the Grand Canal in Yuan Dynasty and Ming dynasty (1368–1644) further complicated local water systems. Numerous depressions enlarged and merged into bigger lakes. In the Qing dynasty (1644–1911), these lakes continued to grow. They submerged small rivers, villages, and even entire towns. Eventually, these lakes merged into four big lakes, which came to be called Lake Nansi. In the early seventeenth century, Lake Nansi already shouldered dual functions: as water reservoirs for the Grand Canal and as the water dumping site to collect flood water from the Yellow River and all rivers nearby. Being the lowest in altitude of the four lakes, Lake Weishan grew even faster because it received surplus water from the other three lakes.[8]

During the rapid growth of Lake Weishan, there were constant floods. Local people suffered tremendously. The worst was yet to come. In 1851, the Yellow River breached at Fengxian county. The torrent quickly swallowed the Peixian and Yutai counties, both were located in the west bank of Lake Weishan. Even the magistrate of Peixian had to move to Xiazhen, in the east bank of Lake Weishan. Next year, an earthquake occurred. Having witnessed plenty of disasters and unable to make a living, many Peixian residents saw no hope in their homeland and left.[9] In a few years, a great deal of the west bank of Lake Weishan became unoccupied and uncultivated.

The rescue came rather suddenly. In 1855, the Yellow River flooded again and changed the course to the north, disrupted the Grand Canal, and flowed through the Shandong province into the sea. This change almost magically saved the Lake Nansi area. Lake Weishan shrank because it no longer collected the Yellow River surplus and no longer served as water reservoir for the Grand Canal. As a result, more lakeside land emerged, and, more troubles ensued.

Refugees from southwestern Shandong, victims of the new Yellow River course, were the first groups who came to take over the unoccupied land in the west bank of Lake Weishan. Many originated from the same villages, traveled together, settled down in large groups, and formed villages along the west bank of Lake Weishan. Those villages tended to be well organized. Often, several, or even several dozens, of them formed a community called *Tuan* which had its own elected leader and local defense. Government officials in Peixian county allowed the immigrants to farm the unclaimed lakeside land, with the promise of paying taxes and rents. Improved ecology in Lake Weishan drew back departed Peixian locals. When they returned, they found their abandoned land was taken by *Tuan* people. In the decades to follow, the two sides fought badly.[10] The casualties were counted in thousands.[11] The grudge between *Tuan* (Shandong origin) and Peixian locals (Jiangsu origin) carried on into the Republic of China (1911–1949).[12] In the late 1930s, the CCP's infiltration of the area further complicated the administration conflicts.

The Creation of Weishan County and a New Dam

In history, Lake Weishan was mostly under the jurisdiction of Peixian county of Jiangsu province. Xiazhen in the east bank of Lake Weishan was the seventh district of Peixian county. Peixian approximated Yutai county of Shandong province: Tongshan (a county of Jiangsu province) neighbors Tengzhou county of Shandong province. When the Sino-Japan War (1937–45) began, the CCP established Peixian-Tengzhou border county among the borders of Jiangsu, Shandong, and Anhui. The CCP operated several guerilla factions in the region. During the Civil War (1946–49), the CCP assigned its Shandong branch to administrate the city of Xuzhou and the Lincheng, Peixian, and Tongshan counties, most of which were previously governed by Jiangsu province.[13]

When the CCP won the Civil War and founded the People Republic of China in 1949, it divided Jiangsu Province into Northern Jiangsu and Southern Jiangsu provinces. Only in 1952, the CCP decided to reinstate Jiangsu Province and ordered Shandong province to return the land originally affiliated to Jiangsu. In 1953, Shandong province agreed to let Tengxian and Xuzhou go, but in return, it demanded the jurisdiction to govern the surface of Lake Weishan, and the thirty villages along the lake that were traditionally parts of Peixian and Tongshan. Communist officials in Shandong province had for years held control over the border region; many Shandong natives ranked high in the party ladder.[14] The newly established Jiangsu province quickly yielded to Shandong's request, without consulting the counties that were involved. In 1953, both provinces signed the interprovincial agreement, consenting to give Lake Zhaoyang and Lake Weishan to Shandong, who established Weishan county to administer Lake Nansi. The surface of Lake Weishan and state-owned lakeside land thus fell under Shandong's jurisdiction. The lakeside land in the west bank formed the border of Weishan county, which practically became the border of Jiangsu province and Shandong province. Any lakeside land without deeds belonged to the state, no matter how long farmers had cultivated it: although farmers were allowed to continue farming the land. Local residents could continue their customary practices such as fishing, planting reeds, and so on. Weishan county will administrate lake resources and lakeside land.[15] In August of 1953, the State Council approved the establishment of Weishan county.

This new Weishan county created many problems. First of all, it deviated from the customs, yet local residents and local counties were not consulted. Second, the language was ambiguous. It emphasized that local residents, many of whom were Jiangsu natives, could continue their lake-related businesses as before, but the lake was to be put under the exclusive administration of Shandong province. More importantly, the landside was not a fixed border. As we have seen, the size of Lake Weishan has gone through dramatic changes in history. It will continue to change, to enlarge or shrink, in accordance with the natural conditions and government projects. Thus the border of Jiangsu and Shandong will continue to shift. Moreover, Lake Nansi is of strategic importance to Jiangsu province. It irrigated more than 2 million mu[16] of farming land in Jiangsu; consequently it collected multiple river waters from Jiangsu. The west bank of the lake is rich in coal mines as well. Giving the lake administration to Shandong province was an enormous loss to Jiangsu. However, in the first half of the 1950s, those issues were mostly overlooked, probably because the water level kept rising.

In the 1951 land reform, the government issued deeds to originally privately owned land, amounted to 93,000 mu, most of which was above 32.5 meter sea level—the then lake surface level. The rest of land was owned by the state, but previous tenants were allowed to farm the land, which amounted to 150,000 mu.[17] In 1953, the water level rose to 33 meters. From 1953 to 1956, the lakeside land in Peixian was shrinking dramatically: the taxable land dropped to one-third from 1953 to 1955.[18]

In 1957 one devastating flood occurred. In July, the rainfall in Lake Nansi was 3.5 times of the average, and was particularly intense in Tengxian next to Lake Zhaoyang. Water from multiple rivers and hills flooded into the lakes, ultimately congregating in Lake Weishan. In a month the water level of Lake Weishan rose from 31 meters to 36.29 meters, far exceeding its capacity. The whole Weishan county, excepting a few hill tops and high land, was submerged in the water: 410,000 mu farming land was flooded, 28 people died, all lake resources were destroyed.[19] This monstrous flood stimulated the idea of building a dam to control the water.[20]

After the 1957 flood, the Ministry of Water Conservancy, along with Jiangsu and Shandong provinces, discussed plans to build a dam on Lake Nansi. However, it was Shandong province alone that designed the dam and commenced the construction. The hidden negotiations are not known yet, but it is likely that Jiangsu Province was not pleased. This new dam was called Erjiba Dam. It would give Shandong strong upper hand over Jiangsu, controlling the dam, the water, the irrigation, and the transportation on Lake Nansi. The construction of the dam could also advance Shandong officials' political careers. It was at the wake of Great Leap Forward (1958–1962) that a great deal of irrigation projects were put forward, Erjiba Dam was one of them. Erjiba Dam was poorly designed. The water gate of the dam was off the center, a second, a third, and a fourth gate, had to be added in the following three decades. The construction was launched in June 1958, an extremely odd timing because it usually rains badly in July, and summer is always the busy season for peasants. Indeed summer was the least ideal time to start an irrigation project. However, to make a political statement, the construction commenced regardless. Unsurprisingly, heavy rains in July quickly soaked everything, so the project halted until October. In 1960, the water gate Red Flag #1 was installed and the project was completed.[21] During the building of the dam, 210,000 mu of arable land on the Jiangsu side was submerged. When the dam was finished, Shandong province got hold of the overwhelming portion of the lake's water reserves and made farmers in Peixian county unable to irrigate their crops in drought.[22]

Land Disputes and Officials' Changing Loyalties in Mao's China

The Erjiba Dam divided Lake Nansi virtually into two lakes, upper lake at water level 34 meters and the lower lake (where Lake Weishan locates) at water level 32.5 meters. The dam blocked the water from upper lake, compounded by a significant drought in 1959, the water level of Lake Weishan dropped sharply. Consequently, 180,000 mu "new" lakeside land emerged in the west side of the lake, which in history belonged to Peixian county. In fall 1959, Peixian county established the "headquarters of striving to farm the lakeside land" and organized 20,000 Peixian residents to plough those land, with no authorization from Weishan county. In October, Weishan county too called its residents to cultivate the land, and demanded Peixian to return their ploughed land. Peixian county appealed to Jining prefecture of Shandong province, Weishan county's superior. In October, Xuzhou prefecture (superior of Peixian county, Jiangsu province) and the Jining prefecture discussed the issue and ordered Peixian to withdraw from farming the lakeside land and to make self-criticism for violating the 1953 agreement. Peixian officials bended. It made self-criticism, acknowledged Weishan county's jurisdiction over lakeside land and lake resources, and promised not to make the same mistake.[23] Jiangsu provincial leaders then broadcasted Peixian's self-criticism to educate party members and forbade Peixian residents from pursuing the lakeside land. The latter were furious, and made many appeals to the Xuzhou prefecture and Jiangsu province.[24] In 1959, when the disputes over Lake Weishan first occurred, local people took the initiatives, but officials in Peixian county, Jining prefecture, and Jiangsu province all yielded to the pressure from Shandong and chose to cooperate with the neighbor. It seems officials were more eager to please their superiors, rather than to defend local interests.

Chinese peasants were catastrophically hit during the Great Famine (1959–1961), and people in Lake Weishan were no exception. Desperate for survival, both Peixian and Weishan residents had their eyes on the lakeside land. In July, 1961, Weishan county distributed all the lakeside land along Lake Weishan and Lake Zhaoyang, including the land originally belonging to Peixian residents who had land deeds, to the communes, schools, and other organizations of Weishan county. Weishan county established an agricultural farm in the west of Lake Weishan, and encouraged Weishan residents in the east bank to walk dozens of miles to farm the west bank of the lake.[25] In fall, Peixian county declared to withdraw its self-criticism, and asserted that the 1953 agreement was not reasonable, emphasizing that history and custom should be honored. It demanded either to reinstate the old Peixian territory, or to take Wei River in the middle of Lake Weishan as the border. Peixian county came up with the slogan "March to the lake" (*xiang dahu jinjun*) and again organized local residents to farm the lakeside land.[26]

In August, 1961, the Departments of Civil Affairs in both Shandong and Jiangsu provinces, officials of Xuzhou and Jining prefectures, of Peixian and Weishan counties, convened several meetings, but failed to reach any consensus. In October, the vice governors of both provinces met in Xuzhou (Jiangsu province). The meeting lasted for twenty days, yet no agreement was struck. Then the meeting moved to Ji'nan (Shandong province), and the first secretary of Shandong Province (no.1 leader of Shandong province) attended. It seems some consensus was coming up. However, skirmish burst out on site. The state farm of Peixian county organized 400 people to plant crops in the lakeside land. In November, Jiang Fangzan, the head of Wanglou Production Brigade of Weishan county, ordered to fire at Peixian residents, killed one and injured two. The killer claimed that he was not guilty of murdering because he was ordered to kill. A common saying was, "Strike, the commune will take the responsibility if there is a death."[27] It seems that starting in the early 1960s officials at the county level and below leaned to protect local interests and defy orders from above. They also had no hesitation of engaging violence.

This killing ignited decades of feuds between Weishan and Peixian residents, both were known for their "toughness." Residents in Peixian had long been practicing Kongfu, calling Peixian "hometown of Kongfu." Residents in Weishan often took hunting as side work and many owned duck guns, bird guns, and hunting guns. From the mid-nineteenth century, residents of both counties did not get along well. Once they started fighting, they could hardly halt.[28]

Erjiba Dam also altered the lake production and water consumption conditions. Before the dam was constructed, Lake Weishan was too deep to plant reeds. But with Erjiba Dam holding much water, Lake Weishan became ideal for reed production. Increasingly, the Peixian-Weishan struggle involved with lake resources. In 1964, Peixian county announced it was to administrate Lake Weishan and established fifteen local stores to purchase lake resources.[29] Holding control of Erjiba Dam, Shandong province could restrict the water volume flowing into Lake Weishan, thus often impairing the irrigation in Jiangsu, which worsened their relationship. Seeds of enmity were planted deeply and tasted badly. Villages, communes, even counties, actively defended their local interests, ignored orders from above and no longer were bounded by their obligations to the superiors. Between 1961 and 1966, more than 200 armed fights broke out, sometimes tens of thousands people were engaged and hundreds were injured.[30]

For example, in spring 1965, the state farm of Peixian county mobilized over 2,000 people to dig a new channel only 300 steps away from Wanglou Production Brigade of Weishan county, which almost led to a bloody fight.[31] In the same year, East China Bureau, the direct superior of both Shandong and Jiangsu Provinces, sent down a work team to investigate and intervene. To make a fair judgment, the work team excluded personnel from Weishan county, Peixian county, Shandong province, and Jiangsu province, only including two comrades from Jining and Xuzhou prefectures. The participants from Jining and Xuzhou prefectures each defended their native interests. After forty days of field investigation, the work team reinstated the 1953 agreement and endorsed Weishan county's authority over the lakeside land and the surface of Lake Weishan, although it required Weishan county to allow Peixian residents to use the lake.[32] Both Peixian and Weishan counties refused to accept the decision.[33] It seemed that in the mid-1960s, most officials from villages to provinces preferred to defend local interests, rather than to bend to the superiors.

Another extreme drought occurred in 1966, struggles for water resources turned more violent. Even state farms and local militia participated and gradually formed the main forces. Armed fights hence were better organized, carried out in larger scale, and became more lethal. In 1966 alone, more than twenty cases of armed fights broke out, with more than sixty people injured.[34] It was in the height of the Cultural Revolution (1966–1976) that governments were in chaos. So in spring 1967, Premier Zhou Enlai asked the Nanjing Military Division to solve the conflict. In May 1967, delegates from Nanjing Military Division, Jinan Military Division, East China Bureau, Shandong province, Jiangxi province, Jining Military division, Weishan county, Xuzhou Military division, Peixian county, convened a meeting in Nanjing.

With the forceful power of the army, after eighteen days, an agreement, called the Nanjing Accord, was reached. It again confirmed Weishan county's jurisdiction over Lake Weishan, although using the water level mark as the border division. The State Council and Central Military Committee both endorsed the Nanjing Accord and demanded for its execution. However, the accord was not a real solution. Of the eighteen days of meeting, participants spent two-thirds of the time to study Maoism, as featured in the Cultural Revolution. The organizers applied the language of class struggles and blamed capitalism and self-serving localism for the causes of the conflicts. Extremely alarmed by the ideological agenda and being vulnerable to those labels, local participants from both Jiangsu and Shandong dared not overtly defend their interests, therefore a conclusion was quickly struck. But neither side wholeheartedly accepted the decision.[35] Main organizers of the meeting were soldiers who knew little about the history and local situation. The 6063 Army unit was assigned to monitor the execution of the accord. Although the unit was stationed in Xuzhou (Jiangsu province), it was affiliated to Jinan military division (Shandong). Again, the decision was in favor of Shandong province.[36]

The political atmosphere of the Cultural Revolution gave people more power. Grassroots officials, with strong support from below, simply denied the solution. When the work team arrived with counties to announce the Nanjing Accord, communes and brigades of Peixian county organized people to protest in public, distributed flyers, made posters, charging "the Nanjing Conference was a black meeting . . . the conflict over lakeside land was triggered by a small group of capitalists in Shandong." Local residents criticized, even attacked the work team members. They were planning large-scale campaigns to occupy lakeside land and grab lake resources. In 1967, hundreds of villagers from Peixian robbed the Xuecheng Military Department and used the newly acquired weapons to seize crops from Weishan county.[37]

The fight reached an apex in 1973. Dianzi village of Peixian had been growing reeds in one corner of Lake Weishan for decades, amounted to 1,600 mu in 1967. However, in 1968, Weishan county claimed its ownership of the lake surface and gave that reed zone to Dajuan brigade of Weishan county, even issued the deed. Since then Dianzi village and Dajuan brigade frequently ran into armed fight over the reeds. In October 14, 1973, Dajuan brigade summoned more than 100 boats, equipped with guns and attacked Dianzi village. The attack left four Dianzi villagers dead, three permanently paralyzed, and two dozens of injured. Shocked by the incident, Jiangsu provincial officials forbade Peixian county to take revenge and halted the reed harvest, affirming that local leaders would take accountability for any violations from below. Shandong provincial officials made apology for the incident. The court of Weishan county sentenced Duan Youguang, the head of Dajuan brigade, to three years of sentence. Officials of both provinces convened and reached a tentative agreement of the distribution of reeds for the year. However, they failed to make any progress on the long-term solution.[38]

Escalation of Disputes and Networking in Deng's Reform

In 1978, Deng Xiaoping launched his economic reform. Deng's reform decentralized the fiscal structure and allowed local government to control more of the local revenues. It strengthened people's interest in local resources and changed the central-local relations. As a result, local governments had more incentives to protect local markets and revenue sources.[39]

Conflicts between Peixian and Weishan counties over Lake Weishan intensified. Multiple armed fights broke out in 1979, and grew worse in 1980. In the armed fights of October 9 and 10, 1980, three Peixian residents were shot to death and forty-seven were injured. The State Council dispatched the Ministry of Civil Affairs and the Ministry of Water Conservancy to investigate the disputes. In November, the joint work team submitted the report to the State Council. The work team believed the prolonged disputes were originated the creation of Weishan county in 1953, and the territory boundary was not clear. The work team proposed to divide the border by the middle line of Lake Weishan, west to Peixian, east to Weishan county. However, Vice Premier Wan Li, who was a Shandong native and worked in Shandong during the revolutionary years, did not approve the proposal. Instead, he demanded the proposal to be fully consulted with Shandong and Jiangsu officials. Of course, Shandong insisted on the 1953 agreement and vetoed the proposal. No consensus was reached.

In September, 1981, another vice premier, Yang Jingren, also a Shandong native, arrived Xuzhou attempting to solve the border dispute. After hearing the reports from county and provincial officials of both sides, Yang emphasized cooperative attitudes, collective benefits, and safety concerns. He prioritized the confiscation of weapons from local residents and militias, but made little progress on the border arrangement. Hundreds of guns were confiscated. Then local residents began to burn reeds as a way of revenge. In 1983, the State Council dispatched another work team, head by Cui Naifu, the minister of civil affairs, to handle the issue. Before Cui's departure for Lake Weishan, Vice Premier Wan Li pointed out to him that "in order to thoroughly resolve this problem, the State Council has to make decisions. After having taken into account of all gains and losses, it seems better to put all villages involving in disputes under the administration of Shandong Province."[40]

Following the tone set by Wan Li, in 1984 and 1985, the State Council and the CCP Central Committee issued three high-level official orders relating to the disputes over Lake Weishan. The first report allowed Peixian residents to keep their reeds and valliseria spiralis, but stressed that Lake Weishan should be under the jurisdiction of Weishan county; the issue of public security was the responsibility of Weishan county. To reduce the source of disputes, the second report recommended fourteen villages of Peixian county under disputes to be transferred to Weishan county; and lake fisheries to be under the administration of Weishan county. The third report divided reeds and lakeside land between Peixian and Weishan counties. But even with Beijing's intervention, those central documents failed to resolve the disputes. In nature, those documents were not clearly defined, often did not coordinate with the other documents. Above all, both Jiangsu and Shandong provinces only accepted the articles favorable to its side and rejected the unfavorable ones. They frequently impeded the implementation, if not openly resisted. Jiangsu province, particularly, complained Shandong's networking with the central leaders.[41]

For example, in 1986, the Fengle village of Peixian submitted one statement to Weishan county, declaring that although the State Council in 1984 had demanded the Fengle village to give up its right over lake resources, but the State Council had failed to provide adequate compensation, thus the village asserted that it still owned the right over lake resources. The village mobilized a strong force ready to act. To prevent any possible armed conflicts, Fengle village sent the formal notice to Weishan county. Between October and December 1986, two large-scale fire arsenals and several armed fights broke out, 32,000 mu reeds were burned and 14 people were injured.[42] Such feud grew more intense. For example, in June 1990, Fengle village organized hundreds of residents, more than forty tractors, and hundreds of vehicles, rushed to harvest the crops of disputed lakeside land. Residents from Weishan county intervened, which led to an armed fight. Three Fengle residents were shot dead. The dead's families refused to bury the bodies, demanded criminal investigation, and made several appeals to Beijing. Three years later, Beijing sent down delegates to persuade the families to cremate the bodies and paid the families financial compensation. But the murderers could not be identified, so local court sentenced two suspects two years in prison to calm the Peixian residents. The feud intensified further.

In the late 1990s, when the central government was surveying the land to define the borders, disputes over Lake Weishan got worse. In August 2000, seven Fengle villagers shot one Weishan resident dead. Two months later, more than twenty Fengle villagers, armed by military rifles and hunting guns, shot three people in Weishan county to death. These incidents alarmed Beijing. The minister of civil affairs decided not to include the Lake Weishan area in the mapping project, stating that it was necessary to get consent from cadres of different ranks, particularly at the county and township level, before the border was defined.[43] Therefore, there was no definite border between Shandong and Jiangsu over Lake Weishan. It remains so today.[44]

Conclusion

Disputes over Lake Weishan reveal a variety of forms of political corruptions in China. First of all, they exposed the CCP's long trend of making arbitrary decisions regardless of local customs. The Lake Weishan area had long been a hotbed for armed fights and territorial disputes; mutual distrusts and animosity were widespread between residents of Peixian and of Shandong. Yet Shandong provincial leaders cared little about the history. They did not bother to consult with local residents, simply decided to create a new county in charge of the lake area, which was at odds with the tradition. After the plan was approved by Beijing and Weishan county was established, it became extremely difficult to amend it.

In the long course of disputes, the absence of legal intervention was astonishing. In the early 1950s, following the Soviet system, the CCP established a legal system composed of three major branches: the public security, the public Procuratorate, and the court. The public Procuratorate had functions of prosecuting criminal cases, prosecuting public officials' wrongdoing as well as monitoring law enforcement. But in the late 1950s, the CCP downplayed the function of public Procuratorate. At the county levels, the three branches were integrated into "area responsibility," in which one agency took charge of affairs previously under the three jurisdictions, often that agency was the police chief.[45] Police chiefs followed the instructions of local governments. Public Procuratorate rarely prosecuted any party officials. Hence local governments were often the sole authority. Whenever disputes occurred in Lake Weishan, for example, local residents either appealed to local governments or took care of things by themselves, they rarely filed lawsuits in the courts.

Governments, from townships to provincial level, seldom, if not never, bothered to consult courts. Only when death or severe injuries were incurred, police would investigate, and courts may pursue trials. However, it was again often local governments' decisions on how to investigate and how to judge. Predominately, the legislation systems of Weishan and Peixian counties tended to endorse their own side, colliding with each other on the jurisdiction, and often hampering each other's investigations. As a result, it was extremely difficult to investigate those armed fights. Many suspects of the mass violence were not justly prosecuted at all.[46]

At the very top level, CCP leaders in Beijing liked to bend the law as they saw fit. When they attempted to interfere the disputes, they were inclined to diminish the legal responsibility, particularly to the cold cases. For example, in 1981, Vice Premier Yang Jingren instructed that the past violence during the disputes could be handled with mercy although the future murderers shall be sentenced more strictly. In 1983, Cui Naifu asserted that the murderers from the old time could be overlooked, only the cases of the past two years shall be investigated. In 1984, the tone turned even softer. The State Council stated that for the injuries and death cases over the lake disputes since 1978, with the exception of some intentional murders, no criminal investigation shall be carried out.[47] Those statements boldly violated the legal principle that "there shall be laws to abide by, everyone should abide by the law, the law must be enforced strictly, and those who violate the law must be dealt with,"[48] but no one questioned them. Local residents, aware of the likelihood of getting away from criminal investigation, grew more violent, hence more injuries and murders ensued.

One form of corruption was nepotism and native connections. The CCP had established the base areas in Shandong province long before in Jiangsu province, thus more high-ranking CCP officials were from Shandong province than from Jiangsu. The best examples were Wan Li and Yang Jingren, both vice premiers in the early 1980s and both have ruled in favor of Shandong province over the disputes. Here comes one of the major drawbacks of the communist bureaucracy: it relied on personal networks rather than being an impersonal bureaucracy. A modern bureaucracy is supposed to be an impersonal, rule-governed administration.[49] But the Communist system under Mao was not. Some of this phenomenon must have been derived from history: in China's imperial past, power had been vested in a system run by personnel. But predominately, China's Communist system was rooted in the "mobile networks of personal links," a feature of the Soviet system.[50]

The deeper problem was whom Chinese officials served. In China, Communist officials were, and still are, labeled "People's Servant" and supposed to "serve the people." But in reality often the opinions of the people mattered little. The promotions of government officials were nominated by the superiors, thus the most crucial requirement for promotion was to develop the support of a network, preferably superiors and even leading politicians. Personal networks and patron-client ties were crucial to understand the operation of communist system.[51] But at times, the dynamic between "serve the people" and "serve the superiors" gets more complicated. Chinese officials now and then switched their loyalties between the local people, the superiors, and other factors. The case of disputes over Lake Weishan exhibits several such turns.

In the early 1950s, Chinese Communist regime was penetrating the society. A series of political, economic, and cultural movements were launched to establish a top-down political system and nurture communist ideology. Private ownership of land and property carried stigma and could be dangerous. Agricultural cooperativization was underway. Thus local residents' aspirations for land and wealth were curbed substantially. During this period, the water level of Lake Weishan kept rising, it submerged more lakeside land and created none, thus the land was not as much of a source of contention. It seems that at this stage, local residents, cadres at village, county, municipal, and provincial levels all bended to the orders from above. They were willing to serve the interests of the "public" as Beijing represented. Under the spirit of Great Leap Forward, Shandong province launched the Erjiba Dam project, which completely changed the ecological environment, created new lakeside land. Meanwhile, the chaos in the Great Leap Forward and the following Great Famine substantially impaired local people's faith in the government. In the early 1960s, the People's Commune Movement waned, but the communes remained and became the basic political and economic units that controlled production materials and protected their members. Disillusioned by the communist ideology and having witnessed much of the hunger and death, many communes had learned to define and defend their own interests. As new lakeside land emerged, villages (or communes) often armed by their own militias, became the major force to claim the source. Cadres at county levels, for example, those of Weishan and Peixian counties, chose to side with villages under their jurisdictions, but not firmly. Officials at the provincial level were still loyal to the orders from above. For example, in 1959, Jiangsu province forced Peixian county to make self-criticism and to withdraw the latter's claim of lakeside land, and Peixian county submitted.

As the conflicts intensified, local communities got more involved, grew bolder, and began to defy their superiors. Political chaos in China in the 1960s–1970s further weakened the central authority and strengthened the local interest groups. As the Cultural Revolution commenced, government authority plunged and the officials themselves could've easily become victims of people's power. Local people grew more violently and used armed force to defend, or expand, their interests. Out of desperation, Beijing appointed local armies to intervene, who knew little about the local conditions and failed the mission as well. At this stage, officials at the county level had switched their loyalties to local interests, willing to resist orders from their superiors. As Deng's Reform began, even provincial governments joined the counties to defend the local interests, constantly defying the orders from Beijing.[52]

The disputes over Lake Weishan demonstrate how local governments at different levels had changed their loyalties, redefined their job description, and acted accordingly, in order to get promoted or to simply survive. Such activities, in my opinion, were the main form of corruptions under Mao's China.

NOTES

1. Ministry of Civil Affairs and National Administration of Surveying, Mapping and Geoinformation ed., *1:400 wan zhonghua renmin gongheguo xingzheng quhuatu* (1:400 Map of the Administrative Divisions of the PRC) (Beijing: Zhongguo ditu chubanshe, 2002).

2. "Guanyu chuban 1:400 wan zhonghua renmin gongheguo xingzheng quhuatu youguan wenti de tongzhi" (Notification on the relevant issues concerning the publication of the Map of Administrative Divisions of the People's Republic of China, November 8, 2002. See Lei Tian, "Centralized-Minimalist Government: The Lake Weishan Issue and the Chinese Mediatory System of Government," in *The History and Theory of Legal Practice in China: Toward a Historical-Social Jurisprudence*, eds. Philip C.C. Huang and Kathryn Bernhardt (Leiden: Brill Academic Pub, 2014), 311.

3. Ting Gong, *The Politics of Corruption in Contemporary China: An Analysis of Policy Outcomes* (Westport, CT: Praeger Publishers), 8.

4. Xiaobo Lu, *Cadres and Corruption: The Organizational Involution of the Chinese Communist Party* (Stanford: Stanford University Press, 2000), 12.

5. Ting Gong, *The Politics of Corruption in Contemporary China,* 153.

6. Shandong sheng weishan xian defang shizhi bianzhuan weiyuanhui ed., *Weishanhu zhi* (Local History of Lake Weishan) (Shandong: Huanghe chubanshe, 2010), introduction.

7. *Weishanhu zhi,* 2–3.

8. Jining shi zhengxie wenshi ziliao weiyuanhui he Weishan xian zhengxie wenshi ziliao weiyuan hui eds., *Weishan hu* (Lake Weishan) (Shandong, 1990), 6–7.

9. Hou Yangjun and Zhangbo, "Weishanhu ximian yimin shulue" (Brief summary of the immigration of the westside of Lake Weishan), *Qilu Journal*, 1992, no. 2, 110–14.

10. Hou Yangjun and Zhangbo, "Weishanhu ximian yimin shulue."

11. Hu Qiwei, *Minguo yilai Yi Shu Si liuyu huanjing bianqian yu shuili jiufen (Water environment variance and water conservancy/irrigation works dissension in Yi, Shu and Si drainage area since Republic of China)*, Dissertation, Fudan University, 2007, 86–87.

12. Hou Yangjun and Zhangbo, "Weishanhu ximian yimin shulue."

13. Hu Qiwei, *Minguo yilai Yi Shu Si liuyu huanjing bianqian yu shuili jiufen,* 111.

14. According to the analysis of CCP's 19th Congress member, out of 204 members, 30 of them were from Shandong province, which exceeded all other provinces in China. Such a dominance was rooted in early years of the PRC, because Shandong province was the old liberated region and supplied many cadres to conquer south China, then stayed and administrated south. http://www.worldjournal.com/5243930/article-%E3%80%9019%E5%A4%A7%E3%80%91%E4%B8%AD%E5%A7%94%E7%B1%8D%E8%B2%AB-%E5%B1%B1%E6%9D%B1%E5%8D%A030%E4%BA%BA%E6%8E%92%E7%AC%AC%E4%B8%80/, access November 12, 2017.

15. Shandong sheng defang shizhi bianzhuan weiyuanhui ed., *Shandongsheng zhi—minzheng zhi* (Local History of Shandong Province: Civil Affairs) (Shandong: Shandong remin chubanshe, 1992), 341.

16. 1 mu = 1/6 acre.

17. Ding Xiujuan, *Jianguo hou Weishanhu diqu de shengji hutian huchan jiufen qingkuang yanjiu* (The Study of interprovincial disputes about lake farmland and lake productions in the Weishan Lake area after the foundation of the new China), Master's thesis, Shandong University, 2007.

18. Hu Qiwei, *Minguo yilai Yi Shu Si liuyu huanjing bianqian yu shuili jiufen*, 119.

19. *Weishan hu,* 37.

20. *Weishan hu*, 49–53.

21. *Weishan hu*, 49–53.

22. Rongxing Guo, *Cross-Border Resource Management*, 201.

23. Ding Xiujuan, *Jianguo hou Weishanhu diqu de shengji hutian huchan jiufen qingkuang yanjiu*, 23.

24. Hu Qiwei, *Minguo yilai Yi Shu Si liuyu huanjing bianqian yu shuili jiufen*, 120.

25. Hu Qiwei, *Minguo yilai Yi Shu Si liuyu huanjing bianqian yu shuili jiufen,* 120.

26. Ding Xiujuan, *Jianguo hou Weishanhu diqu de shengji hutian huchan jiufen qingkuang yanjiu*, 23.

27. Ding Xiujuan, *Jianguo hou Weishanhu diqu de shengji hutian huchan jiufen qingkuang yanjiu*, 46.

28. Hu Qiwei, *Minguo yilai Yi Shu Si liuyu huanjing bianqian yu shuili jiufen*, 107–108.

29. Hu Qiwei, *Minguo yilai Yi Shu Si liuyu huanjing bianqian yu shuili jiufen*, 124.

30. Ding Xiujuan, *Jianguo hou Weishanhu diqu de shengji hutian huchan jiufen qingkuang yanjiu,* 47.

31. Chen Zhong-yuan, "Historical analysis of conflict and harmony in Weishan Lake region," *Journal of US-China Public Administration*, 2008, 5, 34.

32. Hu Qiwei, *Minguo yilai Yi Shu Si liuyu huanjing bianqian yu shuili jiufen*, 128.
33. Hu Qiwei, *Minguo yilai Yi Shu Si liuyu huanjing bianqian yu shuili jiufen*, 128–29.
34. Ding Xiujuan, *Jianguo hou Weishanhu diqu de shengji hutian huchan jiufen qingkuang yanjiu*, 24.
35. Chen Zhong-yuan, "Historical analysis of conflict and harmony in Weishan Lake region," *Journal of US-China Public Administration,* 34.
36. Hu Qiwei, *Minguo yilai Yi Shu Si liuyu huanjing bianqian yu shuili jiufen*, 129.
37. Ding Xiujuan, *Jianguo hou Weishanhu diqu de shengji hutian huchan jiufen qingkuang yanjiu*, 26.
38. Hu Qiwei, *Minguo yilai Yi Shu Si liuyu huanjing bianqian yu shuili jiufen*, 130–33.
39. Rongxing Guo, *Cross-Border Resource Management*, 217.
40. "Comrade Wanli's Speech at the Meeting of Report Delivered by Comrade Cui Naifu of Minister of Civil Affairs on the Issues Concerning the Resolution of the Disputes over lake Weishan," recorded material provided by office of Lakeside land, Peixian county, cited from Rongxing Guo, *Cross-Border Resource Management*, 211.
41. "Comrade Wanli's Speech at the Meeting of Report Delivered by Comrade Cui Naifu of Minister of Civil Affairs on the Issues Concerning the Resolution of the Disputes over lake Weishan," recorded material provided by office of Lakeside land, Peixian county, cited from Rongxing Guo, *Cross-Border Resource Management*, 210–14.
42. Ding Xiujuan, *Jianguo hou Weishanhu diqu de shengji hutian huchan jiufen qingkuang yanjiu*, 31.
43. Ding Xiujuan, *Jianguo hou Weishanhu diqu de shengji hutian huchan jiufen qingkuang yanjiu*, 34–35.
44. Ding Xiujuan, *Jianguo hou Weishanhu diqu de shengji hutian huchan jiufen qingkuang yanjiu*, 31–35.
45. Xiaobo Lu, *Cadres and Corruption: The Organizational Involution of the Chinese Communist Party*, 79–80.
46. Ding Xiujuan, *Jianguo hou Weishanhu diqu de shengji hutian huchan jiufen qingkuang yanjiu*, 42.
47. Ding Xiujuan, *Jianguo hou Weishanhu diqu de shengji hutian huchan jiufen qingkuang yanjiu*, 48.
48. The Third Plenary Session of Eleventh Central Committee of the CCP published the guideline which has been widely accepted as the fundamental legal principle.
49. Joseph Strayer, *On the Medieval Origins of the Modern State* (Princeton, NJ: Princeton University Press, 1970).
50. Gail Kligman and Katherine Verdery, *Peasants under Siege: The Collectivization of Romanian Agriculture, 1949–1962* (Princeton, NJ: Princeton University Press, 2011), 189.
51. Xiaojia Hou, *Negotiating Socialism in Rural China—Mao, Peasants, and Local Cadres in Shanxi 1949–1953* (Ithaca, NY: Cornell East Asia Series, 2016).
52. Chen Zhong-yuan, "Historical Analysis of Conflict and Harmony in Weishan Lake Region."

BIBLIOGRAPHY

Chen, Zhong-yuan. "Historical analysis of conflict and harmony in Weishan Lake region." *Journal of US-China Public Administration,* 2008, 5.

Ding, Xiujuan. *Jianguo hou Weishanhu diqu de shengji hutian huchan jiufen qingkuang yanjiu* (The Study of interprovincial disputes about lake farmland and lake productions in the Weishan Lake area after the foundation of the new China). Master's thesis. Shandong University, 2007.

Gong, Ting. *The Politics of Corruption in Contemporary China: An Analysis of Policy Outcomes.* Westport, Connecticut: Praeger Publishers, 1994.

Guo, Rongxing. *Cross-Border Resource Management, Volume 10.* Netherland: Elsevier Science, 2005.

Hou, Xiaojia. *Negotiating Socialism in Rural China—Mao, Peasants, and Local Cadres in Shanxi 1949–1953.* Ithaca, New York: Cornell East Asia Series, 2016.

Hou, Yangjun and Zhang Bo. "Weishanhu ximian yimin shulue" (Brief summary of the immigration of the westside of Lake Weishan). *Qilu Journal*, 1992, no. 2.

Hu, Qiwei. *Minguo yilai Yi Shu Si liuyu huanjing bianqian yu shuili jiufen* (Water environment variance and water conservancy/irrigation works dissension in Yi, Shu and Si drainage area since Republic of China). Dissertation. Fudan University, 2007.

Jining shi zhengxie wenshi ziliao weiyuanhui he Weishan xian zhengxie wenshi ziliao weiyuan hui, eds. *Weishan hu* (Lake Weishan). Shandong: Jining shi diyi yinshuchang, 1990.

Kligman, Gail and Katherine Verdery. *Peasants under Siege: The Collectivization of Romanian Agriculture, 1949–1962.* Princeton, NJ: Princeton University Press, 2011.

Lu, Xiaobo. *Cadres and Corruption: The Organizational Involution of the Chinese Communist Party.* Stanford: Stanford University Press, 2000.

Ministry of Civil Affairs and National Administration of Surveying, Mapping and Geoinformation, ed. *1:400 wan zhonghua renmin gongheguo xingzheng quhuatu* (1:400 Map of the Administrative Divisions of the PRC). Beijing: Zhongguo ditu chubanshe, 2002.

Shandong sheng difang shizhi bianzhuan weiyuanhui, ed. *Shandongsheng zhi—minzheng zhi* (Local History of Shandong Province: Civil Affairs). Shandong: Shandong remin chubanshe, 1992.

Shandong sheng weishan xian defang shizhi bianzhuan weiyuanhui, ed. *Weishanhu zhi* (Local History of Lake Weishan). Shandong: Huanghe chubanshe, 2010.

Strayer, Joseph. *On the Medieval Origins of the Modern State.* Princeton, NJ: Princeton University Press, 1970.

Tian, Lei. "Centralized-Minimalist Government: The Lake Weishan Issue and the Chinese Mediatory System of Government." In *The History and Theory of Legal Practice in China: Toward a Historical-Social Jurisprudence*, eds. Philip C.C. Huang and Kathryn Bernhardt, 309–43. Leiden: Brill Academic Pub, 2014.

Chapter 7

Power versus Law

Anticorruption in Shaanxi during Jiang Zemin's Era

Dongyu Yang

CHINA'S ERA OF JIANG ZEMIN

China in the 1980s was in an awkward phase of rapid market economic development accompanied by an inherent planned economic model, also known as Deng Xiaoping era. Jiang zemin was elected to the standing committee of the Political Bureau of the CPC (Communist Party of China) Central Committee and general secretary of the CPC Central Committee in the Fourth Session of the Thirteenth Plenary Session of the CPC in June 1989. At the Fifth Plenary Session of the 13th CPC Central Committee in November, he was elected chairman of the CPC Central Military Commission at same year. In March 1990, at the third meeting of the Seventh National People's Congress, he was also elected chairman of the Central Military Commission of the People's Republic of China. In March 1993, he was elected president of the People's Republic of China at the first session of the eighth National People's Congress.

Throughout the 1990s, it entered the period of Jiang Zemin, often referred to as the Communist Party's Third-generation Core Leadership.[1] Jiang was also the principal founder of Three Represents Theory.[2] Under his leadership, China's reform and opening up and modernization continue to move forward. Modernization construction has made rapid development in the 1990s, by 2000 the GDP reached more than 1 trillion US dollars, per capita gross domestic product of about $800.[3]

In the 21st century, Jiang Zemin put forward China's three major tasks to be completed and the New Three-step strategy, the construction of the Communist Party of China put forward new requirements for Three Represents

Theory, the formation of new ideas for China's development in the new century. He also made decisions to establish the socialist market economy, the development of the national economic and social development 9th Five-Year plan and the 2010 long-range goal of the proposed.

Based on practical experience since the reform and opening up, he also comprehensively discussed the Twelve Relations that need to be handled correctly in China's economic and social development. In a report at the Fifteenth National Congress of the Communist Party of China, he made a series of major deployments to the twenty-first century to build socialism with Chinese characteristics. Significant progress has been made in the reform of the economic system. It is certain that the common development of various economic components with public ownership is the basic economic system in the primary stage of Chinese socialism. The realization of public ownership can be diversified, and the non-public economy is an important part of the socialist market economy. In the political system reform, to further expand the democracy, to better guarantee the people's democratic election and democratic policy-making, democratic management and democratic supervision, and adhere to lawfully, strive to build a democratic politics of socialism with Chinese characteristics.

In September 2004, the Fourth Plenary Session of the 16th CPC Central Committee adopted a decision to agree to Jiang Zemin's resignation as chairman of the Military Commission of the CPC Central Committee. In March 2005, the second plenary meeting in the 3rd meeting of the Tenth National People's Congress decided to agree to Jiang Zemin's resignation as chairman of the Central Military Commission of the People's Republic of China. During the Jiang Zemin's reign, the fight against corruption also achieved periodic results, for example, the famous corruption case of Chen Xitong, former member of the Political Bureau of the CPC Central Committee and Beijing Municipal Party secretary, was investigated and sentenced in accordance with the law.

Corruption is a social and historical phenomenon. From the point of view of world history, almost all countries that have corruption, also have anticorruption. However, different countries, different historical periods, due to differences in economic development, political systems, historical and cultural traditions, and other aspects, the manifestation and characteristics of corruption are different. In the specific period from the old economic system to the new socialist market economy system, the reform is at the critical stage of the overall promotion and key breakthrough. As the old planned economic system and the new market economic system, the old norms and new norms, the old ideas and new ideas, coexist and collide with each other in quite a period of time, change pattern of rights and interests and in addition, mechanisms, institutions, and the system are imperfect, as well as factors such as poor management and supervision for power transformation and corruption provide a breeding ground for the soil and conditions.

Since 1978, China began to reform and open up, especially after the Chinese 11th CPC Central Committee Third Plenary Session(December 18 to 22, 1978, Beijing) and the 12th National Congress of the Communist Party of China (September 1 to 11, 1982, Beijing), in the future, adhere to the Four Cardinal Principles and the reform and opening up under the overall guidance of the principle, persist in taking economic construction as the center, step by step comprehensive reform and opening up, in various economic, political, defense, and foreign affairs have made significant achievements. Among them, economic construction is particularly prominent. Compared with 1978, the gross domestic product and the average income of both urban and rural residents have roughly doubled. Past nine years have seen the most vigorous economic development, the most rapidly growing national strength, improvement in people's average lifespan since the founding of the People's Republic of China. However, with the rapid economic development and poor social supervision system, corruption has also has also increased and has reached alarming proportions, impeding social progress, economic development, and political stability of public. After just ten years of reform and opening, China has launched a vast national "anticorruption storm."

As with any other countries, corruption is an encumber on China's economic development and a disaster for social stability because it distorts economic decisions and undermines social law, which are crucial points for a stable and prosperous society. Therefore, corruption is intolerable behavior. In his career of a lifetime, Jiang Zemin has fought with corruption in one way or other. He believes that corruption not only will erode people's moral, but also is the biggest stumbling block to China's full potential as a great power.

Jiang Zemin stepped up the fight against corruption during his tenure, and some powerful figures were caught. The owner of one of China's most popular cigarette factories, known as king of China's tobacco, has been sentenced to life imprisonment for embezzling 3.5 million dollars; a deputy minister of public security, the head of the anti-smuggling operation, was arrested on suspicion of colluding with smugglers. The vice governor of Jiangxi province was found to have taken bribes ninety times, an amount of up to $650,000, becoming the highest-ranking official to be executed in China since 1949.

Jiang Zemin played *a key role* during this important event. When the news was broadcast, Xinhua's comments reflected Jiang's view that only the death penalty could be used to defend the country's laws, appease public anger, regroup the party discipline and anticorruption. And he said that in socialist China no person shall be above the law, no special party members can escape the party discipline, and no illegal or criminal, no matter how high-ranking he is and how powerful he is, could not escape legal punishment.

The most shocking corruption cases occurred in the port city of Xiamen, in Fujian province. The case involving smuggling unprecedented number of billions of dollars is huge; it would become the largest scandal in China in the past fifty years. The contraband involved items ranging from fuel oil to shoes to luxury cars, the tariff up to 100 percent, which makes these products particularly popular. Many sectors in CPC, government, military cooperated with this Yuanhua Company, in the most rampant criminal activity period, the company offered a considerable proportion of the fuel to China's entire retail market.

In the anticorruption event, Zhu Rongji (then China's premier) was an ally of Jiang Zemin; he told the investigation team *that to catch a big fish, you have to put the shrimp*. Those who accept small bribes and agreed to cooperate and expose big bosses were to be exempt from punishment. The Discipline Inspection Commission has even established a witness protection system to protect whistleblowers, which is rare in China's judicial system. Zhu's famous quote is: *prepared 100 coffins, 99 loaded corrupt officials, and one more for myself.*[4]

As early as in 2000, in the fifth plenary meeting of the CPC Central Discipline Inspection Commission, Jiang Zemin, Li Peng, Zhu Rongji, Li Ruihuan, Hu Jintao, Li Lanqing, Wei and seven other Politburo Standing Committee members were present, once again a clear declaration that CPC leadership attaches great importance to a clean government and anticorruption work. Jiang Zemin made an important speech at the meeting. In this speech, he required to take new methods and measures for the works of new century. He even published a book *Jiang Zemin on Clean Government and Fight Corruption*[5]. Wu Guanzheng, member of the Standing Committee of the Political Bureau of the CPC Central Committee and the secretary of the Central Discipline Inspection Commission pointed out at the press conference that Jiang Zemin's anticorruption theory is on the basis of summing up the experience of the CPC's history and practical experience. It is a series of important conclusions that an important political task for the whole party is to firmly oppose and prevent corruption, to prevent and control corruption as a systematic project to grasp. This chapter profoundly expounds that the strategic position of the party to build a clean government and its main task of anticorruption work policy and other major problems in the fundamental purpose have important guiding significance.[6]

The Anticorruption Situation of Jiang Zemin Era in Shaanxi Province

Profile of Shaanxi Province

Shaanxi Province, referred to as *Shaan* or *Qin*, is located in the hinterland of China, the middle reaches of the Yellow River, between the eastern longitude

105° 29'–111° 15' and the northern latitude 31°42'–39°35'. Its eastern neighbors are Shanxi and Henan, and its western neighbors are Ningxia and Gansu, in the south it connects to Sichuan, Chongqing, and Hubei, and in the north to Inner Mongolia. It is an important place to connect the eastern, central, northwestern and southwestern regions of China. The geodetic origin of China is in Yongle town, Jingyang county, Shaanxi Province. It has a population of 379.287 million (2016), with a land area of 20.58 million square kilometers.

Shaanxi is one of the important cradles of China and Chinese culture. There were more than ten regimes and dynasties or capitals in Shaanxi, such as the Qin, Han, and Tang dynasties, for more than 1,000 years. Huangdi mausoleum, Terracotta Warriors, Yan'an pagoda, Qinling, and Huashan are the spiritual and natural signs of Chinese civilization, revolution, and geography. High-tech industry, energy chemical industry, national defense technology industry, forest fruit industry, animal husbandry, and tourism are the six leading industries in Shaanxi province.

There have 10 prefecture-level cities, 1 demonstration area, and 107 county-level administrative divisions in Shaanxi province. Shaanxi region is long and narrow, high-lying in the north and south, low in the middle, and has a variety of terrain plateau, mountains, plains, and basins. Qinling Mountains in Shaanxi has many nationally known ridges, such as Huashan, Taibai Mountain, Zhongnanshan, and Lishan. As China's north-south climatic dividing line, the Qinling mountains traverse the whole province.

Shaanxi spans three climatic zones; the climate in the north and south are quite different. The northern Shaanxi has subtropical climate, the Guanzhong region and most other regions north of Shaanxi province have warm temperate climate, and the region along the Great Wall of northern has mesothermal climate. The seasons are as follows: spring is warm and dry, with less precipitation, rapid and unstable temperature rise, and windy and sandy weather; summer is hot and rainy, sometimes there is summer drought; autumn is cool, wetter, and the temperature drops fast; winter is cold and dry, with low temperature and some rain and snow.

The province's annual average temperature is 9 °C–14 °C, from south to north, decreasing from the east to west: in northern Shaanxi it is in the range of 7 °C–12 °C, in the Guanzhong region, 12 °C–14 °C, and in the southern region, 14 °C–16 °C. It has an average annual rainfall of 340–1240 mm. The amount of precipitation in north Shaanxi is less than that in the south. Southern Shaanxi is a moist area, Guanzhong region is a semi-moist area, and northern Shaanxi is a semiarid area.[7]

Administrative Division of Shaanxi Province

Shaanxi province has jurisdiction over 10 prefecture-level cities, 1 demonstration area, and 107 county-level administrative divisions.

Xi ‘an city has jurisdiction over eleven municipal districts and two counties, they are Xincheng District, BeilinDistrict, Lianhu District, Yanta District, Weiyang District, Baqiao District, Yanliang District, Lintong District, Chang’an District, Gaoling District, Huyi District, Zhouzhi County, and Lantian County. Baoji city has jurisdiction over three municipal districts and nine counties, they are Weibin District, Jintai District, Chencang District, Fengxiang County, Qishan County, Fufeng County, Mei County, Long County, Qianyang County, Linyou County, Feng County, and Taibai County. Xianyang city has jurisdiction over two municipal districts, a county-level city, and ten counties, they are Qindu District, Weicheng District, Xingping City, Sanyuan County, Jingyang County, Qian County, Liquan County, Yongshou County, Bin County, Changwu County, Chunhua County, Xunyi County, and Wugong County. Tongchuan city has jurisdiction over three municipal districts and one county, they are Wangyi District, Yintai District, Yaozhou District, and Yijun County. Weinan city has jurisdiction over two municipal districts, seven counties, and two county-level cities, they are Linwei District, Hancheng City, Huayin City, Huazhou District, Tongguan County, Dali County, Heyang County, Chengcheng County, Pucheng County, Baishui County, and Fuping County. Yan’an city has jurisdiction over two municipal districts and eleven counties, they are Baota District, Ansai District, Yanchang County, Yanchuan County, Zichang County, Zhidan County, Wuqi County, Ganquan County, Fu County, Luochuan County, Yichuan County, Huanglong County, and Huangling County. Yulin city has jurisdiction over two municipal districts, a county-level city, and nine counties, they are Yuyang District, Hengshan District, Shenmu City, Fugu County, Jingbian County, Dingbian County, Suide County, Mizhi County, Jia County, Wubao County, Qingjian County, and Zizhou County. Hanzhong city has jurisdiction over two municipal districts and nine counties, they are Hantai District, Nanzheng District, Chenggu County, Yang County, Xixiang County, Mian County, Ningqiang County, Lueyang County, Zhenba County, Liuba County, and Foping County. Ankang city has jurisdiction over one municipal district and nine counties, they are Hanbin District, Hanyin County, Shiquan County, Ningshan County, Ziyang County, Langao County, Pingli County, Zhenping County, Xunyang County, and Baihe County. Shangluo city has jurisdiction over one municipal district and six counties, they are Shangzhou District, Luonan County, Danfeng County, Shangnan County, Shanyang County, Zhenan County, and Zhashui County. Yangling Demonstration Zone has jurisdiction over one district: Yangling District.[8]

The Rebuilding and Establishment of the Anticorruption Agency in Shaanxi

In the late 1980s, the CPC Central Committee decided to fight against corruption according to the actual situation, and restored the country’s administrative supervision system accordingly. After arrested some corrupt government officials in the early of new China, such as Liu Qingshan, Zhang Zishan, etc. the corruption actions have been generally restricted. According to the experiments, the Central Committee of CPC took anti-corruption works as the top priority of with strict, heavy and quick investigation, and deployed for anti-corruption work. During his tenure as the general secretary of CPC, Jiang Zemin visited Shaanxi four times and gave encouragement and support for anticorruption work in Shaanxi province. In terms of anticorruption, the country not only invested a lot of resources significantly; but also increased efforts to punish corruption, so with the number of investigations rising, the estimated number of corruption cases and the corruption level have become high.

Since the Third Plenary Session of the 11th CPC Central Committee, the CPC Shaanxi Provincial Committee, the CPC Shaanxi Provincial People's Government and the CPC Shaanxi Provincial Commission for Discipline Inspection shall follow the guidelines, policies and work arrangements of the Central Committee for Discipline Inspection of the CPC Central Committee on anti-corruption works, at same time, they will combine with the actual situations on Shaanxi, and pay special attention to the economic construction, then will strengthen party conduct and clean government, conscientiously fulfill the four functions of "protecting, punishing, supervising and education", and maintain political stability, promote reform and opening up to ensure the sound development of economic development. Thus, the discipline inspection departments at all levels are restored and strengthened. November 12, 1978, the CPC Shaanxi Provincial Committee decided to set up the CPC Shaanxi Provincial Temporary Commission for Discipline Inspection, then on December 1, Shaanxi Provincial Party Committee issued a circular requiring local, municipal, and county party committees and enterprises government above the county level set up the party's discipline inspection commission.

In April 1983, according to the notice of the CPC, Shaanxi Provincial Temporary Commission for Discipline Inspection was changed to the Discipline Inspection Commission of Shaanxi Province and was one of the six provincial leaders of the provincial government. On April 17, 1983, Luo Wenzhi was elected the secretary of the Discipline Inspection Commission of Shaanxi Province. On June 15, 1983, the provincial party committee forwarded the report of the Discipline Inspection Commission of Shaanxi Province on strengthening the organization of discipline inspection at all levels, demand for real reinforcement the organization construction of the discipline inspection departments at all levels, improve discipline inspection at all levels of the organization; enrich the cadres of power in discipline inspection departments at all levels; strengthen leadership at all levels of commission for discipline Inspection. On March 4, 1985, the provincial commission forwarded *the views of the Discipline Inspection Commission of Shaanxi Province and the Organization Department of the Provincial Party Committee on strengthening the organizational construction of the province's discipline inspection institution* and *the Discipline Inspection Commission of Shaanxi Province report on a few specific issues of strengthening discipline inspection work*, the requirements were as follows: (1) equip leaders and strengthen the leadership, according to the Central demand; (2) perfect discipline inspection institution and improve the quality of the discipline inspection team; (3) improve working conditions of discipline inspection institutions. During this period, the province's discipline inspection work had gradually improved and become sound.[9]

The Major Steps to Carry Out Anticorruption from 1988 to 2003

In 1988, the Discipline Inspection Commission of Shaanxi Province, after three months of full investigation, submitted to the Shaanxi Provincial Party Committee the report on *the work style building in the province*. According to the report, in addition to the objective historical reasons, the growth and spread of corruption has another important reason: we haven't established a set of effective under the trade (market) economic conditions, management practices and supervision and control mechanism. After the reform and opening up, the old planned economy system did not adapt. In the new situation, establishment of a new supervision and restraint system is the fundamental measure and guarantee to carry out against corruption. According to the report, the Shaanxi Provincial Party Committee developed *a decision to keep the non-corrupt,* while the provincial people's government also formulated and issued a decision on *building a non-corrupt government*, formed the original integrity of the codes and the provisions of the political party and government offices. After *the decision to keep the non-corrupt* was issued, the cities and countries all over the province formulated the relevant rules; this is the initial start of a clean and disciplined work.

In 1988, the Shaanxi Provincial Party Committee and People's Government has laid out the work ideas about the construction of clean government, system construction and mechanism construction, then they put the mechanism construction in a prominent position, namely paid special attention to *two open and one oversight* as the main content of *one line, one area, one point and one school* (one line means Fertilizer monopoly line in the province, one area means Baoji municipal party and government organs, one point means Xi 'an Xincheng district basic management departments, law enforcement departments, and utilities departments, one school means Xi 'an Petroleum Institute) of experimental works, the relevant measures such as open and check, report, investigate were introduced into the experimental works.

In early 1990, the Shaanxi Provincial Party Committee and People's Government decided to comprehensively promote the experimental experiences in building a clean government system and mechanism, focus on building the clean government in the courtyard of the Shaanxi Provincial Party Committee and People's Government, the eight industry sectors such as bank, taxation, industry and commerce, electric power, public security, food, water conservancy, supply and marketing, as well as ten areas/places that the local, city party and governments were located in.

In 1991, it further expanded the construction of the anticorruption system to twenty-two key industries, all achieved good results and provided the practical basis for the mechanism of anticorruption. In early 1992, the Discipline Inspection Commission and Supervision Department of Shaanxi Province summarized the working experience in previous years, starting with the functional structure and running program of anticorruption work, they focused on the institutional measures adopted in the construction of clean government, in particular, the report on the implementation of the report system and the open system above the county level in the whole region is summarized, so that the four systems have been formed:

1. Reporting system for leading cadres and their families on major issues;
2. People's understanding and supervision system for matters related to the masses and party committees, governments and relevant functional departments;
3. Review system for the state organs and their staff;
4. Party conduct clean and government construction responsibility system.

The Discipline Inspection Commission and Supervision Department of Shaanxi Province wrote a special report on this to the CPC Shaanxi Provincial Committee. The four terms reporting system is the result of summarizing the experiments of the Discipline Inspection Commission and Supervision Department of Shaanxi Province, it is also the inevitable outcome of the reform. Its universal implementation has brought good results not only to the construction of the provincial clean government, but also to the construction of anticorruption mechanism in Shaanxi which is at the forefront of the country.[10]

In 1992, it set up and implemented the avoidance system of party and government organs' leader and cadres in Shaanxi province, to overcome the phenomenon of *husband and wife working in same office, father and son using same room in the office, grandson giving his grandfather tea to drink, and relatives by marriage using one table*, these are not conducive to the construction of clean government and the scientific management of cadres. This system contents are mainly three points:

1) avoidance of assignment: it rules the leaders in the party committee, the government, the commission for discipline inspection, public security, court, procuratorate, and the leadership position of cadres; relatives of superiors

may not serve in direct subordinate positions to superiors generally they may not work in the same department.

2) avoidance of the public affair: it rules the leaders of the party and government organs shall not participate in any business work related to their appointment or dismissal or file management of cadres, nor shall they direct or imply the influence or intervention of others. In the work of cadre appointment and dispensing, salary raise, party membership, assess to title, appraisal and recruitment, if the person involved is a relative of a leading cadre they should be avoided or else active explanation should be provided.

3) avoidance of rural cadastral: the avoidance system is also recognized by the central government and implemented nationwide.[11]

In 1993, the whole country to earnestly and substantially implement No. 6 document of Central Committee of the CPC, according to the spirit of the second plenary session of Central Committee for Discipline Inspection of CPC and the third plenary session of the 14th CPC Central Committee carried out anticorruption struggle, supported the key projects, and promoted the reform and opening up development, which then achieved obvious results. From September to December 1993, national discipline inspection and supervision organs completely closed 48,794 cases within the Party, gave disciplinary action against 42,195 people, including three provincial-level cadres, 69 hall (bureau) level cadres, 1,143 county (division) level cadres. And government closed 15,172 cases, gave administrative disciplinary to 16,169 people, including 22 hall (bureau) level cadres, and 271 county (division) level cadres. The national procuratorial organ seized 6,790 cases of embezzlement and bribery involving over 10,000 yuan (RMB); this is a 2.1 times increase compared to that over the same period in 1992. The number of crimes involving embezzlement of more than 50,000 yuan was 1,748; this is a rise of 2.7 times compared to that over the same period in 1992. There were 715 cases of economic crimes at the county level or above, 6.8 times more than that over the same period in 1992, including 61 in the office (bureau) level, 11 times that over the same period in 1992. The court accepted 13,110 cases of economic crimes, an increase of 25.67 percent from 1992.[12]

The Influential Anticorruption Cases in Shaanxi

1. On August 26, 1993, the party group of the People's Bank of Shaanxi province held an enlarged party committee, then in late September, they convened a meeting of the secretaries of the Party Leadership Group and head of discipline inspection group in the whole Shaanxi people's bank system in order to organize and deploy the anticorruption struggle of the Shaanxi people's banking system.

a. The party groups on multiple levels of province, city, and county have held democratic consultations, then the members of division level and above cadres took the self-examinations. During the self-examination for the division level and above cadres, the cadres took part-time job within the industry, bought company's stocks, accepted securities, souvenirs, native products and entertain during their works. According to the requirements, those problems made promptly corrected.
b. The financial systems in the province has been carefully checked all the charges since last year, identified a total of 28 projects arbitrary charges, the cumulative amount of 960,000 yuan. Cancel "lending credit assessment fees" and other fourteen items fees, to the end of this year, it checked and returned the amount of 36,900 yuan.
c. People's Bank of Shaanxi provinces and the specialized banks jointly organized six inspection teams; a special inspection was conducted on six local and city banks and twelve county branches of the bank to effectively stop and correct the arbitrary charges.
d. To investigate of key economic cases in the financial system of the province. By the end of 1993, the province's People's Bank investigation and all kinds of economic cases were eleven cases, completely closed four cases, the transfer of the judiciary four cases, three cases are being investigated.[13]

2. In 1993, Xi'an Lianhu district committee and district government of Shaanxi province issued the notice on "the recent strengthening of the anticorruption and clean government to promote the implementation of views" and "the eight measures for the integrity and self-discipline of leaders in the district level," asking leading cadres to self-check, and hold timely investigations and punish all kinds of illegal and disciplinary cases. By the end of 1993, there were thirteen cases investigated in the whole district; except one case which was transferred to be dealt with in the relative unit, nine cases were completely closed related to nine persons, of which six persons were given punishments by the Party discipline agencies and two persons faced expulsion from the Party. Fourteen departments were identified to be involved in arbitrary charges, involving a cumulative amount of 1,090,000 yuan. A total of thirty-eight projects facing arbitrary charges were canceled and an amount of 710,000 yuan was returned. A total number of thirty-seven unqualified city management staff and coordinators was dismissed. The three fine collecting units were gotten rid of in Erfu street, Western gate and Yuxiang gate. These problems were solved that the Party and government organs separated with its subordinate economic entities, and Party and government officials work part-time in economic entities. The Party and government officials who use public funds to travel abroad have been cleaned up.[14]

3. On September 17, 1993, the Water Resources Department of Shaanxi Province held a meeting of cadres above the level of division head, and made the concrete deployment of anticorruption:
   a. The officers above the level of division-head should firmly adhere to the discipline requirements of the "five forbids,"[15] and conscientiously carry out self-inspection.
   b. Check and completely close two to three major and important cases.
   c. Clean-up and stop all sorts of arbitrary charges as well as the unhealthy practice of public funds from (border) tourism.
   d. Deepen the water "321" clean system,[16] and implement billing the home, effectively reducing unreasonable burden on farmers to irrigate.

In addition, the cases of Yang Feng, former deputy director of the Shaanxi Provincial Economic Commission, who misappropriated 4.22 million yuan of public funds to do business for their families and of Zhao Jingzhang, former director of the Shaanxi Provincial Economic Commission, who was involved in trading of money and power to illegal groups abroad resulting in twenty-three people running away were being investigated.

The Anticorruption Situation in Xi'an

In 1994, Xi 'an Customs established a leadership team for clean government construction, and hired several special supervisors for clean construction of the Customs, issued *the Selected Documents of Clean Government Rules*, so that the leaders of departments lead by example to be anti-corruptible and exercise self-control, and conscientiously accept the inspection and guidance of local party and government leaders and enhance the integrity of the whole staff. When the anticorruption work inspection team of the provincial party committee and the provincial government went to the Customs office to inspect the anticorruption work, they think this unit is very distinctive and has typical significance, because it can focus on the industry characteristics, and not only improve the customs officer's quality, but also pay attention to the establishment of regulations, then organically combine the construction of clean government with the reform of customs business and modern technology management.[17]

In 1995, Xi'an anticorruption works had made new progress. The city discipline inspection organs handled a total of 9,393 cases (the masses petitioning and reporting cases), thereinto, 1,666 cases were preliminarily reviewed, and 1,337 cases were completely closed; 345 cases were on file for investigation out of which 266 cases were completely closed. In new cases on file for investigation, there were 5 cases of bureau-level cadres, 18 cases of county and division-head level cadres. Party and administration disciplinary measures were taken against 274 persons in whole city, including Party disciplinary measures against 154 persons, administration disciplinary measures against 169 persons, punishment for 12 cadres above the county level, transfer to judicial organs and criminal processing for 14 people; direct economic losses of 6.17 million yuan were incurred. Between 1991 and 1995, during the 8th five-year plan, the city discipline inspection organs handled a total of 48,309 mass petitioning and reporting cases, 1,779 cases were on file for investigation and 1,700 cases were completely closed. Party disciplinary punishments were given to 1,520 people, of which 66 cadres were above the county level.[18]

In May 1995, the municipal Party committee and government issued the file of "the notice to strictly prohibit and stop recreational activities and banquet using public funds." The departments of each district, county, and city level made some corresponding systems. Late May and late September, the municipal commission for discipline inspection organized public security, supervision, culture, industry and commerce departments to conduct inspections four times, totally checking 126 restaurants and singing clubs, and investigating a few violators. According to inspecting information, the recreational activities and banquets using public funds had been convergent, so that the turnover of those restaurants had decreased by about 30 percent. In 1995, the City Commission for Discipline Inspection, Municipal Supervision Bureau dealt with Liu Xinqian, who was deputy mayor of Gaolin County, standing member of Zhouzhi County Party Committee and executive vice county mayor of Zhouzhi County from 1988 to 1994, because he was involved in embezzlement, accepted bribes, gifts, totaling more than 26,370 yuan. Liu Xinqian was arrested according to law, expelled from the party, and removed from office.

In 1995, the Shaanxi branch of the Bank of China carefully organized cadres above the section-head level in compliance with the "old and new five items"[19] to make self-check and self-correction, then they focused on investigating and punishing the cases that persons used public funds to participate in high-end consumer entertainment activity and occupied over-standard vehicle. They implemented the responsibility system for preventing economic cases, to strengthen security facility, institution building, defense skills training, and other security work; it effectively prevented the occurrence of major and big cases.[20]

In 1996, a clean government construction supervision mechanism was established in Ankang area. They invited 13 enforcement supervisors to listen to mass opinions and suggestions on the police station's enforcement, and convened regular meetings of the enforcement supervisors to solicit opinions from all parties. Police officers signed letters undertaking responsibility to "not violate discipline" and to "not violate the alcohol prohibition," and formulated and launched the police and people's contact card, distributed more than 600 copies to the people, and heard their opinions and suggestions. The internal supervision mechanism should be established every quarter. They set up income and expenditure systems, resolutely eliminate the occurrence of misappropriation of embezzlement, and all the penalties of the whole year, about total of 40,550 yuan, were handled in the financial departments of the district. They actively participated in the activities of "Aimen cup" and the evaluation works, these works are highly valued and fully affirmed by the regional public security department and the higher authorities.[21]

The Anticorruption in Other Regions

In 1997, Traffic Police Jiangbei Squadron of Shaanxi Ankang Municipality implemented the system of police officers hanging their name tag during working time, and widely accepted public supervision. They hired supervisors, set up police discipline report boxes and installed mirrors, all as part of an effort to enhance the policemen's image. Team of police officer's integrity, has rejected more than 3000 yuan in cash, goods rejected six times, refused to entertain 39 times.[22]

From 1997 to 2001, due to the increased surveillance efforts against corruption, achieved good results for investigating cases, the discipline inspection teams of Shaanxi Coal Industry Bureau and Shaanxi Coal safety supervision Bureau were awarded the Shaanxi Provincial Commission for Discipline Inspection "Advanced units for handling cases" title. In this period, the disciplinary inspection department received a total of 1,614 reports from the masses, related to 35 bureau-level cadres and 184 division-head-level cadres. There were 225 cadres punished by Party discipline, including warning for 87 people, serious warning for 67 people, removal from Party posts for 8 people, probation for 29 people, expelling 26 people from the party. There were 267 cadres punished by administration discipline.[23]

In 1998, the anticorruption measures in Shaanxi national tax system (The IRS) were:

1. Clean-up and clearing of public funds to install 425 residential telephones, and with public funds equipped with 698 mobile phones. After the auction and sale for some goods, they recovered the funds 636,000-yuan, annual savings bill 1.0152 million yuan.
2. Strict implementation of the approval system for various meetings, streamlining of the number of meetings, conference expenditure compression, limiting its size, strict implementation of standards and public meetings' settlement costs. According to statistics, the province's tax system canceled (consolidated) 337 conferences or meetings to save funds 1.3223 million yuan.

3. Stopping public funds for entertainment: the amount of entertainment expenses throughout the year in the province's tax system reduced by 14.1 percent compared to the previous year. Carrying out administrative fees rectification work. The State tax authorities at all levels in the province have seriously checked and rectified the administrative institutional fees that have occurred since 1994. Then, they take corresponding measures to correct the problems of fee collection, management, and non-standard use in the inspection.[24]

In 2000, Shanyang County of Shaanxi Province continued to strengthen the work style of cadres, regulated the behavior of political leaders, firmly stopped extravagance and waste, and organized 304 county branches, totally 5,398 party members and cadres, to participate in the warning education events. During this period, there were a total of 128 cases on file for investigation, 123 cases completely closed, and 109 persons punished. Therein, Party disciplinary action was taken against 73 persons, 44 persons were given administration punishment. After handling these cases, they saved 1,562,300 yuan economic losses. In 2001, the county checked and cleared public funds to purchase 24 mobile phones. By discount handling, funds of 6,652 yuan were recovered. They established a special account "20700581" for party members' and cadres' cleaning and self-regulation. Then they recovered 500RMB in this year, the two section-head and five division-head level cadres were carried out the responsibility for accountability. In 2002, because of using public funds to give gifts and misappropriation of project funds, 3 persons were investigated. Two hundred and fifty-seven administrative examination and approval matters were canceled. In combination with the tax reform, township financial funds were collected and paid at the county level. In 2003, they carried out the inspection and correction work in the county, 14 cars should not hang the public security license plate made remediation. They organized educational activities for hard struggle, and canceled reception fee of towns and villages. In 2004, they strived to improve cleanup of four items: They cleaned up arrears of public fund and restaurants 1.3327 million yuan; meanwhile, they cleaned 17 pieces of privately occupied public property, and 7 vehicles that party and government organs and leading cadres' illegal purchased, pick off 35 police plates on non-police vehicles; and the Party and government cadres quitted from part-time jobs in enterprises. Then, they carried out education and rectification activities, and handled the leading cadres they accepted cash, securities and payment vouchers, it is amount 6 cases and returned 3,000yuan.[25]

Special Anticorruption Cases of Shaanxi in 2001

Case 1, On June 22, 2001, the Intermediate People's Court of Baoji city, Shaanxi province, publicly sentenced the defendants Xu Baosheng and Xia

Jialing to death for bribery and embezzlement, at the same time, they were deprived political rights for life. Xu Baosheng was the general manager of Baoji Yigao Industry and Trade Co., Ltd., and Xia Jialing was the general manager of Baoji Financial Securities Co., Ltd. During their tenure, Xu Baosheng and Xia Jialing illegally accepted RMB 3.7 million in cash, while Xu Baosheng illegally accepted RMB 1414.97 million worth of a Rolex watch. The two defendants jointly embezzled 4.7 million yuan of public funds from Baoji Financial Securities Company for profit-making activities of their private companies.[26]

Case 2, In October 2001, Xi 'an Intermediate People's Court handed down the first trial judgment of the former general manager of Wensen Company in Xi 'an Medical University, Xue Dongbo, who used his position to issue fake drug prescriptions and documents to cheat, steal and embezzle 2.45 million yuan of public funds. Xue Dongbo was sentenced to death penalty, a two-year suspension of execution, deprivation of political rights for life, and concurrently confiscate all personal property. During the trial, the court found that from 1994 to 1997, Xue used the name of 76 doctors of the hospital to forge 758 prescriptions for hospitalized patients, which was embezzled by the hospital for more than 1.73 million yuan. In addition, Xue Dongbo also embezzled more than 720,000 yuan of public funds by means of repeated reimbursement and false documents.[27]

Case 3, On October 25, 2001, the Intermediate People's Court of Xianyang city, Shaanxi province, tried the case of Wang Liguang, the former chairman of Rainbow Display Co., Ltd., and Chen Dezhi, the former general manager of Rainbow Display Co., Ltd. Wang Liguang was the chairman of Rainbow Company before he was arrested, Chen Dezhi was the general manager of Rainbow Company before he was arrested. At the beginning of 1993, Wang Liguang told Wang Mou to use the funds to buy shares, Wang Mou was an employee of the Securities Department of the company. In March 1996, Wang Liguang instructions agent Wang to sell shares, and earned RMB 2.91 million. Then Wang Liguang and Chen Dezhi agreed to, in addition to repay the principal and interest of the two factory "slush fund" and stock cost, the rest of the money totally more than 1.325 million yuan were privately divided by Wang Liguang, Chen Dezhi, Zhai, Wang Mou and Wang Mou-mou, Hou Mou, Zhang Guoqiang (the chief accountant of company, he has sentenced because of embezzlement), there eight persons gained 160,000 yuan per person, then it remained 45,000 yuan, Wang Liguang, Chen Dezhi and their families used in their vacation tour.[28]

Case 4, In November 2001, Wang Zhusheng, the former director of the Political Department of the Public Security Bureau of Xi 'an city, Shaanxi province, was sentenced to two years in prison and three years of probation by the first trial of Xi 'an Intermediate People's Court for abuse of power. The court heard that Wang had agreed to release the man, Min Feng, in violation of the law, to work in the secretary section of the political department secretariat of the Public Security Bureau. In December 1999, Wang Zhusheng, even agreed to allow Min Feng to join the Communist Party of China, leading to Min Feng's mixing with the party. In May 2000, Wang also agreed with the Public Security Bureau to propose Min Feng to serve as deputy chief of the secretary section of the secretariat.[29]

Case 5, On November 5, 2001, Xi'an Intermediate People's Court made the first-instance judgment,mainly for Mai Zhaohui, the former Vice President in Bank of China Xi 'an branch, jointly embezzled more than 670,000 yuan of public funds with Zhao Jun, who was the fund cadre of Planning Department in the bank, and on the crime of accepting bribes and huge unidentified property. Mai Zhaohui found guilty of embezzlement, bribery, huge unidentified property, etc., grafted and sentenced to 20 years imprisonment, confiscation of 550,000 yuan. Accomplice Zhao Jun found guilty of corruption, embezzlement of public funds was sentenced to 15 years imprisonment, confiscation of 30,000 yuan. Between 1997 and 1999, Mai Zhaohui corrupted "private coffer" of public funds 67 million yuan together with Zhao Jun by provincial and municipal bank mergers period. Zhao Jun actually got 4.6 million yuan in public funds from corruption, in addition to separate embezzlement of public funds more than 90,000 yuan, embezzlement 740,000 yuan for individuals buying and selling stocks. During be the vice president of the bank, Mai Zhaohui in charge of duties by approving loans convenience, accepting bribes 230,000 yuan, 150,000 US dollars and stock 300,000 yuan (face value). In addition, Mai Zhaohui cannot explain the legal sources about home RMB deposits, securities and foreign currency deposits amounting to 111.8 million yuan and 5,250 Hong Kong dollars.[30]

Case 6, On November 8, 2001, Shaanxi Provincial Public Security Department issued an arrest warrant, offering a reward of 100,000 yuan for catching Yu Meilan, a criminal suspect who absconded with more than 70 million yuan of public funds. Yu Meilan was a retired worker of the Rainbow Group 4400 Factory Labor Service Company. In the second half of 1997, with her husband Wu Weiren (had been arrested), Yu Meilan embezzled more than 70 million yuan for individual stocks, and he fled after the case.[31]

Case 7, On November 12, 2001, Yan'an Intermediate People's Court of Shaanxi Province held a pronouncement in Yan Chang county, the first trial sentenced the former deputy general manager of Yanchang Oilfield Administration Fengyuan Industrial Company Zheng Daping death, deprived of political rights for life and confiscation of personal property. Court trial ascertained: Zheng Daping served as manager of Yanchang Oilfield Administration Yongping Labor Service Company, the deputy general manager of Fengyuan Industrial Company. From 1997 to before he arrested, Zheng

Daping ordered, collusion his subordinate staffs: Wang Hailian, Zhao Lanzhen, Shi Jianxiong and social unemployed Zhang Youjiang, by taking false invoices, false accounts, write-off borrowing money and other IOUs, false impersonator of public funds, more than 20 times, they totally embezzled 3.24 million yuan.[32]

Case 8, On November 30, 2001, Weinan Intermediate People's Court of Shaanxi Province pronounced the verdict: Ding Shuliang, the original Fuping County Public Security Bureau, was sentenced to seven years in prison and fined 30,000 yuan in the first trial for covering up and conniving at the crime of criminal underworld organization and bribery. From April 1999 to February 2001, the gangsters in Fuping County, Dong Tianyun and Gu Jianjun, etc., members of the underworld of Fuping county, paid bribes to Ding Shuliang, the former director of the Public Security Bureau of Fuping county, the deputy director, Chen Wenzhong, Hui Xiazhi and Zhai Shifu, the former director of the local police station of Dancun for many times, with the amount of more than 280,000 yuan, making it an umbrella for their underworld organizations. Dong Tianyun, Gu Jianjun and other evidentiary criminal activities have obstructed the official business 5, instigated trouble 19, intentionally hurt 5. The body of the victim consists of 2 seriously injured and 5 lightly injured. Dong Tianyun and Gu Jianjun collected more than 4 million yuan through illegal violence and other means.[33]

Case 9, On November 15, 2001, the Intermediate People's Court of Xi 'an sentenced Peng Guojun to death for embezzlement, deprived him of political rights for life and confiscated 50 thousand yuan of property. Guo-Junpeng in Shaanxi province in 1995 the People's Police School as a cashier, beginning in 1997, Guo Junpeng (police superintendent, class 3) to misappropriate the school students clothing fee and so on more than 20 million to lend friends, because friends can't return after borrowing, Guo Junpeng was eager to lend the unit of money secretly accounts fill and level up, unexpectedly will hopes in Casino. Later, he met Yao Xiaoxu, a prostitute from northeast China, in the ballroom, and became even more crazy about gambling. From July 1998 to July 2000, he embezzled 6.67 million yuan of public funds from the school and lost most of the money to Casino.[34]

Case 10, Fan Taimin, the former director of the Public Security Bureau of Baoji city, Shaanxi province, who was suspected of accepting bribes, was prosecuted by prosecutors to the Intermediate Court of Baoji city on Dec 25, 2001. A joint investigation team formed by the Shaanxi provincial commission of discipline inspection and the provincial procuratorate identified Fan Taimin as the director, the deputy director and director of the office of the Public Security Bureau of Baoji city, asking for and accepting more than 100,000 yuan in bribes. Receive a gift of over $300,000; Illegal possession of an enterprise four rooms and one hall housing; From 1994 to 1999, he instructed others to make false tax invoices of more than 200,000 yuan for reimbursement in the subordinate units and set up "private coffer" for his own control and use in violation of financial and economic discipline. He spent more than 40,000 yuan on gifts and illegally participated in profit-making activities for huge profits.[35]

Case 11, On December 27, 2001, Lan Rong (28 years old) was sentenced to death by the Intermediate People's Court of Weinan city, Shaanxi province, for embezzlement. The court found that Lan Rong cheated the depositor's deposit capital of 3.3383 million yuan, and interest of 136.774 million yuan, a total of 351.9374 million yuan, by drawing out the original bank card of the depositor's deposit, tearing off the seal of "settlement," stamping the "official seal of business," and filling the withdrawal voucher falsely. Still use other professional finical methods, embezzle depositor capital 802.595 million yuan. The forfeiture of depositors' deposits amounted to 11,544,600 yuan.[36]

Conclusion

In conclusion, corruption is a common social and historical phenomenon. From a historical point of view, almost all countries have been breeding grounds of corruption, and there have been a variety of appropriate anti-corruption practices. Just because of different countries, there are different phases of economic development, and different political systems, their historical and cultural traditions and other reasons, the performance in the form of corruption, the nature, characteristics of corruption are difference.

During the Jiang Zemin era, the corruption characteristics were as follows: (1) The corruption activity showed higher rate. Since August 1993, after the deployment of the CPC Central Committee for anticorruption work, the number of people reporting has significantly increased, number of major cases has doubled, and the amount of crime is growing. (2) The corrupt form of money and power trading was prominent. New models of abuse of power, such as "power trading," "power and sex trade" and so on, have evolved. (3) Corruption permeated all levels of society and spread rapidly. In terms of socialization, group and high-level, the cases of senior cadres in the subject of corruption are on the rise. (4) Other areas of concern include a general expansion of corruption in luxury; there is the rise of local corruption cover up owing to local protectionism, and so on.

Against the aforementioned corruption information, Jiang Zemin government consider the situation, carefully study the governance program, put clean government position on the important work, and take countermeasures to cope with and against corruption. In particular, practicable promote the governing system construction, gradually solve the problem, focusing on the legal track cure prevention. At the same time, focus on strengthening guidance on anticorruption propaganda and public opinion, encourage people to correctly understand the situation the struggle against corruption; to combine the fight against corruption and the reality of reform, to prevent and overcome the negative lazy state; in addition, seek domestic anticorruption work and the International Anticorruption (Incorruption department) standards to contact and support each other, and actively learn proven methods and excellent system of bribery from foreign anticorruption and eliminating bribery, explore and summarize the successful experience of existing anticorruption to guide the legal system governing system construction, development, and gradually out of a socialist market economy to adapt to new ways of anticorruption.

NOTES

1. Please refer to *Jiang Zemin*, The Central People's Government official website of the People's Republic of China, http://www.gov.cn/test/2007–11/21/content_811768.htm [Reference date 2017–10–25]; *Resume of Jiang Zemin*, Xinhua Net [Reference date 2015–3–25]; *Resume of Jiang Zemin*, People.com.cn [Reference date 2015–3–25].

2. Hu Jintao, *Address on the Semina of studying SELECTED WORKS OF JIANG ZEMIN*, Xinhua Net [Reference date 2015–3–25].

3. Lengrong, *China under Jiang Zemin's leadership (serial 1)*, Perple.com.cn [Reference date 2001–7–06)], http://www.people.com.cn/GB/guandian/29/173/20010706/505085.html.

4. To study *SELECTED WORKS OF JIANG ZEMIN* and promoting the construction and anticorruption work of CPC, *Economic Daily*, August 23, 2006; http://theory.people.com.cn/GB/40557/69447/69448/4731486.html.

5. The CPC Central Discipline Inspection Commission [edit]: *Jiang Zemin on clean government and fight corruption* (Beijing: Fang Zheng Press, 2003).

6. The Press Conference about *Jiang Zemin on clean government and fight corruption*, September 27, 2003; http://www.people.com.cn/GB/shizheng/1024/2113138.html.

7. The local chronicles office in Shaanxi province, *the situation of Shaanxi province*. http://www.sxsdq.cn/sxsq/201610/t20161020_679566.html.

8. The local chronicles office in Shaanxi province, www.sxsdq.cn/sxsq/xzjz/201610/t20161020_679569.html.

9. Edited by the Editorial Committee of the local chronicle office in Shaanxi province, and the party history research office of CPC Shaanxi Provincial Committee, *the local chronicles of Shaanxi province· the chronicles of CPC* volume 47, the fifth, *the Discipline Inspection Committee of CPC Shaanxi Province and its work,* Chapter 3 *construction of party style and clean government* (Xi'an; Shaanxi People's Press, 2002). http://www.sxsdq.cn/sqzlk/xbsxsz/szdyl/zggcdzx/.

10. Xi 'an Yearbook Compilation Committee: *Xi'an yearbook 1993* (Xi'an: Shaanxi People's Press, 1993), 37.

11. Editorial board of the annals of Chinese spiritual civilization: *1992 yearbook of Chinese spiritual civilization* (Beijing: Beijing Yanshan Press), 81.

12. Edited by General Office and research office of the Central Commission for Discipline Inspection: *Compilation of the work report of the CPC Central Committee for Discipline Inspection since the fourteenth National Congress of the CPC* (Beijing: Chinese Fangzheng Press, 2015), 44.

13. Memorandum: *Looking Back 1993*, Shaanxi Financial, 203rd issue.

14. Xi 'an Yearbook Compilation Committee: *Xi'an yearbook 1993* (Xi'an: Shaanxi People's Press, 1993), 302.

15. Xi 'an Yearbook Compilation Committee: *Xi'an yearbook 1993* (Xi'an: Shaanxi People's Press, 1993), 302.

16. The speech of Liu Shuji, Li Futing: *To deploy the Shaanxi water conservancy system to fight against corruption*, Shaanxi Water Conservancy, 5th issue, 1993, 4.

17. Edited by the editorial committee of the local chronicles office in Shaanxi province: *Shaanxi yearbook 1994* (Xi'an: Shaanxi Yearbook Agency, 1994), 265.

18. Xi 'an Yearbook Compilation Committee: *Xi'an yearbook 1995* (Xi'an: Shaanxi People's Press, 1995), 201.

19. The Central Government's five regulations on the integrity and self-discipline of cadres at the level of party and government organs (office) and the "new five regulations" issued in 1994.

20. Edited by the editorial committee of the local chronicles office in Shaanxi province: *Shaanxi yearbook 1995* (Xi'an: Shaanxi Yearbook Agency, 1995), 325.

21. The editorial agency of the economic yearbook of Ankang region: *Ankang region economic yearbook* (Xi'an: Sanqin Press, 1996), 155.

22. The editorial agency of the ecnomic yearbook of Ankang region: *Ankang region economic yearbook* (Xi'an: Sanqin Press, 1997), 154.

23. Edited by Shaanxi Economic and Trade Commission: *Shaanxi economic and trading yearbook 2002* (Xi'an: Xi'an Map Press, 2002), 199.

24. Edited by the editorial committee of the local chronicles office in Shaanxi province: *Shaanxi yearbook 1998* (Xi'an: Shaanxi Yearbook Agency, 1998), 127.

25. Wu Weining: *Shanyang yearbook (2005–2006)* (Party History and Local Chronicles Office of Shanyang County, Shanyang county printing development co. LTD, 2008).

26. Tianjie: *Shaanxi anticorruption big cases record in 2001*, Shaanxi Audit, 2nd issue, 2002.

27. Tianjie: *Shaanxi anticorruption big cases record in 2001*, Shaanxi Audit, 2nd issue, 2002.

28. Tianjie: *Shaanxi anticorruption big cases record in 2001*, Shaanxi Audit, 2nd issue, 2002.

29. Tianjie: *Shaanxi anticorruption big cases record in 2001*, Shaanxi Audit, 2nd issue, 2002.

30. Tianjie: *Shaanxi anticorruption big cases record in 2001*, Shaanxi Audit, 2nd issue, 2002.

31. Tianjie: *Shaanxi anticorruption big cases record in 2001*, Shaanxi Audit, 2nd issue, 2002.

32. Tianjie: *Shaanxi anticorruption big cases record in 2001*, Shaanxi Audit, 2nd issue, 2002.
33. Tianjie: *Shaanxi anticorruption big cases record in 2001*, Shaanxi Audit, 2nd issue, 2002.
34. Tianjie: *Shaanxi anticorruption big cases record in 2001*, Shaanxi Audit, 2nd issue, 2002.
35. Tianjie: *Shaanxi anticorruption big cases record in 2001*, Shaanxi Audit, 2nd issue, 2002.
36. Tianjie: *Shaanxi anticorruption big cases record in 2001*, Shaanxi Audit, 2nd issue, 2002.

BIBLIOGRAPHY

CPC Central Disciplinary Inspection Commission. *Jiang Zemin on Cleaning Government and Fighting Corruption*. Beijing: Fang Zheng Press, 2003.

Editorial Board of the Annals of Chinese Spiritual Civilization. *1992 Yearbook of Chinese Spiritual Civilization*. Beijing: Beijing Yanshan Press, 1993.

Editorial Committee of the Local Chronicles Office in Shaanxi Province. *Shaanxi Yearbook 1995*. Xi'an: Shaanxi Yearbook Agency, 1996.

Editorial Committee of the Local Chronicles Office in Shaanxi Province. *Shaanxi Yearbook 1996*. Xi'an: Shaanxi Yearbook Agency, 1997.

Editorial Committee of the Local Chronicles Office in Shaanxi Province. *Shaanxi Yearbook 1997*. Xi'an: Shaanxi Yearbook Agency, 1998.

Editorial Committee of the Local Chronicles Office in Shaanxi Province. *Shaanxi Yearbook 1998*. Xi'an: Shaanxi Yearbook Agency, 1999.

Editorial Committee of the Local Chronicles Office in Shaanxi Province and the Party History Research Office of CPC Shaanxi Provincial Committee. *The Local Chronicles of Shaanxi Province the Chronicles of CPC*, volume 47, the fifth, the Discipline Inspection Committee of CPC Shaanxi Province and its work, Chapter 3 construction of party style and clean government. Xi'an: Shaanxi People's Press, 2002. http://www.sxsdq.cn/sqzlk/xbsxsz/szdyl/zggcdzx/. Accessed on October 12, 2017.

General Office and Research Office of the Central Commission for Discipline Inspection. *Compilation of the Work Report of the CPC Central Committee for Discipline Inspection since the Fourteenth National Congress of the CPC*. Beijing: Chinese Fangzheng Press, 2015.

Jiang, Zemin. *Resume of Jiang Zemin*. http://www.gov.cn/test/2007-11/21/content_811768.htm. Accessed on October 25, 2017.

Jiang, Zemin. "Press Conference on Cleaning Government and Fighting Corruption," Beijing, September 27, 2003. http://www.people.com.cn/GB/shizheng/1024/2113138.html. Accessed on November 20, 2017.

Leng, Rong. *China under Jiang Zemin's Leadership* (serial 1). http://www.people.com.cn/GB/guandian/29/173/20010706/505085.html. Accessed on January 6, 2017.

Liu, Shuji and Li Futing. "To Deploy the Shaanxi Water Conservancy System to Fight against Corruption." *Shaanxi Water Conservancy*, 5th issue, 1993.

"Promoting the Construction and Anticorruption Work of Communist Party of China." *Economic Daily*, August 23, 2006. http://theory.people.com.cn/GB/40557/69447/69448/4731486.html. Accessed on September 18, 2017.

Shaanxi Economic and Trade Commission. *Shaanxi Economic and Trading Yearbook, 2002*. Xi'an: Xi'an Map Press, 2003.

Shaanxi Economic and Trade Commission. *Shaanxi Economic and Trading Yearbook, 2003*. Xi'an: Xi'an Map Press, 2004.

Shaanxi Economic and Trade Commission. *Shaanxi Economic and Trading Yearbook, 2004*. Xi'an: Xi'an Map Press, 2005.

Shaanxi Economic and Trade Commission. *Shaanxi Economic and Trading Yearbook, 2005*. Xi'an: Xi'an Map Press, 2006.

Shaanxi Provincial Office. The Situation of Shaanxi Province. http://www.sxsdq.cn/sxsq/201610/t20161020_679566.html. Accessed on October 12, 2017.

Shaanxi Provincial Office. The Situation of Shaanxi Province. www.sxsdq.cn/sxsq/xzjz/201610/t20161020_679569.html. Accessed on October 12, 2017.

Xi'an Yearbook Compilation Committee. *Xi'an Yearbook, 1993*. Xi'an: Shaanxi People's Press, 1994.

Xi'an Yearbook Compilation Committee. *Xi'an Yearbook, 1994*. Xi'an: Shaanxi People's Press, 1995.

Xi'an Yearbook Compilation Committee. *Xi'an Yearbook, 1995*. Xi'an: Shaanxi People's Press, 1996.

Xi'an Yearbook Compilation Committee. *Xi'an Yearbook, 1996*. Xi'an: Shaanxi People's Press, 1997.

Xi'an Yearbook Compilation Committee. *Xi'an Yearbook, 1997*. Xi'an: Shaanxi People's Press, 1998.

Chapter 8

Runaway Chinese Officials and International Chase

Yue Li and Chen Liu

INTRODUCTION: CORRUPTION AND PUNISHMENT

China's reform movement, which began in the 1980s has not yet contributed significantly to its democratic transformation or social stability. The new leaders in the 1990s focused on liberal economic reform while discouraging and even stifling political reform. As a result, economic interest groups successfully established an alliance with the Chinese Communist Party (CCP) officials to effectively control economic policy-making and to share political governance.[1] More and more CCP members have increased the private enterprise sector from 12 percent of the total party membership in 1993 to 17 percent in 1997, and more than 20 percent in 2002.[2] The entrenchment of the power-capital establishment institutionalizes corruption as a logical consequence of China's economic development. In the 2000s, corruption has become one of the key elements of the power-capital institution with three ways of connecting politics and business: making money by abusing power; seeking power by paying bribe, and pursuing power and/or money by pawning intellectual capital.[3]

The officials who controlled the resources, public land management, limited quotas of materials, and other valuable assets constituted one of the major power-interest groups. Benefiting from the monopolization of land, resources, and bank notes, their way of transferring their power to capital was to take bribes and demand rents. For instance, in 2000, due to bribery and embezzlement, China lost as much as 3.7 billion yuan *renminbi* (RMB) (about $610 million) in revenue. Consequently, the power-interest groups have gradually spread from the upper class to the middle class, which is demonstrated by the high percentage of income not accounted for by traditional means, or grey income of 6.2 trillion yuan RMB (about $1 trillion), which was 12 percent of the GDP in 2011. The growth of grey income represents the extensive scope of corruption in China. Instead of reinvesting profits in domestic enterprises, assets under the power-capital economy are usually transferred overseas.[4]

The transferred resources are seldom invested in overseas enterprises: rather, they are placed in individual savings accounts, or used for the purpose of facilitating immigration of family members, education of their children or relatives, purchase of houses, and so on, because owners of these assets know that most of their income is illegally obtained. In 2000, the amount of cash sent overseas from China totaled $48 billion. By 2011, that number reached $65 billion, and China had become the country with the fourth largest outflow of capital in the world, after Venezuela, Mexico, and Argentina.[5] According to a report by the People's Bank of China (China's central bank) in 2008, more than 18,000 government officials and state-owned enterprise CEOs escaped from China, taking 800 billion yuan RMB (about $133 billion) in cash to foreign countries since the mid-1990s.[6]

In recent years, Chinese leaders such as Hu Jintao (1942–) (in power 2002–2012) and Xi Jinping (1953–) (in power 2012–2022) have paid special attention to political scandals, corruption, and mismanagement both in the government and in the party. Many cases involved the collection of bribes for the procurement of licenses or the manipulation of regulations. In 2005–2006, prosecutors investigated, detained, and charged more than 6,000 officials. One major case was the arrest and sentence of the CCP Politburo member and Shanghai Party Committee secretary, Chen Liangyu (1946–), in 2006. Chen was charged with corruption and misuse of the city's pension fund. He was responsible for 3.45 billion yuan RMB ($439.4 million) from funds that had been siphoned off from the Shanghai Social Security Pension Fund for illicit loans and investments. The Shanghai party committee and city government advocated the prosecution and hearing of Chen's case, including a threat to remove the chief prosecutor from his office. But the prosecutor won the case, and in 2007 Chen was dismissed from all of his positions in the party and city government. The court then agreed with the prosecutor to relocate the case from Shanghai to the northern city of Tianjin. In November 2008, Chen was convicted and sentenced to eighteen years in prison by the Tianjin Court.[7]

The years of 2012–2014 witnessed one of the greatest challenges the CCP had ever experienced. The dramatic escape of the police chief, Wang Lijun (1959–), from the city of Chongqing, seeking protection from the US Consulate General in Chengdu, provincial capital of southwestern Sichuan, shocked the world. This escape has led to the exposure of many more scandals within the Party. Wang's boss, Bo Xilai (1949–), party chief and mayor of Chongqing and a member of the Politburo, is reported to have been deeply involved in huge illegal financial transactions, retaliation against his opponents, and even murder (and cover-up). On July 26, 2012, Gu Kailai (1958–), Bo's wife, was charged with "intentional homicide." By August 20, she was convicted for the murder of British businessman Neil Heywood because of "economic conflict." On September 28, 2012, Bo Xilai was officially expelled from the CCP. In November, he was stripped of all his positions in the Party, the government, and the National People's Congress (NPC). On July 25, 2013, the Municipal Court of Ji'nan City, eastern Shandong province, sued Bo for corruption, bribery, and power abuse. On September 22, the Ji'nan Court decided its verdict, convicted him, and sentenced Bo to life in jail for his crimes.[8] The Chinese government continues its anticorruption campaign under Xi Jinping's leadership, who has announced the "Eight Rules" to officials and has emphasized tough penalties against corruption, including the death penalty.

The Great Escape of Corrupted Officials

To avoid discipline and punishment in China and protect their cash and properties overseas, more and more corrupted officials looked for opportunities to flee the country and travel overseas. Initially, China's reform and opening up to the outside world provided chances for the corrupted officials to flee overseas. With the deepening of China's reform and opening up, traveling overseas as tourists, business trips, and cultural and educational exchanges became popular in the 1990s and became a new norm in the 2000s. In 2003, more than 20 million Chinese tourists traveled overseas, overtaking Japan for the first time. In 2012, the total business-travel spending reached $135 billion. Chinese business-travel spending was the highest in the world by 2014, overtaking the United States. At the same time, carrying stolen money and fleeing overseas developed some new elements of corruption to evade sanctions in the domestic legal system.[9]

Secondly, the dramatic increase in China's market economy and economic power has become an economic support for the accumulation and removal of huge amounts of corrupt funds to foreign lands. The rapid economic development brought about by the reform and opening up stimulated the corrupted officials to take even more opportunities to attain and remove illegally received funds.

Thirdly, the globalization of electronic communications and e-finance, and the relaxation and removal of controls on international commercial flows have provided technological advantages for the transfer of assets overseas. Since the 1990s, commercial use of the revolution in the modern communications industry has reduced the costs of international transactions. At the same time, it has also promoted the globalization of the economy and facilitated the flow of money more conveniently and rapidly. In order to strengthen economic ties among the countries of the world, the gradual removal and relaxation of international commercial flow control have provided conditions for increased cross-border transfer of assets by corrupt officials.

In the 1990s, corrupt Chinese officials fled to foreign countries as the safest way to evade laws and responsibilities. In particular, developed countries such as the United States, Australia, and Canada have become a paradise for fugitives. Forty corrupt officials fled to the United States, and twenty-six corrupt officials to Canada, accounting for 66 percent of the total. In 1999, Lai Changxing, the main culprit in the largest smuggling case in China, fled to Canada. In 2001, several major suspects in the case of major corruption in Yu Zhendong, Xu Chaofan, and Xu Guojun fled to the United States. The escape of corrupt Chinese officials overseas is a special phenomenon that has arisen in the process of economic globalization in a transitional society. Its characteristics are described below.

From the perspective of the escape, state-owned enterprises and financial chief executives are responsible for corrupt officials in government departments who avoid prosecution by leaving China. The supervision and restriction mechanism of state-owned enterprises is not perfect. There is no necessary supervision and restriction on such major issues as appointment and dismissal of personnel, business decision-making, and financial management. This provided a convenient condition for SOE executives to abuse their power and made SOEs the hardest hit by corrupt officials. As an industry engaged in currency circulation, securities trading, and credit financing, the financial industry is an important carrier for expanding business and transferring risks in other industries. All of these provide plenty of room for corruption in the financial industry. When the oversight mechanism is not perfect, some heads of financial institutions use their powers to engage in corrupt activities such as taking bribes and embezzlement of public funds, accumulating huge amounts of illicit funds and property, which they then take abroad.

With the intensification of anticorruption activity in China, top government officials are in challenging situations. Government officials control the distribution of social resources and may become the targets of blackmail. For example, some have ignored other officials illegally seizing huge amounts of assets. In order to evade the penalties of domestic laws, the men who ignore corruption often choose to take huge sums of money to flee the country and avoid prosecution and implicating others. Prior to fleeing the country, the fugitives generally take steps such as diverting and collecting funds, arranging the relocation of dependents, preparing passports, and finally choosing a time to flee. By embezzling, accepting bribes, misappropriating state-owned assets, and other means, huge amounts of assets have been attained and transferred through various legal and illegal means.

The first step in creating an overseas financial haven is to create a banking account or purchase properties overseas. A report by the People's Bank of China, entitled "Research on Ways and Means of Transferring Assets to Other Countries by Corrupt Elements in Our Country," shows that the transfer of corrupt assets to other countries is mainly through cash smuggling, illegal banking, cross-border exchange, foreign trade, projects, and payment of offshore financial centers to transfer assets overseas.

The second step is to arrange for dependents to move out of the country prior to the corrupted officials leaving China themselves. Studying abroad, visiting relatives, joining tourist groups, and using fake documents are the common means by which they arrange for their family members to leave the country. The purpose is to prepare a life for the corrupt officials themselves and to obtain legal status abroad. The documents required to prepare for going abroad are the key to the corrupt officials' ability to cross the border. In addition to the normal passports, due to public security, many passports are handled illegally. For example, forged passports and altered passports are created through unlawful means, and fake IDs are processed in order to obtain valid passports. These documents allow corrupt officials to hide their identity, which would smooth out their escape and eventual resettlement abroad. Finding the right opportunity to flee is the most vital part of the process. Corrupt officials will choose the appropriate way to escape from time outside. For example, one might ostensibly go abroad to reunite with his family, but actually plan to flee and never return to the motherland, or use other opportunities to go abroad and remain there to avoid investigation.

Methods to Transfer Illegal Assets

The main reason these corrupt officials are successful in fleeing abroad is the lack of experience in communication and cooperation between China and the rest of the world. Especially in the area of international anticorruption cooperation, Chinese authorities do not have enough experience. First, these countries and China did not sign an extradition treaty. Besides, these Western countries have a sound judicial system and generally take a long time to complete the judicial process. Law enforcement officials from some Western countries also have an ideological bias toward China. Therefore, extradition of corrupt officials back to China is a very difficult matter. Corrupt officials make use of the legal loopholes in these countries to plan their cases before they start. If their corrupt practices are discovered or they have a feeling that they will be, they will immediately flee to other countries.

The transfer of illegally obtained money by corrupt officials to overseas property is essentially cross-border money laundering. For example, they set up fake (or shell) companies or underground banks to transfer their assets offshore. They could also have sent business agents or relatives who had immigrated earlier to foreign countries to transfer assets overseas. Or they could transfer funds directly through illegal banks. For example, Cheng Kejie received more than 40 million yuan of bribes, which was handled directly by Hong Kong businessman Zhang Jinghai, who transferred the illegal money to Hong Kong.

Some use their children by sending them to study abroad, or sending their families to settle in overseas countries to transfer corrupt assets. For example, when the Fujian provincial government announced that Zhou Jinwu, former deputy director of the Trade and Industry Bureau, was the mayor of Taijiang District, his wife had already obtained a green card. Later, Zhou Jinhuo repeatedly used this convenience to transfer corrupt assets overseas.

Thirdly, demanding that bribes be directly paid to an overseas entity. Bribe holders abroad will be sent stolen money directly into the account, then spend the money on housing and other immovable property. For example, Zhou Lianguo, former governor of Beijing's Haidian District, arranged for his wife, Lu Xiaodan, to go to Hong Kong and HSBC to open an account, and asked the trustee to accept huge amounts of bribes into the bank account. A more secure and covert way does not involve cash, but instead the corrupt official will arrange for their children to study and travel abroad, providing other means to cover for their financial transactions.

Cash itself can also be smuggled, carried on the person or in luggage and transported out of the country. Alternatively, they can use a few specialized errands to smuggle cash back and forth at border crossings in small quantities. The smuggled cash can then be deposited into bank accounts surreptitiously. For example, Chen Xin, a staff member of the Industrial and Commercial Bank of China's Jiulongpo sub-branch in Chongqing, rushed to the cities of Chengdu, Guangzhou, Haikou, and Zhanjiang within sixty-eight days after taking possession of illegal public funds. Finally he fled to Vietnam. In 2002, XIE Bing-feng and MAI Rong-hui, loan officers at the Danzao Office of Bank of China Nanhai Branch, carried huge sums of smuggled money into Thailand after the bankruptcy of the embezzled bank.

Another way is to use credit card tools to transfer assets overseas. Corrupt officials or their specific affiliates will transfer funds across borders by spending or withdrawing large amounts of credit cards abroad. For example, with MasterCard or Visa, and even with UnionPay credit card spending abroad is simple and very convenient. Domestic repayment fees are generally lower than those obtained by other means are and the probabilities of detection are extremely low.

A final way in which corrupted funds may be laundered internationally is through the purchase and transfer of paintings, antiques, and other works of art. In recent years, Qi Baishi, Chen Yifei, and other people's calligraphy and painting works have fallen under suspicion for this kind of activity, since the price has been artificially high, and antique auction prices have repeatedly broken the artificially high prices. Corrupt officials, by carrying these paintings and calligraphies or antiques out of the country and selling them, can achieve the goal of disguised transfer of corrupt assets. Assets may also be transferred overseas through balance of payments projects. For example, cross-border transfer of capital projects can be realized mainly through the current account of RMB.

There are three forms of current capital flow. The first one is the fraud escaping the trade project, Fulfilling Funds in Fictitious Foreign Trade Contacts. Corrupt officials, for example, collude with unscrupulous companies, use fake import declarations and other commercial documents to defraud a foreign exchange, or remit multiple foreign exchange purchases with the same set of documents. In the corruption case of the Bank of China's Kaiping Branch, Yu Zhendong and Xu Chaofan, among others, realized large sums of money through various forms of control over foreign companies, company transactions, fake transactions, or connected transactions transfer. The second is the transfer of funds through internal manipulation and transfer of prices by multinationals or group companies. For example, multinational corporations rely on global branch networks to formulate "higher than" or "lower than" the accounting costs of commodities, transfer of assets and labor costs, and the transfer of funds abroad. The third is based on the real trade project background, the import price record high, and the export price low report. For example, when companies import machinery, equipment, and raw materials, import prices are reportedly inflated and paid to overseas exporters in the form of discounts with a higher percentage. They then receive rebates into their hands and keep the illegal gains abroad. When exporting, the price of export commodities will be drastically lowered or the difference between the loan amount and the exporter's account deposited overseas shall be kept in the form of an invoice amount far lower than the actual transaction amount, or deposited directly into the account of the corrupt officials outside the territory.[10]

China's "Skynet" and International Hunt

In April 2015, the Central Anticorruption Commission of the CCP launched the "Skynet project," which is an important project to capture the corrupt criminals hiding abroad and bring them back to China for justice. Through the integrated use of police agencies, prosecutors, diplomatic means, and financial instruments, China has concentrated time and effort on arresting corrupt personnel, cleaning up illegal documents, cracking down on illegal banks, recovering the assets involved in the cases and persuading the suspects to return to China. There are several special teams in Skynet, which are led by the Organization Department of the CCP Central Committee, the Supreme

People's Procuratorate, the Ministry of Public Security, and the People's Bank. The Central Organization Department will conduct a thorough examination and handling of the illegal handling and holding of documents by leading cadres. Colleagues, responsible for examination and approval, perform the custodial part of accountability.

The Supreme People's Procuratorate takes the lead in carrying out special international chase recovery and duty-seeking activities on job-related crimes, and focuses on arresting criminal suspects who have absconded outside their posts. The Ministry of Public Security took the lead in carrying out the special operation "Operation Fox 2015," focusing on arresting suspects involved in the flight of job crimes and corruption cases. The People's Bank of China and the Ministry of Public Security launched a special campaign to crack down on the transfer of stolen goods to foreign countries by using offshore companies and illegal banks, focus on the illegal bank criminal activities, and the use of offshore accounts to help others transfer stolen money abroad.

The Skynet project was greatly assisted by the governments of the United States, Australia, Singapore, Cambodia, and other countries and regions. Wang Qishan mentioned in the report of the Seventh Session of the Eighteenth Central Commission for Discipline Inspection that since 2014, 2,566 people have been repatriated and the amount of stolen money recovered has reached 8.64 billion yuan. With the further development of anticorruption, the Skynet project continues. Skynet sent a strong signal to the corrupt elements within and without China, and forms a powerful deterrent effect.

The Red Arrest Warrant is an international circular issued by INTERPOL and is targeted at fugitives who have been issued arrest warrants by their national legal authorities and are required to extradite members. In accordance with the unified deployment of Skynet action, INTERPOL Central Bureau of China announced the red wanted arrests on 100 suspected flight criminals to increase global arrests. The focus group of 100 people, including those fleeing national staff and persons involved in major corruption cases, who have evidence against them and fugitives who have been issued a Red Arrest Warrant by INTERPOL and are being pursued on a global scale. The chief of the Central Anticorruption Coordination Group's Office for International Pursuit said that it is an important measure for the Skynet project to help find fugitives suspected of crimes and people involved in major corruption cases. Doing so is conducive to strengthening international cooperation and enhancing the efficiency of pursuing and catching up stolen goods.[11]

On November 16, 2016, under the overall planning and coordination of the Central Office for the Coordination of Anticorruption Coordination Group on International Pursuit and Removal of Clutches, Yang Xiuzhu, the first most wanted, surrendered to China. She used to be the deputy director of the Zhejiang Provincial Department of Construction, and she is now the first of 100 fugitives. In the first half of 2015, China National Central Bureau released a list of government officials involved in crimes and fled abroad, as well as officials involved in important corruption cases. Yang Xiuzhu was the first person on the list of China's Skynet.[12]

The Case of Yang Xiuzhu

Yang Xiuzhu was born in 1946 and had a unique life. In 1961, she worked at Wenzhou Food Service Company and began to sell bread in the bakery department. During the "Cultural Revolution" of 1966–1976, Wenzhou was famous throughout the country for fighting and violence. Yang Xiuzhu, the bread-maker's caster, started the "revolutionary career" of making her own breakfast and using aggressive characters with radical attitude. In 1967, a large-scale armed struggle took place in Wenzhou. As the result, a "joint" rebel faction (a conservative actually opposed to Mao Zedong's line) was adopted until the end of the Cultural Revolution in October 1976. Yang joined the organization and officially entered the political arena.

After the Cultural Revolution, Yang Xiuzhu started to approach the top of the provincial party committee and adopted a rather special approach. In 1977, she became part of the Metropolitan Women's Federation as a deputy director of the fifth executive committee. She tried to reach out to political celebrities. In 1981, Yang became the deputy chief of the Western District Government in the city of Wenzhou. In 1984, Yang Xiuzhu was the director of the Women's Federation of Wenzhou, and was also promoted to the deputy director of the Wenzhou Urban Construction Bureau.

This period is precisely the beginning of Wenzhou's rapid economic development, and Yang Xiuzhu's corruption began at the same time. In 1984, she was in charge of Wenzhou Urban Construction Bureau. In 1989, Yang was promoted to the director of Wenzhou City Planning Bureau. In 1993, she became assistant to mayor of Wenzhou. In 1995, Yang Xiuzhu as vice mayor of Wenzhou was in charge of urban construction. In 1998, Yang Xiuzhu was promoted to be the deputy director of the Zhejiang Provincial Department of Construction. At that time, it was a period of fast development in Wenzhou and urban construction in Zhejiang Province, which provided great convenience for her corruption, until April 2003 when she absconded.

Yang Xiuzhu has a distinct character, good at high-level contacts. She can grasp the key points of the problem, and is courageous. In order to promote her daughter, using the "three contacts" means, she established contact with the higher authorities (provincial and municipal leading cadres), approached supporters (municipalities and powerful personnel) to the lower levels, and engaged influential organizations in the social field, carefully deploying plans on the ground.

Yang Xiuzhu's earliest known source of fortune is her role in the transformation of old homes in Wenzhou. In the late 1980s, she was also the head of the planning office of the director of the renovated headquarters in Wenzhou. The transformation of old houses in Wenzhou is different from the rest of the country. Because of the lack of government investment, all public buildings in Wenzhou, such as Wenzhou Airport and the expressways between Wenzhou townships, have been funded by private funds over the years. Because there is no government investment in the transformation of old houses, owners basically rely solely on private fund-raising to solve or demolish, which gave her a lot of room for profit. The typical case is the Renmin Road reconstruction project led by Yang Xiuzhu. That year, Yang sold the land at a price less than half the market price to an overseas Chinese buyer in Wenzhou, who lacked the financial strength and real estate development qualifications. The move caused great resentment to ordinary people in Wenzhou. Real estate was thriving in Wenzhou at that time, housing prices rose violently, the relevant departments had played to support the phenomenon of real estate false prosperity. During the process of relocation, damage to households occurred frequently, but was shielded each time because of the need to introduce foreign investment. Ironically, the notorious transformation of the old city turned out to be the "main political merit" of Yang's promotion to deputy director of the Zhejiang Provincial Department of Construction. This project undermines the visual beauty of downtown Wenzhou and has caused traffic jams.

In 1989, Yang Xiuzhu was found guilty of fraud when she was promoted to deputy director of the Planning Bureau by the director. It was reported that her junior high school diploma was changed to a university diploma, but the report was ignored. Once her subordinates identified issues related to housing and children attending school, Yang can solve them through real estate developers. During her tenure at the Planning Bureau, Yang held many official positions in sales. She promoted eleven county-level cadres successively, eight of whom were investigated for various reasons.

In 1993, Yang Xiuzhu was appointed mayor of Wenzhou as assistant to the "Jin Wen" railway deputy commander. Railway Housing Development Corporation, Wenzhou Railway Real Estate Development Company, Wenzhou Real Estate Development Company, and Wenzhou Municipal Construction Supporting Municipal Engineering Company are the project companies that helped Yang Xiuzhu to embezzle. The important posts of the companies were all occupied by the relatives of Yang or by people she trusted. "A human has become a god, and this woman Yang's livestock and pets have also followed her flying to the sky," the people in Wenzhou commented. Yang, her relatives, and her trusted people, who were promoted by Yang, are now in jail.

In 1994, Yang Xiuzhu was transferred to the Wenzhou District as the commander of the "Jin Wen" railway headquarters as well as an assistant to the mayor of Wenzhou. In the following year, she became the vice mayor of Wenzhou in charge of urban construction. In accordance with the procedure, the deputy mayor needs to be elected by the municipal people's congress, but Yang Xiuzhu was notorious in Wenzhou, It was impossible for her to win the election of the people's congress. Yang Xiuzhu resolved the housing problems for the NPC Standing Committee members and built a new building for the municipal people's congress which was satirized by local residents as the "mayor's building."

In 1996, Yang Xiuzhu, using the money she had embezzled from the real estate renovation over the years, bought a five-story building in midtown Manhattan near the Empire State Building and Times Square via a relative, which was about $5 million at that time. In 1998, Yang Xiuzhu was transferred to the provincial city construction department as the deputy director. In the same year, Du Yuesheng, former cadre of the Construction Bureau who had been retaliated against by Yang Xiuzhu because of the investigation of the "mayor's building" as a violation building, said that during the investigation, the infrastructure for the "Mayor's House" of "Yang Er Road" project was not approved. Without a construction permit, the sources of funds for finding and bidding were not legal. Yang Xiuzhu then personally called the leadership of the Construction Bureau and asked them not to intervene. At the same time, Yang Xiuzhu called Du Yuesheng and said, "Municipal leaders are very concerned about you." Du Yuesheng did not accept, and continued to investigate the matter. But it was not long before he was demoted to become the CPPCC's secretary general.

International Cooperation

On April 20, 2003, Yang Xiuzhu, then deputy director of the Zhejiang Provincial Department of Construction, fled to the United States with her daughter, son-in-law, and grandson from Shanghai Airport via Singapore. In February 2004, the procuratorial organ in Zhejiang Province issued the "Red Wanted Order" through Interpol. Yang Xiuzhu was arrested in the Netherlands on May 31, 2005. On August 2, 2011, other people involved in the "Yang Xiuzhu Case" returned to China to surrender. On November 16, 2016, Yang Xiuzhu returned to China and surrendered. On July 28, 2017, the Hangzhou Intermediate People's Court held a public hearing of the corruption and bribery of Yang Xiuzhu, the first suspect of the "100 Red Wanted Persons." Yang Xiuzhu pleaded guilty in court for repentance. Finally, the court announced the adjournment, and at the elective sentencing on October 13, 2017, Yang was sentenced to eight years imprisonment and fined 800,000 yuan.

Yang Xiuzhu's brother, Yang Guangrong, deputy general of the railway construction company manager, was also charged in a bribery case. In February 2003, Wenzhou City Procuratorate found through investigation that a local dealer once gave bribes to Yang Guangrong. In March, personnel of the Anticorruption Bureau of Zhejiang Procuratorate took away Yang Guangrong and took away all accounts of the railway development company. On April 20, Yang Xiuzhu felt that things had come to an end, so he ran away. On November 23, 2004, Yang Guangrong was charged with stealing 180,000 yuan because of bribery and sentenced to ten years and six months. On June 14, 2003, a Zhejiang Provincial Procuratorate directly involved in the "search network" operations in Wenzhou targeted Lin Hsuan-hua, who had been hiding for a long time. He was formerly the accountant of the Wenzhou Municipal Planning Bureau and was once promoted to be the deputy commander of the "Home Security Engineering Command" of Wenzhou Municipal Committee. Also arrested with Lin Suhua were those involved in the case involving Gao Yunguang, deputy director of the reconstruction headquarters of Wenzhou City, who had been arrested already. Almost all the executives of the railway development company, including Yang Guangrong, have been put on investigation and gradually tried.

In mid-November 2004, Teng Deshou, former deputy director of Wenzhou Planning Bureau, took 140,000 yuan of bribes and was sentenced to ten years' imprisonment. Shortly after, Lin Guochun, the former general manager of the railway development company, was sentenced to ten years in prison for taking bribes. So far, the following have been investigated: former directors of the Wenzhou Municipal Bureau of Land and Gardens, Wu Changliu and Yang Bangzhen; former deputy director Ye Xiaoqing; former general manager of Wenzhou Construction Group, Yu Xiaotang; land requisition director of the Land and Resources Bureau of Wenzhou City, Wang Shoufa; former managers of the land Development Company, Zhuang Yaoguang; and some others. Wenzhou City Supervision Bureau staff said that the Yang Xiuzhu series of cases in Wenzhou only achieved initial results and identified 253 million yuan involved in corruption and bribery.

In February 2003, Wenzhou City People's Procuratorate of Zhejiang Province found through investigation that a local dealer once paid Yang Guangrong, brother of Yang Xiuzhu and manager of Wenzhou Railway Real Estate Development Company. In March the same year, law enforcement officials of the Zhejiang Provincial People's Procuratorate arrested Yang Guangrong. During the course of the investigation, law enforcement officers found that Yang Xiuzhu, then deputy director of the Provincial Department of Construction, was the culprit in her term as deputy mayor of Wenzhou.

After Yang Xiuzhu learned of the incident, she felt that she was going to be put on file for investigation soon and started planning to run away. In April 2003, Yang Xiuzhu lied at her workplace that she needed to visit her sick mother and boarded a flight with her daughter, son-in-law, and grandson at Shanghai's Pudong Airport and through Hong Kong fled to Singapore to start her escape. In May the same year, the Zhejiang Provincial Commission for Discipline Inspection formally investigated Yang Xiuzhu.

After investigation, law enforcement officers found that Yang Xiuzhu was involved in corruption involving a significant amount of money. Among the other people who have been investigated and dealt with on a case-by-case basis, there are two officials at the departmental level, eleven officials above the level, and seven officials at the section level. More than 100 people were investigated and evidence collected.

For more than thirteen years since becoming a fugitive in April 2003, Yang Xiuzhu has fled to Hong Kong, Singapore, France, the Netherlands, Italy, and the United States and has applied for political asylum in France, the Netherlands, and the United States. On April 20, 2003, Yang Xiuzhu, then deputy director of the Zhejiang Provincial Department of Construction, fled to Singapore and chose to remain in Singapore, with a large Chinese population and no language barrier.

On May 9, 2003, Yang Xiuzhu traveled from Singapore to Rome, Italy, and then fled to France. The relevant departments of China put forward their requests for judicial assistance to France as soon as possible. In July, through the International Criminal Police Organization, Yang Xiuzhu was issued a "Red Wanted Arrest Order." After escaping to the Netherlands, Yang Xiuzhu was hiding in a dark and damp basement in Rotterdam. In May 2005, at the request of the Chinese judicial authorities, the Dutch police promised to arrest Yang Xiuzhu on the grounds of suspected illegal immigration.

In May 2014, just a night before the repatriation of the judiciary in the Nordic countries, Yang Xiuzhu escaped from the Netherlands Immigrant Migration Center. After being removed to France, Italy, Canada, and other countries, and holding a fake Dutch passport, she traveled with a Canadian local tour group into the United States by train. During this period, China provided evidence and clues to the US side through the JLG Anticorruption Working Group in China and the United States and made a request for assistance.

In May 2014, Yang Xiuzhu fled to New York City with a fake passport. After receiving a request for mutual legal assistance from China, the United States arrested and detained Yang Xiuzhu. In July, Yang Xiuzhu filed a political asylum application with the US government, and the case was transferred to the immigration court for trial. In December the same year, at the twelfth plenary meeting of the joint Sino-US Law enforcement cooperation group, both China and the United States identified Yang Xiuzhu as the number one pursuit case.[13]

In June 2015, the New York Immigration Tribunal conducted its first hearing in which Yang Xiuzhu applied to the US government for asylum. While carrying out criminal prosecutions against Yang Xiuzhu's entry using fake passports and suspected money-laundering crimes, the US justice department also hired lawyers to handle Yang Xiuzhu's application for asylum and the evidence provided by China on Yang Xiuzhu's alleged corruption in China. The fact that France and the Netherlands denied Yang Xiuzhu's asylum application became an important factor.[14]

On September 18, 2015, Yang Jinju, brother of Yang Xiuzhu, was repatriated by the US police, which formed a powerful psychological deterrent to Yang Xiuzhu. As long-term jail life was very difficult, having no hope about her asylum applications, she increasingly wished to return to her motherland. On July 11, 2016, Yang Xiuzhu applied to the United States for withdrawal of asylum applications, formally proposed to return to China and to surrender and unconditionally accept China's judicial sanctions. In August, the US Immigration Tribunal ruled to agree to Yang Xiuzhu's withdrawal of her asylum application and dispatched a court order. On November 16, 2016, Yang Xiuying, the suspect who absconded overseas for thirteen years and who was ranked first on the list of "100 Red Wanted Persons," returned to China, surrendering herself.

After the hearing, the court found that from December 1996 to May 1999, the defendant, Yang Xiuzhu, took advantage of her position to illegally possess, for the purpose of misappropriating public funds, a total amount of 1,905 million yuan. For misusing the trust of units and individuals to seek benefits, receive property, equivalent to RMB 7,344,300 yuan,[15] on October 13, 2017, Hangzhou Intermediate People's Court of Zhejiang Province publicly announced the case of corruption and bribery of the top suspect Yang Xiuzhu on the list of "100 Red Wanted Persons" and sentenced the defendant for the crime of embezzlement to six years in a row and to pay 500,000 yuan. The Court sentenced her to six years in prison for accepting bribes and sentenced her to a fine of 300,000 yuan; and decided to sentence her to eight years imprisonment and a fine of 800,000 yuan. From the recovery of Yang Xiuzhu's corruption and bribes, they received a total of 2,639 million yuan.[16]

IMPACT OF THE INTERNATIONAL CHASE

Yang Xiuzhu's case is strong proof of China's rising international status. As the number one suspect in China's "100 Red Wanted Persons," ending her thirteen-year life in flight and returning to China surrendered, Yang Xiuzhu's influence and deterrence to the lives of corrupt officials who still flee abroad is clear to see. Yang Xiuzhu once stated that "even if [we] die, we should stay in the United States." However, she voluntarily returned to China surrendering herself. A great attitude shift like this not only shows that the sanctions that she cannot escape Chinese law even if she fled abroad are indications of the strictness of Chinese laws, but also reflects the determination and will of the entire Chinese people against corruption in the CPC and the People's Republic of China. This shows that China has enjoyed an increase in its international status and respectability.

Yang Xiuzhu's case brought to justice illustrates the unanimous and firm determination of the Central Committee in fighting corruption in China. Yang Xiuzhu's return to China once again refreshed the transcripts of China's overseas reclamation, demonstrating the clear attitude and firm determination of the CPC Central Committee with Xi Jinping at its core to uphold anticorruption policy and not allow corrupt elements to go unpunished. From the extraordinary irony of the people in satirizing the case of "Yang Xiuzhu," the collapse of the saying of "overseas paradise for avoiding crime," and the outstanding achievements of overseas pursuit, all Chinese people can see that after the 18th NPC, the Central Committee of the CCP pursues a strong opposition to corruption, which is endorsed by all the Chinese people.

The case of Yang Xiuzhu is a vivid warning and education course for other government officials. Yang Xiuzhu's example is a landmark case for corrupt officials who have fled overseas. Although Yang Xiuzhu was only a departmental-level corrupt official, she had fled with more than 125 million yuan for a total of thirteen years since 2003; she had fled to many countries and had caused great social repercussions. Yang Xiuzhu's case is a tremendous deterrence to corrupt elements both at home and abroad and is instrumental in preventing other government officials attempting similar crimes.

At the Third Plenary Session of the 18th Central Commission for Discipline Inspection held in January 2014, General Secretary Xi Jinping emphasized that "the work of international pursuit of retreat must be properly grasped, and all relevant departments should step up negotiations and not allow other countries to become corrupt. No matter where the corrupt elements are hiding in the world, the Chinese judiciary must also arrest them, no matter how many years they take to cut off the corrupt elements." General Secretary Xi Jinping's important speech is a prelude to the project of pursuing corrupt elements outside China. These actions make the public in China more intuitively and profoundly feel the determination of anticorruption form the Eighteenth NPC. "Tiger Hunting" and "Fighting Flies" have become a national policy and international efforts have been taken in overseas pursuit of the 100 Red Wanted Persons. These projects have shown both strength and determination. If the interests of the country and people are harmed, no matter where the perpetrators are hidden, they will also be arrested and brought to face justice. This is a trial for such people as Yang Xiuzhu and a deterrent to those who wish to become Yang Xiuzhu. The example of Yang Xiuzhu illustrates that government officials must abide by the laws and traditions, and respect the common people. People walking on the evil path cannot see the light.

NOTES

1. Julia Kwong, *The Political Economy of Corruption in China* (Armonk, NY: M. E. Sharpe, 1997), 12–14.

2. Xiaobing Li, *Modern China: Understanding Modern Nation* (Santa Barbara, CA: ABC-CLIO Publishing, 2016), 93.

3. Zhaohui Hong, *The Price of China's Economic Development: Power, Capital, and the Poverty of Rights* (Lexington: University Press of Kentucky, 2015), 26–31.

4. Kerry Brown, *The New Emperors: Power and the Princelings in China* (London: I. B. Tauris, 2014), 181–185.

5. Orville Schell and John Delury, *Wealth and Power: China's Long March to the Twenty-first Century* (New York: Random House, 2013), 64–65.

6. *Renmin ribao* [People's Daily], October 18, 2018, 1–2.

7. For more details on Chen Liangyu's case, see Qiang Fang and Xiaobing Li, *Power versus Law in Modern China: Cities, Courts, and the Communist Party* (Lexington: University Press of Kentucky, 2017), 151–159.

8. For more details on Bo Xilai's case, see Xiansheng Tian, "When Chongqing Challengers Beijing: The Bo Xilai Case," in *Evolution of Power: China's Struggle, Survival, and Success*, eds. Xiaobing Li and Xiansheng Tian (Lanham, MD: Lexington Books, 2014), 323–350.

9. Chen Lei, "Common Characters of Fleeing Corrupted Officials and Some Practical Counter Measures," *Zhengfa luntan* [Tribune of Political Science and Law] 1 (2009): 26–43.

10. "Lesson Learned from Bringing the Most Wanted Yang Xiuzhu from Overseas to Justice," *Lingdao zhiyou* [Leadership Guidance], no. 4 (2017): 47–49.

11. "The Red List of the 100 Overseas Most Wanted," *The Disciplinary Committee of the CCP Central Committee*, April 22, 2015.

12. "The Truth about the Most Wanted," *Zhongguo Jinying bao* [China's Commercial Daily], December 19, 2015.

13. "The First One on the Red List of the 100 Overseas Most Wanted Arrested in the U.S.," May 29, 2015, http://news.china.com.cn Assessed on November 22, 2017.

14. "The First One on the Red List of the 100 Overseas Most Wanted Returned back to China," November 17, 2016, http://news.china.com.cn Assessed on November 24, 2017.

15. "The Disciplinary Committee of the CCP Central Committee Contacts the U.S. Government on the Cases of Yang Xiuzhu and Cheng Muyang," January 16, 2016, http://news.china.com.cn Accessed on January 5, 2018.

16. "The Court Sentencing of Yang Xiuzhu," http://news.china.com.cn Assessed on November 20, 2017.

BIBLIOGRAPHY

Brown, Kerry. *The New Emperors: Power and the Princelings in China.* London: I. B. Tauris, 2014.

Chen, Lei. "Common Characters of Fleeing Corrupted Officials and Some Practical Counter Measures." In *Zhengfa luntan* [Tribune of Political Science and Law] 1 (2009): 26–43.

Disciplinary Committee of the CCP Central Committee. "The First One on the Red List of the 100 Overseas Most Wanted Arrested in the U.S." May 29, 2015. http://news.china.com.cn. Assessed on November 22, 2017.

———. "The First One on the Red List of the 100 Overseas Most Wanted Returned back to China." November 17, 2016. http://news.china.com.cn. Assessed on November 24, 2017.

———. "The Red List of the 100 Overseas Most Wanted, April 22, 2015." From http://news.china.com.cn. Assessed on December 10, 2017.

Fang, Qiang, and Xiaobing Li. *Power versus Law in Modern China: Cities, Courts, and the Communist Party*. Lexington: University Press of Kentucky, 2017.

Hong, Zhaohui. *The Price of China's Economic Development: Power, Capital, and the Poverty of Rights*. Lexington: University Press of Kentucky, 2015.

Kwong, Julia. *The Political Economy of Corruption in China*. Armonk, NY: M. E. Sharpe, 1997.

"Lesson Learned from Bringing the Most Wanted Yang Xiuzhu from Overseas to Justice." In *Lingdao zhiyou* [Leadership Guidance], no. 4 (2017): 47–49.

Li, Xiaobing. *Modern China: Understanding Modern Nation*. Santa Barbara, CA: ABC-CLIO Publishing, 2016.

Renmin ribao [People's Daily], October 18, 2018.

Schell, Orville, and John Delury. *Wealth and Power: China's Long March to the Twenty-first Century*. New York: Random House, 2013.

Tian, Xiansheng. "When Chongqing Challengers Beijing: The Bo Xilai Case." In *Evolution of Power: China's Struggle, Survival, and Success*. Edited by Xiaobing Li and Xiansheng Tian, 323–50. Lanham, MD: Lexington Books, 2014.

"The Court Sentencing of Yang Xiuzhu." http://news.china.com.cn. Assessed on November 20, 2017.

"The Disciplinary Committee of the CCP Central Committee Contacts the U.S. Government on the Cases of Yang Xiuzhu and Cheng Muyang." January 16, 2016. http://news.china.com.cn. Assessed on January 5, 2018.

"The Truth about the Most Wanted." In *Zhongguo Jinying bao* [China's Commercial Daily], December 19, 2015.

Chapter 9

The Language of Sarcasm and Irony

Corruption Exposed in Popular Rhymes

Helen Xiaoyan Wu

China in the post-Mao Zedong (1893–1976) era has witnessed economic reform along with endemic corruption. Among the many forms of corruption in all walks of life, it is the corruption committed by high-ranking officials that has been subject to increasingly significant state and mass media attention. Even so, such reports only represent the tip of the iceberg. In this situation, literature, anonymous popular rhymes in particular, has turned more corruption-driven than ever before. An article appeared in the *Procurators' Daily* (*Jiancha Ribao*, March 21, 2002) headlined "There's No Harm in Listening to *Minyao*," appealing to senior officials to sit less in their offices listening to empty reports and go more frequently into the masses for *minyao* (popular rhymes), which can help prevent and root out the problem of corruption.

This research will first outline official corruption in China since the late 1970s and review the publications of *minyao* generated by corruption. This will demystify the myth that popular rhymes targeting corruption, a sensitive topic, are not officially published in print. The research then examines the popular rhymes about corruption from the people's perspective and in the name of officials, followed by some poems created by officials themselves and which are supported by the real-life corruption cases reported in the media. This is followed by a discussion of the tradition that anonymous verses spread widely whenever corruption becomes serious, and the social value that this type of rhymes has in contemporary anticorruption efforts. In conclusion, this chapter argues that *minyao* help to understand today's China. Furthermore, they are not merely a popular literary genre, but rather, truly depict what has been happening in the country.

1. THE EMERGENCE OF PRESENT-DAY POPULAR RHYMES ALONG WITH CORRUPTION

Popular rhymes and official corruption go side by side in China. Everyone loves this type of genre which is satirical, sociopolitical, vivid, and occurs in a timely manner.

1.1 The Rise of Corruption in the Past Four Decades

Of all the dictionary definitions about corruption which is usually regarded as the abuse of power for private gain, the one defined by Transparency International seems to fit exactly what Xi Jinping described metaphorically as "tigers and flies," referring to officials in major and relatively minor cases of corruption in China:

> Grand corruption consists of acts committed at a high level of government that distort policies or the central functioning of the state, enabling leaders to benefit at the expense of the public good. Petty corruption refers to everyday abuse of entrusted power by low- and mid-level public officials in their interactions with ordinary citizens, who often are trying to access basic goods or services in places like hospitals, schools, police departments and other agencies.
>
> Political corruption is a manipulation of policies, institutions and rules of procedure in the allocation of resources and financing by political decision makers, who abuse their position to sustain their power, status and wealth.[1]

This definition is absolutely correct. During the student-led Tiananmen Square protests of spring 1989, demonstrators indignantly shouted "Down with official profiteering!" (*Daodao guandao!*) because the "double price track" government policy had been adopted since the late 1970s, in which the government controlled key sectors of the economy while allowing private enterprises limited control over the other sectors. Taking advantage of the legacy of the Mao-time planned economy being transitioned to the "socialist market economy," officials-turned-profiteers and their contacts secured raw materials for production and scarce goods at the government-fixed prices and sold them at much higher prices in the market.

The June 4 incident of the Tiananmen movement in 1989 brought to the end of the then popular neologism *guandao* (official profiteers; official profiteering) in all publications in China, replaced by "economic crimes" (*jingji fanzui*), a term preferred by the authorities that cleverly avoided the naked truth of official corruption. The euphemism suggests that anyone may commit corruption, not necessarily officials revealed in *guandao* in plain language. Since then, corruption has only worsened, to the point of the "life or death" struggle of the government of the Communist Party of China (CPC), warned by all the CPC general secretaries from Jiang Zemin (1989–2002 in power), to Hu Jintao (2002–2012 in power), to the current general secretary, Xi Jinping,[2] who has vowed to fight both "tigers and flies,"[3] meaning to crack down on senior Party and state leaders as well as lowly government functionaries.

Indeed, the number of Party secretaries and (deputy-) ministers at the national ministerial level of the State Council, (deputy-) governors at the provincial level, as well as (vice-) mayors who had been exposed as corrupt has become larger and larger every year. According to the statistics provided by the *Legal Daily* (*Fazhi Ribao*, December 20, 2017), with a cartoon, in recent years, the ministry- and provincial-level "tigers" or senior officials sentenced for corruption were, respectively, four in 2014, sixteen in 2015, thirty-four in 2016, and thirty-nine in 2017.[4] During the first half of 2018, another twenty-eight such "tigers" were sentenced, which was eight senior officials more than the number in the same period in 2017.[5] Of all the five first six months in the past five years, the cases on file for investigation and prosecution of corrupt officials are 193,000 in 2014, 220,000 in 2015, 256,000 in 2016, 271,000 in 2017, and 302,000 in 2018.[6] The figures support what a popular rhyme described:

[R1] Arresting Corrupt Officials
If every official is arrested one after another,
Some of them may be innocent;
If every other official is arrested,
Some of the guilty may have been slipped through.[7]

Interestingly, the *People's Daily*, the CPC mouthpiece, ridiculed the saying and considered the large growing numbers as an anticorruption achievement.[8] Xinhua News, China's official press agency, holds that the CPC's new anticorruption effort, including fifty-eight officials at the national ministry, provincial, and higher levels punished in 2017 alone, has caught the world's attention and therefore deserves praise.[9]

1.2 Review of *Minyao* Published since the Late 1970s

From the late 1970s onward, as corruption started to spread, so did *shunkouliu* satirizing corruption. *Shunkouliu*, also called *minyao*, is translated as "slippery jingles" and "folk rhymes," respectively, in an article by Perry Link and Kate Zhou. In fact, these two authors do not believe that there is a perfect term in English that covers the Chinese original. While it is wise for them to entitle their essay "*Shunkouliu*: Popular Satirical Sayings and Popular Thought,"[10] "popular rhymes," which is closest to *minyao* in Chinese (*min* means the people or folks; *yao* means ballad or rhyme) is preferred in this research. Depending on the length and the literary value, *shunkouliu* or *minyao* could be equivalent to ballads, doggerel, folk songs, jingles, limericks, or satirical verses in English. Some anticorruption *minyao* have truly been performed as songs, and more were created after popular songs although most are not sung. They are extremely popular, enjoyed by ordinary people and government officials alike. They are poetic and easy to remember. What is even more incredible is they are almost all anonymous! The names that one may see in publications are mostly compilers or collectors of the rhymes rather than the poets. The authors could be anyone apart from literati. In this chapter, the Chinese term "*minyao*" may be used interchangeably with the English translation "popular rhymes" or rhymes in short, and occasionally satirical poems or verses.

Contrary to the common belief that *minyao* are only found online or even thought to be underground literature before the internet was widely used in the 1980s and early 1990s, there are in fact dozens of published books and numerous issues of periodicals about popular rhymes satirizing corruption, all of which are the focus of this chapter. Of course, they are also found online in most cases. The most authoritative of such books is perhaps published by the China Archives Press (Zhongguo Dang'an Chubanshe) in Beijing under the State Archives Administration, by the authors Shu Jian and Zuo Yu in 1994, entitled *Dangdai Shunkouliu yu Shehui Redian Saomiao* (*Contemporary Popular Rhymes and the Scanning of the Hot Spots in Society*), with lengthy commentaries criticizing corruption in forty sections. Lu Wen's *Baixing Huati—Dangdai Shunkouliu* (*The Ordinary People's Sayings: Contemporary Popular Rhymes*) by the same publisher in 1998, is another book in which almost one thousand rhymes are collected under fifty hot topics, with fifty cartoons, providing backgrounds, comments, and food for thought. The year 1999 saw a set of four books with the title *Fengci Shi yu Manhua Xilie Congshu* (*Serial Books of Satirical Verses and Cartoons*) by Wang Shigui, published by the Inner Mongolia People's Publishing House. In addition, the following books, listed chronologically, are worthy of attention:

- *Lidai Mingjia Bopishi Quhua: Guaishi* (*Witty Remarks on Satirical Verses after the Famous Ones in History: Weird Poems*), by Zhou Zhengju (Chengdu: Bushu Shudian, 1997). Disguised by the study of well-known poems in past dynasties, there are some modern-day topical rhymes about corruption included.
- *Minyao Yu* (*The Language of Popular Rhymes*) by He Qun (Beijing: Xinhua, 1998). Again, a few present-day poems with a sharp edge are to be found in it.
- *Baixing Huati—Dangdai Minyan* (*The Ordinary People's Sayings: Voice of the People Today*) by Yi Ren (Beijing: Zhongguo Wenlian, 1999). The author was a senior journalist who paid numerous unannounced visits to

various people and recorded their conversations as private diaries, including many popular rhymes related to complaints.

- *Dingxin Yuyan Guantou—Minyao Qiaopi Dapaidang* (*The New Taste of Language: A Grand Display of Popular Rhymes with Wisecracks*), by Su Guanqun and Liu Xiulan (Hohhot: Inner Mongolia People's, 1999). In the name of the appreciation of the wisdom of words, almost all the rhymes are about corruption, mingled with some quotable quotes from China and abroad.
- *Liuxing Minyao* (*Popular Rhymes*) by Zhen Yan (Hohhot: Yuanfang, 2001). With twenty-four categories of some of the sharpest rhymes of the time, this collection is perhaps the boldest even by today's standard when corruption has been going from bad to worse in the past two decades.
- *Dangdai Minyan Minyao* (*Contemporary Proverbs and Popular Rhymes*), by Jiang Yinnan (Shanghai Cishu, 2005). The collection is full of mild social satire during the Mao time but a small portion about the late twentieth century.
- *Dangdai Hanyu Saoyu Yanjiu yu Yingyi* (*The Contemporary Chinese Language of Complaints: Research and English Translation*), by Guo Guiling (Shanghai: Xuelin, 2008). On the pretext of studying a particular type of Chinese language, numerous popular rhymes are analyzed linguistically, sociopolitically, and translated into English.
- *Dangdai Zuixin Liuxing Shunkouliu Daquan* (*A Complete Collection of the Latest Popular Rhymes*), by Dai Qixiao (Shanghai University Press, 2010). It is a collection of existing less critical rhymes from the internet.
- *Xin Guofeng* (*New Airs of the Country*), by Zhu Wenhua (Guilin: Guangxi Normal University Press, 2011). The title reminds the reader of Guofeng (Airs of the States) from the *Book of Songs*, the oldest existing collection of Chinese poetry, comprising 305 works dating from the eleventh to sixth centuries BCE, in which there is a part under the name of Airs of the States. The lyrics of this part are ancient folk songs which record the voice of the common people who speak of love and courtship, soldiers on campaign, farming and housework, and last but not least, political satire and protest.
- *Shunkouliu Chutan* (*Preliminary Studies of Popular Rhymes*), by Liu Bingyin (Wuhan: Central China Normal University Press, 2011). This is the most academic and scholarly book of the day even though the author emphasized that he is merely a "grassroots scholar." He started the book project after collecting over ten thousand popular rhymes.
- *Renjian Wanxiang Shunkouliu* (*Popular Rhymes about All Worldly Things*), by Wu Weigen (Beijing: Jindun, 2013). Like all books that select the less sharp rhymes, this publication by the Jindun [Gold Shield] Press run by the People's Liberation Army General Logistics Department is still worth noting.

- *Shihua Ciguozi* (*Current Affairs Satirized by Poetry and Painting*), by Jiang Mo and Zhang Jiashu (Dalian, [Liaoning]: Dalian, 2014). The book claims the integral combination of news and views with two forms of art: critical poems and cartoons.

One interesting author is Chi Bei'ou, pen name of Tan Wenrui (1922–2014), who served as the editor-in-chief of the *People's Daily*. He kept on publishing more than half a dozen books of rhymes after retirement, among which *Shitai Jitan* (*The World through Criticism*) with cartoonist Ding Cong (1916–2009) in 2009 and *Jiushi Lao Dadang: Chi Bei'ou Fang Cheng Fengshi Manbi* (*Old Partners at 90: Chi Bei'ou and Fang Cheng Satirize the World with Literary Notes and Sketches*) with another cartoonist Fang Cheng in 2012 contain quite a number of rhymes against corruption. All the poems were composed by himself, using his well-known pen name instead of being anonymous. Although these books contain less serious criticism and more light humor, they were published by the People's Daily Press, an indication of openness to a certain degree in the reform era compared with the tight control of the freedom of speech and the freedom of the press under Mao's leadership.

The satirical verses are so popular that they are published beyond mainland China. Hong Kong and Taiwan have published their collections, such as *Minjian Shunkouliu Xuancui* (*A Fine Selection of Folk Rhymes*), complied by Dong Xianrui and Liu Chunguang (Hong Kong: Hong Kong Wenhua Jiaoyu, 2004) and *Zhongguo Xianxiang Zhongguo Xiaohua* (*China: Phenomena and Jokes*) by Huang Wenxiong and Chen Yuewen (Taipei, [Taiwan]: Yushanshe, 2008). Are some of the satirical verses published abroad in English? The answer is yes. *Understanding China through Cartoons* by C.E. Bled (1985) is one such book published in Ottawa, capital of Canada. Those cartoons, many of which included rhymes, had been published in the *People's Daily* and *China Daily* in the early 1980s and were collected into a book in English, with a French edition as well.

Many magazines and literary journals also publish rhymes about corruption and anticorruption, such as the following:

- *Fengci yu Youmo* (*Satire and Humor*), a weekly since January 1979; many excellent rhymes were chosen for four books by Ying Tao, et al. (1999) to mark the twentieth anniversary of the tabloid under the *People's Daily*.
- *Minzu Wenxue* (*National Literature*), run by the Chinese Writers Association, had a special issue in December 1999, entitled *Bainian Minyao* (*A Century of Popular Rhymes*), for the millennials.
- *Zawen Yuekan* (*Essays Monthly* [1985–2003]; *Essays Semimonthly* [2004–present]), run by the *Hebei Daily*, carries not only satirical essays but also

verses against corruption, including many after the works of renowned poets in the Tang (618–907), Song (960–1279), and Yuan (1271–1368) dynasties. The articles are claimed to be "academic writing" (*xueshu wenzhang*) by the publisher.[11]

On the whole, most of the popular rhymes collected in printed books and periodicals are chosen prudently, and only sometimes list their authors' names. Some sharp poems with a political punch appear to be disguised as something else, cloaked in linguistic and literary studies, or historical and folklore research, or mixed with ancient satirical verses to better blunt their message and avoid making a straightforward criticism of present-day corruption. While they need to meet the demands of society and also make a profit, due to the sensitive nature of corruption involving officials publishers may understandably feel obliged to practice self-censorship.

One may wonder what the difference is between the popular rhymes posted on the internet and those published by officially approved state-run publishing houses in China. According to my observations, there used to be a noticeable gap between those online, sharper, racier, quicker and juicier, and those in print publications, more serious and "cleaner." However, since Xi Jinping came to power in late 2012, rhymes published in books and periodicals are mostly still searchable on the internet, but often not vice versa on the websites registered inside the Chinese Mainland. Many or perhaps most of the extremely critical ones that were only found online have disappeared, while many of them have been kept on overseas websites. The situation makes the hardcopies published in mainland China seem more precious.

2. CORRUPTION REFLECTED IN POPULAR RHYMES

The latest 2016 edition of the *Xiandai Hanyu Cidian* (*Dictionary of Modern Chinese*), an authoritative one-volume dictionary of Standard Mandarin Chinese, refers to *minyao* as folk rhymes or ballads, especially of the topical and political type. Thousands of such popular rhymes have sprung up like mushrooms as corruption flourishes, but selections covering three aspects will be discussed below under the topics of public opinion, witty sarcasm, and poetic justice.

2.1 Public Opinion: Rhymes Uncovering Corruption

[R2] Ten Classes of People of the 1990s
The first class of people are public servants.
Their wives and children enjoy a happy life.

The second class of people are those in government organizations.
They take turns going abroad to have real fun.
The third class of people are the ones who get contracts.
Their eating, drinking, and merry-making can all be reimbursed.
The fourth class of people are those in hiring and leasing.
They travel from one scenic spot to another with their mistresses.
The fifth class of people take kickbacks.
Their embezzlement and bribe-taking are never enough.
The sixth class of people are government functionaries wearing uniform caps.
Delicacies of every kind can be created whenever they want.
The seventh class of people are surgeons.
You must give them red packets of money if you want to stay alive.
The eighth class of people are car drivers.
They follow their leaders to wining and dining.
The ninth class of people are the self-employed.
After deceiving Zhang, they bluff Li or anybody.
The tenth class of people are the "Masters."
They carry their lunch boxes and learn from Lei Feng.[12]

The message of this piece is that corruption has become an epidemic in which people at all strata of society are involved. Among them, cadres or officials take the lead, as targeted in class one, class two, and class six. The broad masses, who were once elevated as the "Masters" of the country by Mao, have sunk to the bottom during the reform era. Without power and privilege, they must live a plain life like Lei Feng (1940–1962), an ordinary soldier who served the people warm-heartedly and sacrificed his young life at his post at the age of twenty-two. There have been several versions of the "Ten Classes of People" since the 1970s. All seem to have sarcastically developed Mao's well-known "Analysis of the Classes in Chinese Society" in 1925, in which he maintained that class distinctions were essential for his revolution. The version above paints a vivid picture of the 1990s, and can also be heard as a *xiangsheng* (comic dialogue) set to rock music, which is a new form of performing art especially enjoyed by young people.

[R3] A New People's Public Servant
By Chengyao Qianjin

He wore a Mao suit and a pair of black sunglasses.
He walked with a measured tread, with his belly projecting conspicuously.
His every move and act looked calm and magnanimous.
When he went out, he sat in a Red Flag car, with police cars leading the way.
His young secretaries were all around him and his entourage looked after him.
There was no lack of flatterers, and there were countless toadies.

Before he entered the conference hall, a rapid round of applause was heard.
In my mind I envied him and ventured to greet him.
"May I ask who you are and where you are serving as an official?"
Learning I was a nobody, he showed on his face
that I was not worth another glance.

"I'm a people's public servant and I'm now a cadre at the township level.
I look a bit old, but it's not owing to my age.
It's all because I work very hard and exert myself all day long.
I'm busy with daytime meetings and I supervise various things at evening dances.

I handle big and small official business and I inspect every village.
There're numerous receptions and banquets, all offering wine and liquor.
I drink to the point of being dazed and muddled, but
still have to grit my teeth to hold on.
I dare not fritter away my time and can never be relaxed.

I'm fully aware as an official I must be at the head of my people.
However tiring and troublesome, I'm willing to
represent the people as their master."
I immediately stare at him in astonishment and start to vomit.
He's so thick-skinned that, damn, I've got to hand it to him.[13]

In China's anti-corruption campaigns, the corrupt official at the township level described above belongs to the category of "flies," corrupt minor government officials. Even though they are not high-ranking "tigers," the number of these low-level bureaucrats is huge and they have close contacts with ordinary people who are frustrated by them and hate them.

[R4] Cowardly Officials
By Wen Xuesi
Once a winecup is raised, policy becomes flexible.
Once a gift is given, the system can be relaxed;
Once a girl's bright eyes smile, the principles are lost;
When their friends ask for favors, they just say okay.[14]

Of all the corrupt officials exposed, from the high-ranking ones such as Lu Wei, who was the deputy head of the Propaganda Department of the CPC and who, in February 2018, was expelled from the CPC and his post for serious corruption,[15] to the petty officials who can embezzle hundreds of millions of yuan,[16] none of them can avoid wining and dining, taking gifts, having extramarital women, either at public expense or paid for by private entrepreneurs, and consequently, shady deals are made.

[R5] Corrupt Officials
By Wen Xuesi
There are never enough snakes, scorpions, and turtles and tortoises to sample.
Wine flows freely but it's never enough to get drunk on.
There are never enough pornographic movies to watch.
There are never enough young girls and secretaries to sleep with.
There are never enough gambling places and dance halls to make them feel tired.
There are never enough heroin and opium to snort.
There are never enough rolls of money to be interested in.
Life imprisonment is not long enough to make them regret.[17]

The baldness of this rhyme published in 2006 is shocking, but is all true. In an article published in December 2017 by Tao Zhiguo, the Party secretary of the Commission for Discipline Inspection of the CPC of Jilin Province, he described corrupt officials as "five evil cadres" (*wu du ganbu*) in wining, dining, whoring, gambling, and embezzling.[18] Do they regret when serving a sentence or before being executed? Let us see what Wen Qiang (1955–2010) said from the bottom of his heart just before his capital punishment on July 7, 2010, for serious corruption,

> Everyone says that I embezzled so much money and amused myself with so many women. Anyone in my position would embezzle so much and amuse himself with so many women, and even much more. For those female students, if I didn't amuse myself with them, others would. I merely did what insiders would do according to the game rules.[19]

Wen Qiang was the former Chongqing Public Security Bureau's executive deputy head for sixteen years and head of the city's Judicial Bureau. His crimes included accepting bribes, with his wife, worth 16.25 million yuan, possessing other 10.62 million yuan from sources that he could not explain, protecting the underworld in Chongqing, and raping a female university student.[20] When it came to his death sentence, he said the above in all honesty.

[R6] Just Guess How Things Look
By Guo Lihe

One
He and she didn't know each other before,
But they became intimate at first sight.
They sing and cuddle,
And are melted together in dancing.
They caress each other,
Like passionate lovers.
They "love" their "hearts out,"
But aren't they just playing games?

Two
"Model," "Outstanding" or "Excellent". . .
They love to consume the best of the best,
But never foot a penny of the bills.
He always talks about being honest and clean,
And he's most "obsessed" with anticorruption.
He has won big honors with titles such as
His deeds were unexpectedly exposed.
Can he make concessions to avoid trouble?

Three
But he still hangs about in hotels . . .
He raised money to buy a Toyota Crown car;
That caused much complaint from the people.
The "public servant" looked calm and natural, and
The "masters" sighed sorrowfully, but what could they do?
They've not got their wages for months,
The informants' reports seem to be going nowhere;
Why does nobody come to investigate?

Four
He uses the "F-" word whenever he starts to talk . . .
His quality is really terrible;
He knows nothing about whatever he does,
But he is good at boasting and flattering!
Each fat post "must be his";
He left the story on everyone's lips to warn the world.
Who gave the official post
To this "Excellent Talent"?[21]

What a good question! The judicial authorities admitted that of all the corrupt officials purged, 80% were being promoted at the very time they were committing corruption (*bian fu bian sheng*).[22] Wang Shouye, one of the five deputy-commanders and a member of the National People's Congress, Vice-Admiral, was sentenced to death in spring 2006, given a two-year reprieve, and had his sentence commuted to life imprisonment in December 2006. He was reported to the authorities by one of his five mistresses, all from the People's Liberation Army (PLA), China's armed forces. He embezzled hundreds of millions of yuan, but for four out of the five years that he was embezzling, he was awarded the titles of "Excellent Communist Party Member" and "Excellent Cadre" in the PLA.[23]

[R7] How the "Scrap Iron" Was Tempered
The Portrait of a Certain Public Servant
By Yang Handuan

He obtained his Party membership by pretence and deceit;
He secured his official position by handing over red packets of money;
He bought his diploma on the street;
He had his secretary make up his political achievements . . .

He grabbed money through bribes;
He got his villas through the rich;
He met his mistresses at singalong parlors;
He caught VD by travelling abroad . . .

He was exposed to the public by a petty thief;
He had money from bribes loaded by the truckload;
He confessed with much hesitation;
He went to jail weeping and wailing . . .

He became corrupt inevitably;
He was caught accidentally;
His supervision existed in name only;
The "scrap iron" was tempered by hidden rules.[24]

The title of this four-stanza rhyme was obviously made after the famous *How the Steel Was Tempered*, a Soviet socialist novel by Nikolai Ostrovsky (1904–1936). The Communists who were praised as strong as steel are now satirized as "scrap iron" in twenty-first-century China. Do corrupt officials actually pick up sexually transmitted diseases after going abroad? There is no detailed news in this regard but this popular rhyme could not be groundless or it would not have been published in the *Beijing Daily* in 2007. Hong Kong and Macao are not officially considered abroad but "outside of the border" (*jingwai*) of the Chinese Mainland. Hu Changqing (1948–2000), while serving as the vice governor of Jiangxi Province, flew to Hong Kong and Macao several times for sightseeing as well as having sex with prostitutes, using a pseudonym.[25] A *People's Daily* website released an article on an official's "way of whoring," that is, "gambling locally but whoring outside the locality." The author reported that some corrupt officials were enthusiastic about going to all parts of China and even abroad to "look for young women" (*zhao xiaojie*), a euphemism for prostitutes. In addition to the "tiger" type of high-ranking officials such as Hu Changqing, the *People's Daily* and *China Daily* websites have also published that a deputy mayor of a county, having learned that he had contracted AIDS, provided a list of over thirty females who he had sex with, most of whom were teachers and public servants.[26]

2.2 Witty Sarcasm: Rhymes in the Name of Corrupt Officials

Corrupt officials have their own justification or perverted logic to defend themselves. There are popular rhymes that sound funny and sarcastic and mimic the tone of those officials. In their minds all they do, be it sitting in a fancy car, keeping dubious relationships with female secretaries, occupying more housing, wining and dining, and taking material things, are for the sake of the people they serve, as [R8] and other rhymes reveal. They may be afraid of being investigated by the CPC internal disciplinary process at the designated time and place, called *shuanggui* (double designation) in Chinese, described implicitly in the last line of [R9]. The "tigers and flies" punished may feel wronged as is seen in [R10], but they always have an excuse for their behavior as vividly depicted in [R11]. For those who have not been caught, they would rather embezzle more "Even though I'm disciplined today; even if I'm jailed tomorrow!" because the cost of the punishment of one official is small compared with the huge benefits his family gets, implied in [R12] and [R13] below.

[R8] It Is Hard to Be an Official

To be an official is hard and it's hard to be an official.
Let me tell you what the difficulties are.

When my jeep was exchanged for a car,
All the masses complained.
It wasn't really what I wanted.
As the leader, how could the money not make my heart ache!

Everyone else rides in a Santana,
So a jeep will indeed make me lose face.
My loss of face is trivial,
But I must consider our enterprise's image.

They say I've been dishonest and behaved indecently,
And my secretaries are more gorgeous than beauties.
In fact, what do they know about that?
Only if they're pretty can they work for public relations.

I feel at ease and relaxed in a dance hall,
As if I were twenty years younger.
Without the secretaries to help me,
How can the leader manage an enterprise?

They say I have housing privileges.
Let me clear up the mystery.
I spare no effort in the performance of my duty.
I haven't taken care of my family matters for years.

I sacrifice my family life for the sake of everyone.
I feel ashamed facing my wife and children.
Only by giving four apartments to my three sons,
Can my conscience feel a bit at ease.

They say I wine and dine excessively.
Talking about that, it makes me feel sad.
Do I eat and drink for myself?
Isn't that for solving the business problems?

Can I afford not to invite the leaders from upper levels?
To promote our products, I have to wine and dine them first.
Is that not considered a contribution?
I end up getting hypertension and diabetes.

They say I embezzle and accept bribes.
This is a total frame-up.
Everyone comes to me for help,
Because the masses trust me.

I exert myself to the utmost for others.
I actually don't take much money for doing so.
A motorcycle, a fridge, and a big colour TV,
I just use them for a while and will return them some day.

I've worked with all my heart for the enterprise.
Everyone still says I'm a corrupt official.
I get no thanks for my kind-heartedness.
Wouldn't you say it's hard to serve as an official?[27]

[R9] "I Have a Strange Habit"
By Li Fuping

I have a strange habit—
If I ride in a car which is not first class, my behind gets sore;

I have a strange habit—
If my secretaries are not beautiful, people think I have no taste;

I have a strange habit—
If there's no meeting for two days, I get distracted;

I have a strange habit—
If there's no banquet for three days, I become uneasy;

I have a strange habit—
When I talk, I only like to say half what I mean;

I have a strange habit—
I often accept a slip of paper as money;

I have a strange habit—
State affairs and family affairs are mixed together when I'm handling them;

I have a strange habit—
Things of an open nature are dealt with in secret.

I have a strange habit—
Whatever I say in public doesn't mean anything;

I have a strange habit—
I rush abroad even in my dreams;

I have a strange habit—
My spirits are low and I'm inefficient in the daytime;

I have a strange habit—
I become stimulated to play on and on in the evening;

I have a strange habit—
I always like to hear flattery;

I have a strange habit—
I dislike what the people say and take it as nonsense;

I have a strange habit—
I break out in a cold sweat in the middle of the night;

I have a strange habit—
My legs tremble at the sight of the national emblem. . . .[28]

[R10] Some Official's "Complaints"
By Xu Lin

People say that I'm corrupt and that I embezzle.
This really makes me feel wronged.

It's just that my car is a bit of a luxury;
It's just that my Western-style house is a bit upscale.

It's just the banquets that I eat are a bit fancy;
It's just the clothes that I wear are a bit expensive;

It's just the travels abroad that I take are a bit more;
It's just the money that I spend on the "image projects" is a bit more;

It's just the gifts that I give to my superiors out of respect are a bit more;
It's just the money that I take for doing things for others has increased a bit more;

It's just the help that I give to my children doing business has become a bit frequent;
It's just the intimacy that I give to the girls is a bit too much . . .

Times are developing and our thinking must be liberated a bit more;
It's hard to be an official and you must understand a bit more!

I only have "new trends" compared with before.
Aren't your reports to the authorities going "too far"?[29]

[R11] A Corrupt Official's Confession
By Liu Deliang

I accepted nineteen thousand in cash that day
All because I drank too much at noon;

I went to bed with "her"
As it was too cold outside.

It's true that I accepted US dollars
Because I was going to Washington;

The owner sent me the remuneration
Because my calligraphy is expensive.

There's also the case of jewels
Because my wife asked for them;

The standard for wining and dining at public expense was high,
But I didn't take anything home at all.

In a word I'm innocent.
I've just had bad luck this year.

The corrupt officials' confessions are laughable.
In the end they are still in handcuffs.[30]

[R12] The Strange Phenomena in the Officialdom
By Yu Zhibo

While I'm still an official, I'd rather drink another cup of wine;
While I'm still an official, I'd rather take another pack of cigarettes;

While I'm still an official, I'd rather visit another prostitute;
While I'm still an official, I'd rather embezzle another amount of money;

While I'm still an official, I'd rather make another inspection tour;
While I'm still an official, I'd rather promote another official;

While I'm still an official, I'd rather change cars once more;
While I'm still an official, I'd rather pray to the temple gods once more;

While I'm still an official, I'd rather curry favor with someone once more;
While I'm still an official, I'd rather celebrate another Chinese New Year;

Loyalty and filial piety, and traditional virtues,
Marx, Lenin, Mao, and Deng, all put aside.

Even though I'm disciplined today;
Even if I'm jailed tomorrow![31]

[R13] The Confession of an "Idle Official"
By Yang Yuchen

Some officials work hard and become out of breath;
They have endless daily affairs to attend to and make errors.
Some officials don't worry too much;
They feel free and easy with a good reputation spreading far and wide.

If you want to know the secret of it,
Listen to the words of an "idle official"—

An official must be broad-minded;
When there are difficult problems, leave most of them for subordinates to do.
If you don't arrogate power to yourself and you're democratic,
It will free yourself to gamble for a couple of times.

An official must dare to delegate his power;
Let the secretaries do the hard work.
If they do well, it's to your credit; if it's not, leave it alone;
It will free yourself to "investigate" by lake fishing.

An official must make room for someone better qualified;
Good things should be passed to your wife so she controls them.
Pillow talk is soothing to lull you to sleep;
"Rich water should stay in one's own fields"—keep all benefits for yourselves.

A term in an official position flies by;
I must eat, drink and be merry without missing anything.
When it's time to enjoy myself freely, I'll just enjoy myself;
Even if I'm dismissed from office, I'm still willing to do so.[32]

2.3 Poetic Justice: Rhymes by Officials Themselves

Some officials are not merely corrupted by power, but also possess a talent for composing poems or writing poetically. If a publisher could publish an anthology of poems by corrupt officials someday, it would contribute quite largely to combating corruption and building a clean government, and it would be educational as well. Seven verses or poetic couplets are examined below.

[R14] The Demons
By Tohti Sabir
The demons put on masks;
And became fairy maidens.
They covered my eyes.
I thought I was having beautiful dreams and
Thought I was in paradise.
I only woke up after I fell
From the high rock down to the abyss.
Ah, everyone, be vigilant.
Don't let demons keep pestering you.[33]

This poem was composed by Tohti Sabir (1933–2017), an ethnic Uyghur, vice chair of the Xinjiang Uygur Autonomous Region, in repentance. His position was equivalent to a vice governor of a province. His corrupt act was that he assisted two women who obtained scarce materials for profiteering through his *guanxi* or connections. The bribes and kickbacks he received during 1987–1989 were worth 6,342 yuan and 82,000 yuan from them, respectively, which was an extremely low amount by the standard then, not to mention today. However, like almost all corrupt officials, he had illicit affairs with one of the women and another girl who was younger than half of his age. When asked who the demons were in the poem he referred to, he said "that type of woman," with a deep sigh. What was he lamenting for? One could only assume that it was for the Party and government posts that he was removed from. However, he was exempted from prosecution. Interestingly, the state media still addressed him as "Comrade" in the Party's decision on him in September 1989 and in the obituary about him in February 2017.[34]

[R15] By Li Chenglong

One
Born of a humble social status and a poor boy,
I have been honest since I was a child . . .
I did not handle great undertakings foolishly,
But I was just stupid in a moment of weakness.
Once I took a wrong step in life, I fell into utter disrepute.
I committed a serious blunder.

Two
When money covered my eyes, I felt dizzy.
Crazy about higher official ranks, I sank to the depths.
Hanging on to fame and wealth,
I finally became a criminal.
Fame and fortune are just like dirt;
Wealth and honors are but floating clouds.
If you can give me a hand to rescue me,
I'll be reborn and suffer hardships to pay for my humiliation.[35]

The two poems above were the work of Li Chenglong (1952–2000) while in jail. He was the Party secretary of Yulin City and later served as the vice-mayor of Guigang, Guangxi Zhuang Autonomous Region. It has been reported that after corrupt officials are arrested, they like to emphasize that they were born into poor families. "I am the son of peasants," most of the corrupt officials have said when writing confessions. Li Chenglong was one more. He blamed his corruption on being "just stupid in a moment of weakness." His second poem looked more artistic, yet in it he still blamed money instead of criticizing himself more profoundly. His crime was that he accepted 3.74 million yuan, US$25,000, HK$10,000 as bribes. In addition, he had 5.68 million yuan, some HK dollars, US dollars and New Taiwan dollars, as well as jewelry the acquisition of which he was unable to explain. Investigators also found 10 password boxes in which he put all the photos of the women he had had relationships with, together with pornographic magazines. He was expecting the cloud to have a silver lining, as in "If you can give me a hand to rescue me" in one line, but was sentenced to death in early 1999 and executed in spring 2000.[36]

[R16] Motto
By Ding Yangning
If I became an official without making a fortune,
I wouldn't do that even if I were invited to.
If I became an official without taking money,
I wouldn't have the capital for my retirement.[37]

[R17] Poem from Jail
By Ding Yangning
Three years have flown by like an arrow.
I ruined my career in a flash.
I shouldn't have sought after fame and wealth,
Putting aside the Party's heavy responsibilities.[38]

Ding Yangning, the Party secretary of Zhenghe, a poor county in Fujian Province, had the nickname of "The Red Packet Secretary" as he expected money sent to him in an envelope whenever he was asked to do something. In less than three years in the late 1990s, he accepted sixty-eight bribes worth half a million yuan, US$2,300, and other materials from seventy-two people worth 15,000 yuan. In return, he recommended seven people to higher-level government departments and personally promoted dozens of cadres to higher positions. In the second poem written in prison, his self-reflection that he should not have sought after fame and wealth seemed to the point, but that came too late. He was sentenced to life imprisonment in March 2000. His motto, which has remained true among all corrupt officials in poor and rich areas, has been quoted in many anticorruption books as a negative example of an official.[39]

[R18] By Cheng Kejie
The Communist Party's kindness to me is as huge as a mountain.
Li Ping's feelings toward me are as deep as the sea.[40]

The most senior official executed for corruption so far is Cheng Kejie (1933–2000), a member of the Zhuang ethnic group. Together with his mistress Li Ping, he accepted 41 million yuan in bribes when he served as the vice-chair of the Standing Committee of the National People's Congress and the chair of Guangxi Zhuang Autonomous Region. Ironically, while Cheng was busy embezzling money intended for their future life together, Li had another lover in Hong Kong. When Cheng was sentenced to death in July 2000, she was able to keep her own life by exposing his crime.[41] As pleasant to the ear as the couplet is, Cheng and Li used each other and Li had the last word.

[R19] By Zhang Zonghai
A flower in the purple bamboo forest,
Roses and peonies are not as beautiful.
I'd like to go forward and pick it,
But I'm afraid it may wither and won't sprout.[42]

Zhang Zonghai was a member of the Party Commission and the director of Communications (*xuanchuan buzhang*) of Chongqing, and he was a good poet despite coming from a peasant family. He had three requirements for those who sought women for him: she must be university educated; she must be pretty; and she must be unmarried. This poem was composed in 2003 on the spur of the moment when he was in the five-star Hilton hotel in Chongqing with Xie Yufen, a teachers college student who also worked in a foot massage parlor where they met. Was he really in love with her? No, Xie was not the only woman. He was enthusiastic about gambling, too. It was after he lost more than a hundred million yuan in gambling in Macao that he was arrested, during which only three items were found in his briefcase: money, Viagra tablets, and condoms. Even when he was studying at the Central Party School of the CPC, he kept up extramarital relationships with quite a few women. In 2005, he was sentenced to fifteen years in prison.[43]

[R20] A Poem of Repentance
By Bao Guiping
Gambling—the poison that ruined my aspirations first;
My desire, hard to fulfill; awaiting me was the sharp sword.
Embezzlement—the devil's rope that wound around my body and broke my soul;
Once the nightmare woke me up, I was already at the cliff's edge.
Love affairs—the sharp teeth that snapped at my heart and changed my nature;
Looking back, astonished, I'm entering the gates of hell.[44]

This rhyme was composed by Bao Guiping, chief of the Labor and Social Security Bureau of Weiyang District, Yangzhou City of Jiangsu Province. After being sentenced to seven years in jail and confiscation of property worth 50,000 yuan, he expressed his sorrowful regret poetically, "I was ruined by gambling, stumbled over greed, and fell down in love affairs." The literary quality of this poem is high, yet the quality of this "fly" category of official is below that of many ordinary people.

In a satirical sketch entitled "New Standard Questions and Answers," Ling Ri raised eight questions and answered them sarcastically. Two of the questions and answers are quoted below:

Q: What two qualities must officials possess?
A: First, the temperament of a poet. They must possess fearlessness and great imagination, which, for instance, can be embodied when reporting the "statistics." Second, the temperament of a philosopher. They must thoroughly know the vocabulary and principles of dialectics, managing to be extremely fluent whenever they speak. For instance, they can see some "good things" in the "bad accidents" that have happened.
Q: What is bedding composed of?
A: To ordinary people, that only includes pillows, mats, and quilts, but to some cadres, it also must include "girls."[45]

The seven poems displayed above confirm that each of those officials literally possessed the temperament of a poet. From the big "tigers" Tohti Sabir of Xinjiang and Cheng Kejie of Guangxi, to the low- and middle-level "flies" Li Chenglong, Zhang Zonghai, and Bao Guiping, all of them, except Ding Yangning of [R16] and [R17], perhaps, were involved with women. They all deserved the punishment they received one way or another.

3. POPULAR RHYMES, AN HONORABLE TRADITION WITH A MODERN SIGNIFICANCE

Broadly speaking, the value of *minyao* lies in their social, historical, and literary aspects. In today's China, *minyao* play a very positive role in exposing corruption and promoting anticorruption education.

First, *minyao* criticize officials' evil practices of the day. Since the very beginning, *minyao* have been an important part of Chinese political culture. When compiling the *Book of Songs*, Confucius (581–479 BCE) put those about the "*feng*" from the fifteen states in Part One of the three-part anthology. The 160 songs in the first part, out of 305 songs in total, are regarded as the most popular poems throughout the centuries down to the present day. The word "*feng*" in Chinese contains a range of meanings, from practice, custom, atmosphere to attitude, and to news, information, and so on. The system of folk song and ballad collection since the Zhou dynasty (1044–256 BCE) was primarily aimed at collecting the people's opinions about the practices, customs, and atmosphere, and all types of news in society related to the rulers. Officials were sent to various regions to listen to what the ordinary people were thinking of, and resentful of, in order to modify government policies.

Confucius attached the importance of the *Book of Songs* to his disciples and said, "Why is it that none of you study the *Songs*? For the *Songs* will help you to incite people's emotions, to observe their feelings, to keep company, to express your grievances."[46] Zhu Xi (1130–1200) and other most renowned commentators on the Confucian classics in history elaborated the fourth function, "to express your grievances" (*keyi yuan*), as meaning one can "criticize the government above" (*ci shang zheng*).[47] Therefore, that *minyao* strongly reflect the people's criticism of the bad practices of government is a fine tradition with a long history. Grievances (*yuan*) and criticism (*ci*) are certainly prominent in contemporary *minyao*.

Second, *minyao* give vent to the people's dissatisfaction. *Minyao*, which traditionally circulated from mouth to mouth, could have seen a steep decline at a time when the media are developing rapidly. On the contrary, in today's China, *minyao* are spreading far and wide, both orally and in the media. Where there is little space for grievances and criticism in the media, there are *minyao* circulating through various ways. People from all strata of society, including government officials, are involved in retelling and spreading them. The less the mainstream media reflect public opinion, the more *minyao* could emerge. In addition, the existence of *minyao* as a phenomenon lies in the nature of bureaucratic corruption as well as social problems. If the issues are not solved or not addressed, the *minyao* concerning them will continue to exist, and new *minyao* satirizing them may be created. Likewise, if the problems are dealt with and solved, the *minyao* in question may stop circulating. In other words, the more versions of *minyao* concerning certain problems that are not solved, the more responses will be found among the people. The various versions of "The Ten Groups of People" mentioned in [R2] are typical of such a phenomenon because, up to now, the description of the ten groups of people still rings true.

Third, *minyao* may serve somehow as a consolation. To a large extent, the present-day *minyao* have a function of self-entertainment. Some people try to explain things away when ridiculed, or laugh at themselves. *Minyao* circulate on various occasions, particularly during feasts at wining and dining tables. Officials, who are often guests of dinners, participate in spreading the *minyao* that make fun of themselves. Is it not ridiculous? Well, many people take *minyao* at dinner time as jokes as if they were playing drinkers' wager games (*xing jiuling*). In Chinese culture, wining and dining in a convivial atmosphere is often denoted by the term "*renao*," literally "hot and lively." Drinking games have long been part of this atmosphere. Literary games, part of the drinking games, including the spontaneous composition of poems, require excellent Classical Chinese and have consequently fallen into disuse. Instead, nowadays, popular verses using vernacular are not uncommon. Two rhymes that encourage diners to eat and drink read,

[R21] We don't embezzle or take bribes,
Why should we feel guilty about wining and dining?[48]

[R22] As long as I don't take bribes,
Why should I worry about a stomach full of liquor?[49]

The above two examples, which were particularly popular before Xi Jinping took power in 2012, show that some people think that they may be corrupt if they pocket something, yet they are clean if they just eat and drink. Once the atmosphere is enlivened, many more *minyao*, political or pornographic, are exchanged.

The question remains why those who are poked fun at, such as officials and the *nouveax riches*, are delighted to "disgrace" themselves by spreading the *minyao*? The answer is that although most *minyao* may be satirical and resentful, yet, they are also humorous, bantering, or teasing. *Minyao* are like what Confucius said when he praised the first poem, "The Cooing" (*Guanju*), in the *Book of Songs*, "Pleasure not carried to the point of debauch; grief not carried to the point of self-injury."[50] Another reason lies in the fact that most *minyao* involving sociopolitical affairs are general. As long as the officials themselves are not identified in the *minyao*, they might as well enjoy their circulation.

4. CONCLUSION

The state media like to say that corruption is a cancer to which no society can be immune, at home or abroad. Of course it is not wrong to claim that. Two citizens in China demonstrate below their international vision as well.

[R23] On the Top Ten Social Hazards
By Li Yuezhong and Zhu Yuanqing
Talking about the No. 1 social hazard,
The whole world recognizes corruption.
It fundamentally causes grave harm to the state and the people.
If corruption is not eliminated, the country will grow weak.[51]

However, despite massive anticorruption efforts, China's scores on Transparency International's Corruption Perceptions Index have made slow progress since Xi Jinping came to power: 39 in 2012, 40 in 2013, 36 in 2014, 37 in 2015, 40 in 2016, and 41 in 2017, with two years scoring even worse, ranking 77 among 180 countries or regions across the world in 2017, far behind Hong Kong and Taiwan ranking 13 and 29, respectively, in the same year.[52] So much work remains to be done!

Also according to the state media, "Revitalizing the Chinese nation has been the greatest dream of the Chinese people since the beginning of modern times. It is called the Chinese Dream. It is a dream of prosperity, of national renewal, and of happiness."[53] The intensifying anticorruption campaign undertaken under Xi Jinping's leadership should be aimed at achieving this goal.

With the improvement of the standard of living and the rise of the educational level, the Chinese people have become less tolerant toward official corruption. While the state media emphasize the bright future of the Chinese Dream, ordinary people want to link the dream with anticorruption as a precondition. Below is one rhyme that reflects what the people think:

[R24] A Chinese Ballad: The Chinese Dream
By Cui Shizhong
The East is red; the sun is rising.
The Chinese Dream is shining.
It shines on our heroes and the masses.
They both strive to revive the country.
Anticorruption comes first.
All the people must take action to foster a healthy society.[54]

This rhyme may not be literary in the Chinese original, but "anticorruption comes first" is the common expectation of the Chinese people.

An article by Liu Xiaochun in *New Orient* (*Xin Dongfang*), the journal of the Communist Party School of Hainan Province, holds that "whereas intellectuals are having unprecedented trouble explaining society, the explanations about society and life by the common people are showing their grassroots wisdom. The current *minyao* among the people reflect a kind of emotion in society."[55] To understand Chinese culture and society better, particularly the officialdom in the past four decades, *minyao* are indispensable. At the time when the Chinese Dream has been made prominent by Xi Jinping, the study of *minyao* becomes even more significant because *minyao*, whether in its traditional or modern sense, are more a reflection of the voice of the ordinary people in society.

NOTES

1. https://www.transparency.org/what-is-corruption#define.
2. All the three general secretaries of the CPC mentioned the life or death struggle of the Party and the state, for example, http://en.people.cn/200211/12/eng20021112_106666.shtml, http://cpc.people.com.cn/GB/164113/15049679.html, and http://www.chinadaily.com.cn/china/2015–02/06/content_19513645.htm.

3. http://cpcchina.chinadaily.com.cn/special/cleanparty/2013–01/29/content_16184813.htm.

4. http://www.legaldaily.com.cn/index_article/content/2017–12/20/content_7425949.htm?node=5955.

5. http://www.ccdi.gov.cn/toutiao/201807/t20180720_175998.html.

6. Ibid.

7. "Zhua Tanguan" (Arresting Corrupt Officials), http://www.readers365.com/xiezuobaodian/224.htm; the English translation of the rhyme is mine; the same hereafter for all the rhyme translation.

8. *Renmin Ribao* (*People's Daily*), June 29, 2016, http://news.china.com/focus/cpc95/11179148/20160629/22955334_all.html.

9. Xinhua News Agency, January 14, 2018, http://www.ccdi.gov.cn/yaowen/201801/t20180114_161833.html.

10. Perry Link, Richard P. Madsen, and Paul G. Pickowicz, *Popular China: Unofficial Culture in a Globalizing Society* (Lanham, Boulder, New York, and Oxford: Rowman & Littlefield, 2002), 89–109.

11. http://zwyk.fabiao.com/.

12. "Jiushi Niandai Shideng Ren" (Ten Classes of People of the 1990s), in Quan Weirun and Wang Zhenhua, *Yaogun Shunkouliu* (*Popular Rhymes with Rock & Roll*), audio cassette tape, n.d., http://zhidao.baidu.com/question/137312902.html?qbl=relate_question_0&optimi=4.

13. Chengyao Qianjin, "Xin Renmin Gongpu" (A New People's Public Servant), *Zawen Yuekan* (*Essays Semimonthly*), 2nd half of July 2005, 27, repr. from *Fengci yu Youmo* (*Satire and Humor*), http://www.eywedu.com/Zwykzx/zwxb2005/zwxb20050753.html.

14. Wen Xuesi, "Nuoguan" (Cowardly Officials), *Zawen Yuekan*, 2nd half of August 2006, 53, repr. from *Yidian Didai* (*A Little Area*), http://www.eywedu.com/Zwykzx/zwxb2006/zwxb20060852.html.

15. http://news.jcrb.com/jxsw/201802/t20180214_1842485.html.

16. http://www.chinanews.com/gn/2014/11–14/6773181.shtml.

17. Wen Xuesi, "Tuanguan" (Corrupt Officials), http://www.eywedu.com/Zwykzx/zwxb2006/zwxb20060852.html.

18. http://zgjjjc.ccdi.gov.cn/bqml/bqxx/201712/t20171205_113180.html.

19. http://redchinacn.net/portal.php?mod=view&aid=1243.

20. https://baike.baidu.com/item/%E6%96%87%E5%BC%BA/1445988.

21. "Shixiang Jingcai" (Just Guess How Things Look), *Zawen Yuekan*, 2nd half of December 2006, 33, repr. from *Shanxi Jiating* (*Shanxi Families*), September 11, 2006, http://www.eywedu.com/Zwykzx/zwxb2006/zwxb20061258.html.

22. http://news.china.com.cn/2013–06/06/content_29040195.htm.

23. http://history.people.com.cn/n/2013/0121/c198865–20269345.html and https://baike.baidu.com/item/%E7%8E%8B%E5%AE%88%E4%B8%9A/30552.

24. Yang Handuan, "Feitie Shi Zenyang Liancheng de—Mou Gongpu Xiezhen" (How the "Scrap Iron" Was Tempered—The Portrait of a Certain Public Servant), *Zawen Yuekan*, 2nd half of Sept. 2007, 54, repr. from the *Beijing Ribao* (*Beijing Daily*), June 25, 2007, http://www.eywedu.com/Zwykzx/zwxb2007/zwxb20070950.html.

25. He Nenggao, *Hu Changqing: Duoluo de Zhengtan Liuxing* (*Hu Changqing: A Fallen Meteor in the Political Arena*) (Beijing: People's Court, 2006), 345–50.

26. http://www.people.com.cn/GB/32306/33232/10332253.html and http://finance.people.com.cn/nc/GB/15415409.html.

27. "Zuo Guan Nan" (It Is Hard to Be an Official), Zhen Yan, *Liuxing Minyao* (*Popular Rhymes*) (Hohhot: Yuanfang, 2001), 145–47.

28. Li Fuping, "Wo You Yige Guai Xiguan" (I Have a Strange Habit), *Zawen Yuekan*, 2nd half of Aug. 2004, repr. from *Luoyang Wanbao* (*Luoyang Evening News*), http://www.eywedu.com/Zwykzx/zwxb2004/zwxb20040868.html.

29. Xu Lin, "Mou Guanyuan 'Baoyuan'" (Some Official's "Complaints"), *Zawen Yuekan*, 2nd half of October 2004, 11, repr. from *Dazhong Manhua* (*Popular Cartoons*), July 10, 2004, http://www.eywedu.com/Zwykzx/zwxb2004/zwxb20041055.html.

30. Li Deliang, "Tanguan Zibai" (A Corrupt Official's Confession), *Zawen Yuekan*, 2nd half of Feb. 2006, 26, repr. from *Xinxiang Ribao* (*Xinxiang Daily*), http://www.eywedu.com/Zwykzx/zwxb2006/zwxb20060254.html.

31. Yu Zhibo, "Guanchang Guaizhuang" (The Strange Phenomena in the Officialdom), *Zawen Yuekan*, 2nd half of July 2006, 54, repr. from *Dahe Bao* (*Dahe Daily*), April 26, 2006, http://www.readers365.com/Zwykzx/zwxb2006/zwxb20060763.html.

32. Yang Yuchen, "'Xianguan' de Zibai" (The Confession of an "Idle Official"), *Zawen Yuekan*, 2nd half of December 2006, 44.

33. Tohti Sabir, "Mogui" (Demons), in *Honghuo: Tanguan Qingfu Xianxiang Jingshu Lu* (*Women Are the Bane of Men: Warning against the Phenomenon of Corrupt Officials with Mistresses*) by Qin Wei and Zeng Ge (Lhasa: Tibet People's, 2003), 19.

34. http://news.163.com/17/0220/10/CDNB1JA8000187VE.html.

35. Li Chenglong, quoted in Guo Zhenya, "Tanguan Shi Dianping" (On the Poems Composed by Corrupt Officials), *Zawen Yuekan*, 2nd half of February 2005, 43, repr. from the *Jinwan Bao* (*Tonight Newspaper*), November 23, 2004, http://www.eywedu.com/Zwykzx/zwxb2005/zwxb20050239.html.

36. http://www.baike.com/wiki/%E6%9D%8E%E4%B9%98%E9%BE%99, and http://cpc.people.com.cn/GB/64093/64103/5707487.html, http://opinion.people.com.cn/GB/1036/3330098.html.

37. Ding Yangning, "Zuoyouming" (Motto), quoted in Guo Zhenya, ibid.

38. Ding Yangming, "Yu zhong shi" (Poem from Jail), quoted in Guo Zhengya, ibid.

39. http://www.people.com.cn/GB/channel1/11/20000331/26991.html, http://hlj.rednet.cn/c/2008/01/17/1420984.htm, and http://lagua.108qi.com/bxcz/20141011/16059_2.html.

40. Zhang Shan, "Tanguan Weishenme Yao Chanhui?" (Why Would Corrupt Officials Repent?), *Fan Fubai Daokan* (*Anticorruption Herold*), April 2005, 12.

41. Ibid., http://en.people.cn/english/200007/31/eng20000731_46885.html, and http://en.people.cn/english/200008/09/eng20000809_47734.html.

42. Hao Qing, "Zhang Zonghai he Tade Mimi Qingren" (Zhang Zonghai and His Secret Lover), *Jiancha Fengyun* (*Procuratorial View*) no. 15, 2006, 30–31.

43. Ibid., http://news.cri.cn/gb/3821/2004/07/23/301@241843_4.htm, and http://www.people.com.cn/GB/paper68/12417/1116679.html.

44. Bao Guiping, "Chanhui Shi" (A Poem of Repentance), *Jiancha Ribao,* August 19, 2008, http://cpc.people.com.cn/GB/64093/64371/7688218.html.

45. Ling Ri, "Xin Biaozhun Wenda" (New Standard Questions and Answers), *Zawen Yuekan*, February 2001, 27.

46. Arthur Waley, tr., *The Analects of Confucius* (New York: Random House, 1938), 212.

47. https://baike.baidu.com/item/%E5%85%B4%E8%A7%82%E7%BE%A4%E6%80%A8.

48. Shu Jian and Zuo Yu, *Dangdai Shunkouliu yu Shehui Redian Saomiao* (*Contemporary Popular Rhymes and the Scanning of the Hot Spots in Society*) (Beijing: China Archives, 1994), 7.

49. Ibid.

50. Arthur Waley, tr., 99.

51. Li Yuezhong and Zhu Yuanqing, "Shuoshuo Shehui Shi Da Hai" (On the Top Ten Social Hazards), *Zawen Yuekan*, February 2001, 29.

52. https://www.transparency.org/news/feature/corruption_perceptions_index_2017#table.

53. China International Publishing Group and China Academy of Translation, *Keywords to Understand China* (Beijing: New World, 2016), 3.

54. http://blog.sina.com.cn/s/blog_68d1554d010181tv.html.

55. Repr. from *Wenhui Dushu Zhoubao (Wenhui Reading Weekly)*, June 6, 2002, 14.

BIBLIOGRAPHY

Baidu Baike (Baidu Encyclopedia). Accessed August 7, 2018. Wang Qiang. https://baike.baidu.com/item/%E6%96%87%E5%BC%BA/1445988; Wang Shouye. https://baike.baidu.com/item/%E7%8E%8B%E5%AE%88%E4%B8%9A/30552; Xing Guan Qun Yuan (To incite, observe, keep, and express something) https://baike.baidu.com/item/%E5%85%B4%E8%A7%82%E7%BE%A4%E6%80%A8.

Baike (Encyclopedia). Accessed August 7, 2018. "Li Chenglong." http://www.baike.com/wiki/%E6%9D%8E%E4%B9%98%E9%BE%99.

China Daily. Accessed August 7, 2018. February 6, 2005. http://www.chinadaily.com.cn/china/2015–02/06/content_19513645.htm.

China International Publishing Group and China Academy of Translation. *Keywords to Understand China*. Beijing: New World, 2016.

CRI [China Radio International] Online. Accessed August 7, 2018. July 23, 2004. http://news.cri.cn/gb/3821/2004/07/23/301@241843_4.htm.

Cui, Shizhong. "Zhonghua Minyao: Zhongguo Meng (A Chinese Ballad: The Chinese Dream)," Sina Weibo, Accessed August 7, 2018. February 2, 2013. http://blog.sina.com.cn/s/blog_68d1554d010181tv.html.

Fan Fubai Daokan (*Anticorruption Herold*), April 2005.

Fazhi Ribao (*Legal Daily*). Accessed August 7, 2018. December 20, 2017. http://www.legaldaily.com.cn/index_article/content/2017–12/20/content_7425949.htm?node=5955.

Fu, Zhiping. *Congzheng Daode Jianshe Dangyuan Ganbu Duben* (*A Reader for Communist Officials' Moral Reconstruction*). Beijing: People's Daily Press, 2012. Accessed August 7, 2018. https://books.google.ca/books?id=nYApDwAAQBAJ&pg=PT212&lpg=PT212&dq=%E4%B8%81%E4%BB%B0%E5%AE%81%EF%BC%8C&source=bl&ots=8i9CNZy7Wt&sig=qApYx2bP_gwT5u8J3nOL1n9V7uM&hl=en&sa=X&ved=0ahUKEwiK9pe91bbZAhVDXq0KHURiAZQQ6AEIJzAA#v=onepage&q=%E4%B8%81%E4%BB%B0%E5%AE%81%EF%BC%8C&f=false.

He, Nenggao. *Hu Changqing: Duoluo de Zhengtan Liuxing* (*Hu Changqing: A Fallen Meteor in the Political Arena*). Beijing: People's Court, 2006.

Hong Wang (Red Net). Accessed August 7, 2018. January 17, 2008. http://hlj.rednet.cn/c/2008/01/17/1420984.htm.

Hongse Zhongguo Wang (RedChinaCn.net, in Chinese). Accessed August 7, 2018. January 11, 2012. http://redchinacn.net/portal.php?mod=view&aid=1243.

Jiancha Fengyun (*Procuratorial View*), no. 15, 2006.

Jiancha Ribao (*Procuratorial Daily*, in Chinese). Accessed August 7, 2018. February 4, 2018. http://news.jcrb.com/jxsw/201802/t20180214_1842485.html.

Link, Perry and Kate Zhou. "*Shunkouliu*: Popular Satirical Sayings and Popular Thought." In *Popular China: Unofficial Culture in a Globalizing Society*, edited by Perry Link, Richard P. Madsen, and Paul G. Pickowicz, 89–109. Lanham, Boulder, New York, and Oxford: Rowman & Littlefield, 2002.

Qin, Wei and Zeng Ge. *Honghuo: Tanguan Qingfu Xianxiang Jingshu lu* (*Women Are the Bane of Men: Warning against the Phenomenon of Corrupt Officials with Mistresses*). Lhasa: Tibet People's, 2003.

Quan, Weirun, and Wang Zhenhua. *Yaogun shunkouliu* (*Popular Rhymes with Rock & Roll*, in Chinese), audio cassette tape, n.d. Accessed August 7, 2018. http://zhidao.baidu.com/question/137312902.html?qbl=relate_question_0&optimi=4.

Renmin Ribao (*People's Daily*), English website. Accessed August 7, 2018. July 31, 2000. http://en.people.cn/english/200007/31/eng20000731_46885.html; August 10, 2000. http://en.people.cn/english/200008/09/eng20000809_47734.html; November 12, 2002. http://en.people.cn/200211/12/eng20021112_106666.shtml.

Renmin Ribao (*People's Daily*, in Chinese) and *Renmin Wang*, the website of Accessed August 7, 2018. 2 Sept. 1989. http://dangshi.people.com.cn/GB/146570/198300/200214/200216/12451312.html; March 31, 2000. http://www.people.com.cn/GB/channel1/11/20000331/26991.html; July 7, 2004. http://www.people.com.cn/GB/paper68/12417/1116679.html; April 18, 2005. http://opinion.people.com.cn/GB/1036/3330098.html; May 9, 2007. http://cpc.people.com.cn/GB/64093/64103/5707487.html; August 19, 2008. http://cpc.people.com.cn/GB/64093/64371/7688218.html; November 6, 2009. http://www.people.com.cn/GB/32306/33232/10332253.html; July 1, 2011. http://cpc.people.com.cn/GB/164113/15049679.html; January 21, 2013. http://history.people.com.cn/n/2013/0121/c198865–20269345.html; June 29, 2016. http://news.china.com/focus/cpc95/11179148/20160629/22955334_all.html.

Shu, Jian and Zuo Yu. *Dangdai Shunkouliu yu Shehui Redian Saomiao* (*Contemporary Popular Rhymes and the Scanning of the Hot Spots in Society*). Beijing: China Archives, 1994.

Transparency International. Accessed August 7, 2018. https://www.transparency.org/news/feature/corruption_perceptions_index_2017#table; https://www.transparency.org/what-is-corruption#define.

Waley, Arthur, tr. *The Analects of Confucius*. New York: Random House, 1938.

Wenhui Dushu Zhoubao (*Wenhui Reading Weekly*), June 6, 2002.

Xiezuo Baodian (Readers 365, in Chinese). Accessed August 7, 2018. http://www.readers365.com/xiezuobaodian/224.htm.

Xinhua News Agency (in Chinese). Accessed August 7, 2018. January 14, 2018. http://www.ccdi.gov.cn/yaowen/201801/t20180114_161833.html.

Xinjiang Ribao (*Xinjiang Daily*, in Chinese), via NetEase. Accessed August 7, 2018. February 20, 2017. http://news.163.com/17/0220/10/CDNB1JA8000187VE.html.

Zawen Yuekan (*Essays Monthly* [before 2004], and *Essays Semimonthly* [since 2004], in Chinese). Accessed August 7, 2018. February 2001, 27 and 29. 2nd half of August 2004. http://www.eywedu.com/Zwykzx/zwxb2004/zwxb20040868.html; 2nd half of October 2004. http://www.eywedu.com/Zwykzx/zwxb2004/zwxb20041055.html; 2nd half of February 2005. http://www.eywedu.com/Zwykzx/zwxb2005/zwxb20050239.html; 2nd half of July 2005. http://www.eywedu.com/Zwykzx/zwxb2005/zwxb20050753.html; 2nd half of February 2006. http://www.eywedu.com/Zwykzx/zwxb2006/zwxb20060254.html; 2nd half of July 2006. http://www.readers365.com/Zwykzx/zwxb2006/zwxb20060763.html; 2nd half of August 2006. http://www.eywedu.com/Zwykzx/zwxb2006/zwxb20060852.html; 2nd half of December 2006, 44. 2nd half of December 2006. http://www.eywedu.com/Zwykzx/zwxb2006/zwxb20061258.html; 2nd half of September 2007. http://www.eywedu.com/Zwykzx/zwxb2007/zwxb20070950.html.

Zhen, Yan. *Liuxing Minyao* (*Popular Rhymes*). Hohhot, Inner Mongolia: Yuanfang, 2001.

Zhongguo Jijian Jiancha Zazhi (*China Discipline Inspection and Supervision Semimonthly*, in Chinese). Accessed August 7, 2018. 1st half of December 2017. http://zgjjjc.ccdi.gov.cn/bqml/bqxx/201712/t20171205_113180.html.

Zhongguo Wang (www.china.com.cn, in Chinese). Accessed August 7, 2018. 6 June 2013. http://news.china.com.cn/2013–06/06/content_29040195.htm.

Zhongxinshe (China News Service, in Chinese). Accessed August 7, 2018. 14 November 2014. http://www.chinanews.com/gn/2014/11–14/6773181.shtml.

Zhongyang Jiwei Guojia Jianwei Wangzhan (Website of the Central Commission for Discipline Inspection of the Communist Party of China and the National Supervisory Commission of the People's Republic of China, in Chinese). Accessed August 7, 2018. 20 July 2018. http://www.ccdi.gov.cn/toutiao/201807/t20180720_175998.html.

Chapter 10

Corruption during China's Golden Ages

Case Studies in the Han and Tang Dynasties

Stella Y. Xu

Most scholars agree that because of the Han and Tang dynasties' consolidation of political power, cultural prosperity, and social stability, these dynasties are golden ages in Chinese history. Yet corruption, which is not uncommon in many administrations and societies, was present even in these dynasties, and so it may be asked why and how corruption occurred during China's golden ages, and how similar or different were their corruption cases in terms of the social background, motivation, and manner of those involved during these periods? In addition, how did the Han and Tang, during which governmental control was relatively strong, try to prevent corruption, and identify, prosecute, and punish officials involved in corruption? It could be said that the government, with its legal codes and policies to prevent corruption, and corrupted officials are like a cat and mouse who keep on tracking and evading each other. Indeed, Han emperors realized the potential problems of corruption and issued edicts to legally prevent the possibility of corruption. A well-known example of their severe penalties for corruption was that punishment was extended to three generations through the stipulation that the descendants of corrupted officials could not be appointed to government positions.

Nonetheless, corruption still occurred. Examples of corruption included illegally taking land from powerless farmers, taking unclaimed public land, taking bribes, manipulating and intervening in the legal system for one's own interest, and withholding soldiers' stipends in the case of military generals. Both the Han and the Tang dynasties strengthened the supervision system and intensified the punishment for corruption, though its rulers found out that it is an endless cycle between the committing of crimes and the establishment of severe laws to prevent these crimes. The corruption cases and anticorruption policies during the Han and Tang dynasties certainly have become some of the best reference points on the subject of corruption for later periods in China.

CORRUPTION DURING THE HAN DYNASTY

The Han dynasty (206 BCE–220 CE) started as a referendum on the failure of the Han's powerful predecessor, the Qin dynasty (221–206 BCE). The apparently strong Qin dynasty only lasted fifteen years, and one of the primary concerns for the new Han rulers was that they should learn from the failures of the Qin. As a result of substantial political adjustments being made from the Emperor Gaozu (r. 202–195 BCE) to the Emperor Wudi (r. 141–87 BCE) eras, the Han dynasty became more stabilized and structured. Emperor Wudi is often remembered as one of the most accomplished emperors in Chinese history, and a role model to be emulated by later emperors. Emperor Wudi's most notable accomplishment was his successful military campaigns against the Xiongnu, Nanye, and Weiman Chaoxian. In addition, he was firm in establishing clean and accountable governance: one thing that Emperor Wudi could not tolerate was corruption.

One of the first Han officials who was punished for corruption was Li Cai李蔡 (186–118 BCE), who worked for the Han emperor Wudi. A cousin of General Li Guang (119 BCE), Li Cai joined the army along with his cousin, and later became an assistant to General Wei Qing (?–106 BCE) in the Han dynasty's military campaign against the Xiongnu. Li Cai was granted the title Marquis of Le'an for his military achievements. He served as prime minister from 121 BCE, and helped Emperor Wudi with managing bureaucracy, currency, and the state monopoly of salt and iron.

As the second prime minister of Emperor Wudi's reign, Li Cai received from the emperor 20 mu (3.3 acres) of land that could be used for a burial site. However, Li Cai managed to acquire more land than he was granted and sold it for a high price. Despite his prominent rank and previous achievements, Li Cai was arrested, and committed suicide before he could be taken away for interrogation. His fief was also confiscated and abolished.[1]

Compared to more severe cases of corruption in later periods, Li Cai's case was relatively minor; it was a single episode, and he was not involved in other similar crimes. More importantly, his case was not fully investigated due to his sudden suicide. Nonetheless, it is worth noting because it was one of the first corruption cases of the Han dynasty which occurred during Emperor Wudi's reign. Moreover, Li Cai was cast aside immediately despite his prior reputation and affirmed competence in military and bureaucratic service to the emperor. The emperor was not hesitant to arrest him as soon as he heard of the allegation; though the circumstances, and whether this was a proved case of corruption, remained unclear, it nonetheless showed Emperor Wudi's undisputed intolerance of corruption.

The second corruption case during the Han period was more conspicuous, with far more clear evidence involved. Chuyu Chang 淳于长 (?-8 BCE) was initially from an unknown family, but his father married a lady Wang, whose younger sister Wang Zhengjun 王政君 later became the queen of the Han emperor Yuandi (r. 49/48–33 BCE). With the marital connection to the royal family, all male members of the Wang family soon became high-ranking officials, and the prestige also extended to other more distant family members.

When one of the Wang brothers, Grand General Wang Feng was seriously ill, Chunyu Chang took great care of him.[2] Wang Feng then recommended Chunyu Chang to the emperor so that Chunyu could gain access to the royal family. Chunyu soon won the favor of Emperor Chengdi (r. 33–7 BCE) and got promoted to the position of minister of the Royal Grand Guard 卫尉.[3] Chunyu got to know the emperor so well that he often took care of the most difficult issues on behalf of the emperor. It also became common knowledge that if anyone had any special request, they should approach Chunyu first so that later they could get what they want from the emperor.

Chunyu soon became the most powerful figure in court. He even meddled with the emperor's family issues. When Emperor Chengdi fell in love with a young lady and made her the new queen, the abdicated Queen Xu hoped to resume her position by bribing Chunyu. Chunyu took a tremendous amount of money in bribes from Queen Xu, and used her money to support his extravagant lifestyle.

Chunyu did not realize that there was someone watching him vigilantly from behind. Wang Mang 王莽 (45 BCE–23 CE, r. 9–23 CE) was from the Wang family and had been waiting for his chance to ascend to the top position in the court. When one of the senior Wangs was about to die, Wang Mang reported all horrible crimes Chunyu had committed.[4] When the report reached the Han empress dowager and emperor, all of them were shocked and enraged, but they still spared Chunyu's life. Chunyu was removed from his position and returned to his fief. But Chunyu could not give up his ambition, and he decided to bribe his former foe Wang Li to speak for him. The emperor was suspicious of Wang Li speaking in favor of Chunyu. After a thorough interrogation, the emperor became furious over what Chunyu had done, and how Chunyu had tried to bribe Wang Li to get back to power. This was the last straw that led to the complete downfall of Chunyu and his whole family. Chunyu was executed in prison, his son was killed, and his other family members were relocated outside of the capital city.[5]

Chunyu was able to get access to power through his connection to the emperor's in-laws and was promoted to the top rank of court officials. It is ironic that his rise and downfall were all related to his connections to the Wang family. His prominence started when he took great care of his ailing maternal uncle who was very impressed with his sincerely offered care and on his deathbed recommended him to the emperor. The emperor was very protective of him during his first conviction and only gave him minimal punishment. It was the second conviction that led to his death penalty. There is no question that Chunyu was an evil official who deserved his penalty; on the other hand, the reason his crime was revealed was rather because of power struggles going on in the court. It was Wang Mang, another ambitious young man from the Wang family, who had secretly collected evidence of Chunyu's crime and reported it to one of the senior Wang family members. The investigation, prosecution, and final execution of Chunyu were more of a power struggle than an authorized formal legal process. More ironically, the one who took credit for Chunyu's downfall, and who was also promoted to the high rank of Grand Marshall Da Xima 大司马 for his efforts, was Wang Mang, who himself later staged a coup, and founded a new dynasty, the Xin (9–23 CE).[6]

Corruption during the Tang Period

The transition period as the Sui gave way to the Tang dynasty in the late sixth century is similar to the Qin-Han transition in many ways. The Tang rulers also took great care not to repeat the mistakes of the Sui dynasty. The bureaucrats in the early Tang period were relatively honest and clean. The second emperor, Tang Taizong (r. 626–649), was more conscious of making a good government and society, and he was also recognized as one of the most accomplished emperors in Chinese history. Tang Taizong's reign was acclaimed as the Heyday Reign of Zhenguan 贞观之治, one of the most peaceful and prosperous phases in Chinese history. This was also a period during which there were few cases of corruption. More interestingly, Emperor Taizong also developed a unique way of punishing corruption: public humiliation.

In 627, Taizong found out that one of his most trusted ministers who had helped him during the critical early years, Zhangsun Shunde 長孫順德 (?–?), was taking bribes from his subjects. Zhangsun was a relative of Emperor Taizong's wife. Initially a military officer in the Sui dynasty, Zhangsun was supposed to be dispatched to northeast China to wage war; instead, Zhangsun fled to Taiyuan and became a loyal and entrusted general in service to Li Yuan, who later became Emperor Taizu (r. 618–626 CE) and founded a new dynasty, the Tang. More importantly, Changsun helped Li Shimin during the Xuanwumen coup to eliminate Li's ambitious brothers; this paved the way for Li Shimin to achieve supreme power. Once Li Shimin was enthroned as

Emperor Taizong, Zhangsun was granted land with 1,200 tenant families and female servants, and was allowed to sleep overnight in the forbidden area in the Tang palace, which was a great honor given exclusively to a small handful of people.

When Emperor Taizong heard allegations that Zhangsun was taking bribes, Taizong was greatly surprised and disappointed: "Zhangsun Shunde was the one who helped found the new dynasty. He is my in-law relative, and his official rank and salary should be far more than sufficient (for his disposal) . . . why would he succumb to a scandal of taking bribes?" Shocked and displeased, Emperor Taizong nonetheless took an action that surprised everyone in court: he awarded Zhangsun a dozen rolls of silk in front of all the court officials.[7] When Taizong's other ministers asked why Taizong would reward him for breaking the law, Emperor Taizong replied: "If he (Zhangsun) is someone who knows shame, giving him a reward for breaking the law is more effective than giving him a penalty; if he cannot understand this, he is no different from beasts, so why would I even bother to kill him?"[8]

Apparently, this anecdote was meant to show the wisdom of Emperor Taizong for achieving the goal of warning his officials without using physical punishment. However, Taizong opted to do this more out of a sense of favoritism toward someone who had worked for him for a long time. This is a typical case of prioritizing loyalty over justice, and his personal authority took precedence over the legal code. It may not have brought about a serious outcry in this particular single case, but it definitely set a bad precedent for not following proper legal procedures in a corruption case. Zhangsun later was involved with someone who plotted a rebellion, and was demoted to a commoner. Later Taizong sent someone to visit him and, pitying him, resumed his rank and returned his former land to him. Taizong continued to care for him, and even awarded him a posthumous title.

This was not the only such case during Taizong's reign. A local general, Chen Wanfu, was on an official trip to the Tang capital in 632. When he stayed overnight at a governmental lodging, Chen took a few *dan* of wheat bran without permission. Though it was only a misdemeanor, it was illegal possession of governmental property. Emperor Taizong was furious but opted for a different type of penalty. He called Chen to the court and awarded Chen a few *dan* of wheat bran, with the stipulation that Chen had to carry it home by himself. All the court officials laughed at and scorned Chen, who was publicly humiliated and left court fully shamed.[9]

With the diminishing power of the Tang central government since the Anshi Rebellion in 755, the corruption cases started to get far worse. Yuan Zai 元载 (?–777 CE) was from a humble background and was initially a diligent, intelligent scholar. He passed the Civil Service Examination and served two emperors, Emperor Suzong (r. 756–762 CE) and Emperor Daizong

(r. 762–779 CE). Yuan Zai was particularly favored by Emperor Daizong because Yuan helped Daizong eliminate two notorious eunuchs of that period. However, after that was accomplished, Yuan Zai became arrogant, took bribes, and lived extravagantly. He built multiple palace-like residences, killed his opponents ruthlessly, and accumulated a tremendous amount of property. During his fourteen-year tenure as prime minister, it became a common rule that whoever wanted a new appointment or promotion had to talk to Yuan, and Yuan did not hesitate to take any amount of bribe. Emperor Daizong was initially reluctant to kill him, and even made the effort to warn him privately so that he would stop his corrupt activities. One brave court official, Li Shaoliang, recorded all of Yuan's misdeeds and reported to the emperor. Yuan responded by having Li Shaoliang and a few of Yuan's other opponents beaten to death at court.

Finally Yuan Zai was arrested. Yuan also has a notorious wife, Wang Wenxiu, and along with their three sons, they were all ordered to commit suicide.[10] Among numerous precious treasures Yuan Zai had accumulated, a famous anecdote noted that 800 *dan* (approximately 64 tons) of black pepper had been found in Yuan's storehouse. Black pepper was introduced to China through the Silk Road, and from then until the Ming dynasty, the black pepper consumed in China was mostly imported from South and Southeast Asia.[11] During the Ming dynasty, there were cases in which black pepper had been used as substitute payment for officials' salaries.[12] Occasionally the unit price of black pepper even exceeded that of gold, and there was always much greater demand than there was supply. Therefore, black pepper became a symbol of wealth to equal gold and precious stones. The amount of black pepper Yuan Zai had stocked must have far surpassed even that of the royal palace. Yuan and his family had been so notorious for corruption that no one was sympathetic to them when they were arrested and punished.

Anticorruption during the Han and Tang Periods

Corruption has long been a persistent issue for governance. Rulers have deliberated over, for one thing, how to recruit, retain, and evaluate capable, accountable, and uncorrupted officials; for another, they have debated about how to develop proper legal systems to prevent corruption, to punish corrupted officials, and to warn officials from falling into any potential temptation. Since the ruling classes have long noted the danger and consequences of corruption, they have also been careful to monitor and try to contain corruption. The Han dynasty finalized evaluation protocols for officials, and hoped to use this system to sustain a group of pure, accountable, and uncorrupted officials. It was in the Han dynasty that legal codes specified corruption as one of the key areas about which officials must be supervised and evaluated.[13]

The Han legal code specified that the penalty for corruption was the second severest one, only next to that for rebellion. If an official was alleged to have taken ten units of gold (one unit gold is equivalent of ten thousand coins), the official would get the death penalty, the body would be discarded and displayed in the market, and his descendants could not be appointed to official positions for up to two or three generations.[14]

During that period a series of policies to prevent corruption was also developed. One of the longest-lasting regulations designed to prevent corruption, the avoidance system, was initiated during the Han. This was a three-pronged law: officials could not be appointed to their hometown area; officials who were related to each other by marriage could not supervise each other; and officials who were relatives or related through marriage could not be appointed to the same area or the same department. There was also an interlink assurance system, which means that whenever an official committed a crime, his supervisors and his inferiors would also get punished, especially those who knew of the crime but opted not to report it.[15]

During the Han dynasty, institutional supervision was also further strengthened. Emperor Wudi divided China proper into thirteen supervision areas and appointed a special supervisor for each area.[16] To maximize the collection of information, the first secret report box was invented and used during the Han's Xuandi (74–49 BCE) era. The Han official Zhao Guanghan 赵广汉 commissioned the manufacture of a secret report box which had a small opening, and only allowed letters to be put in but not taken out; use of this secret report box was later extended to a larger area.[17]

The other major policy change during the Han Xuandi era was to raise salaries for lower-level officials. Emperor Xuandi justified the pay raise as he understood that the workload of lower-level officials was tremendous but came with very low compensation. He restricted the raise to lower-level officials whose salaries were less than 100 *dan*.[18] In the Tang period, the law regarding corruption cases became even more severe. The Tang legal code stipulated that any corrupt officials whose bribe exceeded fifteen rolls of silk would be sentenced to death. In practice, they often used the punishment "beat to death in court," which meant that criminals would be beaten to death in front of all the court officials. The penalty also extended to family members: all family property would be confiscated, family members would become slaves, and their descendants could not be appointed to important posts, so that this policy of punishment for the whole family would continue for generations.

During the Tang there were also regulations to block corruption through immediate family members or other relatives of officials.[19] If their relatives took bribes, the officials would be demoted. If the officials knew about the corruption, then they would be punished as conspirators; if they were totally unaware of the crime, the official would be punished for negligence and tolerance of corruption, and the official's penalty would be reduced to a lesser level. In any case, the official would be punished if his family members or relatives had taken a bribe. On the other hand, despite the establishment of severe penalties for corruption, there were still cases of family members or relatives taking the chance that they would not get caught for bribery.

Another venue that was often contaminated by corruption cases was the recommendation system. By the Tang dynasty, the Civil Service Examination was already implemented to recruit qualified candidates; however, the traditional recommendation system still existed and was in wide use. In order to prevent any corruption in the process of the recommendation system, the government developed an interlink system between the recommender and the recommended. In other words, the recommender needed to take responsibility in case the person he recommended proved to be incapable for the job or became involved in criminal activity later on.

In 812, the Secretariat-Chancellery reported: "If the recommended magistrate abuses his power, and becomes involved in corruption, the one who recommended him should be demoted or suspended."[20] In 817, a subsequent report noted, "If the stated facts in the recommendation letter were inaccurate, without proper evidence of qualification, and if the recommended official proved to be incapable of doing work, and also became involved in criminal activity once he took office, the recommender should be punished. In minor cases the recommender should be suspended; and in worse cases the recommender should be demoted."[21] In 894, the Secretariat-Chancellery stated: "If the recommended one takes a bribe worth up to one hundred *guan*, the recommender should be demoted; if the bribe is worth over one hundred *guan*, the recommender should be relocated to a remote small county."[22] This policy put the onus of responsibility on the recommender, requiring him to recommend a pure, uncorrupted, and accountable person; otherwise the recommender himself would have been punished for any crimes the person he recommended had committed.

Corruption and anticorruption efforts both have a long history. Despite the overall effectiveness of Han and Tang governance, corruption cases occurred in a variety of circumstances. The government continued to develop new laws and regulations to monitor and prevent corruption. Successes and failures with those policies were taken seriously in later periods and had a long-term impact on Chinese politics and society.

NOTES

1. Ban Gu, *History of the Han Dynasty*: 93.63.
2. Ibid.

3. Weiwei was one of the nine major governmental posts during the Qin and Han periods.
4. Ban Gu, *History of the Han* Dynasty: 99; Biography of Wang Mang.
5. Ibid., 98.
6. Ibid.
7. Liu Xu, *Old History of the Tang Dynasty*: 58.
8. Ouyang Xiu, *New History of the Tang Dynasty*: 30.
9. Wu Jing, *Essentials of Government in the Zhenguan Reign*: 6. 26.
10. Liu Xu, *Old History of the Tang Dynasty*: 68; Ouyang Xiu, *New History of the Tang Dynasty*: 70.
11. https://www.zhihu.com/question/28089289/answer/39352875, Accessed on January 20, 2018.
12. During the reign of Ming emperor Xuanzong, inflation became a serious issue due to the over-issuing of paper currency, and black pepper was used for the payment of salaries.
13. Ban Gu, *History of the Han Dynasty*: 72. Shen Weiwei, "Qinhan shidai jiancha de jingyan yu jiaoxun," *Falüwenhua*, January 27, 2017.
14. Ban Gu, *History of the Han Dynasty*: 66, 23.
15. Fan Ye, *History of the Latter Han Dynasty*: 60.
16. http://www.360doc.com/content/07/0803/07/24920_650420.shtml, Accessed on January 20, 2018.
17. http://www.360doc.com/content/09/0304/08/78382_2704377.shtml, Accessed on January 20, 2018.
18. Ban Gu, *History of the Han Dynasty*: 8.
19. Zhangsun Wuji, *Tang Code with Commentaries*: 38.
20. Dong Hao, *The Complete Works of the Tang Dynasty* (*Quan Tangwen*): 974.
21. Ibid., 965.
22. Wang Fu, *Institutional History of the Tang Dynasty*: 75.

BIBLIOGRAPHY

Ban Gu, 2016. *History of the Han Dynasty* (*Hanshu*). Beijing: Zhonghua shuju.

Cai Jingxian. *History of Corrupt Officials in Ancient China* (*Zhongguo gudai tanguan zhuan*). Huhehaote: Neimenggu renmin chubanshe, 2014.

Dong Hao, 1990. *The Complete Texts of the Tang Dynasty* (*quantangwen*). Shanghai: Shanghai guji chubanshe.

Fan Ye, 2000. *History of the Latter Han Dynasty* (*Hou Hanshu*). Beijing: Zhonghua shuju.

Lewis, Mark Edward. *The Early Chinese Empires: Qin and Han*. Cambridge: Harvard University Press, 2009.

———. *China's Cosmopolitan Empire: The Tang Dynasty*. Cambridge: Harvard University Press, 2012.

Liu Xu, 1975. *Old History of the Tang Dynasty* (*Jiu Tangshu*). Beijing: Zhonghua shuju.

Ouyang Xiu, 1975. New History of the Tang Dynasty (*Xin Tangshi*). Beijing: Zhonghua shuju.
Sima Qian, 1982. Historical Records (*Shiji*). Beijing: Zhonghua shuju.
Twitchett, Denis ed. *The Cambridge History of China vol. 3 Sui and T'ang China 589–906*. Cambridge: Cambridge University Press, 1979.
Wang Chunyu, ed. *Zhongguo fantan shi*中國反貪史. Beijing: Renmin chubanshe, 2013, Vol 1.
Wang Fu, 1991. *Institutional History of the Tang Dynasty* (*tanghuiyao*). Shanghai: Shanghai guji chubanshe.
Wu Jing, 1978. *Essentials of Government in the Zhenguan Reign* (Zhenguan zhengyao). Shanghai: Shanghai guji chubanshe.
Zhangsun Wuji, 1999. *Tang Code with Commentaries* (*tanglu shuyi*). Beijing: Falü chubanshe.

Part IV

NEW CENTURY, NEW STRUGGLE

Chapter 11

Hu Jintao's Anticorruption Action (or non-action)

The Bo Xilai Case and After

Xiansheng Tian

INTRODUCTION

Chongqing is one of the largest cities both in China and in the world. As an important municipality behind Beijing, Tianjin, Shanghai, and so on, Chongqing stands farther away from the power center of China. It was there, however, that the CCP under Hu Jintao encountered one of the greatest challenges it had ever experienced in its ninety-plus years of history. The dramatic escape of a powerful police chief, Wang Lijun, from Chongqing City and his effort in looking for protection by American consulate general in Chengdu City shocked the whole world as well as the Chinese Communist Party itself as the first ever case in which a high-ranking official of the People's Republic of China seeked assistance from a foreign diplomatic mission. The event, however, is actually just the tip of the iceberg. Later investigations lead to the exposure of a lot more scandals within the Party. Wang's boss in Chongqing, Bo Xilai, a member of the Party's Politburo and one of the rising stars within the party ranks (rumored to be the contender for top leadership positions), is reported to have been deeply involved. Bo's "popular" campaigns of "Singing the Red songs and Smashing the Black (唱红打黑)," retaliation against his political opponents, suspicious relations with the Chinese military, huge illegal financial transactions, and even murder (and cover-up of it), can all be described as obvious signs of defiance to the authority of Beijing. Hu Jintao, the CCP general secretary, and his central leadership, in Bo's eyes were weak and not doing enough to maintain the Party's monopoly on power as well as betraying the Maoist revolutionary enthusiasm (at least seems to be so superficially). As a member of China's "princelings" group, his personal ambition to become at least one of the top leaders, if not the highest, is also believed to have played a huge role. The Bo Xilai incident, obviously, has become a real challenge to the Party. The event has made many (top leaders included) believe that the long overdue political reform can't be postponed any longer. The actions taken by the central leadership (namely Hu Jintao) have taken the attention of the world when the anticorruption campaigns quickly took place, including the removal of Bo Xilai. With the Xi Jinping administration taking over the leadership in 2012, hundreds of thousands high-ranking official have been removed from their offices so far.[1]

However, it seems the stories of Chongqing has not finished. Just recently (summer of 2017), Bo Xilai's replacement as the party chief in Chongqing, Sun Zhengcai, has also been taken down by the central leadership on various charges. Sun has also been reported to be at least one of the top contenders for the highest positions within the Party. Does Chongqing indeed have a certain curse for these officials as popular rumors go? Does the anticorruption campaign launched continuously reflect the power struggle within the Communist Party leadership and that corruption is only a convenient excuse? Did the Hu Jintao administration try but fail to do anything to curb the rampant corruption among the officials? Will the ongoing campaign under Xi Jinping's leadership lead to political reforms or is it simply a way for him to consolidate his power? Based on available information, this chapter will try to trace some of these events to have a better understanding of what actually happened and the significance of such events to the future of the new generation of CCP leadership as well as the position of China in the world. Some of the most recent developments, including the Xi Jinping administration's reactions to these events, the powerful anticorruption campaigns during the last few years, and the possibility of suggested political reforms, will also be discussed.

Recall the "Wang Lijun Incident": Major Players

In early 2012, news began to spread, at first not via official news channels in China but on internet, that popular and powerful police chief of Chongqing City, Wang Lijun, had entered the Consulate General Office of the United States in Chengdu, a nearby city, on the evening of February 6. Many believed that he was looking for asylum from the Americans. A few days earlier, before Wang fled to US Consulate, Chongqing city government had officially announced that the police chief had been relieved of his police duty and shifted to another job, an obvious sign that he had lost the favor and confidence of his boss, the Communist party chief of Chongqing, Bo Xilai. The internet, especially the Sina Weibo, the Chinese counterpart of Twitter, was flooded with all kinds of "rumors," including stories that will well fit into any

James Bond movie, about how Wang evaded the police force he helped to reform and escaped his own city by disguising himself as a woman. According to some reports, Chongqing mayor, Huang Qifan, rushed to Chengdu, with up to seventy police vehicles surrounding the US Consulate, and tried to convince Wang to come out voluntarily. According to US State Department spokesman, Wang did leave "of his own volition" after a night's stay, though he refused to go back to Chongqing. Instead, he was picked up by the national security authorities from Beijing on February 7. Some stories described that the local police and the national security officials even engaged in heated arguments and even confrontation before Wang left the US Consulate. It was "rumored" again that Wang had carried a "mysterious box of papers" when he walked into the consulate. He also exposed to his American hosts during his thirty-six-hour stay that he escaped Chongqing because he worried that his life was in danger. Wang had been in charge of the investigation regarding an English businessman's death, and his boss's wife, Gu Kailai, was a suspect. He also let Americans know that several of his assistants in the investigation team had been tortured or have even disappeared, and were presumably dead. Although many of these stories were quickly deleted by the Chinese authorities, it could not stop even more people from wondering what had driven Wang on the run and from digging deeper into these events to find answers.[2]

On February 8, the Chongqing government announced that Mr. Wang had been suffering from stress because of "long-term over-work, a state of anxiety and indisposition" and was receiving "vacation-style medical treatment."[3] Of course by this time everyone understood that he was under investigation and in detention. The "rumor" of Wang's defection was confirmed on February 9 by China's official news channels. Many of the earlier "rumors" would also be proved later to be true. With international attention added, Wang's drama soon became the tip of the iceberg of much larger and more complicated events that would shock the whole world as well as the CCP itself. Bo Xilai, who was widely supposed to become a Politburo Standing Committee member later that year, attended China's annual parliamentary session in Beijing as if nothing had really happened. He even talked to reporters, insisting on his wife's innocence. But by the session's end, Chinese premier Wen Jiabao made it clear, though not directly, that the central leadership under Hu Jintao was not happy with Bo's handling of the Wang Lijun incident. Bo's position no longer seemed secure. On March 15, all Chinese news media announced the Party's decision: Bo Xilai had been removed from his office of Chongqing City's party chief. Officials of central government later confirmed his removal because of the Wang Lijun incident. Bo's images, with his handsome smile, disappeared from the public view. On March 26, the United Kingdom confirmed that it has asked the Chinese government to reopen the case of the murder of Neil Heywood, the English businessman who died in Chongqing in 2011. Soon after that, on April 10, Chinese authorities officially announced that Bo Xilai had been stripped of all his Communist Party posts and his wife was under investigation in connection with Heywood's death.[4]

The world was amazed to watch the development of events in China. More and more people by now had come to the conclusion that the so-called Wang Lijun incident was not just another story of a corrupt official falling down like hundreds before him. Many believed that the Wang Lijun incident would be the biggest challenge facing the Chinese Communist Party since decades ago when the Party's vice chairman, General Lin Bio, betrayed Mao and fled the country and then died mysteriously in a plane crash on his way to Russia in 1971. The people of China as well as the world would be dazed and puzzled in the following months by the big shake-up that exposed the highest-level political divisions among top leaders in China, wondering what had really happened and what would be the next.

The fifty-two-year-old Wang Lijun started his career in law enforcement in 1984 from the lowest level in the Inner Mongolia region and then in Liaoning Province. Through his hard work Wang moved up the ladder to become a local police chief. He earned himself the tough guy image by powerfully enforcing the law against organized crimes, though many people argue that his action there actually hurt a lot of good people, including those who dared to expose scandals of government officials. His "achievements" in Liaoning even became the theme of a popular TV series entitled "Iron-Blooded Police Spirits." His achievement and loyalty also earned him his boss's trust. Bo Xilai, mayor of Dalian City and then Party chief of Liaoning Province, would take Wang to his new job in Chongqing when Bo became Chongqing City's Party chief as well as the Party's Politburo member. Wang would reach the peak of his career as well as his downfall in Chongqing, all because of the ups and downs in his relations with his boss, Bo Xilai.

Bo Xilai belongs to a group popularly known group in China as the "princelings." The princelings, like the current Chinese leader, Xi Jinping, are children of the revolutionary leaders of Mao's times. Bo Xilai's father, Bo Yibo, is one of the top communist leaders who served under Mao Zedong to help establish the People's Republic of China in 1949. With the privileges that only princelings could enjoy, Bo Xilai attended a top school in Beijing with children of other communist leaders. During Mao's Great Proletarian Cultural Revolution (1966–1976), Bo joined the infamous "Red Guards" to attack anything he considered not revolutionary enough, including condemning his own father for betraying Mao. It was reported that he even broke his father's ribs to demonstrate his revolutionary spirit during one of the "condemnation meetings." While the senior Bo was purged from his party and government positions, the son was sent later to be "re-educated" by the Chinese peasants, like tens of millions of other young people in later years of the Cultural Revolution. He then met and married his first wife, Li Danyu, also the child of an elite family, in 1976 and they had their first son the next year.

When the Cultural Revolution finally came to its end in 1976 when Mao died and his loyal followers, known as the "Gang of Four," were purged, the country began to come back to its normal life. The senior Bo would come out again to join the top circle of leadership headed by Deng Xiaoping. Beside his "open door" policy and economic reforms, Deng and his colleagues also had another consensus in early 1990s: To avoid the country from falling into chaos like Mao's Cultural Revolution, the party policy should be built upon agreement of a group of top leaders instead of only one. These "consensus builders" also seemed to agree on another idea: Each high-ranking communist leader should "contribute" one of his children to the Party's future leadership. The idea is said to have been first proposed by none other than Bo Yibo himself.[5] This idea pretty much paralleled what these old communist veterans believed: that their own children were the most reliable as the regime's successors, since the two Party chiefs in 1980 (Hu Yaobang and Zhao Ziyang) had both failed to follow closely what the old revolutionaries thought to be the correct line of policies. Bo Xilai's fast-track career seems to have started from here.

Bo Xilai had studied at the prestigious Beijing University, very possible with his father's influence, and majored in world history. He also joined the Communist Party himself in 1980, and later on earned a master's degree in journalism from the Chinese Academy of Social Sciences in 1982. Then he started working as the deputy party secretary of a county in Liaoning province. During the same time period, many other "princelings" were also taking the same road. The current Chinese leader, Xi Jinping, the son of another revolutionary veteran Xi Zhongxun, started his political career in Zhending County in Hebei Province while Liu Yuan, the son of former CCP vice-chairman and president of China, would become the mayor of Zhengzhou City in Henan Province. They all made steady progress upward, working through different levels of party and government offices. Bo moved up the ladder in Liaoning Province in mid-1980s when he was appointed the mayor of coast city Dalian (Westerners would know this city by the nearby Port Arthur that is located on the tip of Liaodong Peninsula) before becoming the governor of the province in 2004 and China's minister of commerce in 2007. However, it was during his time in Dalian that Bo built up his early fame as a tough and energetic administrator. It was also during these years that he divorced his first wife and married Gu Kailai who also has a distinguished background.[6]

Gu Kailai also studied at Beijing University like Bo did, though years later. As the youngest child of another prominent revolutionary family, Gu later became a successful lawyer and, according to recent reports, handled huge amount of suspicious assets domestically and internationally. She even published a well-received book titled *Winning A Lawsuit in America* that was later on turned into a TV miniseries. The couple has only one son, Bo Guagua, who recently finished his graduate studies at Harvard University's Kennedy School of Government (after finishing his earlier studies in England's most expensive private school, Harrow, and Oxford University), though his extravagant lifestyle and the sources of his income have raised a lot of brows despite his strong denial. Gu's success stories just echoed her husband's. After being appointed mayor of coast Dalian City, Bo Xilai's name gradually became well known—he was credited for the successes of the city, one of the cleanest with booming economic activities, which was frequently used to showcase China's economic boom since Deng Xiaoping's "Reform and Open-Up" policy came into place in the early 1980s. Dalian City is the place where Bo and his police chief Wang started and strengthened their relationship. When Bo was promoted to become the governor of Liaoning Province, Wang was also moving up along. In 2004, Bo became China's minister of commerce in 2007, a new member of the most powerful Politburo before moving on Chongqing city.[7]

It is also in Dalian that the Bo family got to know Neil Heywood. According to the *New York Times*, Heywood was born in 1970 and enjoyed a privileged education at Harrow School and later on at Warwick University. He was described by his friends as "charming but elusive" and "a maverick since his school days."[8] He came to China in early 1990s, learned to speak fluent Mandarin Chinese, married his Chinese wife Wang Lulu (the couple would have one son and one daughter), and started his business career. He established several companies, working as a consultant to help foreign businesses (including Aston Martin) that were trying to invest in China's booming economy. Some speculations circulating on internet earlier stated that Heywood was also an undercover agent for the British intelligence service. But such speculations were quickly dismissed by the English government. However, it seems those who knew him all agree that Heywood "did have an ability to work through contacts and build relationships."[9] That is where the Bo family's relations with Heywood started. It was reported that Heywood fully used his connections in Britain to help Bo Guagua attend schools in Britain, first Harrow and later Oxford. This relationship has become the focus of speculations of the whole event.

Neil Heywood was found dead in a hotel room in Chongqing on November 15, 2011. The cause of death cited in an official report from Chongqing police was "overconsumption of alcohol" though his friends insisted that he drank only occasionally. His body was quickly cremated soon after, with his family's approval. The Bo family and Heywood are believed to have close business relations, according to later reports, only to see such relations strain in 2010. Journalist Tom Reed wrote in the *Times* that Heywood once "worried" about such strained relations with Bo and even "considered fleeing China with his family." The *Wall Street Journal* also cited an unnamed friend as saying that Heywood had passed documents relating his relations with Bo family to a lawyer in Britain as an "insurance policy," though so far no such evidence has surfaced. *Reuters* also reported that the English businessman had threatened to expose a plan by Gu Kailai to move huge amount of money abroad.[10] With Wang Lijun's defection into US Consulate, Heywood's relations with the Bo family and how the English businessman actually died became the focus of many people, both inside and outside China. The British government asked the Chinese authorities to reopen the case. The investigation and the trials that followed would lead to Bo's expulsion from the Party and jail times for him and his wife. But one thing is clear: It is not just another corruption scandal and Bo's fall was not only because of Heywood's death.

The Chongqing Model: A Challenge to Beijing?

Bo Xilai is described by foreign correspondents as "flamboyant," "charismatic," and "suave," and as someone who enjoys the limelight with his signature smile in front of cameras, something which set him apart from the typical images of other top communist leaders in China (his boss, Party general secretary, Hu Jintao, is famous for his "poker face").[11] His leadership styles as well as the policies he tried to put into place are also different from those of other communist leaders. While serving as the Party boss in Dalian and later the whole province of Liaoning, Bo tried and successfully installed his policies, attracting foreign investments, starting construction projects, planting trees and grass (locals call it "Xilai grass"), and made many other popular moves. He also made a lot of enemies. According to some reports, he mercilessly chased down his political opponents. Many people, including journalists, businessmen, and government officials, even common folk, who were not willing to cooperate with him, would also face harassment, prison time, and death threats. His actions won praises from the left and the populace, but raised a lot of eyebrows too, especially among the top leaders in Beijing.

Ever since Deng Xiaoping started his reforms in the 1980s, the Communist leadership's major concerns have shifted away from Mao's revolutionary campaigns toward the economic growth of the country. Deng's insistence on development (he believed it to be the "hard truth") allowed "some people to get rich first." However, it opened the door for widespread corruption among government officials and businessmen (many of whom were children of the officials). The 1989 pro-democracy movement initiated by young college students was actually an anticorruption movement from the first place before the slogans shifted their focus on independent news media and political reforms.

Deng's crackdown on the movement and his continued effort at promoting economic development, as we can see today, actually sent a strong signal to everyone that so long as you are not challenging the Party's position and policies, you are free to do whatever to get rich.

Into the twenty-first century, the new Party leadership is no longer around a strong man like Mao or Deng. Instead, consensus (or compromise?) of a group of top leaders became the routine. Jiang Zemin, and later on Hu Jintao, all had to rely on the Politburo's group decisions which followed Deng's idea of giving the economic growth (or GDP) the highest priority. But the rampage of corruption, the abuse of power by local officials, and the government's grand plan to industrialize as well as urbanize the country with numerous construction projects that would force millions of people to relocate also caused new problems. Mass protests (popularly known in China as 群体事件 or "mass incidents") by peasants who lost their land, homeowners who are forced to move without proper compensation, unemployed workers whose factories were "privatized," migrant workers whose paychecks are delayed, and those who believe their right of religious beliefs are suppressed by the government became commonplace. Simply put, the booming economic development only made the gap between the rich and the poor wider, leading to many people's discontent. The rampant corruption among officials added more fuel on the fire. The year of 2006 is the last time when the Chinese government published the numbers of mass demonstrations, petitions, or riots. In that year, it is reported that more than 85,000 such events took place across the whole country. According to scholars' estimate, the year of 2011 saw more than 180,000 such incidents.[12] Clearly, such incidents have become the major concerns of the Party leadership while "maintenance of stability" would become the priority of the Party since the beginning of the new century. Deng's popular 1980s–1990s policy of "Getting rich is glorious" and "Letting some to get rich first" seems to have accomplished its mission and some other policies are badly needed to keep the Party's rein on the power and society.

Bo Xilai's Chongqing model seems to offer an option, or more optimistically, a potential solution, for the problems facing China. Taking full advantage of his revolutionary bloodline as a member of the "princelings," Bo started to put into practice a number of populist campaigns as far back as his days in Dalian but mostly in Chongqing. A campaign he launched in Chongqing demonstrated his skillful use of modern technology and people's yearning for the "simpler," less corrupt years of Mao's times. Bo personally sent out mass text messages to the phones of city folks with his favorite Mao quotations, calling upon people to keep in mind the old but much valued communist ideals of earlier times in the newly developed economy. He also personally promoted another campaign of "Singing the Red Songs." Tens of thousands of people, factory workers, students, government employees are organized to pick up some of the revolutionary songs of Mao's times and compete among different groups (he even personally took some of the winning groups to sing in other regions of the country, including Beijing). In Chongqing, all prime-time commercial advertisings are banned on TV, replaced by revolutionary movies, patriotic songs, or other propaganda programs promoting revolutionary spirit. Tens of thousands of trees are planned in and around the city (again, "Xilai trees"), low-income public housing projects rise up, city's infrastructure is improved.[13]

Alongside the "Singing the Red Songs" is Bo's second campaign, "Smashing the Black," a movement aimed at cracking down on the "mafia-like organized crimes" as he called them that had been bothering the city and its people for quite a while. While serving as the party boss in Chongqing, Bo beefed up the police force with Wang Lijun as the chief, provided more police services, and used this newly reformed police force to help his anti-crime campaigns. According to one official report, from 2009 to March 2012 when Bo was relieved of his official positions, Chongqing government had investigated more than 80 organized crime rings, prosecuted and sentenced 1,297 people, and issued a number of death penalties.[14] Among the condemned were the newly rich, the group that has gained the people's hatred or jealousy for the wealth they have accumulated in a short time. Personal properties, businesses, and cash worth of hundreds of millions dollars were confiscated, some of which was used to "modernize" his police force and city's infrastructure projects but a pretty large amount of it simply "disappeared" later. Bo's political enemies were also included in this group. For example, the former vice commissioner of public safety, Wen Qiang, was sentenced to die for reported corruption and providing protection for organized crimes. It still remains in the dark how much is involved and how many people are in trouble simply because they are not in Bo's favor. Many reports after Bo's downfall actually show that numerous people have been wrongly charged and their properties illegally taken.

But Bo's "Chongqing Model" featured by his "Singing the Red Songs" and "Smashing the Black" campaigns apparently fit into quite a lot people's desires. In their eyes, Bo Xilai simply became "a champion" of the common folks and "a crusader" against corruption, greed, and inequality. Many also believe that his action in Chongqing is a direct criticism of his predecessors in Chongqing as well as the Beijing government for not doing enough to fight against rampant corruption in China.[15] Even after Bo's downfall in 2012, many in Chongqing still insist that Bo had done the right things. American travelers' reports from China seem to back up such claims: "Wang gave people a sense of safety and Bo gave us hope," Chongqing folks would say. Such feelings among Chongqing people are pretty widespread, "they are not perfect, but they really did something."[16] One commentator vividly describes these campaigns. Bao Tong, the former assistant for former Party general secretary Zhao Ziyang before the 1989 Tiananmen Incident, recently pointed out that Bo Xilai actually understands the Party's traditional policy much better than we believe. According to Mr. Bao, Bo's "Singing the Red" is good at promoting the Party's absolute control over the power while "Smashing the Black" can be easily used to eliminate any opposition groups or individuals. As for the common folks, "Singing the Red" will discipline the people to obey the Party absolutely while "Smashing the Black" only makes them willing thugs (打手) of the Party. Bo actually learned the core ideas of Mao's theories, relying on mass movement to replace the rule of law.[17] The powerful anticorruption campaigns led by the Xi Jinping administration actually share a lot of similar features.

Such campaigns, of course, also established Bo Xilai as the symbolic leader of China's New Left group, those who continuously criticize the government, especially the central leadership under Hu Jintao and Wen Jiabao, for letting go of much-valued communist ideals while only promoting capitalist development of market economy. Beijing leaders are not happy to see this. When Bo Xilai took his Chongqing singing groups to perform in Beijing city before the Wang Lijun incident, not a single member of the Politburo attended. On the last day of 2012, by when the news of Wang's defection had already become widespread, Chinese premier Wen Jiabao (surely with the backing of Hu Jintao) openly criticized Chongqing, warning that campaigns in that city could only bring back the bad memories of Mao's Cultural Revolution and Chinese people would not allow that kind of catastrophe to happen again. He also made it clear that the Chongqing Municipal Party Committee and government must "reflect seriously and learn from the Wang Lijun incident." The next day, on April 10, 2012, the Chinese news agency Xinhua officially announced Bo's downfall. He was stripped of all his Party and government positions and his wife would go on trial for Heywood's murder.[18]

Gu Kailai on Trial and Downfall of Bo Xilai

On July 26, Gu Kailai and her aide Zhang Xiaojun were charged with "intentional homicide," according to Xinhua News Agency, and by August 20 both of them would be convicted for the murder of Neil Heywood because of "economic conflict." Earlier rumors that Heywood wanted a bigger cut of Gu's hidden treasures that she wanted to move overseas with Heywood's help seem to be confirmed. When the deal did not go through, Gu stated that Heywood threatened to kidnap her son. Gu suffered a "mental breakdown," according to China's state media, and decided to get rid of Heywood. She had lured Heywood to Chongqing for another round of negotiation, and had, with the help of her assistants (some reports say with Wang Lijun's help), met Heywood in the Chongqing hotel and drank with him. When Heywood, who is no drinker, had got drunk, Gu and her assistant had poured poison into Heywood's mouth.[19] According to one news report, one Chongqing local official, Xia Delian, provided Gu Kailai's assistants with the poison, "Sanbudao," and seven persons who were involved were later arrested.[20]

Everything still looks foggy even after the trial, with a lot of evidence and witnesses' testimonies never released to the public. It is not clear if the murder was committed by Gu behind the back of Bo Xilai or if Bo was also a co-plotter. According to one Chinese-American scholar, Chen Liming, Gu let the court know that she had told Wang Lijun everything about this murder but did not know Wang had recorded their conversation, though nobody knows if Gu informed her husband or what her husband did upon learning about it. It is also unclear what Wang did after Gu's confession to him. Some "rumors" state that Wang went to see his boss with the recorded conversation and an angry Bo slapped Wang in the face, and soon after that Wang was relieved from his office as the police chief.[21] One newly published book, *A Death in the Lucky Holiday Hotel: Murder, Money and An Epic Power Struggle in China* (《中國權貴的死亡遊戲》) by Pin Ho and Wenguang Huang, argues that Wang actually has his backers in Beijing, even among Politburo Standing Committee members. What Wang did, defection to American Consulate, was actually suggested by one of the princelings in Beijing as part of a bigger plan to get rid of Bo Xilai. Also, Wang worried that he would never be able to escape from Sichuan Province which Bo Xilai ruled very much like an independent kingdom. That explains why Wang decided to go to the Americans. With his own life in danger, it seems like a good choice: even if his application for political asylum was rejected, his information regarding Heywood's murder would surely arouse Western media's interest as well as Beijing's attention. In other words, Wang's behavior would surely cause the new leadership group under Xi Jinping to take action: since what Bo Xilai is doing in Chongqing is part of his and his supporters' plan to prevent Xi from successfully taking over the Party's leadership, Xi and his followers would surely move forward to protect Wang. Wang is a winner, according to the authors of the book: he saved his own life and ruined Bo Xilai's political career.[22]

The points of the book are jeered by others. One famous Dalian businessman, ninety-year-old Yu Yunsheng, disagrees. Yu had known Bo and Gu when they were in Dalian. According to Yu, Gu Kailai was a person with strong personality who always tried to control others, including her husband. As a lawyer, Gu had given Bo lots of help, including legal advice. Politically ambitious, Gu is famous for her involvements in many issues in Dalian, big and small. Yu also points out that Bo Xilai's bias against other communist leaders coming from the background of the Communist Youth League (Tuan

Pai团派) is well known. Many people still remember his "purge" of these officials when he was Dalian city's Party boss. The event itself, Yu insists, is just another round of confrontation between the "princelings" and "Tuan Pai" that has been going on for years. Bo and Gu were simply too ambitious and behaved too wildly and overstretched themselves.[23] There are other "rumors," including those that Gu had developed an affair with Heywood as her husband is a famous womanizer. With her strong personality, she demanded Heywood to divorce his wife and swear loyalty to her. Other reports described how Gu delivered "an insane" speech to a group of Chongqing police officials, wearing a major general's uniform of the People's Liberation Army and claiming she was under secret orders from China's Ministry of Public Security to protect Wang Lijun.[24] There are simply so many stories, different version of stories, that there is no way one can prove or confirm any of them. The Party's control over China's news media and the powerful firewall of China's internet service can easily filter off any news the Party does not want its people and the outside world to know, even today.

On August 20, 2012, Gu Kailai's trial in Hefei, China, was over. She received a suspended death sentence for her murder of Heywood (which meant, after two years in prison, hers may turn into a life sentence, according to the tradition in China's legal system). In many reports about the trial, all following the court spokesman, Gu was described as "cooperative" with the court and decided not to contest the charges, blaming her action (poisoning Heywood) on a "mental breakdown." Gu was said to be willing to "accept and calmly face any sentence" for her crime. Her assistant, Zhang Xiaojun, who used to work at Bo's home as an orderly, was charged alongside Gu. China's official news channels announced that he poisoned Heywood together with Gu Kailai. He also appeared to be cooperative, admitting his involvement in the murder and even wanted to apologize to Heywood's family members. He received a nine-year prison sentence.[25]

The former police chief, Wang Lijun, also faced his trial in Chengdu, Sichuan Province. The trial started in secret on September 17 and finished next day. Nobody outside the court knows the details. On September 24 Wang was convicted and received prison sentence for defection (two years), power abuse (two years), bribe-taking (nine years), and bending the law for selfish ends (seven years), but the court decided to give a combined fifteen-year sentence. His "political rights" was also stripped for one year. According to Xinhua News Agency, Wang knew "perfectly well" that Gu was a suspect of Heywood's murder but deliberately covered it up, though he later abandoned his effort to conceal her crime when the relations between the two turned sour. While Gu Kailai worried about her crime being exposed, Wang felt very uncomfortable when Gu let too many people know about the event. That is why Wang decided to report it to his boss, Bo Xilai. According to one witness, the boss "angrily rebuked" his police chief upon hearing his report that Gu Kailai was a chief suspect of Heywood's murder. That is also where the boss slapped his police chief in the face and relieved him from his office. The run-in between the two led to Wang's "rearranging" of the Heywood's case file while some of his close fellow officers were put under "illegal investigation." When Wang finally concluded that his own life was endangered, he made up his mind to go to the Americans for help and protection, thus the beginning of the drama.

However, his sentence is widely believed to be very much lenient than expected as in China bribe-taking can carry the death penalty depending on the amount involved and the seriousness of the case. Wang was accused of accepting cash and property worth 3.05 million Chinese yuan (US$480.000) for personal favors. He received a lighter sentence because he "fully co-operated" with the investigators. Few people know what he did and how exactly he "cooperated" though people tend to believe that his evidence helped the court to convict Gu Kailai. Wang decided not to contest the charges and had no plan to lodge an appeal. He was also reported to have made an apology at the end of his trial by saying "I hope the serious impact (caused by my acts) both at home and abroad would be eliminated through the trial. Meanwhile, I hope the trial will issue a warning to society and let more people draw lessons from me. For the Party organizations, people and relatives that have cared for me, I want to say here, sincerely, 'I'm very, very sorry. I've let you down.'"[26] Later, four high-ranking policy officials in Chongqing were also put on trial and found guilty of helping Wang Lijun in mishandling Heywood's murder case. Each of them were convicted and sentenced to different jail terms.

Bo Xilai's downfall became a sure thing on April 10, 2012, when the official Xinhua News Agency issued a statement regarding Bo: "As Comrade Bo Xilai is suspected of being involved in serious discipline violations, the Central Committee of the Communist Party of China (CPC) has decided to suspend his membership of the CPS Central Committee Political Bureau and the CPS Central Committee, in line with the CPC Constitution and the rules on investigation of CPC discipline inspection department."[27] The investigation by the CPS Discipline Department stated that Bo had seriously violated the Party's rules and abused his power while serving on different positions in Dalian City, Liaoning Province, Department of Commerce, and Chongqing City. In the case of Heywood's murder, Bo is charged of using his office to disrupt the investigation and of making huge mistakes. He also misused his positions for personal gains, directly or indirectly through his family members in taking huge amount of briberies. He was also charged for maintaining illegal sexual relations with many females, and misused persons against the personnel policies, causing serious consequences and greatly hurting the reputations of the Party and the State.[28] In the following days, all official news channels began pouring out large amount of articles, editorials, and comments that all pledged to support the Party's decision on Bo Xilai. Chongqing government itself also issued its own statement in support of the decision by the central leadership under Hu Jintao. *People's Daily* carried a front page headline reading, "Our nation is a nation of socialist rule of law and the authority of the law cannot be trampled."[29] This is very much like what happened in the past whenever the Party made any important decision or policy changes.

Despite the government efforts in controlling the flow of information regarding Bo's case, "rumors" continued to circulate in China and the world through the spring and early summer of 2012, puzzling everyone. Among all this, the rumor about a coup in Beijing on March 29 caught a lot people's attention. It goes that some troops loyal to Bo Xilai and his supporter Zhou Yongkang who is in charge of China's security troops, tried to rescue Bo from custody but failed. The Chinese government moved quickly to delete the news and punished those who were responsible for spreading it. So far there is no detailed information regarding this coup.[30] It was also reported by *New York Times* that Bo Xilai had run a wire-tapping network across Chongqing, with his officials listening into phone calls of Party and government officials, including that of President Hu Jintao. A group of veteran Party members, according to another report, wrote collectively to President Hu demanding him to sack not only Bo Xilai but also his backer, Zhou Yongkan, who was considered the pushing hand behind the curtains to revive a movement to lead China back to Mao's time.[31] Again, few people know if any of these are simply rumors (谣言) or "predictions far ahead of their time (遥遥领先的预言)" at the moment, but the downfall of Zhou himself later on seems to have confirmed such an event.[32]

Through the summer trials of Gu Kailai, Zhang Xiaojun, and Wang Lijun, the prosecutors were careful not to mention anything about Bo Xilai as if he had nothing to do with the cases of his wife and his police chief. But everybody knew his days were numbered. On September 28, Bo Xilai was officially expelled from the Communist Party of China. He was also stripped of all his positions in the Party, the government, and the National People's Congress (NPC). He would have no more immunity from prosecution as a deputy later in October and early November. The only thing left now was when Bo Xilai will face justice in court. For quite a while there was no news regarding Bo's trial, probably an indication that the top leaders still had different opinions on how to handle the Bo Xilai incident.[33] Then in 2013, Bo was found guilty of corruption, stripped of all his assets, and sentenced to life imprisonment for his involvement along with his wife Gu Kailai in the murder of British businessman Neil Heywood, who allegedly had close financial ties with the two.[34]

Impact and Consequences

It seems that one consensus can be surely reached by almost everyone, including those who still openly oppose it. That is, the information flow on internet has indeed broken the Chinese government monopoly, or has at least posed a great challenge for the future government control despite the huge government spending on the issue. The strongest firewall as well as many other government censorship measures to control the internet and people's access to information can only be said to have been partially successful while people's confidence in the official news channels has reached to its lowest point in years. People simply prefer to believe in rumors rather than what the government says.

The popular "Weibo," the Chinese counterpart of Twitter, is one of the most influential channels from which hundreds of millions of Chinese receive their information. It played an important role in challenging the government control on information flow. As early as March 2012, some Weibo users began to report on the Wang Lijun incident and even a possible military coup in Beijing. Such "rumors" were quickly deleted by the government "internet police" and the persons involved were picked up. Even the internet servers like Sina and Tencent were disciplined by authorities for spreading "rumors." But such actions only aroused even more people's interest.[35] Such phenomenon was also confirmed by other international observers. For example, *Wall Street Journal* reported that some Sina Weibo users' accounts were simply deleted by the server with a statement saying that "criminal elements have used Sina Weibo to create and spread malicious rumors online for no reason, producing a terrible effect on society" and those involved have "already been dealt with by public security organs according to the law."[36] The widespread public interest in the issue and the unprecedented participation by the public, through unofficial news channels and other social-media websites has indeed become a serious challenge to the government monopoly on information. It seems at least partially true that gone are the days when the Party decided what it wanted people to know and what to be kept in secret from the public. The decentralization of news sources is sure to put more pressure on the Party to start some reforms to meet the new changes or challenges. The new rising star of WeChat (a cell phone chat group app.) since a few years ago has made things even harder for the government to control the flow of information, although tougher measures are taken by the government in dealing with the spread of "rumors."[37]

So far the Party's response to the event is still a reflection of its longtime tradition and there is not much improvement. Beside censorship and monitoring the internet doing the "necessary" deletions, the official news media continues its old measures of "leading the public opinions": headlines, editorials, reports that have little to do with the most urgent events, and so on, would try to divert people's attention and to promote "positive" news only. The official channels also urge people to ignore "rumors" and give a lot more emphasis on "stability," a tune that has continued since Jiang Zemin was in power and was carried on during last ten years by Hu Jintao/Wen Jiabao team. In April 2012 when the Wang Lijun incident was catching people's attention, almost all newspapers in China carried headlines like "Conscientiously Follow Party Discipline and National Law." It was reported, as many longtime China observers predicted, all the newspapers and other forms of news media were ordered by the government to follow the sources of Xinhua reports only.[38] Developments in other areas indeed helped this effort by the Chinese government. Confrontations between China and its neighboring countries, such as the conflicting claims by China and Japan on Diaoyu Island (in Japan, Senkaku Islands) and conflicts between China and Philippines in the South China Sea quickly diverted people's attention. Large-scale anti-Japanese demonstrations would grab headlines and people's interest in the Bo Xilai case gradually faded out, if not totally. The mass demonstration aiming at South Korea for its agreement to install American anti-missile system in the face of North Korea's continuous nuclear missile experiments also kept people's attention. It seems the Party, once again, successfully handled the issue like it had been doing during the last sixty-plus years after it got into power in 1949, though many continued to believe that the Bo Xilai case is far more than just another case where a corrupt official fell down by accident.

Many observers in China and other countries tend to agree on another issue. The Bo Xilai case is a reflection of the fierce struggle between different factions within the Chinese Communist Party, that is, between the "princelings" and "Tuan Pai" (those who rise up in the Party leadership through the line of Communist Youth League), or among "princelings" themselves (both Bo Xilai and current CCP leader, Xi Jinping, belong to this group) over the power. The princelings, children of old communist leaders of Mao's generation, has long been regarded as the most privileged group in China and their bonds seem to have formed long before the name "princelings" were cast on them.[39] Regarding the party leadership under Jiang Zemin and Hu Jintao as not "orthodoxy" enough and taking advantage of people's discontent with the huge gap between the rich and poor during the last two decades of economic reforms, the princelings were simply not willing to sit idle although the reforms during these years also brought them huge accumulation of wealth. Blaming the Party leaders for "playing a game of passing around a time bomb" (抱着定时炸弹击鼓传花) through their "maintenance of stability," the members of princelings group openly challenged the center. Since 2010 and especially in 2011, they formed into a core group, many active duty military officers (such as General Liu Yuan, son of former Chinese president, Liu

Shaoqi and General Zhu Chenghu, grandson of the Red Army founder, Zhu De), and openly criticized the top leaders.

A book published in April 2011 caught many people's attention. Entitled *Changing Our Cultural History Perspective,* the book traced the problems China was faced with currently and strongly criticized the Hu Jintao-Wen Jiabao administration for stubbornly doing nothing but maintaining "stability." Calling the top leaders "Soft and gutless" and blaming them for having led China into a whole series of "political and social crises," the author predicted that the future leadership, with their high ideals, would not allow that to continue. They would be determined to raise the banner of "New Democracy" and their political wisdom will help solve all the problems China has to deal with. The author of the book, Zhang Musheng, received whole-hearted support from many princelings. General Liu Yuan even drafted the long Preface of the book and quite a few princelings, including several PLA generals, attended the ceremony at the book's publication. In the book, Zhang vividly describes the developments during the last twenty years, and has pointed out pretty accurately that China during the last two decades has seen "corrupt officials set up the stage for profiteers to play, with government power commercialized, administration schemed, and local government turning into mafia-like organizations."[40] The author gives Bo Xilai's "Chongqing Model" pretty high remarks, calling Bo's "Singing Red Songs" campaign an effort to lead people to recall Mao's Yen'an years when the Communists were the most popular among the common people and his "Smashing the Black" campaign as giving people a chance and a place to vent their anger.

Bo Xilai, apparently, belongs to the new leadership group with "very high ideals," according to the author's definitions, though Bo's name has never been mentioned. In the author's eyes, "Chongqing Model" is a wonderful experiment where his "New Democracy" theory can be carried out. As observers pointed out, the so-called Chongqing Model has two major features: the land reform both in the countryside and the city, and the promotion of socialist public ownership with government's close control over economic affairs, although the spotlight is taken by Bo's "Singing the Red Song" and "Smashing the Black" campaigns. But obviously, the author got himself into a hard-to-explain situation—while he believes the governments have already turned into mafia-like organizations, Bo's "Smashing the Black" campaign can lead to nothing else but even more abuse of power, or in another Chinese phrase, "黑打," meaning literarily, "smashing like mafia does.[41] Apparently, the author and his "New Left" colleagues failed to explain. After the downfall of Bo Xilai, the "New left" camp did not stop promoting their ideas except for a short period of silence—the government also silenced their website, Utopia (乌有之乡) for a short time. News of pro-Bo petitions and even demonstrations were reported in different areas from time to time.

Of course, the top leaders in Beijing are not happy about all this. They know clearly what these "New Left" elements are talking about and understand very well what the backers behind them really want. Facing the end of his own career as the Party leader, Hu Jintao of course needs to think about what legacy he is going to leave behind. It is not surprising for anyone to imagine Hu's worry that his own achievements during his tenure would be undone by his successors. Reportedly always overshadowed by his predecessor, Jiang Zemin, and faced with numerous challenges as the top leader, Hu Jintao is never a really happy man as many believe. With his background as a member of "Tuan Pai," Hu understands correctly he lacks support from the princelings. Moving his way up through years along the Party leadership ladder, Hu has never been a bold reformer either. What he has been doing through his ten years in office is to try his best to maintain what the Party has already achieved. His signature "poker face" image is well known, and his push to keep the status quo while the country is facing more and more challenges in terms of social instability, environment disasters, and the increasing gap between the rich and the poor lead many to believe he is simply no good at dealing with these challenges. That also explains why Bo Xilai and the like want to take advantage of the situation to replace him.[42] The downfall of Bo Xilai, starting with the Wang Lijun incident, some people would argue, is a good thing for the Hu Jintao-Wen Jiabao administration. The incident itself, along with more scandals exposed after, simply give Hu Jintao a good opportunity to argue that what Bo Xilai did in Chongqing as well as his challenge to the central leadership is just exactly what China should try to avoid, that is, the return back to Mao's Cultural Revolution. Premier Wen Jiabao's speech in spring 2012 condemning Bo Xilai and his followers seems to prove that. What Bo Xilai did is not necessarily what he truly believes, people would argue. He was simply taking advantage of people's discontent to realize his political ambition.[43] This would also help Hu Jintao to link hands with incoming leaders like Xi Jinping (another princeling) to form a certain kind of alliance so that the Party's 18th Congress would see a successful transfer of power. What happened in November 2012 when such transfer of power indeed took place without too much trouble seems to have confirmed this. And the crisis appears to have passed also, at least momentarily.

However, things are not that simple and a very real challenge is still there. The Bo Xilai incident exposed that Bo and his wife have accumulated huge amount of wealth and have been involved in many multimillion financial or construction projects. It simply confirms people's beliefs that corruption among high-ranking officials has gone beyond control and the Party's promise to crack down on such officials has not worked. It is commonplace in China to see relatives or friends of Party and government officials' become billionaires, involving themselves busily in the country's oil, electricity, insurance, or even diamonds. Then in late October 2012 another heavy-duty bombshell came.

On October 25, *New York Times* carried a report by its journalist, David Barbosa (Chinese name 张大卫), revealing the huge amount of wealth, up to $27 billion worth, owned by then the Chinese premier Wen Jiabao's family members. Though the report, as well as other reports by Bloomberg, never says Wen Jiabao himself is involved, it frankly exposed how many Chinese high-ranking officials and their family members were taking advantage of their offices and special networking for the personal gains. Even President Xi Jinping's family does not escape from spotlight—Xi's daughter is reported to be a student at an Ivy League university in the United States and his other relatives are also involved in hidden wealth. Reports on officials' scandals and downfalls are not new in China. People have seen the downfall of two Politburo members (Chen Xitong and Chen Liangyu, Party bosses in both Beijing and Shanghai) in recent years. But Premier Wen Jiabao had always given people the impression of a "pro-people" and more honest official. If Wen and his family can be that corrupt, who else can be clean? Wen Jiabao, through his family lawyer, issued a statement to deny *New York Times'* charges and promised possible future legal actions. But so far there is no news of any such actions. The timing of the report at such a sensitive moment (Bo Xilai's downfall and the convening of the Party's 18th Congress where power transfer would take place) is very important. Despite Chinese government's protests, blaming Mr. Barboza of attempting to "defame" China with "ulterior purposes," people tend to take it to the heart. For his reporting, David Barboza was granted with the 2013 Pulitzer Prize on international reporting.[44]

Doubtlessly, the report also puts a huge question mark in front of every Chinese, many of whom actually praised Barboza's report, citing the fact that the Communist Party's new leadership can no longer carry on the ineffective crack down campaigns that just "kill the flies but let go the tigers." Many also believe that the whole event, especially Wang Lijun's defection to the Americans, forces the Chinese leaders to take action. If Wang Lijun did not escape into Chengdu US Consulate, no international attention would ever occur, which in turn would never become a big issue in China. Wang could simply fall out from public scenes like many other corrupt officials before him, or he might even "disappear" before he could reach Chengdu. Wang, simply put, can be said to have done something good for China by helping the Party avoid a bloody power struggle or preventing more people like Bo Xilai from committing more crimes.[45] The new leadership is sure to take a few cues from the Bo Xilai incident.

Since taking the leading position at the Party's 18th Congress, which was postponed from October to November 2012 (most possibly because of Bo Xilai incident), Xi Jinping has been trying to establish a new image. Soon after becoming the new Party general secretary, he ordered the party officials to keep their meetings short and "with no empty rhetoric or gobbledygook." Serving as the chairman of the Central Military Commission, Xi Jinping also ordered the Chinese military to follow his "prohibition" orders, banning liquor, which the Chinese military consumes a lot every year. Xi believes such consumption a big waste and a chance for corruption. Such moves by the new administration have won praises in China, but many also point out that all this is far from enough to deal with China's problems. For example, the Party's absolute control on the flow of information continues and the situation actually becomes worse than before when journalists, publishers, and common folks who dare to go beyond the line are continued to be disciplined, forced to shut down, or simply sent to jail. His speeches while touring China's southern city, Shenzhen, gives a lot of emphasis that the Chinese Communist Party under his leadership "will neither take the old way nor the 'evil ways.'"[46] Such a speech sent a mixed signal, to say the best. Not taking the old way obviously refers to Mao's revolutionary campaigns, but what does he mean by "evil ways?" Many believe that he is talking about the Western-style democracy. Then what way is he going to take?

One thing remains clear to everyone, including Xi Jinping himself: the urgency for political reform in China. The last ten years have seen the Hu Jintao-Wen Jiabao administration becoming increasingly "stability obsessed" and refusing to undertake any significant political reforms. The economic boom during the last thirty years does not smooth people's discontent when the gap between the rich and the poor widens to dangerous levels and news about scandals of corrupt officials become daily routines. The Communist leaders are very clear that such social upheavals are the major reasons why dynasties were overthrown since ancient times in China. The international environment makes things even more complicated—the "Color Revolutions" and "Jasmine Revolutions" across the world during the first decade of the twenty-first century alarmed them. They also understand very well and very correctly that the Chinese Communist Party is no longer what it used to be—an energetic and highly disciplined revolutionary party. Coming into power as the representative of the poor with the anticorruption, pro-equality, and democratic banners, the Chinese Communist Party has become *the* establishment that needs to justify its own legitimacy. In one single generation, the Party, since Deng Xiaoping's reforms started, has turned itself into the representative of the wealthiest in China. It has become more and more difficult for the Party to make its Marxist rhetoric fit into China's reality today or just defend the status quo. With corruption reaching the highest-level leadership in China, the Bo Xilai incident simply makes it impossible for the Party to postpone reforms that are long overdue.

It is also the Party's collective belief, many party members insist, that policy-making in China cannot return to Mao's time when one top leader's opinion could decide everything—consensus must be reached among the small group of top leaders—Politburo Standing Committee members in this case. The Bo Xilai incident fully exposes the rifts among the top leaders despite the efforts by the Party to keep the seamless image of unity.[47] Then how to initiate political reform while maintaining the Party's unity and its control over the society has become the top issue for the new leadership under Xi Jinping, who has to make some most difficult decisions the Party has ever faced. The year of 2013 saw the new president of China delivering some inspiring speeches in which Xi Jinping continued to promote his version of "the Chinese Dream," the great rejuvenation of Chinese nation. He also warned the Party and the people that without reforms China would see the death of the Party and the Nation ("亡党亡国"), something totally different from what his predecessor, Hu Jintao, said at the Party's 18th Congress in November 2012. In his report to the Party's Congress, Hu repeatedly mentioned his famous "Three Confidences" in "our way, our theory, and our system," which are sharply different from what Xi is telling us. Although Xi's own "Chinese dream" and his warnings sound contradictory, they surely demonstrate that he is pretty determined to do something. The Bo Xilai incident, once again, simply leaves him not much time or room to postpone before it is too late.

Unofficial discussions and debates on how to start and carry out the political reform have been going on for quite some time, though the central leadership never presents any timetable or blueprint. One of the most discussed issues is the "rule of law." Bo Xilai incident shows clearly, even for the most conservative members of the Party, that without rule of law, abuse of power cannot be stopped and absolute power can only lead to absolute corruption—Communists are no exceptions. The Party's continued efforts at maintaining the status quo can only encourage more corruption and have no way to meet the increasing demands from the people for transparency, equality, and civil rights. It can't even satisfy the demands from within the Party. It seems everyone, including Xi, agrees that without the rule of law, China will have no future.[48] But to go that way will put the Party itself at danger. Suggestions and efforts to demand the Party and government leaders to make their properties known to the public have never succeeded. Zhao Ziyang's last try in 1989 only made his downfall faster as the Party's general secretary. In the case of the Bo Xilai incident, if prosecutors insist on exposing everything, it will very possibly lead to more investigations involving more high-ranking officials. Considering the fact that there are already many scandals, the consequence may be disastrous—the image of the "always correct" Party will be damaged and people's confidence in the Party will be gone, and the Party's control over the nation will also be in jeopardy. The famous "Panama Papers" that came out in 2016 has led to the downfalls of quite a few government leaders in different countries. It also leaked quite a few names of the Chinese leaders and family members who have connections with shell companies overseas where they hide their huge wealth. The Xi administration, however, successfully put it aside by closely monitoring the internet, WeBo, and WeChat. Few people in China even know of the event.[49]

The Chinese Communist Party's history has numerous political, organizational, and policy crises, from the "Ten Struggles on Political Lines" of Mao's times to the 1989 Tian An Men incident. Each time after a crisis, the Party seems to be always able to "pick itself off the ground, reconstituted its armor and reinforced its flanks" and "outlasted, outsmarted, outperformed or simply outlawed its critics," as one American commentator's pointed out.[50] But this time, Xi will face more taunting challenges, as many people predicted, "To reform means suicide, not to reform means a slow death." Of course Xi Jinping will not agree. He does not lack advisors. During the times of his two predecessors, Jiang Zemin and Hu Jintao, numerous laws were put into place. Although these laws and rules have failed to be successfully enforced, they do provide a basis from where Xi can have a jump start with his new reforms. So far, Xi Jinping has frankly admitted all the problems that have been bothering the Party and the country, including the rampant corruption among officials. He also repeatedly promises that the new administration will surely start necessary political reforms, including those in China's constitution, government systems, and legal education as well as the democratization within the Party.[51] In one sense, the Bo Xilai incident has forced the Party and its leaders into a situation where they have no other way out but to look for changes and reforms to remain in the game.

Unfinished Stories of Chongqing

Five years had quickly passed by when the Chinese Communist Party was preparing its 19th national congress that took place in October 2017. Once again, Chongqing city, which is now known for the disgraceful removal of its party boss, Bo Xilai, caught people's attention. In July of the year (2017), Chinese news media, quickly followed by all news channels across the world, reported that Sun Zhengcai, Bo Xilai's successor as the municipality Communist Party secretary in Chongqing, was removed from the position for "serious violations of party discipline," a phrase that may mean taking bribes as an official or not following the party line or anything in between.[52]

By the time this chapter is about to conclude, many things that were labeled as "rumors" since 2012 have been proved to be true. For example, former CCP leader Hu Jintao has been rumored controversially to be powerless in fighting his anticorruption campaigns while in office, with many officials around him appointees from his predecessor (Jiang Zemin). By the time he was finally able to remove Bo Xilai in 2012, with the help of his successor Xi Jinping, Hu had done very little, if nothing, to stop the party officials under him from forming into different interest groups and use their offices for personal gains. It was rumored that Hu, with tears in his eyes, gave his farewell speech at the Party's 18th congress in which he criticized other high-ranking officials, especially his predecessor Jiang Zemin who refused to give up his title as the chairman of the Central Military Commission （中央军委）so as to continue his influence within the party and the military. Hu made sure that he would step down from all his positions within and out of the party, namely, that of CCP secretary general, president of People's Republic of China, and chairman of Central Military Commission.[53]

However, it is not correct to say that Hu Jintao had done nothing to stop the corrupt officials within the party and the government. He was weak as the party leader, a point almost everybody agrees on. That does not mean he never tried. Hu actually tried and indeed succeeded in removing one of his challengers in the Politburo, Chen Liangyu. In the summer of 2006, all major news channels reported that Chen was suspended from his post in the Political Bureau of the Chinese Communist Party and of the Central Committee, as well as the party boss of Shanghai. The Central Commission for Discipline Inspection of the CCP announced that Chen had "authorized the handing over of the city's pension fund to business contacts to invest in their property development" and "other discipline violations, such as helping to further the economic interests for illegal entrepreneurs, protecting his staff who severely violated laws and discipline, furthering the interests of family members by taking advantage of his official posts," and live a life of personal excess including keeping eleven mistresses in addition to his wife. The amount involved in the Shanghai social security fund scandal is more than £2.45 billion and Chen was also accused to have accepted £170, 000, according to British reporters.[54]

This action by Hu Jintao, we can argue, seems much like a counter offensive against his predecessor, Jiang Zemin, and his "Shanghai Gang." Jiang, functioning as the CCP secretary general, was famous in 1995 for taking out another Politburo member, Chen Xitong (not related to Chen Liangyu), who was believed to belong to the group with its power base in Beijing city. As *New York Times*' Joseph Kahn pointed out, Hu Jintao certainly would not have taken action against Chen Liangyu unless he considered Chen Liangyu to have become an obstacle to his political control or his policy agenda.[55] The widely accepted rumor is that the Hu Jintao-Wen Jiabao (Premier) team's orders could only be heard and carried out in Beijing (政令不出中南海) and Hu simply hated that. To reduce the local resistance, with many local official appointees by Jiang Zemin, it is understandable that Hu-Wen team would try their best to smash the political clique that had been tied closely to Jiang Zemin, and Chen Liangyu was simply coming at the right moment. The downfall of Chen Liangyu seemed to signal the rising authority of Hu Jintao, though analysts generally agreed that Hu had to compromise by agreeing not to reverse as many of Jiang Zemin's pro-market policies as he would like.[56]

All these earlier analysis regarding the power struggle between the Beijing leadership and "Shanghai Gang" has been labeled as rumors. But it is true, as we see today, that Jiang Zemin and his followers had been able to hold on to all the major offices of Shanghai for fifteen years, avoiding the rotation system that applied in every other provinces. Shanghai, according to the analysis, became "one of the least transparent governments and the most tightly controlled media environments" in China. To send a signal, Hu actually warned that "whoever it is, no matter how high their positions, anyone who violates party rules or national law will be severely investigated and punished."[57] Hu had tried. But his efforts were mostly negated by the strong network of the Jiang group.

It is just Hu Jintao's weak grip on power, especially his control (or simply no control) of the military, that inspired his successor, Xi Jinping, to launch an all-out "purge" of the Chinese military and the party itself. Serving as a member of the Central Military Commission, Xi personally witnessed how the appointees by Jiang Zemin on the commission, Guo Boxiong and Xu Caihou, took power away from Hu and make all major decisions of the military. With his isolation among his deputies not only in the military but also within the party, Hu Jintao actually had little room to maneuver, just watching Guo and Xu as well as their followers to abuse their power and encourage corruptions, even with many military ranks for sale.[58]

After witnessing Hu's bitter experience, Xi was determined to get something done. Since he took power in 2012, many top officials of the party, military, and government have been going down in Xi Jinping's anticorruption campaign. The list is long. It includes the chief of the CCP Committee on politics and law （政法委）, two vice chairmen of the Central Military Commission, and the chief of the CCP Central Committee's main office （中央办公厅）among many others. Along with them, hundreds of officials on different levels, including more than one hundred generals of the People's Liberation Army, have also been removed. Many of the cases today usually have billions of dollars involved, much larger than during the Hu years. The ranks of the officials involved are also higher than before. Quite a lot of such news were also first labeled as rumors by the Chinese authority at the time, but later on proved to be true. Sun Zhengcai is just one of quite a few provincial-level officials that have gone down recently. But his downfall does have different meanings. It was rumored (proved true too) that he was designated to be the party's next top leader after Xi Jinping's tenure is over by 2022.[59]

There is no curse in Chongqing city, where both Bo and Sun who were, respectively, contenders for the CCP top positions fell. Scholarly analysis or popular "rumors" all focus on one major point: Are the popular anticorruption campaigns by Xi Jinping to crack down on "flies" (lower-ranking officials) and "tigers" (high-ranking officials) simply power struggle among communist leaders? It seems to be so at least superficially: all the officials removed from their positions are either appointed/promoted during the Jiang administration or did not show enough loyalty to the new "Xi center" (another term used in recent months to describe the CCP leadership under Xi Jinping). There might be other reasons, of course, as both Hu and Xi as the party chiefs agreed and repeatedly emphasized that allowing such corruption to go on meant the collapse of the party and the government. Sun's sudden removal from his office also contradicts with the earlier promotion of his office in Chongqing: throughout the year of 2016 the party's mouthpiece, *People's Daily*, had been running news, editorials, reports as well as commentaries regarding Chongqing, all in positive light. Does this suggest that Xi Jinping is not happy with his colleagues on the Politburo, especially those in charge of the party's propaganda machines (namely, Liu Yunshan)? Considering Xi's recent actions in removing quite a few officials from the party's propaganda department and government offices that control China's news media, such "rumors" could be proved true once again.[60]

The future policies of the CCP would be determined at the Party's 19th Congress that will be in session in late October 2017. Several things seem to be certain even before the meeting starts. Apparently Xi is determined to consolidate his power, making himself very much like Mao Zedong, the founding father of the CCP. There are "rumors" that Xi is going to take the position of a decision maker at the Central Military Commission, replacing the current "collective decisions" pattern. Xi seems to be pretty sure too that he will end the appointment/designation procedure of future successors for the party leadership. There is possibility that he might even help his close friends and comrades-in-arms like Wang Qishan (China's anticorruption Tsar) to bypass some earlier regulations of the party, such as "Qishang Baxia" (七上八下),[61] to make sure his anticorruption campaign (or his effort to strengthen his power) will continue, though many people disagree.[62]

The outside world seems all agree that the Party's 19th Congress will surely recognize Xi's absolute control over the Party, government, and the military. However, what he is going to do with this power remains a big question mark. Is he going to continue Mao's leftist policy to keep the authoritarian rule or use his newly consolidated power to move China in a new direction, for example, to promote China's constitutional reform in order to build a more democratic society (as some people wished and totally dismissed by others), or at least some limited democracy within the Communist Party to avoid future power struggle? Will his anticorruption campaign finally save the party? Is he going to build true "rule of law" instead of "rule by law" (with the CCP above the law) in China? All this remains to be proved in the near future. So far as we can see, Xi Jinping is stressing more on his "China Dream" (making China a wealthy and powerful country) through his "One Belt, One Road" program instead of the political reforms that have long been overdue. As the number two economic power today in the world aiming at surpassing the United States soon, any decisions by Xi Jinping and his communist colleagues (with the CCP membership reaching 89 million by 2017) will have huge impact on the rest the world besides the everyday life of more than 1.4 billion Chinese people.[63]

NOTES

1. Reports on the downfall of Chinese officials during the last few years are so numerous that people are no longer feeling excited or bother to care. Many sources both in China and wider world, however, have been keeping on reporting. According to some reports, more than 1,340,000 Communist Party members and officials both in the party and the government have been removed from their offices since 2013, with many ended up in jail. *Radio France International* has a summary of the reports on Oct. 9, 2017. See at http://en.rfi.fr/asia-pacific/.

2. In our internet age, no government can control the flow of information like in the past, even in China where government censorship is still stubbornly persisting. Typing into any major news media website, such as CNN, ABC, CBS, *New York Times,* or BBC, one would be flooded with reports on the issue. Many unofficial sites also provide all kinds of information, though Chinese government always tries to define such reports as "rumors" which frequently proved to be otherwise. This chapter relies pretty much on such official and unofficial news sources to find related information regarding these events, as there is no "real" versions of the story yet or stories already there still need to be verified. The following websites may help anyone interested to continue their research:

http://www.breakingviews.com/review-the-real-story-of-bo-xilais-ruin/21068767.article;

http://topics.nytimes.com/top/reference/timestopics/people/b/bo_xilai/index.html;

http://www.cnn.com/2012/10/26/world/asia/china-politics-bo;http://topics.bloomberg.com/bo-xilai/;

http://www.reuters.com/article/2013/02/21/us-china-politics-bo-idUSBRE91K0D520130221;

http://www.bbc.co.uk/news/world-asia-china-17673505;

http://abcnews.go.com/topics/news/world/bo-xilai.htm;

http://news.xinhuanet.com/english/china/2012-09/28/c_131880079.htm; http://en.boxun.com/tag/bo-xilai/, and many others.

3. Lauren Higers, "The Unraveling of Bo Xilai: China Loses A Populist Star." *Harper's Magazine* (March 2013), pp. 38–45.

4. Please check the time lines of Bo Xilai scandal at Committee to Protect Journalists website at http://cpj.org/reports/2013/03/challenged-china-media-censorship-timeline-bo-xilai.php and BBC http://www.bbc.co.uk/news/world-asia-china-17673505.

5. Higers, "The Unraveling of Bo Xilai," p. 40.

6. There is more discussion on Bo Xilai's "princeling" status at BBC website at http://www.bbc.co.uk/news/world-asia-china-17673505 as well as many Chinese sites, though all the stories need to be verified.

7. Ibid.

8. To find more information regarding Heywood, check the *New York Times* archives at its website at http://topics.nytimes.com/top/reference/timestopics/people/b/bo_xilai/index.html.

9. Ibid.

10. See at http://www.bbc.co.uk/news/world-asia-china-1769025.

11. See at http://www.bbc.co.uk/news/world-asia-china-19709555.

12. Such estimates are done by different groups, such as Tsinghua University. The current number, many believe, can only be higher. See Higers, "The Unraveling of Bo Xilai," p. 41.

13. Ibid. Years after his downfall, many folks in Chongqing still recall the "better times" when Bo was their city leader.

14. See article, "薄王数百亿资金黑幕 法院痛彻心扉" (博讯北京时间2013年3月20日 转载财经网) at http://boxun.com/news/gb/china/2013/03/201303200445.shtml#.UV5ih8rna0M. Many of these cases are under investigation again today. Numerous reports are showing that Bo and his followers were simply using the government offices they control to wrongly charge people and illegally take away their properties.

15. Higers, "The Unraveling of Bo Xilai," p. 41. One may also check China's New Left website, Utopia (乌有之乡) at http://www.wyzxsx.com/ to find more of its defense for Bo Xilai.

16. Peter Hessler, "Return to River Town." *National Geographic* (March 2013), p. 96.

17. 鲍彤，"不再唱红打黑还是坚持唱红打黑？ 十八大有两种选择"(Bao Tong, "To Continue the 'Singing the Red' and 'Smashing the Black' or Not: The Two Choices for the Party's 18th Congress." See at http://my.cnd.org/modules/wfsection/article.php?articleid=3348.

18. Quoted by Higers, "The Unraveling of Bo Xilai," p. 41. Please check out all news reports on Wen's speech and the Party Central Committee's decision on different websites. The general translation is like "As Comrade Bo Xilai is suspected of being involved in 2 serious discipline violations, the Central Committee of the Communist Party of China (CPC) has decided to suspend his membership of the CPS Central Committee Political Bureau and the CPS Central Committee, in line

with the CPS Constitution and the rules on investigation of CPC discipline inspection departments."

19. The story is based on many similar reports, though with slight differences from each other. Since the trial never allowed the details to get out of the courtroom, all of this still need future confirmation. Examples of such doubts include (1) How many people were present when Gu murdered Heywood in his hotel room? Two or Four? (2) What kind of poison was used? (3) Where did this poison come from? One high-ranking Chinese coroner, Wang Xuemei, was reported to blog that she had high doubt about what the court reports said regarding the poison (cyanide). (4) Were there any other persons involved? See 1700319 http://boxun.com/news/gb/china/2013/04/201304020319.shtml#.UV5hgsrna0M.

20. Ibid.

21. There are different versions of this encountering between Bo and Wang. Some insist Wang wanted to use the recording to blackmail Bo and Gu, or for other purposes. But no strong evidence shows up so far.

22. 何頻、黃文合著，《中國權貴的死亡遊戲》，美國公共事務出版社, April 2013. See comments at http://www.amazon.com/Death-Lucky-Holiday-Hotel-ebook/dp/B00B6TVDEG/ref=dp_kinw_strp_1or at http://www.mingjingnews.com/2013/01/blog-post_2783.html.

23. 姜维平 (Jiang Weiping), "薄谷蹦得太欢，自己跳进锅里" (Interview with自由亚洲电台 Radio Free Asia). Carried by http://www.aboluowang.com/2013/0405/296532.html.

24. Higers, "The Unraveling of Bo Xilai." *Harper's Magazine* (March, 2013), p. 44.

25. Please check all major news channels, especially China's Xinhua News Agency website, for reports on the trial and sentences. See note 1 for useful addresses.

26. Ibid, pay special attention to reports at http://www.cnn.com/2012/09/23/world/asia/china-wang-lijun-verdict.

27. See at Xinhua News Agency's website at http://news.xinhuanet.com/english/china/2012/.

28. Ibid. Please also refer to all major news channels both in China and those of other countries.

29. Higers, "The Unraveling of Bo Xilai," p. 44.

30. See reports from all major news channels, especially at http://www.cnn.com/2012/09/23/world/asia/china-wang-lijun-verdict.

31. See BBC reports at http://www.bbc.co.uk/news/world-asia-china-17673505.

32. Yuwen Wu, "Profile: China's Fallen Security Chief Zhou Yongkang," at http://www.bbc.com/news/world-asia-china-26349305.

33. According to China's official news channels, the Standing Committee of the 11th National People's Congress (NPC) announced the termination of Bo Xilai's post as the NPC deputy on October 26. The 7th Plenary Session of the 17th Central Committee of the Communist Party of China (CPC) officially endorsed the decision made by the Political Bureau to expel Bo from the Party on November 4. See comments at http://www.cnd.org/my/modules/wfsection/article.php%3Farticleid=33523.

34. Xiansheng Tian, "When Chongqing Challenges Beijing: Bo Xilai Case," in *Evolution of Power: China's Struggle, Survival, and Success*, eds. Xiaobing Li and Xiansheng Tian (Lanham, MD: Lexington Books, 2014), 327–330.

35. See at the website of Committee to protect Journalists for detailed information at http://cpj.org/reports/2013/03/challenged-china-media-censorship-timeline-bo-xilai.php.

36. See at WSJ website at http://online.wsj.com/article/SB10001424052702303459004577364190134631110.html.

37. That includes the 2017 rule that if a member of the chat group is caught spreading the rumor, the whole group's account may be closed and the group leader would take the legal responsibility.

38. *People's Daily* and other major newspapers on April 13 and *People's Liberation Army Daily* on April 6. Also check the Wall Street Journal's reports on such events. See at http://online.wsj.com/article/SB10001424052702303459004577364190134631110.html.

39. See article by John Garnaut, "Power Shot: A rare photograph sheds new light on China's important social network," at http://www.foreignpolicy.com/articles/2013/02/27/power_shot_china_princelings.

40. 张木生(Zhang Musheng): ". . . 现在中国已经形成了'贪官搭台，奸商唱戏，权力市场化，执政产业化，地方政府黑帮化'。" See discussions at http://chinainformzen.blogspot.com/2011/05/general-liu-yuan-says-read-zhang.html, http://sjfm.xilu.com/2011/0301/news_556_143803.html, http://news.sina.com.cn/c/sd/2011-10-28/114723377991.shtml, and http://www.delex.com/pub/dsr/Delex%20CSA-special%20Report%20on%20Gen%20Liu%20Yuan's%20Preface%20Translation.pdf.

41. Ibid. There are numerous sites that carry such kind of discussions and comments.

42. Please refer to other chapters of the book to find more information regarding the Jiang Zemin and Hu Jintao administrations and their policies.

43. See the *Radio of Free Asia* interview with Wan Runnan and other reports at http://www.boxun.com/news/gb/china/2012/09/201209080220.shtml.

44. Please see information regarding David Barboza at the *New York Times*' website and other comments at http://topics.nytimes.com/top/reference/timestopics/people/b/david_barboza/index.html and http://www.cnd.org/my/modules/wfsection/article.php%3Farticleid=35730.

45. 华正平, "支配中国政治游戏的核心内容" (Hua Zhengping, "The Core Essence that Dominate Political Games in China") at http://www.cnd.org/my/modules/wfsection/article.php%3Farticleid=32982.

46. See Hu Jintao and Xi Jinping speeches and comments at http://theory.people.com.cn/n/2012/1109/c148980-19534438.html, http://news.ifeng.com/mainland/special/zhonggong18da/content-2/detail_2012_11/09/19003067_0.shtml, https://www.youtube.com/watch?v=x9ko3Gd4hnM, http://china.caixun.com/xrz/20121116-CX038vn2.html and many other sites.

47. Hannah Beech, "Big Brotherhood." *Time* (October 22, 2012), p. 42.

48. 巩胜利：废谷保薄，显露中国"天机" (Gong Shengli, "Abandon Gu to protect Bo")? See at http://www.cnd.org/my/modules/wfsection/article.php%3Farticleid=33523.

49. Details can be seen at http://www.scmp.com/news/hong-kong/article/1943463/chinese-dominate-list-people-and-firms-hiding-money-tax-havens-panama; http://

www.bbc.com/news/world-asia-35962326; https://www.economist.com/news/china/21696504-panama-papers-embarrass-chinas-leaders, and other sources.

50. Richard McGregor, "China's Private Party." *The Wall Street Journal* (May 15–16, 2010), p. W2.

51. 华世平 (Shiping Hua), "习近平时代法治将占有突出地位"(Rule of Law will Take the Priority Position in the Xi Era). See at http://www.rmlt.com.cn/qikan/2013-05-02/81448.html.

52. See reports by *Reuters* and Channel News Asia/Asia Pacific, "Former party boss of China's Chongqing under investigation." The former Communist Party boss of the Chinese city of Chongqing, Sun Zhengcai, is under investigation for suspected serious violations of discipline, the official Xinhua news agency said on Monday at http://www.channelnewsasia.com/news/asiapacific/former-party-boss-of-china-s-chongqing-under-investigation-9059012. Many other news channels also followed the report.

53. Please see reports from different news sources at https://www.theatlantic.com/china/archive/2013/03/was-hu-jintao-a-failure/273868/; https://asia.nikkei.com/Features/China-up-close/Is-Hu-Jintao-about-to-go-toe-to-toe-with-Xi; https://www.theguardian.com/world/hu-jintao; http://www.scmp.com/news/china/article/1734663/hu-jintaos-weak-grip-chinas-army-inspired-president-xi-jinpings-military and others. Pay attention to the comments on Hu's weak grip on China's military.

54. *China Daily*, "Shanghai party chief sacked for graft (2006-09-25) at http://www.chinadaily.com.cn/china/2006-09/25/content_696159.htm and *The Telegraph*, "Shanghai Communist Party boss jailed" at http://www.telegraph.co.uk/news/worldnews/1584736/Shanghai-Communist-Party-boss-jailed.html.

55. Joseph Kahn, "Shanghai Party Boss Held for Corruption." *The New York Times* (September 25, 2006) at http://www.nytimes.com/2006/09/25/world/asia/25china.html.

56. See again at http://www.telegraph.co.uk/news/worldnews/1584736/Shanghai-Communist-Party-boss-jailed.html.

57. Jonathan Watts, "Shanghai's Communist Party Chief Sacked in Corruption Purge." *The Guardian* (September 25, 2006) at https://www.theguardian.com/world/2006/sep/25/china.jonathanwatts.

58. Minnie Chan, "Hu Jintao's Weak Grip on China's Army Inspired Xi Jinping's Military Shake-up: President's Predecessor 'Isolated' by Deputies Who Acted as Proxies for Jiang Zemin." *South China Morning Post* (March 11, 2015) at http://www.scmp.com/news/china/article/1734663/hu-jintaos-weak-grip-chinas-army-inspired-president-xi-jinpings-military.

59. See *China Digital Times's* report, "Provincial Leaders Shuffled Ahead of 2017 Transition" at http://chinadigitaltimes.net/2016/08/provincial-leaders-shuffled-ahead-2017-transition/. Also see at http://www.chinavitae.com/biography/Sun_Zhengcai.

60. See at *Channel News Asia*, at http://www.channelnewsasia.com/news/asiapacific/former-party-boss-of-china-s-chongqing-under-investigation-9059012. Also see at http://www.aboluowang.com/2017/0906/989369.html.

61. "Qishang Baxia" (七上八下) is the rule set up by the Jiang Zemin administration in 1990s which requires Politburo members to step down when they are

sixty-eight years old and those who haven't reached that age limits to remain in the ruling bodies. Lower-ranking official have lower age limits.

62. As for Wang Qishan himself, rumors are rampant. For example, a Chinese businessman/billionaire taking refuge in the United States has been broadcasting many scandals of the Wang family and his close followers, including the reports that Wang's own wife and sister-in-law are already holding American passports and one of China's large airline companies has already come under the control of Wang's family members. All this, of course, is collectively dismissed by the Chinese authority as simply rumors. Efforts have been made by the Chinese authority to make deals with American government to deport Guo Wengui back to China to face trials. People need patience to wait and see if these exposed scandals are true or not. We may never know what happened exactly though. It is also true that it is very difficult, if not totally impossible, to get any reliable information regarding the CCP infighting, as the party controls all the news Medias in China and any negative reporting or simply displeasure regarding government policies can be easily detested and censored. Even internet is closely monitored by hundreds of thousands of China's "internet police." Any dissidents who dare to challenge the party authority could easily see their WeMo (a Chinese version of Twitter) or WeChat accounts closed or police knocking on their doors.

63. Before this chapter went to the chief editor, the CCP 19th Congress concluded. Many of the points of analysis proved to be true. For example, Xi Jinping indeed consolidated power to become the strongest CCP leader just after Mao Zedong, and a campaign to promote his popularity is underway. Please see reports both in English and Chinese regarding Xi Jinping's new "titles." See Javier C. Hernández, "China's 'Chairman of Everything': Behind Xi Jinping's Many Titles" in *The New York Times*, October 25, 2017. at https://www.nytimes.com/2017/10/25/world/asia/china-xi-jinping-titles-chairman.html. Also see at https://www.express.co.uk/news/world/867015/Xi-Jinping-chinese-president-powerful-title-chairman-mao-tse-tung; http://indianexpress.com/article/world/china-xi-jinping-mao-zedong-communist-party-of-china-4911021/; and http://www.scmp.com/news/china/policies-politics/article/2117421/xi-jinpings-latest-grandiose-title-aims-take.

BIBLIOGRAPHY

Armstrong, Paul. "Police Chief at Heart of Bo Xilai Scandal Jailed for 15 Years." *CNN* Online. Last modified September 24, 2012. https://www.cnn.com/2012/09/23/world/asia/china-wang-lijun-verdict.

Beech, Hannah. "Big Brotherhood." *Time,* October 22, 2012.

"Bo Xilai: News about Bo Xilai, Including Commentary and Archival Articles Published in the New York Times." *The New York Times.* Accessed July 27, 2018. https://www.nytimes.com/topic/person/bo-xilai.

"Bo Xilai Scandal: How News Breaks in China." Committee to Project Journalists. Accessed July 27, 2018. https://cpj.org/reports/2013/03/challenged-china-media-censorship-timeline-bo-xilai.php.

"Bo Xilai Scandal: Timeline." *BBC* Online. Last modified November 11, 2013. https://www.bbc.co.uk/news/world-asia-china-17673505.

Chan, Minnie. "Hu Jintao's Weak Grip on China's Army Inspired Xi Jinping's Military Shake-up: Sources." *South China Morning Post* online. Last modified March 11, 2015. https://www.scmp.com/news/china/article/1734663/hu-jintaos-weak-grip-chinas-army-inspired-president-xi-jinpings-military.

Chao, Loretta and Josh Chin. "China Escalates Crackdown on Internet Amid Scandal." *The Wall Street Journal* online. Last modified April 25, 2012. https://www.wsj.com/articles/SB10001424052702303459004577364190134631110.

"Chinese President Xi Jinping to Become as Powerful as Chairman Mao Tse-tung." *Sunday & Express* online. Last modified October 16, 2017. https://www.express.co.uk/news/world/867015/Xi-Jinping-chinese-president-powerful-title-chairman-mao-tse-tung.

"David Barboza." Accessed 7/28/18: https://www.nytimes.com/by/david-barboza.

Gan, Nectar. "Why China is Reviving Mao's Grandiose Title for Xi Jinping." *South China Morning Post* online. Last modified October 30, 2017. https://www.scmp.com/news/china/policies-politics/article/2117421/xi-jinpings-latest-grandiose-title-aims-take.

Garnaut, John. "Power Shot: A Rare Photograph Sheds New Light on China's Important Social Network." Last modified February 27, 2013. http://www.foreignpolicy.com/articles/2013/02/27/power_shot_china_princelings.

"General Liu Yuan Says: Read Zhang Musheng's 'Changing Our Cultural History Perspective'." *China Reader* online. Last modified May 23, 2011. http://chinainformzen.blogspot.com/2011/05/general-liu-yuan-says-read-zhang.html.

Lau, Stuart. "Chinese Dominate List of People and Firms Hiding Money in Tax Havens, Panama Papers Reveal." *South China Morning Post* online. Last modified May 10, 2016. https://www.scmp.com/news/hong-kong/article/1943463/chinese-dominate-list-people-and-firms-hiding-money-tax-havens-panama.

Lauren, Higers. "The Unraveling of Bo Xilai: China Loses a Populist Star." *Harper's Magazine*.

Javier C. Hernández, "China's 'Chairman of Everything': Behind Xi Jinping's Many Titles" in *The New York Times*, October 25, 2017. https://www.nytimes.com/2017/10/25/world/asia/china-xi-jinping-titles-chairman.html.

Hessler, Peter. "Return to River Town." *National Geographic*, March 2013.

"Hu Jintao." *The Guardian* online. Accessed July 28, 2018. https://www.theguardian.com/world/hu-jintao.

Kahn, Joseph. "Shanghai Party Boss Held for Corruption." *The New York Times* (New York), September 25, 2006. http://www.nytimes.com/2006/09/25/world/asia/25china.html.

McGregor, Richard. "China's Private Party." *The Wall Street Journal* (New York), May 15–16, 2010.

Nakazawa, Katsuji. "Is Hu Jintao about to go toe-to-toe with Xi?" *Nikkei Asian Review* online. Last modified February 11, 2017. https://asia.nikkei.com/Features/China-up-close/Is-Hu-Jintao-about-to-go-toe-to-toe-with-Xi.

"Panama Papers: China Leaders' Relatives Named in Leaks." *BBC* online. Last modified April 4, 2016. https://www.bbc.com/news/world-asia-35962326.

Pin Ho, and Huang Wengguang. *A Death in the Lucky Holiday Hotel: Murder, Money, and an Epic Power Struggle in China*. New York: Public Affairs, 2013.

"Profile: Bo Xilai." *BBC* Online. Last modified September 22, 2013. http://www.bbc.co.uk/news/world-asia-china-19709555.

"Provincial Leaders Shuffled Ahead of 2017 Transition." *China Digital Times*. Accessed July 28, 2018. https://chinadigitaltimes.net/2016/08/provincial-leaders-shuffled-ahead-2017-transition/.

PTI. "Chinese President Xi Jinping's New Title Aims to Take Personality Cult to Next Level: Experts." *The Indian Express* online. Last modified October 28, 2017. https://indianexpress.com/article/world/china-xi-jinping-mao-zedong-communist-party-of-china-4911021/.

Schiavenza, Matt. "Was Hu Jintao a Failure?" *The Atlantic* online. Last modified March 13, 2013. https://www.theatlantic.com/china/archive/2013/03/was-hu-jintao-a-failure/273868/.

Spencer, Richard. "Shanghai Communist Party Boss Jailed." *The Telegraphy* online. Last modified April 10, 2008. https://www.telegraph.co.uk/news/worldnews/1584736/Shanghai-Communist-Party-boss-jailed.html.

"The Panama Papers Embarrass China's Leaders." *Economist* online. Last modified April 7, 2016. https://www.economist.com/asia/2016/04/07/the-panama-papers-embarrass-chinas-leaders.

Watts, Jonathan. "Shanghai's Communist Party Chief Sacked in Corruption Purge." *The Guardian* (London: UK), September 25, 2006. https://www.theguardian.com/world/2006/sep/25/china.jonathanwatts.

Wu, Yuwen. "Profile: China's Fallen Security Chief Zhou Yongkang." *BBC Chinese* online. Last modified October 12, 2015. http://www.bbc.com/news/world-asia-china-26349305.

Xinhua News Agency. "Shanghai Party Chief Sacked for Graft." *China Daily* online. Last modified September 25, 2006. http://www.chinadaily.com.cn/china/2006-09/25/content_696159.htm.

BIBLIOGRAPHY (CHINESE SOURCES)

鲍彤. "不再唱红打黑还是坚持唱红打黑？ 十八大有两种选择."自由亚洲电台. Last modified August 29, 2012. https://www.rfa.org/mandarin/pinglun/baotong/bt-08292012092352.html.

CK. "万润南：中共度过了十八大常委安排的危机." 博讯新闻网. Last reprinted from 自由亚洲电台 September 8, 2012. https://boxun.com/news/gb/china/2012/09/201209080220.shtml.

"薄王数百亿资金黑幕 法院痛彻心扉." 博讯新闻网 online Last reprinted from 财经网 March 20, 2013. http://boxun.com/news/gb/china/2013/03/201303200445.shtml#.UV5ih8rna0M.

CND《华夏文摘》编辑. “华正平: 支配中国政治游戏的核心内容.” *CND* 刊物和论坛 online. Last modified July 8, 2012. http://hx.cnd.org/2012/07/08/%E5%8D%8E%E6%AD%A3%E5%B9%B3%EF%BC%9A%E6%94%AF%E9%85%8D%E4%B8%AD%E5%9B%BD%E6%94%BF%E6%B2%BB%E6%B8%B8%E6%88%8F%E7%9A%84%E6%A0%B8%E5%BF%83%E5%86%85%E5%AE%B9/.

巩胜利. “废谷保薄，显露中国’天机’？——评中国法院判结 ‘薄谷开来案’以及 ‘薄熙来案’ 的未来走向.” *Epoch Times* online. Last modified September 4, 2012. http://www.epochtimes.com/gb/12/9/4/n3674907.htm.

华世平. “习近平时代法治将占有突出地位.” 中国共产党新闻网 online. Last modified May 3, 2013. http://theory.people.com.cn/n/2013/0503/c112851-21356799.html.

姜维平. “薄谷蹦得太欢，自己跳进锅里.” 阿波罗新闻网. Last modified April 5, 2013. http://www.aboluowang.com/2013/0405/296532.html.

刘源. “为什么要改造我们的文化历史观---读张木生” 人民论坛, 2010年第22期.

“刘云山冀联手孙政才 曾给党媒下特别指示.” 阿波罗新闻网 online. Last modified September 6, 2017. http://www.aboluowang.com/2017/0906/989369.html.

“杀海伍德的是谷开来，或另有其人？” *Boxun.com*. Last modified April 2, 2013. http://boxun.com/news/gb/china/2013/04/201304020319.shtml#.UV5hgsrna0M.

张欢. “张木生：再举新民主主义大旗” last modified October 28, 2011. http://news.sina.com.cn/c/sd/2011-10-28/114723377991.shtml.

ADDITIONAL WEB SOURCES USED FOR GENERAL RESEARCH

http://en.rfi.fr/asia-pacific/.

http://www.breakingviews.com/review-the-real-story-of-bo-xilais-ruin/21068767.article.

http://topics.nytimes.com/top/reference/timestopics/people/b/bo_xilai/index.html.

http://www.cnn.com/2012/10/26/world/asia/china-politics-bo.

http://topics.bloomberg.com/bo-xilai/.

http://www.reuters.com/article/2013/02/21/us-china-politics-bo-idUSBRE91K0D520130221.

http://www.bbc.co.uk/news/world-asia-china-17673505.

http://abcnews.go.com/topics/news/world/bo-xilai.htm.

http://news.xinhuanet.com/english/china/2012-09/28/c_131880079.htm.

http://en.boxun.com/tag/bo-xilai/.

https://en.wikipedia.org/wiki/Bo_Xilai.

http://en.people.cn/.

Chapter 12

The New Leadership Fights the Old Battle

Eight Regulations

Xiaoxiao Li

When Xi Jinping started anticorruption campaign right after 18th CCP National Congress before end of 2012, many thought this was just another short-term movement after which life would become normal as before. Five years later, anticorruption has proofed to be a major institutional building achievement under Xi Jinping's leadership. So people realized that anticorruption in China is not a movement but has become the core of institutional building under Xi Jinping's leadership and will always be on the way to guard against corruption activities, especially by high-ranking government officials and CCP members. Xi's Eight Regulations plays an important role in monitoring the daily activities of government officials at all layers of government in every sector. The regulations have set up strict rules to be followed by every official in China and are the basic standards for the official promotion evaluations. Those who first viewed Xi's anticorruption approach as a temporary and short-term movement that swept over like a tornado have to admit that after five years of his first term efforts, what Xi Jinping has been trying to do is clearly a necessary process of institutional building and will be continuously strengthened along the way of Chinese economic development and national rejuvenation. From the above citations we can feel different concerns from different generations of leadership when they discussed about the anticorruption issue. Xi Jinping paid more attention on institutional building and tried hard to rule by law. This chapter briefly reviewed the background of Xi Jinping's institutional building efforts on anti-corruption. Of course, Xi's final purpose is to stress the legality of CCP leadership in China. We should expect that more corrupted officials would be taken accountable when CCP Nineteenth National Congress completed in second half of October 2017.

BACKGROUND: OLD BATTLE FIELD

According to *Merriam-Webster*, the definition of the term "corruption" is dishonest or illegal behavior especially by powerful people such as government officials or police officers or inducement to do wrong by improper or unlawful means such as bribery. Based on Chinese official terminology, the core element of the definition of corruption in current China is the notion of use of public power and public resources for private interests. In China, the corruption by government officials usually includes such forms as graft, bribery, fraud, embezzlement, extortion, smuggling, and tax evasion.[1] Such practices can be further categorized into three types: *Black* corruption includes clearly illegal practices aimed to increase personal wealth, and constitute an "economic crime." *Grey* corruption happens when the practices is done through legal, semi-legal, and illegal ways, such as profit-making by favoring clients with personal connection, or extravagance and waste in work-related expenses. *White* corruption pertains to the "common practice" of using favoritism and personal connections in recruitment, promotion, and resource allocation, and so on.[2]

Many people consider official corruption in China a systemic crime caused by the one-party system. They think that this is true because "power will intoxicate the best hearts, as wine the strongest heads." "No man is wise enough nor good enough to be trusted with unlimited power," as the saying goes. In China, the Chinese Communist Party (CCP) is the leading party and controls everything, so naturally the corruption in China is generated from many sources and spreads over the entire society. But this assumption ignores the fact that for the past thirty years the CCP Discipline Inspection Commission (DIC), an internal sector of the CCP, responsible for discipline supervision and enforcement over government officials' activities and taking anyone accountable for wrong doing, has made distinctive progress in improving its anticorruption institution and enhancing its authority, independence, integrity and professionalism.[3] We figured out two principle sources from which official corruption deprive are greed coupled with abundant opportunities for profit-making and a weak legal environment replete with outdated rules and regulations. Some people take this as one of the mistakes made by Deng Xiaoping who encouraged some people to get rich first after which these rich people would help those with bad fortune to become rich. Deng Xiaoping never mentioned which group of people should get rich first, and as not all people start from the same point, those who are in higher social and political positions or those who control the recourses utilized their power to get rich.

Corruption is certainly one of the biggest challenges faced by governments and policy-makers in all countries, whether fully developed to highly underdeveloped.[4] It is common to find corruption in all social systems during times of social transition, because the period a country is under significant economic restructuring and social status changes is also the time for corruption to grow in officialdom, as in Great Britain in the eighteenth century, the United States in the nineteenth century, or Singapore and Hong Kong in the twentieth century. The United Nations reported after investigation in 109 countries that a country with average personal income between $265 and $1000 is at its highest social upheaval and unstable stage. This is the time for the biggest changes in social economy and ideological formation.

Since 1982, the first year China fought with crime in the economic sector, China has investigated more than 1 million cases and closed more than 20,000 cases related to leaders at county or division levels. The cases related to officials at city or department levels amounted to more than 1,000, and more than twenty cases involved officials at provincial or state ministry levels by 2004. From 1992 to 2002, more than 1.5 million Communist Party members, including those at state, provincial, municipal, and city levels, were investigated, sentenced, fined, or jailed by the CCP Discipline Commission, the CCP Investigation Bureau, and courts. Some high-ranking officials were sentenced to jail or even given the death penalty, and some significant cases were disclosed to the public, with the criminals being punished severely. In July 1998, Chen Xitong, who had been a member of the Politburo and mayor of Beijing, was sentenced to sixteen years in prison for official corruption. In February 2000, Hu Changqing, who was the vice governor of Jiangxi province, was sentenced to death and executed in March the same year. Wang Leyi, a former deputy director general of China Customs, was sentenced to twelve years in prison.[5] China has shown its people that the central government has been making continuous efforts to control official corruption. The tragedy of severe acute respiratory syndrome (SARS) called much attention to the social and political problems caused by officialdom. The quick spread of SARS disclosed the inefficiency of the Chinese style of officialdom, hurt badly the people's confidence in the central government, and ruined China's international reputation as a country responsible for its people. The lesson learned is that it will only cause panic and distrust among people if the government tries to hide simple truths, which is simply a manipulation of power.

During the first two decades since 1978, other forms of official corruption among government officials and conglomerate state-owned enterprises and financial institutions also existed that have caused severe damage to the Chinese economy and to people's confidence in dealing with businesses in China. Smuggling and fraud raise the question of social honesty in China. The central government has also made serious efforts to totally destroy such kinds of economic or financial kingdoms. For example, the Yuanhua smuggling case in Fujian province caught the attention of the central government, which had to send several thousand staff to investigate and completely destroy the network Yuanhua Company had operated for years. Such network was among the local government officials, customs officers, public security leaders, many of whom were sentenced to prison or even received death penalty. Other ill-famed cases were those of Yinguangxia and Lantian, two companies that cheated shareholders with false information and carried on insider trading to skim shareholders' money for their own benefits.[6]

There are several characteristics of the way the Chinese government controls official corruption and fraud in China. First, the leadership of CCP remains a crucial force of guidance in fighting corruption; second, the government adopts the traditional approach of fighting case-by-case war, with emphasis on those cases that have the worst influence and outcomes to the society; third, the government is seeking people's participation in monitoring state officials; and fourth, new laws are being established to limit officials' power.

China has a feudal history of several thousand years. The feudalistic thoughts have been rooted in the society and inherited in CCP bodies, too. These thoughts legitimize the absolute power of officials; however, the economic reform since 1978 have opened people's mind and enlightened them about Western systems. China is in an early stage of social transition during which many weaknesses have be revealed. Deng Xiaoping has suggested that the government should have two hands functioning effectively, one hand to bring about economic development and the other the ideological standstill of socialist faith. Ironically, the world experienced China's unexpected economic development and China encountered peaceful transformation of ideology. So the battle against official corruption and fraud in China is being implemented under a special mix of social conflicts and contradictions inherited from the past. But as time goes on, and following the examples of Western developed countries, China gradually found its own most effective way to control official corruption and fraud.

After the beginning of the post-Mao reform period in 1978–1979, China experienced a marked worsening of corruption. In this period, the scale of corruption increased exponentially as officials cashed in on their ability to manipulate the allocation of valuable resources, including land and capital, in return for bribes valued at hundreds of thousands of Chinese renminbi.[7] In 1995 Transparency International (TI) ranked China the fourth most corrupt country in its Corruption Perceptions Index. This became one of the reasons of 1989 Tainanmen incident when thousands of people and young students flushed into streets in hundreds of Chinese municipal cities and cried for removal of the corrupted officials and for institutional building of modern civil society.

Since the mid-1990s, it has been admitted officially that corruption-related crimes in China are pandemic. Although the media frequently report on petty cases of corruption, such reports only touch the tip of the iceberg. More and more reports and disclosed cases reveal how officials up to the national level tactfully seek personal gain and angle for fame and power at the expense of the public. Faced with the increasingly high-profile official corruption exposed from the 1990s, the second and third generation of CCP leadership started buildup of institutional monitoring of the activities of officials as well as that of their family members and working staff linked to them during the officialdom. Among the disclosed cases were institutional, legal, moral, or sociocultural ones. However, all corruptions are associated with officials in the CCP, the state, and its state-owned enterprises, including provincial party secretaries, governors, and Pulitburo standing committee members. Some scholars assumed that the officials' motivation in risking embezzling money when they already enjoy very many privileges is that they are preparing for the demise of Chinese communism.[8]

Some scholars have made statements about the corruption status in China that corruption has become a major social and political issue in China since 1978 when Chinese authorities began to implement the policy of "reform and opening."[9]

The market-oriented economic reform of China since 1978 is a gradually advancing process that has followed its own path of evolution. With the goal of establishing a socialist market economy having been finally settled in 1992, the long-term coexistence of the planned and market economies became an important feature of economic transition which contributed to the large-scale growth of corruption. The coexistence of dual economic systems during the whole transition period provides plenty of incentives and opportunities for corrupt practices. Regulating economic activities in the new period of coexistence of the planned and market economies is a totally new task and a major challenge for the Chinese government. Legislation often lags behind changing economic situations and must be revised frequently, thus increasing the difficulty of law enforcement. The prior technique of utilizing direct administrative control to restrain the autonomy of economic actors has become less effective, while learning to skillfully use indirect macro-control means is a slow and long process. Until this transformation is complete, the inevitable loopholes and weakness in economic regulation will encourage corruption. For example, contemporary regulation prohibits all public institutions from engaging in business activities or establishing satellite companies, but allows the trade unions of institutions to engage in such activities, thus opening a door for such activities since all such institutions have their own trade unions. The loopholes in and weaknesses of regulatory policies and institutions, certain policy failures, and a lack of experience and technology in the anticorruption agencies in tackling new forms of corruption all contribute to the growth of corruption. The incompleteness of political reform and the weakness of the current political system undermine anticorruption efforts which, in turn, promote further proliferation of corruption.

In the face of rising corruption, the weakness of the political system has become increasingly evident. The lack of effective mechanisms of checks-and-balances makes it very difficult to supervise senior officials, the lack of independence of existing anticorruption agencies undermines their anticorruption efforts, although the moving force in anticorruption efforts has come mainly from the top leadership, the news media and the public also play a very limited role. So during the second and third generation of CCP, although some cases related to high-ranking officials and army generals were disclosed, people could not help noticing that anticorruption efforts resulted only in accelerating increase of corruption cases. China needs institutional building to actually contain corruption activities by the officials.

New Leadership

Shortly after he took power by end of 2012, Xi Jinping launched a far-reaching anticorruption campaign, vowing to maintain a "zero-tolerance attitude toward corruption" and to "look into every case involving corruption."[10] As of October 2017 from November 2012, more than 100,000 people have been indicted for corruption, and 120 high-ranking officials, including 5 national-level leaders, have been targeted. The campaign has shown no sign of stopping yet, and is said to become the "new normal" that anticorruption will always be on the way.

Xi Jinping has rapidly amassed more power than his predecessors. He has overawed his rivals and shaken up the party-state hierarchy with a thorough anticorruption campaign. The first two years of the administration of Xi Jinping proved much more eventful and at times more exciting than expected. He has waged the largest anticorruption crackdown since the end of the Cultural Revolution in 1976. Since the Eighteenth Party Congress, Xi Jinping has continued to mothball political and institutional reforms. Xi Jinping is the first top leader since the Cultural Revolution to give equal importance to economic construction and ideological pursuits. Xi Jinping came to power at the Eighteenth Congress of the Chinese Communist Party (CCP) in late 2012. Both Chinese and Western experts have touted the "Chinese model"—the "Beijing Consensus" or "Chinese Socialism 3.0" as a viable alternative to laissez-faire capitalism.

Since taking over as secretary general of the CCP at the 18th party congress in 2012, the world saw Xi Jinping crack down on corruption within government and establish new institutions to consolidate his own position. Scholars noticed that Xi Jinping's anticorruption drive stands out for three characteristics: (1) This time a much higher number of officials has been punished and many more provinces and government departments have been implicated in graft cases than in the past. (2) In targeting former Politburo Standing Committee member Zhou Yongkang and other entrenched interests, Xi Jinping has rooted out corruption by moving from the periphery to the inner circle. His purge is more expansive and reaches into higher echelons than ever before, including senior figures of vice state leader level such as Zhou Yongkang, Xu Caihou (the former vice chairman of the Central Military Commission), and Su Rong (vice chairman of China's parliamentary advisory body). (3) The CCP's Central Commission for Discipline Inspection strikes on its own initiative, deploys inspection teams to arrest people in a secretive and swift manner, and announces the cases immediately after netting the suspects. This time, the degree of unprompted initiative, swiftness, and transparency by far exceeds what we have seen in the past.

On February 2, 2016, *the People's Daily* made comments on major anticorruption events after CCP 18th National Conference. We can clearly feel the importance and guiding power of only little more than 600 words stipulating how CCP members should improve their working style and maintain a close contact with the masses, that is, Eight Regulations. On December 6 in the same year, vice party secretary general of Sichuan province, Li Chuncheng, was under investigation, which started the anti-corrupted tiger war. Three years later, such action received mass support and disclosed a number of corrupted tigers.

From January 21 to 22, 2013, Xi Jinping made an important speech for the first time for more scientific and effective prevention of corruption and combating corruption and building a clean government to a higher level. This speech made clear that anticorruption will focus on tigers and flies alike which means that it will not only take those high-ranking officials accountable for their corrupted activities but also actually resolve those unwholesome tendencies and corruptions.

From April to May 2013, Central Commission for Discipline Inspection restructured its internal organization and enlarged its discipline inspection offices from eight to ten and established a whole new office of law enforcement and effective supervision. This was the first internal organization restructuring of Central Commission for Discipline Inspection that lifted the curtain of discipline and inspection system reform. This restructuring focused on internal reform with integration of inside resources to complete its function transformation.

On April 19, 2013, major Chinese mass media websites, such as Peoples' Daily, Xinhua net, Sinanet all uniformly on their front page web supervision space linked to Discipline Inspection, Procuratorial, Court, Territorial Resources, and website www.12380.gov.cn which is specifically set up to monitor officials' unlawful behaviors.

From November 9 to 12, 2013, the CCP 18th National Congress Third Session was held in Beijing and passed Decision on Overall Deepening Reform to strengthen anticorruption systemic construction and system guarantee. This document ordered for two responsibility implementation, to push forward discipline and inspection systemic reform, to realize full scale inspection coverage, and to fine tune anticorruption institutional build-up.

On March 26, 2015, China started its "Skynet Operation" to pursue those escaped corrupted officials from other countries and the dirty money they transferred from China to the overseas accounts, and on April 22, China announced Red Notice to first 100 corrupted officials that reflected China's confidence to take all corrupted officials accountable no matter where they were hiding.

On August 13, 2015, CCP Central Committee published CCP Regulation on Inspection Work. In October, CCP published CCP Integrity and Self-Discipline Guidelines and CCP Disciplinary Measures which supplement Eight Regulations and streamlined discipline inspection application procedures.

From December 4, 2012, to end of August 2017, China has disclosed and resolved 184,000 cases against Eight Regulations, punished 250,000 CCP member officials including 136,000 party and government discipline treatments of which 20 were of provincial leaders.

An eight-point regulation (in simplified Chinese 八项规定) was a document adopted in a meeting of the Political Bureau of the Communist Party of China (CPC) Central Committee**,** the country's top-ruling body, on Tuesday, December 4, 2012. The document made explicit requirements on how Political Bureau members should improve their work style in eight aspects, focusing on rejecting extravagance and reducing bureaucratic visits, meetings, and empty talk.

The requirements, the first detailed guidance for a new working style adopted after the election of the Political Bureau members in November 2012, were issued to strengthen ties between the people and officials, whose malpractices, including corruption and power abuse, have distanced them from ordinary citizens. The Political Bureau, which has twenty-five members, includes the top decision makers, such as State leaders, Party chiefs of several key provincial-level regions, ministers and top army officials. The meeting, presided over by Xi Jinping, general secretary of the CCP Central Committee, was held less than three weeks after the 18th CCP national congress, which convened on November 8–14, 2012. The CCP vowed at the keynote congress to "always work hard and practice economy." It also promised to reject the practices of extravagance, formalism, and bureaucracy.

As the fifth-generation new leader, Xi Jinping has consistently stressed the importance of more work and less talk, many commentators and experts say. Zhu Lijia, professor at the Chinese Academy of Governance, said the measures reflect Xi Jinping's consistent principles on the Party's working style. As early as 2010, Xi told CCP Central Committee Party School in a speech that there was a great deal of room for improvement in many speeches by officials, as they contained too much jargon and empty words. He reiterated his stance in his first speech as the general secretary of the CCP Central Committee on November 15, 2012, when he also addressed ending bureaucracy and pomp. On a visit to the National Museum of China later that year, Xi Jinping again told officials that empty talk harms the nation, while hard work strengthens the country.

Eight Regulations also clearly reflect Xi Jinping's strong will to fight for the final win of the old battle and survival of CCP in the time to come. The document states that the Chinese leaders must keep in close contact with the grassroots. They must understand the real situation facing society through in-depth inspections at grassroots. Greater attention should be focused on places where social problems are more acute, and inspection tours must be carried out more thoroughly. Inspection tours as a mere formality should be strictly prohibited. Leaders should work and listen to the public and officials at the grassroots, and people's practical problems must be tackled. There should be no welcome banner, no red carpet, no floral arrangement, or grand receptions for officials' visits. All meetings and major events should be strictly regulated, and their efficiency should be improved. Political Bureau members are not allowed to attend ribbon-cutting or cornerstone-laying ceremonies, or celebrations and seminars, unless they get approval from the CCP Central Committee. Official meetings should get shortened and be specific and to the point, with no empty and rigmarole talks. In order to improve the governance, the issuing of official documents should be reduced. All official visits abroad should only be arranged when needed in terms of foreign affairs with fewer accompanying members, and on most of the occasions, there is no need for a reception by overseas Chinese people, institutions and students at the airport. This requirement differs greatly from both of his predecessors'. As a common practice in China, whenever officials visit places or on their way, there would be traffic controls for a certain period of time which would cause traffic jams and arouse complaints. Eight Regulations requires that there should be fewer traffic controls when leaders travel by cars to avoid unnecessary inconvenience to the public. There should be fewer traffic controls arranged for the leaders' security of their trips to avoid unnecessary inconvenience to the public. This document also makes such requirement that the media must not report on stories about official events unless there is real news value. The regulations also ban worthless news reports on senior officials' work and activities and have said such reports should depend on work needs, news value, and social effects. In China, there is a tradition that whenever there is a grand ceremony the officials' appearance would add value, so the organizers of such event would like to pay lump sum money to the officials for their participation. Eight Regulations states that leaders should not publish any works by themselves or issue any congratulatory letters unless an arrangement with the central leadership has been made. Official documents without substantial contents and realistic importance should be withheld. Publications regarding senior officials' work and activities are also restricted. Cars and fancy hotels in China are treated as a kind of privilege and symbol of importance. Owing to this, many officials pay very close attention to what car they would be seated in and how many star hotels they would stay in. Eight Regulations pointed out clearly that leaders must practice thrift and strictly follow relevant regulations on accommodation and cars.

Analysts have said that although these measures target senior Party members, they also send a strong message to Chinese society. They have pointed out that the measures address issues that the public resent the most, such as tedious meetings and frequent traffic disruption by cars transporting officials. "The measures have set a good example. Its wording and phrasing are clear, to the point and easy to understand." Some have stressed although that Party officials who violate the measures will be investigated, the requirements may get better results if the State Council, China's cabinet, can adopt similar measures and make them legally valid. Right after Eight Regulation went public, more than twenty-five provinces and municipal cities also announced their own regulations, many of which add more items based on local realities. Some concern that the new measures are welcome but it will still take the supervision of media and society to help implementation. At first, it will not be difficult for the top leadership to carry out the new requirements. But responses from officials at the grassroots should be big concern as they may have become accustomed to a certain lifestyle.

Chinese mass media put forward many positive attitudes toward CCP Eight Regulations. *People's Daily*, the CCP's flagship newspaper, made a commentary on Wednesday, December 5, 2012, that, given the profound changes that the Party, the country, and the world are facing today, we should realize the utmost importance of improving work style, the "improvements in the Party's work style will win people's hearts." Fewer meetings and traffic controls for the officials mean there will be smoother traffic in cities, and less media coverage on officials will leave room for more news dedicated to public welfare. The implementation of any aspect of the regulations will be translated into benefits for the masses.

The comments from common viewers went viral after the release of a statement that reveals the requirements. On China's media platforms similar to Twitter, such as Sina Weibo service, netizens were upbeat about the prospect of imminent changes to China's culture of officialdom, which often features speeches of tedious jargon, expensive banquets, and routine pomp.

The mass hope these requirements are pragmatic and will overhaul the practices of China's officials if implemented well. The public reactions to Eight Regulations vary reflecting strong skepticism and doubt about whether these requirements are wholly met. While gauging the potential effect that the regulations will have in improving relations between officials and the public as well as addressing social problems such as corruption, many people took a wait-and-see attitude as they need to see how the leadership would carry out their new orders. We do see several of the requirements are considerably pragmatic. It can make a difference to some officials' work style if they are implemented and only when the officials match actions to their words, can the society experience a real transformation. As the institutional system buildup, it is necessary to enforce public supervision and hold violators of the regulations legally responsible, in a bid to ensure the regulations are followed. The key is to implement the regulations in a top-down manner.

Institutional Buildup

The anticorruption institutions and systems in different countries vary substantively due to differences in their political institutions, legal systems, historical traditions, and characteristics of corruption.[11] Some analysts found that after 18th National Conference, the corrupted officials were taken accountable through several channels. First, the corrupted officials were disclosed by the central inspection team during routine investigation for "tiger and flies." After 18th National Conference, the central CCP strengthened anticorruption enforcement by sending inspection team to each province and relied heavily on the local people. According to one report on April 3, 2014, twenty central inspection teams investigated eleven provinces and nine government agencies in two different rounds of investigations since May 2013. More than eighty corrupted officials were found guilty and taken legally accountable, of which nine were provincial- and ministerial-level officials. Other major corrupted officials at the same or even higher levels such as Su Rong were legally taken through such inspection teams.

Second, many corrupted officials were disclosed by real-name reporting applications on government websites. On May 12, 2013, the Ministry of Supervision announced that the director of China National Energy Bureau was under investigation. He was disclosed by a media reporter. China Resource president Song Lin was reported by Economic Reference that he intentionally favored one company in Shanxi province and caused the loss of national assets amounting to more than several billion in Chinese currency.

Third, another way to disclose the corrupted officials is through regular investigation of implementation of Eight Regulations. On December 5, 2014, Central Commission for Discipline Inspection announced a summary table that listed activities not in compliance with Eight Regulations between December 4, 2012 and October 31, 2014. Central Commission for Discipline Inspection altogether found 67,737 events of incompliance with Eight Regulations and took 89,585 persons accountable, about 10 percent of whom were high-ranking government officials.

Fourth, some corrupted officials were disclosed during the CCP education programs at local levels. As to those officials who did not treat people fairly but favored only their relatives and friends, damaging CCP reputation and causing loss of national interests, the relevant government agencies punished such flies with urgency.

Fifth, CCP has set up a system that all officials should disclose their own assets value. The system is called Personal Important Events Report Form. Many corrupted officials lied and tried to hide many personal owned wealth, such as vice governor of Jiangxi province Yao Mugen who did not disclose his more than ten personal houses and could not tell how he had such a big amount of money to purchase the houses. Those officials already in their government positions were replaced and those who were in the promotion plan were taken down from the promotion list.

The last, but not least, method is through the corrupted officials' links to disclose a group of corrupted officials in certain relations with the one in disclosure. Wang Qishan, the secretary general of Central Commission for Discipline Inspection, said anticorruption is not only a protracted war but a war of annihilation as well. So since the finish of 18th CCP National Conference, Central Commission for Discipline Inspection organized few such anticorruption wars of annihilation and totally destroyed five corrupted gangs led by Zhou Yongkang, The Highest-ranking corrupt officials ever caught in CCP history including "Sichuan Clique," "Petrolium Ties," "Public Security Favorites," "Secretarial Gang," and "Family Corruption Group." Many high-ranking corrupted officials who were sacked after 18th CCP National Conference were Zhou Yongkang's subordinates such as Li Chuncheng, Guo Yongxiang, Li Chongxi, Ji WEnlin, Jiang Jiemin, Wang Yongchun, Li Dongsheng, Wu Changshun, and Qin Yuhai, and so on.

So we can see that regulations and legal anticorruption acts to contain government officials and CCP members in leading positions publicly announced and enforced; encouragement of common people or related staff to report on certain website, phone numbers, and mail addresses of official corruptions; regular central CCP investigation (inspection team) groups to each region, province, state-owned enterprise, municipal city to collect information and evidences of designated officials for their corruptions and other illegal activities; revision of CCP Constitution; routine study and circulation of CCP anticorruption educations are the approaches that have been actively utilized in the process of institutional building of anticorruption system.

Prospects in the New Era

On October 17, 2017, in his report to 19th CCP National Congress, Xi Jinping announced Xi Jinping Thought on Socialism with Chinese Characteristics for a New Era.[12] This conference sets forth the basic policy for upholding and developing socialism with Chinese characteristics in the new era, and establishes the goal of securing a decisive victory in building a moderately prosperous society in all respects and then embarking on a journey to fully build a modern socialist China. The Congress also sets out an overall plan for advancing the great cause of socialism with Chinese characteristics and the great new project of Party building in the new era.

As socialism with Chinese characteristics has entered a new era, Xi reiterated that CCP must get a new look and make new accomplishments. As the saying goes, it takes a good blacksmith to make good steel. For CCP to unite the people and lead them in carrying out the great struggle, advancing the great cause, and realizing the great dream, all CCP members must unwaveringly uphold and improve CCP leadership and make CCP still stronger. In doing so, it is important to ensure CCP self-governance to be exercised fully and strictly which is a journey with no end. According to the evolution of human history, the future of any political party or any government is determined by whether it enjoys public support. In this respect, CCP must guard against and correct with resolve the practices the people oppose and resent. The whole CCP must be soberly aware that the governance environment CCP faces currently is complex, and that so too are the factors undermining CCP's advanced nature and purity; prominent problems of impurity in thinking, organization, and conduct within CCP have not been solved root and branch. So Xi Jinping warned that CCP must fully recognize the long-term and complex nature of the tests confronting them as they relate to governance, reform and opening up, the market economy, and the external environment. Xi stated frankly that CCP must also fully recognize the intensity and severity of the dangers of a lack of drive, incompetence, disengagement from the people, inaction, and corruption. So their work must focus on solving problems, maintain strategic resolve, and ensure strict self-governance.

Xi Jinping Thought paved the way and raised the general requirements for CCP institutional building in the new era as: to uphold and strengthen overall leadership and ensure that they exercise effective self-supervision and practice strict self-governance in every respect; to strengthen their long-term governance capacity and their advanced nature and purity as the main thrust; to enhance the institutional political building as the overarching principle; to hold dear their ideals, convictions, and purpose as the underpinning; and to harness their enthusiasm, intuitive, and creativity as the focus of efforts; to make all-round efforts to see their institutional political building enhanced, their theory strengthened, their organizations consolidated, their conduct improved, and their discipline enforced, with institution building incorporated into every aspect of CCP political building.[13]

In Xi Jinping Thought, Xi clarified his determination with hard efforts to combat corruption and continue to improve the efficacy of institutional building so as to enjoy people's support and be able to withstand all potential tests. He prioritized the institutional building to ensure his strong authority and central control power by asking CCP members to strictly observe discipline and rules that every member must hold the CCP Constitution in great reverence, act in strict accordance with the code of conduct for intraparty political life under new circumstances, and make intraparty activities more politically oriented, up-to-date, principled, and effective. While doing this they must guard against the rules of business dealings eroding intraparty conduct, and foster a healthy political atmosphere of integrity within the CCP leadership. We must improve and implement the systems of democratic centralism, and practice both democracy-based centralism and centralism-guided democracy. This means we should both give full play to democracy and practice centralism on this basis. We must foster values like loyalty, honesty, impartiality, adherence to fact, and integrity; guard against and oppose self-centered behavior, decentralism, behavior in disregard of the rules, a silo mentality, unprincipled nice-guyism, and sectarianism, factionalism, and patronage. We must resolutely oppose double-dealing and duplicity. All Party members, especially high-ranking officials, must strengthen their Party consciousness, political awareness, and political ability. We must regard it as our fundamental political responsibility to be loyal to the Party, share the Party's concerns, fulfill our obligations to the Party, and work for the people's well-being, and forever preserve the political character of Communists.

Studying carefully Xi Jinping's 3.5-hour report, one can easily feel his ambitions in the new era for his understanding and the definition of the shared ideal of socialism with Chinese characteristics which he stressed as source of strength and ideological mind. He stressed the importance as well as urgency, and ordered to form the theoretical foundation of CCP solidarity and unity, in this way, to gain a good command of the CCP Constitution, CCP regulations, and related major policy addresses and to meet CCP standards. To realize that mission, they would launch a campaign on the theme of "staying true to the founding mission (不忘初心)" to enable all members, especially officials at and above the county and director level, to arm themselves with the Xi's new theories and become more purposeful in working tirelessly to accomplish the CCP's historic mission in the new era.

Xi Jinping's idea for institutional building in all areas including anticorruption embodies a very important process, that is, find a contingent of competent and professional officials because he needs his officials as a central pillar of strength for his cause. In his mind, such officials must adhere to the principle of the CCP supervising officials; select officials on the basis of both integrity and ability, with priority given to integrity, and on the basis of merit regardless of background; and ensure that those who are dedicated, impartial, and upright should be appointed. Xi asked for the implementation in earnest of the criteria for evaluating good officials. In selecting and appointing officials, they should adopt the right approach, with emphasis on political performance. They would only promote and put in important positions those officials who do well according to the following criteria: they maintain political integrity, think in terms of the big picture, follow the leadership core, and keep in alignment with the central CCP leadership, that is, Xi Jinping's leadership; they have full confidence in the path, theory, system, and culture of socialism with Chinese characteristics; they uphold the authority of the Central Committee and faithfully follow Xi's theories, lines, principles, and policies; and they are loyal, have moral integrity, and demonstrate a keen sense of responsibility. With this, they aim to see that in every field the creativity of talent is given great expression and their ingenuity and expertise flow freely.

The institutional building cannot depart from the construction of primary-level organizations. Primary-level organizations do the groundwork to ensure Xi's lines, principles, policies, decisions, and plans are implemented. The scope of primary-level work is to ensure in enterprises, villages, CCP, and government departments, schools, research institutes, sub-districts, communities, and social organizations the officials play a key role in communicating and overseeing community-level social governance, uniting and mobilizing the people, and promoting reform and development.

To reach the target and realize mission in the new ear, Xi stipulated that they should work hard to improve official conduct and enforce discipline. Xi set up the danger that once they become disengaged from the people, they will lose all. In improving official conduct, they should focus on maintaining the close bond with the people, keep them firmly in mind, develop a closer affinity with them, and keep working to foster stronger public support for their governance. The officials are required to earnestly address all issues the people are strongly concerned about, and resolutely correct any behavior that undermines the people's interests. The officials should lead by example in consolidating and building on the advances made in implementing the central CCP leadership's eight-regulations decision on improving officials' conduct. All the officials should continue to address the practice of formalities for formalities' sake, bureaucratism, hedonism, and extravagance, and oppose mind-sets and acts of privilege seeking. In order to assure the success of anticorruption, the officials will focus on strengthening the enforcement of political and organizational discipline, and use this to prompt stricter observance of discipline on upholding integrity, on interacting with the people, and regarding work and life. Xi urged that they would conduct four forms of oversight over discipline compliance,[14] identify problems early and correct them while they are nascent. The relevant organizations with the power to supervise officials will be given corresponding power to take disciplinary action as called for, and accountability for overseeing discipline compliance will be tightened up. To further contain any corrupt activities, they will raise officials' awareness of discipline and strengthen discipline enforcement, and demand that officials hold discipline in awe and respect, do not cross the line, and become used to working and living under oversight and constraints.

All these institutional building requirements are for the purpose of securing a sweeping victory in China's fight against corruption because the people resent corruption most; and corruption is the greatest threat China faces at present. So Xi called for immediate action to have the resolve and tenacity to persevere in the never-ending fight against corruption. Only by intensifying efforts to address both the symptoms and root causes of corruption—by making sure that officials are honest, government is clean, and political affairs are handled with integrity—can China avoid history's cycle of rise and fall and ensure long-term stability. Currently, the fight against corruption remains grave and complex; so they should remain as firm as a rock in their resolve to build on the overwhelming momentum and secure a sweeping victory. As institutional building is a long process and continuous test of one's determination and final success, Xi proposed that they would continue to see that there are no no-go zones, no ground is left unturned, and no tolerance is shown for corruption. China would impose tight constraints, maintain a tough stance and a long-term deterrence, punish both those who take bribes and those who offer them, and prevent interest groups from arising within the CCP. This is also related closely with the primary-level organizations, so China would institute a system of disciplinary inspection for city and county level in an intensified effort to address corruption that occurs on the people's doorsteps. Wherever offenders may flee, they will be brought back and brought to justice.

As Xi focused on rule by law, he also mentioned the importance of working for the adoption of national anticorruption legislation and creating a corruption reporting platform that covers both disciplinary inspection commissions and supervision agencies. The target is to strengthen deterrence so officials don't dare to, strengthen the cage of institutions so they're unable to, and strengthen their vigilance so they have no desire to commit acts of corruption. Xi draws a big picture in his thought that the political environment in China will, through their tireless efforts, like seas fallen calm and rivers running clear, be clean and free of corruption.

Based on experiences from many other countries, China in its institutional building for effective and long-term anticorruption has a plan to improve the oversight systems. Such system will strengthen checks on and oversight over the exercise of power, and ensure that power is exercised under public oversight, in broad daylight, and in an institutional cage. The system needs to strengthen top-down organizational oversight, improve bottom-up democratic oversight, practice peer oversight, and tighten regular supervision over officials in positions of leadership. The intensified political inspection is to identify problems and ensure that deterrence works; this system also includes an oversight network that facilitates coordination in disciplinary inspections conducted at different levels. For that goal, China would deepen reform of the national supervision system, conduct trials throughout the country, and establish supervisory commissions at the national, provincial, prefectural, and county levels, which work together with the CCP disciplinary inspection commissions as one office while keeping their own identity.[15] This will ensure that supervision covers everyone working in the public sector who exercises public power. A national supervision law will be formulated. Supervisory commissions will be given responsibilities, powers, and means of investigation in accordance with law. The practice of "*shuanggui*"[16] will be replaced by detention. To fulfill all these jobs, China will establish an authoritative, efficient oversight system to integrate intraparty oversight with oversight by state organs, democratic oversight, judicial oversight, public oversight, and oversight through public opinion. All this will create a powerful synergy for conducting oversight and important process of institutional building for anticorruption.

Conclusion

Xi Jinping moves toward building a superior-subordinate relationship between him and the other members of the Politburo Standing Committee. The present concentration of power in Xi Jinping's hands runs counter to the collective leadership China's top echelons exercised during the Hu Jintao era. This phenomenon of power concentration is the joint product of three factors. First, China presently faces greater internal and external pressures than during the early Hu Jintao era and therefore needs a strong leader. China's challenges include maintaining a medium to high economic growth rate; alleviating social contradictions resulting from the wealth gap; containing the escalation of ethnic uprisings in the Xinjiang region and Tibet; preventing the United States from encircling China and discouraging the Southeast Asian countries from teaming up and following America's lead. Second, Xi Jinping has lived through the times of Mao Zedong worship and the tumultuous Chinese Cultural Revolution. These experiences have given him a resolute and persevering character that craves national revival and admires charismatic leadership. Yet it has also enabled him to understand the hardships of social underdogs, the workings of realpolitik as well as the importance of the rule of law. Third, as Hu Jintao has completely retired from the political stage and

Jiang Zemin is at an advanced age, Xi Jinping faces relatively little resistance from within the party against the concentration of power in his hands.[17]

Since the start of the twenty-first century, China has placed in a more prominent position the work of combating corruption and building a clean government, adopted the principle of addressing both symptoms and root causes of corruption, enforcing comprehensive treatment, giving simultaneous stresses to punishment and prevention while giving priority to prevention, and establishing the national anticorruption strategy by setting up and perfecting a system of punishment and prevention of corruption to comprehensively promote this undertaking.[18]

As a whole, the trend of China's corruption prevention work develops from special prevention for individual corruption to prevention in key areas focusing on administrative examination and approval, financial management and cadre and personnel system reform, then to all-round prevention marked with the establishment and improvement of corruption punishment and prevention system. According to UN report, on September 13, 2007, China established the National Bureau of Corruption Prevention to coordinate the work of corruption prevention in various aspects and pragmatically implement Article 6, "Each State Party shall, in accordance with the fundamental principles of its legal system, ensure the existence of a body or bodies, as appropriate, that prevent corruption," of UN Convention against Corruption.

Many people were concerned after the announcement of standing committee member names after CCP 19th first national session. There are only seven standing committee members which means that Xi Jinping would continue his leadership after CCP 20th National Conference and there is no existing successor. This is quite different from his two predecessors, Jiang Zemin and Hu Jintao, who were at that position for two terms based on China's Constitution.

So this may lead to two folds of concerns. One is that Xi wants to continue his policy after two terms of CCP leadership but fears that no existing standing committee member would be doing that when he is gone. The other is that if he can keep a clear mind when in power for so long and so many people around him have shown intention to be lifting the sedan chair. Either one would turn the current favorable development trend over and raise uncertainty for China's new era, if there is no institutional buildup to carry on anticorruption efforts and transparency in political operation system of CCP. We can only hope that Xi pays more attention and strives harder to establish a more democratic social system that can oversee potential political turmoil and contain corruption in a way which leads to rejuvenation of China in the next 100 years to come. Right before completion of this chapter, Xi Jinping put out a proposal for establishing a new anticorruption agency with sweeping powers to sidestep the courts and lock up anyone on the government payroll for months without access to a lawyer.[19] This new National

Supervision Commission is under the State Council. The 19th CCP National Congress appeared to strengthen Xi Jinping's authority and usher in a new era of strongman rule in China, laying out a vision of society under the all-encompassing control of the party. The new proposed commission would take over from the party watchdog, but with broader investigative reach. As the current CCP DIC's focus has been limited to Communist Party members, the new proposed commission would be empowered to examine anyone on the public payroll, including more than 62 million government employees, many of whom are not party members. Some scholars assume that this new proposed commission will strengthen the leadership of the party through the form of rule of law. But referring to the beginning part of this chapter, how should we entrust a leader with unlimited power?

NOTES

1. Chan & Gao, Old Wine in New Bottles: A Country Level Case Study of Anticorruption Reform in the People's Republic of China, *Crime, Law and Social Change*, 2008, 49–117.
2. Daniel C.K. Chow, Why China's Crackdown on Commercial Bribery Threatens U.S. Multinational Companies Doing Business in China, *Arizona Journal of International &Comparative Law*, 2014, Vol. 31, No. 3.
3. Yong Guo, Historical Evolvement and Future Reform of the China Communist Party Discipline Inspection Commission, Research Report to Center of Anticorruption Studies and Seminar, 2008.
4. Nicholas D'Amico, Corruption and Economic Growth in China, John Corral University, Spring 2015, http://collected.jcu.edu/.
5. The Name List of Government Officials Sentenced in Five Years, *Beijing Youth Daily*, 2003.
6. The Report of Investigation on Anticorruption in China, Beijing Legal System Daily, 2002.
7. Andrew Wedeman, Growth and Corruption in China, 2012, Vol. 11, No. 2.
8. Xiaoyan Wu, *Anticorruption Literature and Television Dramas, China Today, Jing Luo edits*, (GreenWood Press, 2004), 27–28.
9. Zengke He, Corruption and Anticorruption in Reform China, http://www.wiapp.org/acpapers/a62.html.
10. China Daily, http://www.chinadaily.com.cn/china/2016-07/01/content_25936928.htm.
11. Yong Guo, Historical Evolvement and Future Reform of the China Communist Party Discipline Inspection Commission, Research Report to Center of Anticorruption Studies and Seminar, 2008.
12. During 19th CCP National Congress, CCP summarized Xi Jinping's first term in office as CCP leader as very successful, bringing the end of almost forty years of economic reform and open-door policy and bringing forward a New Era for China's

continued development and becoming one of the world powers by 2050. So this term is used to refer the coming years under Xi Jinping's leadership, most probably long after CCP 20th National Congress.

13. Xi Jinping Report at 19th CCP National Congress, October 18, 2017, see also at http://news.xinhuanet.com/english/special/2017-11/03/c_136725942.htm.

14. The four forms are (1) Criticism and self-criticism activities and oral and written inquiries which are to be conducted regularly, to ensure that those who have committed minor misconduct are made to "redden and sweat"; (2) Light penalties and minor organizational adjustments to official positions, which are to be applied in the majority of cases; (3) Heavy penalties and major adjustments to official positions, which are to be applied in a small number of cases; and (4) Investigation and prosecution, which are to be undertaken in a very small numberofcasesinvolvingseriousviolationsofdisciplineandsuspectedcriminalactivity.

15. According to the *New York Times*, China delivered a proposed draft of new anticorruption agency under the State Council which is separated from CCP DIC whose main targets are CCP members. The new agency mainly oversees 62 million government employees many of whom are not CCP members.

16. A form of intraparty disciplinary action that requires a Party member under investigation to cooperate with questioning at a designated place and at a designated time.

17. Kou Chien-wen, Xi Jinping's Anticorruption Campaign Alters China's Power Structure, Taiwan Brain Trust, Newsletter #26, 2016.

18. https://www.unodc.org/documents/treaties/UNCAC/WorkingGroups/workinggroup4/2011-August-22-24/ pdf.

19. Chris Buckley, In China, Fears that New Anticorruption Agency will be above the Law, *New York Times*, November 29, 2017, see also at https://www.nytimes.com/2017/11/29/world/asia/china-xi-jinping-anticorruption.html?_r=0.

BIBLIOGRAPHY

April, Yazini. Will China's Reforms Impact FOCAC? *Africa Institute of South Africa*, February 2016.

Blackwill, Robert D. and Campbell, Kurt M. Xi Jinping on the Global Stage Chinese Foreign Policy Under a Powerful but Exposed Leader. Council on Foreign Relations, Council Special Report No. 74 February 2016.

Buckley, Chris. In China, Fears that New Anticorruption Agency will be above the Law. *New York Times*, November 29, 2017, see also at https://www.nytimes.com/2017/11/29/world/asia/china-xi-jinping-anticorruption.html?_r=0.

CCP Third Plenary Session of the 18th CPC Central Committee, Establishing a Sound System for Punishing and Preventing Corruption Work Plan (2013–2017), December 2012.

Chan & Gao. Old Wine in New Bottles: A Country Level Case Study of Anticorruption Reform in the People's Republic of China. *Crime, Law and Social Change*, 2008.

China Daily. http://www.chinadaily.com.cn/china/2016-07/01/content_25936928.htm.

Chow, Daniel C.K. Why China's Crackdown on Commercial Bribery Threatens U.S. Multinational Companies Doing Business in China. *Arizona Journal of International &Comparative Law*, Vol. 31, No. 3, 2014.

Country Watch Inc. *China Country Review*. 2017.

D'Amico, Nicholas. *Corruption and Economic Growth in China*. John Corral University, Spring 2015, http://collected.jcu.edu/.

Deng, Xiaoping. *Selected Works of Deng Xiaoping*. Foreign Language Press, 1995.

European Council on Foreign Relations. *Xi's Army: Reform and Loyalty in the PLA*. March 2016.

Guo, Yong. Historical Evolvement and Future Reform of the China Communist Party Discipline Inspection Commission. Research Report to Center of Anticorruption Studies and Seminar, 2008.

He, Zengke. Corruption and Anticorruption in Reform China, http://www.wiapp.org/acpapers/a62.html.

https://www.unodc.org/documents/treaties/UNCAC/WorkingGroups/workinggroup4/2011-August-22-24/pdf.

Information Office of the State Council of the People's Republic of China, White Paper on China's Efforts to Combat Corruption and Build a Clean Government. December 2010, Beijing.

Kallio, Jyrki. Xi Jinping at Mid-Term and Beyond. *The Finnish Institute of International Affairs*, January 2017.

Kou, Chien-wen. Xi Jinping's Anticorruption Campaign Alters China's Power Structure. Taiwan Brain Trust, Newsletter #26, 2016.

Lam, Willy Wo-Lap. *Chinese Politics in the Era of Xi Jinping—Renaissance, Reform, or Retrogression?* Routledge, 2015.

Leung, James. Xi's Corruption Crackdown. *Foreign Affairs*, Vol. 94, No. 3, 2015, 32–38. Academic Search Complete. Web. November 8, 2015.

Li, Jia. *Xi Jinping's Tiger Hunt: Fighting Corruption or Fighting Enemies?* National Chengchi University, July 2016.

Li, Xiaobing and Tian, Xiansheng. *Evolution of Power-China's Struggle, Survival, and Success*. Lexington Books, 2014.

Liu, Zhifeng. *Problem Report on China Political System Reform*. China Film Publishing House, 1999.

Lu, Xin and Soboleva, Elena. Personality Cults in Modern Politics: Cases from Russia and China. CGP Working Paper Series 01/2014.

Luo, Jing. *China Today-an Encyclopedia of Life in the People's Republic*. Greenwood Press, 2004.

McMillan, John. Introduction to Anticorruption Law and Policy in Australia. China-Australia Human Rights Technical Cooperation Program, Tianjin, China, May 26–27, 2008.

Menzel, Donald C. Corruption in China: Tigers and Flies Beware. The New China: Contemporary Life and Governance, https://www.smashwords.com/books/view/352367.

Panda, Jagannath P. *China's Transition under Xi Jinping*. Pentagon Press, 2016.

Pope, Jeremy. Confronting Corruption: The Elements of a National Integrity System. *The Transparency International*, 2000.

Smith, Richard C. Anticorruption Enforcement is Escalating Worldwide. *Law 360*, May 27, 2015. https://www.law360.com/articles/659365/anti-corruption-enforcement-is-escalating-worldwide.

The Name List of Government Officials Sentenced in Five Years. *Beijing Youth Daily*, 2003.

The Report of Investigation on Anticorruption in China. *Beijing Legal System Daily*, 2002.

Wallace, Jeremy. The New Normal: Reform, Information, and China's Anticorruption Crusade in Context. May 13, 2015.

Wang, Mengkui. *Key Issues in China's Development (2006–2020).* China Development Press, 2006.

Wedeman, Andrew. *Growth and Corruption in China.* China Research Center, Vol. 11, No. 2, 2012. https://www.chinacenter.net/2012/china_currents/11-2/growth-and-corruption-in-china/.

Wedeman, Andrew. "Xi Jinping's Anticorruption Campaign and the Third Plenum" in https://www.cecc.gov/sites/chinacommission.house.gov/files/CECC%20Roundtable%20-%20Corruption%20in%20China%20-%20Andrew%20Wedeman%20Written%20Statement.pdf.

Wu, Xiaoyan. Anticorruption Literature and Television Dramas. *China Today*, Jing Luo edits. GreenWood Press, 2004.

Xi, Jinping, Report at 19th CCP National Congress, October 17, 2017.

Xi, Jinping, Report at 19th CCP National Congress. October 18, 2017, see also at http://news.xinhuanet.com/english/special/2017-11/03/c_136725942.htm.

Zhang, Shuguang. *China's Institutional Change.* Shanghai People Publishing House, 1996.

Zhou, Jinghao. Will the Communist Party of China be Able to Win the Anticorruption Battle? *Contemporary Chinese Political Economy and Strategic Relations: An International Journal*, Vol. 2, No. 3, December 2016, 1007–48.

Chapter 13

Xi Jinping's Anticorruption in a Historical Perspective

Qiang Fang

XI'S ANTICORRUPTION

Before Xi Jinping[1], son of former vice premier Xi Zhongxun, took power in late 2012, he had largely been little known to the West, which was in stark contrast to the flamboyant Bo Xilai, the Party secretary of Chongqing, who had led a rather populist movement of "Singing the Red [Songs] and Striking the Black [mafia]." However, shortly after Xi Jinping was made the most powerful leader of the Chinese Communist Party (CCP),[2] he quickly embarked on an anticorruption campaign whose scope and scale are both unprecedented in the history of the People's Republic of China (PRC).

The whole episode began in February 2012 with a surprising attempt of Wang Lijun, the chief of Chongqing Public Security Bureau, to seek political asylum at the United States Consulate in Chengdu, Sichuan province. As a longtime faithful protégé of Bo Xilai, Wang had played a key role in Bo's high-profiled campaign ostensibly against corrupt officials and local mafia. But a dispute over the alleged murder of an English businessman by Bo's wife led to a fatal struggle between the two men.[3] The sudden incident of Wang Lijun offered Xi Jinpin excellent ammunition to attack Bo Xilai, a more popular and ambitious competitor whose late father was also a leading figure in the CCP, and initiated a sweeping anticorruption campaign.

In November 2012, within days after taking the leadership, Xi cautioned Party officials to be "solid for shaping iron (*datie haixu zishenying*)."[4] He also told officials that the Party was in jeopardy due to the rampant corruption that "eating away at the Party's authority and effectiveness."[5] In early December, Li Chuncheng, vice Party secretary of Sichuang Province, was taken away by the Central Disciplinary Commission (CDC) and became the first corrupt "tiger" under Xi's campaign.[6]

According to *ChinaFile*, an online magazine run by Asia Society, an NGO based in New York, at least 146 senior officials and 1,316 lower-ranking officials had been under investigation, expelled from the CCP, or tried and convicted between 2012 and 2015. *ChinaFile* also discovered that Xi Jinping had hardly cracked down corrupt officials during his tenures as Party leader in Fujian, Zhejiang, and Shanghai. In Fujian, for instance, a province racked by a major notorious smuggling case in Xiamen in the 1990s, only two senior officials had been punished.[7]

Invoking Chinese official reports, journalist Tania Branigan argued in early 2015 that more than 100,000 officials had been punished since Xi took power.[8] Despite the disparity of the number of punished officials, it is conspicuous that Xi's anticorruption campaign has been widespread that arguably exceeds any other periods in the PRC.

Some corrupt cases exposed by public media are quite astonishing in terms of the scale of graft and bribes. In one case, when central inspectors searched the home of Ma Chaoqun, a lower-ranking official in Qinhuangdao, Hebei province, they were shocked to find stored cash of over 120 million RMB (20 million USD), 40 pounds of gold, and 68 apartments. Another corrupt official named Wei Pengyuan, who was the vice head of the Coal Department of the National Energy Bureau in Beijing, was searched. The inspectors dug out over 100 million RMB in his home. Of the sixteen machines used to count the cash, four of them were destroyed because of too much cash.[9]

One of the biggest "tigers" captured in the anticorruption is Admiral Gu Junshan, former vice head of the Logistic Department of the Chinese military. According to the Caijin net, an influential website with profound connections to the Chinese central government, Gu had been involved in a graft totaling 20 billion RMB (3.3 billion USD). After his property was confiscated, inspectors had to use four trucks to carry Gu's treasures and two trucks to carry thousands of bottles of Maotai, one of China's top liquor brands. Gu's mansion in his hometown was said to be like a palace.[10]

Xi's massive anticorruption movement has had tremendous physical and psychological impacts on officials. Partly to avoid facing the inhuman interrogations by the CDC inspectors and partly to aim to protect their families and government collaborators, many officials have chosen to commit suicide. According to one source, there were about sixty-eight officials who had killed themselves during the entire tenure of Xi's predecessor Hu Jintao (2003-2012). Yet two years after Xi Jinping took power, at least seventy-seven officials have committed suicide.[11] During Xi's first year in power, only seven officials died because of suicide. In 2014, the number of suicide soared to thirty-nine. Up to April 2016, 120 officials had committed suicide and most of them were of lower ranks.[12] Having fewer allies and feeble protection from the top, these lower-ranking officials would be more vulnerable than powerful princelings such as Bo Xilai and Ling Jihua, chief adviser of former president Hu Jintao, who could manage to escape death penalty despite much worse crimes and corruption.[13]

Aside from his drastic anticorruption, Xi Jinping has also tried to transform the "political culture" inside Chinese government.[14] In December 2012, Xi announced an "Eight-point Code (*baxiang guiding*)," which required officials to reconnect with the masses through the banning of using luxury cars, eliminating lavish gifts, and reducing pomp banquets, ceremonies, bureaucratic visits, and meetings.[15] These new policies to curb prodigious official waste and extravagance immediately won popular support. Most people I had met in China between 2012 and 2014 praised Xi's anticorruption policies. Officials in the public sectors (e.g., government, universities) have to follow strict rules in spending. Many official aberrations have resulted in disciplinary punishment or even dismissal.[16]

Conventional Views on Xi's Campaign

Starting from late 2012, Xi Jinping's anticorruption has triggered extraordinary interest among scholars in the West. Many of them have evaluated the campaign through different perspectives. Roughly speaking, there are about six interconnected types of scholarly view.

One of the most representative and widely accepted views is that Xi Jinping's anticorruption is largely selective. According to Murong Xuechun, a Chinese dissident writer, the primary target of Xi's campaign has been his political enemies or power challengers rather than an unselfish crackdown of all corruptions,

> The anticorruption push is more of a Stalinist purge than a genuine attempt to clean up the government. Charges are framed with reference to party regulations, not the law. Investigations are run by K.G.B.-type cadres, not the regular judicial system. China's media does not report on cases until they are made public, after which there is a barrage of almost identically worded reports used to incriminate the suspect. Most telling of all, the purge has mainly targeted specific party factions, while those groups that support and pledge loyalty to Mr. Xi appear untouched.[17]

In agreeing with Xuechun's view, He Qinglian, a renowned economist and political observer who sought asylum in the United States several years ago, argues that China's ongoing anticorruption has been monopolized by Xi Jinping and his adherents and any non-official involvement will be prohibited. "The only purpose of a monopolized anticorruption," He Qinglian writes, "is to make it convenient for a selective anticorruption." She further asserts that the highly corrupt Chinese government almost cannot accommodate upright persons, which makes it mandatory for the government to monopolize anti-corruption. A monopolized anticorruption will allow the Chinese government to pick its targets and not to harm its allies in the same boat by a "friendly fire." Otherwise, anticorruption will give rise to political upheaval.[18]

In addition, political scientist Minxin Pei questions the objectives of Xi's anticorruption as "no princelings (scions of veteran CCP leaders) who have become kleptocrats in their own right have fallen."[19] Zhou Yahui, a political commentator, makes it more explicit to classify CCP officials into two categories: the princeling party (*taizidang*) and the civilian party (*pingmindang*). The former refers to officials who were born into provincial-level official families and the latter are officials whose parents hold positions below the county level. Unlike princelings whose promotion is largely based on family and personal network, most civilian party officials are pragmatists. They have little interest in Party ideology and most of them acquire promotion in the Party through individual efforts and talents. "Up to now," Zhou writes, "Xi's anticorruption has only struck down two princelings (Bo Xilai and Gu Kailai) and the reasons are that Bo's father once had a bad relationship with Xi's father and Bo himself has tried to challenge Xi's authority in the Party." Zhou goes on to claim that the goal of Xi's anticorruption is safeguarding the dictatorship of the Party-state under princelings. Therefore, Xi's anticorruption is selective whose purpose is to attack officials belonging to the civilian party and replace them with princelings.[20]

The second view argues that Xi's anticorruption is a movement, which echoes late chairman Mao Zedong's political movements. For example, Zhang Lun, associate professor at Ecole Normale Supérieure de Cachan, a French university, believes that Xi's goal of anticorruption is a combination of both political control and gaining people's support. In that regard, Xi was successful in the first two years. But the consequence of Xi's "movement-type (*yundongshi*)" anticorruption appears to be increasingly evident. Due most likely to the harsh anticorruption, the Chinese bureaucratic system virtually ceases to function because many officials are reluctant to work. This could be an answer for the current slowdown of Chinese economy. Zhang alarms Xi that China's anticorruption has arrived at a crossroad. If Xi's anticorruption is sincere, he should take a fresh direction. In other words, Xi Jinping should increase and strengthen the roles of a civil society, media, and legal system. Unfortunately, Xi's actions have proved that he will not pursue that "new" direction after the Chinese government has arrested rights lawyers and tightened its grip on public media.[21]

Like Zhang Lun, an editorial of the *World Journal*, a Chinese-language newspaper based in New York City, also calls Xi's anticorruption a political movement. The editorial discovers many "surprising" similarities between campaigns of Xi's anticorruption and the anticorruption of Jiang Jingguo, son of Republican leader Chiang Kai-shek, in 1948. "Even Xi's words like attacking both tigers and flies are borrowed from Jiang Jingguo," the editorial notes. Both Jiang and Xi have vowed that they would punish all corrupt officials no matter how powerful they are and how higher their positions are. However, both of them quickly encounter a "bottleneck": Jiang Jingguo's anticorruption was blocked by Kong Lingkan, the son of Chiang Kai-shek's brother-in-law and one of the most powerful figures in the Republic of China, whereas the public exposure made by his political adversaries of the grave family corruption committed by former top leaders such as Deng Xiaoping, Wen Jiabao, Hu Jintao, Li Peng, and Xi Jinping has discredited Xi's anticorruption. The editorial further argues that the anticorruption movement led by an enlightened ruler or upright officials remains an old-type and will not succeed. It is because both the supervisor (the Party) and the one to be supervised (i.e., corrupt officials) are living in the same family. If both the player (corrupt officials) and the referee (the Party) are the same person, the CCP would not fight corruption to the end.

Finally, the editorial offers a caveat to Xi Jinping that in China today when people can no longer be duped, it is hard for the CCP and the populace to have the impression that Xi's anticorruption is fair and not the result of a power struggle.[22]

Similar to those holding the view of selective anticorruption, the third group of observers asserts that Xi's anticorruption is a sheer power struggle. He Pin, the founder of the *Mingjing Weekly*, a publication focusing on Chinese politics, says that, although many top officials such as Zhou Yongkang, Bo Xilai, and Xu Caihou have been punished, the fundamental cause of their fall is not their corruption but is their alliance that has threatened Xi Jinping's power. The more corrupt families such as Jiang Zemin, Li Peng, Wen Jiabao, Zeng Qinghong and the like have largely been exempted. Xi Jinping's anticorruption has now entered a stalemate and cannot proceed on. If the CCP wants to investigate those most powerful families, CCP's institution and legitimacy will face "immense crisis."[23]

Likewise, Yu Jie, a dissident Chinese Christian, sharply denounces Xi's anticorruption campaign as a means not as much to create a stable society and clean politics as to establish his own authority and attack his political enemies.[24] Invoking the views of political scientist Gordon Chang, Si Yang, another observer, writes that, because China does not have an independent judiciary and so far no relative or friend of Xi Jinping has been imprisoned, ordinary people have reason to believe that Xi's anticorruption is merely a "movement of political purge."[25]

The fourth view argues that the primary purpose of Xi's anticorruption is to propel the reform in China that has been stymied. In his article, Samson Yuen writes, "It has long been held that Party factionalism and vested interests, especially in the state-owned sectors, have made the economic reforms proposed in the Third Plenum of the 18th Party Congress difficult to implement." Once he has got rid of corrupt officials, Xi could replace them with pro-reformist allies. A *Reuters* report suggests that Xi Jinping hopes that "removing corrupt officials and those resisting changes" will allow him to consolidate his grip on power and implement "difficult economic, judicial, and military reforms" that he believes to be vital to continue CCP's rule.[26]

While Zheng Yongnian, a political scientist at Singapore National University, refrains from saying that Xi's anticorruption is a power struggle, he points out that the ongoing anticorruption is part of Xi's large effort to strengthen his power, which is quite important for him to "push through unfinished market reforms." Unless he has become a paramount leader in China, further reform is out of the question.[27]

The fifth scholarly view on Xi's anticorruption is that Xi Jinping is being endeavored to alter the debauched and wasteful political culture in China. According to Macabe Keliher and Hsinchao Wu, since the beginning of China's open policy and reform in the late 1970s, political corruption has grown "exponentially" as a side effect of the reform. Given greater autonomy and capacity in developing and implementing regional projects and economic policies, a culture of bribery, graft, misappropriation, and nepotism has been nurtured and propagated among officials. The anticorruption campaign kicked off by Xi Jinping along with his stringent orders to sharply curtail government spending on luxury banquet, gifts, and travels have "created the possibility not only of stamping out corruption, but also, more importantly, of transforming the political culture."[28]

The last view on Xi's anticorruption comes from the Chinese official media. Due to the fact that most overseas comments have questioned the nature and actual purpose of Xi's anticorruption, the Chinese official media deem it imperative to rebut those doubts and charges. In the latest issue of *Qiushi* (Seeking Truth), a conservative mouthpiece of the CCP, Shi Ping (a penname of editorial) sharply accuses some Western media and critics of having regarded China's ongoing anticorruption as a power struggle. "If [Western people] look at our current anticorruption with colored eyeglasses," Shi Ping writes, "[they] will come up with a distorted conclusion."

According to Shi Ping, behind the overseas view may be because those people do not understand China's anticorruption. But more likely those people purposely want to denigrate and misrepresent. Using a familiar official rhetoric, Shi Ping criticizes some Western states of having raised the "so-called anticorruption issue" in many international meetings in the past. But after Xi Jinping launched the anticorruption campaign, those Western states, instead of applauding China's efforts, continue to charge the Chinese government with a power struggle. "In their perspective, corruption is a problem while anticorruption is also a problem. Their prejudice and animus [toward the CCP] are ingrained," Shi Ping remarks.

In defense of Xi's anticorruption, Shi Ping stresses that the anticorruption is not a "power struggle" nor does it have the "House of Cards."[29] In conclusion, Shi Ping states that the CCP will deepen the anticorruption campaign, which will spread to all levels and all corners from governments to military and from central ministries to provincial, city, and county governments. Whatever his high official rank and powerful connection, no corrupt official will be able to escape the punishment of Party discipline and state law. Until then, the (Western) talk of "so-called selective anticorruption" will collapse without being attacked.[30]

A Critique of Existing Views

Those overseas comments are made either by Chinese dissidents or by sinologists. With one exception, most of the comments have cast doubt on Xi Jinping's anticorruption campaign. They have portrayed Xi's anticorruption as a movement, a power struggle, a political purge, or an overall selective campaign whose targets are merely his political enemies or challengers. Each of the assertions has its merit as it touches one or more of the nature of Xi's anticorruption. But all of them have certain imperfections.

For instance, the argument that Xi's anticorruption is selective is partially correct because it ignores the fact that the anticorruption is so comprehensive that it has spread to many other social, economic, and political realms. While it may be true that most of the high-ranking officials, such as Zhou Yongkang, Bo Xilai, and Xu Caihou, who have been attacked are Xi's political foes, the "Eight-point Code" proposed and implemented in late 2012 has been highly popular among ordinary people. The code indiscriminately restricts spending in the public sector including, among other things, all levels of government, universities, state enterprises, hospitals, and libraries. In addition to limiting lavish banquets, travel, and gifts, the code also aims to reduce government benefits such as government vehicles, banquet fees, and supplements of gas, bath, and haircut. Many officials I have met in Chinese governments and universities in the past two years have complained that they have lost many benefits and have to spend more from their own pockets.

Two years ago, when I visited a university in Shanghai, one official told me that liquor was no longer covered by the university in treating guests because of the Eight-point Code. One official had to bring a bottle of liquor from his home. Last summer, a university official in central China said that the new regulation allowed only one college official to have free dinner with guests and any other official present had to pay their own food. Such new policies would have been inconceivable before Xi Jinping became the Party secretary.

Since the initiation of the code, many officials have been punished for crossing the line. Accordingly, if Xi's anticorruption is merely selective and only attack his enemies, why would he bother to promulgate the Eight-point code that may cause widespread discontent among officials? Despite wide animosity may come out as a result of the code, Xi Jinping could reap more political fruits as the code is extremely welcome among commoners who have for years frowned on excessive government spending. As taxpayers, commoners find it reasonable for them to vent their anger over the shocking government extravagance and misspending of their hard-earned money. They believe that the unrestricted government spending is one of the crucial causes of social inequality and vices.[31]

Additionally, advocates of "selective anticorruption" seem not to have paid much attention to the urgency and necessity of Xi's anticorruption. Although both Jiang Zemin and Hu Jintao had cracked down official corruption and punished high-profile officials such as Beijing mayor Chen Xitong and Shanghai Party secretary Chen Liangyu, most corrupt officials including close relatives and associates of Jiang and Hu were largely untouched. So long as officials were trusted or threw their lot to Jiang and Hu, they would feel safe no matter how corrupt they were. A good example is Zeng Qinghong, vice chairman under Jiang Zemin. In 2010, one Australian newspaper disclosed that Zeng's son had bought a mansion with $32.4 million, one of the most expensive mansions in that country.[32] Later it was revealed that the money was paid by Jiang Jiemin, former CEO of Chinese National Petroleum Corporation.[33] Another is Wen Jiabao, the liberal premier under Hu Jintao. In 2012, the *New York Times* published a detailed account of the hidden treasure totaling $2.7 billion held by Wen's family.[34] Wen Jiabao quickly denied the report and threatened to sue the *New York Times*. But the lawsuit does not ensue and reporters from the *New York Times* are subsequently banned to enter China.[35]

If the corruption on the top has been so serious, there will be little doubt that bribes and grafts are nearly unchecked on the local level. Worse, after capitalizing on the lower wages and redundant free labor for almost thirty years, Chinese economy began to show signs of slowdown in the later tenure of Hu Jintao. On the one hand, more factories have been forced to close or transfer to interior provinces or other countries due to increasing labor cost; on the other, the gap between rich and poor has reached the highest level in PRC history. Skyrocketing housing prices and the ever-rising costs of buying food, seeing a doctor, and attending a college add to the pains and displeasure of the commoners in both urban and rural areas. For them, all their plights have been caused by rampant official corruption. If the corruption problem is not to be addressed swiftly and properly, the CCP will lose the legitimacy of its rule. As Minxin Pei has argued, "Such endemic corruption has fortuitously created a rare opportunity for Mr. Xi to make an immediate mark after rising to the top."[36]

To champion Xi's anticorruption, both Samson Yuen and Zheng Yongnian have asserted that Xi wants to utilize anticorruption to make the reform "easier" or to deepen the "unfinished market reform."[37] This argument fails to indicate the extent of market reform to which Xi Jinping's anticorruption tries to propel. Since Xi's takeover in 2012, China's economy has been on a downward spiral with the decline of annual GDP growth rate. While Xi has tried to grapple with the inefficiency of the state company, so far no decisive and tangible action has been taken. Instead of stimulating the market reform or making the reform easier, Xi's other new policies such as the "Seven Don't Mentions (*qibujiang*)," resisting Western values, forbidding "improper discussion of the Party central (*wangyi zhongyang*),[38] and arbitrary detainment of rights lawyers" have further tightened the control of political and academic freedom, which, contrary to the argument of Yuen and Zheng, will impede market reform. It is because a healthy market economy needs free flow of not only funds but also ideas and values. But more important, market reform requires the rule of law and not the rule by law.[39]

In an article entitled "Corruption, Anticorruption, and the Transformation of Political Culture in Contemporary China," Macabe Keliher and Hsinchao Wu see the ubiquitous practice of bribes and favors as a serious problem in China today. Both authors note that it is vital for the CCP to "weed out corrupt officials because everyone is corrupt." Yet, their argument that Xi Jinping has succeeded in altering the Chinese political culture may be farfetched. According to the authors, the political culture including bribery, graft, misappropriation, and nepotism has been "nurtured by the Chinese economic reform."[40] In other words, the corrupt culture has ostensibly accompanied the reform. However, history tells us that such a corrupt culture is by no means a side effect of the recent reform. It exists in almost all major periods in the history of China if not in the rest of world. One of the key reasons for the fall of most Chinese dynasties is political corruption, which entails all the features elaborated by the two authors. Thus, the so-called political culture that Xi has tried to transform is actually ingrained in Chinese political history and is not something relatively "new" in the reform period, albeit it is true that the corrupt culture has aggravated since the late 1980s.

Moreover, both Keliher and Wu seem to be in agreement with Shi Ping, the official view of the CCP, that Xi Jinping's anticorruption crackdown "punishes the worst offenses and has sent a shudder throughout the bureaucracy."[41] Shi Ping states that Xi's anticorruption is not selective and all corrupt officials will be punished in compliance with the Party discipline and the state law regardless of their ranks, fields, and backgrounds.[42]

As we have seen, despite their seemingly forceful argument and pledge, Keliher, Wu, and Shi Ping will find it difficult to deny that Xi's anticorruption campaign has up to date only targeted corrupt officials of either his political opponents or relatively lower-ranking officials. None of the "big tigers" related to former leaders has been investigated or punished despite that their corruption is reportedly close to or more serious than those who have been charged and sentenced to prison. Aside from Zeng Qinghong and Wen Jiabao whose family corruption has been exposed by Western media, various sources have also revealed the tremendous corruption committed by scions of previous leaders such as Deng Xiaoping, Jiang Zemin, Li Peng, and Hu Jintao.[43] One good example is Li Xiaolin, daughter of former premier Li Peng, a key decision maker of the crackdown of the Tiananmen demonstration in 1989. As the head of the State Grid Corp of China, the largest state-run electricity provider in the world, Li Xiaolin has been quite bold in her boasts of her personal capacity and showoff of her expensive apparels and jewelries in national conferences.[44] In 2015, some Chinese media reported that a water company whose bottled water had been a mandatory purchase for all passengers boarding high-speed trains for seven years was under investigation by the government. Without intimate and mysterious connection to the Chinese Ministry of Railroad, the water company would not have enjoyed seven years of stable business and enormous profits. It is not until the incarceration of Liu Zhijun, minister of the Chinese Railroad Ministry, in 2013 that the investigation of the water company finally began. Unfortunately, the investigation has gone nowhere as the result has never been disclosed by the government. One can extrapolate that the company must have strong background inside the CCP that Xi Jinping is unwilling or unable to touch.[45] As Michael Forsythe reports, Xi Jinping himself did not have a strong track record in attacking corruption during his years as governors when there "have not seen as many top officials fall in corruption campaigns as neighboring provinces."[46]

Finally, as a major mouthpiece of the CCP, Shi Ping may not want to heed the newly reported corruption cases such as the big explosion in Tianjin (August 2015) and the "man-made" landslide in Shenzhen (December 2015) both of which may have killed hundreds of people respectively. According to some overseas media, the two incidents resulted from local government corruption.[47] While some lower-ranking officials have been detained, no top officials in Tianjin and Shenzhen resign or take full responsibility. Shi Ping may also turn a deaf ear to the new corruption generated by Xi's government. In the summer of 2015, around two hundred right lawyers who had assisted helpless aggrieved petitioners sue the government were detained by police under alleged charges of instigating the overthrow of the PRC. Neglecting foreign protests, Chinese courts recently sentenced some of the lawyers into prison.[48] The attack and imprisonment of rights lawyers serve to manifest a tip of the iceberg of the judicial corruption in the PRC, which not only has not been touched by Xi's campaign, but also has worsened under Xi.

Consequently, due to the nearly impunity of many "big tigers" and the incompleteness of serious anticorruption cases, one has some legitimate reasons to wonder why Xi's anticorruption can be said to be impartial and thorough if the "worst" corrupt officials are still at large and living in peace and comfort.

Anticorruption in Chinese History

To better assess the effectiveness and impact of Xi's sweeping anticorruption movement, it is worth placing it into a larger historical context by contrasting Xi's movement with other equally notable and comprehensive anticorruption campaigns in the Tang, Ming, and Qing dynasties. I would argue that Xi's ongoing anticorruption is in many respects, good or bad, partial or sweeping, akin to some enlightened rulers in the history.

According to historian Bu Xianqun, since the late Xia dynasty (ca. 2070–1600 BCE), the semi-legendary dynasty, corruption has been blamed for the fall of most dynasties. To check corruption, Chinese rulers have taken pains and numerous measures to deal with corruption. The earliest anticorruption arguably began in the Zhou dynasty (1100–256 BCE) and *Lu Xing* (The Punishment of Lu), the earliest law against corruption, was promulgated in the ninth century BCE.[49]

In the Tang dynasty (618–907 CE), Tang Taizong (r.627–649), the founding emperor of the Tang and one of the "most enlightened and law-abiding rulers of all Chinese history," adopted stringent policies against corrupt top officials and even royal relatives.[50] In 642, Dang Renhong, a highly esteemed general and longtime adherent of Tang Taizong was accused of taking bribes worth millions of dollars. According to the Tang Code, Dang should be executed for his crime. To save the life of his old associate, Tang Taizong begged his officials for Dang's sake,

> Yesterday, I read the memorial from the Supreme Court that Dang should be executed. I felt sad to see Dang executed at such an old age . . . I tried to save his life, but [Supreme Court officials] disagreed. Today, I want to violate the law and implore you to save his life.

Several days later, Tang Taizong summoned all officials above the fifth rank to the court. He told them that law was something that heaven rendered to the ruler and accordingly should not be kept as privately owned by the ruler. Tang Taizong continued, "Today, my attempt to use my personal power to pardon Dang Renhong breaks the state law and betrays heaven's [will]."

Tang Taizong decided to punish himself for the law violation by eating only vegetable for three days as a way of seeking apology from heaven. Although top officials said that the ruler had the power to give life to and take life from any official, Tang Taizong remained firm on self-punishment for infringing the state law.[51] In this case, Tang Taizong, the throne and the most powerful person in the empire, could, like many other rulers in history, have easily exonerate a top general. Yet, he instead chose to beg his officials for forgiveness for his law violation, which was rare in Chinese history.

In another case, Li Daozong was not only a close royal relative of Tang Taizong but he had also fought bravely along with Taizong in battles to establish the Tang dynasty. After Tang Taizong was enthroned, Li Daozong continued to fight successfully against northern Turks. His military merits won him a title of king in the year of 638. Driven by insatiable greed for treasure and money, Li Daozong was not satisfied with his rewards and stipends. He took more bribes that led to his own imprisonment. Upon hearing the news about Li Daozong, Tang Taizong told his intimate officials that he would not labor the subjects for his personal pleasure even though he, as the emperor, owned all the empire and treasure. The best way to check endless human desire was human reason. "While Li Daozong enjoys high stipend and rewards," Tang Tiazong noted, "he is still greedy and people feel pathetic for his punishment. How despicable it [Li Daozong's greed] is!" Later, Tang Taizong deprived Li Daozong of all his official titles and cut the size of his fief.[52] This case shows that Tang Taizong would tolerate not even his close relative and able general for corruption.

Tang Taizong was known to be strict on corruption. In 648, one year before his death, Tang Taizong reportedly had investigated and disciplined over 1,000 officials for corruption.[53] Due to Tang Taizong's determined intolerance of any corruption, top officials and royal families were said to have become "upright" and dared not violate state law.[54]

The second prominent ruler to be discussed here is Ming Taizu (r.1368–1398). Like Tang Taizong, Ming Taizu is also the founding father of the Ming dynasty (1368–1644). Growing in an impoverished peasant family, Ming Taizu had been outraged by the corruption, bullying, and extorting of the local Yuan officials. For him, part of the reason for the fall of the Yuan dynasty (1279–1368) was its laxity of law.[55] Before he created his dynasty, Ming Taizu had already adopted strict rules against any official violation of law.

After establishing his dynasty, Ming Taizu was intent on utilizing drastic and merciless means to suppress official corruption. To some extent, his anti-corruption measures such as slicing (*lingchi*) and skinning (*bopi*) were among the cruelest in Chinese history.

In 1393, Ming Taizu issued an order to publicize *Brief Notes to Alarm Corruption* (*xingtan jianyaolu*) and he wrote the Introduction. In the Introduction, Ming Taizu said that among the four types of people (gentlemen, farmers, artisans, and merchants), gentlemen were the most privileged, while farmers were the most miserable. But "officials/gentlemen are not sympathetic with farmers' plight and some of them even exploit and abuse farmers. [Those officials] have no humane heart at all," Ming Taizu wrote. The book also stipulated that any official who had taken a bribe of more than sixty taels would be executed.[56]

Shortly after the Ming dynasty was established, many generals reportedly "become arrogant and willful" and some top officials had taken land illegally and had bullied local people.[57] To counter increasing official corruption, Ming Taizu launched a series of massive and relentless anticorruption campaign. Any official and royal relative would be severely punished regardless of his official rank. In 1362, when Hu Dahai, a famous general and a childhood friend of Ming Taizu, was leading an army attacking a major enemy city, his son had broken the law that banned alcohol drinking. Ming Taizu immediately ordered to execute the violator. An official reminded him that the execution might have adverse impact on Hu Dahai. But Ming Taizu was not persuaded. He said that he would rather let Hu Dahai betray him than see anyone violate his law. He then killed the son of General Hu Dahai with his own sword.[58]

Prime Minister Hu Weiyong had been a longtime follower of Ming Tiazu. Credible and capable, Hu was promoted to prime minister in 1374, the highest-ranking official post and a bridge between the emperor and court officials. Once he became the most powerful official, Hu allegedly turned haughty and autocratic. All state issues, big or small, important or trivial, Hu would deal with them without reporting to Ming Taizu. Some issues were involved in official promotions and demotions, others were related to officials' life and death. If any official memorial was unfavorable to him, Hu would intercept it and not report to Ming Taizu. Because of his power, people who sought official positions or wanted to obtain promotion as well as many others such as dissatisfied meritorious officials and soldiers flocked to Hu's home. They gave Hu all kinds of expensive treasures including gold, silk, horses, and artifacts. The serious corruption and the clique that Hu had formed gradually alarmed Ming Taizu. In 1380, Ming Taizu decided to take action. He charged Hu Weiyong with being "autocratic and creating a clique" and executed Hu, his family, and followers. To prevent future prime ministers from following Hu's suit, Ming Taizu abolished the position of prime minister and directly controlled the court.[59]

In 1393, six years before his death, Ming Taizu launched another brutal anticorruption against his beloved general Lan Yu. Lan Yu was a cousin of

Chang Yuchun, the most audacious warrior in the founding of the Ming. During the early years of the Ming, Lan Yu rose to become the most important general to defend the northern border and defeat the Mongol army. However, like many other generals, Lan Yu's highly accomplished career amplified his ambition and greed. Even after Ming Taizu enacted a law to curb the behavior of his top officials, Lan Yu allegedly continued to hire and adopt thousands of servants and "sons." In one case, Lan Yu and his followers seized a commoner's land by force. The commoner sued Lan Yu to the imperial inspector. When the inspector summoned Lan Yu to his office, Lan Yu beat and expelled the inspector. Lan Yu also asked his servants to buy large amount of salt, a violation of the state monopoly of salt trade. Lan Yu's arrogance, greed, and corruption forced Ming Taizu to attack him with one of the biggest massacres in Chinese history. More than 15,000 people had died as a result of the Lan Yu case and many of them had been sliced to death.[60]

Besides executing top officials for corruption and arrogance, Ming Taizu also punished his close relatives for corruption. According to the official Ming history, in 1382, princess Anqing, Ming Taizu's favorite daughter, married Ouyang Lun. But Ouyang Lun repeatedly sent people to smuggle tea out of the country for profit, which was against the Tea Law in the early Ming. Due to his status as the son-in-law of Ming Taizu, no official dared to question and stop him. Moreover, a servant of Ouyang Lun asked local officials to summon dozens of civilian carts for his personal use. He also reportedly beat and humiliated a local official. Unable to stand the shame, the local official reported directly to Ming Taizu. Upon hearing the news, Ming Taizu was so infuriated that he ordered Ouyang Lun to commit suicide and had his servant executed.[61]

Zhu Wenzheng was Ming Taizu's nephew who had closely followed his uncle in wars before the establishment of the Ming dynasty. In particular, Zhu Wenzheng made a great achievement in a decisive battle against Chen Youliang, Ming Taizu's most formidable enemy. Because of his military accomplishments, Ming Taizu granted Zhu Wenzheng the title of Grand General and promoted him to be the governor of Jiangxi province. But Zhu Wenzheng thought that his reward was not enough to match his achievements. Dissatisfied, Zhu Wenzheng chose to live in a licentious lifestyle and did not care about commoners. He also allegedly hired vicious staff to search and forcefully grab pretty women in the province to his home. After satisfying his sexual pleasure, those women would be thrown into a well alive. Local people were afraid of suing him because he was the emperor's nephew. Until one day, a brave official lodged an accusation against Zhu Wenzheng. Upon hearing the news that Zhu Wenzheng had been convicted, the empress tried to plead for mercy for him. Therefore, Ming Taizu did not kill his nephew but instead deprived him of all his official titles and sent him back to his hometown to guard the ancestors' tombs. When Zhu Wenzheng attempted to escape, Ming Taizu ordered his nephew to kill himself.[62]

Despite his unprecedented relentlessness and unselfishness in anticorruption, Ming Taizu later lamented that corruption could not be exterminated as one corrupt official was punished in the morning and in the evening another official would become corrupt. He then ordered to kill any corrupt official no matter how much bribe he had taken.[63]

The last ruler is Jiaqing (r. 1796–1820), an emperor of the late Qing dynasty (1644–1911). Jiaqing's father was Qianlong (r. 1735–1796), the longest living emperor in Chinese history. While the middle of the Qianlong reign was the heyday of the Qing dynasty, his later years were battered by official corruption and rebellions. When Jiaqing was crowned, Qianlong was still alive and thus Jiaqing had to tie his hands on anticorruption. It was not until 1799 after his father finally died that Jiaqing gained full power to fulfill his plan. The first and primary target of corruption was He Shen, a grand councilor and Qianlong's favorite official and servant. Born in poverty, He Shen joined the government as a low-rank official in 1769. But he quickly won the favor of Qianlong and was promoted to be a grand councilor, the most powerful official in the Qing.

With the favor of Qianlong, He Shen had in several decades amassed incredible amount of treasure and properties. According to the *Official History of the Qing*, He Shen was able to "sense the will of Qianlong" and used it for his own gains. If any official refused to side with him, He Shen would "find an opportunity to incite Qianlong's anger so as to fabricate charges against him." To help allies who had been accused of taking bribes, He Shen would "deliberately postpone the investigation and wait until Qianlong's rage to subside." Although the salt industry and river projects were usually lucrative, He Shen's insatiable demands greatly drained off their profits. After uprisings broke out in Sichuan and Hubei provinces triggered by local official misgovernment, the suppression was unsuccessful as most generals who had aligned with He Shen "wasted military funds and lived in extravagance."

While he was still the apparent heir, Jiaqing had already been quite aware of He Shen's corruption and malice. After he was enthroned in 1796 due to Qianlong's voluntary abdication, Jiaqing refrained from punishing He Shen because of Confucian filial piety. In early 1799, Qianlong died, one official seized the opportunity by charging He Sheng with corruption and law violations. Jiaqing promptly ordered to detain He Shen and asked top officials to investigate the case. Soon an edict listed twenty crimes that He Shen had allegedly committed. Most of the first fourteen crimes denounced He Shen's improper or irreverent behaviors, rites, and activities that only emperors or kings could enjoy. For example, the third crime said that He Shen rode his horse through the left gate of the Summer Palace (*yuanmingyuan*) and past the Guanming Hall. The fourth crime was that He Shen took a palace maid as his concubine, a right reserved for the emperor. The fifth crime criticized He Shen for not feeling melancholy when Qianlong was sick.

From crimes fifteen to twenty, the edict focused on He Shen's shocking and unparalleled corruption and, again, his disrespectful behaviors. A couple of crimes referred to his possession of over 200 pearl bracelets and numerous jades that far exceeded the imperial inventory; in He Shen's homes, investigators found silver and clothes totaling millions of taels and hoarded public gold of 30,000 pounds; He Shen was also accused of competing with commoners by owning many pawnshops and money shops; even his servant named Liu Quan had property that was worth over 200,000 taels along with many big pearl bracelets. He Shen's egregious corruption and disrespect sufficed to warrant his death. Because He Shen was a former grand councilor, Jiaqing ordered him to commit suicide instead of being executed in the market.[64] The crackdown of He Shen was the largest anticorruption effort under the Jiaqing reign, which scared other corrupt officials and, to some extent, slowed down the decline of the Qing.

XI'S ANTICORRUPTION IN A HISTORICAL COMPARISON

If we place Xi Jinping's anticorruption into the large context of Chinese history, we will find some similarities between him and one or all of the three dynastic rulers. In the first place, both Xi Jinping and rulers in the Tang, Qing, and especially the Ming dynasties have conducted an anticorruption from top to bottom rather than by commoners from the bottom, which would threaten the ruling party. Like Ming Taizu who relied mostly on the Imperial Embroidered Army (*jinyiwei*) to deal with corruption, Xi Jinping assigns the CDC to undertake the task.[65] By using the central organs that have often abused their power, both Ming Taizu and Xi Jinping have intentionally skipped the formal judicial system. Part of the reason may be that the judicial system is inefficient or uncooperative. More important, none of the rulers in the dynasties and China today has ever thought about establishing an independent and institutional framework against corruption.[66] For them, an independent anticorruption institution is an anathema that is worse than official corruption as it requires a profound overhaul of the political system on which their power depends. Without an independent political and judicial anticorruption mechanism, both Xi and his dynastic counterparts have to count on their trustworthy followers to attack and replace corrupt officials. In so doing, the seeds of future corruption are planted.

Secondly, both Xi Jinping and the emperors, no matter how enlightened they are, have used anticorruption to consolidate their power. In some respects, Xi and Jiaqing are more alike than Tang Taizong and Ming Taizu. As founding fathers, Tang Taizong and Ming Taizu have tremendous power and authority and their dynasties at the beginning were much healthier. But Jiaqing and Xi Jinping belong to rulers in the middle period who inherit (not found) a state that is very corrupt and is full of political and economic crises. One the one hand, people are dissatisfied with economic downturn and official corruption; on the other, both Jaiqing and Xi see their hands constrained by former rulers and top officials. In that regard, anticorruption would be a double-edged sword that could help them regain popular support and attack principal political adversaries.

Thirdly, while Xi and Jiaqing's anticorruption campaigns are overshadowed in terms of comprehensiveness, determination, or harshness by Tang Taizong and Ming Taizu, they (especially Xi's) nonetheless have made more significant inroads against corruption than their immediate predecessors.[67]

Despite their similarities, Xi's anticorruption also differs in several places from dynastic rulers. For instance, in contrast to dynastic rulers, Xi's power is far more limited and untenable. Unlike dynastic rulers who are emperors and have almost absolute power (Jiaqing after 1799) in the empire, Xi finds his power eclipsed by many former presidents who are still alive and, through their allies, still exert enormous influence in politics. Being restricted in power, Xi has been unable to assault the "biggest tigers" even if he had the intent. If he risks taking the step, Xi may end up facing the same fate as former Soviet leader Nikita Khrushchev who lost his power in a political coup in 1964. Hence, while Tang Taizong could discipline 1,000 corrupt officials in one year and punish an old follower and a royal relative who had been a prominent military commander, Ming Taizu was able to force his son-in-law and nephew to commit suicides and killed top officials such as a prime minister and a famed military general, and Jiaqing, the weakest of the three, could arrest and kill He Shen, the most corrupt and powerful grand councilor, Xi Jinping has yet to show the stamina to punish highly corrupt top officials (e.g., Zeng Qinghong) and the relatives of former leaders (e.g., Deng Xiaoping, Wen Jiabao, Li Peng, Jiang Zemin, etc.). There is no denying that Xi has toppled many powerful corrupt officials such as Bo Xilai, Zhou Yongkang, Ling Jihua, and Xu Caihou, yet his anticorruption has been dismissed as selective as most of those fallen officials are his political foes and more corrupt ones are still at large.

Another difference between Xi and dynastic rulers is that dynastic rulers would allow subjects and officials to complain against corrupt officials who had violated their rights. In the reigns of Ming Taizu and Jiaqing, both emperors had even encouraged aggrieved people to register skipping-level complaints (*yuesu*, banned by law since the Tang) against any official misconduct.[68] But Xi insists on relying mostly on CDC or central inspectors directly under his order to supervise officials and conduct investigations. Many of the "imperial commissioners" have reportedly used extralegal means in their interrogations resulting in scores of official suicides.[69] In the meantime, Xi has tightened the grip on public media particularly the booming social media, forced popular bloggers to make self-denunciations at the CCTV, secretly "kidnapped" Hong Kong booksellers publishing anti-Xi Jinping gossip books, and has shut down relatively outspoken media such as the *Southern Weekend* and *Yanhuang Chunqiu*.[70] Recently, Xi has also created a new ban on "improper discussion of the Party central," a reminiscence of the "literary inquisition" in the dynasties and the Cultural Revolution, to ward off any official from criticizing his policy. All of these new policies will inevitably undercut Xi's ongoing anticorruption efforts and leave little room for Xi to justify his intent of anticorruption against mounting suspicions and questions from overseas media and even his own nationals.

An Impossible Mission

The corruption that Xi Jinping and his cohorts have attempted to tackle has many facets rather than just one. The one people have talked about most is official corruption including, inter alia, taking bribes, misgovernment, lavish living style, and wasting public funds. But in fact, there are many other corruptions some of which may be more serious than official corruption. For example, judicial corruption is one thing that legal scholars and public media have chastised for many years. Social corruption (giving and accepting gifts, expensive banquets), corruption in hiring and promoting staff/officials regardless of ability (especially in banks and governments), and economic corruption (government-company entanglement) are other typical corruptions. The worst and imbedded corruption is institutional corruption (*zhidu fubai*), which is the root of a corrupt, hierarchical, authoritarian, and incompetent political system. The institutional corruption is nothing new in China today. It has been a diehard and fundamental system since as early as the Qin dynasty (221–206 BCE) and it gradually turned to be more stiff and dictatorial in the Ming and Qing dynasty when the rulers were increasingly paramount whereas officials became more subservient.[71]

Since late 2012, hundreds of officials have been detained and punished. But Xi Jinping's anticorruption has focused more or less on official, economic, and social corruptions and he has yet to show any sign to target other corruptions especially the institutional corruption. After top officials in the clique of Zhou Yongkang, Xu Caihou, and Bo Xilai have fallen down, many of their vacant positions have been filled by officials close to Xi Jinping instead of being selected through a fair and democratic method.[72] In this regard, Xi's anticorruption, like those in the Tang, Ming, and Qing, has failed to touch the root of Chinese corruption. Once Xi's anticorruption campaign dies down, corruption will retrieve its strength because its root is left intact and unharmed. However limited its intent and scope, Xi's anticorruption has drawn strong protests from many retired leaders and incumbent officials that he cannot ignore. According to Ji Shenying, author of *Party Remnants: The Lurker of the New "Gang of Four"* (*yudang: xinsirenbang deqianfuzhe*), Wang Qishan, the head of the CDC and Czar of Xi's anticorruption campaign, proposed "four patterns (*sizhong xingtai*)" in Fujian in September 2015, signaling the end of Xi's anticorruption.[73] The Xinhua News Agency, a key Party voice, reported that Wang stressed the importance of anticorruption in disciplining the Party. But Wang also said that it was incorrect to equate rectifying the Party with anticorruption.

In his words, Wang urged officials to prioritize discipline and rules and follow the Party central in their thinking, undertaking responsibility, and methods. Unlike his previous harsh tones against corrupt officials, Wang now suggested that Party discipline and organizational solution would be primary means in the future in dealing with corrupt officials. Only a small fraction of officials would face severe punishment and demotion. "The purpose of the four patterns," Wang stated, "is to rescue [malfeasant officials] and avert future crimes. We must morph the [past] bifurcation of either good Comrades or criminals to genuinely reflect the strict demands and loving concern of Party members."[74]

Wang Qishan's "Four Patterns" represents a departure from what Xi's anticorruption promised three years ago. It signifies the end of the first stage of anticorruption. Instead of unswervingly fighting both "tigers and flies," Xi's anticorruption will very likely shift its attention to "flies" more than to "tigers," much less the "big tigers." Some observers have denounced Wang's talk as "surrendering to the 'big tigers'." A researcher at Beijing University told reporters that Wang's "four patterns" tried to use criticism and warning rather than punishment to save most corrupt officials. Only "very minimal" number of officials would be investigated for serious crimes.[75]

If Wang Qishan's new direction mirrors the view of his boss Xi Jinping, it demonstrates that Xi's anticorruption has lost momentum. Indeed, starting from 2016, the pace of anticorruption has expressly slowed down and only a few high-profile top officials have been punished and most of them are still affiliated with Zhou Yongkang or Ling Jihua. None of the "bigger tigers" such as Zeng Qinghong and Li Xiaolin have been punished despite some rumors that they were under arrest and investigation by the CDC.[76]

While many ordinary Chinese people may feel disappointed at Wang Qishan's latest soft tone of anticorruption, it is doubtless that Xi's three-year anticorruption will become an impossible mission even if Xi and Wang were endeavored to proceed on their anticorruption initiative. It is true that Xi and Wang have punished many top corrupt officials, but the more the anticorruption campaign deepens, the more obstruction the campaign will encounter. With the embarrassing exposure of enormous corruption related to former leaders and Xi's own family, Xi's anticorruption efforts will attract more doubts than trust. Additionally, as more officials have either lost power or committed suicide, Xi will risk facing the danger of losing official support. In the PRC, few officials, if there is any, are honest and incorruptible. The reason is that Chinese people have no power to choose government officials and accordingly officials do not feel the need to woo people's support. To secure their power or obtain promotion, Chinese officials have to align with or bribe their superiors. In some cases, although public media, especially the central media, can occasionally exert their supervisory function on local officials and expose some minor corruptions, they have no audacity to publicize corruption or malfeasance of top officials (at the provincial level). As we have discussed before, Chinese judiciary has no independence and thus cannot make potent and impartial supervision or judgment against official corruption. The institutional corruption ingrained in Chinese history will not be eliminated without a major political reform. Even rulers as merciless as Ming Taizu has failed to completely uproot official corruption. Having no determined intent to cope with China's fundamental institutional problems, Xi's anticorruption is doomed to failure from its inception. Nevertheless, Xi still wants to fulfill his plan to solve China's problem of corruption through a silenced public, arbitrary arrests, and an apparently selective crackdown, which would merely make his goal less likely to prevail. Unlike Tang Taizong and Ming Taizu whose more powerful, balanced, and thorough anticorruption help clear the path for their centuries-long dynasties, Xi Jinping will be at best like emperor Jiaqing whose anticorruption, albeit praiseworthy to some degree, cannot prevent the states they govern from declining.

NOTES

1. This chapter was previously published as Q. Fang, "Xi Jinping's Anticorruption from a Historical Perspective" in *Modern China Studies*, 24 (2), 2017, pp. 112–138.

2. Macabe Keliher and Hsinchao Wu, "Corruption, Anticorruption, and the Transformation of Political Culture in Contemporary China" in *The Journal of Asian Studies*, 75 (1), February 2016, pp. 5–18: 2.

3. For Bo Xilai's campaign and the case of Wang Lijun see Qiang Fang and Xiaobing Li, *Legal Asymmetry: Power vs. Law in Urban China* (forthcoming, University Press of Kentucky, 2017); Samson Yuen, "Disciplining the Party: Xi Jinping's

Anticorruption Campaign and its Limits" in *China Perspectives*, 2014/3 (2014); *The Rise of Environmentalism*; pp. 41–47; Steven L. Myers and Mark Landler, "Frenzied Hours for U.S. on Fate of a China Insider" in *The New York Times*, April 17, 2012.

4. Han Feng and Ma Xueling, "An Analysis of Xi Jinping's Anticorruption Comments: Talking Harshly Against Corruption in all Key Points (*Xi Jinping fanfu lunshu shuli: Guanjiedian junlisheng fanfu*)" in *The People's Net*, January 13, 2015, http://finance.people.com.cn/n/2015/0113/c1004-26371554.html.

5. Michael Forsythe, "Database Tracks 'Tigers and Flies' Caught in Xi Kinping's Corruption Crackdown" in *The New York Times*, January 21, 2016.

6. Han Feng and Ma Xueling, January 13, 2015.

7. In the 1990s when Xi Jinping was the governor in Fujian province, Lai Changxing, the head of Xamen Yuanhua Corp had smuggled millions of tons of oil to make himself one of the richest men in China. He had also bribed local officials at both provincial and municipal levels. After the case was investigated in 2001, Lai exiled to Canada and was extradited back to China in 2012. For ChinaFile see Michael Forsythe, January 21, 2016; for Fujian corruption see Karby Leggett, "In a Land Where Bribes are Commonplace, A Chinese Millionaire Pushed the Envelope" in *The Wall Street Journal*, November 23, 2001,

8. Tania Branigan, "The Guardian Politburo, Army, Casinos: China's Corruption Crackdown Spreads" in *The Guardian*, February 2015.

9. "More than 120 Provincial Level Officials Have Fallen since the Eighteenth Plenary, Where is the Money Resulting from the Anticorruption? (*Shibada yilai 120yu shengbuji luoma, fanfu zhuihui zijin qunaerle*)" in *Wujie News*, December 31, 2015.

10. Zhang Yuxue, "Former Vice Head of the Logistic Department Gu Junshan is Exposed to be Involved in a Case of more than 20 billion (*Yuanzonghouqingbu fubuzhang Gu Junshan beibao shean 200 duoyi*)" in *Caijin net*, April 1, 2015.

11. Choi Chi-yuk, "Chinese Officials Facing Corruption Charges are Being Tempted by Suicide" in *South China Morning Post*, June 15, 2016.

12. Yu Le, "Anticorruption Resulting in Hard Times for Officials? Suicides among High-ranking Officials Breaks Record," June 13, 2016. http://china.dwnews.com/news/2016-06-13/59745814.html.

13. Both Bo Xilai and Ling Jihua were born into the privileged "Red Families (*hongerdai*)" who enjoy deep and enormous connections in the central government. While their crimes would suffice to death penalties, they were able to survive with only life sentences. For more information about the trials of Bo and Ling see Simon Denyer, "China's Ousted Official Bo Xilai Convicted of Corruption" in *The Washington Post*, September 22, 2013; Chun Han Wong, "Chinese Court Issues Life Sentence to Former Presidential Aide for Corruption" in *The Wall Street Journal*, July 4, 2016.

14. Macabe Keliher and Hsinchao Wu, 2016.

15. Samson Yuen, 2014.

16. Sha Lu, "Several Officials of the Development and Reform Commission have been Punished due to Violations of the Rules Regarding Banquet with Public Money and Accepting Gifts (*Fagaiwei duoming guanyuan gongkuan chihe weigui shouli beichufen*)" in *Xinjingbao*, April 17, 2016.

17. Murong Xuechun, "Xi's Selective Punishment" in *The New York Times*, January 16, 2015.

18. He Qinglian, "Government Monopolized Anticorruption Explicitly Reveals the Backwardness of China's Institutions (Zhengfu longduan fanfu tuxian zhongguo zhidu luohou)" in *The Voice of America*, February 7, 2014.

19. Minxin Pei, "China's War on Corruption Could Hasten Communist Party's Decline" in *Nikkei Asian Review*, May 19, 2015.

20. Zhou Yahui, "The Objective of Xi Jinping's Anticorruption is to Deal with Civilian Party (Xi Jinping fanfude mubiao shiduifu pingmindang)," August 15, 2014. www.boxun.com.

21. Zhang Lun, "The Increasing Appearance of the Drawbacks in China's Movement-type Anticorruption (*Zhongguo yundongshi fanfu biduan riyi chengxian*)" in *The French International Broadcast*, February 8, 2015; Ji Shenying, *The Remaining Members: The Lurker of the "New Gang of Four"* (*Yudang: xinsirenbang deqianfuzhe*) (Hong Kong: Neimu chubanshe, 2015), Chapter 2.

22. Editorial, "Is Xi Jinping's Movement-type Anticorruption going to Face Failure (Xin Jinping yundongshi fanfu mianling qiangong jingqi)?" in *The World Journal*, February 18, 2014.

23. Yang Ming, "A Review of CCP's Anticorruption in 2015 and a Prospect of 2016 (2015nian zhonggong fanfu huigu ji2016nian zhanwang)" in *The Voice of America*, December 17, 2015; for a similar argument also see Samson Yuen, 2014.

24. Yu Jie, "Why Can Xi Jinping's Authoritarian Anticorruption not to Succeed (Xi Jinpingde jiquanshi fanfu weiheshi yuanmu qiuyu)?" December 14, 2015. http://www.storm.mg/article/75811.

25. Si Yang, The Voice of America, July 29, 2014. http://www.voachinese.com/content/xijinping-next-challenge-20140728/1966601.html.

26. Samson Yuen, 2014: 44.

27. Zheng yongnian, *China Entering the Xi Jinping Era* (London: Routledge, 2015), 19–20.

28. Keliher and Wu, 2016: 5–7.

29. House of Cards is a Hollywood movie that depicts the relentless political struggle and conspiracy in American politics.

30. Shi Ping, "Fanfubai bushi quanli douzheng (Anticorruption is not Power Struggle)" in *Qiushi*, July 2016.

31. This is based on my recent trips to China in the past three years and talks with some relatives and friends in Chinese governments regarding the Eight-point Code.

32. The Australian newspaper is *Sydney Morning Herald*. See Zhong Chenfang, "People Unhappy to See the Remodeling of a Sydney Mansion by Zeng Qinghong's Son (*Zeng Qinghong zhizi Xini haozhai gaijian yincemu*)" in *Voice of America*, June 19, 2014; also see Odsseus Patrick, "For a Century, the Mansion Sat above Sydney Harbor. Then China's Nouveau Riche Arrived" in *The Washington Post*, June 17, 2014.

33. "250 million Jiang Jiemin Bought an Australian Mansion for Son of Zeng Qinghong" in *The World Journal*, February 15, 2014.

34. David Barboza, "Billions in Hidden Riches for Family of Chinese Leader" in *The New York Times*, October 25, 2012.

35. Andrew Jacobs, "China Appears Set to force Times Reporter to Leave" in *The New York Times*, January 27, 2014.

36. Minxin Pei, "Crony Communism in China" in *The New York Times*, October 17, 2014.

37. Samson Yuen, 2014: 44; Zheng Yongnian 2015: 20.

38. See Sebastian Veg, "China's Political Spectrum under Xi Jinping" in *The Diplomat*, August 11, 2014; Dan Levin, "China Tells Schools to Suppress Western Ideas, with One Big Exception" in *The New York Times*, February 9, 2015; Felicia Sonmez, "Free Speech in China Gets an Unlikely State-Media Backer" in *The Wall Street Journal*, February 17, 2016.

39. For the differences between the rule of law and the rule by law see Qiang Fang and Roger Des Forges, "Were Chinese Rulers above the Law? Toward a Theory of the Rule of Law in China from Early Times to the Present" in *Stanford Journal of International Law*, 44 (1), 2007, pp. 101–146.

40. Macabe Keliher and Hsinchao Wu, 2016.

41. Ibid.

42. Shi Ping, 2016.

43. David Barboza and Sharon Lafraniere, "'Princelings' in China Use Family Ties to Gain Riches" in *The New York Times*, May 17, 2012; Emily Rauhala, "As Panama Leaks Spread, China's 'Red Nobility' Would Rather Not Talk about it" in *The Washington Post*, April 7, 2016.

44. Sneha Shankar, "Li Xiaolin, Former Chinese Premier Li Peng's Daughter, Hid over $2M In HSBC Swiss Account" in *The International Business Times*, February 10, 2015.

45. "Chinese Luxury Water? Tibet 5100 Aims High" in *The Washington Post*, October 5, 2012; He Long, "Behind Railway Bureau Cancels Free High-Speed Train Water: Tibet5100 Wholesale Price is Higher than Retail Price (*Tiezong quxiao gaotie mianfeishui beihou: Xizang5100 caigoujia gaoyu lingshoujia*)" in *Yangcheng Evening News*, July 28, 2015.

46. Michael Forsythe, "Database Tracks 'Tigers and Flies' Caught in Xi Jinping's Corruption Crackdown" in *The New York Times*, January 21, 2016.

47. Andrew Jacobs, Javier C. Hernandez, and Chris Buckley, "Behind Deadly Tianjin Blast, Shortcuts and Lax Rules" in *The New York Times*, August 30, 2015; Editorial Board, "A Deadly Landslide Exposes the Depths of China's Corruption and Censorship" in *The Washington Post*, December 29, 2015.

48. Josh Chin, "Chinese Lawyer Sentenced to Seven Years in Prison" in *The Wall Street Journal*, August 4, 2016.

49. Bu Xianqun, *Corruption and Anticorruption in Chinese History (Zhongguo lishishangde fubai yufanfubai)* (Fujian: Lujiang chubanshe, 2014), 62.

50. Denis Twitchett, "How to Be an Emperor: T'ang T'ai-tsung's Vision of His Role" in *Asia Major* (3rd Series), 9(1/2), (1996), pp. 1–10.

51. Sima Guang, The Comprehensive Mirror for Aid in Government (*Zizhi tongjian*) (Beijing: Zhonghua shujü, 1956), juan 196.

52. Liu Xu, *The Old History of the Tang* (*jiutangshu*) (Beijing: Zhonghua shujü, 1975), juan 60.

53. Zhu Yuyang and Gui Jie, "A Record of State Governing under Tang Taizong: Discussing How the Tang Dynasty Opposed Corruption (*Tang Taizong zhiguo fengyunlu: tantao tangchao ruhe fanfu*)" in *The China Youth Daily*, August 22, 2014.

54. "Scholars Talk about Ancient Anticorruption: 'Beating Tigers' was Most Forceful in the Early Tang and Ming Dynasties (*Xuezhe tangudai fanfu: Tang zhenguan shiqi he Mingchu 'dahu' zuimeng*)" in *The China Youth Daily*, February 13, 2015.

55. Edward Farmer, *Zhu Yuanzhang and Early Ming Legislation* (Leiden: E.J. Brill, 1995), 2; John Dardess, *Confucianism and Autocracy* (California: University of California Press, 1983), 187.

56. Zhang Zhiguang, "Anticorruption in Chinese History (*Zhongguo lishishang defanfu*)" in *Shanghai guancha*, May 29, 2014.

57. Wu Han, *A Biography of Ming Taizu* (*Ming Taizuzhuan*) (Tianjin: Baihua wenyi chubanshe, 2001), 265.

58. Wu Han, 2001: 267.

59. Wang Tianyou and Xu Daling, *Sixteen Ming Emperors* (Mingchao shiliudi) (Beijing: Zijincheng chubanshe, 1991), 31; Wu Han, 2001: 271.

60. Wang Tianyou and Xu Daling, 1991: 34; Wu Han, 2000: 266.

61. Zhang Tingyu, *The History of the Ming* (*Mingshi*) (Beijing: Zhonghua shujü, 1974), juan 121.

62. Wang Lei, "Ming Taizu Zhu Yuanzhang's Anticorruption did not Exempt Relatives: He Killed his Own Nephew and Son-in-Law for the Cause of Anticorruption (*Ming Taizu Zhu Yuanzhang chengtan bubiqin: weifanfu chusi qinzhizi yuqinnuxu*)" in *Fenghuang lishi*, July 1, 2014. http://news.ifeng.com/a/20140701/40965124_0.shtml.

63. Sun Deyue, "Zhu Yuanzhang Lamented: Why Can Corrupt Officials not be Exterminated (Zhu Yuanzhang gantan: tanguan weihe shabujue)?" March 1, 2015. http://blog.people.com.cn/article/1425168463506.html.

64. Zhao Erxun, *The Draft History of the Qing* (*qingshigao*) (Beijing: Zhonghua shuju, 1982), juan 319.

65. Samson Yuen, 2014: 45.

66. Minxin Pei, 2015; Samson Yuen, 2014: 47.

67. Jiaqing's forefathers such as Kangxi, Yongzheng, and Qianlong, though all of them had attacked corruption, none of them had charged and killed top officials like He Shen.

68. For a complete study on the Chinese complaint systems see Qiang Fang, *Chinese Complaint Systems: Natural Resistance* (London: Routledge, 2013).

69. Mu Xiaoyi, "China Sees High Frequency of Official Suicides: [Officials] Would Rather Meet the Death God than Lao Wang (Zhongguo guanyuan zisha shijian pinfa: ningjian yanwang bujian laowang)" in *The Voice of America*, March 26, 2016.

70. For China's recent crackdowns on public media see Beina Xu, "Media Censorship in China" in *Council on Foreign Relations*, April 7, 2015; William Wan, "China Broadcasts Confession of Chinese-American Blogger" in *The Washington Post*, September 15, 2013; Tom Phillips, "China Behaving Like 'Gangster' State with Bookseller Kidnap, Say Hong Kong Politicians" in *The Guardian*, June 17, 2016.

71. For a good study on the rise of rulers' power and the decline of official status see Lin Qian, *Power and Law in Traditional China* (*Chuantong zhongguo dequanyufa*) (Beijing: Law Press, 2013).

72. "Xi Jinping's Followers Appointed in Military is Exposed to Firmly Control Five Key Positions (*Xi Jinping junzhong qinxin buju baoguang wenkong wuda buwei*)" in *China Examiner*, August 18, 2015; "Xi Jinping Frequently Promotes Favorites in the Layout of the Nineteenth Part Congress" in *The World Journal*, May 29, 2016.

73. Ji Shenying, *Party Remnants: The Lurker of the New "Gang of Four"* (*yudang: xinsirenbang deqianfuzhe*) (Hong Kong: Neimu chubanshe, 2015), Chapter 2.

74. Wang Qishan, "Grasping and Utilizing the 'Four Patterns' in Supervising and Disciplining" in *The Xinhua News Agency*, September 26, 2015.

75. Ji Shenying, 2015: Chapter 2.

76. Yang Fan, "The Latest Hearsay: Zeng Qinghong's Secret Detention Place is Exposed (*Zuixin chuanwen: Zeng Qinghong mimi guanya didian baoguang*)" in *Secret China*, July 13, 2014. http://m.secretchina.com/node/546794.

BIBLIOGRAPHY

1968. *Verifiable Records of Qing Shengzu* (*Daqing shengzu shilu*) vol. 39.

1984. *Documents of the Guangxü Reign* (*Guangxüchao donghualu*). Beijing: Zhonghua shujü.

Alexander, Herbert E. 1984. "Making Sense About Dollars in the 1980 Presidential Campaigns" in Michael J. Malbin, ed., *Money and Politics in the United States: Financing Elections in the 1980s*. New Jersey: Chatham House Publishers.

Anticorruption White Paper (*fantanfu baipishu*), United and Self-Strengthening Association in the Republic of China, June 30, 2010.

Arnsdorf, Isaac. "Trump Rewards Big Donors with Jobs and Access." *Politico*, December 27, 2016.

Ballhaus, Rebecca and Mulins, Brody. "Corporations Bet on GOP Senate Control." *The Wall Street Journal*, November 7, 2016.

Barboza, David. "Billions in Hidden Riches for Family of Chinese Leader." *The New York Times*, October 25, 2012.

Barboza, David and Lafraniere, Sharon. "'Princelings' in China Use Family Ties to Gain Riches." *The New York Times*, May 17, 2012.

Bartlett, Beatrice S. 1990. *Monarchs and Ministers: The Grand Council in Mid-Ch'ing China, 1723–1820*. Berkeley: University of California Press.

Berg, Larry L., Hahn, Harlan and Schmidhauser, John R. 1976. *Corruption in the American Political System*. New Jersey: Central Learning Press.

Blinder, Alan. "U.S. Ends Corruption Case Against Former Virginia Governor." *The New York Times*, September 8, 2016.

Bodde, Derk. 1967. *Peking Diary: 1948–1949 A Year of Revolution*. Minnesota: Fawcett Publications.

Branigan, Tania. "The Guardian Politburo, Army, Casinos: China's Corruption Crackdown Spreads." *The Guardian*, February 2015.

Bu, Xianqun. 2014. *Corruption and Anticorruption in Chinese History (Zhongguo lishishangde fubai yufanfubai)*. Fujian: Lujiang chubanshe.

Chen, Zhiping. "The Seeing Clearly the Customary Fees of Late Qing Learning Officials in the Case of Wang Kaitai (*cong Wang Kaitaian kanqing qingmo xueguande lougui*)" in *Zhongguo shehui jingjishi yanjiu*, Vol. 3, 2013, pp. 84–7.

Chin, Josh. "Chinese Lawyer Sentenced to Seven Years in Prison." *The Wall Street Journal*, August 4, 2016.

Choi, Chi-yuk. "Chinese Officials Facing Corruption Charges Are Being Tempted by Suicide." *South China Morning Post*, June 15, 2016.

Cohen, Paul. "Changes over Time in Qing History: The Importance of Context" in *Late Imperial China*, Vol. 37, No. 1, June 2016, pp. 10–3.

Condon, George E., Jr. "Disgraced Congressman Randy 'Duke' Cunningham is a Free Man Again." *The Atlantic*, July 10, 2014.

Confessore, Nicholas and Luo, Michael. "Perry Mines Texas System to Raise Cash." *New York Times*, August 20, 2011.

Dardess, John. *Confucianism and Autocracy*, California: University of California Press.

Deng, Yuwen. "Comment." *The New York Times*, May 9, 2017.

Denyer, Simon. "China's Ousted Official Bo Xilai Convicted of Corruption." *The Washington Post*, September 22, 2013.

Eastman, Lloyd E. 1984. *Seeds of Destruction: Nationalist China in War and Revolution, 1937–1949*. Stanford: Stanford University Press.

Editorial Board. "A Deadly Landslide Exposes the Depths of China's Corruption and Censorship." *The Washington Post*, December 29, 2015.

Elliot, Mark C. 2001. *The Manchu Way: The Eight Banners and Ethnic Identity in Late Imperial China*. Stanford: Stanford University Press.

Fang, Qiang. "Hot Potatoes: Chinese Complaint Systems from Early Times to 1898" in the *Journal of Asian Studies*, Vol. 68. No. 4, November 2009, pp. 1105–35.

———. "A Silent 'Revolution': The Late Qing Reform on the Jumping Appeals" in *The Journal of Asian History*, Vol. 46, No. 1, 2012, pp. 97–116.

———. 2013a. *Chinese Complaint Systems: Natural Resistance*. U.K.: Routledge.

———. 2013b. *A Short History of Chinese Petition* (*zhongguo shangfang zhidu shihua*). Beijing: China Youth Press.

Fang, Qiang and Des Forges, Roger. "Were Chinese Rulers Above the Law? Toward a Theory of the Rule of Law in Chinese History" in *Stanford Journal of International Law*, Vol. 44. No. 1, 2017, pp. 101–146.

Fang, Qiang and Li, Xiaobing. 2017. *Power Versus Law in Modern China: Cities, Courts, and the Communist Party*. Lexington: University Press of Kentucky.

Farmer, Edward. 1983. *Zhu Yuanzhang and Early Ming Legislation*. Leiden: E.J. Brill, 1995, 2.

Fenby, Jonathan. 2004. *Chiang Kai-shek: China's Generalissimo and the Nation he Lost*. New York: Carroll & Graf Publishers.

Ferguson, Charles H. 2012. *Predator Nation: Corporate Criminals, Political Corruption and the Hijacking of America*. Crown Publishing Group.

Feuer, Alan. "Why Are Corruption Cases Crumbling? Some Blame the Supreme Court." *The New York Times*, November 17, 2017.

Forsythe, Michael. "Database Tracks 'Tigers and Flies' Caught in Xi Jinping's Corruption Crackdown." *The New York Times*, January 21, 2016.

Forsythe, Michael. "Database Tracks 'Tigers and Flies' Caught in Xi Kinping's Corruption Crackdown." *The New York Times*, January 21, 2016.

Fu, Zhengyuan. 1993. *Automatic Tradition and Chinese Politics*. Cambridge: Cambridge University Press.

Gao, Hong. "The Fundamental Cause of Lost 1895 War is Qing Corruption (*jiawu zhanzheng shibaide genben yuanyinshi Qingchaode fubai*)" in *The Journal of Qiqihaer Normal College*, Vol. 5, 1995, pp. 158–60.

Gao, Hua. 2011. *How the Red Sun Rises?* (*gongtaiyang shiruhe shengqide*). Hong Kong: Hong Kong Chinese University Press.

Goodpaster, Gary. 2002. "Reflections on Corruption in Indonesia" in Timothy Lindsey and Howard W. Dick, eds., *Corruption in Asia: Rethinking the Governance Paradigm*. Australia: The Federation Press.

Gore, Al. 2013. *The Future: Six Drives of Global Change*. New York: Random House Publishing Group.

Guy, R. Kent. 2017. *Qing Governors and Their Provinces: The Evolution of Territorial Administration in China, 1644–1796*. Seattle: University of Washington Press.

He, Qinglian. "Government Monopolized Anticorruption Explicitly Reveals the Backwardness of China's Institutions (Zhengfu longduan fanfu tuxian zhongguo zhidu luohou)." *The Voice of America*, February 7, 2014.

Helderman, Rosalind S. and Vozzella, Laura. "Va. Gov. McDonnell on Two-Way Street with Chief Executive of Struggling Company." *The Washington Post*, March 30, 2013.

Ho, Ping-ti. 1964. *The Ladder of Success in Imperial China*. Columbia: Columbia University Press.

Hofstadter, Richard. 1989. *The American Political Tradition and the Men Who Made it*. New York: Vintage Books.

Hucker, Charles. 1966. *Censorial System of Ming China*. Stanford: Stanford University Press.

Ingraham, Christopher. "Somebody Just Put a Price Tag on the 2016 Election. It's a Doozy." *Washington Post*, April 14, 2017.

Jacobs, Andrew. "China Appears Set to Force Times Reporter to Leave." *The New York Times*, January 27, 2014.

Jacobs, Andrew, Hernandez, Javier C., and Buckley, Chris. "Behind Deadly Tianjin Blast, Shortcuts and Lax Rules." *The New York Times*, August 30, 2015.

Ji, Shenying. 2015. *Party Remnants: The Lurker of the New "Gang of Four"* (*yudang: xinsirenbang deqianfuzhe*). Hong Kong: Neimu chubanshe.

———. 2015. *The Remaining Members: The Lurker of the "New Gang of Four"* (*Yudang: xinsirenbang deqianfuzhe*). Hong Kong: Neimu chubanshe.

Keliher, Macabe. "Administrative Law and the Making of the First *Da Qing Huidian*" in *Late Imperial China*, Vol. 37, No. 1, June 2016, pp. 55–108.

Keliher, Macabe and Wu, Hsinchao. "Corruption, Anticorruption, and the Transformation of Political Culture in Contemporary China" in *The Journal of Asian Studies*, Vol. 75, No. 1, February 2016, pp. 5–18.

Ketcham, Ralph, ed. 2006. *Selected Writings of James Madison*. Indianapolis: Hackett Publishing.

Leggett, Karby. "In a Land Where Bribes are Commonplace, A Chinese Millionaire Pushed the Envelope." *The Wall Street Journal*, November 23, 2001.

Levin, Dan. "China Tells Schools to Suppress Western Ideas, with One Big Exception." *The New York Times*, February 9, 2015.

Li, Boyuan. 2013. *Exposure of the Official World* (guanchang xianxingji). Zhejiang: Zhejiang chuabn jituan.

Li, Chunmei. 2005. "A Preliminary Study on the Customary fee Income of Governors in Early Qing (*shitan qingchao qianqi dufude lougui shouru*)" in *The Journal of Neimenggu Social Science*, Vol. 26, No. 4, July.

Liang, Hong, ed. 2003. *The Ancient Book* (*shangshu*). Hunan: Shidai wenyi chubanshe.

Lichtblau, Eric. "Lawmakers' Ties to Toyota Questioned at Start of Inquiries." *The New York Times*, February 23, 2010.

Lin, Qian. 2013. *Power and Law in Traditional China* (*Chuantong zhongguo dequanyufa*). Beijing: Law Press.

Liu, E. 2017. *The Travels of Lao Can* (laocan youji). Zhejiang: Zhejiang wenyi chubanshe.

Liu, Xu. 1975. *The Old History of the Tang* (*jiutangshu*). Beijing: Zhonghua shujü.

Lubman, Stanley. 1999. *Bird in a Cage: Legal Reform in China after Mao*. Stanford: Stanford University Press.

Ma, Jun. "Corruption Defeated Late Qing Army: Elite Eight Banners Could not Ride Horses and Half of them Fell (*fubai jikua qingjundui: baqi jingbing buhui qima shiren shangma banshuluo*)." *Wenhui dushu zhoubao*, December 13, 2010.

Marcus, Robert D., Burner, David, and Marcus, Anthony eds. 2007. *American Firsthand: Vol II. Readings from Reconstruction to the Present*. New York: Bedfor/St. Martin's.

Markon, Jerry. "Ex-Rep. Jefferson (D. La) Gets 13 Years in Freezer Cash Case." *The Washington Post*, November 14, 2009.

Meisner, Maurice. 1996. *The Deng Xiaoping Era: An Inquiry into the Fate of Chinese Socialism, 1978–1994*. New York: Hill & Wang.

———. 1999. *Mao's China and After: A history of the People's Republic*. New York: Free Press.

Murong, Xuechun. "Xi's Selective Punishment." *The New York Times*, January 16, 2015.

Myers Steven L. and Landler, Mark. "Frenzied Hours for U.S. on Fate of a China Insider." *The New York Times*, April 17, 2012.

Ni, Shawn and Van, Pham Hoang. 2006. "High Corruption Income in Ming and Qing China" *Journal of Development Economics*.

Nie, Da. "Corruption behind the Frivolity: The Relationship between Governmental and Cultural Corruption in the Dream of Red Mansion (*fuhua beihoude fubai: cong Hongloumeng kan guanchang fubai yuminfeng fubai deguanxi*)." *Zhongguo jijian jianchabao*, November 14, 2014.

Niu, Chuangping and Niu, Jiqing, eds. 2000. *Verifiable Records of the Economic Criminal Cases of Qing First and Second Ranking Officials (Qingdai yierpin guanyuan jingji fanzui anjian shilu)*. Beijing: Zhongguo fazhi chubanshe.

Pei, Minxin. "Crony Communism in China." *The New York Times*, October 17, 2014.

———. "China's War on Corruption Could Hasten Communist Party's Decline." *Nikkei Asian Review*, May 19, 2015.

———. 2016. *China's Crony Capitalism*. Harvard: Harvard University Press.

Park, Nancy E. "Corruption in Eighteenth-century China" in *The Journal of Asian Studies*, Vol. 56, No. 4, November 2017.

———. 2016. "Unofficial Perspectives on Torture in Ming and Qing China" in *Late Imperial China*, Vol. 37, No. 1, pp: 17–54.

Patrick, Odsseus. "For a Century, the Mansion Sat above Sydney Harbor. Then China's Nouveau Riche Arrived." *The Washington Post*, June 17, 2014.

Perdue, Peter C. 2010. *China Marches West: The Qing Conquest of Central Eurasia*. Harvard: Harvard University Press.

Phillips, Tom. "China Behaving Like 'Gangster' State with Bookseller Kidnap, Say Hong Kong Politicians." *The Guardian*, June 17, 2016.

Prazniak, Roxann. 1996. *Of Camel Kings and Other Things: Rural Rebels against Modernity in Late Imperial China*. Lanham: Rowman & Littlefield.

Rauhala, Emily. "As Panama Leaks Spread, China's 'Red Nobility' Would Rather not Talk About it." *The Washington Post*, April 7, 2016.

Reed, Bradly. 2000. *Talons and Teeth: County Clerks and Runners in the Qing Dynasty*. Stanford: Stanford University Press.

Rowe, William T. 2010. *China's Last Empire: The Great Qing*. Harvard: Harvard University Press.

Schrecker, John E. 1991. *The Chinese Revolution in Historical Perspective*. New York: Praeger.

Seagrave, Sterling. 1986. *The Soong Dynasty*. New York: Harper & Row Publishers.

———. 1992. *Dragon Lady: The Life and Legend of the Last Empress of China*. New York: Vintage Books.

Sha, Lu. "Several Officials of the Development and Reform Commission have been Punished due to Violations of the Rules Regarding Banquet with Public Money and Accepting Gifts (*Fagaiwei duoming guanyuan gongkuan chihe weigui shouli beichufen*)." *Xinjingbao*, April 17, 2016.

Shankar, Sneha. "Li Xiaolin, Former Chinese Premier Li Peng's Daughter, Hid over $2M In HSBC Swiss Account." *The International Business Times*, February 10, 2015.

Sheridan, James E. 1966. *Chinese Warlord: The Career of Feng Yu-hsiang*. Stanford: Stanford University Press.

Shi, Minglei and Li, Xueyin. "An Investigation of Gifts on the Teachers' Day (*jiaoshijie songli diaocha*)." *Xinjingbao*, September 10, 2013.

Shi, Ping. "Fanfubai bushi quanli douzheng (Anticorruption is not Power Struggle)." *Qiushi*, July 2016.

Sima, Guang. 1956. *Comprehensive Mirror for Assisting Government* (*zizhi tongjian*). Beijing: Zhonghua shuju.

Smith, Richard J. 2005. *The Qing Dynasty and Traditional Chinese Culture*. Rowman & Littlefield.

Sonmez, Felicia. "Free Speech in China Gets an Unlikely State-Media Backer." *The Wall Street Journal*, February 17, 2016.

Spence, Jonathan. 1981. *The Gate of Heavenly Peace: The Chinese and Their Revolution, 1895–1980*. New York: Penguin Books.
———. 1991. *The Search for Modern China*. New York: W.W. Norton & Company.
———. 2001. *Treason by the Book*. New York: Viking Press.
Sun, Yat-sen. 1981. *The Complete Works of Sun Yat-sen* (*Sun Zhongshan quanji*). Beijing: Zhonghua shuju.
Teachout, Zephyr. 2014. *Corruption in America: From Benjamin Franklin's Snuff Box to Citizens United*. Harvard: Harvard University Press.
Thiessen, Marc A. "Crony Capitalism Exposed." *The Washington Post*, November 14, 2011.
Tipton, Frank B. 2008. *Asian Firms: History, Institutions and Management*. U.K.: Edward Elgar Publishing.
Transparency International. "Corruption Perfections Index 2015." https://www.iaca.int/images/news/2016/Corruption_Perceptions_Index_2015_report.pdf.
Twitchett, Denis. 1996. *How to Be an Emperor: T'ang T'ai-tsung's Vision of His Role*, *in* 9 Asia Major 1–3, 92–97. 3rd ed.
Veg, Sebastian. "China's Political Spectrum under Xi Jinping." *The Diplomat*, August 11, 2014.
Vogal, Ezra F. 1969. *Canton under Communism: Programs and Politics in a Provincial Capital, 1949–1968*. Harvard: Harvard University Press.
Wakeman, Frederic jr. 1985. *The Great Enterprise: The Manchu Reconstruction of Imperial Order in Seventeenth-century China*. Berkeley: University of California Press.
———. 2003. *Policing Shanghai: 1927–1937*. Stanford: Stanford University Press.
———. 2003. Spymaster: *Dai Li and the Chinese Secret Service*. Stanford: Stanford University Press.
Wan, William. "China Broadcasts Confession of Chinese-American Blogger." *The Washington Post*, September 15, 2013.
Wang, Qishan. "Grasping and Utilizing the 'Four Patterns' in Supervising and Disciplining." *The Xinhua News Agency*, September 26, 2015.
Wang, Tianyou and Xu, Daling. 1991. *Sixteen Emperors in the Ming Dynasty* (*mingchao shiliudi*). Beijing: Zijincheng chubanshe.
Wong, Chun Han. "Chinese Court Issues Life Sentence to Former Presidential Aide for Corruption." *The Wall Street Journal*, July 4, 2016.
Wu, Han. 2000. *Biography of Zhu Yuanzhang* (*Zhu Yuanzhangzhuan*). Zhejiang: Baihua wenyi chubanshe.
———. 2001. *A Biography of Ming Taizu* (*Ming Taizuzhuan*). Tianjin: Baihua wenyi chubanshe.
Xu, Beina. "Media Censorship in China." *Council on Foreign Relations*, April 7, 2015.
Yang, Fan. "The Latest Hearsay: Zeng Qinghong's Secret Detention Place is Exposed (*Zuixin chuanwen: Zeng Qinghong mimi guanya didian baoguang*)." *Secret China*, July 13, 2014. http://m.secretchina.com/node/546794.
Yang, Hegao. 1979. *Selected Works of Ancient Politics and Law (gudai zhengfa wenxuan)*. Beijing: Beijing zhengfa xueyuan.

Yang, Jia Lynn, Hamburger, Tom and ElBoghdady, Dina. "Ways Investors Gain 'Political' Facing Public Scrutiny." *The Washington Post*, May 9, 2013.

Yuen, Samson. "Disciplining the Party: Xi Jinping's Anticorruption Campaign and its Limits." *China Perspectives*, Vol. 2014, No. 3, 2014.

Zeleny, Jeff and Thee-Brenan, Megan. "New Poll Finds a Deep Distrust of Government." *The New York Times*, October 25, 2011.

Zhang, Jixin. 2016. *Things Seen and Heard about Bureaucracy in both the Daoguang and Xianfeng Reigns* (*daoxian huanhai jianwenlu*). Beijing: Zhonghua shuju.

Zhang, Lun. "The Increasing Appearance of the Drawbacks in China's Movement-type Anticorruption (*Zhongguo yundongshi fanfu biduan riyi chengxian*)." *The French International Broadcast*, February 8, 2015.

Zhang, Tingyu. 1974. *The History of the Ming* (*Mingshi*). Beijing: Zhonghua shujü.

Zhang, Yuxue. "Former Vice Head of the Logistic Department Gu Junshan is Exposed to be Involved in a Case of more than 20billion (*Yuanzonghouqingbu fubuzhang Gu Junshan beibao shean 200 duoyi*)." *Caijin net*, April 1, 2015.

Zhang, Zhiguang. "Anticorruption in Chinese History (*Zhongguo lishishang defanfu*)." *Shanghai guancha*, May 29, 2014.

Zhao, Erxun. 1982. *The Draft History of the Qing* (*qingshigao*). Beijing: Zhonghua shuju.

Zheng, Yongnian. 2015. *China Entering the Xi Jinping Era*. U.K.: Routledge.

Zhong, Chenfang. "People Unhappy to See the Remodeling of a Sydney Mansion by Zeng Qinghong's Son (*Zeng Qinghong zhizi Xini haozhai gaijian yincemu*)." *Voice of America*, June 19, 2014.

Zhou, Yahui. "The Objective of Xi Jinping's Anticorruption is to Deal with Civilian Party (Xi Jinping fanfude mubiao shiduifu pingmindang)." August 15, 2014. www.boxun.com.

"*Zhu Yuanzhang chengtan bubiqin: weifanfu chusi qinzhizi yuqinnuxu*)." *Fenghuang lishi*, July 1, 2014. http://news.ifeng.com/a/20140701/40965124_0.shtml.

Zhu, Yuyang and Gui, Jie. "A Record of State Governing under Tang Taizong: Discussing How the Tang Dynasty Opposed Corruption (*Tang Taizong zhiguo fengyunlu: tantao tangchao ruhe fanfu*)." *The China Youth Daily*, August 22, 2014.

Conclusion

Anticorruption: A Global Thorny Task

Qiang Fang and Xiaobing Li

CORRUPTION IS A GLOBAL ISSUE

In this book, most chapters have discussed corruption and anticorruption in modern China from a variety of perspectives. They have shown that China, whatever the polity is a dynasty or a republic, has been battered by serious corruption in most, if not all, modern periods. As Xiaobing Li has argued, bureaucratic corruption in the later Republic was so widespread and uncontrollable that it finally cost Chiang Kai-shek his regime in China. The anticorruption campaigns launched by rulers in both the family-state Qing (e.g., Qianlong and Jiaqing) and the Party-states such as the Republic of China (e.g., Yuan Shikai, Jiang Jinguo's anticorruption) and the People's Republic of China (early PRC) have largely failed due to either the gravity, unrestraint, or the prevalence of the corruption. Since Deng Xiaoping kicked off its sweeping reform in 1978, official corruption has become increasingly serious and has drawn enormous discontents from the populace. Today, four decades after the reform and nearly six years after Xi Jinping launched his anticorruption campaign, corruption in China remains a constant challenge, which is like an incurable cancer that has deeply penetrated almost all parts of the nation such as judiciary, military, academia, companies, charity, hospitals, and even elementary schools.[1] The authoritarian nature of communist China plus capitalism and the slogan "being rich is glorious" only worsens bureaucratic misconducts and social corruption.

In dynastic or republican China alike, rulers or the central governments have promulgated draconian laws against corruption. In the Qing dynasty, for example, a "dirty graft" of as little as eighty taels of silver would suffice to a deferred capital punishment. To clamp down unbridled official corruption, Qing and republican rulers have executed many high-ranking officials such as former grand councilor Heshen in the Jiaqing reign, the Beijing mayor under Yuan Shikai (chapter 3), seasoned communist cadres Liu Qingshan and Zhang Zishan in the early PRC (chapter 6), and the recent life sentences of Bo Xilai and Sun Zhengcai (chapter 11), both of them were former Politburo members. Yet, those high-profiled anticorruption cases have nonetheless failed to thwart bureaucratic corruption, much less to uproot the basis of corruption.

In the conclusion, we would like to examine corruption beyond China's boundary. Some of the questions to be addressed are: Is China the only country that suffers official corruption? Does China have the worst corruption in the world? To what extent are forms and severity of corruption in China similar to other countries? Do democratic nations have less corruption than their authoritarian counterparts? Will democracy be the only solution to solve political corruption?

To be sure, corruption is anything but limited to China. It was and still is a thorny problem all nations have to grapple with and no nation can boast that it is immune to corruption. According to the annual report of the Transparency International, an international nongovernmental organization based in Berlin, Germany, no country is "corruption free." The most incorruptible states such as Denmark and New Zealand score about 90.[2] According to José Ugaz, chair of the Transparency international, corruption remains a big problem of the world and "6 billion people live in a country with a serious corruption problem."[3] The corruption index testifies that democracy may not have less corruption than authoritarianism. Many traditional democratic states including the United States (No.18) and Japan (No.20) are more corrupt than Singapore (No.7) whose one-party rule has long been a target of the West. Moreover, while China is widely regarded as an authoritarian country with grave corruption, its democratic neighbor India does not perform better and had the same score as China in the 2016 corruption index of the Transparency international.[4]

In particular, to better grapple the fundamental human problem of corruption, we want to conduct a relatively in-depth analysis on the political and social corruptions in the United States, a nation whose territorial size is comparable to that of China and whose politicians and people have often touted their long and stable democracy and freedom. As the most powerful democratic country in the world, the United States has always been a model of democracy and, however selective, selfish, and inconsistent, a relatively staunch defender of freedom and democracy in the world. Yet, when we have the chance to look into the political and social corruption within the United States, we are astonished to ferret out far-reaching and deeply rooted corruption in almost all social circles. Charles H. Ferguson, a political observer, denounces the United States politics as being dominated by money. "Starting around 1980, American society began to undergo a series of deep shifts," Ferguson points out, "Deregulation, weakened antitrust enforcement, and technological changes led to increasing concentration of industry and finance. Money began to play a larger and more corrupting role in politics."[5]

The width and depth of corruption in the United States testifies that corruption is never confined to an authoritarian polity. Rather, it is a global disease or epidemic that has gripped all states and all polities. Most democratic states may have better check on corruption than states ruled by either dictators or one political party, but they are not able to eliminate corruption. As Lord Acton's often cited admonition tells us, "Power tends to corrupt and absolute power corrupts absolutely."[6] So long as power exists in a state, there will be certain form of corruption.

Illegal Corruption in the United States

Like China, US government and state laws have outlawed many forms of corruption. One of them is for politicians to take bribes from companies or businessmen in exchange for political favor. Also like China, many elected officials from both Republican and Democratic Parties could not resist the temptation to take bribes from corporations. In November 2005, Randy Cunningham, a Republican congressman of California, pleaded guilty to charges of tax evasion and conspiracy to commit bribery, mail fraud, and wire fraud. Cunningham was accused of using his powerful position on the House Appropriations and Intelligence Committees to "steer lucrative contracts" to those who would help him enjoy an extravagant lifestyle. The bribes taken by Cunningham totaled at least $2.4 million. Disgraced and powerless, Cunningham was sentenced by a local court to 100 months in prison in 2006. In 2014, when he was released, Cunningham was seventy-two years old.[7]

When Cunningham was imprisoned in 2006, his sentence was then the longest. But that record stayed only three years when in 2009 prosecutors sentenced former democratic congressman William Jefferson of Louisiana to thirteen years of prison. During his tenure as the co-chairman of congressional caucus on Nigeria and Africa trade, Jefferson reportedly had capitalized on his position to "direct more than $400,000 in payoffs, relating to business ventures he helped arrange in Africa, to companies he set up in family members' names." In 2009, according to a *Washington Post* report, when the FBI launched a raid to his Washington office, $90,000 was uncovered in his freezer.[8]

The above two cases involve elected politicians from both major parties who have used their power to take bribes from companies for personal luxurious lifestyle or profits. This sort of corruption is explicit and illegal resulting in years of incarceration for both lawmakers. As a matter of fact, there are numerous other bureaucratic misbehaviors or misconducts whose legal status is blurred. They appear to be more covert and, with the vocal advocate from powerful political and judicial officials, those kinds of corruption are deemed legal or, in the words of George Washington Plunkitt, the former head of the powerful Democratic Tammany in New York City, "honest graft."[9] It is not surprising that such legal corruption exists in both past and present and in many polities, if not all, be they authoritarian or democratic.[10]

Legal Corruption in the United States

Elections and Money

In the United States, money and elections are deeply intertwined and no politician can be elected without money. The higher the election, the more the money involved. More than 200 years ago, Gouvermeur Morris, one of the founding fathers of the United States, warned the deadly relationship between money and power that, "wealth tends to corrupt the mind and to nourish its love of power."[11]

Long before the Supreme Court lifted the limits of private money from corporations and labor unions to congressional and presidential elections in 2010, money had played an important if not decisive role in political campaigns. In the words of Herbert E. Alexander who studies the 1980 elections, the 1980 presidential election was the "most expensive" in the nation's history, which cost $275 million to elect a president and challengers usually spent more money than the incumbents.[12] After the Supreme Court rendered the green light to private money on grounds that "uncoordinated corporate spending was archetypal political speech and such spending did not corrupt candidates or the political system,"[13] both Republican and Democratic parties use all means to seek donations from companies or unions. Accordingly, corporations and labor unions quickly use their monetary power to exert more influence on elections and politicians. The money spent in recent political campaigns has easily dwarfed that in previous presidential election. In the election of 2016, a total of $6.5 billion has been spent by candidates and the presidential campaign alone cost nearly $1 billion.[14] According to Rebecca Ballhaus and Brody Mulins, corporations generally "split their PAC money fairly evenly between Republicans and Democrats" for fear that the incumbent survives.[15] On February 5, 2016, an editorial of *USA Today* argued that money tended to play a more crucial role in the election of House representatives than in Senate Elections or the presidential elections. It noted,

> One key reason that so few incumbent members are ever defeated is that they have access to money not available to challengers. Special interest groups

> shower incumbents with money because they have watched them vote and have a good idea how responsive they will be to donor's interests in the future. Challengers represent more of a gamble.[16]

While it is true that money per se does not warrant a successful campaign, the increasing influence of money cannot be more explicit. As a popular Chinese saying aptly notes, "[a man] accepting things (e.g., money or gifts) from others will be obsequious," the elected politicians of all parties in the United States who have taken donations will more likely fall to the prey of their money donors or at least will reward their donors with profits or government posts. For example, during the 2016 presidential election, despite Donald Trump's claim that he would not be manipulated by donors because he funded his own campaign, after Betsy DeVos and her family donated $10.4 million including $445,000 to Donald Trump's joint fundraising committee or Trump Victory and one of the super PAC supporting him, Trump offered his appreciation by appointing DeVos to be the head of the education department, albeit she having no working experience in education whatsoever. Likewise, Andy Puzder, the labor secretary appointed by Trump had spent $160,000 to Trump Victory and more than $600,000 to other Republicans.[17]

Like presidents, some governors have also rushed to reward their donors after successful elections. According to a *New York Times* report, John McHale, a businessman from Austin Texas, gave $50,000 to Governor Rick Perry in 2009 who was then seeking a third term and he did it again in 2010. In May 2010, to reward the financial support of his donor, an economic development fund administered by the governor's office in Texas handed $3 million to G-Con, a pharmaceutical start-up that Mr. McHale helped get off the ground. At least two other executives with connections to the firm had also given Mr. Perry tens of thousands of dollars.[18]

The money politics in the United States has been under fire from many politicians, media, and commoners. Most of them argue that the increasing role of money in politics has corrupted and undermined democracy. Former vice president and Nobel Peace Prize laureate Al Gore worries that the US democracy has been hacked by money because the "democratically elected national legislature" is now "incapable of passing laws without permission from the corporate lobbies and other special interest that control their campaign finances."[19] In 2015, Jimmy Carter, former president, lashed out at the flawed US political election: "Now [the United States] is just an oligarchy," he said, "with unlimited political bribery being the essence of getting the nominations for president or to elect president. And the same thing applies to governors and US senators and congressmen." Bernie Sanders, the Democratic presidential candidate whose campaign had been scuttled by his own party, states that the "millionaire class and the billionaire class increasingly own the political process and they own the politicians that go to them for money."

It is not without irony that, although Donald Trump has accepted donors' money during his presidential campaign and has rewarded them with government posts after a successful election, he chastised the US political system as "a broken" one in 2016,

> I gave to many people, before this, before two months ago, I was a businessman. I give to everybody. When they call, I give. And do you know what? When I need something from them two years later, three years later, I call them, they are there for me. And that's a broken system.

Most Americans share the views and criticism that money plays a critical role in political campaigns. Around 85 percent of Americans reportedly say that the United States needs to either "completely rebuild" or make "fundamental changes" to the campaign finance system.[20] According to one ordinary observer whose first name is Scott, the American political system is one of bribery and "if you don't have the money you don't get any representation in Washington. Democracy is dead." Another observer was "saddened" to see that the presidential election in the United States "has come down to who has the most money."[21]

However radical some of the comments are, it is true that the integrity of political campaigns in the United States has been deeply corroded by money.

Congressmen and Corporations

Aside from lawfully encroaching political campaigns in the United States, money also becomes a powerful link between congressmen/government officials and corporations. And the bigger problem is that this sort of cronyism is legal or at least referred to as "honest grafts."

According to a *Washington Post* report on November 14, 2011, several congressmen had made sizable fortunes through the valuable but confidential information obtained in congressional meetings. In September 2008, for instance, after a "terrifying closed-door meeting with congressional leaders," Democratic congressmen Jim Moran, a member of the Appropriations Committee, "dumped his shares in ninety different companies," which was his most "active trading day" of the year. In another case, Republican representative Shelly Capito of West Virginia, allegedly "dumped $100,000 and $250,000" in Citigroup stock the day after the briefing. During the Obama administration, many government officials capitalized on their power to make profits or cultivate good relations with donors. It is reported that

"$16.4 billion of the $20.5 billion in loans granted went to companies either run by or primarily owned by Obama financial backers, individuals who were bundlers, members of Obama's National Finance Committee, or large donors to the Democratic Party." That is a staggering 71 percent of the loan money.[22]

Some journalists have questioned the legality of the insider-trading liability. But Congress has a "more freewheeling culture in which lawmakers and their staffs view the open exchange of information as being part of the political tradition of the legislative branch." Legal experts said no one appeared to be breaking the law in the meetings whose details have surfaced. Laws dictate that sensitive information must be material and nonpublic to qualify as "insider."[23] Making money by being the insider is exactly what Plunkitt called "honest graft," which is lawful and played in the gray area.

Worse than the profits made through an insider role is the mutual beneficial and protection between congressmen and corporations. In some cases, the collaboration has resulted in lethal outcomes. In February 2010, the *New York Times* exposed that some lawmakers in Congress who possessed large sums of Toyota stocks might "taint" the inquiries on the investigations over Toyota's defects that had caused several fatal accidents. The report said that more than a dozen lawmakers had owned stock in Toyota since 2008, "valued, in some cases, at tens of thousands of dollars." Representative Jane Harman, a California Democrat, held Toyota stocks valued at $116,000 to $315,000. Ms. Harman served on the House energy committee, which would begin a public examination of Toyota's problems at a hearing. Due to the conflict of interest, it should be without doubt that this congresswoman would unlikely risk the loss of her stock value by punishing Toyota.[24]

In a well-publicized case in 2016, the Supreme Court acquitted Robert McDonnell, a former Virginia governor, who was indicted in 2013 for corruption charges. During his tenure as the governor, Mr. McDonnell allegedly had accepted the financial contribution for his daughter's wedding from Jonnie R. Williams Sr., the CEO of a pharmaceutical company. Three days before his daughter's wedding, the governor's wife had touted and promoted the medicine made by Williams' company. But the Supreme Court, by ignoring the lucid quid pro quo in this case, overturned the corruption charge three years later on grounds that the behavior of the Republican governor McDonnell "qualifies as public corruption," which, as the Justice Department interpreted later, should not be deemed as a crime.[25] The Supreme Court's exoneration of corrupt politicians has reportedly increased since the 1999 and in the words of reporter Alan Feuer, the court has "eroded the country's body of corruption laws."[26] Therefore, more than one hundred years after Plunkitt bragged his "honest graft," many bureaucratic misconducts and collaborations between politicians and corporations that normally are unlawful and criminal in many, if not most, other countries including authoritarian states remain largely legal and protected by law in the United States. Partly because of the political corruption and endless contests between the two parties, people in the United States generally have hold a highly negative view and trust of the government. In 1973, a special public opinion survey found that between 1966 and 1973 "all major political institutions of the United States government suffered a serious loss of public trust." The federal government had the biggest decline of confidence of 22 percent from 41 percent to 19 percent. Congress and the Supreme Court also witnessed similar loss ranging from 12 percent to 18 percent.[27] According to a report in 2011, as high as 89 percent of Americans said that they did not trust the government to do the right thing and 84 percent of them disapproved the work of Congress.[28]

The abovementioned legal corruption cases in the United States, however, are only a tip of the iceberg of lawful bureaucratic corruption. In actuality, legal corruption is definitely not restrained in the interrelations between politicians and corporates and it is so prevalent that it has penetrated profoundly into numerous social, economical, and academic sectors such as college acceptance, charities, and federal tax levies. Behind all these legal corruption is money. For example, billionaire Warren Buffet once urged Congress to raise taxes on the super-rich people like him because his federal tax bill, which was about 17.4 percent of his taxable income, was in fact "a lower percentage than was paid by any of the other twenty people in our office."[29] In the so-called Ivory Tower, which should be corruption-free regardless of it being legal or illegal. But recently some newspapers reveal that Ivy League schools such as Harvard University have secretive acceptance rules that invariably favor the rich and powerful. "If you can donate $1 million to Harvard," a report says, "you will be qualified to become a member of the powerful Committee of University Resources (COUR)." While over 50 percent of applicants who have perfect SAT scores have been turned down by Harvard, the kids of 336 out of 424 COUR members have been accepted. Children of some Chinese leaders such as Xi Jinping and Bo Xilai are able to study at Harvard without having to take the stiff tests as most other students have to. So long as his or her parents have money or power, it is not difficult for the student, however lower his or her scores are, to be accepted by top schools like Harvard.[30]

Chinese Corruption versus US Corruption

As we have shown, corruption in modern China is quite serious and it has corrupted almost all the social cells. We have also known that corruption is not limited on Chinese territory. Rather, it is a global thorny problem that no country can claim to be exempted. Even the United States, the mother of modern republic whose people often take pride in their democratic government and the rule of law, have seen both illicit and lawful corruption. One of the key differences between Chinese corruption and American corruption is that some bureaucratic-business grafts in China are culpable but they become lawful in the United States. Another difference is that China inflicts far more severe punishments including life sentence and execution over corrupt officials than the United States. In that regard, CCP and the Qing dynasty are more rigorous against corruption than the United States.

Yet, despite widespread and deep encroachment of money in political campaigns, cronyism, and mutual benefits between corporate and politics, the United States still possesses a much better mechanism in confining and curbing political corruption than China. In China, from the Qing through the People's Republic, political corruption has been rampant and the amount of average corruption is considerably big especially in the reform era. One thing is common in modern China that the ruling family or party is so omnipotent that no political, legal, or military force has been able to exercise any effective check of corruption. Five years after communist leader Xi Jinping initiated the anticorruption campaign, the campaign is far from successful. Corruption continues to appear daily in the newspapers and some critics have the legitimate reason to believe that the ongoing anticorruption is mostly selective because, as the self-exiled billionaire Guo Wengui has claimed, bigger corrupt officials are still on the top.[31]

Unlike China, the democratic United States has numerous relatively cogent and forceful means to rein in political corruption and prevent it from becoming more unrestrained, open, or serious. One effective means is the quasi-independent public media. Mostly privately owned, public media enjoy constitutional rights and protection that allow them to conduct bold and independent investigations. Many corrupt cases including the Watergate scandal have been uncovered by journalists. Another powerful means to check political corruption is the judiciary, which has the same power as the presidency and Congress and thus could use its legal leverage to punish corruption. Despite its little credibility and efficacy, the legislature with its contentious parties could play a certain role in curbing corruption by exposing and attacking each other. In addition, the mostly independent states and local governments in the United States also help the country avert the top-bottom and collective corruption in China. Due to the farsighted design of its founding fathers, the United States does not see corruption cases entailing colossal amount of bribes or grave systematic bureaucratic corruption similar in scale and scope to what have happened in recent China.

Although, as we have mentioned, a relatively matured democracy and the rule of law like the United States would not be sufficient to eradicate corruption for good, they could do a better job than most authoritarian polities or states whose ruling elites are above the law in avoiding unbridled or systematic government corruption. As James Madison, the de facto father of the American constitution in the late eighteenth century, correctly argued that a government "must first . . . control the governed; and in the next place, obliged to control itself."[32] Thus, if the communist regime of China genuinely wants to curb its corruption, a determined political and legal reform will be inevitable to confine the ruling party within the law. However painful the reform will be, it is still better than a total disruption as seen in the late Qing and late Republican period.

NOTES

1. According to Chinese newspaper, most elementary school students have to give gift to their teachers. See Shi Minglei and Li Xueyin, "An Investigation of Gifts on the Teachers' Day (*jiaoshijie songli diaocha*)" in *Xinjingbao*, September 10, 2013.
2. For the annual report of each country's corruption index see https://www.transparency.org/country.
3. Transparency International, "Corruption Perfections Index 2015" in https://www.iaca.int/images/news/2016/Corruption_Perceptions_Index_2015_report.pdf.
4. Both China and India scored 79 in the 2016 report. https://www.transparency.org/news/feature/corruption_perceptions_index_2016.
5. Charles H. Ferguson, *Predator Nation: Corporate Criminals, Political Corruption and the Hijacking of America* (Danvers: Crown Publishing Group, 2012), 3.
6. For Lord Acton's famous dictum see https://acton.org/research/lord-acton-quote-archive.
7. George E. Condon Jr, "Disgraced Congressman Randy 'Duke' Cunningham is a Free Man Again" in *The Atlantic*, July 10, 2014.
8. Jerry Markon, "Ex-Rep. Jefferson (D. La) Gets 13 Years in Freezer Cash Case" in *The Washington Post*, November 14, 2009.
9. Robert D. Marcus, David Burner, and Anthony Marcus eds., *American Firsthand: Vol II. Readings from Reconstruction to the Present* (New York: Bedfor/St. Martin's, 2007), 76–84.
10. In the Qing dynasty, many forms of gift or even extortion such as *menbao* were legal and even the emperor could not change the tradition. See Sun Yat-sen, 1981: 1. 95–7; Li Chunmei, 2005: 26–30; and Nancy E. Park, 1997: 967–1005.
11. Cited in Richard Hofstadter, *The American Political Tradition and the Men Who Made it* (New York: Vintage Books, 1989): 11.
12. Herbert E. Alexander, "Making Sense About Dollars in the 1980 Presidential Campaigns" in Michael J. Malbin, ed., *Money and Politics in the United States: Financing Elections in the 1980s* (New Jersey: Chatham House Publishers, Inc, 1984), 11–37: 11.
13. Cited in Zephyr Teachout, *Corruption in America: From Benjamin Franklin's Snuff Box to Citizens United* (Harvard: Harvard University Press, 2014), 7.
14. Christopher Ingraham, "Somebody Just Put a Price Tag on the 2016 Election. It's a Doozy" in the *Washington Post*, April 14, 2017.
15. Rebecca Ballhaus and Brody Mulins, "Corporations Bet on GOP Senate Control" in *The Wall Street Journal*, November 7, 2016.

16. Editorial, "Money Can't Buy You Love or the Presidency" in *USA Today*, February 5, 2016.

17. Isaac Arnsdorf, "Trump Rewards Big Donors with Jobs and Access" in *Politico*, December 27, 2016.

18. Nicholas Confessore and Michael Luo, "Perry Mines Texas System to Raise Cash" in the *New York Times*, August 20, 2011.

19. Al Gore, *The Future: Six Drives of Global Change* (New York: Random House Publishing Group, 2013), 104.

20. Jon Schwarz, "'Yes, We're Corrupt': A List of Politicians Admitting That Money Controls Politics" in *The Intercept*, July 30, 2015.

21. Readers' comments recorded by the *New York Times*, February 1, 2012.

22. Marc A. Thiessen, "Crony Capitalism Exposed" in *The Washington Post*, November 14, 2011.

23. Jia Lynn Yang, Tom Hamburger, and Dina ElBoghdady, "Ways Investors Gain 'Political' Facing Public Scrutiny" in *The Washington Post*, May 9, 2013.

24. Eric Lichtblau, "Lawmakers' Ties to Toyota Questioned at Start of Inquiries" in *The New York Times*, February 23, 2010.

25. See Rosalind S. Helderman and Laura Vozzella, "Va. Gov. McDonnell on Two-Way Street with Chief Executive of Struggling Company" in *The Washington Post*, March 30, 2013; and Alan Blinder, "U.S. Ends Corruption Case Against Former Virginia Governor" in *The New York Times*, September 8, 2016.

26. Alan Feuer, "Why Are Corruption Cases Crumbling? Some Blame the Supreme Court" in *The New York Times*, November 17, 2017.

27. See Larry L. Berg, Harlan Hahn, and John R. Schmidhauser, *Corruption in the American Political System* (New Jersey: Central Learning Press, 1976), 60.

28. Jeff Zeleny and Megan Thee-Brenan, "New Poll Finds a Deep Distrust of Government" in *The New York Times*, October 25, 2011.

29. Reuters Staff, "Stop Coddling the Super-rich-Buffet" in Reuters, August 15, 2015. https://www.reuters.com/article/buffett-tax/stop-coddling-the-super-rich-buffett-idUSL3E7JF0ZY20110815.

30. "A Precise Count of the Cover Rules Adopted by American Elite Universities in Accepting Students (*xishu meiguo jingying daxue zhaosheng deqianguize*)" in *The Southern Weekend*, December 9, 2013.

31. A former businessman and agent of the Chinese State Security Bureau, Guo Wengui has launched relentless attack in his public talks on youtube and tweets against some top communist leaders, their relatives, and business partners.

32. Ralph Ketcham, ed., *Selected Writings of James Madison* (Indianapolis: Hackett Publishing, 2006), 122.

BIBLIOGRAPHY

1968. *Verifiable Records of Qing Shengzu* (*Daqing shengzu shilu*) vol. 39.

1984. *Documents of the Guangxü Reign* (*Guangxüchao donghualu*). Beijing: Zhonghua shujü.

Alexander, Herbert E. 1984. "Making Sense About Dollars in the 1980 Presidential Campaigns" in Michael J. Malbin, ed., *Money and Politics in the United States: Financing Elections in the 1980s*. New Jersey: Chatham House Publishers.

Anticorruption White Paper (*fantanfu baipishu*), United and Self-Strengthening Association in the Republic of China, June 30, 2010.

Arnsdorf, Isaac. "Trump Rewards Big Donors with Jobs and Access." *Politico*, December 27, 2016.

Ballhaus, Rebecca and Mulins, Brody. "Corporations Bet on GOP Senate Control." *The Wall Street Journal*, November 7, 2016.

Barboza, David. "Billions in Hidden Riches for Family of Chinese Leader." *The New York Times*, October 25, 2012.

Barboza, David and Lafraniere, Sharon. "'Princelings' in China Use Family Ties to Gain Riches." *The New York Times*, May 17, 2012.

Bartlett, Beatrice S. 1990. *Monarchs and Ministers: The Grand Council in Mid-Ch'ing China, 1723–1820*. Berkeley: University of California Press.

Berg, Larry L., Hahn, Harlan and Schmidhauser, John R. 1976. *Corruption in the American Political System*. New Jersey: Central Learning Press.

Blinder, Alan. "U.S. Ends Corruption Case Against Former Virginia Governor." *The New York Times*, September 8, 2016.

Bodde, Derk. 1967. *Peking Diary: 1948–1949 A Year of Revolution*. Minnesota: Fawcett Publications.

Branigan, Tania. "The Guardian Politburo, Army, Casinos: China's Corruption Crackdown Spreads." *The Guardian*, February 2015.

Bu, Xianqun. 2014. *Corruption and Anticorruption in Chinese History (Zhongguo lishishangde fubai yufanfubai)*. Fujian: Lujiang chubanshe.

Chen, Zhiping. "The Seeing Clearly the Customary Fees of Late Qing Learning Officials in the Case of Wang Kaitai (*cong Wang Kaitaian kanqing qingmo xueguande lougui*)" in *Zhongguo shehui jingjishi yanjiu*, Vol. 3, 2013, pp. 84–7.

Chin, Josh. "Chinese Lawyer Sentenced to Seven Years in Prison." *The Wall Street Journal*, August 4, 2016.

Choi, Chi-yuk. "*Chinese officials facing corruption charges are being tempted by suicide*." *South China Morning Post*, June 15, 2016.

Cohen, Paul. "Changes over Time in Qing History: The Importance of Context" in *Late Imperial China*, Vol. 37, No. 1, June 2016, pp. 10–3.

Condon, George E., Jr. "Disgraced Congressman Randy 'Duke' Cunningham Is a Free Man Again." *The Atlantic*, July 10, 2014.

Confessore, Nicholas and Luo, Michael. "Perry Mines Texas System to Raise Cash." *New York Times*, August 20, 2011.

Dardess, John. *Confucianism and Autocracy*, California: University of California Press.

Deng, Yuwen. "Comment." *The New York Times*, May 9, 2017.

Denyer, Simon. "China's Ousted Official Bo Xilai Convicted of Corruption." *The Washington Post*, September 22, 2013.

Eastman, Lloyd E. 1984. *Seeds of Destruction: Nationalist China in War and Revolution, 1937–1949*. Stanford: Stanford University Press.

Editorial Board. "A Deadly Landslide Exposes the Depths of China's Corruption and Censorship." *The Washington Post*, December 29, 2015.

Elliot, Mark C. 2001. *The Manchu Way: The Eight Banners and Ethnic Identity in Late Imperial China*. Stanford: Stanford University Press.

Fang, Qiang. "Hot Potatoes: Chinese Complaint Systems from Early Times to 1898" in the *Journal of Asian Studies*, Vol. 68. No. 4 (November) 2009, pp. 1105–35.

———. "A Silent 'Revolution': The Late Qing Reform on the Jumping Appeals" in *The Journal of Asian History*, Vol. 46, No. 1, 2012, pp. 97–116.

———. 2013a. *Chinese Complaint Systems: Natural Resistance*. U.K.: Routledge.

———. 2013b. *A Short History of Chinese Petition (zhongguo shangfang zhidu shihua)*. Beijing: China Youth Press.

Fang, Qiang and Des Forges, Roger. "Were Chinese Rulers Above the Law? Toward a Theory of the Rule of Law in Chinese History" in *Stanford Journal of International Law*, Vol. 44, No. 1, 2007, pp. 101–146.

Fang, Qiang and Li, Xiaobing. 2017. *Power Versus Law in Modern China: Cities, Courts, and the Communist Party*. Lexington: University Press of Kentucky.

Farmer, Edward. 1983. *Zhu Yuanzhang and Early Ming Legislation*. Leiden: E.J. Brill, 1995, 2.

Fenby, Jonathan. 2004. *Chiang Kai-shek: China's Generalissimo and the Nation he Lost*. New York: Carroll & Graf Publishers.

Ferguson, Charles H. 2012. *Predator Nation: Corporate Criminals, Political Corruption and the Hijacking of America*. Crown Publishing Group.

Feuer, Alan. "Why Are Corruption Cases Crumbling? Some Blame the Supreme Court." *The New York Times*, November 17, 2017.

Forsythe, Michael. "Database Tracks 'Tigers and Flies' Caught in Xi Jinping's Corruption Crackdown." *The New York Times*, January 21, 2016.

Forsythe, Michael. "Database Tracks 'Tigers and Flies' Caught in Xi Kinping's Corruption Crackdown." *The New York Times*, January 21, 2016.

Fu, Zhengyuan. 1993. *Automatic Tradition and Chinese Politics*. Cambridge: Cambridge University Press.

Gao, Hong. "The Fundamental Cause of Lost 1895 War is Qing Corruption (*jiawu zhanzheng shibaide genben yuanyinshi Qingchaode fubai*)" in *The Journal of Qiqihaer Normal College*, Vol. 5, 1995, pp. 158–60.

Gao, Hua. 2011. *How the Red Sun Rises? (gongtaiyang shiruhe shengqide)*. Hong Kong: Hong Kong Chinese University Press.

Goodpaster, Gary. 2002. "Reflections on Corruption in Indonesia" in Timothy Lindsey and Howard W. Dick, eds., *Corruption in Asia: Rethinking the Governance Paradigm*. Australia: The Federation Press.

Gore, Al. 2013. *The Future: Six Drives of Global Change*. New York: Random House Publishing Group.

Guy, R. Kent. 2017. *Qing Governors and Their Provinces: The Evolution of Territorial Administration in China, 1644–1796*. Seattle: University of Washington Press.

He, Qinglian. "Government Monopolized Anticorruption Explicitly Reveals the Backwardness of China's Institutions (Zhengfu longduan fanfu tuxian zhongguo zhidu luohou)." *The Voice of America*, February 7, 2014.

Helderman Rosalind S. and Vozzella, Laura. "Va. Gov. McDonnell on Two-Way Street with Chief Executive of Struggling Company." *The Washington Post*, March 30, 2013.

Ho, Ping-ti. 1964. *The Ladder of Success in Imperial China*. Columbia: Columbia University Press.

Hofstadter, Richard. 1989. *The American Political Tradition and the Men Who Made it*. New York: Vintage Books.

Hucker, Charles. 1966. *Censorial System of Ming China*. Stanford: Stanford University Press.

Ingraham, Christopher. "Somebody Just Put a Price Tag on the 2016 Election. It's a Doozy." the *Washington Post*, April 14, 2017.

Jacobs, Andrew. "China Appears Set to force Times Reporter to Leave." *The New York Times*, January 27, 2014.

Jacobs, Andrew, Hernandez, Javier C., and Buckley, Chris. "Behind Deadly Tianjin Blast, Shortcuts and Lax Rules." *The New York Times*, August 30, 2015.

Ji, Shenying. 2015. *Party Remnants: The Lurker of the New "Gang of Four" (yudang: xinsirenbang deqianfuzhe)*. Hong Kong: Neimu chubanshe.

———. 2015. *The Remaining Members: The Lurker of the "New Gang of Four" (Yudang: xinsirenbang deqianfuzhe)*. Hong Kong: Neimu chubanshe.

Keliher, Macabe. "Administrative Law and the Making of the First *Da Qing Huidian*" in *Late Imperial China*, Vol. 37, No. 1, June 2016, pp. 55–108.

Keliher, Macabe and Wu, Hsinchao. "Corruption, Anticorruption, and the Transformation of Political Culture in Contemporary China" *The Journal of Asian Studies* Vol. 75, No. 1, February 2016, pp. 5–18.

Ketcham, Ralph, ed. 2006. *Selected Writings of James Madison*. Indianapolis: Hackett Publishing.

Leggett, Karby. "In a Land Where Bribes are Commonplace, A Chinese Millionaire Pushed the Envelope." *The Wall Street Journal*, November 23, 2001.

Levin, Dan. "China Tells Schools to Suppress Western Ideas, with One Big Exception." *The New York Times*, February 9, 2015.

Li, Boyuan. 2013. *Exposure of the Official World* (guanchang xianxingji). Zhejiang: Zhejiang chuabn jituan.

Li, Chunmei. "A Preliminary Study on the Customary fee Income of Governors in Early Qing (*shitan qingchao qianqi dufude lougui shouru*)" in *The Journal of Neimenggu Social Science*, Vol. 26, No. 4, July 2015.

Liang, Hong, ed. 2003. *The Ancient Book* (*shangshu*). Hunan: Shidai wenyi chubanshe.

Lichtblau, Eric. "Lawmakers' Ties to Toyota Questioned at Start of Inquiries." *The New York Times*, February 23, 2010.

Lin, Qian. 2013. *Power and Law in Traditional China* (*Chuantong zhongguo dequanyufa*). Beijing: Law Press.

Liu, E. 2017. *The Travels of Lao Can* (laocan youji) (Zhejiang: Zhejiang wenyi chubanshe).

Liu, Xu. 1975. *The Old History of the Tang* (*jiutangshu*). Beijing: Zhonghua shujü.

Lubman, Stanley. 1999. *Bird in a Cage: Legal Reform in China after Mao*. Stanford: Stanford University Press.

Ma, Jun. "Corruption Defeated Late Qing Army: Elite Eight Banners Could not Ride Horses and Half of them Fell (*fubai jikua qingjundui: baqi jingbing buhui qima shiren shangma banshuluo*)." *Wenhui dushu zhoubao*, December 13, 2010.

Marcus, Robert D., Burner, David, and Marcus, Anthony, eds. 2007. *American Firsthand: Vol II. Readings from Reconstruction to the Present*. New York: Bedfor/ St. Martin's.

Markon, Jerry. "Ex-Rep. Jefferson (D. La) Gets 13 Years in Freezer Cash Case." *The Washington Post*, November 14, 2009.

Meisner, Maurice. 1996. *The Deng Xiaoping Era: An Inquiry into the Fate of Chinese Socialism, 1978–1994*. New York: Hill & Wang.

———. 1999. *Mao's China and After: A history of the People's Republic*. New York: Free Press.

Murong, Xuechun. "Xi's Selective Punishment." *The New York Times*, January 16, 2015.

Myers, Steven L. and Landler, Mark. "Frenzied Hours for U.S. on Fate of a China Insider." *The New York Times*, April 17, 2012.

Ni, Shawn and Van, Pham Hoang. 2006. "High Corruption Income in Ming and Qing China" in *Journal of Development Economics*.

Nie, Da. "Corruption behind the Frivolity: The Relationship between Governmental and Cultural Corruption in the Dream of Red Mansion (*fuhua beihoude fubai: cong Hongloumeng kan guanchang fubai yuminfeng fubai deguanxi*)." *Zhongguo jijian jianchabao*, November 14, 2014.

Niu, Chuangping and Niu, Jiqing, eds. 2000. *Verifiable Records of the Economic Criminal Cases of Qing First and Second Ranking Officials (Qingdai yierpin guanyuan jingji fanzui anjian shilu)*. Beijing: Zhongguo fazhi chubanshe.

Pei, Minxin. "Crony Communism in China." *The New York Times*, October 17, 2014.

———. "China's War on Corruption Could Hasten Communist Party's Decline." *Nikkei Asian Review*, May 19, 2015.

———. 2016. *China's Crony Capitalism*. Harvard: Harvard University Press.

Park, Nancy E. 1997. "Corruption in Eighteenth-century China" in *The Journal of Asian Studies*, Vol. 56, No. 4, November.

———. 2016. "Unofficial Perspectives on Torture in Ming and Qing China" in *Late Imperial China*, Vol. 37, No. 1, pp. 17–54.

Patrick, Odsseus. "For a Century, the Mansion Sat above Sydney Harbor. Then China's Nouveau Riche Arrived." *The Washington Post*, June 17, 2014.

Perdue, Peter C. 2010. *China Marches West: The Qing Conquest of Central Eurasia*. Harvard: Harvard University Press.

Phillips, Tom. "China Behaving Like 'Gangster' State with Bookseller Kidnap, Say Hong Kong Politicians." *The Guardian*, June 17, 2016.

Prazniak, Roxann. 1996. *Of Camel Kings and Other Things: Rural Rebels against Modernity in Late Imperial China*. Lanham: Rowman & Littlefield.

Rauhala, Emily. "As Panama Leaks Spread, China's 'Red Nobility' Would Rather not Talk About it." *The Washington Post*. April 7, 2016.

Reed, Bradly. 2000. *Talons and Teeth: County Clerks and Runners in the Qing Dynasty*. Stanford: Stanford University Press.

Rowe, William T. 2010. *China's Last Empire: The Great Qing*. Harvard: Harvard University Press.

Schrecker, John E. 1991. *The Chinese Revolution in Historical Perspective*. New York: Praeger.

Seagrave, Sterling. 1986. *The Soong Dynasty*. New York: Harper & Row Publishers.

———. 1992. *Dragon Lady: The Life and legend of the Last Empress of China*. New York: Vintage Books.

Sha, Lu. "Several Officials of the Development and Reform Commission have been Punished due to Violations of the Rules Regarding Banquet with Public Money and Accepting Gifts (*Fagaiwei duoming guanyuan gongkuan chihe weigui shouli beichufen*)." *Xinjingbao*, April 17, 2016.

Shankar, Sneha. "Li Xiaolin, Former Chinese Premier Li Peng's Daughter, Hid over $2M In HSBC Swiss Account." *The International Business Times*, February 10, 2015.

Sheridan, James E. 1966. *Chinese Warlord: The Career of Feng Yu-hsiang*. Stanford: Stanford University Press.

Shi, Minglei and Li, Xueyin. "An Investigation of Gifts on the Teachers' Day (*jiaoshijie songli diaocha*)." *Xinjingbao*, September 10, 2013.

Shi, Ping. "Fanfubai bushi quanli douzheng (Anticorruption is not Power Struggle)." *Qiushi*, July 2016.

Sima, Guang. 1956. *Comprehensive Mirror for Assisting Government* (*zizhi tongjian*). Beijing: Zhonghua shuju.

Smith, Richard J. 2005. *The Qing Dynasty and Traditional Chinese Culture*. Rowman & Littlefield.

Sonmez, Felicia. "Free Speech in China Gets an Unlikely State-Media Backer." *The Wall Street Journal*, February 17, 2016.

Spence, Jonathan. 1981. *The Gate of Heavenly Peace: The Chinese and Their Revolution, 1895–1980*. New York: Penguin Books.

———. 1991. *The Search for Modern China*. New York: W.W. Norton & Company.

———. 2001. *Treason by the Book*. New York: Viking Press.

Sun, Yat-sen. 1981. *The Complete Works of Sun Yat-sen* (*Sun Zhongshan quanji*). Beijing: Zhonghua shuju.

Teachout, Zephyr. 2014. *Corruption in America: From Benjamin Franklin's Snuff Box to Citizens United*. Harvard: Harvard University Press.

Thiessen, Marc A. "Crony Capitalism Exposed." *The Washington Post*, November 14, 2011.

Tipton, Frank B. 2008. *Asian Firms: History, Institutions and Management*. U.K.: Edward Elgar Publishing.

Transparency International. "Corruption Perfections Index 2015" in https://www.iaca.int/images/news/2016/Corruption_Perceptions_Index_2015_report.pdf.

Twitchett, Denis. 1996. *How to Be an Emperor: T'ang T'ai-tsung's Vision of His Role*, *in* 9 Asia Major 1–3, 92–97. 3rd ed.

Veg, Sebastian. "China's Political Spectrum under Xi Jinping." *The Diplomat*, August 11, 2014.

Vogal, Ezra F. 1969. *Canton under Communism: Programs and Politics in a Provincial Capital, 1949–1968*. Harvard: Harvard University Press.

Wakeman, Frederic jr. 1985. *The Great Enterprise: The Manchu Reconstruction of Imperial Order in Seventeenth-century China*. Berkeley: University of California Press.
———. 2003. *Policing Shanghai: 1927–1937*. Stanford: Stanford University Press.
———. 2003. Spymaster: *Dai Li and the Chinese Secret Service*. Stanford: Stanford University Press.
Wan, William. "China Broadcasts Confession of Chinese-American Blogger." *The Washington Post*, September 15, 2013.
Wang, Qishan. "Grasping and Utilizing the 'Four Patterns' in Supervising and Disciplining." *The Xinhua News Agency*, September 26, 2015.
Wang, Tianyou and Xu, Daling. 1991. *Sixteen Emperors in the Ming Dynasty* (*mingchao shiliudi*). Beijing: Zijincheng chubanshe.
Wong, Chun Han. "Chinese Court Issues Life Sentence to Former Presidential Aide for Corruption." *The Wall Street Journal*, July 4, 2016.
Wu, Han. 2000. *Biography of Zhu Yuanzhang* (*Zhu Yuanzhangzhuan*). Zhejiang: Baihua wenyi chubanshe.
———. 2001. *A Biography of Ming Taizu* (*Ming Taizuzhuan*). Tianjin: Baihua wenyi chubanshe.
Xu, Beina. "Media Censorship in China." *Council on Foreign Relations*, April 7, 2015.
Yang, Fan. "The Latest Hearsay: Zeng Qinghong's Secret Detention Place is Exposed (*Zuixin chuanwen: Zeng Qinghong mimi guanya didian baoguang*)." *Secret China*, July 13, 2014. http://m.secretchina.com/node/546794.
Yang, Hegao. 1979. *Selected Works of Ancient Politics and Law (gudai zhengfa wenxuan)*. Beijing: Beijing zhengfa xueyuan.
Yang, Jia Lynn, Hamburger, Tom and ElBoghdady, Dina. "Ways Investors Gain 'Political' Facing Public Scrutiny." *The Washington Post*, May 9, 2013.
Yuen, Samson. "Disciplining the Party: Xi Jinping's Anticorruption Campaign and its Limits." *China Perspectives*, Vol. 2014, No. 3, 2014.
Zeleny, Jeff and Thee-Brenan, Megan. "New Poll Finds a Deep Distrust of Government." *The New York Times*, October 25, 2011.
Zhang, Jixin. 2016. *Things Seen and Heard about Bureaucracy in both the Daoguang and Xianfeng Reigns* (*daoxian huanhai jianwenlu*). Beijing: Zhonghua shuju.
Zhang, Lun. "The Increasing Appearance of the Drawbacks in China's Movement-type Anticorruption (*Zhongguo yundongshi fanfu biduan riyi chengxian*)." *The French International Broadcast*, February 8, 2015.
Zhang, Tingyu. 1974. *The History of the Ming* (*Mingshi*). Beijing: Zhonghua shujü.
Zhang, Yuxue. "Former Vice Head of the Logistic Department Gu Junshan is Exposed to be Involved in a Case of more than 20 billion (*Yuanzonghouqingbu fubuzhang Gu Junshan beibao shean 200 duoyi*)." *Caijin net*, April 1, 2015.
Zhang, Zhiguang. "Anticorruption in Chinese History (*Zhongguo lishishang defanfu*)." *Shanghai guancha*, May 29, 2014.
Zhao, Erxun. 1982. *The Draft History of the Qing* (*qingshigao*). Beijing: Zhonghua shuju.
Zheng, Yongnian. 2015. *China Entering the Xi Jinping Era*. U.K.: Routledge.

Zhong, Chenfang. "People Unhappy to See the Remodeling of a Sydney Mansion by Zeng Qinghong's Son (*Zeng Qinghong zhizi Xini haozhai gaijian yincemu*)." *Voice of America*, June 19, 2014.

Zhou, Yahui. "The Objective of Xi Jinping's Anticorruption is to Deal with Civilian Party (Xi Jinping fanfude mubiao shiduifu pingmindang)." August 15, 2014. www.boxun.com.

"*Zhu Yuanzhang chengtan bubiqin: weifanfu chusi qinzhizi yuqinnuxu*)" in *Fenghuang lishi*, July 1, 2014. http://news.ifeng.com/a/20140701/40965124_0.shtml.

Zhu, Yuyang and Gui, Jie. "A Record of State Governing under Tang Taizong: Discussing How the Tang Dynasty Opposed Corruption (*Tang Taizong zhiguo fengyunlu: tantao tangchao ruhe fanfu*)." *The China Youth Daily*, August 22, 2014.

Index

About the Contributors

Dr. Qiang Fang is a professor of East Asian History at the University of Minnesota Duluth and also a visiting professor at China University of Geosciences. He serves as the president of Chinese Historians in the United States (CHUS) for 2017–2019 and the editor-in-chief of a book series entitled "China: From Revolution to Reform" published by Amsterdam University Press. Apart from a coauthored book (first author) entitled *Power versus Law in Modern China: Cities, Courts, and the Communist Party* (University Press of Kentucky, 2017), his monograph entitled *Chinese Complaint Systems: Natural Resistance,* co-edited book with Xiaobing Li entitled *Modern Chinese Legal Reform: New Perspectives*, and co-edited book *Oumei xuezhe yanjiu zhongguo falushi lunwen xuanyi* [Selected Articles of Chinese Legal History by Western Scholars] were published by Routledge (2013), the University Press of Kentucky (2013), and China Law Press (2017), respectively. Another book in Chinese entitled *Zhongguo shangfang zhidu shihua* [*A Short History of Chinese Petition*] was also published in 2013 by China Youth Press, one of China's prominent national presses. In addition, he has published many articles regarding Chinese law, history, and politics in major journals such as *Stanford Journal of International Law*, *Modern Chinese Studies, Collected Papers of History Study*, *Journal of Asian History*, *Education about Asia*, and *Stanford Journal of East Asian Affairs*. In 2009, his article entitled "Hot Potatoes: Chinese Complaint Systems from Early Times to 1898" was published by the *Journal of Asian Studies*. Some of his articles have been published in edited volumes. Currently, he is working on a book project tentatively entitled *The Making of a Communist Judiciary in China, 1927–1965*.

Dr. Xiaojia Hou received her PhD in history from Cornell University in 2008, and her undergraduate and master's degrees in history from Peking

University. She is currently an associate professor at the Department of History, San Jose State University. Her research agenda centers on China's socialist transformation in the 1950s, particularly on the lives of ordinary Chinese who wrote little and were rarely written about. Her monograph *Negotiating Socialism in Rural China—Mao, Peasants, and Local Cadres in Shanxi 1949–1953* was published by the Cornell East Asian Series (Ithaca, New York) in 2016. She has published two peer-reviewed book chapters, one article, multiple book reviews and article reviews, in English and in Chinese language. She has served as peer reviewer for several academic journals, in English and in Chinese. Recently, her research interest has turned to how politics intertwined with environment in China. She is now working on two projects. One is about a lost province in China called Pingyuan; the other is on the ill-fated Weishan Lake.

Dr. Sherman Xiaogang Lai is an adjunct professor at the Department of Political Science at Royal Military College of Canada (RMC). His current research is on Chinese government's maritime-related polices such as China's maritime economy, naval strategy, Arctic policy, overseas fisheries, foreign policy, and fiscal policy is an extension of doctoral and postdoctoral research on Republican China, focusing on the formation of the two opposing party-states of Guomindang (Nationalists) and Communists. His publications cover a wide range of topics from Chiang Kai-shek and Britain prior to the end of the First Burma Campaign in 1942 (Routledge, 2015) and the formation of Communist fiscal-military party-state in Shandong province (Brill, 2011) to the dilemma of China's currant naval and maritime policy (CMSEC, 2015) and the birth of China's post–Cold War military strategy (JMSS, 2016). These research projects are based on his broad international experience. He is a BA graduate in history from Nankai University in Tianjin and obtained his MA at Chinese Academy of Sciences. He joined the Chinese army and worked as a translator, sub-editor, and researcher in the Academy of Military Science. He also served as a foot soldier in the frontline of Sino-Vietnamese War and as a Chinese contingent member in the United Nation's peacekeeping mission in Western Sahara. After having immigrated to Canada, he was admitted to Royal Military College's MA program of War Studies and PhD program at Queen's University at Kingston. He then went to Oxford University and Stanford University for his postdoctoral research. In addition to the publications in English mentioned above, he has a significant amount of publications on World War II in Chinese language. To his English-speaking readers, his research offers insights into the workings and dynamics of the Communist fiscal-military party-state of China, a kind of knowledge that helps outsiders comprehend and interpret relevant policies of the Chinese government as well as behaviors of concerned Chinese officials. To his Chinese-speaking readers, Lai's publications and research enabled them to observe China and China-related events in a global and historical perspective.

Dr. Xiaobing Li is a professor and the chair of the Department of History and Geography and the director of the Western Pacific Institute at the University of Central Oklahoma. He served as the Council Chair of the United Societies of China Studies (USCS) in 2016–2017 and as the president of Southwestern Association of Asian Studies (AAS) from 2004 to 2006. He is currently the editor of the *Journal of Chinese Military History* and *Western Pacific Journal*. He has authored, edited, and co-edited books, both in America and in China, including *Urbanization and the Party Survival* (Lexington Books, 2017); *Modern China: Understanding Modern Nations* (ABC-CLIO, 2016); *Ethnic China: Identity, Assimilation, and Resistance* (Lexington Books, 2015); *China's Battle for Korea* (Indiana University Press, 2014); *Oil: A Cultural and Geographic Encyclopedia of Black Gold* (ABC-CLIO, 2014); *Evolution of Power: China's Struggle, Survival, and Success* (Lexington, 2013); *Modern Chinese Legal Reforms* (University Press of Kentucky, 2013); *China at War* (ABC-CLIO, 2012); *Civil Liberties in China* (ABC-CLIO, 2011); *Voices from the Vietnam War* (UPK, 2010); *New Historiography in the Contemporary West* (in Chinese; Shanghai: Lexicographical Press, 2008); *A History of the Modern Chinese Army* (UPK, 2007); *Voices from the Korean War* (UPK, 2004); *Taiwan in the 21st Century* (University Press of America, 2003); *Chinese Immigrants in the United States* (in Chinese; Chengdu: Sichuan People's Press, 2002); *Mao's Generals Remember Korea* (University Press of Kansas, 2001); and *Asia's Crisis and New Paradigm* (UPA, 2000).

Dr. Xiaoxiao Li is a faculty member in China Studies at the University of Oklahoma with a PhD in contemporary world history at Northeast Normal University of China. He taught macro and micro economics as well as international management courses at University of Central Oklahoma from 2007 to 2011 and US-China Trade Relations in 2017. Before he began his college teaching career, he worked as the director of international marketing for China CEE and Power Cost Inc of USA; general manager of Asian Projects for Smith Cogeneration Management in 2001–2008; deputy chief of Xinjiang Carpet and Arts & Crafts Imp-Exp Corporation in 1996–1999; and general manager of Joint Venture Lejia Carpet Corporation in 1994–1997. Among his major administration and business achievements was the construction of a 550-megawatt gas turbine power plant in China between 2001 and 2007. In May 2013 and 2015, he was invited by Hubei Development and Reform Commission to investigate Hubei new rural construction pilot projects.

Yue Li works as researcher at the Economic and Technology Research Institute, China National Petroleum Corporation (CNPC), Beijing. She received her degrees from China Agricultural University in 2009 and the University of Central Oklahoma in 2012. She also received her NBA from China University of Petroleum in 2016.

Chen Liu works as account manager of Bank of Kunlun in Beijing. He received his degree from Hunan University in 2007. After his graduation, he had worked as Project Manager at China Petroleum Technology and Development Corporation (CPTDC) for eight years, mainly responsible for the project of supplying oil equipment to the foreign clients of CNPC.

Dr. Patrick Fuliang Shan is a professor in the Department of History at Grand Valley State University, where he teaches Chinese history, East Asian history, and world history. He earned his PhD from McMaster University, MA from Liaoning University, and BA from Henan University. His monograph entitled *Taming China's Wilderness: Immigration, Settlement, and the Shaping of the Heilongjiang Frontier, 1900–1931* (Ashgate, 2014) probes the history of China's northeastern frontier during the crucial period of historical transformation. He has published over a dozen research articles on twentieth-century Chinese history in *Journal of Social History, Frontiers of History in China, Peace and Conflict Studies, Asian Ethnicity, American Journal of Chinese Studies, American Review of China Studies, and Chinese Historical Review*. He has contributed several chapters to books, wrote many encyclopedic articles, and published over thirty critical review essays. In the past decade, he has focused on Yuan Shikai for a particular scholarly exploration. Consequently, he has written a critical biography of Yuan Shikai (to be published). Besides the above-mentioned publications in English, he has also published in Chinese on various historical topics in the past thirty years. He has translated scholarly works from Chinese to English and from English to Chinese, and promoted US-China academic exchanges. Because he was a co-author of the first mainland Chinese written biography of General Claire Lee Chennault, he was invited to be the keynote speaker for the 64th Flying Tigers' Annual Reunion held in Grand Rapids in 2005. He served as president of the Chinese Historians in the United States (CHUS, 2009–2011), a member of the board of the Historical Society for Twentieth Century China (HSTCC, 2011–2014), and the coordinator of the East Asian Studies Program at Grand Valley State University (2013–1016). Since 2012, he has served as an associate editor of *American Review of China Studies*, a peer-reviewed scholarly journal published in the United States.

Dr. Xiansheng Tian finished his undergraduate studies in English at the Henan University in China in 1981 and worked there till 1987 when he started his studies at the State University of New York-Cortland to finish his master's degree in History in June 1989. From 1989 to 1994 he studied at Oklahoma State University and received his PhD in History. Since 1996 he has been teaching at Metropolitan State University of Denver and earned his tenure there in 2001. His publications and research topics include American diplomatic history, US-China relations during and after World War II, and US-China-Taiwan relations. His coedited books, *Urbanization and Party Survival in China: People vs. Power* and *Evolution of Power: China's Struggle, Survival, and Success*, were published by Lexington Books in 2016 and 2013. His monograph, *Patrick J. Hurley and US-China Relations, 1944–1945*, was published in 2008 (University Press of the South, New Orleans). Besides presenting at academic conferences and contributing to many journals and books, he also coedited two other books, *Taiwan in the Eyes of Chinese-American Scholars: Critical Analysis of Taiwan Society in the 21st Century* (Taipei Xiuwei Press, 2005) and *New Historiography in the Contemporary West, 1987–2007* (Shanghai Cishu Press, 2008). He served on the Boards of Directors of the Association of Chinese Historians in the United States (CHUS, 1999–2005) and the Association of Chinese Professors in Social Sciences (ACPSS, 2003–07), and functioned as the latter's executive vice president from 2005–2007. He is also on the editorial board of *American Review of China Studies* since 2006.

Dr. Helen Xiaoyan Wu, received her PhD in Chinese political culture and sociolinguistics, and is an associate professor at the University of Toronto. She has co-authored two Chinese language textbooks (2013 and 2016) and one textbook of Chinese Canadian writers (summer 2017). The topics of the book chapters and articles she has published include sociolinguistics, the sociology of language, politics, and society in contemporary China (e.g., women and official corruption), Chinese linguistics, classical Chinese, rhetoric, literary criticism, poetry and satirical verse, folk rhymes, sayings and proverbs, song lyrics, translation, and translation studies, as well as pedagogy.

Dr. Stella Y. Xu is an associate professor of history at Roanoke College in Virginia, where she teaches East Asian history. She received her PhD at the University of California at Los Angles. Her essays and book reviews have appeared in *Korean Studies*, *Journal of Korean Studies*, *Pacific Affairs*, *ASIANetwork Exchange: A Journal for Asian Studies in the Liberal Arts*, *Women and Social Movement in the United States, 1600–2000*, and *Japanese*

Studies Association Journal. Her book, *Reconstructing Ancient Korean History: The Formation of Korean-ness in the Shadow of History* (Lexington Books) was published in June, 2016.

Dr. Dongyu Yang is a professor in the Department of History and Research Fellow at the Institute of China's Frontier and Ethnic Minorities at Shaanxi Normal University, Xi'an. He received his PhD form Shaanxi Normal University in 2006 and was a postdoctoral candidate in the Institute of Ethnology and Anthropology (IEA) in 2007, China Academy of Social Sciences (CASS). He has published five books and more than twenty articles on anthropology and history of Chinese medicine both in China and America. Among his publications is a book chapter titled "Maternal and Children Healthcare in Ethnic Minority Towns of Xinjiang," in Urbanization and Party Survival in China: People vs. Power, edited by Xiaobing Li and Xiansheng Tian and published by Lexington Books in 2017. Currently Professor Yang is a visiting scholar at the University of Central Oklahoma, USA.

Dr. Zhiguo Yang was trained as a historian both in China and in the United States. He received his master's degree from the Peking University and his PhD from the University of Maryland, College Park. Prior to being appointed as professor of history at the University of Wisconsin-River Falls in 2010, he had taught world and East Asian history at George Mason University, Truman State University, Gettysburg College, and West Texas A&M University. With a teaching and research specialty in modern Chinese history and the history of China-US relations, he has published several articles on topics of Chinese nationalism, Chinese consumer culture in the twentieth century, the role of retired American military personnel in the economic development of Taiwan in the 1950s, the history of beer brewery industry in Qingdao, and the history of post-WWII interactions between Chinese civilians and American marine troops stationed in Qingdao, North China. Currently, he is finishing an article exploring the relationship between the labor movement in Japanese-owned cotton mills and the Nationalist effort to consolidate the Chinese rule in Qingdao during the period of 1928–1937. He is also a long time member of several organizations for historians, including the Association for Asian Studies (AAS) and Chinese Historians in the United States (CHUS).

www.ingramcontent.com/pod-product-compliance
Ingram Content Group UK Ltd.
Pitfield, Milton Keynes, MK11 3LW, UK
UKHW041128071026
15587UKWH00009B/290

9 781498 574310